TOUCHSTONE

NIKOS KAZANTZAKIS

REPORT TO GRECO

Translated from the Greek by
P. A. BIEN

A Touchstone Book
Published by Simon and Schuster

ORIGINAL GREEK LANGUAGE EDITION ENTITLED
ΑΝΑΦΟΡΑ ΣΤΟΝ ΓΚΡΕΚΟ

A TOUCHSTONE BOOK
PUBLISHED BY SIMON AND SCHUSTER
A DIVISION OF GULF & WESTERN CORPORATION
SIMON & SCHUSTER BUILDING
ROCKEFELLER CENTER
1230 AVENUE OF THE AMERICAS
NEW YORK, NEW YORK 10020
TOUCHSTONE AND COLOPHON ARE TRADEMARKS
OF SIMON & SCHUSTER

ISBN 0-671-22027-6
LIBRARY OF CONGRESS CATALOG CARD NUMBER 65-22535
DESIGNED BY EDITH FOWLER
MANUFACTURED IN THE UNITED STATES OF AMERICA

5 6 7 8 9 10 11 12 13

CONTENTS

INTRODUCTION: THE WRITING OF "REPORT TO GRECO"

by Helen N. Kazantzakis

NIKOS KAZANTZAKIS asked his God for ten additional years, ten additional years in which to complete his work—to say what he had to say and "empty himself." He wanted death to come and take only a sackful of bones. Ten years were enough, or so hc thought.

But Kazantzakis was not the kind who could be "emptied." Far from feeling old and tired at the age of seventy-four, he considered himself rejuvenated, even after his final adventure, the tragic vaccination. Freiburg's two great specialists, the hematologist Heilmeyer and the surgeon Kraus, concurred in this opinion.

The whole of the final month Professor Heilmeyer shouted triumphantly after each visit, "This man is healthy, I tell you! His blood has become as sound as my own!"

"Why do you run like that!" I kept scolding Nikos, afraid that he might slip on the terrazzo and break a bone.

"Don't worry, Lénotska, I've got wings!" he answered. One sensed the confidence he had in his constitution and his soul, which refused to bite the dust.

Sometimes he sighed, "Oh, if only I could dictate to you!" Then, grasping a pencil, he would try to write with his left hand.

"What's the hurry? Who is chasing you? The worst is past. In a few days you'll be able to write to your heart's content."

He would turn his head and gaze at me for a few moments in silence. Then, with a sigh: "I have so very much to say. I am being tormented again by three great themes, three new novels. But first I've got to finish Greco."

"You'll finish it, don't worry."

"I plan to change it. Will you get some paper and a pencil? Let's see if I can manage."

But our combined labor lasted less than five minutes.

"Impossible! I don't know how to dictate. I can think only when the pencil is in my hand."

Ancestors, parents, Crete, childhood years . . . Athens, Crete, travels . . . Sikelianos, Vienna, Berlin, Prevelakis, Moscow . . .

Now I remember another crucial moment in our lives, another hospital, this time in Paris. Nikos gravely ill again with a temperature of 104, the physicians all in a turmoil. Everyone had lost hope; only Kazantzakis himself remained unperturbed.

"Will you get a pencil, Lénotska? . . ."

Still plunged in his vision, he dictated to me in a broken voice the Franciscan haikai he placed in the saint's mouth: "I said to the almond tree, 'Sister, speak to me of God.' And the almond tree blossomed."

Before we departed for China, he left the *Report* in the hands of a young painter, his "midwife" as he called him, because he used to come at the crack of dawn, climb up to Nikos' study, troubled by all the great problems—God, men, art—and begin the interminable *whences, whithers* and *how longs*, whereupon Nikos, laughing, admiring the youth's passion and his violent love for his art, "delivered." He "dropped" ideas and unburdened himself.

"The house might catch on fire," Nikos told him. "I'd rather leave the manuscript with you. If it's burned at this point, I'll never be able to rewrite it. The great shame is only that I never finished it."

But how could he have ever finished it? What had he left undone in those last few months before the journey?

He began the *Report* in the autumn of 1956, upon our return from Vienna. When he needed a change, he took up the translation of Homer's *Odyssey*, which he and Professor Kakridís were working on together.

"We've got to manage to finish it in time so I won't go down to Hades with a lame leg," he used to say half ironically, half with fear.

During these same months, sections from the English translation of his own *Odyssey* kept arriving at frequent intervals, together with entire pages listing words difficult to translate. How much time, how much labor were consumed, also, by that *Odyssey!* Not to mention the numerous publications of his other works in Greek. There were texts which had to be corrected or supplemented; and *Russia*, the manuscript of which had been lost; and Pierre Sipriot of the French radio, who plagued him with his "Colloquies"; and the film; and a trip to India at the invitation of Nehru, which we prepared for but did not take because we feared the many innoculations required.

No, he did not manage to finish the *Report to Greco* in time; he was unable to write a second draft, as was his custom. He did manage, however, to rewrite the entire first chapter and one of the concluding sections: "When the germ of *The Odyssey* formed fruit within me," which he sent before his death to be published in the periodical *Nea Estia*. In addition, he managed to read over his manuscript and to make penciled corrections or additions here and there.

Alone, now, I re-experience the autumn twilight which descended ever so gently, like a small child, with the first chapter.

"Read, Lénotska, read and let me hear it!"

I collect my tools: sight, smell, touch, taste, hearing, intellect. Night has fallen, the day's work is done. I return like a mole to my home, the ground. Not because I am tired and cannot work. I am not tired. But the sun has set. . . .

I could go no further; a lump had risen in my throat. This was the first time Nikos had spoken about death.

"Why do you write as though ready to die?" I cried, truly despondent. And to myself: Why, today, has he accepted death?

"Don't be alarmed, wife, I'm not going to die," he answered without the slightest hesitation. "Didn't we say I'd live another ten years? I need ten more years!" His voice was lower now. Extending his hand, he touched my knee. "Come now, read. Let's see what I wrote."

To me he denied it, but inwardly, perhaps, he knew. For that very same night he sealed this chapter in an envelope together with a letter for his friend Pantelís Prevelakis: "Helen could not read it; she began to cry. But it is good for her—and for me also—to begin to grow accustomed . . ."

It seems his inner daemon had prodded him to abandon the *Faust: Part Three* which he so desired to write, and to lay the keel of his autobiography instead.

The *Report* is a mixture of fact and fiction—a great deal of truth, a minimum of fancy. Various dates have been changed. When he speaks about others, it is always the truth, unaltered, exactly what he saw and heard. When he speaks about his personal adventures, there are some small modifications.

But one thing is certain: If he had been able to rewrite this *Report*, he would have changed it. Exactly how, we cannot know. He would have enriched it, for each day he recalled new incidents which he had forgotten. Also, he would have poured it (so I believe) into the mold of reality. His actual life was full of substance, of human anguish, joy, and pain—"dignity," to put it in a single word. Why should he have changed this life? Not for lack of difficult moments of weakness, flight, and pain. On the contrary, it was precisely these difficult moments which always served Kazantzakis as new steps enabling him to ascend higher—to ascend and reach the summit he promised himself he would climb before abandoning the tools of labor because night had begun to fall.

"Do not judge me by my actions, do not judge me from man's point of view," another struggler once entreated me. "Judge me from God's —by the hidden purpose behind my actions."

This is how we should judge Kazantzakis. Not by what he did, and whether what he did was or was not of supreme value; but rather by what he wanted to do, and whether what he wanted to do had supreme value for him, and for us as well.

I, for one, believe it did. In my thirty-three years by his side I cannot recall ever being ashamed by a single bad action on his part. He was honest, without guile, innocent, infinitely sweet toward others, fierce only toward himself. If he withdrew into solitude, it was only because he felt the labors required of him were severe and his hours numbered.

His round, round eyes pitch black in the semidarkness and filling with tears, he used to say to me, "I feel like doing what Bergson says—going to the street corner and holding out my hand to start begging from the passers-by: 'Alms, brothers! A quarter of an hour from each of you.' Oh, for a little time, just enough to let me finish my work. Afterwards, let Charon come."

Charon came—curse him!—and mowed Nikos down in the first flower of his youth! Yes, dear reader, do not laugh. For this was the time for all to flower and bear fruit, all he had begun, the man you so loved and who so loved you, your Nikos Kazantzakis.

—H.N.K.

Geneva, June 15, 1961.

TRANSLATOR'S NOTE

THE READER will soon discover that I have retained many Greek terms in this translation. I have done this whenever there is no real English equivalent, especially in cases of food and clothing. Sometimes, even when a reasonable equivalent exists, I retain the Greek original out of respect for the increasing number of English-speaking people who know a little of modern Greek life at first hand. These modern philhellenes would wince if they encountered *hors d'oeuvres*, for instance, as a rendering of *mezédhes*. For their sake, I ask other readers to endure temporary mystification with forbearance.

All the modern Greek terms, as well as certain historical allusions, are explained below. They are listed alphabetically for easy reference. In one or two places I have also added explanatory material to the text, but always in square brackets. My transliterations are deliberately inconsistent. Most often I try to approximate the present-day pronunciation, but in certain cases I give precedence to etymology. As a possible aid to pronunciation I include accents where I think they will be of use. These indicate stress only; they do not change the vowel. Pronounce *a* as in father, *e* as in bed, *i* as in machine.

acrite. During the Byzantine era the acrites guarded the frontiers against inroads by the barbarians. They became symbols of heroism and devotion to country, and their deeds, often magnified to supernatural proportions, were immortalized in epic and song.

amané, *pl. amanédhes*. Passionate songs, usually about love, so called because the expression *amán* ("alas") occurs frequently.

antídoro. Bits of consecrated bread distributed to the entire congregation at the end of the service in Orthodox churches. This is instead of communion, literally "instead of the [Lord's] gift."

Boule. The Greek legislature, a term used in both ancient and modern times. The modern pronunciation is *Voulí*.

briki. The special pot used for making Turkish coffee.

Christos anéstakas. This requires some explanation. Greek is rich in expressive suffixes. Adding *áki* to the word *pódhi*, for example, we get *podháki*, or "small foot." Similarly, we can add a suffix to indicate a large foot: *podhára*. Then, if we have a friend with large feet, we can call him a *podharás*. If our friend is a big drunkard, he will be known as a *methýstakas*. On analogy to this last example, the priest in Chapter 28 who says *Christos anéstakas* instead of *Christos anesti* (Christ is risen) is simply trying to say that Christ is so tremendous that He did not simply "rise," He rose in a tremendous way, suitable to His giant stature. He breaks all grammatical rules because he adds the suffix to a verb instead of to a noun.

epitáphios. This is the canopy-like structure, made of flowers, which represents Christ lying in the tomb. It is placed in the church on Good Friday.

foufoúla, pl. foufoúles. The loose, hanging part of the Cretan *vraka* (q.v.).

Friendly Society. A secret society founded in Odessa in 1816 with the purpose of organizing the Greek War of Independence.

"Hold fast, poor Missolonghi." A well-known phrase referring to the heroic resistance of Missolonghi while under siege during the Greek War of Independence (1821 ff.).

kalýmmafko. A covering of black material placed over the hat of Orthodox monks and falling down the back as far as the waist. Sometimes it is gathered into a pyramid over the head. It is similar in purpose to the wimple: it prevents the monk from seeing "the world."

Karaïskakis, Georgios. Important general in the Greek War of Independence. Killed in action, 1827.

katharévousa. The official language of Greece. It is an artificial language constructed by nationalists in the late eighteenth and early nineteenth centuries as a compromise between ancient Greek and the so-called "demotic," the spoken language which evolved naturally during the Hellenistic and Byzantine periods, and the 400 years of Turkish rule. The linguistic nationalists attempted to "purify" demotic of foreign words and to return as far as possible to the vocabulary, syntax, and grammar of the ancient Attic dialect. Though katharévousa is employed today for all official documents, scholarly books, university lectures, etc., demotic survives with undiminished vitality. Since katharévousa has to be learned at the gymnasium, it can be used in an affected way as a sign that one is educated, i.e., superior. This is the basis of the Títyros anecdote in Chapter 5.

Kifissiá. A suburb of Athens, now very fashionable.

koulouri, pl. koulouria. Doughnut-shaped rolls sprinkled with sesame seeds. They are sold in the street by men or boys and are a Greek institution.

kourabiédhes. These are little cookie-like sweets made of flour, sugar, eggs, and mastic. They are baked and then covered with powdered sugar.

kulah. The high round felt hat of the dervishes.

mantinádha, pl. mantinádhes. From Italian *mattinata*. Originally a lover's serenade sung beneath a girl's window. In Crete the mantinadha always takes the form of a rhymed couplet. It is often improvised and is no longer restricted in subject matter.

Megalo Kastro. This is Iraklion, Kazantzakis' birthplace and the chief city of Crete. Megalo Kastro means "great fortress." Iraklion is famous for its walls, built over the period 1462–1570 by the Venetian conquerers.

mezé, pl. mezédhes. Food eaten with wine or raki to prevent intoxication. Usually appetizers such as sardines, olives, cheese, stuffed vine leaves, fish roe, etc.

myzíthra. A soft white cheese somewhat like cottage cheese.

"Over the years, in time, she'll be ours once more." Slogan during the Greek War of Independence, attributed to the archbishop Germanós (Palaion Patron Germanos).

pallikári. A true man, i.e., brave and strong, able to resist pain, etc. The term was originally applied to the foot soldiers accompanying mounted knights, later to any soldier, now to any young man who has soldier-like qualities. In Greece today it is an unqualified term of praise.

papadhiá. Wife of a priest.

Paramythía, Ktetórissa, Bematárissa, Antiphonétria, Esphagméne, Elaiobrótida. Each of these celebrated icons has a legend associated with it. The Esphagméne ("slaughtered one"), for example, is represented with blood flowing from her cheek. The story goes that a certain deacon was so zealous in his desire to tidy the church that he missed his dinner. When he went after hours to the refectory, he was refused even a slice of bread, whereupon he returned to the church and knifed the Virgin in his rage. Blood flowed and the deacon was immediately struck blind, but the Virgin eventually forgave him and restored his sight. The transgressing hand, however, was condemned to be sent to hell at the Second Coming. When the deacon's bones were disinterred, this hand was discovered still intact. A certain pilgrim, assuming that the hand's preservation indicated its holiness, bit off a piece in order to profit therefrom, and straightway fell down dead. The other icons are equally wonder-working.

passatempo. Salted, lightly roasted pumpkin seeds, munched for the purpose indicated in the name.

Prodromos. Theodore Prodromos, called "Prodromos the Poor," was a Byzantine poet (died 1160). The Comneni patronized him for a time, but then their support was withdrawn, and Prodromos died as a monk in great poverty.

Psiloríti. Mountain not far from Iraklion. The ancient Mount Ida.

Stournaras, Nikólaos. Military leader in the Greek War of Independence. He fell at Missolonghi in 1826.

vrakes. Jodhpur-like trousers worn until recently by Cretan men. They are extremely baggy above the knees, being made from an immense amount of material which hangs down loosely.

Zálongon. A cliff in Epirus, famous in Greek history. It was here, on Dec. 18, 1803, that 57 Greek women chose death rather than capture by the Turks. After hurling their babies over the cliff, they formed a circle and danced until each had leaped to her doom.

This translation is in many ways a collaboration, and I wish to record here my indebtedness and sincere thanks to my many fellow workers. Above all to my wife, who with her accustomed patience and good humor answered my endless queries. I am also indebted to Helen Kazantzakis, the author's widow; Nikos Saklambanis of Iraklion, the author's nephew; Pandelis Prevelakis, who carefully checked my rendering of the Terzina in the Epilogue; Emmanuel Kasdaglis, who with infinite care and dedication prepared Kazantzakis' original manuscript for publication; Stephen Mavroyiannis, icon painter; Boule Prousali; Lola Sphairopoulou, and various waiters, fishermen and vineyard-keepers of the village of Aghia Triadha. Lastly, I would like to record my thanks here to Professor Kakridís, Kimon Friar, George Sabbides, Mrs. Chatzidakis of the Benaki Museum, Theodora Koumvakali, Alexander Segkopoulos, Evro Layton, Dr. and Mrs. Atlas, the Yiannakoses, Katherine Kakouri, Michael Antonakis, and Jeff Amory, all of whom in one way or another made my stay in Greece more enjoyable than it otherwise would have been. —P.A.B.

Aghia Triadha, Macedonia August 28, 1964

AUTHOR'S INTRODUCTION

My *Report to Greco* is not an autobiography. My personal life has some value, extremely relative, for myself and no one else. The sole value I acknowledge in it was its effort to mount from one step to the next and reach the highest point to which its strength and doggedness could bring it: the summit I arbitrarily named the Cretan Glance.

Therefore, reader, in these pages you will find the red track made by drops of my blood, the track which marks my journey among men, passions, and ideas. Every man worthy of being called a son of man bears his cross and mounts his Golgotha. Many, indeed most, reach the first or second step, collapse pantingly in the middle of the journey, and do not attain the summit of Golgotha, in other words the summit of their duty: to be crucified, resurrected, and to save their souls. Afraid of crucifixion, they grow fainthearted; they do not know that the cross is the only path to resurrection. There is no other path.

The decisive steps in my ascent were four, and each bears a sacred name: Christ, Buddha, Lenin, Odysseus. This bloody journey from each of these great souls to the next is what I shall struggle to mark out in this Itinerary, now that the sun has begun to set—the journey of a man with his heart in his mouth, ascending the rough, unaccommodating mountain of his destiny. My entire soul is a cry, and all my work the commentary on that cry.

During my entire life one word always tormented and scourged me, the word *ascent*. Here, mixing truth with fancy, I should like to represent this ascent, together with the red footprints I left as I mounted. I am anxious to finish quickly, before I don the "black helmet" and return to dust, because this bloody track will be the only trace left by my passage on earth. Whatever I wrote or did was written or performed upon water, and has perished.

I call upon my memory to remember, I assemble my life from the air, place myself soldier-like before the general, and make my Report to Greco. For Greco is kneaded from the same Cretan soil as I, and is able to understand me better than all the strivers of past or present. Did he not leave the same red track upon the stones?

THREE KINDS OF SOULS, THREE PRAYERS:

1] I AM A BOW IN YOUR HANDS, LORD. DRAW ME, LEST I ROT.

2] DO NOT OVERDRAW ME, LORD. I SHALL BREAK.

3] OVERDRAW ME, LORD, AND WHO CARES IF I BREAK!

PROLOGUE

I COLLECT MY TOOLS: sight, smell, touch, taste, hearing, intellect. Night has fallen, the day's work is done. I return like a mole to my home, the ground. Not because I am tired and cannot work. I am not tired. But the sun has set.

The sun has set, the hills are dim. The mountain ranges of my mind still retain a little light at their summits, but the sacred night is bearing down; it is rising from the earth, descending from the heavens. The light has vowed not to surrender, but it knows there is no salvation. It will not surrender, but it will expire.

I cast a final glance around me. To whom should I say farewell? To what should I say farewell? Mountains, the sea, the grape-laden trellis over my balcony? Virtue, sin? Refreshing water? . . . Futile, futile! All these will descend with me to the grave.

To whom should I confide my joys and sorrows—youth's quixotic, mystic yearnings, the harsh clash later with God and men, and finally the savage pride of old age, which burns but refuses until the death to turn to ashes? To whom should I relate how many times I slipped and fell as I clambered on all fours up God's rough, unaccommodating ascent, how many times I rose, covered with blood, and began once more to ascend? Where can I find an unyielding soul of myriad wounds like my own, a soul to hear my confession?

Compassionately, tranquilly, I squeeze a clod of Cretan soil in my palm. I have kept this soil with me always, during all my wanderings, pressing it in my palm at times of great anguish and receiving strength, great strength, as though from pressing the hand of a dearly loved friend. But now that the sun has set and the day's work is done, what can I do with strength? I need it no longer. I hold this Cretan soil and squeeze it with ineffable joy, tenderness, and gratitude, as though in my hand I were squeezing the breast of a woman I loved and bidding it farewell. This soil I was everlastingly; this soil I shall be everlastingly. O fierce clay of Crete, the moment when you were twirled and fashioned into a man of struggle has slipped by as though in a single flash.

What struggle was in that handful of clay, what anguish, what pursuit of the invisible man-eating beast, what dangerous forces both celestial and satanic! It was kneaded with blood, sweat, and tears; it became mud, became a man, and began the ascent to reach— To reach what? It clambered pantingly up God's dark bulk, extended its arms and groped, groped in an effort to find His face.

And when in these very last years this man sensed in his desperation that the dark bulk did not have a face, what new struggle, all impudence and terror, he underwent to hew this unwrought summit and give it a face—his own!

But now the day's work is done; I collect my tools. Let other clods of soil come to continue the struggle. We mortals are the immortals' work battalion. Our blood is red coral, and we build an island over the abyss.

God is being built. I too have applied my tiny red pebble, a drop of blood, to give Him solidity lest He perish—so that He might give me solidity lest I perish. I have done my duty.

Farewell!

Extending my hand, I grasp earth's latch to open the door and leave, but I hesitate on the luminous threshold just a little while longer. My eyes, my ears, my bowels find it difficult, terribly difficult, to tear themselves away from the world's stones and grass. A man can tell himself he is satisfied and peaceful; he can say he has no more wants, that he has fulfilled his duty and is ready to leave. But the heart resists. Clutching the stones and grass, it implores, "Stay a little!"

I fight to console my heart, to reconcile it to declaring the Yes freely. We must leave the earth not like scourged, tearful slaves, but like kings who rise from table with no further wants, after having eaten and drunk to the full. The heart, however, still beats inside the chest and resists, crying, "Stay a little!"

Staying, I throw a final glance at the light; it too is resisting and wrestling, just like man's heart. Clouds have covered the sky, a warm drizzle falls upon my lips, the earth is redolent. A sweet, seductive voice rises from the soil: "Come . . . come . . . come . . ."

The drizzle has thickened. The first night bird sighs; its pain, in the wetted air, tumbles down ever so sweetly from the benighted foliage. Peace, great sweetness. No one in the house . . . Outside, the thirsty meadows were drinking the first autumn rains with gratitude and mute well-being. The earth, like an infant, had lifted itself up toward the sky in order to suckle.

I closed my eyes and fell asleep, holding the clod of Cretan soil, as always, in my palm. I fell asleep and had a dream. It seemed that day was breaking. The morning star hovered above me, and I, certain it was about to fall upon my head, trembled and ran, ran all alone through the arid, desolate mountains. Far in the east the sun appeared. It was not the sun, it was a bronze roasting tray filled with burning coals. The air began to seethe. From time to time an ash-gray partridge darted out from a ledge, beat its wings, and cackled, mocking me with guffaws. A crow, the moment it saw me, flew up from a declivity on the mountain. It had doubtlessly been awaiting my appearance, and it followed behind me, bursting with laughter. Bending down angrily, I picked up a stone to hurl at it. But the crow had changed body, had become a little old man who was smiling at me.

Terror-stricken, I began to run again. The mountains whirled and I whirled with them, the circles continually contracting. Dizziness overcame me. The mountains pranced around me, and suddenly I felt that they were not mountains but the fossil remains of an antediluvian cerebrum, and that high above me, on my right, an immense cross was embedded in a boulder, with a monstrous bronze serpent crucified upon it.

A lightning flash tore across my mind, illuminating the mountains around me. I saw. I had entered the sinuous, terrifying ravine which the Hebrews, with Jehovah in the lead, had taken thousands of years earlier in their flight from the rich, prosperous land of Pharaoh. This ravine constituted the fiery smithy where the race of Israel, hungering, thirsting, blaspheming, was hammered out.

I was possessed by fear, fear and great joy. Leaning against a boulder so that my mind's whirling might subside, I closed my eyes. All at once everything around me vanished, and a Greek coast line stretched before me: dark indigo-blue sea, red crags, and between the crags the squat ingress to a pitch-dark cave. A hand bounded out of the air and wedged a lighted torch into my fist. I understood the command. Crossing myself, I slipped into the cave.

I wandered and wandered, sloshing through frozen black water. Blue stalactites hung damply above my head; huge stone phalli rose from the ground, flashing and laughing in the torch's glare. This cave had been the scabbard of a large river which, changing course over the centuries, had abandoned it and left it empty.

The bronze serpent hissed angrily. Opening my eyes, I saw the mountains, ravine, and cliffs again. My dizziness had abated. Everything drew to a standstill and filled with light. I understood: Jehovah, in the same way, had tunneled out a passage in the blazing ranges surrounding me. I had entered God's terrifying scabbard and was following—stepping in—His tracks.

"This is the road," I cried in my dream, "this is man's road. The only road there is!"

And as these audacious words flew from my lips, a whirlwind wrapped me round, fierce wings lifted me, and I suddenly found myself at the summit of God-trodden Sinai. The air smelled of brimstone, and my lips tingled as though pricked by numberless invisible sparks. I raised my eyelids. Never had my eyes, never my entrails, enjoyed a sight so cruelly inhuman and so completely in harmony with my heart—waterless, treeless, without a human being, without hope. Here the soul of a proud or despairing man could find ultimate bliss.

I glanced at the boulder on which I was standing. Two deep cavities were gouged out of the granite; they must have been the footprints of the horned prophet who waited for the famished Lion to appear. Had He not commanded the prophet to wait here on Sinai's peak? He had waited.

I waited too. Leaning over the precipice, I listened intently. Suddenly I heard the muffled thunder of footsteps far, very far, in the distance. Someone was approaching; the mountains shook. My nostrils began to quiver. The air all about smelled like the head goat that leads the flock. "He is coming, He is coming," I murmured, tightly girding my loins. I was making myself ready to fight.

Oh, how I had yearned for that moment when I would confront the ravenous beast of the celestial jungle—confront Him face to face, without the brazen visible world intervening and leading me astray! When I would confront the Invisible, the Insatiable, the simple-hearted Father who devours His children and whose lips, beard, and nails drip with blood.

I would speak to Him boldly, tell him of man's suffering and the suffering of bird, tree, and rock. We were all resolute in our desire not to die. In my hand I held a petition signed by all the trees, birds, beasts, and humans: "Father, we do not want you to eat us!" I would give Him this petition, I would not be afraid.

I talked and implored in this way, girding my loins and trembling.

And while I waited, the stones seemed to shift. I heard great breaths.

"Behold Him!" I murmured. "He has come!"

I turned with a shudder. But it was not Jehovah. It was not Jehovah, it was you, grandfather, from the beloved soil of Crete. You stood before me, a stern nobleman, with your small snow-white goatee, dry compressed lips, your ecstatic glance so filled with flames and wings. And roots of thyme were tangled in your hair.

You looked at me, and as you looked at me I felt that this world was a cloud charged with thunderbolts and wind, man's soul a cloud charged with thunderbolts and wind, that God puffs above them, and that salvation does not exist.

Lifting my eyes, I glanced at you. I was about to ask, Grandfather, is it true that salvation does not exist? But my tongue had stuck to my throat. I was about to go near you, but my knees gave way beneath me.

At that point you held out your hand as if I were drowning and you wished to save me.

I clutched it avidly. It was spattered with multicolored paints. You seemed to be painting still. The hand was burning. I gained strength and momentum by touching it, and was able to speak.

"Give me a command, beloved grandfather."

Smiling, you placed your hand upon my head. It was not a

hand, it was multicolored fire. The flame suffused my mind to the very roots.

"Reach what you can, my child."

Your voice was grave and dark, as though issuing from the deep larynx of the earth.

It reached the roots of my mind, but my heart remained unshaken.

"Grandfather," I called more loudly now, "give me a more difficult, more Cretan command."

Hardly had I finished speaking when, all at once, a hissing flame cleaved the air. The indomitable ancestor with the thyme roots tangled in his locks vanished from my sight; a cry was left on Sinai's peak, an upright cry full of command, and the air trembled:

"Reach what you cannot!"

I awoke with a terrified start. Day had already begun. I rose, went to the French doors, and issued onto the balcony with the grape-laden trellis. The rain had abated now, the stones were gleaming and laughing, the leaves on the trees were weighted with tears.

"Reach what you cannot!"

It was your voice. No one else in the world could have uttered such a masculine command—only you, insatiable grandfather! Are you not the desperate, unyielding general of my militant race? Are we not the wounded and starving, the numskulls and pigheads who left affluence and certainty behind us in order to assault the frontiers, following your lead, and smash them?

God is the most resplendent face of despair, the most resplendent face of hope. You are pushing me beyond hope and despair, grandfather, beyond the age-old frontiers. Where? I gaze around me, I gaze inside me. Virtue has gone mad, geometry and matter have gone mad. The law-giving mind must come again to establish a new order, new laws. The world must become a richer harmony.

This is what you want; this is where you are pushing me, where you have always pushed me. I heard your command day and night. I fought as well as I could to reach what I could not. This I had set as my duty. Whether I succeeded or not is up to you to tell me. I stand erect before you, and wait.

General, the battle draws to a close and I make my report. This is where and how I fought. I fell wounded, lost heart, but did not desert. Though my teeth clattered from fear, I bound my forehead tightly with a red handkerchief to hide the blood, and ran to the assault.

Before you I shall pluck out the precious feathers of my jackdaw soul, one by one, until it remains a tiny clod of earth kneaded with blood, sweat, and tears. I shall relate my struggle to you—in order to unburden myself. I shall cast off virtue, shame, and truth—in order to unburden myself. My soul resembles your creation "Toledo in the Storm"; girded by yellow thunderbolts and oppressive black clouds, fighting a desperate, unbending battle against both light and darkness. You will see my soul, will weigh it between your lanceolate eyebrows, and will judge. Do you remember the grave Cretan saying, "Return where you have failed, leave where you have succeeded"? If I failed, I shall return to the assault though but a single hour of life remains to me. If I succeeded, I shall open the earth so that I may come and recline at your side.

Listen, therefore, to my report, general, and judge. Listen to my life, grandfather, and if I fought with you, if I fell wounded and allowed no one to learn of my suffering, if I never turned my back to the enemy:

Give me your blessing!

1

ANCESTORS

I LOOK DOWN into myself and shudder. On my father's side my ancestors were bloodthirsty pirates on water, warrior chieftains on land, fearing neither God nor man; on my mother's, drab, goodly peasants who bowed trustfully over the soil the entire day, sowed, waited with confidence for rain and sun, reaped, and in the evening seated themselves on the stone bench in front of their homes, folded their arms, and placed their hopes in God.

Fire and soil. How could I harmonize these two militant ancestors inside me?

I felt this was my duty, my sole duty: to reconcile the irreconcilables, to draw the thick ancestral darkness out of my loins and transform it, to the best of my ability, into light.

Is not God's method the same? Do not we have a duty to apply this method, following in His footsteps? Our lifetime is a brief flash, but sufficient.

Without knowing it, the entire universe follows this method. Every living thing is a workshop where God, in hiding, processes and transubstantiates clay. This is why trees flower and fruit, why animals multiply, why the monkey managed to exceed its destiny and stand upright on its two feet. Now, for the first time since the world was made, man has been enabled to enter God's workshop and labor with Him. The more flesh he transubstantiates into love, valor, and freedom, the more truly he becomes Son of God.

It is an oppressive, insatiable duty. I fought throughout my life and am fighting still, but a sediment of darkness continues to remain in my heart, and the struggle continually recommences. The age-old paternal ancestors are thrust deep within me; they keep fluctuating, and it is very difficult for me to discern their faces in the fathomless darkness. The more I proceed in my search for the first terrifying ancestor inside me, piercing through the heaped up layers of my soul—individual, nationality, human species—the more I am overcome by sacred horror. At first the faces seem like a brother's or father's; then, as I proceed to the roots, out of my loins bounds a hairy, heavy-jawed ancestor who hungers, thirsts, bellows, and whose eyes are filled with blood. This ancestor is the bulky, unwrought beast given me to transubstantiate into man—and to raise even higher than man if I can manage in the time allotted me. What a fearful ascent from monkey to man, from man to God!

One night I was walking on a high snow-covered mountain with a friend. We had lost our way and been overtaken by darkness. Not a cloud in the sky. The moon hung mute and fully round above us; the snow glistened, pale blue, all the way from the saddle of the mountain, where we found ourselves, down to the plain below. The silence was congealed and disquieting—unbearable. For thousands of eons the moon-washed nights must have been similar, before God likewise found such silence unbearable and took up clay to fashion man.

I preceded my friend by a few paces, my mind enveloped in a strange dizziness. I stumbled like a drunkard as I advanced; it seemed to me that I was walking on the moon, or before man's coming in some age-old uninhabited—but intensely familiar—land. Suddenly, at a turn in the terrain, I spied some tiny lights shining palely in the far distance, near the bottom of a gorge. It must have been a small village whose inhabitants were still awake. At that point an astonishing thing happened to me. I still shudder when I recall it. Halting, I shook my clenched fist at the village and shouted in a furor, "I shall slaughter you all!"

A raucous voice not my own! My entire body began to tremble with fright as soon as I heard this voice. My friend ran up to me and anxiously grasped my arm.

"What's the matter with you?" he asked. "Who are you going to slaughter?"

My knees had given way; suddenly I felt inexpressible fatigue. But seeing my friend in front of me, I came around.

"It wasn't me, it wasn't me," I whispered. "It was someone else."

It was someone else. Who? Never had my vitals opened so deeply and revealingly. From that night onward I was at last certain of what I had divined for years: inside us there is layer upon layer of darkness—raucous voices, hairy hungering beasts. Does nothing die, then? Can nothing die in this world? The primordial hunger, thirst, and tribulation, all the nights and moons before the coming of man, will continue to live and hunger with us, thirst and be tormented with us—as long as we live. I was terror-stricken to hear the fearful burden I carry in my entrails begin to bellow. Would I never be saved? Would my vitals never be cleansed?

Now and then, sporadically, a sweet voice sounds in the very center of my heart: "Have no fears. I shall make laws and establish order. I am God. Have faith." But all at once comes a heavy growl from my loins, and the sweet voice is silenced: "Stop your boasting! I shall undo your laws, ruin your order, and obliterate you. I am chaos!"

They say that the sun sometimes halts in its course in order to hear a young girl sing. Would it were true! If only necessity, spellbound by a songstress down below on earth, could change its course! If only we, by weeping, laughing, and singing, could create a law able to establish order over chaos! If only the sweet voice within us could cover over the growl!

When I am in my cups, or angry, or when I touch the woman I love, or when injustice is strangling me and I raise my hand in rebellion against God, the devil, or the representatives of God or the devil on earth, I hear these monsters bellowing within me and charging against the trap door in order to smash it, rise again into the light, and take up arms once more. I am the latest and most beloved grandchild, after all; aside from me they have no hope or refuge. Whatever remains for them to avenge, enjoy, or suffer, only through me can they do this. If I perish, they perish with me. When I topple into the grave, an army of hairy monsters and aggrieved men will topple into the grave with me. Perhaps this is why they torment me so and are in such a hurry, perhaps this is why my youth was so impatient, unsubmissive, and wretched.

They killed and were killed without respecting the soul, either their own or others'. They loved life and scorned death with the same extravagant disdain. They ate like ogres, drank like calves, did not soil themselves with women when it was a question of going to war. Their torsos were bare in summer, wrapped in sheepskins in the winter. Summer and winter they smelled like animals in rut.

I feel my great-grandfather still fully alive in my blood; of all of them, he, I believe, lives most vibrantly in my veins. His head was shaven above the forehead, with a long braid behind. He kept company with Algerian pirates and flailed the high seas. They established their hideout on the deserted islands of Grabousa at the western tip of Crete. From there they packed on the black sail and rammed the vessels that passed. Some were sailing toward Mecca with a cargo of Moslem pilgrims, others toward the Holy Sepulcher with a cargo of Christians on their way to become hadjis. Whooping, the pirates threw their grapnels and leaped onto the deck, cleavers in hand. Showing no favor either to Christ or Mohammed, they slaughtered the old men, took the young ones as slaves, keeled over the women, and burrowed into Grabousa again, their mustaches full of blood and female exhalations. At other times they swooped down upon the rich spice-laden caiques which appeared from the east. The old men still remembered hearing it said that the entire island of Crete had once smelled of cinnamon and nutmeg because my ancestor, the man with the braid, had plundered a vessel loaded with spices. Not having any way to dispose of them, he had sent them to all the villages of Crete as gifts for his godsons and goddaughters.

I was deeply stirred when a centenarian Cretan informed me of this incident not so many years ago, for without knowing why, I had always liked to keep a tube of cinnamon and several nutmeg seeds with me on my travels, and also in front of me on my writing desk.

Whenever, by listening to the hidden voices within me, I succeeded in following the blood instead of the mind (which quickly pants and halts), I arrived with mystic certitude at my remotest ancestral beginnings. Afterwards, in time, this mysterious certitude was strengthened by palpable signs from everyday life. Although I thought these signs accidental at first and did not pay attention, I was finally able, by blending the voice of the visible world and my hidden inner voices, to penetrate the primordial darkness beneath the mind, lift up the trap door, and see.

And from the moment I saw, my soul began to solidify. It no longer flowed with constant fluctuation like water; a face began to thicken and congeal now around a luminous core, the face of my soul. Instead of proceeding first to the left, then to the right, along ever-changing roads in order to find what beast I was descended from, I proceeded with assurance, because I knew my true face and my sole duty: to work this face with as much patience, love, and skill as I could manage. To "work" it? What did that mean? It meant to turn it into flame, and if I had time before death came, to turn this flame into light, so that Charon would find nothing of me to take. For this was my greatest ambition: to leave nothing for death to take—nothing but a few bones.

Helping me more than anything else to reach this certainty was the soil where my paternal ancestors were born and raised. My father's stock derived from a village called Barbári, two hours from Megalo Kastro. When the Byzantine emperor Nicephorus Phocas retook Crete from the Arabs in the tenth century, he penned those Arabs who survived the slaughter in several villages, and these villages were called Barbári. It was in such a village that my paternal ancestors put down their roots. All of them have Arab traits. They are proud, obstinate, tight-lipped, abstemious, anti-social. Their anger or love they store for years within their breasts, never saying a word, and then suddenly the devil straddles them and they explode in a frenzy. The supreme benefit for them is not life but passion. They are neither good nor accommodating; their presence is insufferably oppressive, not because of others, but because of themselves. An inner demon strangles them. Suffocating, they become pirates or stab their arms in a drunken stupor in order to shed blood and find relief. Or else they kill the woman they love, lest they become her slave. Or like me, their marrowless grandson, they toil to alter the dark weight and turn it into spirit. What does this mean: to turn my barbarous ancestors into spirit? It means to obliterate them by subjecting them to the supreme ordeal.

Still other voices have secretly marked the road to my ancestors. My heart bounds with joy whenever I encounter a date tree. You would think it were returning to its homeland, to the arid dust-filled Bedouin village whose one precious ornament is the date tree. And once when I entered the Arabian Desert on camelback and gazed out over the waves of boundless, hopeless sands extending before me—yellow and rose, mauve toward evening, without a trace of a human being—I was carried away by a queer intoxication. My heart cried out like a she-hawk returning to a nest it had abandoned years, thousands of years, before.

Then there was this: Once I lived all alone in an isolated hut near a Greek village, "shepherding winds" as a Byzantine ascetic used to say; in other words, writing poetry. This little cottage was buried among olive trees and pines, and the boundless, deep blue Aegean was visible between the branches far below me. No one passed except Floros, a simple grease-stained shepherd with a blond beard. He came with his sheep every morning, brought me a bottle of milk, eight boiled eggs, and some bread, then left. Seeing me bent over my paper and writing, he always shook his head. "Saints preserve us! What do you want with all that letter-writing, boss? Don't you ever get tired?" This was followed by peals of laughter. One day he passed in a great hurry, so sullen and enraged that he did not even say good morning. "What's wrong, Floros?" I called to him. He brandished his huge fist. "Damn it, boss, leave me alone! I couldn't sleep a wink last night. But didn't you hear it yourself? Where are your ears? Didn't you hear that shepherd on the mountain over there, devil take him! He forgot to tune the bells of his flock! How could I sleep! . . . . I'm going!"

"Where to, Floros?"

"To tune them, of course. So I can calm down."

As I was saying, one day at dinnertime when I went to the cupboard to get the saltcellar for my eggs, a little salt spilled on the dirt floor. My heart stood still. Lying down hastily, I began to pick the salt up grain by grain; whereupon I suddenly realized what I was doing and grew frightened. Why all this chagrin over a little salt fallen on the ground? What value did it have? None.

Afterwards, on the sands, I ferreted out still other markers which would enable me to reach my ancestors if I followed them. These were fire and water.

I always jump up with concern when I spy a fire burning uselessly, for I do not want to see it perish; I always race to turn off a tap when I see it running without a jug to be filled or a person to drink or a garden to be watered.

I experienced all these strange things, but never combined them with clarity in my mind in order to discover their mystic unity. My heart could not bear to see water, fire, or salt being squandered; I exulted each time I saw a date tree; when I entered the desert I did not want to leave—but my mind proceeded no further. This lasted many years. In the dusky workshop within me, however, the concern apparently kept working away in hiding. All those unexplained happenings were being secretly joined inside me. As they came to stand one next to the other, they began little by little to take on meaning, and one day, abruptly, as I was ambling idly in a large city without thinking of this meaning at all, I found it. Salt, fire, and water were the three all-precious possessions of the desert! Surely, therefore, it must have been some ancestor inside me—a Bedouin—who jumped to his feet and dashed to the rescue when he saw salt, fire, and water perishing.

A gentle rain was falling on that day in the large city. I remember seeing a little girl who had found shelter beneath the canopy of a doorway. She was selling small bouquets of drenched violets. I stopped and looked at her, but my mind—far away, eased now, extremely happy—was vagabonding in the desert.

All this may be fancy and autosuggestion, a romantic yearning for the exotic and remote; all the strange events I have enumerated may not be strange at all, or may not have the meaning I give them. Yes, this is possible. Nevertheless, the influence of this organized, cultivated hoax, of this delusion (if it is a delusion) that twin currents of blood, Greek from my mother and Arab from my father, run in my veins, has been positive and fruitful, giving me strength, joy, and wealth. My struggle to make a synthesis of these two antagonistic impulses has lent purpose and unity to my life. The moment the indeterminate presentiment inside me became certainty, the visible world round about fell into order and my inner and outer lives, finding the double ancestral root, made peace with each other. Thus, many years later, the secret hatred I felt for my father was able, after his death, to turn to love.

2

THE FATHER

MY FATHER spoke only rarely, never laughed, never engaged in brawls. He simply grated his teeth or clenched his fist at certain times, and if he happened to be holding a hard-shelled almond, rubbed it between his fingers and reduced it to dust. Once when he saw an aga place a packsaddle on a Christian and load him down like a donkey, so completely did his anger overcome him that he charged toward the Turk. He wanted to hurl an insult at him, but his lips had become contorted. Unable to utter a human word, he began to whinny like a horse. I was still a child. I stood there and watched, trembling with fright. And one midday as he was passing through a narrow lane on his way home for dinner, he heard women shrieking and doors being slammed. A huge drunken Turk with drawn yataghan was pursuing Christians. He rushed upon my father the moment he saw him. The heat was torrid, and my father, tired from work, felt in no mood for a brawl. It occurred to him momentarily to turn into another lane and flee—no one was looking. But this would have been shameful. Untying the apron he had on, he wrapped it around his fist, and just as the colossal Turk began to raise the yataghan above his head, he gave him a punch in the belly and sprawled him out on the ground. Stooping, he wrenched the yataghan out of the other's grip and strode homeward. My mother brought him a clean shirt to put on—he was drenched in sweat—and I (I must have been about three years old) sat on the couch and gazed at him. His chest was covered with hair and steaming. As soon as he had changed and cooled off, he threw the yataghan down on the couch next to me. Then he turned to his wife.

"When your son grows up and goes to school," he said, "give him this as a pencil sharpener."

I cannot recall ever hearing a tender word from him—except

once when we were on Naxos during the revolution. I was attending the French school run by Catholic priests and had won a good many examination prizes—large books with gilded bindings. Since I could not lift them all by myself, my father took half. He did not speak the entire way home; he was trying to conceal the pleasure he felt at not being humiliated by his son. Only after we entered the house did he open his mouth.

"You did not disgrace Crete," he said with something like tenderness, not looking at me.

But he felt angry with himself immediately; this display of emotion was a self-betrayal. He remained sullen for the rest of the evening and avoided my eyes.

He was forbidding and insufferable. When relatives or neighbors who happened to be visiting the house began to laugh and exchange small talk, if the door suddenly opened and he came in, the conversation and laughter always ceased and a heavy shadow overwhelmed the room. He would say hello halfheartedly, seat himself in his customary place in the corner of the sofa next to the courtyard window, lower his eyes, open his tobacco pouch, and roll a cigarette, without saying a word. The guests would clear their throats dryly, cast secret, uneasy glances at one another, and after a discreet interval, rise and proceed on tiptoe to the door.

He hated priests. Whenever he met one on the street, he crossed himself to exorcise the unfortunate encounter, and if the frightened priest greeted him with a "Good day, Captain Michael," he replied, "Give me your curse!" He never attended Divine Liturgy—to avoid seeing priests. But every Sunday when the service was over and everyone had left, he entered the church and lighted a candle before the wonder-working icon of Saint Minas. He worshiped Saint Minas above all Christs and Virgin Marys, because Saint Minas was the captain of Megalo Kastro.

His heart was heavy, unliftable. Why? He was healthy, his affairs were going well, he had no complaints regarding either his wife or children. People respected him. Some, the most inferior, rose and bowed when he passed, placed their palms over their breasts, and addressed him as Captain Michael. On Easter Day the Metropolitan invited him to the episcopal palace after the Resurrection, along with the city's notables, and offered him coffee and a paschal cake with a red egg. On Saint Minas's day, the eleventh of November, he stood in front of his house and said a prayer when the procession passed.

But his heart never lightened. One day Captain Elias from Messará dared to ask him, "Why is there never a laugh on your lips, Captain Michael?" "Why is the crow black, Captain Elias?" my father replied, spitting out the cigarette butt he was chewing. Another day I heard him say to the verger of Saint Minas's, "You should look at my father, not at me, at my father. He was a real ogre. What am I next to him? A jellyfish!" Though extremely old and nearly blind, my grandfather had taken up arms again in the Revolution of 1878. He went to the mountains to fight, but the Turks surrounded him, caught him by throwing lassos, and slaughtered him outside the Monastery of Savathianá. The monks kept his skull in the sanctuary. One day I looked through the tiny window and saw it—polished, anointed with sanctified oil from the watch lamp, deeply incised by sword blows.

"What was my grandfather like?" I asked my mother.

"Like your father. Darker."

"What was his job?"

"Fighting."

"And what did he do in peacetime?"

"He smoked a long chibouk and gazed at the mountains."

Being pious when I was young, I asked still another question: "Did he go to church?"

"No. But on the first of every month he brought a priest home with him and had him pray that Crete would take up arms again. Your grandfather fretted, naturally, when he had nothing to do. Once when he was arming himself again I asked him, 'Aren't you afraid to die, Father?' But he neither answered nor even turned to look at me."

When I grew older, I wanted to ask my mother: Did he ever love a woman? I was ashamed to, however, and never found out. But he surely must have loved many women, because when he was killed and the family opened his coffer, a cushion was found there, stuffed with black and brown tresses.

3

THE MOTHER

My mother was a saintly woman. How was she able to feel the lion's heavy inhalations and suspirations at her side for fifty years without suffering a broken heart? She had the patience, endurance, and sweetness of the earth itself. All my forebears on my mother's side were peasants—bent over the soil, glued to the soil, their hands, feet, and minds filled with soil. They loved the land and placed all their hopes in it; over the generations they and it had become one. In time of drought they grew sickly black from thirst along with it. When the first autumn rains began to rage, their bones creaked and swelled like reeds. And when they ploughed deep furrorws into its womb with the share, in their breasts and thighs they re-experienced the first night they slept with their wives.

Twice a year, at Easter and Christmas, my grandfather set out from his distant village and came to Megalo Kastro in order to see his daughter and grandchildren. Always calculating carefully, he came and knocked on the door at an hour when he knew for sure that his wild beast of a son-in-law would not be at home. He was a juicy, vigorous old man, with unbarbered white hair, laughing blue eyes, and great heavy hands covered with calluses—my skin was flayed when he reached out to caress me. He always wore black boots, his Sunday foufoúla, which was deep indigo in color, and a white kerchief with blue spots. And in his hand he always held the same gift: a suckling pig roasted in the oven and wrapped in lemon leaves. When he laughingly uncovered it, the entire house filled with fragrance. So completely has my grandfather blended and become one with the roast pig and the lemon leaves, that ever since those days I have never been able to smell roast pork or step into a lemon orchard without having him rise into my mind, gay and undying, the roast suckling pig in his hands. And I am glad, because although no one else in the world remembers him now, he will live inside me as long as I live. We shall die together. This grandfather was the first to make me wish not to die—so that the dead within me should not die. Since then, many departed dear ones have sunk, not into the grave, but into my memory, and I know now that as long as I live they shall live too.

As I recall him, my heart is fortified with the realization that it can conquer death. Never in my life have I met a man whose face was circuited by such a kindly, tranquil resplendence, as though from a watch lamp. I cried out the first time I saw him enter the house. Dressed as he was in his wide vrakes and red cummerbund, with his luminous moonface and merry manner, he seemed to me like a water sprite, or like an earth spirit who at that very moment had emerged from the orchards smelling of wet grass.

Removing a leather tobacco pouch from beneath his shirt, he rolled a cigarette, reached for the flint and punk, lighted the cigarette, and smoked, gazing contentedly at his daughter, his grandchildren, and the house. At rare intervals he opened his mouth and spoke about his mare that had dropped a colt, about rain and hail, about the overprolific rabbits who were ruining his vegetable garden. I, perched on his knees, threw an arm around his neck and listened. An unknown world unfurled in my mind—fields, rainfalls, rabbits—and I too became a rabbit, slipped out stealthily to my grandfather's yard, and devoured his cabbage.

My mother would ask about this one and that one in the village—how were they getting along, were they still alive?—and grandfather sometimes replied that they were alive, having children, flourishing; sometimes that they had died—another one gone, long life to you! He spoke about death just as he spoke about birth—calmly, in the same voice, just as he spoke about the vegetables and rabbits. "He's gone too, Daughter," he would say. "We buried him. And we gave him an orange to hold in his hand for Charon, also some messages for our relatives in Hades. Everything was done according to order, praised be God." Then he puffed on his cigarette, blew smoke out through his nostrils, and smiled.

His wife was among the departed; she had died many years before. Every time my grandfather came to our house, he mentioned her and his eyes filled with tears. He loved her more than his fields, more than his mare. And he also respected her. Though poor when he married, he had persevered. "Poverty and nakedness are nothing, provided you have a good wife," he used to say. In those days it was the long-established custom in Cretan villages for the wife to have warm water ready for the husband when he returned from the fields in the evening, and for her to bend down and wash his feet. One evening my grandfather returned from work completely exhausted. He sat down in the yard, and his wife came to him with a basin of warm water, knelt in front of him, and reached out in order to wash his dusty feet. Looking at her with compassion, my grandfather saw her hands that had been corroded by the daily household chores, her hair that had begun to turn gray. She's old now, poor thing, he thought to himself; her hair has turned gray in my hands. Feeling sorry for her, he lifted his foot and kicked away the basin of water, upsetting it. "Starting today, Wife," he said, "you're not going to wash my feet any more. After all, you're not my slave, you're my wife and 'lady.' "

One day I heard him say, "She never failed me in anything . . . except once. May God have mercy on her soul."

Sighing, he fell silent. But after a moment: "Every evening, naturally, she stood in the doorway and waited for me to return from the fields. She used to run and relieve me by taking the tools from my shoulder; then we entered the house together. But one evening she forgot. She didn't run to me, and it broke my heart."

He crossed himself.

"God is great," he whispered. "I place my hopes in Him. He will forgive her."

His eyes shiny again, he looked at my mother and smiled.

On another occasion I asked him, "Grandfather, don't you hate to kill the little pigs, don't you feel sorry when we eat them?"

"I do, my boy, God knows I do," he answered, bursting into laughter, "but they're delicious, the little rascals!"

Every time I recall this rosy-cheeked old peasant, my faith in the soil and in man's labor upon the soil increases. He was one of the pillars who support the world upon their shoulders and keep it from falling.

My father was the only one who did not want him. He felt displeased when he entered his house and talked to his son, as though afraid my blood might be polluted. And when the feast was laid out at Christmas and Easter, he did not help himself to any of the roast suckling pig. Nauseated by its odor, he left the table as quickly as possible and began to smoke in order to dispel the stench. He never said anything, except once when he knitted his brows after grandfather had left, and murmured scornfully, "Pfff, blue eyes!"

I learned afterwards that my father despised blue eyes more than anything else in the world. "The devil has blue eyes and red hair," he used to say.

What peace when my father was not at home! How happily and quickly time passed in the little garden inside our walled courtyard. The vine arbor over the well, the tall fragrant acacia in the corner, the pots of basil, marigolds, and Arabian jasmine around the edges . . . My mother sat in front of the window knitting socks, cleaning vegetables, combing my little sister's hair, or helping her to toddle; and I, squatting on a stool, watched her. As I listened to the people pass by outside the closed door and inhaled the odor of jasmine and wet soil, the bones of my head creaked and opened wide in order to contain the world which was entering my body.

The hours I spent with my mother were full of mystery. We used to sit facing each other—she on a chair next to the window, I on my stool—and I felt my breast being filled to satisfaction amid the silence, as though the air between us were milk and I was nursing.

Above our heads rose the acacia; when it flowered, the courtyard filled with perfume. How very much I loved its sweet-smelling yellow blossoms! My mother put them in our coffers, our underwear, our sheets. My entire childhood smelled of acacia.

We talked, had many quiet conversations together. Sometimes my mother told about her father and the village where she was born; sometimes I recounted to her the saints' lives I had read, embellishing them in my imagination. The martyrs' ordeals were not enough for me. I added new ones of my own until my mother began to weep. Then, pitying her, I sat on her knees, stroked her hair and consoled her.

"They went to paradise, Mother. Don't be sad. Now they take walks beneath flowering trees and talk with angels, and they've forgotten all about their tortures. And every Sunday they put on clothes all of gold, and red caps with pompons, and go to visit God."

My mother used to wipe away her tears and look at me with a smile, as though to ask, Is it really true? And the canary in its cage used to hear us, stretch forth its throat, and chirp away with drunken contentment, as if it had descended from paradise, left the saints for a few moments, and come to earth in order to gladden men's hearts.

My mother, the acacia, and the canary have blended in my mind inseparably, immortally. I cannot smell an acacia or hear a canary without feeling my mother rise from her grave—from my vitals—and unite with this fragrance and the canary's song.

I had never seen my mother laugh; she simply smiled and regarded everyone with deep-set eyes filled with patience and kindness. She came and went in the house like a kindly sprite, anticipating our every need without noise or effort, as though her hands possessed some magical, beneficent power which exercised a benevolent rule over everyday needs. As I sat silently watching her, I reflected that she might be the Nereid mentioned in the fairy tales, and imagination set to work in my childhood mind: My father had glimpsed her dancing beneath the moon one night as he passed the river. He pounced, caught hold of her kerchief, and that was when he brought her home and made her his wife. Now my mother came and went all day long in the house, searching for the kerchief so that she could throw it over her hair, become a Nereid again, and depart. I used to watch her coming and going, opening the wardrobes and coffers, uncovering the jugs, stooping to look under the beds, and I trembled lest she chance to find her magic kerchief and become invisible. This fear lasted many years, deeply wounding my newborn soul. It remains within me even today, still more indescribably. It is with anguish that I observe all the people or ideas that I love, because I know they are searching for their kerchiefs in order to depart.

I remember only one occasion when my mother's eyes gleamed with a strange light and she laughed and enjoyed herself as in the days of her engagement, or when she was a free, unmarried girl. It was the first of May and we had gone to Phódhele, a village full of water and orange orchards, so that my father could sponsor a child in baptism. Whereupon, a violent downpour suddenly broke out.

The heavens turned to water and emptied onto the earth, which opened chucklingly and received the male waters deep into its breast. The village notables were gathered with their wives and daughters in a large room in the godchild's house. The rain and lightning entered through the windows, through the cracks in the door; the air smelled of oranges and soil. In and out came the handsels, the wine, the raki, the mezédhes. It began to grow dark, the lamps were lighted, the men grew merry, the women lifted their normally downcast eyes and began to cackle like partridges. Outside the house God was still roaring. The thunder increased, the village's narrow lanes had been transformed into rivers, the stones tumbled down them, laughing wildly. God had become a torrent; He was embracing, watering, fructifying the earth.

My father turned to my mother. It was the first time I ever saw him look at her with tenderness, the first time I heard sweetness in his voice.

"Sing Marghí," he said to her.

He was giving her permission to sing, giving it in front of all the other men. I became angry, though I don't know why. Rising all in a ferment, I started to run to my mother as though wishing to protect her, but my father touched my shoulder with his finger and made me sit down. My mother seemed unrecognizable; her face gleamed as if all the rain and lightning were embracing it. She threw back her head. I remember that her long raven-black hair suddenly became undone and fell over her shoulders, reaching to her hips. She began . . . What a voice that was: deep, sweet, with a shade of throatiness, full of passion. Turning her half-closed eyes upon my father, she sang a mantinadha which I shall never forget. I did not understand at the time why she uttered it, or for whom. Later, when I grew up, I understood. Looking at my father, her sweet voice filled with restrained passion, she sang:

I'm amazed the streets don't blossom when you stroll,
And you don't become an eagle with wings of gold.

I looked the other way to avoid seeing my father, to avoid seeing my mother. Going to the window, I pressed my forehead against the pane and watched the rain fall and eat away the soil.

The deluge lasted the entire day. The night had borne down

upon us; the world outside grew dark, heaven blended with earth, and the two turned to mud. More lamps were lighted. Everyone moved toward the walls. Tables and stools were moved aside to make room; youngsters and oldsters alike were going to dance. Installing himself on a high stool in the middle of the room, the rebecist grasped his bow as though it were a sword, mumbled a couplet beneath his mustache, and began to play. Feet tingled, bodies fluttered their wings, men and women looked at each other and jumped to their feet. The first to step out was a pale, slender woman, about forty years old, her lips tinted orange because she had rubbed them with walnut leaves, her jet-black hair anointed with laurel oil and glistening sleekly. I was frightened when I turned and saw her, because her eyes were circled by two somber blue rings, and the dark, dark pupils shone from deep within; no, did not shine, burned. I imagined for a moment that she glanced at me. I clutched my mother's apron, feeling that this woman wanted to seize my arm and take me away with her.

"Bravo, Sourmelína!" shouted a robust old man with a goatee. Jumping out in front of her, he removed his black kerchief, gave one corner to the woman, took the other himself, and the two of them—transported, their heads held high, their bodies as slender and straight as candles—gave themselves over to the dance.

The woman was wearing wooden clogs; she beat them against the floorboards, beat them down forcefully, and the whole house shook. Her white wimple came undone, revealing the gold florins decorating her neck. Her nostrils flared, sniffed the air; the masculine exhalations all around her were steaming. She bent her knees, pivoted, was about to fall against the man before her, but then all at once with a twist of her hips she vanished from in front of him. The elderly dance-lover neighed like a horse, grasped her in midair, held her tightly; but she escaped again. They played, they pursued each other, thunder and rain vanished, the world sank away, and nothing remained above the abyss except this woman, Sourmelína, who was dancing. Unable to remain on his stool any longer, the rebecist jumped to his feet. The bow went wild, gave up trying to stay in command, and began to follow Sourmelína's feet now, sighing and bellowing like a human being.

The old man's face had turned savage. Blushing deeply, he eyed the woman, his lips quivering. I felt that he was about to pounce on her and tear her to bits. The rebecist must have had the same foreboding, for his bow stopped abruptly. The dance came to a standstill; the two dance-lovers remained motionless, one foot in the air, the sweat gushing off them. The men ran to the old dancer, took him to one side, and massaged him with raki; the women surrounded Sourmelína to keep the men from seeing her. I worked my way in among them; I wasn't a man yet, and they did not stop me. Opening her bodice, they sprinkled orange-flower water over her throat, armpits, and temples. She had closed her eyes and was smiling.

It was then that the dance, Sourmelína, and fear—the dance, woman, and death—blended within me and became one. Forty years later, on the high terrace of the Hotel Orient in Tiflis, an Indian woman got up to dance. The stars shone above her. The roof was unlit; some dozen men stood around her, and you saw nothing but the tiny red lights from their cigarettes. Loaded with bracelets, jewels, earrings, and golden ankle bands, the woman danced slowly, with a mysterious fear, as though performing at the brink of the abyss, or of God, and playing with Him. She approached, retreated, provoked Him, while trembling from head to foot lest she fall. At times her body remained stationary while her arms wrapped and unwrapped themselves around each other like two snakes and coupled erotically in the air. The tiny red lights died out; nothing remained in the whole of the vast night except this dancing woman and the stars above her. Immobile, they danced too. We all held our breath. Suddenly I was terror-stricken. Was this a woman dancing at the brink of the abyss? No, it was our very souls flirting and playing with death.

4
THE SON

WHATEVER fell into my childhood mind was imprinted there with such depth and received by me with such avidity that even now in my old age I never grow tired of recalling and reliving it. With unerring accuracy I remember my very first acquaintance with the sea, with fire, with woman, and with the odors of the world.

The earliest memory of my life is this: Still unable to stand, I crept on all fours to the threshold and fearfully, longingly, extended my tender head into the open air of the courtyard. Until then I had looked through the windowpane but had seen nothing. Now I not only looked, I actually saw the world for the very first time. And what an astonishing sight that was! Our little courtyard-garden seemed without limits. There was buzzing from thousands of invisible bees, an intoxicating aroma, a warm sun as thick as honey. The air flashed as though armed with swords, and, between the swords, erect, angel-like insects with colorful, motionless wings advanced straight for me. I screamed from fright, my eyes filled with tears, and the world vanished.

On another day, I remember, a man with a thorny beard took me in his arms and brought me down to the harbor. As we approached, I heard a wild beast sighing and roaring as if wounded or uttering threats. Frightened, I jumped erect in the man's arms and shrieked like a bird; I wanted to go away. Suddenly—the bitter odor of carob beans, tar, and rotten citrons. My creaking vitals opened to receive it. I kept jumping and pitching about in the hairy arms that held me, until at a turn in the street—dark indigo, seething, all cries and smells (what a beast that was! what freshness! what a boundless sigh!)—the entire sea poured into me frothingly. My tender temples collapsed, and my head filled with laughter, salt, and fear.

Next I remember a woman, Anníka, a neighbor of ours, newly married, recently a mother, plump and fair, with long blond hair and huge eyes. That evening I was playing in the yard; I must have been about three years old. The little garden smelled of summer. The woman leaned over, placed me in her lap, hugged me. I, closing my eyes, fell against her exposed bosom and smelled her body: the warm, dense perfume, the acid scent of milk and sweat. The newly married body was steaming. I inhaled the vapor in an erotic torpor, hanging from her high bosom. Suddenly I felt overcome by dizziness and fainted. Blushing terribly, the frightened neighbor put me down, depositing me between two pots of basil. After that she never placed me on her lap again. She just looked at me very tenderly with her large eyes and smiled.

One summer night I was sitting in our yard again, on my little stool. I remember lifting my eyes and seeing the stars for the first time. Jumping to my feet, I cried out in fear, "Sparks! Sparks!" The sky seemed a vast conflagration to me; my little body was on fire.

Such were my first contacts with earth, sea, woman, and the star-filled sky. Even now, in the most profound moments of my life, I experience these four terrifying elements with exactly the same ardor as in my infancy. Only then, when I succeed in re-experiencing them with the same astonishment, fright, and joy they gave me when I was an infant, do I feel—even today—that I am experiencing these four terrifying elements deeply, as deeply as my body and soul can plunge. Since these were the first forces which I consciously felt occupying my soul, the four joined indissolubly inside me and became one. They are like a single face which keeps changing masks. Looking at the star-filled sky, I sometimes imagine that it is a flowering garden, sometimes a dark, dangerous sea, sometimes a taciturn face flooded with tears.

Every one of my emotions, moreover, and every one of my ideas, even the most abstract, is made up of these four primary ingredients. Within me, even the most metaphysical problem takes on a warm physical body which smells of sea, soil, and human sweat. The Word, in order to touch me, must become warm flesh. Only then do I understand—when I can smell, see, and touch.

In addition to these first four contacts, my soul was also deeply influenced by a fortuitous event. Fortuitous? Such are the prudent, unmanly nebulosities with which the cowardly mind, which quakes lest it utter some nonsense and wound its dignity, characterizes whatever it is incapable of interpreting. I must have been four years old. On New Year's Day my father gave me a canary and a revolving globe as a handsel, "a good hand," as we say in Crete. Closing the doors and windows of my room, I used to open the cage and let the canary go free. It had developed the habit of sitting at the very top of the globe and singing for hours and hours, while I held my breath and listened.

This extremely simple event, I believe, influenced my life more than all the books and all the people I came to know afterwards. Wandering insatiably over the earth for years, greeting and taking leave of everything, I felt that my head was the globe and that a canary sat perched on the top of my mind, singing.

I recount my childhood years in detail, not because the earliest memories have such a great fascination, but because during this period, as in dreams, a seemingly insignificant event exposes the true, unmascaraed face of the soul more than any psychoanalysis can do later. Since the means of expression in childhood or dreams are very simple, even the most intricate of inner wealth is delivered from all superfluity, so that only the essence remains.

The child's brain is soft, his flesh tender. Sun, moon, rain, wind, and silence all descend upon him. He is frothy batter and they knead him. The child gulps the world down greedily, receives it in his entrails, assimilates it, and turns it into child.

I remember frequently sitting on the doorstep of our home when the sun was blazing, the air on fire, grapes being trodden in a large house in the neighborhood, the world fragrant with must. Shutting my eyes contentedly, I used to hold out my palms and wait. God always came—as long as I remained a child, He never deceived me—He always came, a child just like myself, and deposited His toys in my hands: sun, moon, wind. "They're gifts," He said, "they're gifts. Play with them. I have lots more." I would open my eyes. God would vanish, but His toys would remain in my hands.

Though I did not know this (did not know it because I was experiencing it), I possessed the Lord's omnipotence: I created the world as I wanted it. I was soft dough; so was the world. I remember loving cherries more than any other fruit when I was little. I used to fill a bucket at the well, toss them in—red or black, crunchily firm—lean over, and admire how they swelled the moment they entered the water. But when I removed them, I saw to my great disappointment that they shrank. I closed my eyes, therefore, to avoid seeing them shrink, and thrust them—still monstrous, as I imagined—into my mouth.

This insignificant detail exposes in its entirety the method by which I confront reality, even now in my old age. I re-create it—brighter, better, more suitable to my purpose. The mind cries out, explains, demonstrates, protests; but inside me a voice rises and shouts at it, "Be quiet, mind; let us hear the heart." What heart? Madness, the essence of life. And the heart begins to warble.

"Since we cannot change reality, let us change the eyes which see reality," says one of my favorite Byzantine mystics. I did this when a child; I do it now as well in the most creative moments of my life.

Truly, what miracles are the child's mind, eyes, and ears! How insatiably they gobble down this world and fill themselves. The world is a bird with red, green, and yellow feathers. How the child hunts this bird and tries to catch it.

Truly, nothing more resembles God's eyes than the eyes of a child; they see the world for the first time, and create it. Before this, the world is chaos. All creatures—animals, trees, men, stones; everything: forms, colors, voices, smells, lightning flashes—flow unexplained in front of the child's eyes (no, not in front of them, inside them), and he cannot fasten them down, cannot establish order. The child's world is made not of clay, to last, but of clouds. A cool breeze blows across his temples and the world condenses, attenuates, vanishes. Chaos must have passed in front of God's eyes in just this way before the Creation.

When I was a child, I became one with sky, insects, sea, wind—whatever I saw or touched. The wind had a breast then; it had hands and caressed me. Sometimes it grew angry and opposed me, did not allow me to walk. Sometimes, I remember, it knocked me down. It plucked the leaves from the grape arbor, ruffled my hair which my mother had combed so carefully, carried off the kerchief from our neighbor Mr. Dimitrós's head, and lifted his wife Penelope's skirts.

The world and I still had not parted. Little by little, however, I drew myself out of its embrace. It stood on one side, I on the other, and the battle began.

As the child sits on his doorstep receiving the world's dense, turbid deluge, one day he suddenly sees. The five senses have grown firm. Each has carved out its own road and taken its share of the world's kingdom. The sense of smell was the very first to grow firm within me, I remember. It was the first to start establishing order over chaos.

Every person had his distinctive odor for me when I was two or three years old. Before raising my eyes to see him, I recognized him by the smell he emitted. My mother smelled one way, my father another; each uncle had his special odor, as did each woman of the neighborhood. When someone took me in his or her arms, it was always because of his smell that I either loved him or began to kick and reject him. In time this power evaporated. The various smells blended; everyone plunged into the same stink of sweat, tobacco, and benzene.

Above all, I distinguished unerringly between the smells of Christian and Turk. A kindly Turkish family lived across the street from us. When the wife paid a visit to our house, the odor she emitted made me nauseous, and I used to break off a twig of basil and smell it, or else stuff an acacia flower into each of my nostrils. But this Turkish lady, Fatome, had a little girl about four years old (I must have been three) who exuded a strange smell neither Turkish nor Greek, which I found very pleasing. Eminé was white and chubby, with palms and soles dyed with cinchona, and hair done up in tiny, tiny braids with a shell or little blue stone hanging from each to ward off the evil eye. She smelled of nutmeg.

I knew the hours when her mother was away from home. I used to go to our street door at those times and watch Eminé sitting on her threshold chewing gum. I signaled her that I was coming over. But her door had three steps which seemed immensely high to me. How could I ever scale them? I sweated, I slaved, and after a struggle mounted the first. Next, a new struggle to climb the second. Stopping for a moment to catch my breath, I raised my eyes to look at her. She sat on the threshold completely indifferent. Instead of offering her hand to help, she just looked at me and waited without budging. She seemed to be saying, If you can conquer the obstacles, everything will be fine. You'll reach me and we'll play together. If you cannot, turn back! But I conquered them at last after much struggle and reached the threshold where she was sitting. She rose then, took me by the hand, and brought me inside. Her mother was away the entire morning; she hired out as a charwoman. Without losing a moment, we took off our socks, lay down on our backs, and glued our bare soles together. We did not breathe a word. Closing my eyes, I felt Eminé's warmth pass from her soles to mine, then ascend little by little to my knees, belly, breast, and fill me entirely. The delight I experienced was so profound that I thought I would faint. Never in my whole life has a woman given me a more dreadful joy; never have I felt the mystery of the female body's warmth so profoundly. Even now, seventy years later, I close my eyes and feel Eminé's warmth rise from my soles and branch out through my entire body, my entire soul.

Little by little I lost my fear of walking and climbing. Going inside the nearby houses, I played with the children of the neighborhood. The world was growing broader.

When I was five years old, I was taken to some woman vaguely a teacher to learn how to draw *i*'s and *koulouria* on the slate. This was supposed to train my hand so that I would be able to write the letters of the alphabet when I grew older. She was a simple peasant type, short and fattish, a little humpbacked, with a wart on the right side of her chin. Her name was Madam Areté. She guided my hand (her breath smelled of coffee) and expounded on how I should hold the chalk and govern my fingers.

At first I wanted nothing to do with her. I liked neither her breath nor her hump. But then, though I don't know how, she began to be transformed little by little before my eyes: the wart disappeared, her back straightened, her flabby body grew slim and beautiful, and finally, after a few weeks, she became a slender angel wearing a snow-white tunic and holding an immense bronze trumpet. I must have seen this angel on some icon in the church of Saint Minas. Once again the eyes of childhood had performed their miracle: angel and Madam Teacher had become one.

Years went by. I traveled abroad, then returned again to Crete. I called at my teacher's house. A little old lady was sitting on the doorstep sunning herself. I recognized her by the wart on her chin.

When I approached and made myself known to her, she began to weep with joy. I had brought her some presents: coffee, sugar, and a box of loukoums. I hesitated a moment, ashamed to ask her, but the image of the angel with the trumpet had become so firmly established inside me that I could not restrain myself.

"Madam Areté, did you ever wear a white tunic and hold a large bronze trumpet in your hands?"

"Saints preserve us!" the poor old lady cried out, crossing herself. "Me a white jelab, me a trumpet? God forbid! Me a chanteuse!"

And her eyes began to flow.

All things were magically re-kneaded in my yeasty childhood mind; they were brought beyond the reasonable and very close to madness. But this madness is the grain of salt which keeps good sense from rotting. I lived, spoke, and moved in a fairy tale which I myself created at every moment, carving out paths in it to allow me to pass. I never saw the same thing twice, because I gave it a new face each time and made it unrecognizable. Thus the world's virginity renewed itself at every moment.

Certain fruits, especially, had an inexplicable fascination for me, cherries and figs above all. Not simply the fig itself, the fruit, but the fig leaves and their aroma. I used to close my eyes and smell them, turning pale from dreadful bodily contentment. No, not contentment—agitation, fear, tremor, as though I were entering a dark, dangerous forest.

One day my mother took me with her and we traveled to a secluded beach outside of Megalo Kastro, a place where women went swimming. My brain filled with a vast boiling sea. Protruding from this fiery indigo were bodies, very pale, weak, and strange, so it seemed to me, as though they were ill. They were emitting shrill cries and hurling armfuls of water at one another. I could see most of them only as far as the waist; from the waist down they were in the sea. Below the waist they must be fish, I decided; they must be the mermaids that people talk about. I remembered the fairy tale my grandmother told me about the mermaid who is Alexander the Great's sister. Roaming the seas in search of her brother, she asks all the boats that pass, "Is King Alexander alive?" The skipper leans over the gunwale and shouts, "He's alive, my lady, alive and flourishing!" Alas if he says the king is dead, for then she beats the sea with her tail, raises a tempest, and shatters all the boats.

One of these mermaids swimming in front of me rose out of the waves and beckoned. She shouted something at me, but the sea's din was so great that I could not understand her. I had already entered the world of the fairy tale, however, and thinking she was inquiring about her brother, I cried out fearfully, "He's alive, alive and flourishing!" Suddenly all the mermaids shook with laughter. Ashamed, I ran away in a furor. "They were women, damn them, not mermaids," I murmured, and I sat down on a small stone, completely humiliated, with my back turned to the sea.

I thank God that this refreshing childhood vision still lives inside me in all its fullness of color and sound. This is what keeps my mind untouched by wastage, keeps it from withering and running dry. It is the sacred drop of immortal water which prevents me from dying. When I wish to speak of the sea, woman, or God in my writing, I gaze down into my breast and listen carefully to what the child within me says. He dictates to me; and if it sometimes happens that I come close to these great forces of sea, woman, and God, approach them by means of words and depict them, I owe it to the child who still lives within me. I become a child again to enable myself to view the world always for the first time, with virgin eyes.

Both of my parents circulate in my blood, the one fierce, hard, and morose, the other tender, kind, and saintly. I have carried them all my days; neither has died. As long as I live, they too will live inside me and battle in their antithetical ways to govern my thoughts and actions. My lifelong effort is to reconcile them so that the one may give me his strength, the other her tenderness; to make the discord between them, which breaks out incessantly within me, turn to harmony inside their son's heart.

Here is another incredible fact: The presence of my two parents is clearly manifested in my hands. My right hand is very strong, completely lacking in sensitivity, absolutely masculine. My left is excessively, pathologically sensitive. Whenever I recall the breast of a woman I loved, I feel pain and a slight tingling in my left palm. It is almost ready to turn black and blue from the pain, almost ready to manifest an actual wound. When I am alone and watching a bird soar in the air, I feel the warmth of its belly in my left palm. It was in my hands, and only in my hands, that my parents deserted each other and took separate possession, my father in my right hand and my mother in my left.

Here I must add an event which had a profound influence on my life. It was the first spiritual wound I received. Though I am old now, this wound still has not healed.

I must have been four years old. One of my uncles took me by the hand; apparently we were going to see a neighbor in the little graveyard of Saint Matthew's, which lay inside the city walls.

Springtime: camomile had blanketed the graves, a rose bush in one corner was filled with small Aprilish blossoms. It must have been midday; the sun had warmed the ground, the grass was fragrant. The church door stood open. The priest had put incense in the censer and donned his stole. Crossing the threshold, he set out toward the graves.

"Why is he swinging the censer?" I asked my uncle, deeply inhaling the odor of incense and soil.

It was a warm odor and seemed a trifle sickening to me. It reminded me of the smell in the Turkish bath I had visited with my mother the previous Saturday.

"Why is he swinging the censer?" I demanded once more of my uncle, who continued to proceed in silence between the tombs.

"Keep quiet. You'll see in a minute. Follow me."

Turning behind the church, we heard conversation. Five or six women dressed in black were standing around a grave. Two men lifted the tombstone, then one of them stepped into the grave and began to dig. We went close and stood by the open pit.

"What are they doing?" I asked.

"Disinterring the bones."

"What bones?"

"You'll see in a minute."

The priest had placed himself at the head of the grave, where he swung the censer up and down and murmured prayers under his breath. I leaned over the newly dug soil. Mold, putrefaction; I pinched my nostrils. Though I felt sick to my stomach, I did not go away. I waited. Bones? What bones? I kept asking myself, and I waited.

Suddenly the man who was bent over and digging stood up

straight. His torso emerged above the pit. In his hands he held a skull. He cleaned the dirt off it, inserting his finger and pushing the mud out of the eye cavities, then placed it on the lip of the grave, leaned over again, and recommenced his digging.

"What is it?" I asked my uncle, trembling from fright.

"Can't you see? It's a dead person's head. A skull."

"Whose?"

"Don't you remember her? It's our neighbor Annika's."

"Annika's!"

I burst into tears and began to howl.

"Annika's! Annika's!" I cried. Throwing myself on the ground, I grabbed all the stones I could find and started to hurl them at the gravedigger.

Wailing and lamenting, I screamed how beautiful she was, how beautiful she smelled! She used to come to our house, place me on her knees and comb my curls with the comb she removed from her hair. She used to tickle me under the arms, and I giggled, I peeped like a bird.

My uncle took me in his arms, carried me off a little ways, and spoke to me angrily. "Why are you crying? What did you expect? She died. We're all going to die."

But I was thinking of her blond hair, her large eyes, the red lips which used to kiss me. And now . . .

"And her hair," I shrieked, "her lips, her eyes? . . ."

"Gone, gone. The earth ate them."

"Why, why? I don't want people to die!"

My uncle shrugged his shoulders. "When you grow up, you'll find out why."

I never did find out. I grew up, became old, and never did find out.

5

ELEMENTARY SCHOOL

WITH MY EVER-MAGIC EYE, my buzzing bee- and honey-filled mind, a red woolen cap on my head and sandals with red pompons on my feet, I set out one morning, half delighted, half dismayed. My father held me by the hand; my mother had given me a sprig of basil (I was supposed to gain courage by smelling it) and hung my golden baptismal cross around my neck.

"God's blessings upon you, and my blessings too," she murmured, looking at me proudly.

I was like a small sacrificial victim weighted down with ornaments. Within me I felt both pride and fear, but my hand was wedged deeply in my father's grasp, and I bore myself with manly courage. We marched and marched through the narrow lanes, reached Saint Minas's, turned, and entered an old building with a wide courtyard. Four great rooms occupied the corners and a dust-covered plane tree the middle. I hesitated, turning coward; my hand had begun to tremble in the large warm palm.

Bending over, my father touched my hair and patted me. I gave a start, for as far as I could remember, this was the first time he had ever caressed me. Lifting my eyes, I glanced at him fearfully. He saw that I was afraid and withdrew his hand.

"You're going to learn to read and write here so you can become a man," he said. "Cross yourself."

The teacher appeared in the doorway. He was holding a long switch and seemed like a savage to me, a savage with huge fangs. I pinned my eyes on the top of his head to see if he had horns. But I was unable to see, because he was wearing a hat.

"This is my son," my father said.

Untangling my hand from his own, he turned me over to the teacher.

"His bones are mine, his flesh is yours. Don't feel sorry for him. Thrash him and make a man of him."

"Don't worry, Captain Michael," said the teacher, pointing to his switch. "Right here is the tool which makes men."

A pile of heads remains fixed in my memory from those elementary school days, a pile of children's heads glued one to the next like skulls. Most of them must actually have become skulls by now. But remaining in me above and beyond those heads, undying, are my four teachers.

Paterópoulos in the first grade: a little old man, very short, fierce-eyed, with drooping mustache, and the switch constantly in hand. He hunted us down, collected us, then set us out in a row as though we were ducks and he were taking us to market to sell. "The bones are mine, the flesh is yours, Teacher," every father instructed him as he turned over his wild goat of a son. "Thrash him, thrash him until he becomes a man." And he thrashed us pitilessly. All of us, teacher and students alike, awaited the day when these many beatings would turn us into men. When I grew older and philanthropic theories began to mislead my mind, I termed this method barbarous. But when I came to know human nature still better, I blessed, and still bless, Paterópoulos's holy switch. It was this that taught us that suffering is the greatest guide along the ascent which leads from animal to man.

Títyros—"What-cheese"—reigned over the second grade; reigned, poor fellow, but did not govern. He was pale, with spectacles, starched collar and shirt, pointed down-at-heel patent leather shoes, a huge hairy nose, and slender fingers yellowed from tobacco. His real name wasn't What-cheese, it was Papadákis. But one day his father, who was the priest in an outlying village, came to town bringing him a large head of cheese as a present. "What cheese is this, Father?" said the son [using the form *tyrós* instead of *tyrí*, to show off his katharévousa]. A neighbor happened to be at the house. She overheard, spread the word, and the poor teacher was roasted over the coals and given this nickname. What-cheese did not thrash, he entreated. He used to read us *Robinson Crusoe*, explaining each and every word. Then he gazed at us with tenderness and anguish, as though begging us to understand. But we were thumbing through the book and gazing ecstatically at the poorly printed pictures of tropical forests, trees with great fat leaves, Robinson in his broad-brimmed straw hat with an expanse of deserted ocean on all sides. Bringing out his tobacco pouch, poor What-cheese would roll a cigarette to smoke during recess, look at us imploringly, and wait.

One day when we were doing Sacred History, we came to Esau, who sold his birthright to Jacob for a pottage of lentils. When I went home for dinner, I asked my father what birthright meant. "Go ask Uncle Nikoláki," he said, scratching his head and coughing.

This uncle had finished elementary school, which made him the family's most educated member. He was my mother's brother: a stubby little Tom Thumb, bald, with large timorous eyes and monstrous hands all covered with hair. He had married above him, and his jaundiced, venom-nosed wife felt nothing but scorn for him. She was also jealous. Every night she tied his foot to the bedpost with rope to keep him from getting up during the night and going to visit their plump big-breasted servant, who slept downstairs. In the morning she released him. My poor uncle endured this martyrdom for five years, but then the Lord willed that the venom-nose should die (this is why we call Him the All-good) and this time my uncle married a solid, kindhearted, foul-mouthed peasant girl, who did not tie him. He used to come to our house, all elated, and find my mother.

"How are you getting along now with your new wife, Nikoláki?" she inquired.

"Marghí, no need to ask how happy I am! She doesn't tie me."

Afraid of my father, he never lifted his eyes to look him in the face but gazed constantly at the street door, rubbing his hairy hands together. On this day, as soon as he heard that Captain Michael was calling him, he rose from table with his mouth still full of food and sped to our house.

What could the ogre want with me now? he asked himself with irritation, swallowing his last mouthful. How does my poor sister stand him? Recalling his first wife, he smiled contentedly and murmured, "I, at least, was saved. Praise the Lord!"

"Come here," my father said as soon as he saw him. "You went to school. Explain this."

The two of them held council, bending over the book.

"Birthright means hunting costume," said my father after much reflection.

My uncle shook his head.

"I think it means musket," he objected. But his voice was trembling.

"Hunting costume," roared my father. He knitted his brows, and my uncle cowered.

The next day the teacher asked, "What does birthright mean?"

I jumped up. "Hunting costume."

"What nonsense! What ignorant fool told you that?"

"My father."

The teacher quailed. Afraid like everyone else of my father, how could he dream of contradicting him?

"Yes," he said, swallowing hard, "yes, certainly, sometimes, but very rarely, it can mean hunting costume. Here, however . . ."

Sacred History was my favorite subject. It was a strange, intricate and somber fairy tale with serpents who talked, floods and rainbows, thefts and murders. Brother killed brother, a father wanted to slaughter his only son, God intervened every two minutes and did His share of killing, people crossed the sea without wetting their feet.

We did not understand. We asked the teacher, and he coughed, raised his switch angrily, and shouted, "Stop this impertinence! How many times do I have to tell you—no talking!"

"But we don't understand, sir," we whined.

"These are God's doings," the teacher answered. "We're not supposed to understand. It's a sin!"

A sin! We heard that terrible word and shrank back in fright. It wasn't a word, it was a serpent, the same serpent that had beguiled Eve, and it was coming down from the teacher's platform and opening its mouth in order to eat us. We shrank into our desks and did not utter a sound.

Another word which horrified me when I first heard it was *Abraham*. Those two *ah*'s reverberated inside me; they seemed to come from far away, out of some deep, dark, and dangerous well. I whispered "Abraham, Abraham" secretly to myself and heard footsteps and panting behind me—someone with huge bare feet was pursuing me. When I learned that he had taken his son one day in order to slaughter him, I became terror-stricken. Without a doubt he was the one who slaughtered little children, and I hid behind the back of my desk to keep him from discovering me and carrying me off. When the teacher told us that whoever follows God's commandments goes to Abraham's bosom, I swore inwardly to transgress all the commandments in order to save myself from that bosom.

I felt the identical agitation when, in the same subject, Sacred History, I first heard the word *Habakkuk*. This word also seemed extremely dark to me. Habakkuk was a bogeyman who came to lurk in our courtyard every time the darkness fell (I knew just where he crouched: behind the well). Once when I dared to venture all alone into the yard at night, he sprang from behind the well, reached out his hand, and shouted at me: "Habakkuk!" In other words, "Stop! I'm going to eat you!"

The sound of certain words excited me terribly—it was fear I felt most often, not joy. Especially Hebrew words, for I knew from my grandmother that on Good Friday the Jews took Christian children, tossed them into a trough lined with spikes, and drank their blood. Oftentimes it seemed to me that a Hebrew word from the Old Testament—and above all the word *Jehovah*—was a spike-lined trough and that someone wanted to throw me in.

In the third grade we had Periander Krasákis. What merciless godfather gave the name of Corinth's savage tyrant to this sickly runt of a man with his high starched collar to conceal the scrofula on his neck, his skinny grasshopper legs, the little handkerchief always at his mouth so that he could spit, spit, and spit as though breathing his last? This onc had a mania for cleanliness. Every day he inspected our hands, ears, nose, teeth, and nails. He did not thrash, did not entreat; he shook his oversized head which was covered with pimples, and shouted at us:

"Beasts! Pigs! If you don't wash every day with soap, you'll never, never become men. You know what being a man means? It means washing with soap. Brains aren't enough, you poor devils, soap is needed too. How are you going to appear before God with hands like that? Go out to the yard and get washed."

He drove us to distraction for hours on end—which vowels were long, which short, whether to use an acute or circumflex accent—while we listened to the voices in the street—vegetable mongers, kouloúri boys, donkeys braying, women laughing—and waited for the bell to ring so that we could escape. We watched the teacher sweating away at his desk as he repeated the points of grammar over and over again in an effort to make them stick in our minds. But our thoughts were outside in the sun, on pebble warfare. We adored this game and often came to school with broken heads.

One divine spring day the windows were open. A tangerine tree was in bloom across the street, and its perfume entered the classroom. Each of our minds had turned into a blossoming tangerine tree; we could not bear to hear anything more about acute and circumflex accents. A bird came just then, perched on the plane tree in the schoolyard and began to sing. At that point a pale redheaded student who had arrived that year from his village, Nikoliós by name, was unable to control himself. He raised his finger.

"Be quiet, sir," he cried. "Be quiet and let us hear the bird."

Poor Periander Krasákis! One day we buried him. He had rested his head calmly on his desk, palpitated a moment like a fish, and given up the ghost. Terror-stricken at the sight of death right in front of our eyes, we rushed screaming into the yard. The next day we donned our Sunday clothes, washed our hands carefully (in order not to deny him anything at that point) and took him to the old cemetery by the sea. It was springtime; the heavens were laughing, the soil smelled of camomile. The coffin lay uncovered. The dead man's face was full of oozing pimples; it had begun to turn green and yellow. And when his students leaned over one by one to give him the parting kiss, the spring no longer smelled of camomile, but of rotting flesh.

In grade four we had the principal of the school, who both reigned and governed. He was short, as tubby as a storage jar, and had a small pointed beard, gray eyes that were always angry, and bowlegs. "Good God, just look at his legs," we used to say to each other in hushed voices so that he would not hear. "Just look how they wrap around each other. And listen to him cough. He isn't a Cretan!" He had come to us from Athens, freshly educated, apparently bringing New Pedagogy with him. We thought it must be some young woman named Pedagogy [the word *new* in Greek can also mean *young woman*], but when we confronted him for the first time, he was alone. Pedagogy wasn't there; she must have stayed at home. He was holding a small braided cowhide. He lined us up and began to lecture us. We must see and touch whatever we learned, he said, or else draw it on some paper covered with dots. And we were to look sharp. He wasn't going to stand for any nonsense, not even laughing and shouting during recess. We were to keep our arms crossed, and whenever we saw a priest in the street, kiss his hand. "Look sharp, poor devils, because otherwise—see this?" He pointed to the cowhide. "I'm not just talking; you'll see that I mean business!" And indeed we did see. When we were disorderly, or when he felt in a bad mood, he unbuttoned us, lowered our shorts, and thrashed our bare skin with the cowhide. And when he was too lazy to undo the buttons, he lashed us across the ears until blood flowed.

One day I fortified my heart, raised my finger, and asked, "Teacher, where is New Pedagogy? Why doesn't she come to school?"

He bounded out of his chair and removed the cowhide from its hook on the wall.

"Come here, you impudent brat," he cried. "Unbutton your pants!"

He was too lazy to do it himself.

"Here! Here! Here!" he bellowed as he struck. When he had worked up a sweat, he stopped.

"That's where New Pedagogy is," he said. "Next time shut up!"

But he was also a sly little devil, this husband of New Pedagogy. One day he said to us, "Tomorrow I'm going to tell you about Christopher Columbus, how he discovered America. But so you'll understand better I want each of you to be holding an egg in his hands, and whoever doesn't have an egg at home, let him bring some butter."

He had a daughter of marriageable age named Terpsichore: short, but very delectable. Though she had many suitors, he did not want her to marry. "I won't have any such abominations in my house," he used to say. And when the toms came out in January and began miaowing on the pantiles, he got a ladder, climbed onto the roof, and chased them away. "Nature be damned," he murmured, "it has no morals."

On Good Friday he took us to church to do obeisance to the Crucified. Afterwards he brought us back to school to explain what we had seen, whom we had worshiped, and what crucifixion meant. We fell into formation in our seats, tired and disgusted because we had eaten nothing that day except sour lemons and had drunk nothing except vinegar so that we too might taste Christ's suffering. Whereupon, New Pedagogy's spouse began in a deeply solemn voice to explain how God descended to earth, how he became Christ, suffered, and was crucified in order to deliver us from sin. Exactly what this sin was we did not understand very clearly, but we did understand clearly that he had twelve disciples, one of whom—Judas—had betrayed him.

"And Judas was like . . . like whom?"

The teacher left his platform and began to proceed slowly, threateningly, from desk to desk, eying us one by one.

"Judas was like . . . like . . ."

His index finger was extended; he shifted it from pupil to pupil, trying to find which of us Judas was like. We all quailed and trembled lest the terrible finger come to rest upon us. Suddenly the teacher emitted a cry, and his finger halted at a pallid, poorly dressed boy with beautiful reddish-blond hair. It was Nikoliós, the same who the year before in third grade had called out, "Be quiet, Teacher, and let us hear the bird."

"There, like Nikoliós!" cried the teacher. "Identical! The same pallor, the same clothes. And Judas had red hair. Deep red, like the flames of hell!"

When poor Nikoliós heard this, he burst into tears. The rest of us, no longer in danger, eyed him with ferociously hateful glances and passed the word secretly from desk to desk that as soon as school was out we would beat him to a pulp because he had betrayed Christ.

Satisfied at having followed New Pedagogy and shown us tangibly what Judas was like, the teacher dismissed the class. We hemmed Nikoliós in as soon as we reached the street and began to spit on him and beat him up. He ran off in tears, but we pursued him with stones, jeering "Judas! Judas!" at him until he reached his home and slipped inside.

Nikoliós never appeared again in class, never set foot again in school. Thirty years later, when I had returned to Crete after my stay in Europe, there was a knock on our door. It was Holy Saturday. My father had ordered us all new shoes for Easter, and a pale, feeble man with red hair and beard stood on the threshold. He was delivering the shoes, which were neatly wrapped in a colored cloth. He stood shyly on the threshold, looked at me, and shook his head.

"Don't you know me?" he said. "Don't you remember me?"

And as he said this, I recognized him.

"It's Nikoliós!" I cried, clasping him in my arms.

"Judas," he said, and he smiled bitterly.

I often recall the men and women of our neighborhood, and always with terror. Most of them were freakish and half mad; I passed their doors as quickly as I could, because I was afraid. Their brains had gone to pot, perhaps because they were isolated inside the four walls of their houses all year long, boiling in their own juices, perhaps because of their fear of the Turks and their concern for their lives, honor, and possessions, which were in daily peril. Indeed, they heard the old men tell stories about massacres and wars, about the ordeals of the Christians, and their hair stood on end. If someone came along and stopped in front of their doors, they jumped to their feet, stricken dumb with fear. And how could they sleep at night? Their eyes wide open, their ears cocked, they waited for the evil hour which was sure to come.

It really is with terror that I recall the men and women of our neighborhood. Madame Victoria, just a little below our house, sometimes greeted you sweetly with a barrage of tender chitchat impossible to check, sometimes slammed the door in your face and began to curse you behind it.

Opposite her was Madame Penelope. Fat, greasy, getting on in years, she always chewed cloves, apparently to sweeten her breath. She laughed continually, as if someone were tickling her. Mr. Dimitrós, her husband, was a taciturn, hypochondriacal man who took his umbrella every so often and set off for the mountains. Two or three months later he returned in tatters, dying of hunger, his trousers hanging empty around him. When Madame Penelope saw him appear in the distance holding the opened umbrella above him, she burst into laughter. "Here he comes again to fill up his pants," she shouted to the neighbors, and they all split their sides with guffaws.

Farther down the street lived Mr. Manoúsos, a merchant of

consequence but a little touched. Every time he left his house in the morning, he inscribed a cross on the front door with a piece of chalk he held in his hand, and at midday when he came home to eat, he thrashed his sister—regularly, always at exactly the same hour. When we heard her screams, we knew it was dinnertime and we went to the table. Mr. Manoúsos never parted his lips to say good morning; he simply glared at you with a mixture of savagery and fear.

Mr. Andreas the Feeler occupied a large house a little above us, at the head of the street. Rich and pock-marked, he had a fat nose with wide nostrils, which made him look like a calf. Every time he closed his door, he stood and felt it for an hour to make sure it hadn't by chance remained open, all the while murmuring exorcisms to chase away burglars, fire, and sickness. Finally he crossed himself three times and went on his way, looking continually behind him. The children of the neighborhood had noticed that he always stepped on the same stones, and they used to heap mud or horse manure on these stones in order to tease him. But he pushed the piles to one side with his stick and stepped as before.

We also had as our neighbor the excellent Dr. Pericles, the pride of the street. He was a physician freshly arrived from studies in Paris. Blond and handsome, he had gold spectacles, wore a top hat, surely the first "mirabeau" ever to disembark at Megalo Kastro, and made calls to his patients in slippers because (so he said) his feet were swollen. These slippers had been embroidered by his old-maid sister, who exhausted her dowry to pay for his education. He was our family doctor. I used to bend down and admire the embroidery: silken roses surrounded by green leaves. Once when I had temperature and he came to see me, I told him imploringly that if he wanted me to get well, he would have to give me the slippers. And he, with the utmost seriousness—he never deigned to laugh—put them on my feet to determine if they fit. But they were much too large. To console myself, I glued my nose on top of the embroidered roses to see if they smelled. They smelled, but not like roses.

I cannot recall my neighbors without bursting into laughter mixed with tears. In those days men were not cast by the dozen in the same mold. Each was a separate world with his own peculiarities. He laughed differently from his neighbor, talked differently.

Shutting himself up in his house, he kept his most secret desires hidden out of shame or fear, and these desires luxuriated within and strangled him. But he said nothing, and his life took on a tragic seriousness. In addition there was poverty, and as if this were not enough, the pride which demanded that no one discover this poverty. People fed themselves bread, olives, and mustard stems to avoid having to step outside with patched clothes. I once heard a neighbor remark, "A poor man is someone who fears poverty. I do not fear it."

6

THE DEATH OF MY GRANDFATHER

I MUST have still been in elementary school when a shepherd came scurrying from the village to get me and bring me to my grandfather, who apparently was breathing his last. He had asked for me so that he could give me his blessing. It was August, I remember. Torrid heat. I rode on a donkey while the shepherd walked behind holding a forked stick with a nail at the tip. He goaded the animal frequently, drew blood, and the suffering donkey kicked and began to run. I kept turning to the driver.

"Have pity!" I implored him. "Don't you feel sorry for the beast? You're hurting him."

"Only men feel pain," he answered me. "Donkeys are donkeys."

But I forgot the donkey's pain as soon as we reached the vineyards and olive groves. The women were still vintaging and spreading the grapes over the cloth-covered drying areas to become raisins. The world was fragrant, the grasshoppers deafening. One of the vintagers saw us and laughed.

"Why is she laughing, Kyriákos?" I asked the donkey driver (I had learned his name by now).

"She's being tickled and she's laughing."

He spat.

"Being tickled? Who is tickling her, Kyriákos?"

"Demons."

I did not understand, but I felt afraid. Closing my eyes to keep from seeing the demons, I pounded the donkey with my fist to make it carry us by quickly.

Great hairy giants were treading grapes in one of the villages we passed through. Stripped to the waist, they were dancing in the wine press and telling jokes which made them double over with laughter. The ground smelled of must. Women were removing fresh loaves from the ovens, dogs barking, bees and wasps buzzing, the westering sun inclining with a rubicund face as though treading grapes along with the others, completely drunk. I too began to laugh. Whistling, I took the forked stick from the shepherd and started to goad the donkey, thrusting the nail deep into its rump.

By the time we reached my grandfather's house, I was dizzy from fatigue, sun, and grasshoppers. When we arrived and I saw him lying in the middle of the courtyard surrounded by his children and grandchildren, I felt relieved. For night had fallen already, the heat had subsided, and my grandfather lay with closed eyes, unaware of my presence. In this way I escaped the immense hand which reddened my skin wherever it touched me.

"I'm tired," I said to the woman who took me in her arms and lowered me from the donkey.

"You'll have to be patient," she replied. "Your grandfather is going to give up the ghost at any minute. Better stay near him so that you can be the first to receive his blessing."

This blessing I had come such a distance to receive seemed like some miraculous gift, some expensive toy. The dragon's hair mentioned in the fairy tales—that is what it would be! You kept this one hair on your person as a talisman, and in time of great need you burned it, and the dragon came to save you. So I began to wait for my grandfather to open his eyes and give me the dragon's hair.

At that very moment, uttering a cry, he rolled into a ball on the sheepskin which had been spread out beneath him.

"He saw his angel," said an old lady. "He's going to surrender his soul any minute now."

Crossing herself and taking up a piece of wax, she began to warm it in her breath and knead it with her fingers. She was making it into a cross to seal the dead man's lips.

One of his sons rose. He had a thorny jet-black beard. Going inside, he brought out a pomegranate and placed it in his father's palm so that he could take it to Hades.

We all went close and gazed at him. A woman began chanting the dirge, but the son with the thorny beard placed his hand over her mouth.

"Quiet!"

At this point my grandfather opened his eyes and beckoned. Everyone went still closer, his sons in the first circle, the male grandchildren behind them, further back the daughters and daughters-in-law. The moribund extended his hands. An old lady placed a pillow behind his neck. We heard his voice.

"Goodbye, lads," he said. "I ate my share of bread; now I'm going. I filled my yard with children and grandchildren, filled my jugs with oil and honey, filled my barrels with wine—I have no complaints. Goodbye!"

He moved his hands, bidding us farewell. Turning slowly, he looked at each of us, one by one. I had forgotten all about the blessing. I was hidden behind two or three of my cousins, and he did not see me. No one spoke. The old man parted his lips again.

"Give an ear, lads, and listen to my final instructions. Look after the animals—the oxen, sheep, and donkeys. Don't fool yourselves, they have souls just like us, they're men, only they wear hides and don't know how to talk. They're men from way back; give them enough to eat. And look after the olive trees and vines. Be sure you manure, water, and prune them if you want them to bear fruit for you. They're men from way back too, but so far back they don't remember. But man remembers; that's why we're men, after all. . . . Are you listening? Or am I talking to a flock of deaf-mutes?"

"We're listening." "We're listening," replied several voices.

The old man held out his huge hand and called for his eldest son. "Eh, you—Kostandís!"

Kostandís, a curly-haired giant with a gray beard and large bovine eyes, touched his father's hand.

"Here I am, sir. Tell me what you want."

"I've got some select wheat in the small jar. I've been keeping it a long time now, for my memorial offering. Boil it on the ninth day, and mind you put in plenty of almonds (we've enough, thank the Lord) and don't skimp on the sugar, as you usually do. Hear? You're a skinflint and I don't trust you."

"I honor your wishes," answered the eldest son, nodding his head. "Yes, I honor your wishes, but let the others share the expenses. The whole works, provided everyone shares the expenses. We're dealing with a memorial offering and that means money, it's no joke. Then there are the candles, and the priest who has to be paid, and then the gravedigger, don't forget, and then the funeral pies, and the mezédhes and wine for the memorial spread, not to mention all the coffee the women will drink. It means money, I tell you, it's no joke. We'll all share the expenses."

He turned toward his brothers on either side.

"Do you hear? All of us, each his share. Let's get that straight."

The sons grumbled between their teeth. One of them spoke up. "Fine, Kostandís, fine. We're not going to fight over it."

I had slipped into the first circle. As I've already remarked, death was always a strange mystery which lured me. I approached in order to have a close view as my mother's father died.

His eye fell on me.

"Eh, welcome, welcome to the little fellow from Kastro. Bend down so I can give you my blessing."

The old lady who was kneading the wax grasped my head and lowered it. I felt my grandfather's huge heavy paw spread over my entire scalp.

"Bless you, grandson from Kastro," he said. "May you become a man one day."

He moved his lips to say something else, but he was exhausted now, and he closed his eyes.

"Which way does the sun go down?" he asked in an expiring voice. "Turn me that way."

Two of his sons took hold of him and turned him toward the west.

"Goodbye," he whispered. "I'm going."

Uttering a deep sigh, he tautened his legs. His head rolled off the pillow and struck the stones of the courtyard.

"Is he dead?" I asked one of my little cousins.

"Pff, that's the end of him!" he answered. "Let's go and eat."

7

CRETE VS. TURKEY

But what influenced my life incalculably—far more than schools and teachers, far deeper than the first pleasures and fears I received from viewing the world—was something which moved me in a truly unique way: the struggle between Crete and Turkey.

Without this struggle my life would have taken a different course, God surely have acquired a different face.

From the day of my birth I inhaled this terrible visible and invisible battle in the very air I breathed. I saw Christians and Turks cast fierce sidelong glances at each other and twist their mustaches in a furor; I saw Christians barricade their doors with curses as the musket-armed occupation troops patrolled the streets; I heard the old men tell about wars, massacres, heroic deeds, about freedom, about Greece, and I lived all this deeply, mutely, waiting to grow up and understand what it all meant, so that I too could tuck up my sleeves and go to war.

In time I saw clearly. The opponents were Crete and Turkey; Crete was battling to gain freedom, the other trampling on its breast and preventing it. After that everything around me acquired a face, the face of Crete and Turkey; in my imagination, and not only in my imagination but in my flesh as well, everything became a symbol reminding me of the terrible contest. One summer the icon of the Assumption of the Blessed Virgin was brought into the church on the fifteenth of August and placed on a prie-dieu. The Mother of Christ lay with crossed hands. An angel had dashed forward on her right, the devil on her left, both in the hope of winning her soul. The angel had drawn his sword and cut off the devil's two hands at the wrist—they were suspended in mid-air, oozing blood. As I gazed at the icon, my heart swelled with happiness. The Virgin is Crete, I told myself, the black devil is the

Turk, and the snow-white angel is the Greek king. One day the Greek king will cut off the Turk's hands. When? As soon as I grow up, I thought to myself, and my childish breast swelled.

This tender childhood breast began to fill with yearning and hate. I too clenched my tiny fists, ready to enter the fray. I knew full well where my duty resided, with which of the two antagonists, and I was in a hurry to grow up so that I could follow in line behind my grandfather, my father, and make war.

This was the seed. From this seed the entire tree of my life germinated, budded, flowered, and bore fruit. What first truly stirred my soul was not fear or pain, nor was it pleasure or games; it was the yearning for freedom. I had to gain freedom—but from what, from whom? Little by little, in the course of time, I mounted freedom's rough unaccommodating ascent. To gain freedom first of all from the Turk, that was the initial step; after that, later, this new struggle began: to gain freedom from the inner Turk—from ignorance, malice and envy, from fear and laziness, from dazzling false ideas; and finally from idols, all of them, even the most revered and beloved.

In time, after I grew up and my mind broadened, the struggle broadened as well. Overflowing the bounds of Crete and Greece, it raged in all eras and locales—invaded the history of mankind. Battling now were not Crete and Turkey but good and evil, light and darkness, God and the devil. It was always the same battle, the eternal one, and standing always behind the good, behind light and God, was Crete; behind evil, behind darkness and the devil, Turkey. Thus, through the accident of being born a Cretan at a critical moment when Crete was fighting for its freedom, I realized as far back as my childhood that this world possesses a good which is dearer than life, sweeter than happiness—liberty.

My father had a friend, a hoary captain known as Polymantiliás—"Many-kerchiefs"—because he always had so many on him: one covering his hair, another beneath the left armpit, two hanging from his silk cummerbund, and one which he held in his hand and employed to wipe his forehead, which was always sweating. He was a frequent visitor to my father's store. My father ordered him a cup of coffee and a hookah, his juniors gathered around him, he opened his tobacco pouch, stopped up his nostrils with tobacco, sneezed, and began to talk.

I stood off to one side and listened. Wars, assaults, massacres. Megalo Kastro vanished, the mountains of Crete towered before me. The air filled with roaring; roaring from Christians, roaring from Turks. Silver-handled pistols flashed before my eyes. It was Crete and Turkey battling. "Freedom!" cried the one. "Death!" answered the other, and my mind filled with blood.

One day the old captain squinted his eyes at me and weighed me in his glance.

"Crows don't hatch doves!" he said. "Do you understand, my little pallikári?"

I blushed.

"No, Captain," I replied.

"Your father is a pallikári. Like it or not, you'll be a pallikári too."

Like it or not! Those heavy words hammered themselves home in my mind. Crete was speaking through the old captain's mouth. I did not understand his words at the time; only much later did I realize that I had a superior force in me, a force not my own, and that this force was governing me. Though I was ready to give up many times, this force did not let me. What force? Crete!

Indeed, even as a child I managed to conquer fear—out of self-respect: the idea that I was a Cretan. Also because I was afraid of my father. At first I dared not venture into our yard at night. A tiny, glittery-eyed devil was stealthily spying on me in every corner, behind every vase, and at the brim of the well. But my father used to give me a rap, thrust me into the yard, and bolt the door behind me.

The sole fear I had not succeeded in conquering up to that point was the fear of earthquakes. Megalo Kastro often shook to its very foundations. A rumble sounded below in the world's cellars, the earth's crust creaked, and the poor people above went out of their minds. Whenever the wind subsided abruptly, not a leaf moved, and a hair-raising hush settled over everything, the inhabitants of Kastro rushed out of their homes or shops and glanced first at the sky, then at the ground. They did not say a word lest the evil hear and come, but to themselves they thought fearfully, There's going to be an earthquake, and they made the sign of the cross.

One day our teacher, old Paterópoulos, tried to set our minds at ease. "There is nothing to an earthquake, really," he explained. "Don't be afraid of it. It's just a bull beneath the ground. He bellows, butts the earth with his horns, and the ground shakes. The ancient Cretans called him the Minotaur. There's really nothing to it at all."

But after being consoled in this way by our teacher, we found that our terror had increased all the more. The earthquake was a living thing in other words, a beast with horns; it bellowed and shook beneath our feet, and it ate people.

"Why doesn't Saint Minas kill him?" asked chubby little Stratís, the sexton's son.

But the teacher became angry. "Don't talk nonsense!" he shouted, whereupon he left his desk and twisted Stratís's ear to make him keep quiet.

One day, however, as I was racing through the Turkish quarter at top speed because the smell the Turks exuded disgusted me, the earth began to shake again, the windows and doors rattled, and I heard a great clatter, as though from collapsing houses. I stood petrified with fear in the middle of the narrow lane, my eyes riveted to the ground. I was waiting for it to crack and the bull to emerge and eat me, when suddenly a vaulted door swung open, revealing a garden, and out darted three young Turkish girls, barefooted and unkempt, their faces uncovered. Quaking with fear, they scattered in all directions, uttering shrill cries like swallows. The entire lane smelled of musk. Ever since that moment earthquakes began to display a different face for me, one which endured my entire life. It was no longer the fierce face of the bull. They stopped bellowing and began to chirp like birds. Earthquakes and the little Turks became one. This was the first time I saw a dark force merge with the light and become luminous.

Many times in my life, sometimes voluntarily, sometimes involuntarily, I placed an expedient mask over terrors in this same way—over love, over virtue, over illness. This is how I made life bearable.

8

SAINTS' LEGENDS

FREEDOM was my first great desire. The second, which remains hidden within me to this day, tormenting me, was the desire for sanctity. Hero together with saint: such is mankind's supreme model. Even in my childhood I had fixed this model firmly above me in the azure sky.

In those days everybody in Megalo Kastro had roots deeply sunk in both earth and heaven. That was why, after I had learned to read syllables and form words, the first thing I had my mother buy for me was a legend, the *Holy Epistle*. "God's manifestation is a marvelous miracle! A stone fell out of heaven . . ." and this stone broke, and written inside was found: "Woe to him who uses oil or drinks wine on Wednesdays and Fridays!" Clutching the *Holy Epistle* and holding it high above me like a flag, I knocked on our neighbors' doors each Wednesday and Friday—on Madame Penelope's, Madame Victoria's, on old lady Katerina Delivasílaina's. Beside myself with fervor, I bounded into their houses, made a beeline for the kitchen, smelled what was being cooked, and alas the day I caught the scent of meat or fish. I waved the *Holy Epistle* menacingly and shouted, "Woe to you, woe to you!" whereupon the terror-stricken neighbors caressed me and implored me to be still. And one day when I questioned my mother and learned that I had nursed on Wednesdays and Fridays when I was an infant, and had therefore drunk milk on those holy days, I broke into wailing and lamentation.

Selling all my toys to my friends, I purchased the lives of the saints in popular, pamphlet-sized editions. Each evening I sat on my little stool amid the basil and marigolds of our courtyard and read out loud all the various ordeals the saints had endured in order to save their souls. The neighbors congregated around me with their sewing or work—some knitted socks, others ground coffee or cleaned mustard stalks. They listened, and little by little our courtyard began to ring with lamentations for the saints' sufferings and torments. When the canary, suspended beneath the acacia, heard the reading and lamentations, it threw its head back drunkenly and began to warble. With its spices and the trellis overhead, the little garden—so sequestered, warm, and fragrant—seemed like an epitáphios surrounded by women's keening: like Christ's flower-canopied tomb. Passers-by hesitated and said to themselves, Someone has died in there. They went to my father to bring him the sad news, but he shook his head and told them, "It's nothing. Just my son trying to convert the neighbors."

Distant seas unfolded in my childish imagination, boats cast off furtively, monasteries glittered amid rocky crags, lions carried water to the ascetics. My mind brimmed with date trees and camels, strumpets fought to enter the church, fiery chariots rose into the sky, the deserts warbled with women's clogs and laughter, the Tempter came like a kindly Santa Claus and brought gifts of food, gold, and females to the eremites. But they had their eyes riveted on God, and the Tempter vanished.

Be hard, be patient, scorn happiness, have no fear of death, look beyond this world to the supreme good: such was the insuppressible voice which rose from these popular editions and instructed my childish heart. And together with this came a vehement thirst for furtive departures and distant voyages, for wanderings filled with martyrdom.

I read the saints' legends, listened to fairy tales, overheard conversations, and inside me all this was transformed—deformed—into dazzling lies. Assembling my schoolmates or the children of the neighborhood, I passed these lies off as my own adventures. I told them I had just returned from the desert. I had a lion there, and I'd loaded two jugs on his back and we had gone together to the fountain to fetch water; or that outside our door the other day I had seen an angel who plucked out one of his plumes and gave it to me. I even had the plume in my hand ready to show them (we had killed a white rooster at home the other day and I had removed a long white feather). I said in addition that I planned to make the feather into a pen and write.

"Write? Write what?"

"Lives of the saints. My granddad's life."

"Was your granddad a saint? Didn't you tell us he fought the Turks?"

"Isn't that the same thing?" I answered, sharpening the tip of the feather with my clasp knife in order to make it into a pen.

One day in school we read in our primer that a child fell down a well and found himself in a fabulous city with gilded churches, flowering orchards, and shops full of cakes, candies, and toy muskets. My mind caught fire. Running home, I tossed my satchel in the yard and threw myself upon the brim of the well so that I could fall inside and enter the fabulous city. My mother was sitting by the courtyard window combing my little sister's hair. Catching sight of me, she uttered a cry, ran, and seized me by the smock just as I was kicking the ground in order to hurl myself headforemost into the well.

Every Sunday when I went to church, I saw an icon (placed low on the iconostasis) which showed Christ rising from the grave and hovering in the air, a white banner in His hand. On the bottom His guards were fallen on their backs and staring at Him in terror. I had heard many stories about Cretan uprisings and about wars, I'd been told that my paternal grandfather was a great military leader, and as I gazed at the icon, I gradually convinced myself that Christ was indeed my grandfather. I collected my friends around the icon, therefore, and said to them, "Look at my grandfather. He's holding the banner and going to war. And see there on the bottom? The Turks, sprawled on their backs."

What I said was neither true nor false; it overstepped the limits of logic and ethics in order to hover in a lighter, freer air. If someone had accused me of telling lies, I would have wept from shame. The feather in my hands had ceased to be a rooster's; the angel had given it to me. I was not telling lies. I had an unshakable faith that the Christ with the banner was my grandfather and the terror-stricken guards below were the Turks.

Much, much later, when I started writing poems and novels, I came to understand that this secret elaboration is termed "creation."

One day while reading the legend of Saint John of the Hut, I jumped to my feet and made a decision: "I shall go to Mount Athos to become a saint!" Without turning to look at my mother (Saint John of the Hut had not turned to look at his mother), I strode over the threshold and out into the street. Taking the most outlying lanes and running all the way for fear that one of my uncles might see me and take me back home, I reached the harbor, where I approached a caique, the one which was ready to weigh anchor first. A sun-roasted seaman was leaning over the iron bitt and struggling to undo the cable. Trembling with emotion, I went up to him.

"Can you take me with you, Captain?"

"Where do you want to go?"

"Mount Athos."

"Where? Mount Athos? To do what"'

"Become a saint."

The skipper shook with laughter. Clapping his hands as though shooing away a hen, he shouted, "Home! Home!"

I ran home in disgrace, crawled under the sofa, and never breathed a word to anyone. Today is the first time I admit it: my initial attempt to become a saint miscarried.

My misery lasted for years, perhaps even to this day. I was born, after all, on Friday the eighteenth of February, the day of souls, a very holy day indeed, and the old midwife clutched me in her hands, brought me close to the light, and looked at me with great care. She seemed to see some kind of mystic signs on me. Lifting me high, she said, "Mark my words, one day this child will become a bishop."

When in the course of time I learned of the midwife's prophecy, I believed it, so well did it match my own most secret yearnings. A great responsibility fell upon me then, and I no longer wished to do anything that a bishop would not have done. Much later, when I saw what bishops actually do, I changed my mind. Thenceforth, in order to deserve the sainthood I so craved, I wished to avoid all things that bishops do.

9

LONGING FOR FLIGHT

THE DAYS were slow-moving and monotonous in that era. People did not read newspapers; the radio, telephone, and cinema were still unborn, and life rolled along noiselessly—serious and sparing of words. Each person was a closed world, each house both locked and bolted. The goodmen within grew older day by day. They caroused in whispers lest they be overheard, or they quarreled secretly, or fell mutely ill and died. Then the door opened for the remains to emerge, and the four walls momentarily revealed their secret. But the door closed again immediately, and life began noiselessly to grind away once more.

On the annual holidays—Christ's birth, death, or resurrection—all the people dressed, donned their jewelry, and forsook their houses to pour out of every lane. They were headed for the cathedral, which awaited them with gaping doors. Its great candlesticks and chandeliers had been lighted, and the knight and master of the house, Saint Minas, stood on the threshold to receive his dear friends the residents of Megalo Kastro. Hearts opened, misfortunes were put out of mind, names forgotten; all became one. They were slaves no longer. Disputes and Turks did not exist, nor did death. Inside the church, with the mounted Captain Minas as leader, everyone felt part of an immortal army.

Life was deep and stationary in those years. Laughter was minimal then in Megalo Kastro, tears ample, and the undivulged heartaches more ample still. The solid citizens were serious, always looking after their own affairs, the rabble docile: they rose with respect whenever a rich man passed. But all were united by a single shared passion which made them forget their cares and privations and brought them together in brotherhood. They did not divulge this passion, however, because they feared the Turk.

And lo! One day the still waters began to move. A steamship all bedecked with flags was seen to enter the harbor one morning. Those Kastrians who happened to be at the waterfront stood with gaping jaws. What was this multicolored, multiplumed, flag-bedecked boat which had slipped between the two Venetian towers at the harbor's mouth? It was coming close. Saints preserve us! This one said it was a flock of birds, that one, a group dressed for a masquerade, and still another, a floating garden, one of those that Sinbad the Sailor had viewed in warm faraway seas. At that point a huge wild voice cried from the harbor café, "Welcome to the pelerines!" The onlookers suddenly all took a deep breath; they had understood. The boat had come closer meanwhile. Now its cargo was clearly visible: gaudily dressed women, with hats, with plumes, with colorful pelerines, their cheeks dabbed with poppy-colored rouge. At the sight of them the older Cretans crossed themselves and murmured, "Get thee behind me, Satan," spitting onto their chests. What business did the hussies have here? This was celebrated Megalo Kastro; it wasn't going to stand for any such abominations!

An hour later scarlet programs had been pasted to all the walls and the city was informed that these people were a troupe of actors and actresses. It seems they had come to entertain the Kastrians.

To this day I still cannot understand how the miracle happened, but my father took me by the hand and said, "Let's go to the theater and see what the devil this is." Night had already fallen. He held me by the hand and we proceeded harborwards to a poor section which was unknown to me. There were huge sheepfolds and only a few houses. One of the sheepfolds was brightly illuminated. The sound of a clarinet and bass drum came from within. A ship's sail hung over the entrance; you raised it to go inside. Entering, we found benches, stools, and chairs with seated men and women gazing at a curtain in front of them and waiting for it to open. A gentle breeze came from the sea, the air was fragrant, the men and women talking, laughing, and munching peanuts or pumpkin seeds.

"Which is the theater?" asked my father (he too was going to this kind of fête for the very first time). He was shown the curtain. We sat down as well, therefore, and pinned our eyes on this curtain. Written at the top of the canvas in large capitals was

"Schiller's *The Brigands*, a most entertaining play," and just below, "No matter what you see, do not be disturbed. It's all imaginary."

"What does 'imaginary' mean?" I asked my father.

"Hot air," he answered.

My father had his own problems. He turned to ask his neighbor who these brigands were, but too late. Three raps were heard, and the curtain opened. I stared in goggle-eyed amazement. A paradise had unfolded before me: male and female angels came and went, dressed in gaudy costumes, with plumes, with gold, their cheeks colored white and orange. They raised their voices and shouted, but I did not understand; they became angry, but I did not know why. Then two hulking giants suddenly made their entrance. It seems they were brothers, and they began to argue and hurl insults and pursue each other with intent to kill.

My father pricked up his ears and listened, grumbling with dissatisfaction. He squirmed on his chair; he was sitting on hot coals. Drawing out his handkerchief, he wiped away the sweat which had begun to flow from his brow. But when he finally realized that the two gangling beanstalks were brothers at odds, he jumped to his feet in a frenzy.

"What kind of buffoonery is this?" he said in a loud voice. "Let's go home!"

He grabbed my arm and we left, overturning two or three chairs in our haste.

Putting his hand on my shoulder, he shook me. "Don't ever set foot in a theater again, you wretch. Do you hear? Because if you do, I'll tan your hide!"

That was my first acquaintance with the theater.

A warm breeze blew; my mind sprouted grass, my entrails filled with anemones. Spring came with her fiancé Saint George mounted on a white steed, it left, summer came, and the Blessed Virgin reclined upon the fruited earth, that she too might rest after bearing such a son. Saint Dimítris arrived on a sorrel horse in the middle of the rains, dragging autumn behind him crowned with ivy and shriveled vine leaves. Winter pressed down upon us. At home (when my father was absent) my mother, sister, and I lighted the brazier and sat around it roasting chestnuts or chick-peas on the embers. We were waiting for Christ to be born, so that my rosy-cheeked grandfather could come with the roast piglet wrapped in lemon leaves. This is exactly how we imagined winter: like my grandfather, with black boots, white mustachios, and holding a roast suckling pig in its hands.

Time passed; I grew bigger. In the courtyard the pots of basil and marigolds shrank; I mounted Eminé's steps in a single stride now, with no need for her to hold out her hand. I grew bigger, and inside me the old desires grew bigger also, while others, new ones, rose by their side. The saints' legends were too confining; they stifled me. It was not that I had ceased to believe. I believed, but the saints struck me now as much too submissive. They continually bowed their heads before God and said yes. The blood of Crete had awakened inside me. Without elucidating this clearly in my mind, I had a presentiment that the true man is he who resists, struggles, and is not afraid, in time of great need, to say no, even to God.

I could not set any of this new agitation forth in words, but at that stage in my life I had no need of words. I understood unerringly, without help from either my intellect or words. I was overwhelmed with sorrow when I saw the saints sitting with folded arms in front of paradise, calling out, imploring, and waiting for the door to open. They reminded me of the lepers I observed every time I went to our vineyard. They sat just outside the city gate with their eroded noses, missing fingers, putrescent lips, and extended the stumps of their arms to passers-by, begging for charity. I felt not the least bit sorry for them. They disgusted me, and I always turned my head the other way and passed as rapidly as I could. This was the state to which the saints began to decline in my childish mind. Was there no other way to enter paradise? Leaving the dragons and princesses of the fairy tales, I had entered the Theban desert with the beggar-saints, and now I felt I must escape them as well.

My mother made sweets for every important holiday, sometimes kourabiédhes, sometimes loukoums, and at Easter the special paschal cake. I used to put on my best suit and go to distribute them to my aunts and uncles as a way of sending our regards. They, in their turn, welcomed me heartily and presented me with silver coins, supposedly so that I could buy candy and decals. But I ran the next day to Mr. Loukás's tiny bookstore and bought pamphlets about distant lands and great explorers. The seed of Robinson Crusoe had obviously fallen into me. Now it had begun to bear fruit.

I understood only a small part of these new "saints' legends," but their essence filtered down to the depths of my soul. My brain began to open now and be filled with medieval towers, exotic regions, and mysterious islands which smelled of cloves and cinnamon. Savages with red feathers stepped inside me, danced, lighted fires, roasted human beings, and the islands surrounding them smiled like newborn infants. These new saints did not beg for alms. Whatever they desired they took by the sword. I thought to myself, If only a person could enter paradise in this way, on horseback, like those knights! Hero together with saint: that was the perfect man.

My family home grew narrow; Megalo Kastro grew narrow. The earth now seemed like a tropical jungle with colorful birds and beasts, with ripe honey-sweet fruits, and I wanted (so I imagined) to traverse all of this tropical jungle in order to protect a pale damsel in distress. Passing by a café one day, I saw her face. Her name was Genevieve.

In my imagination the saints now merged with the vehement knights who set out to save the world, the Holy Sepulcher, or some maiden. They merged as well with the great explorers, and the ships of Columbus which departed from a tiny Spanish port were the same—and the same wind swelled their sails—as the ships which up to that point had departed within me for the desert, loaded with saints.

When I read Cervantes, still later, his hero Don Quixote seemed to me a great saint and martyr who had left amidst jeering and laughter to discover, beyond our humble everyday life, the essence which hides in back of appearances. What essence? I did not know at the time; I learned later. There is only one essence, always the same. As yet, man has found no other means to elevate himself—none but the routing of matter and the submission of the individual to an end which transcends the individual, even though that end be chimerical. When the heart believes and loves, nothing chimerical exists; nothing exists but courage, trust, and fruitful action.

Years have passed. I tried to establish order over the chaos of my imagination, but this essence, the same that presented itself to me still hazily when I was a child, has always struck me as the very heart of truth. It is our duty to set ourselves an end beyond our individual concerns, beyond our convenient, agreeable habits, higher than our own selves, and disdaining laughter, hunger, even death, to toil night and day to attain that end. No, not to attain it. The self-respecting soul, as soon as he reaches his goal, places it still further away. Not to attain it, but never to halt in the ascent. Only thus does life acquire nobility and oneness.

Such were the flames in which I spent my childhood. The many vicissitudes of the saints and heroes struck me as man's simplest, most realistic course. But these flames joined with still others, greater ones, that were burning Megalo Kastro and Crete in that era of slavery.

Megalo Kastro in those olden heroic times was not a band of houses, shops and alleyways huddled together along a Cretan shore line in front of an incessantly angry sea. Its inhabitants were not a disorderly, headless (or multiheaded) troop of men, women, and children who dissipated all their efforts in the daily concerns: food, children, women. A strict unwritten order governed them. No one lifted a rebellious hand against the harsh law above him. Someone over his head gave the orders. The entire city was a garrison, each inhabitant himself a garrison eternally besieged, and as his captain he had a saint, Saint Minas, the defender of Megalo Kastro. Astride a gray horse, holding a red lance pointed at the sky, the saint remained motionless all day in his diminutive church, upon his icon—fierce-eyed, sunburned, with a short curly beard. All day long, weighed down by the silver ex-votos—hands, feet, eyes, hearts—which the Kastrians had attached to him so that his grace might heal them, he remained immobile, pretending to be only a picture: paint on a piece of board. But as soon as night fell and the Christians gathered in their homes and the lights began going out one by one, he pushed aside paints and silver offerings with a sweep of his hand, spurred his horse, and went out for a ride through the Greek quarters, went out on patrol. He closed whatever doors the Christians had forgetfully left open, he whistled to night owls to return to their homes, he stood outside the doorway and listened absorbedly, with satisfaction, whenever he heard singing. A wedding must be taking place, he murmured. A blessing on the happy couple, and may they bear children to swell the ranks of Christendom. Afterwards he made a tour of the ramparts which gird Megalo Kastro, and at cockcrow, before daybreak, spurred his horse, entered the church with a bound, and climbed onto his icon. Once more he put on a show of indifference. But his mount had perspired, its mouth and flanks were covered with froth, and when Mr. Haralámbis, the verger, came first thing in the morning to dust and polish the candlesticks, he saw Saint Minas's horse drenched in sweat. This did not surprise him, however, for he knew (everyone knew) that the saint patrolled the streets the entire night. Whenever the Turks sharpened their knives and prepared to fall upon the Christians, Saint Minas sprang from his icon once more in order to protect the citizens of Megalo Kastro. The Turks did not see him, but they heard his horse whinnying, recognized the sound, saw the sparks thrown by the horseshoes as they struck the cobbles, and burrowed panic-stricken into their homes.

A few years before, however, they had actually seen him with their eyes. They were preparing another massacre, but Saint Minas had charged toward the Turkish quarter upon his horse. Just as he rounded a street corner he was observed by the half-insane hodja-Moustafáa, who took to his heels and began screaming, "Allah! Allah! Saint Minas is descending upon us!" The Turks opened their doors a crack and peeped out. As they spied the saint with his golden armor, his curly gray beard, his red lance, their knees gave way beneath them and they resheathed their knives.

For the Kastrians, Saint Minas was not simply holy, he was their captain. They called him Captain Minas and secretly brought him their arms to be blessed. Even my father lighted candles for him. God only knows what he must have said to him and what reproaches he heaped upon him for delaying so long to liberate Crete.

He was Christendom's captain. Hassan Bey, the Christians' bloodthirsty antagonist, was his neighbor; his sanctum butted against the church. One night he heard knocking on the wall just above his bed. He understood. It was Saint Minas, threatening him because on that very day he had beaten a Christian almost to death. Captain Minas had grown angry on this account and was knocking now against his wall. Raising his fist, Hassan Bey began to strike the wall in his own right. "Hey there, neighbor," he shouted, "you're right. Yes, by my faith, you're right. But stop knocking down my wall and I'll bring you two goatskins of oil for your watch lamp and twenty okes of wax each year to appease you. We're neighbors; let's not quarrel!" And ever since then Hassan Bey (the dog!) sent his servant each year on Saint Minas's name day, the eleventh of November, and had him unload two goatskins of oil and twenty okes of wax in the churchyard. Saint Minas never knocked on his wall again.

There is a kind of flame in Crete—let us call it "soul"—something more powerful than either life or death. There is pride, obstinacy, valor, and together with these something else inexpressible and imponderable, something which makes you rejoice that you are a human being, and at the same time tremble.

When I was a child, the Cretan air smelled of the Turk's exhalation, the breath of the wild beast. A Turkish yataghan hung suspended over every head. Many years later, when I saw "Toledo in the Storm," I understood what kind of air I inhaled when a child and what angels hung like meteors over Crete.

August was the month I liked best in my childhood, the month I still like best. After all, it brings us grapes and figs, cantaloupes and watermelons. I christened it Saint August. Here is my protector, I told myself; to him I shall address my prayers. When I desire anything, I shall ask Saint August, and he will ask God, and God will give me what I want. Once I took some watercolors and painted him. He proved to be very much like my peasant grandfather—the same ruddy cheeks, the same broad smile—but he was barefooted in a wine press, treading grapes. His legs up to the knees, even as far as the thighs, I painted red with must; his head I crowned with vine leaves. Something was missing, however. What? Regarding him carefully, I placed two horns on his head amid the vine leaves, because the kerchief my grandfather used to wear had two large hornlike knots, one to the right and one to the left.

The moment I drew August and established his features, my confidence in him became established inside me, and each year I waited for him to come and vintage the vineyards of Crete, tread the harvest, and perform his miracle of extracting wine from grapes. For I remember being greatly tormented by this mystery. How could grapes become wine? Only Saint August had the power to perform such a miracle. Oh, if only I might meet him by chance one day in the vineyard we had outside of Megalo Kastro, and ask him to tell me the secret; I could not understand this miracle. The unripe fruit turned into grapes, the grapes into wine, men drank the wine and became drunk. Why? Why did they become drunk? All these seemed frightening mysteries to me. Once when I asked my father, he knitted his brows and replied, "Mind your own business!"

It was in August also that the grapes were laid on the cloth-covered tracts to be dried by the sun and turned into raisins. One year we had gone to our vineyard and were staying in our little country cottage. The air was fragrant, the earth burning, the grasshoppers burning too. They seemed to be sitting on live coals.

It was August fifteenth, the Assumption of the Blessed Virgin, and the workers were on holiday. My father sat at the foot of an olive tree smoking. The nearby neighbors, who had laid out their grapes as well, sat next to him smoking in silence. They seemed worried. Everyone had riveted his eyes upon a tiny, darkly sinister cloud which had appeared mutely at the horizon and begun to advance. I was sitting near my father like the others, and I too watched the cloud. I liked it. Fluffy, colored a dull lead-gray, it grew continually bigger, all the while changing its face and body. Sometimes it resembled a full goatskin, sometimes a black-feathered vulture, sometimes the elephant I had seen in a picture; it swung its trunk back and forth, trying to find the earth below and touch it. A warm breeze blew; the leaves on the olive tree shuddered. One of the neighbors jumped to his feet and extended his arm toward the advancing cloud.

"Devil take it!" he grumbled. "Call me a liar if it doesn't bring us a downpour."

"You'd better eat your words," a pious old man said to him. "The Virgin won't permit it. This is her day."

My father grunted but did not breathe a word. He believed in the Virgin but had doubts about her ability to command clouds.

While they were talking, the sky became completely overcast and the first large, warm drops began to fall. The clouds drew close to the ground; yellow lightning flashes tore mutely across the sky.

"Holy Virgin!" cried all the neighbors. "Help!"

They all jumped up and scattered in every direction, each racing toward his vineyard, where his entire year's supply of raisins was laid out. The air grew continually darker as they ran, black tresses suspended themselves from the clouds, and the squall broke out in earnest. The drain ditches overflowed, the roads began to run like rivers. Mournful voices rose from every vineyard. Some cursed, others called upon the Virgin to take pity on them and intervene. Finally, from every vineyard, behind the olive trees, came cries of lamentation.

I slipped away from our cottage and began to run beneath the downpour, transported by a strange joy resembling intoxication. It was the first time I made the horrible discovery that as soon as great calamities occur, an inexplicable, inhuman joy takes possession of me. When I first saw a fire, the time my aunt Kalliópe's house burned down, I hopped and danced before the flames until someone caught me by the nape of the neck and tossed me out of the way. And when our teacher Krasákis died, I had to force myself not to laugh. It was as though my teacher and my aunt's house had been weights removed from around my neck, relieving me. Fire, deluge, and death struck me as extremely friendly ghosts. I felt I was a ghost from the same family. We were demons one and all, toiling to relieve the earth of its houses and population.

I reached the road, but it was a racing torrent and I could not go across. I just stood there and looked as the half-dried grapes—the whole year's labor—flowed away with the water by the armful, racing toward the sea to perish. The lamentations grew louder. Several women had plunged knee-deep in the water, where they struggled to preserve a few raisins. Others, their wimples removed, stood at the edge of the road pulling out their hair.

I was drenched to the bone. Fighting to hide my joy, I ran back to the house, anxious to see how my father had reacted. Would he be weeping? Would he be cursing or crying out? As I passed the drying area, I saw that all of our grapes were gone.

I found him standing motionless on the threshold biting his mustache. My mother stood behind him; she was weeping.

"Father," I cried, "our grapes are gone!"

"We're not gone," he answered. "Shut up!"

I never forgot that moment. I believe that it served as a great lesson in the crises of my life. I always remembered my father standing calmly, motionlessly on the threshold, neither cursing, entreating, nor weeping. Motionless, he stood watching the disaster and—alone among all the neighbors—preserved his human dignity.

10

MASSACRE

MISFORTUNE is welcome when it comes unaccompanied, we say in Crete, for in truth only rarely does it come unaccompanied. The following day the sky was completely clear. The day before it had had its fling and decimated mankind; today it was laughing. The proprietors toured their vineyards. All the grapes were lost; fistful after fistful could still be seen buried in the mud. At exactly noon my father returned in haste from Kastro. One of his friends had arrived early in the morning, whispered something in his ear, and left. Word had spread that Christians had killed some important aga in a certain village. The Turks were incensed, the Christians had armed themselves. We were going to have another uprising. The Turks were racing to Megalo Kastro to find safety behind the Venetian walls.

I was walking through our vineyard with my mother and sister, collecting the last grapes that still hung on the vines. The heat had reached its zenith, the air was seething. Suddenly we heard shouts and braying in the road. A great tumultuous crowd was passing. The donkeys were laden with kneading troughs, kettles, and Turkish women. Behind them the turbaned men sloshed hurriedly through the mud, some barefooted, some with boots lacking soles. Bellowing, not speaking, they raced toward Kastro.

"Turkish dogs!" growled my mother. Seizing us beneath the armpits, she took us inside.

I hugged her knees.

"Why are they running, Mother?" I asked. "What do they want? Why are you shivering?"

She stroked my hair.

"Oh Lord, what your eyes are about to see, my child! It's a terrible thing to be born a Cretan."

We opened the window a crack and looked out. The horde

receded into the distance, then disappeared behind the olive trees. The road became quiet.

"Let's go," said my father. "Quickly. We've got to arrive before sunset."

My mother seized our hands. My father took his revolver from beneath his pillow. He examined it. It was loaded. Thrusting it in his pocket, he followed behind us.

The sun was about to set as we passed through the fortified gate. But in the lanes it seemed that night had already fallen. People were running hastily, doors being slammed, mothers appearing and calling their children to come in from the streets. Our Turkish neighbor Fatome saw us and did not say good evening.

My father sat down in his accustomed place on the sofa, in the corner near the courtyard window. Mother stood in front of him waiting. She knew that he was about to give orders. He took out his tobacco pouch and rolled a cigarette slowly, leisurely. Then, without lifting his eyes, he said, "No one is to set foot out of the house."

He turned to me with a frown. "Are you afraid?"

"No," I replied.

"And what if the Turks break down the door? What if they come inside and slaughter you?"

I shuddered. I could feel the blade at my throat. I wanted to cry, Yes, I'm afraid, I'm afraid! but my father's eyes were fixed on me and I was too ashamed. Suddenly my breast swelled out. I had felt my heart being filled with manly valor.

"Even if they slaughter me," I said, "I won't be afraid!"

"Good," said my father, and he lit his cigarette.

That past summer when I went to our village to see my grandfather die, I slept with one of my uncles in a melon field. Suddenly, just as I was about to fall asleep, I heard a *crr! crr! crr!* all around me: the creaking of some strange objects. Frightened, I drew close to my uncle. "What's making that creaking noise?" I asked. "I'm afraid." My uncle turned his back to me, irritated because I had awakened him. "Go to sleep, city boy," he said. "Is this the first time you've heard that noise? It's the watermelons growing bigger." Similarly on this day, my father's eyes fixed upon me as they were, I felt my heart growing bigger and creaking.

Megalo Kastro had four fortified gates. The Turks locked them each day at sunset and opened them when the sun came up again. No one could either enter or leave the city all night long, and thus the few Christians inside fell into the rat trap. The Turks could carry out a massacre at night, as long as the gates were locked and bolted, because they were in a majority inside the city and also had the Turkish garrison.

This was when I experienced my first massacre. A few days later, for the first time, my childish mind saw life's true face behind the beautiful mask of sea, verdant fields, fruit-laden vines, wheaten bread, and a mother's smile. Life's true face: the skull.

It was at this time, also, that the seed dropped secretly into my bowels, the seed which was destined, much later, to flower and bear as its fruit my third eye, the inner one: limpid, open day and night, knowing neither fear nor hope.

My mother, my sister, and I sat glued to one another, barricaded within our house. We heard the frenzied Turks in the street outside, cursing, threatening, breaking down doors, and slaughtering Christians. We heard dogs barking, the cries and death râles of the wounded, and a droning in the air as though an earthquake were in progress. My father stood in wait behind the door, his musket loaded. In his hand, I remember, he held an oblong stone which he called a whetstone. He was sharpening a long black-handled knife on it. We waited. "If the Turks break down the door and enter," he had told us, "I plan to slaughter you myself, before you fall into their hands." My mother, sister, and I had all agreed. Now we were waiting.

I believe I would have seen my soul maturing during those hours if the invisible had become visible. I sensed that in the space of just a few hours I had begun to change abruptly from a child into a man.

Thus the night went by. Morning came, the droning subsided, death retired to a distance. Carefully opening our door, we put our heads outside. Several of the neighboring housewives had timidly, stealthily opened their windows. They were examining the street. At that moment the Turkish kouloúri man came by, the one with the small high-pitched voice and no beard on his face. He was hawking in a singsong the cinnamon and sesame rolls he carried on a huge tin tray upon his head. What a pleasure that was! Everything seemed reborn; for the first time, it seemed, we were seeing sky, clouds, and a tin tray laden with fragrant kouloúria. My mother bought me one. I chewed it with indescribable delight.

"Did the massacre go away, Mother?" I asked.

This frightened her.

"Quiet, quiet, my child. Don't mention its name! It might hear you and return."

I wrote the word *massacre* just now and the hairs of my head stood on end, because when I was a child this word was not simply eight letters of the alphabet pasted one next to the other, it was a great droning, and feet kicking down doors, horrible faces with knives between their teeth, women shrieking everywhere in the vicinity, and men loading muskets as they knelt behind their doors. For us who lived as children in Crete in that era, there are also several other words which drip copiously with blood and tears, words upon which an entire people was crucified: *freedom, Saint Minas, Christ, revolution.*

The man who writes has an oppressive and unhappy fate. This is because the nature of his work obliges him to use words; that is, to convert his inner surge into immobility. Every word is an adamantine shell which encloses a great explosive force. To discover its meaning you must let it burst inside you like a bomb and in this way liberate the soul which it imprisons.

Once there was a rabbi who always made his will and tearfully bade farewell to his wife and children before he went to the synagogue to pray, for he never knew if he would emerge from the prayer alive. As he used to say, "When I pronounce a word, for instance *Lord,* this word shatters my heart. I am terror-stricken and do not know if I shall be able to make the leap to the following words: *have pity on me.*"

O for the person able to read a poem in this way, or the word *massacre,* or a letter from the woman he loves—or this Report by a man who struggled much in his life and yet managed to accomplish so very little!

Early the next morning my father took me by the hand.

"Come," he said.

My mother became frightened. "Where are you taking the boy? Not a single Christian has left his house yet."

"Come," my father repeated. He opened the door and we went outside.

"Where are we going?" I asked. My hand was trembling inside his massive palm.

I looked up and down the street. It was deserted except for two Turkish women at the corner who were washing at the tap. The water had turned red.

"Are you afraid?"

"Yes."

"That doesn't matter. You'll get used to it."

Turning the corner, we headed toward the harbor gate. We passed a house that was still smoking and many others with broken doors, blood still on the thresholds. When we reached the main square with its lion-sculptured fountain and the huge old plane tree at the edge, my father stopped.

"Look!" he said, pointing with his hand.

I looked up toward the plane tree and uttered a cry. Three hanged men were swinging there, one next to the other. They were barefooted, dressed only in their nightshirts, and deep green tongues were hanging out of their mouths. Unable to endure the sight, I turned my head away and clung to my father's knees. But he grasped my head with his hand and rotated it toward the plane tree.

"Look!" he ordered me again.

My eyes filled with hanged men.

"As long as you live—do you hear—may these hanged men never be out of your sight!"

"Who killed them?"

"Liberty, God bless it!"

I did not understand. Goggle-eyed, I stared and stared at the three bodies that were slowly swaying among the yellowing leaves of the plane tree.

My father swept his glance around him and pricked up his ears. The streets were deserted. He turned to me.

"Can you touch them?"

"No!" I answered, terrified.

"You can! . . . Come!"

We went close; my father crossed himself hurriedly, repeatedly.

"Touch their feet!" he commanded.

He took my hand. I felt their cold, crusty skin against the tips of my fingers. The night dew was still upon them.

"Kiss them! Do obeisance!" my father now commanded. Seeing

me try to make a break and get away, he seized me beneath the arms, lifted me, bent my head downward, and forcefully glued my mouth to the rigid feet.

He put me down. My knees could not support me. He leaned over and looked at me.

"That was to help you get used to it," he said.

Once more he took me by the hand. We returned home. My mother was standing behind the door waiting anxiously.

"Where in God's name did you go?" she asked, seizing me avidly and kissing me.

"We went to do obeisance," answered my father, and he gave me a trustful look.

The fortified gates remained closed for three days; on the fourth they were opened. But the Turks prowled about the streets, filled the cafés, gathered in the mosques; the seething within them still had not subsided, their eyes were still full of murder. Crete was ready to burst into flames—only a single spark was needed. All the Christians who had children boarded steamships and caiques to depart for free Greece. All who did not have children left Megalo Kastro and took to the mountains.

We were among those who went to the harbor in order to leave. My father led the way, my mother and sister followed him, and I brought up the rear.

"We men must protect the women," my father had said to me (I was not even eight years old). "I'll go in front, you stay behind. And look sharp!"

We passed through neighborhoods which had been burned. Some of the victims still had not been removed; the corpses had already begun to stink. My father bent down at one of the doorways and picked up a stone all splattered with blood.

"Keep it," he said to me.

I had at last begun to understand why my father behaved in this ferocious way. He did not apply the methods of New Pedagogy; he followed the age-old, merciless method which is alone capable of preserving the race. This is how the wolf trains its favorite cub, the firstborn—it teaches it to hunt and kill, and by means of trickery or valor to escape from traps. To my father's ferocious pedagogy I owe the endurance and obstinacy which have always stood by me in times of difficulty. To this ferocity I also owe all the indomitable thoughts which govern me now at the end of my life and which do not condescend to accept comforting from either God or the devil.

"Let's go up to your room and decide," my father said to me before we left home.

He halted in the middle of the room and pointed to the large map of Greece which hung on the wall.

"I don't want either Piraeus or Athens; that's where everyone will congregate. Then they'll start whining that they don't have anything to eat, and they'll beg for help. None of that disgusting business for me! Choose some island."

"Whichever I want?"

"Yes, whichever you want."

Climbing onto a chair, I took all the Aegean islands in with a glance: green dots on the blue sea. Then, starting at Santorini, I promenaded my finger to Melos, Siphnos, Mykonos and Paros. At Naxos I stopped.

"Naxos!" I said. I liked its shape and name. How could I ever foresee at that moment what a decisive effect that accidental, fatal choice was to have on my entire life!

"Naxos!" I repeated, looking at my father.

"Fine," he replied. "Let's go to Naxos."

11

NAXOS

THIS ISLAND possessed great sweetness and tranquility. Everywhere huge piles of melons, peaches, and figs, surrounded by a calm sea. I looked at the inhabitants. Their faces were kindly; they had never been frightened by Turks or earthquakes, and their eyes were not on fire. Liberty here had extinguished the yearning for liberty. Life extended like a sheet of contented, slumbering water which, though turbulent at times, never raised a true tempest. As I walked about Naxos, security was the island's first gift that I became aware of. Security and, a few days later, boredom. We had made the acquaintance of a Mr. Lazaros, a wealthy Naxiot who had a splendid orchard at Engarés, one hour from the main town. He invited us there, and we stayed two weeks. What abundance, what fruit-laden trees, what beatitude! Crete became a fairy tale, a menacing cloud far in the distance with never an alarm, nor shedding of blood, nor struggle for liberation. All this melted away and vanished in the drowsy Naxiot well-being.

I found a pile of books in one of the cupboards of the country mansion. They were yellowed with age. I took them, and each day I sat beneath an olive tree and leafed through them avidly. I gazed at the old, faded illustrations of warriors and ladies, wild beasts and banana jungles. In another book, frozen seas, icebound ships, bear cubs rolling in the snow like tufts of cotton. In another, distant cities with high chimneys, workers, and huge fires.

My mind broadened; the world broadened with it. My imagination was filled with gigantic trees, strange animals, black and yellow people. Several of the phrases I read threw my heart into a ferment. In one of these yellowed books I came across the words, "Happy the man who views the most seas and the most continents." And in another, "Better a bull for a day than an ox for a year." This latter I did not understand very well, but I knew one thing: I did not want to be an ox. Closing the book, I inhaled the warm fragrant air, my eyes fixed upon the fruit-laden apricot and peach trees. I was an insect with still-undeveloped wings, kicking at the soil with its little feet in an effort to fly, even though its heart trembled. Would it succeed or fail? Better be patient, just a little while longer.

I was patient. Without even suspecting this, I was secretly, inwardly preparing for the day when my wings would be ready and I would leave.

But Mr. Lazaros's niece, a twelve-year-old tomboy named Stella, had suspended a swing from the olive tree next to mine. She swung in the air and sang, the movement lifting her dress so that her snow-white, exquisitely round knees glittered in the sunlight. I could not stand to hear her song or look at her knees, and one day in a furor I banged my books down on the ground. She just looked at me and burst out laughing, chewing away on her gum. Very often too she taunted me with mocking songs. I have forgotten all of them except one:

Lower those sable eyes regarding me,
Lower them, my jewel; they are flogging me.

"Stella," I cried angrily, jumping to my feet, "either you leave or I do!"

She tumbled off her swing. "Let's leave together!" she answered, no longer laughing. Then, lowering her voice, "Let's leave together, my poor friend, because on Monday you're going to be shut up in the Catholic school. I heard your father talking with my uncle."

Within the commanding Naxiot citadel which had been inhabited for centuries now by the Frankish conquerors was the celebrated French school run by Catholic priests. My father and I had climbed to it one day. He gazed at it for some time, then shook his head.

"A boy can get a fine education here, but the teachers are Catholic priests, the devil take them! You might turn Catholic."

Though he did not mention the school again, I was aware that the idea was pricking him and that he did not know what decision to make. After supper on the same day that Stella had alerted me, my father took me with him for a walk in the orchard. The moon had risen; everything was tranquil and fragrant.

For quite some time he did not speak. Finally, when it was the hour for us to return to the house, he halted and said, "The revolution in Crete will be a long one. I'm going back there; I can't let my fellow Christians fight while I stroll in orchards. Every night I see your grandfather in my sleep, and he scolds me. I have to go. But meanwhile you mustn't lose any time. I want you to become a man."

He fell silent again, took a few steps, then halted once more.

"Do you understand?" he asked me. "A man—that means useful to your homeland. Too bad you were born for studies and not for arms, but unfortunately there's nothing to be done about it. That's your road; follow it. Understand? Educate yourself in order to help Crete gain her freedom. Let that be your goal. Otherwise, to the devil with education! I don't want you to become a teacher, monk, or a wise Solomon. Get that clear! I've made up my mind, now you make up yours. If you can't help Crete either through arms or letters, you'd do better to lie down and die."

"I'm afraid of the Catholic fathers," I said.

"So am I. The true man fears, but conquers his fear. I have faith in you."

He reflected for a moment, then corrected himself. "No, I don't have faith in you, I have faith in the blood which flows in your veins—the blood of Crcte. Ready now, cross yourself, clench your fists, and on Monday, God willing, we'll go to register you with the Catholics."

It was raining on the day my father and I began the climb to the citadel—a sparse autumn drizzle which dimmed the streets. Behind us the sea was sighing. A gentle breeze kept shanking the leaves from the trees; they fell one by one, yellow and brown, and adorned the wet ascent. The clouds raced over our heads, pursued by a strong wind which must have been blowing up above. I raised my head and gazed insatiably as they ran, joined, separated, and as some let down long gray fringes in an effort to touch the earth. Ever since my childhood I had loved to lie on my back in our yard and watch the clouds. Every so often a bird winged by, a crow, swallow, or dove, and I identified with it so completely that I felt the warmth of its breast in my open palm. "Marghí, I think your son's going to become a dreamer and visionary," our neighbor Madame Penelope said one day to my mother. "He's always looking at the clouds."

"Don't worry, Penelope," my mother answered her, "life will come along and make him lower his gaze."

But it still had not come, and on this day I kept admiring the clouds as I climbed to the citadel. I stumbled and slipped constantly. My father gripped my shoulder as though wishing to steady me.

"Forget the clouds. Keep your eyes on the stones beneath you if you don't want to fall and kill yourself."

A young, withered-looking girl emerged from the vaulted doorway of a large half-crumbling house. She too gazed at the sky. Extremely pale and emaciated, with a face characterized by great nobility, she was tightly wrapped in a ragged shawl and shivering. Afterwards I learned that she belonged to one of the celebrated Catholic families of ruined nobility, all dukes and countesses, who centuries before had conquered Naxos and built this citadel to be their seat—built it at the city's highest point, whence they could look down and watch the Orthodox plebeians toiling for their benefit along the harborfront and in the plain beyond. But now they had fallen into decline, were paupers, their palaces in ruins; and their noble great-great granddaughters starved and grew pale. These girls were unable to find husbands because the men of their class had lost their vigor; they either lacked all desire to marry or were unable to support a wife and children. To marry into humble Orthodox stock, on the other hand, was something these noble ladies would never deign to do. They held their pride forever high, for pride was all they had. . . . The girl looked at the sky for a moment, shook her head, stepped inside again.

I remember everything, absolutely everything that happened as I climbed the citadel that day in order to enter the Catholic school. I can still see the cat sitting on a doorstep in the rain; it was white with orange patches. Also a young barefooted girl holding a brazier of burning coals and running, her face bright red from the reflections.

"Here we are," said my father. He raised his arm and knocked on the huge door.

This was the first and perhaps the most decisive leap in my intellectual life. A magic portal opened inside my mind and conducted me into an astonishing world. Until this time Crete and Greece had been the confined arena in which my struggling soul was jammed; now the world broadened, the divisions of humanity multiplied, and my adolescent breast creaked in an effort to contain them all. Before this moment I had divined but had never known with such positiveness that the world is extremely large and that suffering and toil are the companions and fellow warriors not only of the Cretan, but of every man. Above all, only now did I begin to have a presentiment of the great secret: that by means of poetry all this suffering and effort could be transformed into dream; no matter how much of the ephemeral existed, poetry could immortalize it by turning it into song. Only two or three primitive passions had governed me until this time: fear, the struggle to conquer fear, and the yearning for freedom. But now two new passions were kindled inside me: beauty and the thirst for learning. I wanted to read and learn, to see distant lands, to have personal experience of suffering and joy. The world was larger than Greece, the world's suffering was larger than our suffering, and the yearning for freedom was not the exclusive prerogative of the Cretan, it was the eternal struggle of all mankind. Crete did not vanish from my mind, however. Instead, the entire world unfurled within me to become one gigantic Crete which was oppressed by all sorts of Turks but continually leaping to its feet and seeking liberty. In this way, converting the entire world into Crete, I was able in the early years of adolescence to feel the suffering and pain of all mankind.

This French school had students gathered from the whole of Greece. Since I was a Cretan and Crete was at that time fighting the Turks, I considered it my duty not to disgrace my homeland. I had a responsibility to be first in my class. This conviction, which I believe sprang not from individual pride but from a sense of national obligation, increased my powers, and in no time I surpassed my classmates—no, not I, but Crete. Thus the months slipped by in what was for me a previously unheard-of intoxication, a drunken desire to learn and make progress, to pursue the bluebird which (as I afterwards discovered) is called Spirit.

So audacious did my mind become, that one day I made the

harum-scarum decision that next to every word in the French dictionary I would write the Greek equivalent. This labor took me months, requiring the aid of various other dictionaries, and when I finally finished and the entire French dictionary had been translated, I took it and proudly showed it to Père Laurent, the school's director. He was a learned Catholic priest, reticent, with gray eyes, a bitter smile, and a broad beard half white, half blond. Taking the dictionary, he leafed through it, looked at me with admiration, and placed his hand on my head as though wishing to bless me.

"What you've done, my young Cretan," he said, "shows that one day you will become an important man. You are fortunate in having found your road while so young. Scholarship—that is your road. God bless you."

Filled with pride, I ran as well to the assistant director, Père Lelièvre, a well-fed, fun-loving monk with playful eyes, who used to laugh, tell jokes, and play with us. Each weekend he took us on an excursion to one of the school's country orchards. There, freed from Père Laurent, we wrestled all together, laughed, ate fruit, rolled in the grass, and relieved ourselves of the week's burdens.

I ran, therefore, to find Père Lelièvre and show him my achievement. I found him in the courtyard watering a row of lilies. Taking the dictionary, he turned its pages over very, very slowly and looked at them. The more he looked the more inflamed his features became. Suddenly he lifted the dictionary and hurled it in my face.

"Shame on you!" he screamed. "Are you a boy or a doddering old graybeard? What is this old man's work you've wasted your time on? Instead of laughing, playing, and looking through the window at the girls who pass, you sit like a dotard and translate dictionaries! Away with you—out of my sight! Take it from me that if you follow this road, you'll never amount to anything—never! You'll become some miserable round-shouldered little teacher with spectacles. If you're really a Cretan, burn this damnable dictionary and bring me the ashes. Then I'll give you my blessing. Think it over and act. Away with you!"

I went away completely confused. Who was right, what was I to do? Which of the two roads was correct? This question tortured me for years, and when I finally discovered which road was the correct one, my hair had turned gray. Like Buridan's ass, my soul vacillated indecisively between Père Laurent and Père Lelièvre. I looked at the dictionary with the Greek words written ever so diminutively in the margin in red ink, and as I remembered Père Lelièvre's advice, my heart broke in two. No, I did not have the courage to burn it and bring him the ashes. Many years later, when I finally began to understand, I did throw it in the fire. But I did not collect the ashes, for Père Lelièvre had died long since.

Immediately after my father put me in school and saw me settled, he boarded a caique and departed secretly for Crete in order to fight. Once he sent me a succinct note on paper discolored by gunpowder:

> *I'm doing my duty, fighting the Turks. You fight too: stand your ground and don't let those Catholics put ideas into your head. They're dogs, just like the Turks. You're from Crete, don't forget. Your mind isn't your own, it belongs to Crete. Sharpen it as much as you can, so that one day you can use it to help liberate Crete. Since you can't help with arms, why not with your mind? It too is a musket. Do you understand what I'm asking of you? Say yes! That's all for today, tomorrow, and always. Do not disgrace me!*

I felt the whole of Crete upon my shoulders. If I failed to know my lessons perfectly, to understand a problem in arithmetic, to come out first in the examinations, Crete would be disgraced. I lacked boyhood's insouciance, freshness, and levity. When I saw my classmates laugh and play, I admired them. I should have liked to laugh and play also, but Crete was warring and in danger. Most terrible of all was the fact that teachers and students no longer addressed me by name; they called me "the Cretan," and this was an incessant and even more oppressive reminder of my obligation.

As to turning Catholic, I had no fears. Not because I comprehended which religion was the truest, but because of another factor which, though it seems insignificant, influenced my youthful soul more deeply than any theological doctrine. Every morning we had compulsory mass in the Catholic chapel, a tiny bare room in the center of the school building, frightfully hot in summer, frightfully cold in winter, with two colored statues of plaster, one depicting Christ and the other the Virgin. Abundant clusters of white lilies stood on the High Altar in tall glass vases. These were not attended to often enough. The lilies remained for days in the same water and became so slimy that when I entered the chapel each morning their smell nearly made me vomit. Once, I remember, I fainted. Thus little by little these rotted lilies and the Catholic Church joined in me indissolubly, and ever since, the thought of turning Catholic has made me nauseous.

Nevertheless, the moment arrived (even today I recall it with shame) when I was on the verge of betraying my faith. Why? What devil prodded me? How cunning, how patient this inner devil must be in order to lie in wait behind our virtues, himself assuming the features of virtue, and be certain that sooner or later, without fail, his hour will come!

And indeed, one day his hour did come. The cardinal who inspected Catholic schools in the Levant arrived one morning from Rome. He was wearing a black silk habit with scarlet lining, a broad-brimmed scarlet biretta, sheer scarlet stockings, and had on his finger a large ring set with a scarlet stone. The air around him beamed and filled with fragrance; the moment he made his appearance and stood before us, we were sure he was a monstrous exotic flower which had at that very instant issued from paradise. Lifting his chubby, pure white hand, the one with the gold ring, he blessed us. We all felt a mysterious force descend from the top of our heads down to our very heels, as though we had drunk vintage wine, and our brains became colored deep scarlet.

Père Laurent must have told him about me, because as he was leaving us, he signaled me to follow him. We went up to his room. He had me sit down on a stool at his feet.

"Would you like to come with me?" he inquired in a voice which seemed as sweet as honey.

"Where?" I asked in astonishment. "I'm a Cretan."

The cardinal laughed. Opening a box, he took out a caramel and placed it in my mouth. His own mouth was small, round, and clean-shaven, with thick, bright red lips. Each time he moved his hand, the air smelled of lavender.

"I know, I know," he said. "I know everything about you. You are Cretan, in other words a wild goat. But be patient and listen to me. We shall go to Rome, the Holy City. You will enter a large school to pursue your studies in order to become great and important. Who knows—perhaps one day you'll wear this same cardinal's biretta I now wear. And don't forget that someone from your island, a Cretan, once became Pope—the leader of Christendom, greater than an emperor! Then you will be able to act, to liberate Crete. . . . Do you hear what I'm saying?"

"Yes, yes," I murmured. I had raised my head and was listening avidly.

"This very moment, my child, your life is at stake. If you say yes, you are saved; if you say no, you are lost. What will you become if you remain here? What does your father do?"

"He's a merchant."

"Very well, you'll become a merchant too, at the very most a lawyer or doctor. In other words, nothing. Greece is a province. Come out of the provinces, my child. I've been told a great deal about you; I'd hate to see you perish."

My heart was thumping loudly. Once again two roads were opening before me. Which was I to choose? To whom could I run for help? Père Laurent would push me one way, Père Lelièvre the other. Which road was correct? And what if I asked my father?

Recalling my father, I was terror-stricken. He had just then returned from Crete, stained with gunpowder and seriously wounded in the arm. The muskets were silent now. After so many centuries and so much blood, freedom had placed her gory feet on Cretan soil. Soon Prince George of the Hellenes would arrive and offer the engagement ring, earnest of the time when Crete and Greece would be united forever.

My father had come to see me immediately upon his return from Crete. At first I did not recognize him. His skin was even blacker than before and a smile (the first I had seen) brightened his lips. "How goes it? Did they convert you?" he asked me with a laugh. I turned purple. He placed his huge palm on my head. "I'm only joking. I have confidence in you."

As I recalled my father now in the cardinal's presence, I must have grown livid, for the prelate placed his plump hand tenderly on my hair and asked, "What are you thinking about?"

"What my father would say," I murmured.

"He doesn't have to know; no one has to know. We'll leave secretly, at night."

"And what about my mother? She'll start crying."

" 'He who denies not his father and his mother cannot follow me.' Those are Christ's words."

I remained silent. The face of Christ had fascinated me indescribably ever since my childhood. I had followed Him on the icons as He was born, reached His twelfth year, stood in a rowboat and raised His hand to make the sea grow calm; then as He was scourged and crucified, and as He called out upon the cross, "My God, my God, why hast thou forsaken me?" After that, as one fine morning He rose from the tomb and ascended to heaven, clasping a white pennon in His hand. Seeing Him, I too was scourged, I too was crucified and resurrected. And when I read the Bible, the ancient tales came to life: man's soul seemed a savage, slumbering beast bellowing in its sleep. Suddenly the heavens opened and Christ descended. He kissed this beast, whereupon it sighed sweetly, awakened, and became what it had always been: a superbly beautiful princess.

"All right," I said to the cardinal, kissing his hand, "I shall forsake my father and mother."

"This exact moment, my son, I saw the Holy Spirit descend over your head. You are saved." Saying this, he held out the amethyst he was wearing so that I could kiss it.

We were to depart three days later. I wanted to see my parents and bid them an inner farewell without divulging the secret to them, but the cardinal refused.

"The true man," he said, "is he who leaves his loved ones without saying goodbye."

Desiring to be a true man, I hardened my heart and remained silent. Had I not read in the legends time after time that the ascetics did just this when they departed for the desert? They did not look back to see their mothers; they did not wave goodbye. I was going to do the same.

I was given various weighty books, all bound in gold. I read about eternal Rome and about the Holy Father, the Pope. I grew drunk as I looked at the illustrations: Saint Peter's, the Vatican, the paintings, the statues.

Everything was going well. In my imagination I had already departed, crossed the sea, reached the Holy City, and finished my studies. I was wearing a broad scarlet biretta with a silk fringe, and as I looked at the middle finger of my right hand, I spied the mystic amethyst glimmering in the darkness. . . . At that point, however, destiny suddenly stirred, reached out its hand, and blocked my way. Someone whispered in my father's ear, "The Catholics are taking your son!" It was at night. The fierce Cretan jumped out of bed and roused several boatmen and fishermen he knew. Lighting torches and taking along a can of gasoline, as well as crowbars and pickaxes, they ascended the road to the citadel. There they began to beat on the school door, howling that they would set the place on fire. The monks were panic-stricken. Père Laurent, wearing his nightcap, stuck his head out of the window and shouted and implored, half in French, half in Greek.

"My boy," called my father, waving the lighted torch, "my boy, you papist dogs, or else it's fire and the axe!"

They woke me up. I dressed as fast as I could, they lowered me from the window in a basket, and I fell into my father's arms. He seized me by the nape of the neck and banged me against the ground three times. Then he turned to his companions. "Out with the torches. Let's go!"

It was three days before my father spoke to me. He saw to it that I was bathed, dressed in clean clothes, and that my head was anointed with oil from the Virgin's watch lamp. He had the priest come to sprinkle me with holy water and perform an exorcism to rid me of the Catholic filth. Then he turned to look at me.

"Judas!" he growled between his teeth, and he spat three times into the air.

But God was kind, and a few weeks later came the good news: Prince George of the Hellenes was on his way to Crete to take possession. My father jumped up, prostrated himself three times so that he touched the soil, crossed himself, and headed straight for the barber's. He had never applied a razor to his cheek, but had let his beard flood down over his breast because he was in mourning, in mourning for Crete, which was enslaved. This was also why he never laughed, and why it angered him to see any Christian laugh. In his mind, laughter had degenerated into an unpatriotic act. But now, thank God, Crete was free. He headed straight for the barber's, therefore, and when he returned home, his shaven, rejuvenated face beamed and the whole house was perfumed by the lavender which the barber had poured over his hair.

Then, turning to my mother, he pointed to me and smiled.

"Crete is free, the past forgotten. Let's forgive even Judas!"

A few days later we embarked for Crete. What a triumphant journey that was, and how the sun on that autumn day penetrated to the very depths of our hearts! But oh, how long the ship took to cross the Aegean! Dawn found my father leaning over the bow and gazing toward the south, and if the eyes of man had been able to move mountains, we would have seen Crete like a frigate bearing down upon us.

12

LIBERTY

MY EYES, even now after so many years, still overflow with tears when I recall that day: the day Prince George of the Hellenes, in other words Liberty, set foot on Cretan soil. Mankind's struggle is truly an uninterrupted sacrament. What is this terrestrial crust—so shoddy, unstable, and fissured—that men, those parasites all covered with mud and gore, should crawl upon it seeking their freedom? How moving it is to see Greeks in the vanguard—Greeks!—climbing the unending ascent and opening the way whether with the chlamys and lance, the evzone skirts and muskets of '21, or with their Cretan vrakes!

I remember a certain Cretan captain, a shepherd who reeked of dung and billy goats. He had just returned from the wars, where he had fought like a lion. I happened to be in his sheepfold one afternoon when he received a citation, inscribed on parchment in large red and black letters, from the "Cretan Brotherhood" of Athens. It congratulated him on his acts of bravery and declared him a hero.

"What is this paper?" he asked the messenger with irritation. "Did my sheep get into somebody's wheatfield again? Do I have to pay damages?"

The messenger unrolled the citation joyfully and read it aloud.

"Put it in ordinary language so I can understand. What does it mean?"

"It means you're a hero. Your nation sends you this citation so you can frame it for your children."

The captain extended his huge paw.

"Give it here!"

Seizing the parchment, he ripped it in shreds and threw it into the fire beneath a caldron of boiling milk.

"Go tell them I didn't fight to receive a piece of paper. I fought to make history!"

To make history! The uncultivated shepherd sensed very well what he wanted to say, but did not know how to say it. Or did he perhaps say it in the finest way possible?

The messenger was saddened to see the shredded parchment in the fire. The captain rose. He filled a small basin with milk, cut off half a cheese, brought two barley rolls, then turned to the other and said, "Come here, brother; don't get excited. Eat, drink, and to the devil with citations! Tell them—do you hear?—tell them I don't want payment. I fight because I like it. Tell them that. . . . Do what I say: eat!"

There have been two supreme days in my life. The first was the day Prince George set foot on Crete, the second was in Moscow many years later—the tenth-anniversary celebration of the Russian Revolution. On both of those days I felt that human partitions—bodies, brains, and souls—were capable of being demolished, and that humanity might return again, after frightfully bloody wandering, to its primeval, divine oneness. In this condition there is no such thing as "me," "you," and "he"; everything is a unity and this unity is a profound mystic intoxication in which death loses its scythe and ceases to exist. Separately, we die one by one, but all together we are immortal. Like prodigal sons, after so much hunger, thirst, and rebellion, we spread our arms and embrace our two parents: heaven and earth.

With flowing tears that drenched their martial beards, Cretan captains tossed their kerchiefs in the air; mothers raised their infants high so that they could see the blond giant, this fairy-tale prince who had heard Crete's lamentations centuries earlier and, mounted on a white horse like Saint George, had set out to liberate the island. Cretan eyes were glassily blank after so many centuries' watch over the sea. There he is! No, he still has not appeared, but he shall appear any minute. . . . Sometimes it was a springtime cloud or a white sail that misled them; sometimes, in the depths of night, a dream. But the cloud always scattered, the sail vanished, the dream expired, and once again the Cretans fixed their eyes northward upon Greece, upon Muscovy, upon the merciless, slow-moving Lord.

And now, lo! the whole of Crete quaked, its tombs opened, and a voice resounded from the summit of Psiloríti: "He is coming! He has arrived! Behold him!" Aged captains with deep wounds and silver pistols tumbled out of the mountains; youths came with their black-handled daggers and tinkling rebecs; bells tolled from quivering campaniles. The city had been adorned everywhere with palm leaves and myrtles—and the fair-haired Saint George stood on a pier strewn with laurel, the whole of the Cretan sea glittering behind his shoulders.

The Cretans sang and danced in the taverns, they drank, they played the rebec, but still they did not find relief. Unable to fit any longer inside their bodies, they grasped knives and stabbed themselves in the arms and thighs so that blood would flow and they would be unburdened. In church the elderly Metropolitan stood with raised arms beneath the dome and gazed at the Pantocrator. He wanted to preach but his throat was blocked. Parting his lips, he cried, "Christ is risen, my children"—unable to utter anything else. "He is truly risen!" resounded from every breast, and the cathedral's great chandeliers shook as though from an earthquake.

I was young and inexperienced then; inside me the sacred intoxication did not wear off for an extremely long time—perhaps it has not worn off to this day. Even now in my most deeply joyful moments—when I view the sea, the star-filled sky or an almond tree in bloom, or when I relive my first experience of love—December 9, 1898, the day when Crete's betrothed the Prince of Greece set foot on Cretan soil, flashes undying within me and the whole of my inner breast is adorned, like all of Crete on that day, with myrtles and laurels.

My father took me by the hand in the early afternoon, while Megalo Kastro was still bellowing with joy. Stepping upon myrtles and laurels, we walked the length of the main street. Then we passed through the fortified gate and emerged into open fields. It was winter, but the day was pleasantly warm and an almond tree behind a hedge had produced its first flower. The fields had begun to turn green, deceived by the weather's sweetness, while far off to our left the Selena mountains sparkled with full caps of snow. Though the vines were still dry stumps, the almond's flower, striking out gallantly in the vanguard, had already begun to announce the coming of spring, and the stumps would open once again to liberate the white and black grapes inside them.

A huge man came by with a load of laurel branches. Seeing my father, he halted.

"Christ is risen, Captain Michael!" he exclaimed.

"Crete is risen!" replied my father, placing his palm over his heart.

We continued on our way. My father was in a hurry, and I had to run to keep up with him.

"Where are we going, Father?" I asked, gasping for breath.

"To see your grandfather. March!"

We reached the graveyard. My father gave the gate a push and opened it. Painted on the lintel was a skull over two bones crossed to form an X, the initial letter of Χριστός—Christ—who rose from the dead. We proceeded to the right, beneath cypresses, striding over abject graves with broken crosses and no watch lamps. I was afraid of the dead; I clutched my father's jacket and followed behind him, stumbling constantly.

My father halted at one of the abject graves—a small mound of rounded earth with a wooden cross. The name had been effaced by time. Removing his kerchief, he fell face-downward on the ground, scraped away the soil with his nails and made a little hole in the shape of a megaphone. Into this he inserted his mouth as deeply as he could. Three times he cried out, "Father, he came! Father, he came! Father, he came!"

His voice grew louder and louder. Finally he was bellowing. Removing a small bottle of wine from his pocket, he poured it drop by drop into the hole and waited each time for it to go down, for the earth to drink it. Then he bounded to his feet, crossed himself, and looked at me. His eyes were flashing.

"Did you hear?" he asked me, his voice hoarse from emotion. "Did you hear?"

I remained silent. I had heard nothing.

"Didn't you hear?" said my father angrily. "His bones rattled."

Whenever I recall that day, I thank the Lord for allowing me to be born. And I thank him for allowing me to be born a Cretan and in time to have seen, with my own eyes, Liberty tread the laurel leaves and march up from the harbor gate to Saint Minas's lair. What a shame that man's eyes of clay are unable to discern the invisible! On that day I would have seen Saint Minas leap from his icon and stand at the church door mounted on his horse, the tears running down his sunburned cheeks and gray beard as he awaited the Prince of Greece.

After the joy had finally subsided, after a strong south wind came a few days later and brushed, as I remember, the laurel leaves from the streets, after a fresh rain washed the spilled wine off the sidewalks, life became sober again and our minds shrank back inside their boundaries. The barbers had swept up the beards from their shop floors; the shaved faces of the Christians were sleek and resplendent. From time to time various belated shouts still issued raucously from the taverns. As for myself, I roamed the lanes sopping from rain, and whenever I saw the street in front of me deserted, I screeched and bellowed to find relief. Thousands of generations inside me were screeching and bellowing to find relief.

Never have I felt so deeply that our departed ancestors do not die, that at critical moments they cry out, jump to their feet, and take possession of our eyes, hands, and minds. During those days, all my grandfathers that had been murdered by the Turks, all my grandmothers whom the Turks had tortured by ripping off their breasts, bellowed and screeched from joy whenever the street was deserted and no one could see us. I rejoiced because I had a presentiment, without being able to think this out very clearly as yet, that I too would live on, would be able to think and see even after I died. All that was needed was the continued existence of hearts to remember me.

Through that portal, that gateway decorated with laurel and ancestral bones, I entered my adolescent years. I had ceased to be a child.

13

ADOLESCENT DIFFICULTIES

I SPENT my adolescent years beset by youth's customary difficulties. Two huge beasts awoke inside me, that leopard the flesh, and that insatiable eagle which devours a man's entrails and the more it eats the more it hungers—the mind.

When I was still very young, only three or four years old, I was overcome by a violent curiosity to untangle the mystery of birth. I asked my mother and aunts, "How are babies born, how do they suddenly enter the house? Where do they come from?" I reasoned that some verdant country must exist, perhaps Paradise, where children sprouted like red poppies; every so often a father entered Paradise, picked one, and brought it home. This I turned over and over in my mind without giving it very much credence. As for my mother and aunts, they either failed to answer me at all or else told me fairy tales. But I understood more than they thought, more than I myself thought, and did not believe their tales.

One day during that same period our neighbor Madame Katina died, although still a young woman. When I saw her brought out of her house lying on her back and followed by a large group of people who turned hurriedly into a lane and disappeared, I was seized by terror. "Why did they take her away?" I asked. "Where are they bringing her?" "She died," I was told. "Died? What does that mean?" But no one offered me an explanation. Huddling in a corner behind the sofa and covering my face with a pillow, I began to cry, not from sorrow or fear, but because I did not understand. When my teacher Krasákis died a few years later, however, death had ceased to astonish me. I felt that I understood what it was, and I did not ask.

These two, birth and death, were the very first mysteries to throw my childish soul into a ferment; I kept beating my tender fist against this pair of closed doors to make them open. I saw that

I could expect help from nobody. Everyone either remained silent or laughed at me. Whatever I was to learn I would have to learn by myself.

Gradually the flesh awoke also. My kingdom, which had been composed of premonitions and clouds, began to solidify. I overheard street talk. Although I had no clear understanding what these overheard expressions meant, some of them seemed to be filled with secret and forbidden matter. Thus I set them apart, marked them out in my mind, and repeated them over and over—always to myself—so that I would not forget them. One day, however, one of them escaped me; I pronounced it aloud in my mother's presence. She winced from fright.

"Who told you that naughty word?" she shouted. "Don't say it again!"

Going to the kitchen, she got some ground pepper and rubbed it thoroughly into my mouth. I began to howl; my mouth was on fire. But then and there, to spite her, I secretly vowed that I would continue to say those words, though to myself. For I felt great pleasure in pronouncing them.

Ever since then, however, every forbidden word has burned my lips and smelled of pepper—even now, after so many years and so many sins!

In those faraway times in Crete, puberty awoke extremely late. Blushing deeply from bashfulness, it struggled to hide behind many different kinds of masks. For me, the first of these masks was friendship, a passion for an insignificant classmate, indeed the most insignificant of all my classmates, a short, fat, bowlegged boy with a heavily athletic body and not a jot of intellectual curiosity. We exchanged fiery letters daily. If a single day passed when I did not receive a letter from him, I felt reproachful and often even wept. I used to prowl about his house and observe him by stealth, my heart skipping a beat whenever I saw him emerge. My flesh had awakened but it still did not know what features to give its desire, it still had not sorted out very well what distinguishes male from female. On the other hand, associating with a boy rather than a girl must have seemed much less dangerous to me, much more convenient. When I confronted a woman, I felt a strange antipathy mixed with fear; and when a wind blew and lifted the hem of her dress a little, I turned my head abruptly away, flushing deeply from shame and indignation.

One day—it must have been noontime, for the sun was broiling —I was walking along a narrow, shaded lane on my way home. Suddenly a Turkish woman appeared on the other side of the street. As she passed in front of me, she parted her tunic slightly and exposed her naked breasts. My knees gave way beneath me. Staggering home, I leaned over the basin and vomited.

Many years later, when I discovered my friend's letters in a neglected drawer, I was terrified. Great God, what ardor, what innocence! Without wanting to or being aware of it, this homely, coarsely fashioned classmate had become a mask to hide women from me for a number of years. And I, assuredly, had become the same for him, delaying a little the fatal moment when he would fall into woman's terrible trap. I learned that he did fall eventually—fell and perished.

One summer during vacation this friend and I, together with another classmate, a tight-lipped lad with blue-green eyes and slender limbs, founded a new "Friendly Society." We held sessions in secret, took and received oaths, signed a list of by-laws, and gave our lives a goal: to make uncompromising war on falsehood, servitude, and injustice until the day we died. The world seemed false, unjust, and dishonest to us. We undertook to save it—we three. Isolating ourselves from our other classmates, we always went about together. We drew up plans how to achieve our goal, and distributed to each his battle sector. I was supposed to write plays, my friend would become an actor and perform them, and the third, who had a mania for mathematics, would study engineering and produce a great invention in order to swell the society's treasury and thus enable us to aid the poor and oppressed.

In the meantime, until the arrival of this great moment, we did what we could to remain faithful to our vows. We never told lies, we beat up all the Turkish children we happened to meet in outlying lanes, and we replaced our collars and ties with undershirts striped white and blue, the colors of the Greek flag.

Down at the harbor one winter evening we spied an old Turkish stevedore huddled in a corner and shivering. It was dark already; no one was looking. One of us removed his undershirt, the other his shirt, the third his vest. We gave them to the man. We also wanted to embrace him, but did not dare. Disturbed and ashamed because we had not accomplished our duty to the full, we departed.

"Let's go back and find him," my friend suggested.

"Good! Let's go."

We returned at a run and searched for the old porter in order to embrace him, but he was gone.

On another day we heard that a distinguished Kastrian lawyer had become engaged to a wealthy young lady; their marriage was to take place that Sunday. In the meantime, however, another young lady had arrived from Athens. Poor but very beautiful, she had been the lawyer's girl friend during his student days at the university, and he had promised to marry her. The moment I heard of this scandal, I called the members of the Friendly Society into session. All three of us assembled in my room, boiling with indignation. In accordance with the by-laws of our society, we found it impossible to tolerate an injustice of this sort. After debating for hours what measures to take, we finally came to a decision: the three of us would present ourselves before the Metropolitan and denounce the perpetrator of this immoral act. In addition, we addressed a letter to the lawyer over the signature "Friendly Society," threatening him that if he did not marry Dorothy (this was the Athenian's name) he would have to answer for it both to God and us.

Donning our Sunday best, we presented ourselves before the Metropolitan. He was a feeble, consumptive old man, but as sly as they come. Though the effort of speaking made him gasp for breath, his eyes gleamed like live coals. The icon hanging over his desk depicted a rosy-cheeked well-fed Christ with a part in his hair. A large lithograph of Saint Sophia hung on the opposite wall.

"What's on your minds, boys?" he asked, looking at us with surprise.

"A great injustice, Your Reverence," all three of us began pantingly, in unison, shouting to gain courage. "A great injustice is taking place."

The Metropolitan coughed, spat into his handkerchief, and said in a sarcastic tone, "A great injustice? And is that any of your business? You're schoolboys, aren't you? You should attend to your lessons."

"Your Reverence . . ." began my friend, who was the most accomplished orator of the group, and he related the commonly known scandal in its entirety.

"We won't be able to sleep, we won't be able to attend to our lessons, Your Reverence," he concluded, "unless this injustice is first corrected. The lawyer must marry Dorothy."

The Metropolitan coughed again, put on his glasses, and regarded us for a long time. It seemed to us that a strange sorrow had spread across his face. All three of us waited in agony. Finally he parted his lips.

"You are young," he said, "you are still children. I wonder if God will grant me enough time to see how you regard injustice fifteen or twenty years from now."

He fell silent for a short while; then he murmured, as though talking to himself, "This is the way we all begin."

"Your Reverence," I said at that point, seeing that he was changing the subject, "what should we do to prevent this injustice? Command us. Even if you tell us to throw ourslves into a blazing furnace, my friends and I will do so, just so long as justice triumphs."

The Metropolitan rose.

"Go now with my blessing," he said, giving us his hand to kiss. "You did your duty. That's enough. The rest is my affair."

We left, as happy as could be. "Well done, Friendly Society!" exclaimed my friend, throwing his arms around the third member and myself, who were walking on either side of him.

That Sunday the lawyer married the rich young lady. And we learned subsequently that the Metropolitan had related our visit and indignation to all his friends, doubling over with laughter.

We read all the novels that fell into our hands. Our minds caught fire, the boundaries faded between reality and imagination, between truth and poetry, and it seemed to us that man's soul was capable of undertaking and accomplishing all things.

But the more I felt my mind opening and pushing back the frontiers of truth, the more I sensed my heart filling and overflowing with grief. Life seemed excessively constricting to me. Unable to fit within it, I yearned for death; this alone struck me as boundless and therefore capable of containing me. One day, I recall, a day when the sun was shining and I felt my body healthy and contented, I suggested to my friend that we kill ourselves. I had already written a long letter filled with despair, a kind of testament in which I bade farewell to the world. But my friend refused, and I had no desire to depart all by myself.

So deeply had I been possessed by this undefined, incomprehensible grief that the day arrived when even my friend became intolerable to me. I began to go out by myself in the early evening to walk along the Venetian walls above the waves.

How divine the weather! What a refreshing sea breeze! And the young ladies strolling with silk ribbons in their loosely flowing hair, and the little barefooted Turks hawking jasmine and passatempo in tender girlish voices, and Barbaláris arranging tables and chairs in the café above the sea so that the goodmen could come with their wives, the betrothed youths with their fiancées, to order coffee, orgeat, and a spoonful of jam, while with well-fed satisfaction they saw the sun go down.

But I saw nothing—neither the vast placid sea, nor the graceful promontory of Aghia Pelaghiá in this distance, nor Stroúmboulas, the pyramid-shaped mountain with the Chapel of the Crucified, a minuscule white egg, at its summit. Nor the betrothed youths and their fiancées. My eyes were clouded by tears, tears not related to any personal grief, for my soul had been thrown into a ferment by two terrible secrets our physics teacher had revealed to us that year. I believe the wounds he inflicted have festered ever since.

The first secret, the truly terrible one, was that the earth, contrary to our belief, is not the center of the universe. The sun and the star-filled heavens do not submissively revolve in circles around the earth. Our planet is nothing but a small and insignificant star indifferently tossed into the galaxy, and it slavishly circles the sun. . . . The royal crown had tumbled from the head of Earth, our mother.

I was overcome with bitterness and indignation. Together with our mother, we too had fallen from our place of precedence in heaven. In other words, our earth does not stand as a motionless lady in the middle of the heavens, the stars revolving respectfully about her; instead, she wanders among great flames in chaos, humiliated and eternally pursued. Where does she go? Wherever she is led. Tied to her master, the sun, she follows. We too are tied, we too are slaves, and we follow. So does the sun; it is tied also, and it follows. . . . Follows whom?

In short, what was this fairy tale our teachers had shamelessly prated about until now—that God supposedly created the sun and moon as ornaments for the earth, and hung the starry heavens above us as a chandelier to give us light!

This was the first wound. The second was that man is not God's darling, his privileged creature. The Lord God did not breathe into his nostrils the breath of life, did not give him an immortal soul. Like all other creatures, he is a rung in the infinite chain of animals, a grandson or great-grandson of the ape. If you scratch our hide a little, if you scratch our soul a little, beneath it you will find our grandmother the monkey!

My bitterness and indignation were insupportable. I began to take solitary walks along the shore or through the fields, speeding in order to tire myself and manage to forget. But how could I forget? Bareheaded, I marched and marched, my shirt opened down the front because I was suffocating. Why had we been deceived for so many years, I asked, talking to myself as I proceeded; why had royal thrones been established for human beings and for our mother the earth, only to be pulled down afterwards? Did this mean that the earth was insignificant, that we human beings were insignificant, and that a day would come when all would perish? No, no, I shouted to myself, I refuse to accept it. We must knock against our destiny and knock again, until we open a door and save ourselves.

Unable to endure this any longer, one evening I sought out the physics teacher who had divulged these terrible secrets to us. I went to his house. He was of jaundiced complexion and spoke sparingly, but always in a biting, caustic way. Extremely intelligent, extremely malicious, he had cold eyes and narrow lips that were full of irony. With his low forehead, his hair that nearly reached his eyebrows, he truly resembled a monkey—a sick one. I found him stretched out in a rickety armchair reading. He looked at me and obviously understood my trouble, because he smiled sardonically.

"Why this visit?" he asked. "You must have something important on your mind."

"Forgive me for disturbing you," I gasped, "but I want to learn the truth."

"The truth," replied the teacher with sarcasm. "Is that all! You're asking quite a lot, young man. Which truth?"

"That He took clay, breathed . . ."

"Who?"

"God."

A maliciously dry and cutting laugh unsheathed itself from his narrow, emaciated lips.

I waited. But the teacher opened a little box, took out a piece of candy, and began to chew it.

"Aren't you going to answer me, sir?" I ventured.

"Yes, I am going to answer you," he replied, shifting the candy from cheek to cheek.

A considerable time elapsed.

"When?" I ventured anew.

"Ten years from now, maybe even twenty. After your pigmy mind becomes a real brain. Now it's still much too early. Go home!"

I wanted to cry, Have pity on me, sir, tell me the truth, the whole truth! But my throat was blocked.

"Go home," the teacher repeated, and he showed me to the door.

On my way back, at the street corner, I encountered the archimandrite who was our instructor in religion, a naïve, saintly man, chubby and extremely hard of hearing. Passionately in love with his elderly mother who lived in a little village far from Kastro, he frequently informed us with tearful eyes that he had seen her in his dreams. He possessed little in the way of gray matter, and from excessive chastity even that must have gone soft. Every time the bell rang and the lesson ended, he hesitated for a moment at the exit, then turned around and instructed us in a sweetly supplicating voice, "Above all, my children, be sure to perpetuate your race." We, doubling over with laughter, shouted back loud enough for him to hear, "Don't worry, sir, don't worry!" I did not like this teacher at all. His mind was a sheep; it bleated away and was incapable of easing any of our anxieties. One day when he was expounding the Creed to us, he raised his finger triumphantly: "There is one God—oonne!—because the Creed states, 'I believe in oonne God.' If there were two, it would state, 'I believe in twwoooo Gods.'" We all felt sorry for him, and no one had the cruelty to object.

On another day, however, I found it impossible to restrain myself. He was teaching us about God's omnipotence. I raised my pen.

"Sir," I asked, "is God able to abolish the fact that this pen ever existed?"

The poor archimandrite turned purple. He reflected for a moment, laboring to find some answer. Finally, unable to do so, he seized the lottery box and hurled it in my face. I jumped to my feet.

"That's no answer," I said to him with arrogant seriousness.

He expelled me from school for three days, and that same evening he went to find my father.

"Your son is undisciplined and insolent," he told him. "This boy will come to a bad end. You'd better tighten up on his reins."

"What did he do?"

Such and such: the archimandrite recounted the whole story. My father shrugged his shoulders.

"I care only if he tells lies or gets a beating. As for all the rest, he's a man now, let him do as he pleases."

This, then, was the archimandrite whom I encountered on the street. As soon as I saw him I turned my head the other way so that I would not have to greet him. Just at that moment I was furious; now at last I knew that he and all his ilk had been mocking us for years, mocking us concerning that part of humanity's endeavor which was most sacred.

What days those were when the two lightning flashes tore through my mind—what nights! Unable to sleep, I leaped out of bed in the middle of the night, descended the stairs very, very slowly lest they creak and give me away, opened the street door like a thief, and dashed out into the street. Not a soul in sight, doors shut, lights extinguished . . . I wandered through Kastro's narrow lanes, listening intently to the tranquil respiration of the slumbering city. Sometimes, however, I found several inamoratos singing serenades with guitars and lutes beneath a closed window, their lovelorn dirge, so full of complaint and supplication, ascending beyond the rooftops. The neighborhood dogs would hear, awaken, and begin to bark. But I was scornful of amours and women. I kept asking myself, How can people sing, how is it their hearts are not throbbing to learn what God's nature is, and where we come from, and where we are going. Passing them as quickly as I could, I would reach the bulwark and breathe freely again. The pitch-black sea, thundering in anger below, dashed rabidly against the ramparts and devoured them. The spray mounted the walls and splattered my forehead, lips, and hands, refreshing me. I would stand above the water for hours, feeling that it, not the earth, was my mother, that only the sea could understand my anguish, because it shared this same anguish, it too was unable to sleep. The sea beats its breast, strikes the shores, is struck in turn. Seeking freedom, it toils to crumble the ramparts which loom before it and to pass beyond them. Dry land is tranquil and secure, simplehearted and industrious. It blossoms, bears fruit, and wilts. But it does not feel afraid, for it is secure in its knowledge that, willy-nilly, spring will rise once more from the soil. My mother the sea, however, is not secure; it neither blossoms nor bears fruit, but instead sighs and struggles night and day.

I heard it, it heard me, and we comforted and encouraged each other until nearly daybreak. Then, afraid that the awakening people might see us, I returned home rapidly and lay down on my bed. A bitter, salty contentment flooded my entire body; I rejoiced that I was made not of soil but of sea water.

One of our nearby neighbors possessed a monkey, a shameless red-rumped creature with human eyes. This neighbor had kept company with an elderly bey from Alexandria, and he had given her the monkey as a keepsake. I saw it crouching on a stool in her doorway every time I passed; it was always shelling peanuts, munching them, and scratching itself to get rid of its lice. Formerly I had stopped to observe its actions and laugh. A caricature of man it seemed to me, a merrily shameless creature devoid of mystery—people might gaze at it unconcernedly and chuckle. Now, however, I was horrified. Unable to set eyes on the creature, I changed route. Was this my grandmother? It humiliated the human being. Ashamed and angry, I felt that a kingdom within me was crumbling to ruins.

This my very first grandmother? These my roots? In other words, was it true that God did not bear me, did not fashion me with His hands, breathe His breath into my nostrils? Was I begotten by a he-monkey who had siphoned his sperm from she-monkey to she-monkey? In short, was I a son not of God, but of the monkey?

My disillusion and indignation endured for months. Who knows, perhaps they endure even now. On one side of the abyss stood the ape, on the other the archimandrite. A string was stretched between them over chaos, and I was balancing on this string and advancing in terror. This was a difficult time for me. Vacation had arrived; I shut myself inside the house with a multitude of borrowed books on animals, plants, stars, and remained bent over them night and day like the man who is perishing from thirst and falls face-down by a brook to drink. I did not go outside. I purposely shaved half of my scalp, and when my friends called to have me go for a walk with them, I stuck my head out of the window, pointed to the half-shaved scalp, and said, "Don't you see me? How can I go out in such a state?" Then I threw myself into my studies again, listening with relief to my friends' mocking laughter as they receded into the distance.

The more I filled myself with learning, the more my heart overflowed with bitterness. Lifting my head, I used to listen as my neighbor the monkey screeched. One day it escaped its rope, worked its way into our yard, and climbed the acacia; as I raised my eyes, I suddenly saw it spying on me from between the branches. I shuddered. Never in my life had I observed such human eyes. They were planted upon me, filled with cunning and raillery—round, black, and motionless.

Rising, I pushed away my books. "This is not the way," I cried. "I am going contrary to human nature, am forsaking flesh for shadow. Life consists of flesh, of meat, and I am hungry!" Leaning out of the window, I tossed the monkey a walnut. It caught the nut in mid-air, broke it between its teeth, discarded the shell, and began to chew away insatiably, looking at me in a sneering manner and yelping. It had been trained to drink wine. I flew down to our storeroom, got a cupful, and placed it on the windowsill. The monkey's nostrils quivered avidly. Taking a jump, it seated itself on the sill, thrust its snout into the cup, and began to drink and drink, clacking its tongue with satisfaction. Then it threw its arms around my shoulders and embraced me as if it never wished to disengage itself. It smelled of wine and unwashed flesh. I felt its body heat at my throat. Hairs from its mustache entered my nostrils, tickling me and making me laugh. Its whole body pressed against mine, it kept sighing like a human. Our two warmths joined, the monkey's inhalations followed quietly after my own; we became friends. That night when it left to return to its rope, this embrace seemed to me like a black Annunciation; a dark angel was departing from my window, the messenger of some hairy four-footed God.

The next day I went down to the harbor around suppertime, though previously I'd had no such plan in mind. Stopping at a tavern frequented by fishermen, I ordered wine with a dish of fried smelts as mezé. I began to drink. I do not know if I felt sad, angry, or happy. Everything—monkey, God, starry heavens, human dignity—was tangled within me; it was as though I had placed my hopes in alcohol now to untangle it all for me.

Sipping their wine leisurely in a corner were several fishermen and stevedores, celebrated drunkards all. They saw me and laughed.

"His mother's milk is still on his lips and he's playing the man about town," said one.

"Aping his pa," offered another. "But he's got a long way to go."

When I heard this I became red hot with rage.

"Hey, friends," I shouted, "come here and let me make you drunk!"

They approached, guffawing. I kept filling the glasses to the brim and we downed them in single gulps, one after the other, without food now. The men looked at me with irritation. We neither talked nor sang, but simply drank down the full glasses and stared at each other, anxious to see who would subdue the rest. Their Cretan self-respect had exploded into flames; these fiercely mustachioed winebibbers were ashamed to be defeated by a beardless youth. Nevertheless, they sank to the floor one by one, while I alone remained sober throughout. So great, apparently, was my pain, it triumphed over wine.

The same thing the next night, and the next and the next. I became renowned throughout Kastro as a drunkard who kept company each night with the shiftless fishermen and stevedores of the waterfront.

My friends were delighted to see me running downhill. They had long since been unable to stomach the fact that I felt no desire for their company and kept myself shut up in my house reading—or, more recently, went out for solitary walks, a book in my pocket. I did not play with them, or gossip, or go courting. "He'll butt his head against the stars and smash it in a thousand pieces," they had scoffed, looking upon me with hatred. But now that they saw me drinking and disgracing myself with the barefooted riffraff of Kastro they were delighted. They approached me, perhaps even began to like me, and one Saturday night they brought me by underhanded treachery to the town's best cabaret, the audaciously named "Combatants of '21." A new act had arrived not long before, a troupe of Romanian and French belles who were driving the respectable burghers out of their minds. Each Saturday evening these prudent homeowners slipped secretly into the forbidden, dimly lighted paradise, seated themselves timidly at the most out-of-the-way tables, glanced in every direction to make sure that none of their acquaintances was looking, then clapped their hands to have a painted and perfumed chanteuse come and sit on their knees. In this way these honorable burghers, poor things, were able for a few moments to forget the fault-finding and bickering which accompany a life of virtue.

My friends brought me to the very center and ordered drinks. Along came a fat, billowy Romanian whose sweaty breasts overflowed her unbuttoned silk bodice, a woman of a certain age who knew every trick of the trade. My companions kept refilling my glass; I drank, I became pleasantly happy. Inhaling the acrid female odor, I felt the he-monkey in me awakening. I seized the singer's slipper, filled it again and again with champagne, and drank.

The next day all of Kastro buzzed with the great scandal: the saint, the sage Solomon with his nose in the air, had—alack! alas! —spent the night carousing in a cabaret, imbibing out of a chanteuse's slipper. The end of the world! One of my uncles, mortified by his nephew's ignominious fall, ran to my father and communicated the news to him. But my father just shrugged his shoulders. "In other words he's a man now, he is beginning to become a man," he replied. "All he needs to do is buy the singer a new pair of slippers."

As for me, I rejoiced inwardly because I was transgressing the law, because I was liberating myself from archimandrites and those bugaboos the Ten Commandments, because I was following the firm, sure steps of my hairy forebear.

I had started on the downgrade and I liked it! It was my final year in the gymnasium. I eyed the archimandrite with hatred as he smiled serenely, entrenched in his virtue. Sure about this life and the next, this sheep regarded us, the wolves, with compassion. This I could not stand. I had to disturb his peace, raise a tempest in his blood, erase that moronic smile which suffused his face. One morning, therefore, I did something very wicked. I sent him a short note: "Your mother is gravely ill. She is dying. Hurry to her so that she may give you her blessing." I dispatched it, then proceeded nonchalantly to school and waited. That day the archimandrite did not appear in class. Nor the next, nor the third. Five days later he returned, unrecognizable. His face was bloated and disfigured by an eczema which reached to his throat and armpits. He scratched himself continually, turned fiery red, was unable to speak, and left before the bell rang. For three months he remained bedridden. Then one morning he returned to us, no longer swollen. But he was exhausted, and vestiges of scabs still covered his face. He looked at us tenderly. The smile had suffused his entire face once more, and his first words were "Praise the Lord, my children. He prodded the hand which wrote me the note saying that my mother was gravely ill, and thus he gave me the opportunity to pay humanity's tribute in my turn—to suffer." These words made me wince. Was it therefore so very difficult to triumph over virtue? For a moment I felt like standing up and shouting, Forgive me for I have sinned! But another voice rose immediately within me, a voice full of sarcasm and malice: You are a dog, an archimandrite-dog. You are whipped and you lick the hand that is whipping you. . . . No, what I did was right. I should not repent!

The next day I summoned the members of the Friendly Society. Now that our own minds were enlightened, I told them, it was our duty to enlighten the minds of everyone else. This must be the

Friendly Society's great mission. Wherever we traveled, wherever we halted, each of our words and deeds must have a single, sole purpose—to enlighten.

Whereupon, the enlightening commenced. We had finished the gymnasium and were free. My father, who wanted me to enter politics, sent me to a village to sponsor a child in baptism. I took my two friends with me; here was the perfect opportunity for us to enlighten an entire village. When we sat down at table immediately after the baptism, and the festivities started, my bosom friend, working up steam, began to preach to the villagers and enlighten them. And before all else he spoke to them of the origin of man, declaring that our progenitor was the monkey and that we must not be so conceited to believe in our supposed status as privileged beings created by God.

All the while my friend was delivering his oration, the village priest kept gazing at him with protruding eyes. He did not speak. When the enlightening drew to a close, however, he shook his head with compassion and said, "Excuse me, my boy, for staring at you all the time you were speaking. It's possible, as you say, that all men are descended from the monkey. As for yourself, however, forgive me for saying so, but you are a lineal descendant of the ass."

A shiver ran through my body. I looked at my friend; it was as though I were seeing him for the very first time. With his massive drooping jaw, large cauliflower ears, and peaceful velvety eyes he really did resemble an ass. How had I failed to notice it before? A thread within me snapped. After that day I never sent him another letter and I ceased to envy him.

We endured much in our effort to enlighten mankind on the succeeding days as we roamed through Megalo Kastro or toured the villages. We were called atheists, Freemasons, hirelings. Little by little we began to be hooted and barraged with lemon peels wherever we went, but we held ourselves proudly erect and pressed on through the insults and peels, content in the knowlege that we were witnessing and enduring martyrdom for the sake of Truth. Was this not the way it always happened, we said to one another to console ourselves. What a joy to die for a great idea!

On another occasion the three of us went on an excursion to a market town two hours from Kastro. Famous for its vineyards, this town was spread out at the foot of Yioúchtas, the sacred mountain where (so it was said) Zeus, the father of gods and men, had been interred. But beneath the stones where he reposed, the dead god had still possessed the strength to refashion the mountain above him, and he had altered the position of the rocks, giving them the shape of a gigantic overturned head. One could plainly distinguish the brow, nose, and the long beard which, composed of ilexes, carobs, and olive trees, extended clear down to the plain.

"Even the gods die," said my third friend, the one who hoped to become an inventor in order to enrich the Friendly Society.

"The gods die," I answered, "but divinity is immortal."

"What do you mean?" asked the others. "We don't understand."

"I don't understand very well myself," I answered, laughing. Although I felt that I was right, I was unable to make my thought clear. I fell back on laughter, which has always served as my door of escape in times of danger.

We reached the village. The air smelled of raki and must. The villagers had completed the vintage, placed the must in barrels and extracted the raki from the residuum of skins. Now they were seated in the café or outside on their stone oven-platforms or beneath the poplar trees, drinking raki, playing cards, and relaxing.

Several of them rose to greet us. Placing us at their table, they treated us to three glasses of cherry juice. We struck up a conversation. The three of us had come to an understanding earlier, and little by little we subtly brought the conversation around to the miracles performed by science.

"Can your minds conceive how paper is made and newspapers printed?" we asked. "What a great miracle! A forest is chopped down, the logs are transported to machines that crush them into pulp, and the pulp is turned into paper which goes into the printer's through one door and comes out a newspaper through the other."

The villagers listened with cocked ears; those at adjacent tables rose and sat down at ours. We're doing fine with them, they're being enlightened, we said to ourselves. But at that point a hulking gallows bird came by with a donkeyload of wood. He stopped to hear what was being said.

"Hey, Dimitrós, where are you taking that wood?" someone called to him.

"To make a newspaper!"

Instantaneously, all the villagers, who until then had restrained themselves out of politeness, doubled over with laughter. The whole village rocked with their guffaws.

"I think we'd better leave," I whispered to my friends. "I feel the lemon peels coming."

"Where are you going, boys?" cried the villagers, splitting their sides. "Stay a while and tell us more—we want to laugh." Then they began to follow behind us, shouting:

"Say, which came first, the chicken or the egg?"

"And why does God make tiles stay up without nails?"

"And was wise Solomon a man or a woman? Show your stuff, boys!"

"And why does the spotted goat laugh—can you tell us that?". . .

But we had taken to our heels.

By this time we had grown weary of enlightening mankind by word of mouth. One day we decided to print a manifesto for the masses, a document in which we would clearly and dispassionately state our goal and prescribe the nature of man's duty. Each of us chipped in his savings. We went to the printer Markoulís, who was also known as Mr. Proletariat because he too issued manifestoes meant to rouse and unite the poor—with the purpose of making them a great force which would elect him to the Boule. We went, therefore, and found him. He was middle-aged, with curly gray hair, spectacles, a broad barrel-chested torso, and tiny little bowed legs. A greasy red kerchief was tied around his neck. Taking our manuscript, he began to declaim it aloud with bombastic exaggeration, and the more he read, the more enthusiastic we became. How excellently it was written, how luminously, with what strength! The three of us craned our necks triumphantly, like young cocks about to crow.

"Well done, boys!" declared Markoulís, folding the manuscript. "Mark my words, one day you'll be elected to the Boule and will save our people. Why not join forces, then? I issue manifestoes too. Shake on it!"

But I resisted. "You care only about the poor," I said to him. "We care about everyone. Our goal is bigger."

"But your brains are smaller," retorted the printer, piqued.

"You think you're going to convert the rich also, do you? To wash a nigger is a waste of soap. Listen to me: the rich man is well set up; he doesn't want to change anything, neither God, country, nor his prosperous life. So knock as much as you like on the deaf man's door. You've got to start with the poor, my young cocks, with those who are not well set up, with the oppressed. Otherwise, go find another printer. I'm known as Mr. Proletariat!"

The three of us withdrew to the door to hold council. In no time we reached a unanimous decision. My friend turned to the printer.

"No, we refuse to accept your proposal. We won't make a single concession. Unlike you, we don't distinguish between rich and poor. All must be enlightened!"

"In that case go to the devil, you little fops!" roared Markoulís, and he hurled the manuscript in our faces.

14

THE IRISH LASS

I WAS still not entirely satisfied, however. I liked the road I had taken but felt I had to reach its furthest limits. That year an Irish girl had arrived in Kastro. She gave English lessons. The thirst for learning was aflame in me as always; I engaged her to tutor me. I wanted to learn the language and write manifestoes in English in order to enlighten those who lived outside Greece. Why should we let them remain in darkness? So I threw myself heart and soul into English, that strange magical world. What joy when I began to saunter through English lyric poetry with this Irish girl! The language, its vowels and consonants, had become so many warbling birds. I stayed at her house until late at night. We talked about music, read poetry, and the air between us caught fire. As I leaned over her shoulder following the lines of Keats and Byron, I breathed in the warm acrid smell of her armpits, my mind grew turbid, Keats and Byron disappeared, and two uneasy animals remained in the tiny room, one clothed in trousers, the other in a dress.

Now that I had finished the gymnasium, I was preparing to go to Athens to register at the university. Who could tell if I would ever see her again, this blue-eyed, slightly stooped but fluffily plump daughter of an Irish pastor. As our separation approached, I grew increasingly more uneasy. Just as when we view a ripe fig oozing with sweet syrup, and being hungry and thirsty we avidly stretch forth our hand to strip its rind, and as we strip it our mouth waters; so in the same way I cast furtive glances at this ripe Irish girl and stripped her in my imagination—like a fig.

One day in September I made my decision.

"Would you like to climb Psiloríti with me?" I asked her. "The whole of Crete is visible from the top, and there's a little chapel at the summit where we can spend the night and I can say goodbye to you."

Her ears turned crimson, but she accepted. What deep mystery that excursion involved, what sweetness and anxious anticipation—just like a honeymoon! We set out at night. The moon above our heads was truly dripping with honey; never again in my life did I see such a moon. That face, which had always seemed so sorrowful to me, laughed now and eyed us roguishly while advancing with us from east to west and descending by way of our opened blouses to our throats, and then down as far as our breasts and bellies.

We kept silent, afraid that words might destroy the perfect, tacit understanding achieved by our bodies as they walked one next to the other. Sometimes our thighs touched as we proceeded along a narrow path, but then each of us suddenly, abruptly, drew away from the other. It seemed that we did not wish to expend our unbearable desire in petty pleasures. We were keeping it intact for the great moment, and we marched hurriedly and with bated breath, not, so it seemed, like two friends, but like two implacable enemies: we were racing to the arena where we would come to grips, breast to breast.

Though we had uttered not a single amorous word before this time, though now, on this excursion, we had agreed on nothing, both of us knew full well where we were going and why. We were anxious to arrive—she, I felt, even more than I.

Daybreak found us in a village at the foot of Psiloríti. We were tired, and we went to lodge at the house of the village priest. I told him that my companion was the daughter of a pastor on a distant, verdant island, and that she desired to see the whole of Crete from the mountain's top. The priest's wife, the papadhiá, came to set the table. We ate. Then, sitting on the sofa, we engaged in small talk. First we discussed the Great Powers—England, France, America, Muscovy. Then vines and olives. Afterwards the priest spoke of Christ, who he said was Orthodox and would never turn Protestant no matter what was done to him. And he wagered that if the girl's father had been with us, he would have converted him to Orthodoxy in one night. But the blue eyes were sleepy, and the priest nodded to his wife.

"Fix her a bed so she can get some sleep. She's a woman, after all, and she's tired.

"But as for you," he continued, turning in my direction, "you're a man, a stalwart Cretan, and it's disgraceful for a Cretan to sleep during the day. Come, let me show you my vineyards. There are still some unpicked grapes. We can eat them."

I was ready to drop from fatigue and lack of sleep, but what could I do? I was a Cretan and could not disgrace Crete. We went to the vineyards, ate the leftover grapes, then took a walk in the village. The retorts were boiling away in the courtyards, the liquor being removed. We drank more than enough raki, still warm, and returned home arm in arm, both staggering. It was evening already. The Irish girl had awakened, the papadhiá had killed a hen. We ate again.

"No talking tonight," declared the priest. "Go to sleep. At midnight I'll wake you up and give you my little shepherd as a guide, so you won't get lost."

Going out to the courtyard, he inspected the sky like an astronomer, then stepped back inside with a satisfied air. "You're in luck," he said. "Tomorrow will be gorgeous. Leave everything in God's hands. Good night."

Around midnight the priest seized me by the leg and awakened me. He also awakened the girl, by banging a copper roasting pan above her head. Awaiting us in the yard was a curly-haired shepherd boy with pointed ears and a fierce glance. He smelled of billy goats and cistus.

"Ready!" he said, raising his crook. "Quick march! We want to reach the summit in time for sunup."

The moon was at the zenith, still happy, still full of sweetness. It was cold out; we wrapped ourselves in our overcoats. The Irish girl's tiny nose had turned white, but her lips were richly red. I looked the other way in order not to see them.

It was a fierce mountain. Leaving the vineyards and olive groves behind us, then the oaks and wild cypresses, we reached bare rock. Our shoes lacked spikes; we kept slipping. The Irish girl fell two or three times but got up unaided. We were no longer cold; sweat drenched our bodies. Clenching our lips together to keep from gasping, we advanced in silence, the little shepherd boy leading, the Irish girl in the middle, and myself bringing up the rear.

The sky began to turn bluish white. The crags became visible; the first hawks hovered in the blue-black air in search of prey. And when at last we set foot on the summit, the east was gleaming rosy-red. But I could see nothing in the distance. A thick mist lay all around us, shrouding land and sea. Crete's entire body was covered. Shivering from the frightful cold, we pushed open the chapel's little door and went inside. The shepherd, meanwhile, began to search all about to find dry twigs in order to light a fire.

The chapel was built of stones laid up without cement. We remained alone inside, the Irish lass and myself. Christ and the Virgin gazed at us from the humble iconostasis, but we did not gaze at them. Demons opposed to Christ and Virgin, antichrists, antivirgins, had risen within us. Extending my hand, I seized the Irish lass by the nape of the neck. She inclined submissively—this is what she had been waiting for—and the two of us rolled down together onto the flagstones.

A black trap door opened to swallow me, and I perished within. When I raised my lids, I discovered Christ eying me furiously from the iconostasis. The green sphere He held in his right hand was swaying, as though about to be hurled at me. I felt terrified, but the woman's arms wrapped themselves around me and I plunged anew into chaos.

My knees were shaking when we opened the door to go outside; my hand trembled as it drew back the bolt. I had suddenly been possessed by an age-old fear: God would hurl a thunderbolt to reduce both of us, the Irish girl and myself—Adam and Eve—to ashes. To be sure, it is not with impunity that one defiles the house of the Lord directly in front of the Virgin's eyes. . . . I gave the door a push and bounded outside. Whatever happens, I said to myself, may it happen quickly and let's be done with it. But as I ran outside and saw: Oh, what immense joy, what a miracle this was that stretched before me! The sun had appeared, the mist had lifted, and the entire island of Crete from one end to the other gleamed white, green, and rose—fully naked—surrounded by her four seas. With her three high summits, the White Mountains, Psiloríti and Dhikti, Crete was a triple-masted schooner sailing in the foam. She was a sea monster, a gorgon with myriad breasts, stretched supine on the waves and sunning herself. In the morning sun I distinctly saw her face, hands, feet, tail, and erect breasts. . . . A goodly number of pleasures have fallen to my lot in the course of a lifetime; I have no reason to complain. But this, the sight of the entire island of Crete upon the billows, was one of the greatest. I turned to look at the Irish girl. She was leaning against the little church, chewing a piece of chocolate and calmly, indifferently, licking her lips, which were covered with my bites.

The return to Kastro was dismal. At last we came near; there stood the famous Venetian ramparts with their winged lions of stone. The tired Irish girl drew close in order to lean against my arm, but I could not endure her odor or her leaden eyes—the apple she fed me had covered my lips and teeth with ashes. Moving away brusquely, I refused to let her approach. She, without a word, fell one pace behind me. I heard her sobs. I wanted to turn, clasp her in my arms, and say a kind word to her, but instead I quickened my pace and remained silent. Finally we reached her house. She withdrew the key from her pocket and opened the door. Then she stood waiting on the threshold. Head bowed, she stood waiting. Would I come in or not? Unbearable compassion and a multitude of joyful and sorrowful words rose in me, reaching as far as my throat. But I pressed my lips tightly together and did not speak. I gave her my hand; we separated. The following day I departed for Athens. I had no monkey to give her as a keepsake, but through one of her students I sent her a little dog which liked to snap, a dog I loved. Its name was Carmen.

15

ATHENS

YOUTH is a blind incongruous beast. It craves food but does not eat, is too timid to eat; it need simply nod to happiness, which strolls by on the street and would willingly stop, but it does not nod; it turns on the faucet, permitting time to drain away uselessly and be lost, as though time were water. A beast that does not know it is a beast—such is youth.

My heart breaks when I bring to mind those years I spent as a university student in Athens. Though I looked, I saw nothing. The world, covered by a dense fog of morality, fanciful imaginings, and frivolity, was hidden from my eyes. Youth is bitter, bitter and disdainful; it does not comprehend. And when one begins to comprehend, youth has fled. Who was the Chinese sage who was born an old man with white hair and beard, his eyes filled with tears? As the years went by, gradually his hair turned black, his eyes began to laugh, his heart was relieved of its burdens, and when he finally neared death, his cheeks became those of a virgin and were covered with delicate childish fuzz. . . . This is the way our lives should unfold, the way they would unfold if God pitied mankind.

In Crete I had risen in revolt against my destiny. I had given myself over to wine for one moment, touched the Irish girl for another moment. But this was not my road. I felt that I had sinned. Ashamed and repentant, I returned to solitude and books.

From youth right to old age every word or deed which diverted me from my destiny I considered a sin. What was this destiny of mine, where was it leading me? Since my intellect still could not unravel the mystery, I allowed my heart to decide: "Do this, don't do that. March! Do not halt or cry out. You have a single duty—to reach the limit." "What limit?" I demanded. "Ask no questions. Advance!"

As I listened intently in solitude to my heart's foolhardy and pretentious advice, my cravings grew overluxuriant and nothing of all I saw or heard around me in the celebrated city of Athens was able to satisfy my hunger. The courses at law school failed to answer my soul's needs to the slightest degree, nor did they even satisfy my intellectual curiosity. I felt no pleasure whatsoever in the parties my friends had with girl students or simple little dressmakers. The ashes from the apple the Irish lass had fed me were still resting on my teeth. Once in a while I went to the theater or to a concert and enjoyed myself. But the joy was a surface one which did not change the inner man; as soon as I reached the street again, I forgot. I continued my study of foreign languages. The awareness that my mind was broadening pleased me greatly, but straightway the mysterious tepid wind of youth always blew, and all these pleasures wilted. I craved some other good, something beyond women or learning, beyond beauty—but what?

The two wounds of my adolescence opened frequently. All seemed futile and worthless, since everything was ephemeral and raced into the abyss, incited as a joke by some merciless, invisible hand. I pushed away the refreshing face of every young girl and saw the future crone. The flower wilted; behind the girl's happily laughing mouth I perceived her skull's naked jaws. The world in front of my eyes took on a violently rapid rhythm and crumbled to ruins. Youth seeks immortality, does not find it, will not deign to compromise, and thus rejects the entire cosmos—out of pride. Not all cases of youth, only those which are wounded by truth.

On Sundays I liked to go on solitary outings. I felt that the company of friends—their conversation, jokes, and laughter—debased the sacred silence. The mountains were fragrant with pine and honey. I entered the olive groves and felt my eyes being refreshed. I exchanged a word or two with any peasant who happened to pass—an Albanian, for example, with narrow forehead and a filthy black hat, who smelled of milk and garlic. His words were prosaic, fuddled, full of dark curiosity. These peasants glanced at me out of the corners of their tiny cunning eyes, tormenting their minuscule brains to find out who I was and why I roamed the mountains. A spy? Lunatic? Peddler? They cast rapacious eyes on the sack I carried on my back.

"What are you selling, friend?" they asked. "Bibles? Are you a Freemason, is that it?"

One day when I heard chirping and saw a steel-blue bird fly overhead, I stopped a peasant who was passing by.

"What kind of bird is that, my friend?" I anxiously inquired. "What is it called?"

"Poor fellow, why worry about it," he replied with a shrug of his shoulders. "It's no good for eating."

I used to get up at dawn. The morning star would be dripping onto the earth, a light mist hovering over Hymettus. A cool breeze icicled my face. Larks ascended songfully into the air and vanished in the light. One Sunday in springtime I remember seeing two or three blossoming cherry trees in a red, recently ploughed field. Happiness filled my heart. At that very moment the sun rose, gleaming as on the day it first emerged from God's hands. The Saronic Gulf beamed; Aegina, in the distance, filled with roses in the morning light. Two crows, their wings vibrating like bowstrings, flew by on my right—a good omen.

On one side, white-maned waves like Homeric horses, long-sweeping, refreshing verses of Homer; on the other, Athena's oil- and light-filled olive, and Apollo's laurel, and Dionysus's wonder-working grape all wine and song. And the dry, frugal earth, its stones tinted rose-red by the sun, the mountains flapping bluishly in mid-air, steaming in the light, peacefully, restfully sunning themselves, all naked, like athletes.

I marched, and as I marched, I felt that the entire earth and sky were journeying with me. All the surrounding miracles penetrated me. I blossomed, laughed, vibrated in my turn like a bowstring. How my soul vanished on that Sunday, faded songfully into the morning light, just like the lark!

I climbed to the top of a hill and gazed out over the narrow rose-colored beaches, the sea, the faintly outlined islands. What joy that was! Greece with her virgin body, how she swims through the waves and lifts herself above them, the sun falling upon her like a bridegroom! How she has tamed stones and water, rid herself of matter's inertia and coarseness, and conserved only the essence!

I was roaming in order to become acquainted with Attica, or so I thought. But I was really roaming in order to become acquainted with my soul. I wished to find it and come to know it in trees, mountains, and solitude—but in vain. My heart did not bound with joy, a sure sign that I had not found what I was seeking.

Only once, one day at noon, did I believe I found it. I had journeyed all alone to Sounion. It was summer already, and the resin flowed from the slit bark of the pine trees, filling the air with balm. A grasshopper landed on my shoulder and sat there; for some time we traveled together. My whole body smelled like a pine, I had become a pine. Then, as I emerged from the pine forest, I saw the white columns of the temple of Poseidon, and between them the hallowed sea, a deep scintillating blue. My knees gave way beneath me; I halted. This is beauty, I thought to myself. This is the Wingless Victory, the summit of joy; man can reach no higher. This is Greece.

So great was my joy that for a moment, viewing Greece's beauty, I believed that my two wounds had healed and that this world, even though ephemeral—precisely because ephemeral—possessed value. I believed I was wrong in my attempt to divine the future crone behind the young girl's face; rather, I should re-create and resurrect in the face of the crone the freshness and youth of the girl who no longer existed.

The Attic landscape is truly fascinating in an inexpressible, penetrating way. Here in Attica one feels that everything is subordinated to a rhythm which is simple, sure, and balanced. Everything here possesses an aristocratic grace and ease: the frugal, arid land, the graceful curves of Hymettus and Pentelicus, the silver-leafed olive trees, the slender ascetic cypresses, the playful glare of rocks in the sun, and above all the buoyant, diaphanous, completely spiritual light which dresses and undresses all things.

The Attic landscape determines the lineaments of the ideal man: handsomely well built, taciturn, freed from superfluous wealth; powerful, but capable on the other hand of restraining his power and imposing limits on his imagination. Sometimes the Attic landscape reaches the borders of austerity. But it does not cross them; it stops at a cheerful, good-natured seriousness. Its grace does not degenerate into romanticism, nor, by the same token, its power into asperity. All is finely balanced and measured. Even its virtues do not run to excess, do not break the human mean, but stop at a point beyond which, if they proceeded further, they would become either cruelly inhuman, or divine. The Attic landscape does not swagger, does not indulge in rhetoric, does not degenerate into fits of melodramatic swooning; it says what it has to say with a calm, virile forcefulness. By the simplest means possible it formulates the essential.

But now and again in the midst of this seriousness there is a smile—two or three silver-branched olive trees on a completely arid slope, some refreshingly green pines, oleanders at the edge of a dry, brilliantly white riverbed, a tuft of wild violets between blazing blue-black stones. All opposites join together, mix, and are reconciled here, creating the supreme miracle, harmony.

How did this miracle happen? Where did the grace find so much seriousness, the seriousness so much grace? How was the power able to avoid abusing its force? All this must constitute the Greek miracle.

There came moments, as I roamed through Attica, when I had a premonition that this land could become the highest lesson in civility, nobility, and strength.

After each of my wanderings through the Attic countryside, at first without knowing why, I climbed the Acropolis to view and review the Parthenon. This temple is a mystery to me. I can never see it the same way twice; it seems to change constantly, come to life, undulate while remaining motionless, play games with light and the human eye. But when, after longing to see it for so many years, I confronted it for the very first time, it appeared immobile to me, the skeleton of a primordial beast, and my heart did not bound like a young calf. (Throughout my life this has served me as the infallible sign. When I encounter a sunrise, a painting, a woman, or an idea that makes my heart bound like a young calf, then I know I am standing in front of happiness.) The first time I stood in front of the Parthenon, my heart did not bound. The building seemed a feat of the intellect—of numbers, geometry—a faultless thought enmarbled, a sublime achievement of the mind, possessing every virtue—every virtue except one, the most precious and beloved: it failed to touch the human heart.

I felt that the Parthenon was an even number such as two or four. Even numbers run contrary to my heart; I want nothing to do with them. Their lives are too comfortably arranged, they stand on their feet much too solidly and have not the slightest desire to change location. They are satisfied, conservative, without anxieties; they have solved every problem, translated every desire into reality, and grown calm. It is the odd number which conforms to the rhythm of my heart. The life of the odd number is not at all comfortably arranged. The odd number does not like this world the way it finds it, but wishes to change it, add to it, push it further. It stands on one foot, holds the other ready in the air, and wants to depart. Where to? To the following even number, in order to halt for an instant, catch its breath, and work up fresh momentum.

This sober enmarbled rationality was unpleasing to youth's rebellious heart, which wants to crush everything old and remake the world anew. An excessively prudent dotard it was, who desired with his counsels to give excessively short rein to the heart's impulsion. Turning my back on the Parthenon, I submerged myself in the superb view which extended as far as the sea. The sun stood at the zenith; it was noontime, the culminant hour, devoid of shadows or any play of light; austere, sublime, perfect. I looked at the blazing, brilliantly white city, the hallowed sea sparkling around Salamis, the surrounding mountains which were sunning themselves, bare and contented. Submerged in this vision, I forgot the Parthenon which stood behind me.

But after each new return from Attica's olive groves and the Saronic Gulf, the hidden harmony, casting aside its veils one by one, slowly, gradually revealed itself to my mind. Each time I climbed the Acropolis again, the Parthenon seemed to be swaying slightly, as in a motionless dance—swaying and breathing.

This initiation lasted for months, perhaps years. I do not remember the exact day when I stood completely initiated before the Parthenon and my heart bounded like a young calf. This temple that towered before me, what a trophy it was, what a collaboration between mind and heart, what a supreme fruit of human effort! Space had been conquered; distinctions between small and large had vanished. Infinity entered this narrow, magical parallelogram carved out by man, entered leisurely and took its repose there. Time had been conquered as well; the lofty moment had been transformed into eternity.

I allowed my gaze to creep over the warm, sun-nourished marble. It touched the stones and rummaged through them like a hand, uncovering the hidden mysteries; it clung to them and refused to depart. I saw the seemingly parallel columns imperceptibly incline their capitals one toward the other so that concertedly, with tenderness and strength, they might sustain the sacred pediments entrusted to them. Never have undulations created lines so irreproachably straight. Never have numbers and music coupled with such understanding, such love.

This, I believe, was the greatest joy I experienced in my four years as a student in Athens. Not a single feminine exhalation came to cloud the air I breathed. But I had several friends I liked very much. I went mountain climbing with them, and in summertime we swam together in the sea. We chatted about fleeting everyday things, and occasionally we held parties to which some of them brought their girl friends. We laughed without cause, because we were young; we grieved without cause, again because we were young. We were like fresh unspent bull-calves who sigh because their strength is strangling them.

How many possibilities were held out to each of us! I looked my friends in the eye, one by one, struggling to guess in which direction their strength would blaze a trail. One, when he parted his lips to speak of some idea or mad folly that he loved, caught fire all at once; it was an immense pleasure to hear the great epigrammatic force with which, never stumbling, he enumerated his thoughts. As I listened to him I felt envious, because whenever I opened my mouth to speak, I immediately regretted it. Words came to me with difficulty, and if I happened to advance an argument in support of an opinion I had, the opposite argument, equally correct, always came immediately to mind. Ashamed to tell lies, I fell abruptly silent. . . . Another friend was reserved. Extremely sparing of words, he never opened his mouth except during the law school recitations, and then the professor and all the rest of us listened to him with admiration as he purposely made tangled knots of the problems of justice and then undid them by feats of prestidigitation. Another was a great organizer who ruled the masses. He became involved in politics, organized demonstrations, gave speeches, went to prison, came out again, resumed the struggle. We all said that one day he would doubtlessly become a great statesman. Another, a pale, soft-spoken vegetarian with faded blue eyes and ladylike hands, had by dint of great effort established a club whose emblem was a white lily with the inscription, "The feet cleaner than the hands." He loved the moon. "The moon is the only woman I adore," he used to say. Another was an untouched lily—pallid, melancholy, with large blue eyes and long-fingered hands. He wrote poetry. I have been able to remember very little of this poetry, but when in solitude I whisper the verses to myself, my eyes fill with tears. For one night this young man was found outside the monastery of Kaisarianí, hanging from the branch of an olive tree.

There were many others as well, each with his own individual soul full of closed buds. When are they going to flower, I asked myself, when are they going to bear fruit? Dear God, I implored, let me live long enough to see them, let me live long enough to see, in my own case, which buds will open inside me and what kind of fruit they will form. I looked at my friends with anxiety and unutterable sadness, as though bidding them farewell. For I was afraid that time might be the gale which blows when nature burgeons, afraid that it might blow mercilessly and strip these souls bare.

Departing from Athens, I left two laurel crowns behind me, the only two I was ever awarded in my whole life. The first I received for fencing. It was heavy, interwoven with white and blue ribbons, and composed of laurel supposedly picked in the Delphian gorge. This was a lie. I knew it, everyone knew it, but this lie bathed the leaves in splendor. The second I received in a playwriting competition. I don't know why, but one day my blood caught fire and I wrote an ardent drama full of melancholy and passion. It was about love; I called it *Day Is Breaking*. To be sure, I believed that I was offering the world a superior, more moral morality, a greater freedom, a new light. The professor who was judge, a serious, close-shaven man wearing a high collar, ruled that mine was the best of all the plays submitted. But, giving way to fear, he stigmatized [in irreproachable katharévousa] its audacious phrases and unbridled eroticism. "We give the poet his laurel crown," he said in conclusion, "but we dismiss him from these sacred precincts." I was there in the great university auditorium, a beardless inexperienced student, and I heard. Blushing to the ears, I stood up, left the laurel crown on the judge's table, and walked out.

I had a friend who was an attaché in the Ministry of Foreign Affairs. We had recently made plans to travel together in western

Europe. "You'd better take along the fencing crown," he said to me one day. "We won't be able to get laurel leaves up north, and we'll need them for stew."

I hung the crown on the wall and saved it. Years passed. When our dream finally came true and my friend and I departed for Germany, I took it with me. In two years we had consumed all the leaves in stew.

16

RETURN TO CRETE. KNOSSOS

I RETURNED to Crete for the final summer of my student years. My mother I found seated in her usual place by the window which gave onto the courtyard. She was knitting socks. It was evening, and my sister had begun to water the pots of basil and marjoram. The trellis above the well was laden with bunches of fat, still-unripened grapes.

Nothing in the house had been moved. Everything stood in its place: the sofa, mirror, lamps, and all around on every wall the heroes of '21 with their thick mustaches, hairy chests, the pistols at their waists, wild, passion-governed souls who were capable of doing—and did—both good and evil, according to how their spleen prodded them. Karaiskakis wrote to Captain Stournáras, "Most valiant brother, Captain Nikólaos: I got your letter; I've seen everything you wrote. My prick has trumpets and it also has toubelékia. I play whichever I please!" The toubelékia is a Turkish musical instrument, the trumpet a Greek. These heroes were not pure souls, they were great ones. And great souls are always dangerous.

I often contemplate what a mystery it is that in such dung the blue flower of liberty could have found nourishment and put forth shoots. Hatred, betrayals, dissension, feats of bravery, ardent love for the fatherland, the dance at Zálongon!

Bright and early the next morning I went to find my two classmates, whom I had not seen for four years. The former members of the Friendly Society were unrecognizable. Life had already rolled over them and leveled them flat. When they spoke of the Friendly Society, they burst out laughing. One had a fine voice and was invited to all the marriages, baptisms, and holiday festivities. He ate, drank, and sang. People admired him for his sweet voice and he shared their admiration. He had started along the downgrade; his hands already trembled from too much drink. The other had studied the guitar. He played passionate airs and lively ditties, accompanying his friend. I found both of them well nourished and satisfied, with noses already turning red. They had found employment in a soapworks; they were earning their living, enjoying life, and looking for wives.

I observed them and listened to their words but did not speak—my throat was blocked. Could the flame, then, be reduced to ashes so very quickly? Was the soul so very closely related to the flesh? They knew the dowry of every young girl, where you could eat the fluffiest loukoums, and which tavern had the best wine.

I left feeling sick at heart, as though I had just been at a funeral. The minor virtues, I reflected, are much more dangerous than the minor vices. If these two did not sing and play so well, they would not be invited to parties, would not get drunk, would not fritter away their time, and they might be saved. As it was, singing beautifully, playing the guitar beautifully, they had started along the downgrade.

The next day when I spied them in the distance, I changed my route. I was ashamed because so many friendships and longings had faded in me so quickly, so many great plans to save the world. A wind had blown, and the whole of youth's blossoming tree had been stripped bare. Wasn't this tree of youth going to form any fruit, I wondered. Was this, then, the way flotillas set out to cleave the ocean, only to founder in a domestic trough?

Wandering all alone through the narrow lanes, I returned again and again to the harbor to inhale anew the beloved smell of carob beans and rotted citrons. I always had a book in my hand, sometimes Dante, sometimes Homer. As I read the immortal verses, I felt that man could become immortal and that the world's heterogeneous surface of houses, people, joys, insults—the incoherent chaos we call life—was capable of uniting into harmony.

One day I called at the Irish girl's house. She had left. I passed by a second time, feeling strangely bitter and remorseful concerning what I had done and failed to do. It was as though I had committed a crime and was returning again and again to circle about its victim. I could not sleep. One night as I was passing through the Turkish quarter, I heard a woman singing an oriental amané in a voice full of woefully convulsive passion. The sound was somber, raucous, very deep; it issued from the woman's loins and filled the night with despair and plaintive melancholy. Finding it impossible to proceed, I halted and listened, my head thrown back against the wall. I could not catch my breath. My suffocating soul, unable any longer to fit within its cage of clay, was hanging from my scalp and weighing whether or not to flee. No, the singer's female breast was not being convulsed by love, not by that total mystery the coupling of a man with a woman, not by joy and the hope for a son. It was being convulsed by a cry, a command to break our prison bars of morality, shame, and hope, and to give ourselves over to, lose ourselves in, become one with, the fearful, enticing Lover who lies in wait in the darkness and whom we call God. Listening to the woman's woefully convulsive song on that night, I felt that love, death, and God were one and the same. As the years went by, I became ever more deeply aware of this terrifying Trinity that waits in ambush in the abyss of chaos—in the abyss and in our hearts. It was not a Trinity; it was what a certain Byzantine mystic called a Militant Monad.

The singer fell silent. I drew away from the wall. The world had risen again out of chaos. The houses grew stable, the streets rolled out smoothly in front of me once more, and I was able to walk. I roamed all night long. My mind remained mute; not a single thought came to reduce my disturbance or change its form. Letting my body guide me, I promenaded along the Venetian walls above the sea. The sky was sparkling, everything brilliantly illuminated. The constellations shifted, slid down toward the west, and vanished; my soul vanished with them. A cool, cool breeze blew from the mountains and entered the houses through the cracks around the windows, cooling the sleeping, sweating inhabitants. I could hear the city breathing in the deep silence.

That night I passed the Irish girl's house again. I had been walking for hours, and without wanting to or being aware of it, I found myself going in ever-contracting circles which brought me nearer and nearer to the center, to her house. It was as though a cry remained at that house, an imperious and reproachful cry which called me and which I could not resist. Toward daybreak, however, as I was about to arrive once more in front of her closed windows and doors, a lightning flash tore across my mind and illumined it. This was not a cry, it was the woman's song, the somber, raucous song I had heard that evening as I passed through the Turkish quarter. The song had become deformed now inside me; it had turned into the howl of a lonely, mateless beast which had been abandoned.

Song, beastly howl, the Irish girl's despairing cry—all became a noose around my neck, strangling me. I recalled a grave saying I had once heard from the lips of an elderly Moslem: "If a woman calls you to sleep with her and you do not go, you are damned. God does not forgive this. You'll be placed with Judas at the very bottom of hell." This terrified me. Breaking out into a cold sweat, I headed rapidly homeward, staggering like a wounded animal.

Ascending the stairs on tiptoe so that they would not creak and alert my father, I fell into bed. I was quivering. One moment I felt fiery hot, the next I was shivering. Obviously I had a fever. Sleep came like a poisonous spider and wrapped its web around me. When I awoke toward noon the following day, I was still quivering.

This anguish lasted three days. It was not anguish, it was a heavy lump in the middle of my heart, and my mouth was bitter, poisonously bitter. As I gazed through my window at the acacia in the center of the yard, the fruit-laden arbor, my sister embroidering and my mother coming and going in silence, yoked to her hallowed domestic servitude, the lump rose from my heart to my throat. I was being strangled. I felt as though I had been expelled from heaven. No, not expelled; it was as though I had of my own accord vaulted the celestial railings and fled, an act which I now regretted as I roamed inconsolably outside the closed gates.

On the fourth day I jumped out of bed early in the morning and, without having any clear aim in mind or knowing what I was going to do, took up my pen and began to write.

This turned out to be a decisive moment in my life. Perhaps in this way, on this morning, my inner anguish would open a door for itself and escape. Who could tell (I must have thought this, but without formulating it clearly): perhaps if the anguish became embodied, if words gave it a body, I would see its face and, seeing it, no longer fear it. I had committed a great sin. If I confessed this sin, I would find relief.

I began therefore to mobilize words, to regurgitate the poems, saints' legends, and novels I had read. Pillaging involuntarily from this one and that, I started to write. But the very first words I placed on paper astonished me. I had had nothing like that in mind. I refused to write such a thing; why then had I written it? As though I had not been delivered permanently from my first sexual contact (yet I was certain I had been delivered), I began to crystallize a tale around the Irish girl, a tale full of passion and fanciful imaginings. Never had I spoken such tender words to her, never felt such raptures when I touched her as those I now proclaimed on paper. Lies, all lies, and yet as I enumerated these lies now on the sheet before me, I began to understand to my astonishment that I had indeed tasted great pleasure with her. Were they really true, then, all these lies? Why had I not been aware of this pleasure in the course of experiencing it? Why, now that I was writing it down, did I become aware of it for the first time?

I swaggered as I wrote. Was I not God, doing as I pleased, transubstantiating reality, fashioning it as I should have liked it to be—as it should have been? I was joining truth and falsehood indissolubly together. No, there were no longer any such things as truth and falsehood; everything was a soft dough which I kneaded and rolled freely, according to the dictates of whim, without securing permission from anyone. Evidently there is an uncertainty which is more certain than certitude itself. But one of these is to be found a full story higher than that ground-level construction of humanity's which goes by the name of truth.

This insignificant, slightly stooped Irish girl had become unrecognizable in my work, and as for me, the plucked cock, I had glued to myself huge parti-colored feathers which did not belong to me.

I finished in a few days. Gathering together the manuscript, I inscribed *Snake and Lily* at its head in red Byzantine characters and, getting up, went to the window to take a deep breath. The Irish girl did not torment me now; she had left me in order to lie down on the paper and she could never detach herself from it again. I was saved!

Clouds had covered the sky, the air grown dim; it was raining. The broad vine leaves glistened, the fat grapes beamed glassily. I inhaled the aroma of wet soil, an odor which always reminds me of a newly dug grave. Today, however, the reek of death had been exorcised and my mind was filled with sweet fragrance. A sparrow, drenched from the rain, came and found refuge on the windowsill. On the roof above my head the water cooed and pecked away like a flock of pigeons.

I still clutched the manuscript tightly, as though it were a tiny living creature I did not wish to escape, as though in my fist I held the drenched sparrow—or as though I had made peace with the Irish girl, the ashes had turned back into an apple, and I was holding this apple in my hand.

I went out to the courtyard and walked back and forth in the rain among the flowerpots, tasting in my own right the pleasure felt by a dusty, thirsty tree when the heavens take pity on it and rain begins to fall. Rain has always given me an inexplicable joy—if I weren't ashamed, I would say a sexual one. I feel as though I were earth, thirsty earth; the feminine element within me, a woman hidden deep down in my bowels, awakes and receives the sky as she would receive a man. . . . I walked exultantly beneath the rain; my heart had been unburdened. I did not think of the Irish lass any longer, except as I had refashioned and solidified her with words. She was reclining now, lying down on the paper. The truth which had been storing up anguish in my breast for such a long time was not the real truth; the real truth was this newborn creature of imagination. By means of imagination I had obliterated reality, and I felt relieved.

This struggle between reality and imagination, between God-the-Creator and man-the-creator, had momentarily intoxicated my heart. "Here is my road, here is my duty," I cried out in the courtyard as I paced back and forth beneath the rain. Each man acquires the stature of the enemy with whom he wrestles. It pleased me, even if it meant my destruction, to wrestle with God. He took mud to create a world; I took words. He made men as we see them, crawling on the ground; I, with air and imagination, the stuff that dreams are made on, would fashion other men with more soul, men able to resist the ravages of time. While God's men died, mine would live!

Now I feel ashamed when I recall this satanic arrogance. But then I was young, and to be young means to undertake to demolish the world and to have the gall to wish to erect a new and better one in its place.

My breast was heaving with anguish. Though the old inquietudes sat cowering silently in a corner, new ones began to rise up. The road which suddenly flashed before me was a dangerous and exceedingly steep one. How had it appeared so abruptly, this road which had never occurred to me? Who opened this inner door and beckoned, pointing to it as the supposed gateway to salvation? Did the pain of unfulfilled love do this, or could this door have been opened by the saints from the legends I read as a child? Or by Crete, which, seeing that I could not help her by fighting, placed other weapons in my hands?

In order to change the direction of my thoughts, the next morning, as the Sunday bells tolled and Christians proceeded to Saint Minas's to do worship, I set out for another shrine. I went to pay my respects to Saint Crete, which in recent years had been exhumed from the age-old soil of Knossos.

Crete's mystery is extremely deep. Whoever sets foot on this island senses a mysterious force branching warmly and beneficently through his veins, senses his soul begin to grow. But this mystery has become even deeper and richer since the discovery of this immensely versatile and varicolored civilization until then buried beneath the soil, this civilization filled with such great nobility and youthful joy.

I left the city and took the charming road which leads to the new cemetery. Hearing exclamations and weeping, I quickened my pace. A well-bred merchant of our neighborhood, one of Megalo Kastro's great figures, had died two days before and was being buried in the newly fitted-out cemetery. He had died young; as his friends started to carry him away his wife clung to the coffin and refused to let him leave. I had been passing at that moment. I averted my face to avoid seeing the corpse, because ever since that day in my fourth year when, as you will remember, I observed our neighbor Anníka's bones being removed from her tomb, I have been unable to view a dead body. I am overcome with fear. A hairless, eyeless, lipless Anníka darts out in front of me and rushes forward to seize me, in order to seat me again on her knees. Of course I know this is not true, but I also know that there is something truer than truth itself, and for this reason I grow afraid and quicken my steps every time I see a corpse.

I was surrounded by olive groves and vineyards. The vintage still had not begun; the grapes drooped heavily and touched the soil. The air smelled of fig leaves. A little old lady came along. She halted. Lifting the two or three fig leaves which covered the basket she carried on her arm, she picked out two figs and presented them to me.

"Do you know me, old lady?" I asked.

She glanced at me in amazement. "No, my boy. Do I have to know you to give you something? You're a human being, aren't you? So am I. Isn't that enough?"

Laughing a fresh girlish laugh, she began to hobble along once more toward Kastro.

The two figs were dripping with honey; I believe they were the most delicious I ever tasted. The old lady's words refreshed me as I ate. You are a human being. So am I. That's enough!

A shadow fell next to my own. Turning, I saw a Catholic priest. He looked at me and smiled.

"Abbé Mugnier," he said, holding out his hand. "Would you care to keep me company? I don't know modern Greek, only ancient: Μῆνιν ἄειδε, θεά, Πηληϊάδεω 'Αχιλῆος . . ."

". . . οὐλομένην, ἣ μυρί' 'Αχαιοῖς ἄλγε' ἔθηκε . . ." I continued.

Laughing, we continued to declaim the immortal verses as we proceeded. I learned subsequently that this abbé who laughed and recited, a tuft of gray hair fluttering over his forehead, was celebrated for his sancity and intelligence. In Paris he had led many well-known atheists back to the fold. Endowed with a sparkling mind, he frequented the world, talking and joking with great ladies, but behind this playful, mobile exterior loomed Christ crucified, an immobile, impregnable rock. No, not Christ crucified, Christ resurrected.

The custodian hurried forward to greet us and explain the site. He was a simple, jovial Cretan who wore vrakes and carried a large crook. His name was David. In his many years as custodian and guide at Knossos he had learned much. He spoke of the palace as though it were his home, received us in the capacity of master of the house.

Taking the lead, he extended his crook to indicate the sites.

"Before you is the great royal court, sixty meters long, twenty-nine meters wide. Here are the storerooms with their huge decorated jars. In here the king stocked his produce in order to feed his people. We found sediment from wine and olive oil in the jars, also olive pits, beans, chick-peas, wheat, barley, and lentils. Everything was carbonized by great fires."

We climbed to the upper story. On all sides: short, thick columns colored black and purple. In the passageways we saw wall paintings of flowers, shields, and bulls. We reached the high terrace. The happy domesticated landscape stretched all around us; at the center of the horizon lay Yioúchtas, Zeus's supine head. The half-crumbling, half-restored palace gleamed with brilliance after thousands of years, once more enjoying Crete's masculine sunlight. In this palace one does not see the balanced geometric architecture of Greece. Reigning here are imagination, grace, and the free play of man's creative power. This palace grew and proliferated in the course of time, slowly, like a living organism, a tree. It was not built once and for all with a fixed, premeditated plan; it grew by additions, playing and harmonizing with the ever-renewed necessities of the times. Man was not guided here by inflexible, untrickable logic. The intellect was useful, but as a servant, not a master. The master was something or someone else. What name could we give it?

Turning to the abbé, I revealed my thoughts and asked his opinion.

"You want to know who the master was?" he answered with a smile. "What do you expect a priest to tell you except God? The Cretans' god was the master; He guided their hands and minds, and they created. God was the master builder. And this Cretan god was as nimble and playful as the sea which embraces the island. This is why landscape, palace, paintings, and sea have such a faultless harmony and unity."

Descending the stone stairway, we gazed in silence at the paintings on the walls: bulls, lilies, fish in the blue sea, the flying fish that spread their fins to leap above the waves, as though water, their maternal element, stifled them and they wished to inhale a more rarefied atmosphere. We halted at the theater. Here the guide caught fire.

"This is where the bullfights took place," he said, his face glowing with pride. "But the Cretan bullfights were not like the barbarous ones in Spain. There, so I'm told, the bull is killed and the horses disemboweled. Here the bullfight was a bloodless game.

Man and bull played together. The bullfighter grasped the bull by the horns, the beast became angry and tossed his head high in the air, which enabled the bullfighter to gain momentum and jump with a nimble somersault onto the bull's back. Then he made a second somersault and landed on his feet behind the bull's tail, where a young girl was waiting to clasp him in her arms."

The abbé had fixed his gaze upon the theater's stone tiers, apparently struggling to draw the divine game freshly into the light. I explained the custodian's words to him.

He took me by the arm. We continued on.

"It is terribly difficult to play bloodlessly with God," he murmured.

We stopped at a square column of glazed plaster, at the top of which was incised the sacred sign: the double-edged axe. The abbé joined his hands together, bent his knee for a moment, and moved his lips as though in prayer.

I was astonished. "What—are you praying?" I asked him.

"Of course I am praying, my young friend. Every race and every age gives God its own mask. But behind all the masks, in every age and every race, is always the same never-changing God."

He fell silent, but after a moment: "We have the cross as our sacred sign; your most ancient ancestors had the double-edged axe. But I push aside the ephemeral symbols and discern the same God behind both the cross and the double-edged axe, discern Him and do obeisance."

I was very young at that time. On that day I did not understand, but years later my mind was able to contain those words and make them bear fruit. Then I too began to discern the eternal, immutable face of God behind all religious symbols. And still later, when my mind grew overbroad and my heart overbold, I began to discern something behind God's face as well—chaos, a terrifying uninhabited darkness. Without meaning to, this holy abbé had opened a road for me on that day at Knossos. I took this road, but I did not stop where he would have liked me to stop. Possessed by satanic curiosity, I went further and discovered the abyss.

We sat down between two columns. The fiery sky gleamed like steel. The crickets in the olive groves surrounding the palace were deafening. The custodian leaned against the column, removed his tobacco pouch from beneath his belt, and began to roll a cigarette.

None of us spoke. We sensed the sacredness of moment and place, and knew that silence alone was fitting. Two doves flew above our heads and perched on one of the columns. These were the sacred birds of the Great Goddess worshiped here by the Cretans. Sometimes they are seen sitting on a column, sometimes being held by the goddess between her two milk-swollen breasts.

"Doves . . . " I said softly, as though afraid that they might be scared away by the sound of my voice and leave the column.

The abbé placed his finger over his lips. "Quiet," he whispered.

Though my mind was overflowing with questions, I did not speak. The extraordinary murals passed again before my sight: large almond-shaped eyes, cascades of black tresses, imposing matrons with bare breasts and thick voluptuous lips, birds—pheasant and partridge—blue monkeys, princes with peacock feathers in their hair, fierce holy bulls, tender-aged priestesses with sacred snakes wrapped around their arms, blue boys in flowering gardens. Joy, strength, great wealth; a world full of mystery, an Atlantis which had issued from the depths of the Cretan soil. This world looked at us with immense black eyes, but its lips were still sealed.

What kind of world is this? I asked myself. When will it open its lips and speak? What feats did these forebears accomplish here on the very soil we are now treading?

Crete served as the first bridge between Europe, Asia, and Africa. Crete was the first place in a then totally dark Europe to become enlightened. And it was here too that the Greek soul accomplished its destined mission: it reduced God to the scale of man. Here in Crete the monstrous immovable statues of Egypt or Assyria became small and graceful, with bodies that moved, mouths that smiled; the features and stature of God took on the features and stature of man. A new, original humanity full of agility, grace, and oriental luxury lived and played on the Cretan soil, a humanity which differed from the subsequent Greeks.

As I looked about me at the small domesticated hills, the sparsely leafed olive trees, a slender slowly swaying cypress which rose among the rocks; as I listened to the light harmonious tinkling from some invisible flock of goats and inhaled the fragrant sea breeze that straddled the hill, the age-old Cretan secret penetrated me ever more deeply, I believe, and became less and less obscure. This secret is concerned not with supramundane problems but with everyday ones in all their fervent detail, with the incessantly renewed problems of man's life here upon this earth.

"What are you thinking about?" the abbé asked me.

"About Crete . . ." I replied.

"I too was thinking about Crete," said my companion. "Crete and my soul. . . . If it is given me to be reborn, I should like to see the light again here, on this soil. Some sort of invisible witchcraft exists here. . . . Come, let's go."

Getting up, we threw a final, slow-moving glance at the extraordinary sight. I would see it again, but the abbé whispered with a sigh, "Farewell . . . farewell for the last time."

He waved his hand at the columns, the courtyards, the murals.

"Farewell. From the ends of the earth a Catholic priest came to do obeisance to you. He did obeisance. Now, farewell."

We started back. The terribly hot and dusty road made the abbé tired. We stopped at a little monastery occupied by dervishes who danced every Friday. The arched doorway was green and had an open hand of bronze—Mohammed's sacred symbol—on the lintel. We entered the immaculate courtyard. It was paved with large white pebbles; there were flowerpots and creepers all around the edges, and in the center a huge fruit-laden laurel. We stopped beneath its shade to catch our breath. One of the dervishes saw us from his cell. Approaching, he greeted us by placing his hand over his breast, lips, and forehead. He was wearing a long blue robe and a tall kulah of white wool. His beard was pitch black and pointed; a silver earring hung from his right ear. He clapped his hands. A chubby barefooted boy came and brought us some stools. We sat down. The dervish chatted about the flowers we saw around us, then about the sea, which we observed sparkling between the laurel's lanceolate leaves. Finally he began to speak about dancing.

"If a man cannot dance, he cannot pray. Angels have mouths but lack the power of speech. They speak to God by dancing."

"Father, what name do you give God?" asked the abbé.

"God does not have a name," the dervish replied. "He is too big to fit inside names. A name is a prison, God is free."

"But in case you should want to call Him," the abbé persisted, "when there is need, what name will you use?"

The dervish bowed his head and thought. Finally he parted his lips:

"*Ah!*—that is what I shall call Him. Not Allah, but *Ah!*"

This troubled the abbé. "He's right," he murmured.

The chubby little dervish boy appeared again, this time with a tray containing coffee, cold water, and two large bunches of grapes. A pair of doves flirted and cooed on the roof above us. Were they the same we had seen at Knossos? When we fell silent for a moment, the monasterial air filled with amorous sighs. I turned to the abbé. He was gazing upward at the doves and the sky beyond them, his eyes brimming with tears.

He felt that I was watching him.

"The world is beautiful," he said with a smile. "Yes, it is beautiful in the lands of the sun—wherever you find blue skies, and doves, and grapes. And a laurel above you."

He was eating his grapes one by one in perfect contentment. You could sense that he hoped this moment would never end.

"Even if I were certain I was going to heaven," he said, "I would pray God to let me go by the longest possible route."

So happy did we feel in the courtyard of the Mohammedan monastery, we could not bear to leave.

Other dervishes emerged from the surrounding cells. The younger ones had pale faces and fiery eyes; they seemed in desperate pursuit of God. The old ones, who must have found God, were red-cheeked, their eyes filled with light. They squatted around us. Some unhooked chaplets from their leather belts and started to tell their beads tranquilly, gazing with curiosity at the Christian monk. Others brought out their long chibouks, half closed their eyes, and began contentedly, silently, to smoke.

"What joy this is," whispered the abbé. "How brightly the Lord's face shines here too, behind all these faces!"

He touched my shoulder in an imploring way.

"Please, the dervishes are a religious order. Ask them what their rule is."

The oldest of the group, a man with a long white beard, laid his chibouk on his knee.

"Poverty," he answered. "Poverty. To own nothing, be weighted down by nothing, to journey to God along a flowering pathway. Laughter, the dance, and joy are the three archangels who take us by the hand and lead us."

The abbé turned to me again. "Ask them how they make themselves ready to appear before God. Is it by fasting?"

"No, no," answered a young dervish with a laugh. "We eat, drink, and bless the Lord for giving food and drink to man."

"Well then, how?" insisted the abbé.

"By dancing," replied the oldest dervish, the one with the long white beard.

"Dancing?" said the abbé. "Why?"

"Because dancing kills the ego, and once the ego has been killed, there is no further obstacle to prevent you from joining with God."

The abbé's eyes sparkled.

"The order of Saint Francis!" he exclaimed, squeezing the old dervish's hand. "That's just what Saint Francis did: he danced his way across the earth and mounted to heaven. He used to say, 'What are we but God's buffoons, born to soothe and delight the hearts of men.' So, my young friend, once more you see—always, always the same never-changing God."

"But in that case," I dared to object, "why do missionaries go to the four corners of the world and try to make the natives renounce the mask of God which suits them, in order to put on a foreign mask—ours—in its place?"

The abbé rose.

"I find it very difficult to answer that question," he said. "If, God willing, you should come to Paris to complete your studies, call at my house."

He smiled cunningly.

"Perhaps by then I shall have found the answer."

We said goodbye to the dervishes. They escorted us to the outer door with smiles and bows, once again touching their hands to breast, mouth, and forehead.

On the threshold the abbé said to me, "Tell them, please, that we all worship the same God. Tell them I am a dervish in a black robe."

17

PILGRIMAGE THROUGH GREECE

My father had promised me a year of travel, wherever I wanted to go, if I took my degree with highest honors. The reward was a great one, and I threw myself heart and soul into my studies. One of my friends, a devilishly clever Cretan, was going to take his examinations with me. The crucial day arrived. We started together for the university, both extremely uneasy. I had known everything and forgotten everything. My memory was a void; I felt terrified.

"Do you remember anything at all?" my friend asked me.

"Not a thing."

"Neither do I. Let's go to a beerhall to drink, get soused, and loosen our tongues. That's the way my father went to war—drunk."

"Come on."

We drank, drank some more, began to feel happy.

"How does the world look to you?" asked my friend.

"Double."

"Me too. Can you walk?"

I got up and took a few steps.

"Yes," I answered.

"Then let's go. Roman Law—tremble!"

We set out arm in arm at first, but then each worked up courage and continued on his own two feet.

"Hi, Bacchus my stalwart!" I cried. "Give Justinian and his Novels the old hammer lock. Lay him out cold on the ground!"

"Why call on Bacchus?" my friend asked. "We drank beer, not wine."

"Are you sure?"

"You don't believe me? Let's go back and ask."

We went back.

"Beer, beer," the owner of the establishment assured us, splitting his sides with laughter. "Where are you headed, gents?"

"To take our law exams."

"Wait, I'll come along for the laughs."

He removed his apron and followed behind. The professors were waiting for us. Enthroned as they were, all in a row, they seemed like so many gnats. Our brains spat fire. With immense gusto we answered their questions, answered them with a nonchalance somewhat insolent, mixing in Latin tags with great frequency. Our tongues wagged incessantly, and we both came out with highest honors.

We were overjoyed. My friend planned to establish a law office in Crete and enter politics, while I rejoiced because a door of escape was opening for me. All my life one of my greatest desires has been to travel—to see and touch unknown countries, to swim in unknown seas, to circle the globe, observing new lands, seas, peoples, and ideas with insatiable appetite, to see everything for the first time and for the last time, casting a slow, prolonged glance, then to close my eyes and feel the riches deposit themselves inside me calmly or stormily according to their pleasure, until time passes them at last through its fine sieve, straining the quintessence out of all the joys and sorrows. This alchemy of the heart is, I believe, a great delight which all men deserve.

The canary, the magic bird my father gave me as a New Year's present when I was a child, had become a carcass years before; no, not "become a carcass"—I blush that this expression escaped me—had "passed away" I meant to say, passed away like a human. Or better still, had "rendered its song up to God." We buried it in our little courtyard-garden. My sister cried, but I was calm because I knew that as long as I remained alive, I would never allow it to perish. "I won't let you perish," I whispered as I covered it over with earth. "We shall live and travel together."

When I grew older, left Crete, and wandered over the earth's surface, I always felt this canary clinging to my scalp and singing—singing the identical refrain over and over again, incessantly: "Let's get up and leave. Why are we sitting here? We are birds, not oysters. Let's get up and leave." My head had become a terrestial globe with the canary, perched at its pole, raising its warm throat toward heaven and singing.

I've heard that in the old days the concubines of the harem stood in a row each evening in their garden, freshly bathed and scented, their breasts uncovered, and the sultan came down to make his choice. In his hand he held a little handkerchief which he thrust beneath the armpit of each and then sniffed. He chose the woman whose aroma pleased him the most that evening.

It was like concubines that the various countries lined themselves up in a row before me.

Hastily, avidly, I swept my eyes over the map. Where to go? Which continent, which ocean to see first? All the countries held out their hands and invited me. The world was extensive, praise the Lord, and—let idlers say what they will—man's life was extensive too. We would have time to see and enjoy all countries.

Why not begin with Greece!

My pilgrimage through Greece lasted three months. Even now after so many years my heart throbs with happiness and inquietude when I recall the mountains, islands, villages, monasteries, and coast lines. It is a great joy to travel through Greece and see it, a great joy and an agony.

I traveled through Greece, and gradually I began to see with my eyes and touch with my hands something that abstract thought cannot touch or see: the means by which strength and grace combine. I doubt that these two ingredients of perfection, Ares and Aphrodite, have ever joined together so organically in any other part of the world, have ever joined together so organically as in the austere, ever-smiling land of Greece. Some of her regions are severe and haughty, others full of feminine tenderness, still others serious and at the same time cheerful and gracious. But the spirit passed over all of them and by means of a temple, myth, or hero bequeathed the proper, suitable soul to each. That is why whoever journeys in Greece and has eyes to see with and a mind to think with, journeys in an unbroken magical unity from one spiritual victory to another. In Greece a person confirms the fact that spirit is the continuation and flower of matter, and myth the simple, composite expression of the most positive reality. The spirit has trodden upon the stones of Greece for many, many years; no matter where you go, you discover its divine traces.

Various regions in Greece are dual in nature, and the emotion which springs from them is also dual in nature. Harshness and tenderness stand side by side, complementing each other and coupling like a man with a woman. Sparta is one such source of tenderness and harshness. In front of you stands Taygetus, a hard, disdainful legislator full of cliffs and precipices, while below, stretched out at your feet like a woman in love, is the fruited, seductive plain. On the one hand Taygetus, the Mount Sinai of Greece, where the pitiless god of the Race dictates the most rigid of commandments: life is war, the world is a battlefield, your sole duty is to win; do not sleep, do not adorn yourselves, laugh, or talk; fighting is your sole purpose in life, therefore fight! And on the other hand, at Taygetus's foot—Helen. Just as you begin to grow savage and to disdain the earth's sweetness, suddenly Helen's breath, like a flowering lemon tree, makes your mind reel.

Is this Spartan plain really so tender and voluptuous? I wonder. Is the fragrance of its oleanders really so intoxicating—or does all this fascination perhaps spring from Helen's oft-kissed far-roving body? Certainly Eurotas would not possess its present-day seductive grace had it not flowed as a tributary into Helen's immortal myth. For lands, seas, and rivers, as we well know, join with great beloved names and, evermore inseparable from them, flow into our hearts. Walk along the humble banks of the Eurotas and you feel your hands, hair, and thoughts become entangled in the perfume of an imaginary woman far more real, far more tangible, than the woman you love and touch. The world today is drowning in blood, passions rage in our present-day anarchistic hell, yet Helen, immortal and untouched, stands unmovable in the air of her extraordinary verses while time flows by in front of her.

The soil was fragrant; the dewdrops hanging from the lemon flowers capered in the sunlight. Suddenly a gentle breeze blew and a flower struck my forehead, sprinkling me with dew. A quiver ran through me, as though I had been touched by an invisible hand. The whole earth seemed a freshly bathed, laughing-weeping Helen. She was lifting her veils with their embroidered lemon flowers and, her palm to her mouth, her virginity constantly renewed, following a man, the strongest that could be found. And as she raised her legs with their snow-white ankles, the round soles of her feet gleamed with blood.

What would this Helen have been if Homer's breath had not passed over her? A beautiful woman like countless others who made their passage across this earth and perished. She would have been abducted, just as pretty girls are still frequently abducted in our mountain villages. And even if this abduction had ignited a war, everything—the war, the woman, the slaughter—would have perished if the Poet had not reached out his hand to save them. It is to the Poet that Helen owes her salvation; it is to Homer that this tiny riverbed, Eurotas, owes its immortality. Helen's smile suffuses all the Spartan air. But even beyond this, she has entered our very blood streams. Every man has partaken of her in communion; to this day every woman reflects her splendor. Helen has become a love cry. She traverses the centuries, awakens in every man the yearning for kisses and perpetuation. She transforms every woman we clasp to our breast, even the most commonplace, into a Helen.

Thanks to this Spartan queen, sexual desire assumes exalted titles of nobility; the secret nostalgia for some lost embrace sweetens the brute within us. When we weep or cry out, Helen throws a magic herb into the bitter dram we are drinking, and we completely forget our pain. In her hand she holds a flower whose scent drives off serpents. At her touch ugly children become beautiful. She straddles the goat of the ancient Bacchic rites, shakes her foot with its untied sandal, and the entire world is transformed into a vineyard. One day when the ancient poet Stesichorus uttered an uncomplimentary word about her in one of his odes, he was immediately struck blind. Then, trembling and repentant, he took his lyre, stood up before the Greeks at a great festival, and sang the famous palinode:

What I said about you is not true, Helen;
you never boarded the swift ships,
nor did you ever reach the citadel of Troy.

He wept, holding his hands aloft; and all at once the light, submerged in tears, descended to the corners of his eyes.

Our ancestors held beauty contests in her honor, the "Heleneia." Truly, the earth is a palaestra and Helen the unattainable achievement, the achievement beyond life, perhaps nonexistent, perhaps just a phantom. In one of the mystery cults the tradition confided to initiates was that the Achaeans did not fight at Troy for the true Helen, that only her image was discovered in Troy, that the real Helen had found refuge in Egypt, in a sacred temple where she remained untouched by human breath. Who knows—perhaps we too fight, weep, and kill each other here on earth only for Helen's image. But on the other hand, who knows (the shades in Hades came to life when they drank the blood of a living man)—with all the blood that Helen's shade has drunk over so many thousands of years, will it never be able to come to life again? I wonder. I wonder if the image will not eventually join its flesh, thus enabling us one day to embrace a real, warm body, a true Helen?

Taygetus the fierce warrior and Helen his wife. Inhaling Helen's perfume amidst the oleanders of the Eurotas, I had forgotten myself. I felt ashamed. In order to breathe more virile air I set out one morning to climb Taygetus.

The mountain's cheer, the pine tree's balm, the fiery rocks, the hawks hovering above me, the impregnable solitude—all these fortified my heart. I climbed happily for many hours. Around noontime, however, black clouds gathered overhead. There were muffled thunderclaps. I started back down at a run, feeling the storm approaching behind me. I jumped from stone to stone, raced, compcted with it so that it would not overtake me. But suddenly the pines quivered, the world grew dark, and I was belted by lightning flashes. The whirlwind had caught me. Plunging face-downward on the ground so that I would not fall, I closed my eyes and waited. The whole mountain shook; next to me two pines split in half and thundered down the slope. I smelled the sulphur in the air. All at once the torrent let loose. The wind subsided and huge necklaces of water poured out of the sky. The thyme, savory, sage, and mint, battered by the downpour, threw forth their scents; the entire mountain began to steam.

Getting up, I resumed the descent, rejoicing to have the water thrash my face, hair, and hands. Zeus the Descender was falling with all his might upon Earth, his suffocating wife, who split open with cackling laughter and received the male waters.

Soon the sky cleared. The storm had been a violent descent of the Holy Ghost; now, as the cuckoo began to proclaim, it was finished. At that very moment the sun went down. Far in the distance below me I spied the freshly bathed ruins of the Frankish citadel of the Villehardouins at the top of its hill, above Mistra. The entire sky had turned gold and green.

The next day, proceeding through orchards and cypress groves, I went as a pilgrim to Mistra, the Greek Pompeii. This sacred hill, the birthplace of modern Greece, possesses all the manifest and hidden charms needed to entice even the most difficult of souls: lemon and orange trees, narrow twisting lanes, half-naked children playing in the streets, women going for water, girls sitting beneath blossoming trees and embroidering. Life has begun to cling to this soil again; it is struggling to reclimb the whole of the ancestral hill. This is Mistra's first zone, the green and inhabited one. Proceed farther and the dusty, treeless ascent begins. Striding through crumbled houses, you reach the charming sun-baked Byzantine churches—Perívleptos, Metrópoli, Aghioi Theodoroi, Aphendikó, Pandánassa. This is Mistra's second zone, and it is studded with churches.

I was thirsty. I entered the Pandánassa convent to have the nuns offer me a glass of water. The courtyard was shining, the cells whitewashed and immaculate, the sofas covered with embroidered woolen blankets. The nuns ran to welcome me. Some were young, others stiff from rheumatism, all inordinately pale bacause they must work very hard in order to subsist. They keep vigils, they pray, and they never have enough food to calm their hunger. When they have a free hour, they bend over their handwork and embroider traditional motifs—tiny roses out of red silk thread, crosses, monasteries, vases full of carnations, little cypress trees. You are overcome with sadness when they proudly spread these embroideries before you, as though showing you their dowries. They smile, say nothing, but you know that the bridegroom does not exist.

Pandánassa gleamed in the honey-green twilight like a small Byzantine pyx of ivory, worked with patience and love to house the Virgin's sweetly effluent breath. What unity, concentration, and grace this church possesses, from the cornerstone of the foundation to the erotic curves of the dome! The whole of the charming temple lives and breathes, peacefully, like a warm animate organism. All the stones, carvings, paintings, and nuns exist as organic ingredients of this convent, as though one midday they had all been born simultaneously, from the same procreative shudder.

I had never expected to find such tenderness and warm human understanding in Byzantine paintings. Previous to this I had seen only fierce ascetic forms holding parchments covered with red letters and calling to us to despise nature and flee to the desert; to die in order to be saved. But now here were splendid colors, here were faces of the utmost sweetness. Christ entering Jerusalem on his humble beast, kindly and smiling, the disciples following with palm branches, and the populace gazing at them with ecstatic eyes, as at a cloud which passes and then scatters. . . . And the angel I saw at Aphendikó, a beautiful stalwart the green color of oxidized brass, his curly hair bound in a wide ribbon. With his impulsive stride and firm round knees he resembled a bridegroom heading for— But where was he heading with such joy and haste?

Just at that moment the bell began to ring softly, sweetly, for the Good Friday vigil. I entered the church's warm domed interior. In the center, covered with lemon flowers, was the epitáphios, the sepulchral canopy, and lying dead upon the lemon flowers, He who is incessantly dying, incessantly resurrected. Once He was called Adonis, now Christ. Pale black-robed women were kneeling around Him, bending over Him, bewailing Him. The entire church smelled of wax, like a beehive. I thought of those other priestesses, the Melissae, at the temple of the Ephesian Artemis; also the temple of Apollo at Delphi, built of wax and feathers.

Suddenly the women's laments, the unbearable dirge, broke out in full force. I knew that human suffering was the force which would resurrect God, but here in Helen's kingdom my heart was not at all prepared to wail. Darkness had not fallen yet; I rose and continued to climb this hill with its ruined mansions, its towers sprawled on the ground, and, as a stone crown at the summit, the celebrated citadel of the Villehardouins. The great fortified gate was open, the courtyards deserted. I mounted the crumbling stairs and reached the battlements, forcing a surprised flock of crows to take wing. I looked down at the fertile plain below me and at the smoke which rose from the squat cottages; I could hear the creaking of a cart and a song filled with passion. The atmosphere all around me heaved a sigh. Specters filled the air. The blond daughters of Frankish seigneurs rose from the grave, together with the armor-encased knights who came here to the Peloponnesus in the role of conquerers, married Greek girls, became inoculated with Greek blood, and forgot their homeland. Thanks to our dark-skinned women with their raven-black hair and large eyes, the victors were vanquished.

A few days later I enjoyed another scene. You cross a dry riverbed shaded by plane trees and beflowered by osiers, you climb an austere mountain fragrant with savory and thyme, devoid of villages, people, goats, and sheep—utterly forsaken. Then, suddenly, behind a turn in the terrain, looming unexpectedly before you in the heart of the Peloponnesus is the famous temple of Apollo at Bassae. It is constructed from the same gray stones that compose the mountain, and the moment you face it, you sense the profound correspondence between temple and site. It seems a piece of the mountain, rock of its rock, wedged indistinguishably between the crags—itself a crag, but one over which the spirit has passed. Carved and placed as they are, the columns of this temple express the very essence of all this montigenous austerity and forsakenness. It is as though the temple were the cranium of the surrounding landscape, the sacred mound-circle inside whose sheltered precincts the mind of the site keeps ever-vigilant watch. Here the artistry of the ancients, continuing and expressing the landscape to perfection, does not make you gasp with astonishment. It lifts you to the summit along a human pathway, so gently and dexterously that you do not grow short of breath. You might say that the entire mountain had been longing for eons inside its tenebrous bulk to find expression, and that the moment it acquired this temple of Apollo, it felt relieved. Felt relieved—in other words assumed a meaning, its own meaning, and rejoiced.

Each day as I walked over the Greek land, I realized more clearly that ancient Greek civilization was not a supernatural flower suspended in mid-air; it was a tree that rooted itself deeply in the earth, consumed mud, and turned this mud into flowers. And the more mud it consumed, the more richly elaborate did this flowering become. The ancients' splendid simplicity, balance, and serenity were not the natural, easily achieved virtues of a simple and balanced race. They were difficult exploits, the spoils of painful, dangerous campaigns. Greek serenity is intricate and tragic, a balance between fierce opposing forces which after a toilsome and prolonged struggle succeeded in making peace with one another and in reaching the point prescribed by a Byzantine mystic—effortlessness. In other words, effort's peak.

The factor which renders Greece's mountains, villages, and soil buoyant and immaterial is the light. In Italy the light is soft and feminine, in Ionia extremely gentle and full of oriental yearning, in Egypt thick and voluptuous. In Greece the light is entirely spiritual. Able to see clearly in this light, man succeeded in imposing order over chaos, in establishing a "cosmos"—and cosmos means harmony.

A little old lady emerged from the custodian's hut next to the temple. She held two figs and a bunch of grapes in her palm. They were the first to ripen on this high plateau and she wished to present them to me as a gift. She was a sweet, thin, jovial old lady who surely must have beamed with radiance in her youth.

"What's your name?" I asked her.

"Maria."

But as she saw me grasp a pencil to make note of this name, she extended her wrinkled hand to stop me.

"Mariyítsa," she said with juvenile coquetry. "Mariyítsa."

Since her name was to be perpetuated in writing, she seemed to want to save her other name, the pet one. This would awaken life's sweetest moments in her memory.

"Mariyítsa . . . " she repeated, as though afraid I had failed to hear.

I was glad to see the eternal feminine rooted even in this most ramshackle of bodies.

"What's all this around us?" I asked her.

"Don't you see? Stones."

"And why do people come from the ends of the earth to see them?"

The old woman hesitated a moment. Then, lowering her voice, she asked me, "Are you a foreigner?"

"No, Greek."

Encouraged, she shrugged her shoulders.

"Foreign idiots!" she exclaimed, bursting into laughter.

This was not the first time I saw these old ladies, the ones who watch over ancient temples or famous churches containing wonder-working icons, laugh sacrilegiously at the saints or ancient marble daemons they guard. They associate with them daily, after all, and familiarity breeds contempt.

Old Mariyítsa watched me with satisfaction as I pecked at the pleasantly tart grapes she had given me.

"And what do you think about politics?" I asked, trying to tease her.

"Eh! my boy," she answered with unexpected pride, "we're very high up here, removed from the world, and we don't hear its racket."

We—in other words "the temple and myself." And she had uttered the word *removed* in a proud tone which meant *superior*. I felt glad. The old woman's remark, even more than the temple itself, satisfied my heart to the full.

I walked to and fro beneath the columns. It had rained two days before and pools of water still lay motionless and clear in the hollows of the broken marble. Leaning over, I saw fluffy white clouds pass like ghosts across the water's surface. I had read that divinity had once been worshiped similarly in the Far East, in water-filled hollows over which clouds passed.

As I was returning to the plain, I saw an old man kneeling on the stones. He was leaning over a channel and watching the water run, his face bathed in inexpressible ecstasy. It seemed as though his nose, mouth, and cheeks had vanished; nothing remained but the two eyes which followed the water as it flowed between the rocks. I went up to him.

"What do you see there, old man?" I asked him.

And he, without lifting his head or removing his eyes from the water, replied, "My life, my life which is running out . . ."

All things in Greece—mountains, rivers, seas, valleys—become "humanized": they speak to man in a language which is almost human. They do not torment or crushingly overwhelm him; they become his friends and fellow workers. The turbid, unsettled cry of the Orient grows pellucid when it passes through the light of

Greece; humanized, it is transformed into *logos*—reason. Greece is the filter which, with great struggle, refines brute into man, eastern servitude into liberty, barbaric intoxication into sober rationality. To give features to the featureless and measure to the measureless, balancing the blind clashing forces, such is the mission of the much-buffeted sea and land known as Greece.

To travel through Greece is a true joy, a great enrichment. The Greek soil has been so saturated with blood, sweat, and tears, the Greek mountains have witnessed so much human struggle, that you shudder in contemplating the fact that here, on these mountains and shores, the destiny of the white race—of all mankind—was at stake. Surely it must have been on one of these shores so filled with grace and frolicsomeness that the miraculous transformation of beast into man took place. It must have been on such a Greek strand that Astarte of the multitudinous sowlike breasts cast anchor from Asia Minor and the Greeks, receiving the barbaric and coarsely carved wooden statue, cleansed it of its bestiality, left it with only the two human breasts, and gave it a human body full of nobility. From Asia Minor the Greeks took primitive instinct, orgiastic intoxication, the bestial shout—Astarte. They transubstantiated the instinct into love, the bite into kisses, the orgy into religious worship, the shout into the lover's endearment. Astarte they transformed into Aphrodite.

Greece's spiritual as well as geographical location carries with it a mystic sense of mission and responsibility. Because two continually active currents collide on her land and seas, she has always been a place subjected both geographically and spiritually to incessant whirlpools. This fated location has exerted a fundamental influence on Greece's lot and also the lot of the entire world.

I viewed, smelled, and touched Greece, proceeding all alone on foot, an olivewood staff in my hand and a carpetbag over my shoulder. And as Greece penetrated increasingly within me, I felt with ever-increasing depth that the mystic essence of her land and sea is musical. At every moment the Greek landscape changes slightly and yet remains the same; makes its beauty undulate, renews itself. It has a profound unity and at the same time a constantly renewed diversity. I wonder if this same rhythm did not govern the art of the ancient Greeks, an art which was born in regarding, loving, understanding, and giving concrete expression to the visible world around it. Look at a work of the great classical period. It is not motionless; an imperceptible quiver of life pervades it. Just as the hawk when it hesitates at the zenith of its flight, its wings beat and yet to us it appears immobile, so in the same way the ancient statue moves imperceptibly and lives. In one immortal instant which both continues artistic tradition and makes ready art's future course, it holds the threefold flux of time in perfect equilibrium.

By means of their struggles the Greeks sanctified each region, subordinated each to an exalted meaning which formed its definitive essence. By means of beauty and disciplined passion they converted each region's physical nature into something metaphysical. Pushing aside grass, soil, and stones, they discovered the region's cool, cool soul deep beneath the ground. This soul they embodied sometimes in a graceful temple, sometimes in a myth, and sometimes in a happy indigenous god.

For hours on end I gazed at Olympia's sacred landscape—its nobility and meditative tranquillity, the cheerful, welcoming valley between domesticated foothills which screen it from the fierce north wind, the scorching south wind, and leave it exposed only on the western side toward the water, whence arrives the cool sea breeze, ascending the course of the Alpheus. No other site in Greece incites a feeling of peace and concord in you so gently, so compellingly. With unerring eyes the ancients designated it as the place where all the Greek stocks would meet together in brotherhood every four years, and in so designating it they filled it with meaning and increased its tranquillity and its power to instigate reconciliation.

Greece was torn by jealousies, hatreds, civil wars. Democracies, aristocracies, and tyrannies exterminated one another. The closed gorges, sequestered islands, secluded coast lines, and small independent city-states created a single multiheaded organism rent by mutual hatred; and passions boiled in every breast. Then suddenly, every four years, garlanded heralds, the *spondophoroi*, set out from this sacred valley in summertime and ran to the farthest boundaries of the Greek world. They proclaimed the *hieromenia*, the "sacred month" of the games, declared a general truce, and invited friends and enemies alike to come to Olympia in order to compete.

From the whole of the Peloponnesus and continental Greece, from Macedonia, Thessaly, Epirus, and Thrace, from the shores of the Black Sea, Asia Minor, Egypt, and Cyrene, from Magna Graecia and Sicily, athletes and pilgrims sped to the sacred panhellenic cradle of sport. Slaves were not allowed to set foot here, nor were criminals, foreigners, or women. Only free Greeks.

No other people had comprehended sport's hidden and manifest value so perfectly. When life has succeeded by dint of daily effort in conquering the enemies around it—natural forces, wild beasts, hunger, thirst, sickness—sometimes it is lucky enough to have abundant strength left over. This strength it seeks to squander in sport. Civilization begins at the moment sport begins. As long as life struggles for preservation—to protect itself from its enemies, maintain itself upon the surface of the earth—civilization cannot be born. It is born the moment that life satisfies its primary needs and begins to enjoy a little leisure.

How is this leisure to be used, how apportioned among the various social classes, how increased and refined to the utmost? According to how each race and epoch solves these problems, the worth and substance of its civilization can be judged.

I walked back and forth among the ruins of the Altis, joyfully viewing the shell-bearing stones employed to build the temples. These stones have been smashed by Christians and devastated by earthquakes. Rains and Alphean floods have washed away their stunning iridescence. The statues have been burned for lime; few remain to us, but these suffice to console our minds. I picked two or three sprigs of mint which had sprouted in the hollow where Phidias's gold and ivory statue is reputed to have stood, and the eternal scent filled my fingers.

Man wrestled in this mystic place, but the gods wrestled here before him. Zeus fought Chronos, his father, in order to take away his kingdom. Apollo, the god of light, defeated Hermes in running and Ares in boxing—mind conquered time, light conquered the dark forces of fraud and violence. Heroes were the next to contend here, after the gods. Pelops came from Asia, defeated the bloodthirsty barbarian Oenomaus and wedded his horse-taming daughter Hippodamia. The advanced Ionian civilization, so full of serenity and grace, defeated the unpolished natives of this region, brought the horse under subjection, and solidified man's might.

Another hero, Heracles, having cleaned the Augean stables, came here to offer up great sacrifices to Zeus, the new god. With the ashes remaining from the victims he burned, he raised an altar and proclaimed the first Olympic games. This divine altar was raised continually higher with the ashes from new sacrifices, and Olympia became ever-increasingly the great workshop where the various Greek stocks forged their bronze bodies.

They did not do this simply to make these bodies beautiful. The Greeks never served art for its own sake. Beauty always had a purpose: to be of service to life. The ancients wanted their bodies strong and beautiful so that these bodies might be receptacles for balanced, healthy minds. And beyond this—the supreme purpose—so that they might defend the *polis*.

For the Greeks, gymnastics was a required preparation for each citizen's life as a member of society. The perfect citizen was the man who by frequenting the gymnasium and palaestra was able to develop a body both strong and harmonious, in other words beautiful, and have this body ready to defend the Race. Look at a statue from the classic age and you know at once whether the man portrayed was free or a slave. His body discloses it. A serene bearing, passion that is perfectly disciplined, a beautiful athletic form: these characterize the free man. The slave is always portrayed with abrupt unbridled gestures and a body either fat or sickly. Dionysus, the god of intoxication, stands calmly by while around him the besotted sileni and satyrs, his slaves and inferiors, behave indecently and perform their obscene dances.

Harmony of mind and body—that was the Greeks' supreme ideal. Hypertrophy of one to the detriment of the other they considered barbaric. When Greece began to decline, the athlete's body began at the same time to hypertrophy and to kill his mind. Euripides was among the first to protest; he proclaimed what risks the spirit was running at the hands of athleticism. Later, Galen added his denunciation: "They eat, drink, sleep, evacuate their bellies, and roll in dust and mud—behold what life the athletes lead." Heracles, the great martyr, who in the glorious years passed from exploit to exploit balancing mind and body to perfection, gradually degenerated into the huge-bodied, low-browed "winebibber and ox-eater." And the artists, who in the great eras had created the ideal type of the youthful form, now took to representing the athletic bodies they saw around them with raw realism, heavy and barbaric.

In Greece, as everywhere, once realism begins to reign, civilization declines. Thus we arrive at the realistic, magniloquent, and faithless Hellenistic era, which was devoid of suprapersonal ideals. From chaos to the Parthenon, then from the Parthenon back to chaos—the great merciless rhythm. Emotions and passions run wild. The free individual loses his powers of discipline; the bridle which maintained instinct in strict balance flies from his hands. Passion, emotionality, realism . . . A mystical, melancholy yearning suffuses the faces. The fearful mythological visions become merely decorative. Aphrodite undrapes herself like an ordinary woman, Zeus acquires roguishness and elegance, and Heracles regresses to a brute. After the Peloponnesian war Greece begins to disintegrate. Belief in the fatherland is lost; individual self-sufficiency triumphs. On the stage the protagonist is no longer God or the idealized youth, he is the wealthy citizen with his lascivious pleasures and passions—a materialist, skeptic, and libertine. Talent had already replaced genius; now good taste replaces talent. Art becomes filled with children, coquettish women, realistic scenes, and men either brutal or intellectual.

I climbed the hillock leading to the museum, hurrying to see Praxiteles' Hermes, the feats of Heracles, and the two marvelous pediments which have survived—hurrying, as though afraid that before I arrived, the soil might have swallowed these remains as well. Why? Perhaps because man's lofty toil transgresses the inhuman laws of eternity. (Thus our life and our endeavors acquire a tragic, heroic intensity. We have but a single moment at our disposal. Let us transform that moment into eternity. No other form of immortality exists.)

My heart relaxed when I encountered the museum's great hall. Apollo, Heracles, Nike, the centaurs, and the Lapithae were all glowing peacefully in the morning light, all still alive. I rejoiced. This world of ours follows extrahuman laws. We sense, in these fatal times in which it is our lot to live, that at any moment a bomb might fall and reduce man's most precious memorials to ashes. When we greet a work of art now, our pleasure is tightly interwoven with the danger of everlasting separation which overhangs that work.

Looking at the two great pediments here, you realize how accurately a certain Far Eastern sage formulated the purpose of art when he said, "Art is the representation not of the body but of the forces which created the body." These creative forces rage visibly beneath the transparent surface here, especially in the western pediment. The banquet has just terminated; the intoxicated centaurs have charged in order to seize the women of the Lapithae. One of them sprints forward and embraces a woman, at the same time squeezing her breast with his huge hand. She seems to have swooned from the pain, and also from a mysterious, indescribable delight. Elsewhere the combatants bite and stab one another. The beast has been let loose in a savage outburst of violent passion; age-old scenes somewhere between man and ape-man are revived before our eyes. A mystic tranquillity, however, extends over all this astonishing primitive passion, because standing with perfect composure in the midst of the frenzied people, invisible to all the combatants, is Apollo, his right arm, and only his right arm, stretched out horizontally.

Though the sculptor who created this great scene, a few years before the Parthenon, had already surpassed the virgin awkwardness of the archaic artist, he still had not reached the artistic perfection of the classic moment. He was still in the midst of the assault, he had not touched the summit, and he was burning with a passionate, impatient desire to attain victory. He had smashed one equilibrium but had not reached the next; full of panting impetuosity, he was racing toward the final destination. If this pediment moves us so profoundly, it is because it still has not attained man's highest summit, the summit of perfection. One is still able to discern the suffering, struggling hero.

There is still another pleasure here. On this pediment you distinguish all the ranks of the hierarchy: god, free men, women, slaves, beasts. God stands in the middle, erect and calm, lord of his strength. Though he sees the horror around him, he is not disturbed. He controls his wrath and passion without on the other hand remaining indifferent, for he calmly extends his arm and grants the victory to the party he likes. The free men—the Lapithae—also maintain the human stamp on their faces, maintain it as immobile as they can. They do not howl, do not fall prey to panic. They are men, however, not gods, and a slight pulsation on their lips in addition to a wrinkle on the brow discloses that they are suffering. The women are suffering even more, but their pain merges unspeakably with a dark desire. In spite of themselves they seem glad to be seized by terrifyingly masculine brutes, glad to be shedding blood for their sakes. The slaves, on the other hand, are lounging about with presumptuous familiarity as they watch the others. They lack strict restraint. In the period when this pediment was created, these reclining forms at the edges could not represent gods. The gods would never have wallowed in such a way, never have forgotten their sacerdotal dignity. Finally we have the centaurs, the debauched drunken beasts. Howling and biting, they pounce upon the women and boys. The mind is absent and thus there is no force to impose order upon their strength or nobility upon their passion.

It is an extraordinary moment, this moment in which all the graduated ranks of life preserve their features intact. In this enmarbled moment all the elements coexist: the divine imperturbability, the free man's discipline, the beast's outburst, the realistic representation of the slave. A few generations afterwards the latter two, the lowest elements, were to rule. Realistic passion would spread out and disfigure both the free man and the gods. The rein would be left slack, and art would bolt and decline. From the dynamic tragicality of this Olympic pediment and the divine calm of the Parthenon we would arrive at the unbridled verbalism of Pergamum.

On this pediment we have the pleasure of seeing all the seeds of acme, pro-acme and post-acme coexisting in one conjoint flash. Perfection is a momentary equilibrium above chaos, a most difficult and dangerous balance. Throw a little weight to one side or the other, and it falls.

This pediment grants us still another pleasure. We look at it, and many questions arise. It came into being immediately after the Greek forces defeated the Persians and a happy wave of relief, pride, and strength poured over the entire land. Greece felt its might. The world around it and within it was renewed, gods and men were illuminated with a new light. Now everything else had to be renewed as well: temples, statues, paintings, poems. An everlasting memorial to the Greek victories over the barbarians had to be erected. What sculptural form was this memorial to take?

The great artist looks beneath the flux of everyday reality and sees eternal, unchanging symbols. Behind the spasmodic, frequently inconsistent activities of living men, he plainly distinguishes the great currents which sweep away the human soul. He takes ephemeral events and relocates them in an undying atmosphere. The great artist considers realistic representation a disfigurement and caricature of the eternal.

This is why not only the sculptors but all the great artists of classical Greece, wishing to insure the perpetuation of every contemporary memorial to victory, relocated history in the elevated and symbolic atmosphere of myth. Instead of representing contemporary Greeks warring against the Persians, they gave us the Lapithae and centaurs. Behind the Lapithae and centaurs we discern the two great, eternal adversaries: mind and beast, civilization and barbarism. Thus a historic event, occurring at a specific time, escaped time and bound itself to the entire race and that race's ancient visions. Last of all, it escaped the race and became an undying, panhuman memorial. By means of this symbolic ennoblement the Greek victories were thus elevated into those of all mankind.

All this applies as well to the twelve metopes which embellished the temple of Zeus. They represent the twelve feats of Heracles. Even in the shattered, ruinous state in which they were preserved for us and hung here on the museum walls, how deeply they move us, to what proud heights they elevate the mind! Look how Athena, the human intellect, young as yet but full of vigor, stands by the athlete and aids him. In a similar way, a short while earlier, she must have leaped from the Acropolis to Marathon and Salamis in order to help the Greeks. Further along on the metopes she is seated upon a rock, a little fatigued from her efforts, but proud. Look how she gazes at the athlete as he returns in triumph and offers her the birds of Stymphalus as spoils! Still a little further along, see how tenderly she lifts her hand as, standing behind him, she helps him support the weight of the world.

Though the artist surely wished to hymn the Greeks of his own time, he transferred the praise respectfully to Heracles, the great ancestor and racial chieftain. The hymn seems to be saying, We of this generation did not attain the victory, it was attained by the genius of the race. It was attained by our forebear the obstinate, resolute athlete. Thus symbolically formulated, the hymn expands still further until it embraces the entire species of free man. We Greeks did not attain the victory, it says; it was attained not by our race alone, but by every man who, advancing from exploit to exploit, struggled to conquer beasts, barbarians, and death.

I passed through the museum door and walked a little way onto the pine-shaded patio. Here I was seized by sudden despondency. Would we moderns, I wondered, ever in our turn achieve the balance and the serene, heroic vision of the ancient Greeks? Every pilgrim, after he disengages himself from this Olympic dream, after he emerges through the museum door and faces the sun of our own day, surely, and with anguish, must pose this basic question to himself. For us Greeks, however, the despondency is twofold, because we consider ourselves descendants of the ancients. Thus, willy-nilly, we give ourselves the duty to equal our great ancestors—and even beyond this, every son's duty to surpass his parents.

How pleasant if the Greek could stroll through his country and not hear stern, angry voices beneath the soil! For the Greek, however, a journey through Greece degenerates into a fascinating and exhausting torture. You stand on a spot of Greek land and find yourself overcome with anguish. It is a deep tomb with layer upon layer of corpses whose varied voices rise and call you—for the voice is the one part of the corpse which remains immortal. Which among all these voices should you choose? Each is a soul, each soul yearns for a body of its own, and your heart listens, greatly troubled. It hesitates to make a decision, because the dearest souls are often not the most deserving.

I remember feeling this terrible, age-old struggle between heart and mind one noontime when I stopped beneath a blossoming oleander along the Eurotas, halfway between Sparta and Mistra. My unrestrainable heart charged forward to resuscitate the pallid, death-sealed body of our Byzantine emperor Constantine Palaeologus; to turn back the wheel of time to January 6, 1449, when here on the heights of Mistra he accepted the short-lived, blood-dyed crown of Byzantium. Innumerable ancestral gasps, innumerable racial yearnings prod us to follow our heart's desire, but the mind callously resists. Turning its face angrily toward Sparta, it wishes to toss the pallid emperor into the Kaiadas of time and cohere to the callous Spartan youths—for the mind's wish is precisely what this terrible moment demands of us, the terrible moment in which it was our lot to be born. If we want our lives to bear fruit, we must make the decision which harmonizes with the fearsome rhythm of our times.

When a Greek travels through Greece, his journey becomes converted in this fatal way into a laborious search to find his duty. How is he to become worthy of our ancestors? How can he continue his national tradition without disgracing it? A severe, unsilenceable responsibility weighs heavily on his shoulders, on the shoulders of every living Greek. The name itself possesses an invincible, magical force. Every person born in Greece has the duty to continue the eternal Greek legend.

In the modern Greek no region of his homeland calls forth a disinterested quiver of aesthetic appreciation. The region has a name; it is called Marathon, Salamis, Olympia, Thermopylae, Mistra, and it is bound up with a memory: here we were disgraced, there we won glory. All at once the region is transformed into much-wept, wide-roving history, and the Greek pilgrim's entire soul is thrown into turmoil. Each Greek region is so soaked with successes and failures possessing world-wide echoes, so filled with human struggle, that it is elevated into an austere lesson which we cannot escape. It becomes a cry, and our duty is to hear this cry.

Greece's position is truly tragic; on the shoulders of every modern Greek it places a duty at once dangerous and extremely difficult to carry out. We bear an extremely heavy responsibility. New forces are rising from the East, new forces are rising from the West, and Greece, caught as always between the two colliding impulses, once more becomes a whirlpool. Following the tradition of reason and empirical inquiry, the West bounds forward to conquer the world; the East, prodded by frightening subconscious forces, likewise darts forward to conquer the world. Greece is placed in the middle; it is the world's geographical and spiritual crossroads. Once again its duty is to reconcile these two monstrous impulses by finding a synthesis. Will it succeed?

It is a sacred and most bitter fate. At the end of my trip through Greece I was filled with tragic, unexpected questions. Starting with beauty, we had arrived at the agonies of our times and the present-day duty imposed on every Greek. Today, a man who is alive—

who thinks, loves, and struggles—is no longer able to amble in a carefree way, appreciating beauty. The struggle, today, is spreading like a conflagration, and no fire brigade can insure our safety. Every man is struggling and burning along with all humanity. And the Greek nation is struggling and burning more than all the rest. This is its fate.

The circle closed. My eyes filled with Greece. It seems to me that my mind ripened in those three months. What were the most precious spoils of this intellectual campaign? I believe they were these: I saw more clearly the historic mission of Greece, placed as it is between East and West; I realized that her supreme achievement is not beauty but the struggle for liberty; I felt Greece's tragic destiny more deeply and also what a heavy duty is imposed on every Greek.

I believe that immediately following my pilgrimage through Greece I was ripe enough to begin the years of maturity. It was not beauty which led the way and ushered me into manhood, it was responsibility.

This was the bitter fruit I held in my hand when, returning after my three-month journey, I entered my father's house.

18

ITALY

I RETURNED to my father's house. There, amidst my mother's affectionate silence and under my father's strict eye, I would relive my journey, giving some order to its joys and sorrows. I could no longer escape my responsibility; it had acquired a voice within me now. The ground had spoken and the dead had risen, divulging Greece to me as a huge Crete—it too had been struggling for freedom (such was its destiny) since the beginning of time. What then was my duty? It was to work with her, to throw my life and soul into the struggle at her side.

But from whom, from what, was I seeking freedom? These were difficult questions, and I could not answer them. The one thing I did feel was that my role did not lie in going to the mountains, rifle in hand, and warring against the Turks. My weapons were different. In addition, I still could not determine the identity of my enemies. The only thing I saw clearly was that whatever decision I made, I would accomplish my duty as honorably as possible. Of this I was certain—of my perseverance and honor. Of this, and nothing else.

Remember when the archimandrite went to my father and complained that I did not listen to my teachers? My father—I was there and heard—answered him: "I care only if he tells lies or gets a beating. Those two. As for everything else, let him do as he pleases!" Those words embedded themselves deeply in my mind; I believe my life would never have been the same if I had not heard them. In bringing up his son my father seemed to be guided by some dark and unerring instinct, the instinct of a wolf raising its first-born cub.

I did not leave the house. I had no companions now; the Friendly Society had been a juvenile kite, and its parts were scattered to the four winds. Pushing aside the new concerns which had been tormenting me since my pilgrimage to Greece, I diverted my thoughts by studying the Italian Renaissance and the great souls it had engendered. For I had decided to make a tour of Italy, thereby exhausting the remainder of my father's gift of a year of travel.

Thus, one morning I removed myself again from my family home. My weeping mother asked, "How long will you keep going away? How long?" I wanted to answer (how unfeeling youth is!): As long as I'm alive, Mother; as long as I'm alive. But I restrained myself. I kissed her hand, and the sea carried me off.

To be young and healthy, twenty-five years old; to love no particular person male or female (this would narrow your heart and keep you from loving all things with equal disinterestedness and fervor); to travel on foot, alone, from one end of Italy to the other, with a carpetbag over your shoulder; and for it to be springtime, and then for summer to arrive, and after that autumn and winter laden with fruit and rain—what impudence for man to desire any greater happiness!

I lacked nothing, I believe. The three savage beasts—body, mind, and soul—all exulted similarly; all three were equally contented, their hunger equally appeased. For the entire extent of this honeymoon with my soul I felt, to a greater degree than ever again in my life, that body, mind, and soul are fashioned of the same clay. Only when a person ages or falls into the grips of illness or misfortune do they separate and oppose one another. Sometimes the body wishes to assume command, sometimes the soul raises its own rebellious banner and wishes to flee. And the mind stands by impotently, watching and recording the dissolution. But when a person is young and strong, how united in loving brotherhood these triplets are, how they nurse on the same milk!

I close my eyes. Youth returns; harmony is re-established inside me. The shores and mountains pass freshly before my eyes, and the villages with their slender campaniles and tiny shaded squares —the plane tree, the flowing fountain, the stone benches at the edges and the old men, in the evening, who sit leaning on their sticks conversing quietly: the same things over and over for so many years, so many centuries. The very air around and above them is as old as time. And when I first saw the famous paintings, how my insatiable heart did tremble! I would halt on the threshold with buckling knees, interminably, until finally my throbbing heart subsided and I was able to bear all that beauty. For beauty, as I correctly divined, is merciless. You do not look at it, it looks at you and does not forgive.

I raced from city to city. Paintings, statues, churches, palaces. What greed, what yearning! My hunger and thirst could not be sated. An amorous breeze kept blowing across my temples. Never again in my later life did I feel such sheer bodily delight, either from women, ideas, or contact with God. Abstract concerns not having overwhelmed me as yet, I found pleasure in seeing, hearing, and touching. The inner world was one with the outer. I touched it; it was warm, and it had the same odor as my body. If it had been given me in that period to create my God, I would have fashioned him with the body of an adolescent—like an ancient Kouros, with thick fuzz on his cheeks, solid knees, slender waist, and holding the world on his shoulders as though it were a calf.

Here in Italy the apple of life was firm and unblemished. Greece was entirely different. My pilgrimage through Greece was often painful because that soil was so excessively near to me, so excessively my own. Knowing Greece's sufferings so well, I saw them plainly behind her beautiful face and suffered with her. But Italy was foreign soil. It too had its sufferings, but I did not know them, and if I did, they failed to distress me to such an extent. Here, for me, beauty's face had not a single wound, or so I felt.

I was an unsophisticated provincial still covered with adolescent fluff, who for the first time was walking alone and free in a foreign country, and so great was my joy that sometimes, I remember, I felt terror-stricken. For as I well knew, the gods are envious creatures, and it is *hubris* to be happy and to know that you are happy. In order to exorcise their evil eye, I had recourse to comic schemes for diminishing my happiness. I remember being so elated in Florence that I realized the rights accorded to humans had been overstepped. I had to find some way of suffering, so I went and bought a pair of shoes much too narrow for me. I put them on in the morning, and I suffered so much that I could not walk—I hopped about like a crow. All that morning, until midday, I was miserable. But when I changed shoes and went out for a walk in the afternoon, what joy! I strode along weightlessly; I flew. The world became paradise again. I promenaded along the banks of the

Arno, went past the bridges, and climbed up to San Miniato. A cool breeze blew as evening approached, and the people wore robes of gold as they went by in the sun's last rays. The next morning, however, I donned the narrow shoes and was miserable once more. But the gods had no reason to intervene now. I had clearly paid the tribute they exact from men.

Everything was so childishly simple. Not a single problem bothered me; the apple of life had not a single worm inside. Appearances sufficed; I did not seek to discover if anything existed behind them. An artist of ancient Greece once painted a curtain and invited a rival painter to see and judge his work. "Well, draw back the curtain and let me see the picture!" "The curtain *is* the picture," was the artist's reply. The curtain of mountains, trees, oceans, and people which I now saw before me, that was the picture, and I was enjoying it with an unadulterated, gluttonous joy.

The initial rebelliousness of my adolescent years had vented its force. I had digested the humiliating notions that the earth is not the center of the universe and that man is descended from beasts, is himself a beast more intelligent and immoral than his progenitors. As for the Female, who had come and so roused my blood for an instant, since the moment I laid her out on paper, she had not returned to spoil my harmonious well-being. No matter how much my intellect discourses, proving that women have the same worth, the same soul as men, the age-old heart inside me, the African heart which scorns the Europeanized mind and wants nothing to do with it, repulses women and refuses to trust them or permit them to penetrate deeply within me and take possession. Women are simply ornaments for men, and more often a sickness and a necessity.

I think of Kostandís, a ferocious field warden in Crete who lived as a hermit and never let a female near him. Suddenly the word spread that Kostandís was getting married. "Good God, Kostandís," I said to him, "what's this I hear? Are you really getting married?" And he answered me, "Well, what can I do, boss? I figured, suppose I catch cold, who'd bring me the cupping glass?" And someone else who was marrying in his fifties told me by way of justification, "Well, what's to be done, my boy? You see, I decided I wanted some nice curls on my pillow just like everyone else."

As we said: sometimes a necessity, sometimes an ornament.

During that entire honeymoon in Italy I was free, without metaphysical problems or worries about love. My delights were unsullied.

When I wish to recall those delights now after so many years, however, I am astonished. The most intellectual have deposited themselves within me, become one with me, and are no longer identifiable as memories. From my memory they have passed into my bloodstream, where they live and operate like natural instincts. When deciding something, I often recollect afterwards that it was not I who made the decision but the influence exerted on me by such and such a painting, such and such a fierce tower of the Renaissance, or such and such a line from Dante inscribed in one of the narrow streets of the old part of Florence.

It is not the intellectual delights, but others more corporeal, more proximate to human warmth, that remain stationary in my memory and look at me with great tenderness and sorrow. The end result is that from the whole of that youthful adventure I am left with nothing but a meager plunder, a very meager and humble one indeed: a rose I saw wilting on a hedgerow in Palermo, a little barefooted girl wailing in one of the filthy alleyways of Naples, a black cat with large white patches, sitting in a Gothic window in Verona. It is a mystery what the human memory chooses to preserve from all that is given it. Who was the great conqueror who sighed upon his deathbed, "Three things I longed for in my life and did not have the opportunity to enjoy: a little house on the seashore, a canary in a cage, and a pot of basil"? From my entire Italian journey, two extremely bitter memories settled down within me more than all the rest. Full of reproaches, they will pursue me to the death, even though I am entirely blameless.

This is the first:

It was almost nightfall. The whole day: rain, torrents of rain. Drenched to the bone, I arrived in a little Calabrian village. I had to find a hearth where I could dry out, a corner where I could sleep. The streets were deserted, the doors bolted. The dogs were the only ones to scent the stranger's breath; they began to bark from within the courtyards. The peasants in this region are wild and misanthropic, suspicious of strangers. I hesitated at every door, extended my hand, but did not dare to knock.

O for my late grandfather in Crete who took his lantern each evening and made the rounds of the village to see if any stranger had come. He would take him home, feed him, give him a bed for the night, and then in the morning see him off with a cup of wine and a slice of bread. Here in the Calabrian villages there were no such grandfathers.

Suddenly I saw an open door at the edge of the village. Inclining my head, I looked in: a murky corridor with a lighted fire at the far end and an old lady bent over it. She seemed to be cooking. Not a sound, nothing but the burning wood. It was fragrant; it must have been pine. I crossed the threshold and entered, bumping against a long table which stood in the middle of the room. Finally I reached the fire and sat down on a stool which I found in front of the hearth. The old lady was squatting on another stool, stirring the meal with a wooden spoon. I felt that she eyed me rapidly, without turning. But she said nothing. Taking off my jacket, I began to dry it. I sensed happiness rising in me like warmth, from my feet to my shins, my thighs, my breast. Hungrily, avidly, I inhaled the fragrance of the steam rising from the pot. The meal must have been baked beans; the aroma was overwhelming. Once more I realized to what an extent earthly happiness is made to the measure of man. It is not a rare bird which we must pursue at one moment in heaven, at the next in our minds. Happiness is a domestic bird found in our own courtyards.

Rising, the old lady took down two soup plates from a shelf next to her. She filled them, and the whole world smelled of beans. Lighting a lamp, she placed it on the long table. Next she brought two wooden spoons and a loaf of black bread. We sat down opposite each other. She made the sign of the cross, then glanced rapidly at me. I understood. I crossed myself and we began to eat. We were both hungry; we did not breathe a word. I had decided not to speak in order to see what would happen. Could she be a mute, I asked myself—or perhaps she's mad, one of those peaceful, kindly lunatics so much like saints.

As soon as we finished, she prepared a bed for me on a bench to the right of the table. I lay down, and she lay down on the other bench opposite me. Outside the rain was falling by the bucketful. For a considerable time I heard the water cackle on the roof, mixed with the old lady's calm, quiet breathing. She must have been tired, for she fell asleep the moment she inclined her head. Little by little, with the rain and the old lady's rhythmical respiration, I too slipped into sleep. When I awoke, I saw daylight peering through the cracks in the door.

The old lady had already risen and placed a saucepan on the fire to prepare the morning milk. I looked at her now in the sparse daylight. Shriveled and humped, she could fit into the palm of your hand. Her legs were so swollen that she had to stop at every step and catch her breath. But her eyes, only her large, pitch-black eyes, gleamed with youthful, unaging brilliance. How beautiful she must have been in her youth, I thought to myself, cursing man's fate, his inevitable deterioration. Sitting down opposite each other again, we drank the milk. Then I rose and slung my carpetbag over my shoulder. I took out my wallet, but the old lady colored deeply.

"No, no," she murmured, extending her hand.

As I looked at her in astonishment, the whole of her bewrinkled face suddenly gleamed.

"Goodbye, and God bless you," she said. "May the Lord repay you for the good you've done me. Since my husband died I've never slept so well."

And here is the second memory, the more bitter of the two:

Toward the beginning of spring I arrived at Assisi, Italy's most sacred city. Gardens, rooftops, courtyards, the very air—all were filled with the invisible presence of God's sweet little pauper. It was Sunday. The massive bells of his church were ringing, and the shrill, silver-voiced bells of the Convent of Saint Clare were answering them from the small square opposite. The two of them, Saint Clare and Saint Francis: joined in the air, forever inseparable, with the immortal voices given them by sainthood and death. "Father Francis, when are you finally going to come and see us poor sisters in our convent?" "When the thorns blossom with white flowers . . ." And behold! thorns now blossom everlastingly, and God's two mated doves, forever inseparable, flap their wings eternally over Assisi.

I climbed the narrow streets. Doors kept opening, women emerging. Freshly bathed, perfumed with lavender, their hair carefully combed, they were setting out hurriedly, cheerfully, for church—to see and be seen. In springtime in the lands of the sun the church is the Lord's sitting room; His friends, men and women alike, go there, seat themselves in the rows of chairs, and engage in small talk, at one moment with God, at the next with their neighbors. God's servant comes and goes, habited in white lace and a black or red dress. He rings the little bell and in a sweet voice chants the praises of Saint Francis, the master of the house. Then the guests rise, say goodbye, and head for the door. They have paid their visit to the Saint; now the visit is over. Heaven laughs with satisfaction, and below on earth the taverns open their doors.

I had a letter of introduction to Countess Erichetta which would enable me to stay at her palazzo. She had been described to me as an elderly aristocrat who lived all alone with a faithful servant named Ermelinda and who would be extremely delighted to have my company. Once Assisi's loveliest belle, she had been widowed at the age of twenty-six, and since that time had not known any man. She possessed huge expanses of olive groves and vineyards; formerly she had mounted her mare each morning and gone out to inspect her lands, but now she was old, continually cold, and she simply sat in front of her fire, taciturn and sorrowful, as though regretting her life of chastity. Talk to her, I had been told, look at her as if she were still twenty-six years old, give her a little joy, even if too late.

It was a mild spring day. The swallows had returned, the fields were filled with small white daisies, the breeze warm and fragrant. But the fire was burning in the great mansion and the old countess was seated in a low armchair in front of it, with a kerchief of blue silk over her white hair. Placing my letter on her knees, she turned to look at me. I was flushed and overheated from my climb, my shirt unbuttoned down the front. My knees—I was wearing short pants—glistened in the fireglow. I was twenty-five years old.

"Well?" said the countess, smiling at me. "The whole of Greece has suddenly entered my house. Welcome."

Ermelinda came—the young "adopted daughter" who eventually would receive a dowry from her mistress. Bringing a tray, she prepared settings on a low table, then arranged the milk, butter, toast, and fruit on it.

"I'm very happy," said the countess. "Now I am not alone."

"Nor am I," I answered. "As I sit here, I understand the meaning of nobility, beauty, and kindness."

The countess's pale cheeks flushed, but she said nothing. I saw a flame flash briefly across her eyes. She must surely have thought to herself with anger and complaint, The devil take nobility, beauty and kindness! It's youth that counts, youth, nothing else!

She set aside for me an immense room containing a vast bed with a velvet tester. Two large windows gave onto the street; I could see the courtyard of the Convent of Saint Clare opposite us, with the nuns coming and going in silence, white flaps on both sides of their heads. The campanile, roof, and court were full of doves; the entire convent kept sighing amorously, like one huge female dove. "What do the nuns want with all those doves?" the countess asked me one day. "For shame! Don't they see and hear them; don't they realize how scandalous it is? They should chase them away, or better still, butcher them and eat them—to be rid of them! To let us be rid of them!"

I remained in Assisi three months. Saint Francis and Countess Erichetta held me there, not allowing me to leave. Where was I to go? If the goal of life was happiness, why leave? Where could I find a dearer, surer companion than Saint Francis, whom I went to visit each day in his house, or more charming company than the countess, that living Saint Clare? All day long I sauntered through gay Umbria, following the Saint's tracks through olive grove and vineyard. The entire spring struck me as a Franciscan procession of red, yellow, and snow-white *fioretti:* Saint Francis with his retinue of flowers, rising once more from the soil of Assisi to greet Brother Sun. And Brother Wind as well and Sister Fire and our cheerful little Brother Water . . . and the countess . . . and the happy Cretan lad at her side.

Each evening I returned to the house, tired and content. The fire would be burning, the countess waiting with folded arms in her low armchair, dressed and coiffured, her face lightly powdered. Sorrowful and taciturn as always, she sat with closed eyes, but the moment she heard the door and became aware of my footsteps, her eyes opened. She would indicate the armchair next to her and touch my knee with her extended hand.

"Talk, talk. Open your mouth and do not stop. This is the only joy I have."

And I would open my mouth and talk to her about Crete, my parents, the women of our neighborhood, about the Cretan wars of independence, and Prince George when he set foot on Cretan soil . . . The entire island was adorned with myrtles and laurels; the elderly combatants—with their long white beards, their bodies hewn by sword blows—bowed to kiss the Greek prince's hand; they stumbled over one another; they could not see because their eyes were filled with tears. . . . On other occasions I told her about the Irish girl, about our ascent of Psiloríti, what we did there when we were alone in the little chapel, and our subsequent separation.

"But why, why?" asked the astonished countess. "Didn't the poor dear make you happy?"

"Yes, very happy."

"Well then?"

"But it was precisely because of that, Countess."

"I don't understand."

"More happiness than a young man needs. I was in danger."

"In danger of what?"

"Of one of these two possibilities: either I would grow accustomed to this happiness, whereupon it would lose its intensity and all its glory, or I would not grow accustomed to it and would always consider it as great as before, in which case I would be lost completely. I saw a bee drowned in its honey once, and learned my lesson."

The countess fell into a prolonged meditation.

"You're a man," she said finally. "You don't have only this on your mind, you have other things. But as for us women . . ."

That evening we said nothing else. Both of us gazed into the fire until midnight, in silence.

Sometimes she sent Ermelinda to ask me, "May the countess come to visit you this afternoon?" I would go out immediately to buy sweets and flowers, then return to wait for her. At the prescribed hour she knocked timidly, hesitatingly on my door. I ran to open it for her and she entered, blushing deeply from shyness, as though she were fifteen years old and going out for the first time with a boy. For a considerable while she remained at a loss, unable to speak at all; then, her eyes glued to the floor, she began to respond to me in monosyllables, with an unsure voice. My heart was torn in two. Just look how shyness and maidenhood come again, how in the true woman they survive, undying, and give her a despairing thrice-bitter resplendence in extreme old age!

The day I finally had to leave, the countess threw her arms around my neck and made me swear I would come to Assisi again in order to see her.

"And quickly, quickly." She tried to laugh but could not, and tears welled up into her eyes. "Quickly, because I may have departed by then." She never said *died*, always *departed*.

I kept my word. Quite a few years later I received a message from her confessor, Don Dionigi: "Come. The countess is departing."

I was in Spain; I dispatched a telegram and set out at once.

Holding an armful of white roses, I knocked with trembling hand on the door of her palazzo. Was she alive or dead? Ermelinda opened the door, but I dared not ask her. I gave her the roses.

"The countess is expecting you," she said. "She's in bed; she is unable to walk now."

I found her sitting up in her bed. Her hair had been combed, her jewelry put on, a little rouge placed on her pale cheeks, and a pink ribbon tied around her neck to hide the wrinkles. And she had polished her nails, the first time I'd seen her do so. She spread her arms, and I fell into them. Then I sat down at the bedside and looked at her. How beautiful she still was at the age of eighty; what sweetness and anguish in her eyes!

"I am departing," she said in a low voice, "I am departing . . ."

I was about to open my mouth and protest in order to comfort her, but she grasped my hand as though taking leave of me.

"I am departing . . ." she murmured again.

Night had fallen. Ermelinda entered to light the lamp, but the countess would not let her.

I could see the faint glow of her face in the semidarkness; her eyes had become two large holes filled with night. And as the blackness thickened, I sensed that the countess was silently, hopelessly departing.

A few hours later, toward midnight, she had departed.

19

MY FRIEND THE POET. MOUNT ATHOS

How difficult, how extremely difficult for the soul to sever itself from its body the world: from mountains, seas, cities, people. The soul is an octopus and all these are its tentacles.

Italy occupied my soul, my soul occupied Italy. We were inseparable now; we had merged into one. No force anywhere on earth is as imperialistic as the human soul. It occupies and is occupied in turn, but it always considers its empire too narrow. Suffocating, it desires to conquer the world in order to breathe freely.

Such was my first, my virgin voyage to western Europe. Though I did not immediately realize this at the time, within me the provincial frontiers had begun to dissolve. I saw that the world is richer and wider than Greece, and that beauty, suffering, and strength can assume other countenances besides those given them by Crete and Greece. How many times as I gazed at the beautiful bodies in Renaissance paintings, bodies so resplendent with seeming immortality, was I overcome by unbearable sorrow and indignation because all the divine forms which had been the pretext of those paintings had rotted away and returned to dust; because human beauty and glory maintained themselves in the light of the sun but for a flash. The two great wounds had begun to open again inside me. Ever since that first trip, beauty has always left an aftertaste of death on my lips. As a result, my soul was enriched; it found a new source of rebellion. For the unsophisticated soul of youth does not easily tolerate the sight of beauty being reduced to nothing while God stands by and neglects to lift His hand to make it immortal. If I were God, thinks the young man, I would distribute immortality lavishly, never once permitting a beautiful body or valiant soul to die. What kind of God is this who tosses the beautiful and the ugly, the valiant and the cowardly all on the same dunghill, stamps His foot down on them without distinction, and turns them all to mud? Either He is not just or not omnipotent—or else He simply does not understand! . . . The young man, frequently without knowing it, has secretly begun to fashion within himself a God who will not shame his heart.

When Ernest Renan was once asked if he believed in the immortality of the soul, that cunning old prestidigitator replied, "I see no reason why my grocer should be immortal. Or why I should. But I do see a reason why great souls should not die when they depart the flesh."

This was how I returned to Greece—wounded. I was seething with intellectual revolt and spiritual confusion, all as yet disordered and indecisive inside me. I did not know what I was going to do with my life; before anything else I wanted to find an answer, my answer, to the timeless questions, and then after that I would decide what I would become. If I did not begin by discovering what was the grand purpose of life on earth, I said to myself, how would I be able to discover the purpose of my tiny ephemeral life? And if I did not give my life a purpose, how would I be able to engage in action? I was not interested in finding what life's purpose was objectively—this, I divined, was impossible and futile —but simply what purpose I, of my own free will, could give it in accord with my spiritual and intellectual needs. Whether or not this purpose was the true one did not, at that time, have any great significance for me. The important thing was that I should find (should create) a purpose congruent with my own self, and thus, by following it, reel out my particular desires and abilities to the furthest possible limit. For then at last I would be collaborating harmoniously with the totality of the universe.

If having these metaphysical concerns in one's youth is a disease, I was, at that period, gravely ill.

In Athens there was no one. As for my friends, life's everyday concerns had wizened their minds and hearts.

"We have no time to think," one of them said to me.

"We have no time to love," declared another.

"So you're interested in the purpose of life, are you?" a third said to me, laughing. "Poor fellow, why worry about it!"

I was reminded of the answer the peasant gave me when the

bird flew over our heads and I was so anxious to discover its name. He had looked at me mockingly. "Poor fellow, why worry about it? It's no good for eating."

A man about town who was with my friend stepped forward with a sarcastic glance and chanted:

I'll sing you a song, as daintily as I can,
To shit, eat, fart, and drink, behold the life of man.

As for the intellectuals: petty jealousies, petty quarrels, gossip, and arrogance. I had begun to write in order to divert my inner cry and keep myself from bursting. I used to climb up to the great and dangerous literary wasps' nest at Dexamení Square, sit down in a corner, and listen. I did not gossip, did not frequent taverns, did not play cards—I was insufferable. My first three tragedies were painfully taking on flesh within me. The future verses were still music; they were battling to surpass mere sound and become speech.

Three great figures—Odysseus, Nicephorus Phocas, and Christ—were toiling inside me to acquire faces, to sever themselves from my entrails and be liberated so that I could be liberated too. My whole life I was dominated by great heroic figures, perhaps because I read the lives of the saints so passionately when I was a child, yearned to become a saint in my turn, and after that devoted myself with equal passion to books about heroes—conquerors, explorers, Don Quixotes. Whenever a figure chanced to combine heroism with sanctity, then at last I possessed a model human being. Now, since I myself could not become either a saint or a hero, I was attempting by means of writing to find some consolation for my incapacity.

You are a nanny goat, I frequently told my soul, trying to laugh lest I begin to wail. Yes, a nanny goat, poor old soul. You feel hungry, but instead of drinking wine and eating meat and bread, you take a sheet of white paper, inscribe the words *wine, meat, bread* on it, and then eat the paper.

Whereupon, one day a light shone in the darkness. I had taken solitary refuge in Kifissiá, in a little house surrounded by pine trees. I have never been a misanthrope; indeed, I have always loved people (from a distance) and whenever someone came to see me, the Cretan in me awoke and I took a holiday in order to welcome a fellow human being to my house. For a good while I would enjoy myself, listening to him and entering into his thoughts, and if I could help him in any way, I did so joyfully. But as soon as the conversation and contact became too prolonged, I withdrew into myself and longed to be left alone. People sensed I had no need of them, that I was capable of living without their conversation, and this they found impossible to forgive me. There are very few people with whom I could have lived for any length of time without feeling annoyed.

But one day the light shone. That day, at Kifissiá, I met a young man of my own age whom I loved and respected without interruption, one of the few people I found more agreeable in their presence than in their absence. He was extremely good-looking, and knew it; he was a great lyric poet, and knew it. He had written a long, marvelous poem which I read over and over, finding insatiable delight in its versification, diction, poetic atmosphere, and magical harmony. This poet was of the race of eagles; with the first flap of his wings he reached the pinnacle. Afterwards, when he aspired to write prose as well, I saw that he was truly an eagle, for when he ceased flying and attempted instead to walk upon the ground, he was as heavy and awkward as a walking eagle. The air was his element. He had wings; he did not have a solid, terrestrial mind. He saw far, and dimly. He thought in pictures. Poetic figures, for him, were unshakable logical arguments. When he became embroiled in ratiocination and could not find his way out, either a brilliant image would flash across his mind, or else he would shake with fits of laughter and in this way escape.

But he had great majestic dignity, a rare charm and nobility. When you watched him speak, his blue eyes sparkling ecstatically, or heard him rattle the windows as he recited his poems, you understood what the ancient Greek rhapsodists must have been like, the bards who wandered from palace to palace, crowned with vine leaves or violets, and tamed their still-bestial auditors by means of poetry. Truly, from the very first moment I saw this young man, I felt that he was an honor to the human race.

We became abrupt, immediate friends. So greatly did we differ, we divined at once that each needed the other and that the two of us together would constitute the whole man. I was coarse and taciturn, with the tough hide of a peasant. Full of questions and metaphysical struggles, I remained undeceived by striking exteriors, for I divined the skull beneath the beautiful face. I was devoid of naïveté, sure of nothing. I had not been born a prince; I was struggling to become one. He was jolly, with a stately grandiloquence, sure of himself, the possessor of noble flesh and the unsophisticated, strength-engendering faith that he was immortal. Certain he had been born a prince, he had no need to suffer or struggle to become one. Nor to yearn for the summit, since—of this he was certain also—he had already attained the summit. He was convinced that he was unique and irreplaceable. He would not condescend to compare himself with any other great artist, dead or alive, and this naïveté gave him vast self-confidence and strength.

Once I told him how the queen bee flies into the air on her marriage day followed by an army of drones who try to catch her. One succeeds—the bridegroom. He couples with her, and all the rest fall to the ground and die.

"All the suitors die contented," I said to him, "because they all feel the bridegroom's joy at his nuptials—as though all had been united into one."

But my friend simply burst into thunderous laughter.

"I don't understand what you say at all. The bridegroom has to be me, me and no one else!"

"The spirit is not called *Me*, it is called *All of us*," I replied with a laugh. And I reminded him of the words of a beloved mystic: "I think I am being crowned, whereas others are the victors."

Later, when I knew him better, I said to him one day, "The great difference between us, Angelos, is this: you believe you have found salvation, and believing this, you are saved; I believe that salvation does not exist, and believing this, I am saved."

Lying in ambush deep down inside him, however, was an extremely compelling, extremely tender weakness: he had an absolute need to be loved and admired. If you were able to penetrate his triumphant face and trumpet-voiced self-assurance, you saw a perturbed aristocrat holding out his hand to every passer-by. An old friend of his, a very cynical person, said to me one day, "He plays the sultan, but he is really a sultana."

Many, out of jealousy or an aversion to the pomposity of his outward life, considered him a play-actor and hypocrite; they claimed that he believed in nothing, that all his sayings and doings were lies and ostentation, that he was a peacock with his stunning feathers permanently deployed, but that if you plucked him you would find nothing but a common, insignificant hen.

No, he was not a hypocrite. His outward life—the big talk, the arrogance and bombast, the assurance that he was unique in the world and could perform miracles at will—all this corresponded with absolute sincerity to his profound inward certainty. He did not pretend he was unique; he firmly believed it. He was capable of putting his hand in a fire with the certainty that he would not be burned; he was capable of plunging unconcernedly into battle with the certainty that no bullet could ever touch him. He ate a great deal and boasted of it, because he was certain that whatever *he* ate would be transformed into spirit. "As for the others . . . " he used to say with roars of laughter, "as for the others . . ."

One day while we were strolling through the old part of Athens, he remarked, "I feel so much God in me that if you touch my hand this moment, it will emit sparks."

I said nothing.

"What, don't you believe me?" he asked, seeing me remain silent. "Try. Touch it!" He held out his hand.

I did not want to humiliate him. "Very well," I said. "I believe. Why do I have to try?"

I was naturally convinced that it would not emit sparks. Or was I? Who knows . . . Now I am sorry that I did not try.

Angelos a hypocrite? He would have been had he put on a show of simplicity and modesty. But he was the sincerest person in the world. This I confirmed one day when I observed an incident which passed beyond the limits of the comic and entered the dangerous, fiery domain of lunacy.

We were sojourning in a country house set among pine trees by the edge of the sea. We went for long walks together, read Dante, the Old Testament, and Homer, and he recited his verses to me in his thunderous voice. These were the first days of our acquaintanceship, the time of betrothal. I was overjoyed at having found a person incapable of breathing anywhere but on the most elevated level of desire. We were destroying and rebuilding the world. Both of us knew with certainty that the soul was omnipotent, with the single difference that he thought this of his own soul, I of the soul of all mankind.

Late one afternoon as we were about to take our evening walk and were still standing on the threshold looking at the sea, who should arrive at a run but the village postman. Removing a letter from his sack, he gave it to my friend. Then he leaned against his ear and said in an agitated, frightened voice, "You also have an immense parcel."

But my friend did not hear. His face vermilion, he was reading the letter. He handed it to me.

"Read . . . "

I took the letter and read: "Dearest Buddháki, our neighbor the tailor just died, poor thing. I'm sending him to you. Please revive him." The letter was signed by his wife.

My friend gave me an anguished look. "Do you think I . . . Is it difficult?"

I shrugged my shoulders. "I don't know. At all events . . . Yes, it is very difficult."

But the postman was in a hurry.

"What should I do with the parcel?" he asked, already raising his foot to leave.

"Deliver it!" replied my friend brusquely, and he turned and looked at me again, as though expecting encouragement.

But I felt extremely disturbed and said nothing.

We stood there in silence and waited. The sun was about to set, the sea had turned dark rose. My friend waited, biting his lips.

Soon two villagers appeared carrying a cheap coffin. Inside was the tailor.

"Bring him upstairs!" commanded my friend. His radiant face had darkened.

Once more he turned and looked at me. "What do you think?" he asked again, glaring anxiously right into my pupils. "Do you believe I can do it?"

"Try," I answered. "I'll go for a walk."

I set out along the shore line. Deeply inhaling the aroma of pine and sea, I thought to myself, Now we shall see whether he is a hypocrite or a dangerously venturesome soul ready to desire and attempt the impossible. What will he do: try to resurrect the corpse, or, afraid of looking ridiculous, go off by stealth like a sly fox and creep softly into bed? Tonight we shall see. . . . My heart in a ferment, I walked as quickly as I could, trembling at the thought that my friend's soul should be put to the test in this way before me.

The sun had already plunged below the horizon. From the pine forest came the first sorrowful, tender hooting of owls. The distant mountain peaks began to melt away into the dusk.

I purposely extended my walk, feeling uncomfortable about returning to the house. First and foremost, the presence of the corpse bothered me; I had never been able to confront a corpse without shuddering from fear and loathing. Secondly, I wished to postpone as long as possible the necessity of seeing how my friend would behave in this crucial moment.

When I reached the house, my friend's room, which stood above my own, was ablaze with light. Feeling in no mood for supper, I went to bed. But how was I to sleep? All night long above me I heard a muted bellowing and the creaking of the bed, followed immediately by heavy pacing up and down the room for a considerable period, then the groans and creaking again. All night long. From time to time I heard my friend sigh deeply and open the window, as though suffocating and in need of air. By dawn I had grown tired enough to fall asleep. When I awoke and went downstairs, it was already quite late. My friend was sitting at the table, the milk in front of him untouched. I grew frightened when I saw him. He was deathly pale, his lips ashen; two large blue rings extended around his eyes. I did not speak to him. Perturbed, I sat down at his side and waited.

"I did what I could," he said at last, as though wishing to justify himself. "Do you remember how the prophet Elisha restored the dead man? He lay down with his whole body on top of him, glued his mouth to the corpse's and blew his breath into it, bellowing. I did the same."

He fell silent for a moment, and then: "All night long . . . all night long. In vain!"

I gazed at my friend with amazement and admiration. True, he had entered the realm of the ridiculous, but he had passed beyond it to reach the tragic boundaries of lunacy, and now he had returned and was sitting next to me exhausted.

He got up and went to the door. Wiping his brow, which was

pearled with large drops of sweat, he looked at the sea in front of him.

"Now what's to be done?" he asked, turning to me.

"Call the priest to come and bury him," I replied. "As for us, let's go for our walk along the beach."

I gave him my arm, which was trembling. Removing our shoes and socks, we waded along the shore, refreshing ourselves. Though he did not speak, I could feel him being calmed by the water's coolness and quiet rippling.

"I'm ashamed . . ." he murmured finally. "Does this mean that the soul is not omnipotent?"

"It isn't yet," I replied, "but it will be. You did a wonderfully brave thing in wishing to overstep human boundaries, but it is also a wonderfully brave thing to acknowledge those boundaries fearlessly and without despair. We are going to beat our heads against the bars, then beat them some more; many heads will be smashed to pieces, but one day the bars will break."

"The head that breaks them must be mine—that's what I want," he declared, obstinately hurling a large pebble into the sea. "Mine," he shouted, "mine and no one else's!"

I smiled. This *mine, mine* and *me, me* was my friend's terrible prison, a dungeon without windows or doors.

"Do you know the highest peak a man can reach?" I asked in an effort to comfort him. "It is to conquer the self, the ego. When we reach that peak, and only then, Angelos, we shall be saved."

He said nothing, but he was beating the waves maniacally with his heel.

The atmosphere between us grew heavy.

"Let's go home," he said. "I'm tired."

He was not tired; he was angry.

We did not exchange a single word the entire way back. We walked quickly. A breeze had risen and the sea was sighing. The air felt damp and briny.

When we reached the house, I pointed to my friend's extensive library in an effort to exorcise the unfortunate incident.

"Look," I said, "I'll close my eyes and take a book. The book will decide."

"Decide what?" my friend asked with irritation.

"What we do tomorrow."

Closing my eyes and groping with my hand, I seized a book. My friend snatched it out of my fingers and opened it. It was a large album of photographs: monasteries, monks, campaniles, cypresses, cells atop precipitous cliffs, with the sea raging savagely beneath.

"Mount Athos!" I cried.

My friend's face gleamed.

"Just what I wanted!" he shouted. "I've wanted that for years and years. Let's go!"

He spread his arms and clasped me tightly to his breast.

"Are you ready?" he asked. "Should we put on our seven-league boots—we're ogres, aren't we? Yes, let's put on our seven-league boots to tread the Holy Mountain."

It was raining. The summit of Athos had disappeared behind a wrapping of dense mist. The sea was calm, jellied, muddy. A monastery gleamed brilliantly white amid rain-blackened chestnut trees. The sky had descended to the treetops; the rain was silent and continuous, the kind that saturates the ground. Five or six drenched monks stood on the wharf like cypress trees.

Two monks sat chatting next to us in the rowboat which was bringing us to Daphne, the Holy Mountain's tiny port. The younger of the pair, who had a scanty black beard and carried a heavy sack beneath his arm, was saying, "Just to hear him chant, you forget the world. His voice is sweeter than a father or a mother."

The other replied, "What are you trying to tell me? In our monastery we have a blackbird who sings the 'Lord, I Cried unto Thee' and the 'Christ Is Risen.' He makes your head whirl. We call him Father Blackbird; he comes to church with us, and he fasts the whole of Lent."

"Then he couldn't be a blackbird, Father Lavréndios," the young monk said after reflection, "No, he couldn't be a blackbird."

We set foot upon the sacred ground. The monks standing on the wharf cast trained eyes on each person who debarked, in case a woman dressed in man's clothing should be hidden among the passengers. In the thousand years since the Holy Mountain was consecrated to the Virgin, no woman has ever set foot here, no feminine exhalations have soiled the air, not even those of female animals—ewes, nanny goats, hens, or cats. The air is soiled only by masculine exhalations.

Our two traveling companions had set out behind us, loaded down like mules. They increased their pace in order to catch up.

"Pilgrims?" asked the young monk, smiling. "May Her Grace aid you."

Hermits are always dying to talk. These two, working up steam, chatted about miracles, holy relics, about the ascetics who lift their arms in prayer at the top of great cliffs.

"And as long as they keep their arms raised," said the young one, "you need have no fear that the world will collapse. They hold up the world and keep it from falling."

"Is it true that a woman has never set foot on the Holy Mountain?" I asked.

"Never, never," replied the older of the two, spitting into the air and mumbling "Get thee behind me, Satan! Sometimes a woman is saucy enough to come ashore here dressed as a man. But the monks on watch spot her immediately and send her away."

"How can they tell?" asked my friend with a laugh.

"From the smell," the young monk answered. "Here, ask the Father; he was once a sentry at the wharf."

My friend turned to the old monk. "Do women smell different, holy Father? What do they smell like?"

"Like stinking skunks," answered the old man, quickening his pace.

The rain began to decrease. A wind must have risen in the upper levels of the atmosphere; the clouds broke and a little sunlight appeared. All at once the earth smiled, still bathed in tears, and an extremely pale rainbow suspended itself in the air along with the sun, re-establishing the friendship between sky and wetted soil.

"The Virgin's girdle!" exclaimed the two monks, crossing themselves.

Leaning on our stout oaken walking sticks, our sacks on our backs, we climbed the cobbled road that led to Karyés, passing through a dense forest of half-defoliated chestnut trees, pistachios, and broad-leafed laurels. The air smelled of incense, or so it seemed to us. We felt that we had entered a colossal church composed of sea, mountains, and chestnut forests, and roofed at the top by the open sky instead of a dome. I turned to my friend; I wanted to break the silence which had begun to weigh upon me.

"Why don't we talk a little?" I suggested.

"We are," answered my friend, touching my shoulder lightly. "We are, but with silence, the tongue of angels."

Then he suddenly appeared to grow angry.

"What do you expect us to say? That it's beautiful, that our hearts have sprouted wings and want to fly away, that we've started along a road leading to Paradise? Words, words, words. Keep quiet!"

Two blackbirds darted out from a walnut tree; the wet branches shook and the raindrops splashed our faces.

"The bird kingdom has its monks too—the blackbirds," said the elderly Father. "The Holy Mountain is full of them."

"And what about the stars, Father Lavréndios?" asked the youth. "Do they have their monks too?"

"They used to be monks, all of them, my brother. Here on earth they bore witness to the faith of Christ, were martyred, and rose to Abraham's bosom. Heaven, in case you don't know it, is Abraham's bosom."

I listened to them, admiring man's soul, that force which in its omnipotence has been able to transform all things and subject them to its dream. The faithful have made both heaven and earth whirl around one immortal polestar, Christ, one immutable figure, obliging both to enter His service. Christ, for them, is the Great Answer to every perplexity. All things are explained, illuminated, placed in order, and the soul rests at ease. Questions are asked only by those without faith; they alone struggle, lose their way, and fall into despair.

But a few days after we reached the Holy Mountain, a half-insane ascetic said something which muzzled me. He lived in a state of ecstatic frenzy perched in a cave overhanging the sea.

"Poor, poor man, I see you've lost your wits," I said to tease him.

He laughed. "I gave my wits and received God in return. In other words, I gave a counterfeit farthing and purchased paradise. What do you think, my boy, did I strike a good bargain?"

After a moment's silence, he continued. "And let me tell you something else, for your information. There was once a great king who had three hundred and sixty-five wives in his harem. He was very handsome, and loved to eat and have a good time. One day he went to a monastery, where he saw an ascetic. He looked at him compassionately. 'What a great sacrifice you are making!' he said. 'Your sacrifice is greater,' the ascetic replied. 'How's that?' 'Because I have renounced the ephemeral world, while you have renounced the eternal.' "

Somewhere behind the chestnut trees a nearby bell began to toll vespers. The monks' village came into sight as we rounded a bend in the road. We quickened our pace.

Grocers, vegetable dealers, cooks, peddlers, street cleaners—all of them monks! It was a sorrowful, unbearable village of males, without a woman, without a child, without laughter. Nothing but beards: black, blond, brown, gray, and snow-white, some pointed, some spread out like bell-shaped brooms, others thick, curly, and impenetrable, like healthy cauliflowers.

We went to the Protáton, the residence where the commissioners of the twenty monasteries had their seat. Enthroned in their stalls, they regarded us with sly quick-moving eyes that were full of suspicion. We said who we were—two God-fearing Christians who had the zeal of the Lord and were coming to do homage. We were still young, we said, and before commencing to taste the troubles of the world, before marrying, we had come here to the Virgin's Garden, so that Her Grace might enlighten us and show us the true road. We had come as votaries to Her Grace.

My friend, speaking with his thunderous voice and poetic elevation, became more and more ignited. The monks listened with gaping mouths, some tightly clutching their beards. The more my friend spoke, the more I myself penetrated his meaning and understood the true reason why we had come to the Holy Mountain. Doubtlessly, even my friend had not known it but had found it in the course of speaking.

Leaning over, the monks whispered in one another's ears, then rose in a single body and gave us written permission to tour all the monasteries and hermitages, doing homage at each, and to remain until the Virgin in her grace gave us a sign that our votive offering had terminated.

Our journey began. Ecstatically happy, we traveled from monastery to monastery, miracle to miracle, conversing in muted voices like the ancient pilgrims, about God, man's destiny, and our own particular duty—the three persistent subjects of our entire trip. I kept a diary, recording the day's harvest every evening. Now, forty years later, it has grown yellow with age, but as I turn over its pages, I relive those divine, unbelievable days. Every word, even the most insignificant, brings joys and yearnings back to life inside me, and also youthful anxieties, the frantic schemes my friend and I made to save our souls—all the insolence, nobility, and naïve ingenuousness of youth.

Iviron Monastery, November 19. In the morning, walk along the seashore. A little spring of holy water and the tiny chapel next to it, with the icon of the Virgin inside, blood running from her cheek. Two fishermen-monks drawing the nets. The fish dancing inside.

Back to the monastery. The Portaïtissa—Our Lady of the Gate—what a miracle! Huge woeful eyes, petite wavy mouth, firm chin—joy, sadness, all the delight and pain of humankind.

And at night, what a divine moment when we saw the sea, brilliantly white and sighing, with the moon monstrously huge over it. My friend said that tonight the moon was really fulfilling its vocation: it was illuminating eternity.

We talked in low voices, leaning close to each other. We said that we had to make a radical decision, had to experience eternity at every moment.

Wherever we went we were followed by a pale, silent monk, a sickly creature who coughed, spat, and scratched himself incessantly. But his face was radiant with happiness.

"He must be a lunatic," said my friend.

"He must be a saint," I said. "Don't you see how his face gleams? Just as though some sun were hitting it."

Once we halted and he joined us.

"I am Father Lavréndios," he said. "The fool. You've probably heard about me."

"You are very fortunate," my friend remarked, "for you have entered heaven while still alive. Your face is radiant."

"Praise the Lord," answered the monk, crossing himself. "What others call folly I call paradise. But I had a terrible time opening the door."

"What door?"

"The door to paradise, brother. When I first entered the monastery I trembled and wept from fear. I wept at the thought of heaven, wept at the thought of hell. But one morning I got up and said to myself, Why weep? God is our Father, isn't He? We're his sons, aren't we? Well then, why be afraid? Since that day I've been called a fool."

He took a dry crust from beneath his shirt and gave it to us.

"The bread of the angels," he said. "Eat! Eat, your poor devils, so you too can grow wings!"

Stavronikíta Monastery, November 21. Amazingly high over the sea. The old doorkeeper an ancient wreck from Crete. He seized me by the hand.

"Eh, and who are you?"

"A Cretan!"

"Enter!"

In one of the cells some young novices were learning Byzantine music, picking out the first notes in loud voices. They hold tradition like a lighted candle in their dirty, childish hands.

The sea viewed from the monastery tower: how like a gigantic bow it is, a gigantic bow stretched taut!

Further along in the same monastery, the head of the twelve-year-old Christ, so precociously filled with understanding and divine seriousness. Precipitous, towering forehead, chubby white chest, eyes deep and thoughtful. Truly the Portaïtissa's son. . . . Another icon, a large Saint Nicholas of the Oysters. He had a sizable oyster embedded in his forehead, and his hands seemed to be dripping with brine.

I chatted with the Cretan doorkeeper.

"What made you become a monk?"

"My aunt read me the Gospel one day and said the world was worthless."

Must not forget Father Philemon, who waited on us at table. Body as lithe as a sword of damask steel; like an angel, all flame. He longed to receive orders, greatly enjoyed serving and obeying. His joy was so great that he could not keep from laughing; he laughed constantly.

"When will my turn come to see God?" I asked him.

"It's easy, very easy," he answered. "Just open your eyes and you'll see Him."

Pantocrátoros Monastery. Before daybreak I heard a bewitching melody from the monastery courtyard. The sweetest of sounds. Racing to my window, I saw a monk in the half-light of the dawn. He was wearing the monk's hat with its black kalýmmafko flowing down his back. He carried an oblong block of wood, the portable semantron, which he struck rhythmically with a little hammer. He advanced slowly around the courtyard, going from cell to cell to summon the brothers to matins. My friend, who had awakened also, leaned out of the window at my side, and both of us listened with absorption and contentment. After the semantron stopped, we dressed ourselves and went down to the chapel. Total darkness, except for two cressets burning on the iconostasis in front of the icons of Christ and the Virgin Mother. The air was pungent with wax and rose incense.

The psalms for matins began softly, gently like the rustling of trees, the sighing of the sea. The abbot, a lighted candle in his hand, approached each stall in turn to see if all the brothers had come down; then he dipped the aspergillum in the freezing holy water and vigorously aspersed the forehead of each of the monks. As we strolled in the cloister afterwards, we commented on the life here: what divine rhythm, what a marvelously embossed shell it was, the product of untold generations—but now, inside, the oyster which had created and beautified this shell was dead. "We must reorganize Christian asceticism," we said, taking an oath to do so. "We must blow the breath of creativity into it once more. We must. This is why we came to the Holy Mountain."

Vatopédi Monastery. We approached the celebrated Vatopédi on a tender morning filled with God's loving-kindness, a morning straight from heaven, as though this were the fifth day of the Creation and God still had not fashioned man to spoil His work. The east opened by degrees like a rose, and tiny rosy-cheeked clouds emerged like cherubs from behind the horizon, growing gradually larger, so that they appeared to be descending to earth. A blackbird landed in the middle of the road and looked at us, the dew still upon its wings. But as though it were not a blackbird, but instead a kindly spirit which recognized us, it neither grew frightened nor moved out of our way. A tiny little owl perched on a rock had already grown giddy from the light; it remained peaceful and motionless, waiting for darkness to return.

We did not speak. Both of us felt that the human voice, no matter how sweet and hushed, would reverberate shrill and discordant here, and that all the magic veil which enveloped us would be torn apart. Our faces and hands sprinkled with morning dewdrops as we pushed aside the low-hanging pine branches, we proceeded on our way.

My happiness was choking me. Turning to my friend, I was about to open my mouth to exclaim, What joy this is! But I did not dare. I knew that as soon as I spoke, the sorcery would be dispelled. I remember seeing a fox late one afternoon on Taygetus, above Sparta; it was advancing gingerly with craned neck, its bushy tail held stiffly erect, so that it cast a long purple shadow on the stones. I held my breath lest the animal catch scent of me and run off, but I was not quick enough in restraining my exultation; in spite of myself a tiny, tiny cry excaped me. This the fox heard, and before I even had a chance to see which direction it took, it had vanished. . . . Happiness in man's life, I felt, is always exactly the same.

Suddenly we heard talking and laughter; we had finally reached the monastery. Two well-nourished monks were sitting on a stone bench in front of the outer door, joking with the doorkeeper.

As though we had seen a snake, we halted abruptly. My friend looked at me. "It was a dream," he said, shaking his head. "For an instant we believed that people did not exist."

"What a shame," I answered. "That was the true paradise, far, far superior to the other. Instead of man and wife strolling beneath God's trees, there were two friends. And now, look, we've been expelled—not by an angel who came running with a scimitar, but by a human being armed with a voice."

The two monks had been shouting loudly and bursting into irrepressible laughter as they teased the doorkeeper. But they fell silent the moment they saw us. Clasping their bellies, they rose and held out their hands for us to kiss.

"Welcome," they said. "God be with you."

"You seem to be doing pretty well, holy Fathers," replied my friend, glancing at their paunches and red cheeks. He still could not forgive them for expelling us from paradise.

"We have renounced the false world and its pleasures," said the first, the one with the blond beard.

We kept mum. But the other, the black-bearded monk, snapped, "Why look at us with such surprise? Prayer is more nourishing than meat."

They had come close to us; their breath reeked unbearably of garlic.

"Let's go inside to do obeisance," we said, anxious to escape these two garlic-monks.

Along came the guestmaster, an immaculate blue-eyed monk with a silken white beard and rosy skin, obviously thriving quite nicely. After bidding us welcome, he led the way and we followed. It was a rich monastery, an entire city, with guest rooms, freshly painted doors and windows, electric lights, and orchards overlooking the sea. The monks had left the refectory already and were seated outside their cells digesting their food in the sun. Entering the church, we did obeisance to the renowned icons of the Virgin: the Paramythía, the Ktetórissa, the Bematárissa, the Antiphonétria, the Esphagméne, and the Elaiobrótida. A precious reliquary was opened for us and we kissed the Virgin's Holy Girdle. I remembered the two monks who had brought it to Crete when I was a child. The populace raced to Saint Minas's to do obeisance, filling the monks' little sack with silver metzilies and golden liras, earrings, and wedding bands. I had nothing to give to Her Grace, so I dug in my pocket, found a pencil, and tossed that into the sack.

We went out to the courtyard and climbed to the guest room. A sumptuous meal had been prepared for us, replete with all God's riches.

"We're not doing badly here," said my friend, who loved good food. "Not badly at all—you'd think we were Vatopédi monks!"

"Let's drink the health of poor pauper-Prodromos," I suggested, "poor famished Prodromos. O how jealous he was when he thought of the abbots eating their meals in the monasteries, how his mouth watered! And what a complaint he made to his emperor! Do you remember the lines?"

"Of course I remember:

When I think of the abbots, Sovereign,
I am beside myself, I go out of my mind.
They stuff themselves with first-class fish,
And me they give a stinking tunny!
They swill down Chios wine until they're glutted,
While my poor belly writhes from vinegar!"

My friend chuckled, but a shadow fell over his face immediately. "Shame on us for laughing," he said. "This monastery crushes my heart. Did you see the monks? Well nourished, every one of them! If Christ came back to earth and happened to stop at Vatopédi, O how he'd make the scourge sing over their heads! Come on, let's go."

"Go where? Our hearts are being crushed not only by this monastery but by the whole world—don't you feel that? Everywhere some go hungry while others, glutted, lick their chops; everywhere sheep and wolves. One law in this world is still inviolable: eat or be eaten—the law of the jungle."

"But does this mean that salvation does not exist? Is there no animal sufficiently good and at the same time sufficiently strong so that it will neither eat others nor allow itself to be eaten by others?"

"None, but there might be some day. Thousands of years ago an animal set out to reach this goal, but it has not arrived yet."

"Which animal?"

"The monkey. We are still only at the halfway point—the Pithecanthropus. Be patient."

"God can afford to be patient. He's immortal. What does time cost Him? But man? . . ."

"Man is immortal too," I replied. "Not all of him, though. The immortal part, inside him, can be patient."

We rose from the table and went down to the shore. The sun was about to set; not a leaf was stirring. Two gulls, their wings folded, were pushing the sea happily with their white breasts.

"They must be man and wife," remarked my friend, looking at them with admiration.

"Or two friends," I said, and picking up a pebble from the beach, I flung it in order to separate them.

As I pore over this ancient diary now in my old age and see our quixotic campaigns of that time—the ramshackle lance, worm-eaten shield, tin helmet, the mind filled with nobility and wind—I am unable to smile. Happy the youth who believes that his duty is to remake the world and bring it more in accord with virtue and justice, more in accord with his own heart. Woe to whoever commences his life without lunacy.

We toured the Holy Mountain, and the more we inhaled its atmosphere, the more our hearts caught fire and blazed up in a furor. My god, what decisions we made, what vows we took! How weightlessly we jumped the boulders as we proceeded from monastery to monastery, feeling not solely in our imaginations but with our entire bodies that we were being supported by the wings of angels! Such, surely, is the atmosphere which at times begets lunacy, at times sanctity and heroism. In the years which crushed down upon us afterwards, however, neither my friend nor I ever mentioned those sacred, quixotic hours again. We felt ashamed, not because the flame had subsided—alas! it did not subside—but because our strength proved to be lax, inferior to our desire. We still wanted, as we always had, to create a new and better world, but we saw that we could not do so. I admitted this, but my friend kept it hidden all his life. That was why he secretly writhed and suffered more than I did.

Only once, one evening many years later when a huge harvest moon rose sadly from the sea as we were leaving the convent on Spetsai, I turned to my friend and said to him, "Angelos, do you remember . . . ?" But he became pale—he realized that I had been reminded of the moon at Athos. Placing his hand over my mouth and commanding me to be silent, he quickened his pace.

Now I lean over my old journal once more and thumb through its pages.

Karakállou Monastery. Clouds had covered Athos's foot and summit, leaving free a wide zone of sparkling snow in the middle. It began to rain—sun showers. Our guide ran ahead and fired a rifleshot. The sound of the monastery bells came festively from behind a clump of fir trees, and the abbot, holding the tall crosier symbolizing his office, appeared on the threshold to welcome us, accompanied by the commissioners.

We entered the refectory; it was long and narrow, with columns painted blue and black. The abbot sits at the head of the table, severe, taciturn, black-bearded; above him a fierce Christ with knotted brows, done in black and green paint. In a small elevated pulpit, the lector, a pale monk of tender age, declaims from the lives of the saints in a monotonous, chanting voice. Everyone bends over his plate, no one talks. The abbot scarcely touches his bread and food; then suddenly he takes a small bell standing at his right side and rings it three times. All the monks spring to their feet, still chewing their half-finished meals. The one who is waiting on table runs, prostrates himself before the abbot, and receives his blessing. Then the lector does the same and begs to be forgiven if he read poorly. In comes the Host on a tiny tray, a piece of bread from which each monk pinches off a small bit which he nibbles as holy antídoro.

That night we lay awake talking into the early hours. We told each other that the time was ripe, the world was ripe, for a new way to love Christ. Earlier that day we had met a monk standing outside the monastery graveyard. When we asked him why the paintings over cemetery entrances always represented Christ crucified and not, as would be fitting, Christ rising from the grave, the monk became angry. "Our Christ is Christ crucified," he replied. "In the Gospels did you ever see Christ laugh? He is always sighing, being scourged, and weeping—always being crucified."

Now, unable to fall asleep, we were saying, "The time has come when we must make Christ laugh; yes, must! No more scourgings, weeping, or crucifixions. Christ must bind the strong, happy gods of Greece together inside him; He must assimilate them all. The time has arrived for the Jewish Christ to become a Greek."

"And who shall bring this about—we shall!" exclaimed my friend, raising his hand as though taking an oath.

"Yes, we!" I exclaimed in my turn. I felt at that moment that nothing in the whole world could resist the human soul.

"We'll never separate!" cried my friend. "We'll yoke ourselves together like a pair of oxen to plow the earth!"

Years later we understood. We had yoked ourselves together like oxen, and had plowed the air.

Philothéou Monastery. Marvelous stroll in the fog. Graceful, lanky poplars choked by ivy. A revolting monk named Ioannikios—a bony redhead forever jabbering. Wouldn't stop telling us about a sister of his, Kallirhóe, who was possessed by demons. Apparently he himself had demons inside him; two of them, one called Hodja and the other Ishmael. The accursed creatures always opposed God, opposed Ioannikios. They wanted to eat meat during Lent, and they prodded Ioannikios to descend the stairs on tiptoe at night and go into the kitchen in order to devour whatever food remained from the collation. In addition, each dawn when Ishmael and Hodja—damn them!—heard the semantron, they cried out, "I'm not going! I'm not going!"

We proceeded to the monastery's courtyard. Grass was growing everywhere between the cobblestones, and the surrounding walls and cells were black with dampness and mildew. The chapel stood in the center; we entered to do obeisance to its wonder-working icon, the Virgin of the Tender Kiss. Her cheek is resting with inexpressible tenderness against the cheek of the infant Jesus, and her eyes, incurably sad, are staring into the distance.

"Look carefully into the Virgin's eyes," said the monk who was accompanying us. "What do you see there?"

We went close and looked.

"Nothing," we both answered.

"Whoever has faith sees Christ crucified," declared the monk, casting a stern glance at us.

He opened a silver reliquary containing a long bone.

"Do obeisance! It is Chrysostom's right arm! Cross yourselves!"

Aghias Lavras Monastery. We departed first thing in the morning, anxious to see the famous Great Lavra, the monastery built by the tragic emperor Nicephorus Phocas, who yearned to cast off his crown, take refuge here, and lead the life of an ascetic. But his other yearning—for women—did not permit him, and he continually procrastinated, procrastinated and waited. Until along came his most trusted friend with a sword and cut off his head.

We arrived. Two luxuriant cypresses in the courtyard, one planted by Nicephorus Phocas's confessor, Saint Athanásius, the other by his disciple Euthýmius. Athos, completely snow-capped, hangs over the monastery like the Pantocrator.

We were brought into the sacristy and proudly shown the monastery's treasures—the skull of Basil the Great, the jaw of Theodore Stratelátes, the left arm of Chrysostom, and a multitude of other bones. A gorgeous cross case, adorned everywhere with precious stones and pearls, was opened for us; inside lay a large section of the True Cross. The monk's voice trembled with emotion, but I was reminded of something a certain real Christian once said: "Every piece of wood is 'true,' because from each a cross can be made." Next, Nicephorus Phocas's dress uniform, all gold, with roses and lilies embroidered in silk. And his golden crown, studded with immense green and red jewels. And the Gospel written in his hand. . . . And then a multitude of ancient worm-eaten account books.

My friend and I gasped with admiration, but all this failed to touch our hearts. I remember most deeply of all, and with greater gratitude, the fragrance of the two blossoming medlar trees at the entrance to the library. My entire body rejoiced as it inhaled the medlar's perfume which I so adore, that sweet, peppery aroma more intoxicating than wine, women, or all the world's splendors.

The following morning we set out before dawn for the summit of Athos. The semantron had yet to sing out in the cloister, the birds had yet to awaken. The sky was milky and absolutely clear, with the morning star shining far off in the east like a six-winged seraph.

Short, bowlegged Father Loukás, a former smuggler, went in the lead to show us the way. From time to time he stopped to chat with us about seas, revels, disputes with the Turks. The whole of his previous existence in the world remained like a fairy tale inside him; it seemed to have taken place on some other wilder and more dangerous planet, one filled with shouts, curses, and women. He told and retold this fairy tale of his, relived it, and felt happy. Though he had renounced every aspect of his former life, he had taken it all with him, wrapped inside his frock.

He halted now beneath a large fir tree, anxious to talk.

"We'll stop and rest awhile, lads—all right? Let's exchange a word or two. I'm ready to burst."

He brought out a tobacco pouch hidden beneath his cincture, rolled a cigarette, and opened the conversation.

"Me, the person you see now with the frock, they used to call me Leonidas—Captain Leonidas of Kálymnos, the terror of the Turks. A smuggler I was, a hellion if there ever was one. Now, just how I came to don the frock, that I'll tell you some other time.

Suffice it to say that the smuggler inside me never croaked. How could he, seeing as I stuff him with food and drink as though he were a bey, no matter if he's chained inside me like a boat dog. Loukás eats bread and olives in the refectory with the other monks, but when he goes back to his cell and bolts the door, he sets the table for Leonidas and eats meat. As you can see, we're not one but two. Understand? . . . That's what I wanted to tell you. Sin confessed: sin redressed. I've spoken and I feel better. Now let's go."

"Bravo, Captain Loukás!" exclaimed my friend, splitting with laughter. "You've done a fine job of managing the unmanageable. But don't you ever have a suspicion that all this might be the work of the Tempter?"

"Of course, of course," said the monk, winking his eye cunningly. "I have this suspicion every morning—but by dinnertime I've forgotten it."

"Tie a knot in your handkerchief as a reminder," I suggested.

He took a deep puff on his cigarette; the smoke came out through his nostrils.

"I don't have a handkerchief," he said.

We resumed our climb. Pines, firs, terrifying precipices. The sea, calm today, stretched below in the gentle morning light. As the brightness increased, we were able to make out the divine islands of Imbros, Lemnos and Samothrace in the distance; they seemed to be floating in mid-air, not touching the water.

We reached the snow line. Father Loukás advanced slowly with careful steps. We slid and fell, proceeding with difficulty and danger upon the frozen snow; the mountain was precipitous, cruelly inhuman. Suddenly my friend, who was climbing in front of me, halted, leaned over, and gazed downward into a deep, bottomless chasm. Livid with vertigo, he turned to me and murmured, "Let's go back."

"But wouldn't that be shameful?" I said, looking at him reproachfully. I wanted so very much to reach the summit.

"Yes, yes," he murmured in humiliation. "Forward!" And he began once more to climb.

The sun was high when we set foot on the summit. We were both panting with fatigue, but our faces were resplendent because we had achieved our goal.

We went to do obeisance in the little chapel dedicated to the Transfiguration of Christ. Meanwhile Father Loukás built a fire with the twigs and branches he had collected along the way, then took some coffee from his sack and brewed it. Huddling together behind a large rock because the wind had begun to blow and we were cold, we gazed at the mute, boundless sea in front of us, the islands sailing brilliantly white in it, and far in the distance, the unknown mountains which gave a leaden cast to the air.

"They say you can see Constantinople from this holy peak," declared Loukás, and he gazed out goggle-eyed toward the east in an effort to discern the royal capital.

"Have you yourself ever seen it, Father Loukás?"

The monk sighed. "No. I was never deemed worthy. It seems that our bodily eyes are not sufficient. Others are needed, the eyes of the soul, and alas! my soul is shortsighted."

"But you're able to see God," I said.

"Eh! eyes aren't needed for that," replied the monk. "God is closer to us than our liver and lungs."

My friend had been despondent and silent. Doubtlessly he could not bring himself to forgive his body for momentarily turning coward. Suddenly he was unable to restrain himself any longer. He held out his hand and squeezed mine energetically.

"Please," he said, "forget it. I swear I won't do it again."

Iosaphaíoi, December 6. We spent today, my name day, in the celebrated painting studio of Iosaphaíoi. There are ten painter-monks. Each week one of them takes over the household chores—sweeps, washes, and cooks—while the others paint. Emerging from this studio to be disseminated to the farthest limits of the Orthodox world are the well-combed well-nourished Christs, the beautiful, richly gowned Virgins, the rosy-cheeked, contented saints lacking all sanctity—decalcomanias, all of them. The monks are simple and personable, hospitable and self-respecting; they love fine food, fine wine, and castrated cats. For hours after dinner we sat together and talked in front of the large fire burning in the hearth, we about this world, they about the divine world above. Father Akákios, a short, rotund monk with swollen feet, had spent the entire day painting Saint Antonius, and now, stroking a fat black cat on his knees, he spoke movingly about the saintly eremite. It seems that a girl came to him one day and said, "I have observed all of God's commandments; I place all my trust in the Lord. He will open the gates of paradise for me." Saint Antonius then asked her, "Has poverty become wealth for you?" "No, Abba." "Nor dishonor honor?" "No, Abba." "Nor enemies friends?" "No, Abba." "Well then, my poor girl, go and get to work, because right now you possess nothing."

As I looked at the simple Akákios, who was perspiring from too much food, the fire's great warmth, and the memory of the frightening ascetic, I kept thinking what a rosy-cheeked Antonius he must have been painting all day, and I was possessed by a diabolical urge to say to him, Go and get to work, poor fellow, because right now you possess nothing. But I did not speak. A crust of lard, habit, and cowardice envelops the soul; no matter what it craves from the depths of its prison, the lard, habit, and cowardice carry out something entirely different. I did not speak—from cowardice.

That night when we went to bed, I confessed this to my friend.

"You must have refrained out of courtesy, not cowardice," he said to console me. "Out of pity, because you did not want to sadden such a fine fellow. Perhaps even out of the conviction that your words would have accomplished nothing."

"No, no," I protested. "Even if it's as you think, we must conquer the minor virtues you talk about—courtesy, pity, expediency. I am less afraid of the major vices than of the minor virtues, because these have lovely faces and deceive us all too easily. For my part, I want to give the worst explanation: I say I did it from cowardice, because I want to shame my soul and keep it from doing the same thing again."

The next morning, sitting with the ten befrocked artists in the glassed-in veranda of the hermitage amidst the painted rosy-cheeked saints and chubby Virgins, we drank our milk and munched the tasty wheaten rusks and the rich condiments which accompanied them. The winter sun came in with extreme mildness through the large windows, together with the honey-sweet aroma of pine. We talked and laughed. This was not the Holy Mountain. Christ had been resurrected here; He was laughing along with us. When the monks recounted the miracles performed by the saints, their eyes fluttered from belief (or disbelief) and their faces glowed with a faraway luster.

Father Agápios extended his hand and directed our attention to one of his paintings, which hung on the wall opposite us. He was the youngest of the artists and had a glossy black beard and red lips.

"It is Arsénios the great ascetic," he said, admiring his work. "And the woman you see kneeling at his feet is a beautiful Roman aristocrat who crossed mountains and seas to come and prostrate herself before him. But look how the ascetic is pointing with his finger to the sea and knitting his brows (I want to show that he is angrily repulsing her). 'Go away,' he says, 'and don't tell anyone you saw me—because the sea will become a highway and women will start transporting themselves to my solitude.' 'Pray for me, Father,' implores the woman. 'Woman,' replies the ascetic, 'I shall pray God to make me forget you.' "

The painter turned, gave us a sly look, and asked, "What does that mean: 'I shall pray God to make me forget you'?"

Not knowing what the monk had in mind, we kept still.

"It means that the ascetic was pricked by the woman's beauty; that explains why he sought God's help to make him forget her."

"And did he forget her," asked my friend, winking at the monk.

"Can such things be forgotten?" he answered, but seeing old Habakkuk looking daggers at him, he regretted his words and bit his thick red lips.

Saint Paul's Monastery. Marvelous rowboat ride to Saint Paul's. The sea a thousand colors—pale blue and green, also like mother-of-pearl. Beetling crags of bright bloodlike red; black caves, wild doves, and then all of a sudden level stretches of brilliantly white sand.

Today my friend was in a fine mood; the whole boat shook from his thunderous laughter. I told him to be angry in Chinese, and he began at once, with astonishing readiness, to spout a raging torrent of imaginary Chinese words. I was so pleased that I could scarcely fit in the boat. "Now make love in Arabic," I said to him, and he began with irrepressible passion to confess his love to an invisible Arab lady. Thus, as though in a flash, we reached the port of Saint Paul's and commenced the steep, difficult ascent to the monastery.

The doorkeeper was a Cephalonian. A wily old fellow; also a joker. In order to pass the time, he spent his days seated behind the door with a penknife in hand, carving what appeared to be little wooden Christs, saints, and demons. He looked us over carefully.

"What do you want here, morons?" he asked with a laugh.

"We want to do obeisance, old man."

"Obeisance to what? Are you in your right minds?"

"To the monastery."

"What monastery? There is no monastery—it's finished! The world, that's the monastery. Take my advice and go back to the world!"

We gazed at him with gaping mouths. He really seemed to feel sorry for us.

"I'm only joking," he said at that point. "Step inside. Welcome."

We entered and looked at the cells which circled the courtyard. The monk extended his hand. "Behold God's beehive," he said sarcastically. "Behold the cells. Once they were inhabited by bees who made honey; now by drones, and what a sting they have! . . . May the Lord protect you," he added, and burst out laughing.

We did not breathe a word, but we were sick at heart. Had the sacred monastery been emptied of its hallowed contents to such an extent? Had the monks been left only hollow shells to such an extent, the sacred butterfly having flown from inside them!

With weary feet we climbed the stone stairway which led to the hall set aside for the reception of guests. My friend took hold of my arm compassionately. "Be patient," he said. "Don't feel bad. As long as our souls remain strong, that is all that matters; as long as *they* don't go into decline. Because with the fall of certain souls in this world, the world itself will collapse. These are the pillars which support it. They are few, but enough."

He shook me forcefully. "Hold fast, poor Missolonghi!" he said with a laugh.

We entered the hall. The commissioners, five or six large-sized men with hands crossed over their abdomens, were seated around the abbot. He was enthroned in the center, an elegant figure with a curly black beard, feminine face, white hands, and a headdress of black silk. He held out his hand in an extremely dandyish way for us to kiss, then inquired how the world was getting on, and whether we had brought any newspapers.

"What's happening in England?" asked one of the commissioners. "What's happening in Germany? Do you think we'll have a war?"

"God grant we shall," said another, winking at his neighbor. "I hope the Germans get their faces bashed in."

At these words a fat seven-footer kicked away his chair and sprang to his feet.

"The Germans will gobble them all up in a single gulp—English, French, and Russians. Cut off my nose if I'm wrong! The German is today's Messiah. He will save the world!"

"Sit down, Germanós!" said the abbot, placing his white hand over his mouth to stifle his laughter.

He turned to us. "Don't listen to him. His name is Germanós, which explains why he became a Germanophile. The brothers tease him."

But just as the conversation began to take a calmer turn, the door was kicked open and in flew a bony, gawky beanstalk of a monk with a cracked skull, the blood flowing down his beard and torn frock.

"Holy Abbot," he cried, "look, the antichrists murdered me because I voted for you the other day in the elections."

The abbot rose, deathly pale.

"Get out of here!" he cried. "Can't you see we have visitors!"

But the monk had no intention of leaving. He took off his hat, which was in shreds and dripping with blood.

"I'm going to hang it before the icon of Saint Paul to let him see how far his monastery has fallen."

The commissioners rose in an agitated state and began to cajole him. He resisted, but little by little they hauled him outside. As for us, we seized our opportunity in the meantime. Slipping between the monks, we made our way out of the hall.

We went down to the cloister, where we paced back and forth in silence. The doorkeeper caught sight of us and understood. Forsaking his little saints and demons, he came over to us bursting with jollity.

"Don't feel bad, my friends," he said. "So you saw Father Innocent, did you? I pulverized his head for him, but it'll heal up again, never fear. It's not the first time."

"But do such things happen in the monastery very often?" asked my friend. "In other words, does the devil enter even here?"

"And where else, my boy! No matter what you do, he'll get in somehow. Once upon a time there was a monastery with three hundred and sixty-five monks. Each monk had three suits of armor and three horses, one white, one red, and one black. They patrolled the monastery three times every day in order to keep the devil from entering: in the morning on the white horses, in the afternoon on the red, and at night on the black."

"And did the devil enter?"

The wily monk laughed.

"Are you joking? All the time they were riding around the monastery on their horses, the devil was sitting on the abbot's throne, inside. It was the abbot."

"And what about you, Saint Doorkeeper?" asked my friend. "Have you ever seen the devil?"

"But naturally! Of course I've seen the devil."

"And what's he like?"

"Chubby and beardless, fair and fluffy. Twelve years old."

He looked at us and winked. "You saw our holy abbot, I presume. How did he strike you? His blessings upon you both!"

Bursting with laughter, he entrenched himself again behind the door.

Five or six monks came now and surrounded us. In an effort to make us forget Innocent's smashed head they took us to pay our respects to the saintly relics conserved piously in a silver reliquary —various bones and the gifts of the Magi: gold, frankincense, and myrrh. These they had us bend over to smell. So many centuries, they said, and the gifts had not lost their fragrance—it was a great miracle!

When we emerged into the courtyard and remained alone, the doorkeeper nodded to us. We went over to him.

"They smell, eh?" he said to us amidst guffaws. "A great miracle! If you pour cologne over them, they smell like cologne. If you pour patchouli, they smell like patchouli. And if you pour gasoline, they smell like gasoline. It's a great miracle, I tell you. What did they smell like today?"

"Roses," said my friend.

"Well, they must have must have poured rosewater over them. You see!"

He doubled over the piece of wood he was carving and nearly died laughing.

"Off with you now, or they'll see I'm talking with you and I'll get into hot water. They take me for a madman, I take them for quacks, and the devil, he'll take every last one of us!"

Dionysíou Monastery. We set off by rowboat early in the morning and proceeded toward Dionysíou.

Father Benedict, our boatman, told us it was the strictest monastery on the Holy Mountain. No matter how merry you felt, you could not laugh; no matter how much wine you drank at this monastery, you could not become drunk. And there was a laurel they had planted in the yard, and if you looked at it carefully, you saw Christ crucified on every leaf.

We had a bishop with us. He was going to Daphne, the port, in order to leave.

"The entire universe, Father Benedict, is a cross with Christ crucified upon it. Not just the laurel leaves, but you and I and the very stones of the ground."

This was too much for me.

"Begging your pardon, Bishop, I see Christ everywhere resurrected."

The bishop shook his head.

"You're in a hurry, in a hurry, my child," he answered me. "We shall see the risen Christ, but only after we die. This our earthly passage, now and as long as we live, is a crucifixion."

A dolphin bounded out of the calm waters, very near to us, its firm supple back gleaming powerfully in the sun. It plunged again, reappeared, soared joyfully—the entire ocean was its province. Suddenly another dolphin appeared in the distance and each raced head-on toward the other. Meeting, they frolicked, then all at once swam off side by side with lifted tails, dancing.

I was overjoyed. Extending my arm, I indicated the two dolphins.

"Is Christ crucified or resurrected?" I asked triumphantly. "What do the two dolphins tell us?"

But we had arrived at Dionysíou, and the bishop did not have time to reply.

The moment we stepped into the courtyard, we halted in terror.

We felt we were entering a damp, dark prison for life-termers. The columns around the periphery were squat and black, the arches between them painted a dark orange. Every inch of the walls was covered with savage paintings of the Apocalypse: devils, hell-fire, prostitutes with two rivers of blood flowing from their breasts, hideous dragons with horns—all of the Church's sadistic longing to intimidate men and bring them to heaven not by love but by fear.

The guestmaster came, the monk who looked after visitors. Seeing us glaring in terror at the paintings, he parted his narrow, yellowish lips maliciously—he seemed overcome with hatred at the sight of two well-dressed, thriving men in the flower of youth.

"Open wide your eyes," he said. "Do not screw up your faces in a grimace. Look! Man's body is full of fires, demons, and whores. The filth you see is not the inferno but the bowels of man."

"Man is created in the image of God," objected my friend. "He is not just this filth, he is something else."

"He was," shrieked the monk, "was, but isn't any more. In the world you live in, the soul has become flesh too. Sin holds it to her breast and nurses it."

"What's to be done, then?" I asked. "Is there no door to salvation?"

"There is, there is. But it is a narrow, dark, and dangerous one. A person doesn't enter easily."

"What door do you mean?"

"Behold!"

He extended his hand and indicated the entrance to the monastery.

"We're not ready yet," said my friend, who had found the monk's words irritating. "Later, when we're old and feeble. The flesh is God's work too."

A venomous smile incised the monk's lips.

"The flesh is the work of the devil," he shrieked. "It's time you learned, you emissaries from the world, that God's work is the soul."

Wrapping himself tightly in his robe as though afraid we might touch him, he disappeared beneath an orange vault.

We remained alone in the center of the courtyard.

"Let's leave," said my friend. "It's obvious that Christ does not live here."

The doors to two or three cells opened. Skeleton-like monks appeared, looked at us, murmured something, then closed their doors again.

"There is no love here," insisted my friend. "Let's leave."

"Don't you feel sorry for them?" I asked. "Suppose we remain here a few days and preach the true Christ? What do you say?"

"To them? Impossible! A waste of effort."

"Nothing ever goes to waste. Even if they're not saved, we shall be for undertaking the impossible."

"Are you serious?" asked my friend, looking at me in amazement.

"If only I knew!" I replied, suddenly overcome by great despondency. "Would that I could actually do it! My heart says to me, If you are really a man, stay here and declare war. But alas! the mind—Satan—does not let me."

Two monks made bold to come to us and bring us inside. They took us around the monastery. We saw a fresco of the giant with the head of a wild boar, Saint Christopher, and were shown his monstrous fang. Then they had us do obeisance to John the Baptist's right hand. In the refectory were two fiery red seraphim, both holding a pair of erect lances in each hand, their snow-white feet planted in the green earth; on the left-hand wall a representation of the Virgin seated between two angels, with bright green trees on both sides, birds perched on the branches, and a slender cypress behind each of the angels; on the dome above us the Pantocrator with a ribbon unwinding from his mouth, and upon the ribbon large red letters. Raising their arms, the monks pointed to the Pantocrator.

"Can you make out what the letters say? *Love one another.* Pronounce those words to a dead stick and it will blossom, but pronounce them to a human being and he will not blossom. We are all headed for hell."

The cemetery was simple and charming, like a balcony overlooking the sea. Just five or six wooden crosses gnawed by wind and salt.

Suddenly a flock of white pigeons flew over us, headed for the water. One of the monks, his eyes filled with murder and hunger, threw up his hand rapaciously as though wishing to catch them.

"God, if I only had a gun!" he murmured, his teeth grating from ravenous hunger.

Our pilgrimage was finally drawing to a close. A few days before our departure I set out by myself to climb to Karoúlia, to the wild hermitages wedged between crags high above the sea. Burrowed in caves there and praying for the sins of the world, each far from his neighbor lest he draw comfort from the sight of another human being, live the most savage and saintly ascetics of the Holy Mountain. Each has a little basket hanging down over the water, and the skiffs which chance to pass from time to time draw up to these baskets and toss in a little bread, a few olives—whatever they have—in order to keep the ascetics from starving to death. Many of these savage ascetics go mad. Believing that they have sprouted wings, they fly out over the precipice and hurl downward. The shore line below is covered with bones.

Living at that time among these hermits was Makários the Speleote, a monk renowned for his sanctity. It was to see him that I departed for Karoúlia. I had made the decision the moment I set foot on the sacred mountain. I wanted to bow, kiss his hand, and confess to him. Not my sins—I did not believe I had committed very many up to that point—not my sins, but the satanic arrogance which frequently goaded me to speak insolently of the seven sacraments and the ten commandments, and made me wish to inscribe my own decalogue.

It was nearly noon when I reached the hermitages—black holes in the cliffside, each with its iron cross implanted in the rock. A skeleton emerged from one of the caves, terrifying me. It was as though the Last Judgment was already upon us and this skeleton had issued from the earth before having time to dress itself in all its flesh. Fear and disgust overwhelmed me, but at the same time a hidden, unconfessed admiration. Not daring to go near him, I asked directions from a distance. Without speaking, he extended a desiccated arm and directed me high above to a black cave at the very edge of the cliff.

I began to climb the crags once more, lacerating myself on their sharp edges. When I reached the cave, I leaned over to peer inside. Complete darkness; odor of soil and incense. Gradually I began to distinguish a tiny jug to the right in a cleft in the rock; nothing else. I was about to call out, but the silence within this darkness seemed so hallowed to me, so disquieting, that I did not dare. Here the human voice, I felt, was like a sin, a sacrilege.

My sight finally grew accustomed to the darkness, and as I peered inward with protruding eyeballs, I saw a gentle phosphorescence—a pale face and two emaciated arms—stir in the depths of the cave and I heard a sweet, gasping voice.

"Welcome!"

Working up courage, I entered the cave and proceeded toward the voice. The ascetic was curled on the ground. He had raised his head, and I was able in the half-light to make out his face as it gleamed in the depths of unutterable beatitude—hairless, with sunken eye sockets, gnawed away by vigils and hunger. All his hair had fallen out, and his head shone like a skull.

"Bless me, Father," I said, bowing to kiss his bony hand.

For a long time neither of us spoke. I kept looking greedily at this soul which had obliterated its body, for this was what weighed down its wings and kept it from mounting to heaven. The soul that believes is a merciless man-eating beast. It had devoured him: flesh, eyes, hair—all.

I did not know what to say, where to begin. The ramshackle body before me seemed like a battlefield following a terrible massacre; upon it I discerned the Tempter's scratches and bites. Finally I gathered up courage.

"Do you still wrestle with the devil, Father Makários?" I asked him.

"Not any longer, my child. I have grown old now, and he has grown old with me. He doesn't have the strength. . . . I wrestle with God."

"With God!" I exclaimed in astonishment. "And you hope to win?"

"I hope to lose, my child. My bones remain with me still, and they continue to resist."

"Yours is a hard life, Father. I too want to be saved. Is there no other way?"

"More agreeable?" asked the ascetic, smiling compassionately.

"More human, Father."

"One, only one."

"What is it?"

"Ascent. To climb a series of steps. From the full stomach to hunger, from the slaked throat to thirst, from joy to suffering. God sits at the summit of hunger, thirst, and suffering; the devil sits at the summit of the comfortable life. Choose."

"I am still young. The world is nice. I have time to choose."

Reaching out with the five bones of his hand, the ascetic touched my knee and pushed me.

"Wake up, my child. Wake up before death wakes you up."

I shuddered.

"I am young," I repeated in order to gain courage.

"Death loves the young. The inferno loves the young. Life is a tiny lighted candle, easily extinguished. Take care—wake up!"

He fell silent for a moment, and then: "Are your ready?"

Possessed by indignation and obstinacy, I shouted, "No!"

"Youthful arrogance! You say that and think it is something to boast about. Stop shouting. Aren't you afraid?"

"Who isn't? Yes, I am afraid. And what about yourself, holy Father, aren't you afraid also? You have hungered, thirsted, suffered; you are about to reach the highest step. The door to paradise appears before you. But will this door open and let you in? Will it? Are you sure?"

Two tears rolled from the corners of his eyes. He sighed. Then, after a brief silence: "I am sure of God's goodness. It is this that conquers and forgives man's sins."

"I too am sure of God's goodness. In other words, this might also forgive my youthful arrogance."

"Woe to us if we depended solely on God's goodness. In that case virtue and vice would enter heaven arm in arm."

"And do you believe, Father, that God's goodness is not sufficiently great to allow that?"

As I uttered these words, across my mind flashed the thought—impious perhaps, but, who knows, perhaps thrice-hallowed—that the time of perfect salvation will come, of perfect reconciliation, when the fires of hell will be extinguished and Satan, the Prodigal Son, will mount to heaven and kiss the Father's hand, tears flowing from his eyes. "I have sinned!" he will cry, and the Father, opening wide his arms, will say, "Welcome, welcome, my son. Forgive me for having tormented you so very much."

But I dared not express my thought directly. Instead, I chose an oblique path as a means of conveying it.

"I've been told, Father, that a certain saint—I don't remember now which one—was unable to find repose in heaven. God heard his sighs and summoned him. 'What's the matter? What makes you sigh?' He asked. 'Aren't you happy?'

" 'How do you expect me to be happy, Lord,' the saint answered him, 'when in the very center of Paradise there is a fountain that weeps?'

" 'What fountain?'

" 'The tears of the damned.' "

The ascetic crossed himself with trembling hands.

"Who are you?" he asked in an expiring, deathlike voice. "Get thee behind me, Satan!"

He crossed himself three more times, and spat into the air. "Get thee behind me, Satan," he repeated. His voice had grown firm now.

I touched his knee, which gleamed nakedly in the half-light. My hand froze.

"Father," I said, "I did not come here to tempt you; I am not the Tempter. I am a young man who wants to believe as my peasant grandfather believed, simply and naïvely, without asking questions. I want to, but I cannot."

"Woe is you, woe is you, unfortunate boy. You shall be devoured by the mind; you shall be devoured by the ego—the 'me,' the self. Do you know when the Archangel Lucifer was hurled into hell, the same you defend and wish to save? It was when he turned to God and said, 'Me.'

"Yes, yes, listen, young man, listen and register this well in your mind: One thing only is punished in the inferno—the ego. Yes, the ego, all curses upon it!"

I shook my head stubbornly. "By means of this ego, this awareness of self, man was separated from the beasts. Do not belittle it, Father Makários."

"By means of this awareness of self, man was separated from God. Originally everything was united with God, contented in His bosom. There was no such thing as you, me, and him, no such thing as yours and mine; there were not two, there was one. One cosmos, one Being. This was the paradise you hear about, this and only this. From here we all had our start. This is what the soul remembers; to this it longs to return. Blessed be death! For what do you suppose death is? It is a mule; we mount this mule and depart."

He spoke, and the more he spoke the more brightly luminous did his features become. A sweet, contented smile suffused outward from his lips and invaded his entire face. You could sense that he was submerged in paradise.

"Why are you smiling, Father?" I asked.

"How can I keep from smiling? I am happy, my child. Each day, each hour, I hear the mule's hoofbeats: I hear death approaching."

I had climbed the rocks with the intention of confessing to this fierce life-denier, but I saw that it was still too soon. Inside me, life had not yet volatilized. I greatly loved the visible world. Lucifer gleamed with brilliance in my mind; he still had not vanished into the blinding brilliance of God. Later, I said to myself; later, when I grow old and feeble, when Lucifer grows feeble inside me.

I rose. The old man raised his head.

"Are you leaving?" he asked. "Good luck. God be with you."

And a moment later, mockingly: "Regards to the world."

"Regards to heaven," I retorted. "And tell God it's not our fault but His—because He made the world so beautiful."

Not all of the monks, however, were happy; not all were sure. I remember one especially, Father Ignatius. My friend and I stayed up talking each night after the monks departed for bed and we were left alone in the guest hall. We discussed our great spiritual concerns and the various pathways man could follow in order to reach God. In addition, we struggled to give a more virginal content to this word which had become so trite in the mouths of priests. Once while we were talking—it must have already been midnight—a voice choked with emotion suddenly bounded out of a dark corner.

"May God enable me to sit here and listen to you for all eternity. I want no other paradise!"

It was Father Ignatius. He had been listening to us, huddled in the semidarkness. Assuredly he did not understand very well what we were saying, but he had been moved by the words *God*, *love*, and *duty* which recurred again and again during our conversation, and above all by the tone and warmth of our voices. Also, perhaps, by how pale our faces looked in the lamplight.

We became friends. From that night onward he remained continually in our presence, not speaking, just listening. You could feel his thirst to hear talk which surpassed the conversation the monks had among themselves. On the eve of our departure he called me to his cell. It was late; my friend was tired and had gone to bed.

"I want to confess to you," he said. "Sit down."

He gave me a stool and I seated myself. I looked at him. His sparse, all-white beard gleamed in the moonlight. His black robe had turned green with age; the material was shiny from wear and grease stains. His cheeks were sunken, his face covered everywhere with deep wrinkles, like a plowed field. His thick, prickly eyebrows beetled over his hollowed, jet-black eyes. He smelled of incense and rancid olive oil. The big toe of his right foot protruded through a rip in his large coarsely made shoes.

For a long while he remained silent, as though he had made a decision which he now regretted.

At last he said, "For the love of God, be patient and listen to me. Do not speak or get up to leave until I have finished my confession. Have pity on me."

His voice was trembling.

"Would you like some coffee?" he asked, as though wishing to postpone the difficult moment. But without waiting for a reply he sat down on his humble bed and clasped his beard, pensive and undecided. I pitied him.

"There is no need for you to hesitate, Father Ignatius," I said. "I am a good person, and I know something about human suffering. Speak freely; unburden yourself."

"It's not a question of suffering," he said—suddenly his senile voice took on strength—"not suffering, but joy. Is joy accursed or blessed? For years I've been tormenting myself in an effort to find out, and I can't. That's why I called you. I need help. Do you understand?"

No sooner had he uttered these words than his heart opened. He hesitated no longer now. Crossing himself and focusing his eyes not on me but on the watch lamp burning opposite him, next to the icon of the Crucified, he began.

"My son, for years and years I tried to see God, but without success. For years I prostrated myself—here, look how callused my hands are. For years after that I cried out, Very well, let me not see God, since I am unworthy. But let me be able to feel His invisible presence so that I too may rejoice if only for a split second and know that I am a Christian and that my years in the monastery were not spent for nothing. I cried out, wept, fasted—in vain! My heart was unable to open and let God enter me. Satan had locked it and he held the keys."

Raising his eyebrows so that he could see me, he turned and glanced in my direction.

"Why am I telling you all this?" he asked, as though scolding me. "Who are you? Where do you come from? What is your business here on the Holy Mountain? Why should I trust you and want to tell you this secret you are about to hear, a secret I still have not divulged even to my confessor, and which is weighing me down and plunging me into hell? Why? Why?"

He looked at me perplexedly, waiting for an answer.

"It might be God's will," I replied. "Perhaps God sent me to the Holy Mountain in order to listen to you, Father Ignatius. How do you expect the human mind to know what ways the Lord chooses in order to unburden you of the weight you were talking about."

The monk bowed his head and lost himself for a moment in thought.

"Perhaps . . ." he said finally. Encouraged, he continued now without stumbling.

"So you see, I tortured myself year after year and felt that my life was going to waste. Prayer, fasting, solitude—none of them helped me in the least. I began to have the terrifying suspicion that this was not the road, not the road which would lead me to God. There must be another road, another road, but which? Whereupon, one day the holy abbot ordered me to go and act as supervisor on a dependency the monastery owned near Salonika. It was summer, harvest time, and I had to be there to keep the sharecroppers from cheating us.

"For twenty-one years I had not set foot outside the monastery, had not seen people with children, heard laughter, set eyes on a woman. The plain outside was broiling hot. I was somewhere around forty years old; twenty-one years in prison, and now the gates had opened and I was inhaling clear air. I had forgotten the sight of children rolling on the ground and playing, of a woman going to the fountain with a jar on her shoulder, of young men drinking in the taverns, a sprig of basil behind their ears. At the dependency's door was a woman holding her baby in her arms and nursing it. For an instant—God forgive me—I thought she was the Virgin Mary and I started to bow down to worship her. I hadn't seen a woman for twenty years, I tell you, and my mind was in a daze.

"As for her, she buttoned up her blouse and concealed her breast as soon as she saw me. Then she leaned over to kiss my hand. 'Welcome, Father,' she said. 'Give us your blessing.'

"But I became angry without knowing why. Drawing back my hand, I shouted, 'Don't nurse where men can see you. Go inside!'

"She blushed. Pulling closed the wimple which was wrapped around her head, she hid her mouth. Then, frightened, without breathing a word, she went inside."

The monk closed his eyes, doubtlessly in order to see the doorway, the woman and the unbuttoned blouse.

"Go on," I said, seeing him remain silent for some time.

"This is where the ascent begins," replied the monk, "the upgrade—I mean the downgrade. We agreed that you are going to listen to me without speaking or getting up to leave. It's not my fault, it's Satan's—no, not even his; everything is God's work. Scripture says that if even a single leaf falls, God has cast it down. How much more, then, if a soul . . . I say this to comfort my conscience, but it cannot be comforted. During the day it says nothing, but at night it rises and shouts at me, The fault is yours!

"I told you about the woman who was standing on the doorstep nursing. From the moment I saw her breast, I could find peace no longer. A great ascetic, Saint Antonius, says, 'If you are at peace and hear the call of a sparrow, your heart no longer has its former peace.' Well then, if the call of a sparrow can throw our hearts into a ferment, what is the naked breast of a woman capable of doing! Don't forget, I was still young when I entered the monastery, and I had never known a woman. Why do I say *known*? Had never touched a woman. What was I to do? How could I exorcise Satan? I threw myself into fasting and prayer; I took the whip used for lashing the oxen at threshing time and lashed my body rabidly, until the whole of me became one great wound. Once more in vain, in vain! If the light of the lamp was lowered just a little, I saw a white breast gleaming in the dimness. And one night I had a dream so terrifying that I still shudder when I think of it."

Suddenly he became tongue-tied; his mouth had grown parched.

But I mercilessly demanded, "What was this dream?"

He wiped the sweat from his brow and caught his breath.

"I dreamed of a white breast—not of a body or a woman. Deep darkness, and in the middle of this darkness a white breast, and I, with my robe, my hat, my beard, was pressed to it and . . . nursing!"

He sighed like a calf, then fell silent.

"Go on, go on," I said mercilessly. My longing to hear had triumphed over the kindness within me. It was not curiosity; it was deep commiseration for this unfortunate man who wanted so much to speak but could not.

"Why are you so insistent—don't you pity me?" asked the monk, gazing at me imploringly.

"No," I answered. But I immediately felt ashamed. "Yes, yes, I do pity you, and that is why I insist. You'll see—as soon as you speak, you'll feel relieved."

"You're right. . . . Yes, as soon as I speak, I will feel relieved. Very well then, listen. Each evening this woman, the one I saw the first day on the doorstep, brought me a plate of food and a cup of wine for my dinner. I ate at first, but then left everything untouched for several days. Each morning when she came to take the things back, she hesitated a moment, as though wishing to ask me why I didn't eat. But she never dared. One night, however . . . It was Sunday and she was rested, she hadn't tired herself from mowing in the fields. She had washed her hair and put on her Sunday clothes, a tight-fitting bodice with red embroidery, I remember. It was warm out; she had unbuttoned her blouse a little, and an inch of her throat was showing. She must also have anointed her hair with laurel oil according to the custom of village women, for it smelled sweetly. I don't know why, but she reminded me of the church on Easter day after we've decorated it with myrtles and have strewn laurel leaves over the floor. The air everywhere smelled of laurels and resurrection.

"She put the plate and wine on the table and working up courage—who knows why: because she was bathed? because she was rested? (a bath, some perfume, an undone button—all are capable of aiding the Tempter to cast a person into hell)—in any case, working up courage this time, she did not go away but stood where she was.

" 'Why haven't you eaten these last few days, Father Ignatius?' she asked, her voice full of compassion and concern. To tell you the truth, it was just as if her son had not nursed for some days, and she was worried that he might be ill.

"I gave no answer. Still she did not leave. Do you know why? You are young still, and you don't. It was because the devil inside a woman's womb does not sleep; he works.

" 'You'll ruin your health, Father Ignatius,' she said. 'The body is God's work too, and we must feed it.'

" 'Get thee behind me, Satan,' I murmured to myself, and I refused to raise my eyes to look at the woman.

"Suddenly I uttered a cry as though drowning: 'Go away!'

"The woman became frightened and ran toward the door. But as I saw her nearing it, apparently I became frightened too. I was afraid she might leave me. Dashing forward, I seized her by the hair. I blew out the lamp to keep the Crucified from seeing. The light fled; darkness is Satan's dwelling place. Still holding her by the hair, I threw her down on the bed. I was lowing like a calf; she was silent. I grabbed hold of her bodice, tugged at it, and with one motion undid all the buttons of her blouse.

"How many years have gone by since then? Thirty? Forty? No, none. Time has stood still. Have you ever in your life seen time stand still? I have. For thirty years I have been unbuttoning her blouse and there is no end to it; there is always one more button!

"I kept her with me until dawn, not letting her leave. Good God, what joy that was, what an unburdening, what a resurrection! My whole life I had been crucified; that night I was resurrected. But there was also something else, the terrible part, the part which I believe alone constituted my sin. That is why I brought you here to my cell, to have you untangle the puzzle for me. The terrible part was this: for the very first time I felt God come near me, come near with open arms. What gratitude I felt; what prayers I offered up the whole of that night, right until daybreak; how completely my heart opened and let God enter! For the first time in my life—Oh, I'd read it in Scripture before, but those were just words—for the first time in my inhuman, cheerless life I understood to what degree God is all-good, to what degree He loves man, and how very much He must have pitied him in order to have created woman and favored her with such grace that she leads us to paradise along the surest and shortest of roads. Woman is more powerful than prayer, fasting, and—forgive me, Lord—even than virtue."

He stopped, terrified by the words he had just uttered. Two tears rolled from his tiny eyebrow-engulfed eyes as he cast a frightened glance at the Crucified.

"Forgive me, Christ!" he bellowed, and he closed his eyes so that he would not see the icon.

But presently he recovered somewhat, opened his eyes, and looked at me. I was about to part my lips to say something. I had no idea what, but I could not stand the silence, and the tears which kept rolling from the aged eyes frightened me. But before I had a chance to utter a word, he reached out his hand as though to place it over my lips.

"Wait," he said. "I haven't finished.

"At daybreak the woman got up hastily, dressed herself, then opened the door quietly and left. I shut my eyes and began to weep, lying in bed on my back. But those tears were not like the bitterly rancorous ones I had shed in my cell; they had an inexpressible sweetness about them, because I felt that God was in my room and bending over my pillow. I was certain that if I held out my hand I would touch Him. But I wasn't a doubting Thomas; I had no need to extend my finger to touch Him. A woman had given me this certainty—a woman, I repeat, and not prayer or fasting. It was Woman, God bless her! who brought the Lord into my room.

"Ever since that night thirty, forty, years ago, I have sat and thought to myself, Can sin too be in God's service? Oh, I know what you'll tell me (it's what they all say): Yes, certainly, provided you repent. But I did not repent. I say this openly—let God's thunderbolt fall on me if it will and reduce me to ashes—I did not, and will not, repent! If I had the chance to do it again, I would."

He removed his hat to scratch his head. His white hair spilled down, covering his face. For a short while he remained lost in thought. I sensed that he felt hesitant about carrying this any further, but finally he made his decision.

"Or is it possible that what I did was not a sin? And if it was not, what then is the meaning of original sin, the serpent, and the apple from the forbidden tree? I do not understand; that is why I called you here. Perhaps you understand; that is why I called you. I am clinging to life with the two or three bones left to me. I want to understand before I die. . . . Why don't you say something? It seems that you are just as confused as I am, my child."

What could I say? Was sin in God's service? It was the first time this question had come to torment me. Parallel to the road of virtue was there another wider, more level road, the road of sin, which could lead us to God?

"Father Ignatius," I replied, "I am still too young. I have not had time yet to commit many sins or to suffer very much, and therefore I cannot answer your question. I don't want to set my mind up as the judge; I don't trust it. Nor my heart; I don't trust that either. The one always condemns; the other always pardons. How can I ever decide which is right? The mind says, Father Ingatius, this road of sin which you say leads you to God is much too pleasant and convenient; I refuse to accept it. The heart, on the other hand, says, It is impossible that God should be so cruel and unjust to want man to suffer martyrdom, hunger, nakedness, and humiliation. In other words, are madmen and physical wrecks the only ones capable of entering His house? I refuse to accept this. . . . So you see, Father Ignatius, what conclusion can I draw, believing as I do that both views are right?"

As I was speaking, I thought to myself without voicing my thought, A new decalogue is needed! A new decalogue! . . . Just how this new decalogue would classify the virtues and vices, however, I was unable to discover. What I kept saying over and over to myself was simply this: A new decalogue, a new decalogue is absolutely necessary. Who will give it to us?

The cell's tiny window had begun to glow with a feeble light; from the monastery courtyard came the melodious beating of the wooden semantron as it progressed from cell to cell, summoning the monks to matins.

Father Ignatius glanced at the window.

"Daylight already," he murmured, astonished. "Daylight already . . ."

He dragged himself to a corner. Bending over with groans because of the pains in the small of his back, he picked up a tiny cruet and, going to the Crucifix, poured a little oil into the watch lamp suspended before it. The tiny flame received a new lease on life, illuminating Christ's face, those yellowish, afflicted features with the blood dripping from the crown of thorns onto the brow and cheeks.

The monk kept his eyes pinned on this face for a long time. Then, sighing, he turned to me.

"In short, you have no answer to give me? Nothing?"

His tone was derisive, or so it seemed. I had risen from my stool. Standing next to the monk, I gazed with him at the Crucified. I was tired and wanted to go to sleep.

"Nothing," I answered.

"Oh, well, it doesn't matter," said the monk. He took his staff from the corner, ready to go to matins. Then he placed himself once more in front of the icon to do obeisance. His withered, lifeless face gleamed beneath the lamplight. Lifting his finger, he indicated the Crucified to me.

"He gave an answer," he said.

Just at that moment there was a knock on the cell door. A voice called, "Father Ignatius . . ."

"I'm coming, holy Abbot," replied the monk, and he drew back the bolt.

As I turn over the yellowed pages of my journal, it becomes clear that nothing died. Everything was simply asleep inside me. Look how all has awakened now, how everything rises from the worn, half-indecipherable pages to become monasteries, monks, paintings, and the sea once more! And my friend, he too rises from the soil as he was at that time, handsome, in the flower of youth, with his Homeric laugh, his blue eagle-eye, his breast filled with poems! He gave men more than they were able to receive, he sought from them more than they were able to give, and he died forsaken and sorrowful, having been left with nothing but the bitter smile of a proud, wounded soul. A meteor, he conquered the darkness for an instant and then perished. Such is the way we all shall perish, such the way the earth too will perish; but this fact offers no consolation, nor is it any justification for He who begets and then destroys us.

We had toured the Holy Mountain for forty days. When, completing our circle, we finally returned to Daphne on Christmas Eve in order to depart, the most unexpected, most decisive miracle was awaiting us. Though it was the heart of winter, there in a small, humble orchard was an almond tree in bloom!

Seizing my friend's arm, I pointed to the blossoming tree.

"Angelos," I said, "during the whole of this pilgrimage our hearts have been tormented by many intricate questions. Now, behold the answer!"

My friend riveted his blue eyes upon the flowering almond tree and crossed himself, as though doing obeisance before a holy wonder-working icon. He remained speechless for a long moment. Then, speaking slowly, he said, "A poem is rising to my lips, a tiny little poem: a haïkai."

He looked again at the almond tree.

I said to the almond tree,
"Sister, speak to me of God."
And the almond tree blossomed.

20

JERUSALEM

When I was alone again, I closed my eyes and asked myself what finally remained from the Holy Mountain. Out of so many pleasures and moving experiences, so many questions tormenting my friend and myself, what had finally deposited itself within me? What was I seeking when I went to the Holy Mountain, and what did I find there?

The old wounds inflicted during my adolescence when my teacher divulged the two great secrets to me, that the earth is not the center of the universe and that man is not a privileged creature issuing directly from the divine hand, these old wounds, which had been closed for a number of years, opened once again on the Holy Mountain—the two metaphysical torments: where do we come from and where are we going. One answer had been given by Christ. He brought a balm which healed many wounds. But was this balm able to heal my wounds? For a brief moment the semantron, matins, psalmody, and paintings—the divine rhythm of the ascetic life—had calmed my anguish. Experiencing Christ's struggle at first hand, I felt my own struggle take on courage, sweetness, and hope. But the enchantment was quickly dispelled and once more my soul found itself deserted. Why? What did it lack, whom did it lack? What was my soul seeking when it went to the Holy Mountain, and what did it fail to find there?

As the years passed, I began little by little to have a premonition that I had gone to the Holy Mountain in search of something I have sought throughout my life: a great friend and enemy not of my own stature but bigger, who would enter the struggle at my side. Not a woman, not an idea. Something else. Someone else. This was the thing, the person, my soul lacked; this was why it felt stifled.

Only afterwards, not while I was there, did I realize that I had failed to find this someone on the Holy Mountain. Was precisely this, I wonder, the fruit of my entire journey over Athos?

The only thing I found as I roamed the Holy Mountain was a veteran campaigner (so he seemed to me at first) holding out his wounded hands to the monks who passed. His naked feet were dripping with blood, his cheeks sunken from hunger, his clothes in tatters, revealing his emaciated body. Shivering, his eyes filled with tears, he knocked on every door, but no one admitted him. He was chased from monastery to monastery, and the dogs ran in back of his ragged cloak and barked. One evening I saw him seated on a stone gazing at the desolate sea. I hid behind a fir tree and spied on him. For a long time he remained silent, but then, unable to restrain himself any longer, he suddenly cried out, "The foxes have holes, but I have not where to lay my head!" A flash tore across my mind, I recognized Him and ran to kiss His hand. I had loved Him when I was a small child, had loved Him ever since. Now I searched everywhere, but He had become invisible. Feeling aggrieved, I sat down on the stone where He had been sitting. Oh, if I could only open my heart to Him so that He might enter it and not have to wander homeless and cold! I thought of the philosopher Proclus, who lived at the time when men had ceased to believe in the gods of Olympus and were rejecting them. Proclus lay asleep in a shack at the foot of the Acropolis; suddenly, in the middle of the night, he heard someone knocking on his door. Jumping up and running to see who it was, he discovered Athena standing in full panoply on his threshold. "Proclus," she said, "I am rejected wherever I go. I have come to take refuge in your forehead!"

Would that Christ, in a similar way, could take refuge in my heart!

Returning from Mount Athos, I felt for the first time that Christ wanders about hungry and homeless, that He is in danger, and that now it is His turn to be saved—by man.

I was overwhelmed by great sorrow and compassion. Not wanting to return to a life of tranquility and comfort, I took to the road and marched for days and days through the Macedonian mountains, until I found a dark, miserable, woebegone little village—hovels stuccoed over with oxdung, a flock of children and pigs splashing in the mud. The men looked at me with scowling faces;

when I greeted them, they did not answer. The women, as soon as they saw me, slammed their doors.

This is just the place for me, I said to myself. O my soul, here in this horrible village of horrible people, you will demonstrate if you are able to endure.

The wounded Campaigner did not leave my thoughts. Wanting to mortify my body, I decided to spend the winter in this village.

After no end of trouble I finally succeeded in making an old shepherd comprehend that I was neither a criminal, Freemason, nor madman. He consented to rent me one corner of his hut and to give me a little milk and bread each day. There being more than enough wood, I sat and read in front of the fire. I had nothing with me except the Gospels and Homer; at times I read Christ's words of love and humility, at times the immortal verses of the Patriarch of the Greeks. You should be good, peaceful, forbearing; when you are slapped on one cheek you should turn the other; this life on earth has no value, the true life is in heaven—thus dictated the first. You should be strong, should love wine, women, and war; should kill and be killed in order to hold aloft the dignity and pride of man; love this earthly life, better a slave and alive than a king in Hades—thus dictated the second, the grandfather of Greece.

The Achaeans rose to the edge of my mind, the Achaeans with their large noses, their greaves, their broad callused feet, hairy thighs, pointed beards, long greasy mops of hair, their odor of wine and garlic. And there was Helen promenading untouched and immortal on the walls, radiantly pure in the light, with only the arched soles of her feet submerged in blood; and the gods, enthroned reposefully in the clouds above, passing their time by watching men slaughter one another.

Here in my solitude I pricked up my ears and listened to these two Sirens. I listened to them both. Their talons embedded in my entrails, both were deeply bewitching me, and I had no idea to which of these two Sirens' ghosts I should render up my bones.

There was snow outside; I used to look through the tiny window and watch the falling flakes cover the hamlet's ugliness. Each morning flocks of sheep passed, waking me with their bells. I jumped out of bed and climbed the snow-covered paths with them, exchanging a few words with the shepherd on the subjects of poverty, the cold, the sheep that died. Never once did I hear a shepherd speak of anything pleasant; it was nothing but poverty, the cold, the sheep that died.

On one particular day when everything had been covered with a plump bed of snow, the village chimes began to toll mournfully; someone must have died. The villagers had locked themselves inside their houses. From time to time a mule's bell sounded in the motionless air. Through my window I could see famished crows flying back and forth. I had lighted a fire; the warmth clasped me in a tenderhearted embrace, like a mother. I felt that I was completely happy. But then, suddenly, as though joy were treasonous and a great sin, weeping broke out within me—a tranquil, despairing, tender weeping, as from a mother singing a lullaby to her dead son.

This was not the first time I had heard this inner weeping. Whenever I felt sad, it grew a little milder, sounding to me like the remote humming of bees. Whenever I was happy, however, it raged uncontrollably. I used to cry out in fear, "Who is weeping inside me? For what reason? What have I done wrong?"

Night had fallen. As I gazed into the fire my heart resisted. It refused to join the lamentations. Why should I begin to wail and lament? No great sorrow was crushing my soul. I had quiet and warmth, the house's peasant air smelled of sage and quince, I was sitting before the hearth and reading Homer—I was happy. "I am happy," I cried. "What do I lack? Nothing! Well then, who or what is weeping inside me? What does he want? What does he want with me?"

For a moment I thought I heard a knock on the door. I got up but found no one. The sky was absolutely clear, the stars burning like lighted coals. I leaned over and searched the snow-covered road in the starlight to see if perchance I might discover human footprints. Nothing. I cupped my ear and listened. A dog was barking lugubriously at the edge of the village; it must have seen Charon roaming over the snow. An aged but robust and seemingly immortal shepherd had fallen into a ravine two days before and had spent this entire day giving up the ghost, the whole village bellowing from the thunderous râles of his death agony. Now he was silent, and nothing could be heard except his dog's barked lamentations.

He must have died, I said to myself with a shudder. Death angered me. Consoling words about Second Comings and future existences still had not managed to seduce me; but on the other hand, neither had I acquired the strength to confront death fearlessly.

I plunged once more into Homer, as though seeking refuge at the old grandfather's knees. The immortal verses began to roll like waves again and break over my temples. Across the centuries, I heard the din raised by gods and mortals striking out with their lances; I saw Helen as she walked slowly along the Trojan walls surrounded by the old men of the city, and seeing her, I struggled to forget. But my thoughts were on death. Oh, I said to myself, if only man's heart were omnipotent, powerful enough to wrestle with death! If only it were like Mary Magdalene—Mary Magdalene the prostitute—and could resurrect the beloved corpse!

I felt stricken at heart. Alas, how could I in my turn manage to resurrect Him and find relief! He, I sensed, was the one lying still dead in my entrails, the one who kept weeping. He was struggling to rise, but could not without man's help, and on account of this He felt great resentment toward me. How was I to save Him—and be saved?

My grandfather would have boarded his corsair and sailed out to the straits to ram Turkish sloops, since he held Turks and Jews equally responsible for crucifying Christ. He would have vented his spleen in this way and found relief. My father would have mounted his mare and likewise assaulted the infidels, returning from battle at night to hang the gory turbans of Christendom's foes on our household iconostasis, beneath the icon of the Crucified. In this way he too would have found relief and, in his own fashion, felt Christ being resurrected in his heart. After all, my father was a warrior, and war was his way both of delivering and receiving deliverance.

But what was I, the dregs of our lineage, to do?

High up in the mountains of Crete it sometimes happens, though rarely, that a milksop is born into a family of ogres. The old sire looks him over, looks him over once more, and is at a loss to understand. How the devil did this refuse, this jellyfish, issue from his loins? He calls into council the rest of the beasts he has engendered, his sons, to see what can be done with him. "He is a disgrace to our lineage," roars the old man. "What are we going to make of him, boys? He can't be a shepherd; how can he vault into other sheepfolds to steal? He can't be a fighter; it grieves him to kill. He's a disgrace to our stock; let's make him a schoolteacher!"

I, alas, was the schoolteacher of our family. But why resist? I might as well become resigned to it. No matter how much my ancestors might despise me, I too had my weapons, and I would go to war.

It was snowing out. God was mercifully covering the world's unseemliness with His snow. The rags hanging on the fence around the Macedonian hovel I occupied had become precious white furs, and the dormant thistles had all blossomed. Occasionally you heard a baby's wail, a dog's bark, the voice of a man; but everything became immediately mute once more, and then you heard nothing but silence, the voice of God.

Tossing a log onto the fire and also an armful of laurel branches to make the air fragrant, I bent over my Homer again. But my thoughts were no longer with Achaeans, Trojans, and Olympian gods; the sun-washed vision flitted before my eyes like a butterfly and vanished. Once again I heard my entrails weep.

He was lying inside the sepulcher, expecting the Disciples to run, roll back the stone, crouch in the darkness and call Him, whereupon He would rise again to earth. But no one had come. Feeling aggrieved, He was weeping.

As I stared into the dying flames, I saw the panic-stricken Disciples gathered together in an attic. "The Rabbi is dead, he is dead." They were awaiting nightfall so that they could leave Jerusalem and disperse. But a woman jumped up. She alone refused to accept His death, for Christ had risen within her heart. Barefooted, unkempt, half naked, she ran toward the tomb at the break of day. Certain that she would see Christ, she saw Him; certain that Christ had been resurrected, she resurrected Him. "Rabbi!" she cried, and inside his tomb the Rabbi heard her voice, bounded to his feet, and appeared to her in the dawnlight, walking on the springtime grass.

My brain filled with this vision of resurrection. A slight, extremely sweet fever weighed down my eyelids, and the blood began to throb vigorously at my temples. Just as when a wind blows vigorously, the clouds scatter, reunite, are metamorphosed into men, animals, and ships, so in the same manner inside me, as I huddled next to the fire, my mind blew and the vision within me became dismembered and transformed, turning into human faces clothed in longing and wind. But these faces would likewise quickly disperse into smokelike rings in my head, unless words came—at first timid and uncertain, then continually more impetuous and sure—to jell that which cannot be jelled. I understood: the spermatic, generative wind which had blown into my entrails had taken on substance, become an embryo, and was kicking now in a desire to emerge.

Taking up my pen, I commenced to write and to relieve myself—to give birth.

I did not begin at the beginning. It was Magdalene who sprang out first of all, apprehensive, bathed in tears, her hair undone. She had awakened with a start, before daybreak. She must have seen the Rabbi in her dreams. Like the fowler enticing his prey, she began to call him:

Oh how wonderful! I cannot lift
my head, so fragrant is the air. Arise,
my heart, and beat the ground to force it open!
My earthen shoulders skip like wings, but dawn
is slow in coming, the body oh so heavy.
Do not hasten, soul, before I clothe myself
and go. See, as a bride I dress and preen.
My palms and soles I paint with henna, my eyes
with dilute kohl, and a beauty spot joins my brows.
For as love the earth, so majestic heaven gently
beats my breast, and bowing down, I
accept the Word with joy and lamentation,
as if it were a man. And when by flowering
paths I finally reach your beloved tomb,
like a woman, Christ, forsaken by her lover,
shall I clasp your pallid knees, that never
may you leave me. . . . I shall talk, and clasp
your pallid knees. . . . Though all deny you, Christ,
you will not die, for in my breast I hold
the immortal water; I give it you, and upon the

earth you mount once more and walk with me
in the meadows. I shall sing like the love-struck
bird that sits upon the almond branch in
snowtime and warbles in a rapture, its beak
raised high toward heaven, until the branch sprouts blossoms.

I could not sleep; I was in a terrible hurry, because now that the faces had solidified for an instant, I wanted to be in time to take them—the Apostles, Magdalene, Christ; the mist that becomes corporeal, the lie that becomes truth, the soul that sings from its perch on the highest branch of hope—and stabilize them permanently with sure, firm words.

At the end of a few days and nights the manuscript of the entire drama lay upon my knees. I held it tightly, just as a mother holds her son after childbirth.

Lent had started and Easter was approaching. I began to go for strolls in the fields. The world had become a paradise; the snows of Olympus sparkled in the sunlight while the fields below shone bright green and the returning swallows, like shuttles of a loom, wove spring into the air. Small white and yellow wildflowers, pushing up the soil with their tiny heads, began to emerge into the sunlight in order to see the world above. Someone must have rolled back the earthen tombstones above them: they were being resurrected. Someone? . . . Who? Doubtlessly God, God of the innumerable faces: sometimes a flower, sometimes a bird or a fresh shoot on a grapevine, sometimes wheat.

As I strolled through the blossoming fields, a gentle vertigo transformed time and place around me. I seemed to be walking in Palestine rather than Greece; I could discern the still-fresh traces left by Christ's feet on the frothy springtime soil, while around me towered the holy mountains of Carmel, Gilboa, and Tabor. These were not stalks of wheat springing from the ground until they reached the height of a man, they were Christ springing from the tomb; those were not red anemones, they were Christ's holy blood.

Somebody once asked Rabbi Nahman, "What do you mean when you preach that we should go to Palestine? Surely Palestine is simply an idea, a faraway ideal which Jewish souls must someday reach." Nahman became angry. Driving his staff into the ground, he shouted, "No, no! When I say Palestine, I mean its stones, vegetation, and soil. Palestine is not an idea, it is stones, vegetation, and soil. That is where we must go!"

That is where I must go, I told myself. To see and touch Palestine's warm body, and not simply to enjoy it in my imagination while sauntering over the mountains and fields of Greece; to breathe the air, tread the ground, touch the stones that Christ breathed, trod, and touched; to follow the drops of blood which marked out His passage among men. Yes, I must leave! Perhaps there in Palestine I will find what I sought in vain at the Holy Mountain.

Once more the wind of embarkment blew across my mind. How long would it continue to do so? God grant until my death! What joy to cast off from dry land and depart! To snip the string which ties us to certitude and depart! To look behind us and see the men and mountains we love receding into the distance!

Holy Week was approaching. Throughout all of Christendom Christ would be crucified; the five immortal wounds would reopen, and the heart—Mary Magdalene—would come once more to wrestle with death. What happiness when a man has a heart still like a child's and he can suffer during these days: be unable to eat, sleep, or control his tears when at the vigils he sees the lemon-flower-covered body of his God writhing on the cross! What further happiness when, spring entering through the open windows of the church, he is in love with a girl, his first love, and they have promised to meet at noon of Good Friday to do obeisance together by kissing the Crucified's feet, and he, being so terribly young, trembles because he believes he is committing a sin to join his lips with a woman's upon the body of God.

Closing my Homer, I kissed the immortal grandfather's hand, without daring, however, to lift my head and look him straight in the eye. I was ashamed and afraid before him, because I knew only too well that I was betraying him at that moment: leaving him behind me and taking along his great enemy, the Bible.

Neither heaven nor earth had awakened yet—just a cock on a rooftop, craning its neck toward the east and calling the sun (the night had lasted far too long!) finally to appear.

As though afraid the old grandfather might hear me, I opened the door stealthily, like a thief, and took the road to the harbor in order to set sail. Hordes of men and women had come down from their villages to depart like myself for Palestine and do obeisance at the Holy Sepulcher. I shall never forget that evening of embarkment—the tenderness, the sweetness, the compassion of it! There was a gentle, ruthful drizzle, and if you had raised your head to look at the sky, you would have seen God's face filled with tears.

On the boat itself, greasy quilts and blankets of many colors had been spread out on deck. Throngs of old women were opening their baskets and chewing; the air smelled of fish roe and onions. In the center stood an elderly man with rose-red cheeks and long gray hair. His torso swaying back and forth, he read the Christ story in a loud, chanting voice—Christ's life and passion: how the Bridegroom came to Jerusalem, after that how He and the Disciples ate the bitter Lord's Supper, how the traitorous disciple left hastily, and how Jesus climbed the Mount of Olives, the sweat running from His forehead "like clots of blood."

The little old black-mantled women sighed, swayed their heads, listened with deep emotion, all the while chewing away calmly and noiselessly, like sheep. God, in their simple hearts, was once more taking on flesh, being crucified, saving mankind. A young shepherd, his back turned toward the women, listened intently as he leaned over, penknife in hand, and whittled the head of a bird on the top of his crook.

Suddenly, when Christ's broiling throat finally became unbearably parched and He cried out, "I thirst!" a youngish, rather plump woman jumped up in a frenzy and shouted, "O my son!" How disturbed I felt at hearing the woman's deep, maternal cry, at hearing her call God himself her son!

We had left the Aegean behind us now and were approaching the Near East. Africa lay invisible on our right, Cyprus stood to our left on the horizon. The fiery sea was flashing. Two butterflies flew up above the rigging. A small, famished bird had been following us; it darted forward and ate one of them. When a pale and delicate girl began to scream in protest, someone said, "Forget about it; that's the way it should be. What do you think God is—some delicate lady?"

We were drawing near the sun-baked land where once upon a time a flame had bounded out of a poor cottage in Nazareth, a flame which burned and renewed man's heart. Life today is again in a state of decomposition, just as it was two thousand years ago, but the problems currently shattering the equilibrium between mind and heart are more intricate, the solutions more difficult and bloody. Then, a simple message of utmost sweetness was found, and salvation rose to the earth's surface like the season of spring. No simpler, sweeter message exists. Perhaps this message is capable of saving us even now—who can tell? That was why we were going to Jerusalem: to listen once more to the Son of Mary.

It was nighttime. I stretched out on the deck to go to sleep, but a violent debate had begun to rage in the hold below, and I lent an ear. Someone, a young man, judging from the quality of his voice, was passionately condemning the dishonesty and injustice of present-day economic and social life. The masses went hungry while the great and powerful piled up fortunes. Women sold themselves, priests did not believe, both heaven and the infernal pit were here on earth. The afterlife did not exist; here was where we had to find justice and happiness. . . . Cries rang out: "Yes, yes, you're right!" "Fire and the axe!" Only one person attempted to object. I recognized him by his chanting inflection as the deacon traveling with us. But his voice was drowned in shouts and laughter.

Springing off my pillow, I listened greedily. This ship's hold seemed like a new catacomb in which slaves had assembled once more—today's slaves—to conspire to blow the world up all over again. It was frightening. The purpose of our trip was to worship the sweet, familiar face of God—so gentle, so tortured, so filled with hopes for life everlasting. The little old women were bringing Him consecrated bread, silver ex-votos, candles, tears, and prayers. High up in first class, the carefree faithless talked politics or slept, while here below, deep down in the hold, we were carrying as a terrifying gift the seed of a new, dangerous, and as yet unformed cosmogony.

A beloved and sacrosanct world was in danger; another, a harsh world all mud and flame, was rising full of life from the soil and man's heart. Hidden deep down in the hold, it straddled every boat, and traveled.

The next morning we began to see the Promised Land—a distant line on the horizon at first, invisible in the milky haze; then the low mountains of Judea, gray in the beginning, afterwards light blue, finally vanishing, drowned in the powerful light of day. The little old ladies rose. Gathering together their bundles and tying their black wimples over their heads, they began to cross themselves and weep.

Sand, genial orchards, swarthy, greasy women, prickly pears, date trees; the climb to the holy city in panting buses. Suddenly every heart beat violently. Walls, battlements, fortified gates; odor of dung, spices, and rotted fruit. White jelabs, fierce guttural voices. The shades of all the murdered prophets rose from the soil; the stones came to life and cried out, all covered with blood.

Jerusalem!

I neither desire to recall that Holy Week, nor dare. During those seven days the whole of man's tragic adventure finally became manifest—the hope and love, the betrayal and sacrifice, the cry of "My God, my God, why hast Thou forsaken me?" Not Christ but man—every just and pure man—was being betrayed, scourged, and crucified, without God offering His hand to help. Indeed, had woman's warm heart not been present, God would have left man to lie within the tomb forever. Our salvation hangs upon a thread, upon a cry of love.

One night led to the next, bringing me finally to the holy dawn of Easter Day. The Temple of the Resurrection was buzzing like an immense hive. It smelled of beeswax and human perspiration—the sweaty white, brown, and black armpits of men and women who had slept that night beneath the temple vaults, awaiting the universe-generating moment when the holy light would spring from Christ's Sepulcher. Everywhere a deep acid stench of wax and rancid oil. Underneath the holy icons coffee boiled in little pots and mothers bared their breasts to nurse their infants. The Negresses must have anointed their hair with tallow; it had melted, making them smell like sheep. Their menfolk exuded the insupportable fetor of billy goats.

Wave after wave of pilgrims arrived, filling the temple to overflowing. Some climbed the columns, others straddled the stalls. Still others drooped over the women's gallery, their excited, transfixed eyes riveted to the small tabernacle in the center of the church, from which the holy light would spring at any moment.

Abyssinians and Bedouins, Negroes with fezzes, with multicolored jelabs and flaming rheumy eyes—all the races of mankind—shouting, laughing, sighing. A young man fainted, was lifted up and deposited stiff as a board in the courtyard; a slender elderly Maronite priest clothed in a snow-white soutane and red sash fell to the paving stones foaming at the mouth.

Suddenly the multitude grew silent. The air filled with burning eyes. The Patriarch had appeared, dressed all in gold. Alone, without speaking, he lowered his head and stepped beneath the holy tabernacle at the center of the church. Mothers lifted their children to their shoulders so that they could see; the fellahs stood with hanging jaws. Each second fell like a thick drop upon our heads, the air tautened until it rasped like a drumhead, and behold! a gleam leaped from the sacred canopy, and the Patriarch emerged with a thick bundle of burning white candles in his hand. In a flash the temple was flooded with flames from base to top. All the onlookers, holding their white candles, had dashed toward the Patriarch to receive the light. They put their hands into the flame and rubbed their faces and breasts. The women were shrieking; the men began to dance. Howling, everyone poured out toward the door to leave.

The temple remained empty. The fearful din, the frenzied crowd, the multicolored tatters—all seemed like some exotic dream. Looking down at the floor, however, I ascertained that this entire vision had been true, for below me on the paving stones I saw the certain remains of ecstasy: orange peels, olive pits, and broken bottles.

I went out to the courtyard to breathe fresh air. I longed to go away, to take to the desolate, denuded mountains opposite me and walk and walk, without seeing anything but sun, moon, and stones. For the entire time that mass intoxication raged around me and the faithful rushed forward in a transport, calling Christ—commanding Him—to emerge from the tomb, I had restrained myself and refused to allow my heart to become drunk. The soul, like the body, has its modesty; it refuses to disrobe in public. But as soon as I was alone, I cried to myself, Away, away! To the wilderness! There God blows like a scorching wind; I shall undress and have Him burn me.

"Stay, Madam Soul," said God, "do not leave." "What do you

want of me, Lord?" "I want you to undress, Madam Soul." "Lord, how can you ask such a thing of me? I'm ashamed." "Madam Soul, nothing must stand between us, not even the most delicate of veils. Therefore, madam, you must undress." "Here I am, Lord. I have undressed. Take me!"

Singing to myself these immortal words of a soul in love with God, I set out along the road to the Dead Sea. I longed to see the pit opened by the two sinful cities that were engulfed. The gray, yellow, and rose-red crags steamed as a fierce, gelatinous sun dripped upon them. Every so often a breath of scorching wind filled my mouth and soul with sand. The stones were on fire. Not a flower, not a drop of water, not a single songbird to emit a sound to welcome the passer-by or jeer him away. Suspended above me was God, only God—like a sword.

This God is not Christ, I thought to myself with a shudder. He is not the kind, sweetly speaking son of Mary. He is Jehovah, the terrifying man-eater. I sought the one and found the other. How can I escape at this point from the dark, impenetrable precincts of His silence?

The more the desert swallowed me up, the more my head caught fire. I began to call on God to appear and speak to me. Had He not created me a man? Was not man the animal that asked questions? Well, I was questioning; He ought to reply. I addressed Him softly in the scorching wind. "Lord," I confessed, "I am passing through a difficult moment. What should I do? Place a live coal in my mouth, a word, the simple word which brings salvation. This is why I have descended into this deep well, this well blinded by excessive light—to talk with You. Reveal Yourself!"

I waited and waited. No answer.

Ever since my childhood years when I read the lives of the saints in our family courtyard, I had been burning with the desire to set foot on this soil I was now treading, burning with the desire to tread the soil and stones trodden by Christ, and to hear His voice. I had always had something to say to Him (and still have). He would take pity on me, would He not? Yes, He would answer! As the world rolls along, it changes its questions, anguishes, and devils. Christ might therefore have some new word to cure the new wounds, to give a new and more virile face to love.

Talking to myself in this way, I proceeded, inhaling the same desert air composed of flames and sand that the prophets had inhaled and received into their bowels. As I was arriving at the depths of the funnel, suddenly the Dead Sea gleamed before me, motionless and ashen, like molten lead, filled with slimy, jellied, tarry water; and flowing from it toward Palestine between reeds and tamarisk, was the blue-green River Jordan. Groups of men in long shirts were crossing themselves. A priest stood chanting on the riverbank while they plunged into the sanctified water and became hadjis.

A tavern had been set up along the bank beneath a roof of woven reeds. While an antique phonograph raucously mewed Arab amanédhes, the rotund tavern-keeper, whose jelab was covered everywhere with grease stains, fried lamb livers and accompanied the phonograph in a bellowing voice.

Quickening my pace, I skirted the venomous shore line of the Dead Sea and re-entered the desert, my excited, startled eyes pinned on the lifeless waters as though toiling to discern the twin cities submerged at their bottom. And as I looked, a yellow flash tore across my mind. I saw—saw that some all-powerful foot had come along here, angrily trampling the two cities of Sodom and Gomorrah, and submerging them. I was heart-stricken. One day our own Sodom and Gomorrah would be trampled by some all-powerful foot, and this world which laughed, reveled, and forgot God would be transformed, in its turn, into a Dead Sea. At the end of every period God's foot comes along in this way and tramples the cities of the overindulged belly, the overdeveloped mind.

I felt afraid. (Sometimes it seems to me that this world is another Sodom and Gomorrah just before God's passage above it. I think the terrible foot can already be heard approaching.)

I halted on a low sand dune and gazed for a long time at the accursed water struggling to haul those charming, sinful cities up out of the tarry bowels. I wanted them to shine again for a brief instant in the sunlight, just long enough for me to catch a glimpse of them. Then I would bat my eyelashes once more, and they would vanish.

Sodom and Gomorrah reclined along the riverbank like two whores kissing each other. Men copulated with other men, women with other women, men with mares, women with bulls. They ate and overate from the Tree of Life; they ate and overate from the Tree of Knowledge. Smashing their sacred statues, they saw that they were nothing but wood and stone; smashing their ideas, they saw that they were filled with air. Coming very, very close to God, they said, "This God is not the father of Fear, he is the son of Fear," and they lost their fear. On the four gates to the city they wrote in large yellow letters, THERE IS NO GOD HERE. What does *There is no God* mean? It means there is no bridle on our instincts, no reward for good or punishment for evil, no virtue, shame, or justice—that we are wolves and she-wolves in heat.

God grew angry and called Abraham.

"Abraham!"

"Command me, Lord."

"Abraham, take your sheep, camels, and dogs, your servant men and women, your wife, your son—and leave! Leave. I have come to a decision."

"On your lips, Lord, 'I have come to a decision' means 'I shall kill!' "

"Their minds have grown overinsolent, their hearts overjubilant, their bellies overinflated—I'm sick of them! They build houses out of stone and iron as though they were immortal. They equip themselves with furnaces, make fires, and melt down metals. I laid the desert out as a leprosy over the face of the earth because that's the way I wanted it! And those people down there in Sodom and Gomorrah irrigate the desert, manure it, transform it into a garden. The immortal elements of water, iron, stone, and fire are nothing more now than their slaves. No, I've had enough of them! They ate of the Tree of Knowledge, picked the apples, and they shall die!"

"All of them, Lord?"

"All. Am I not omnipotent?"

"No, Lord, you are not omnipotent, because you are just. You cannot do anything unjust, dishonest, or absurd."

"What can any of you know about just and unjust, honest and dishonest, logical and absurd, you worms made of dust, nourished on dust, and destined to return to dust? My designs are unfathomable; if you could meet them face to face, you would be terror-stricken."

"You are lord of heaven and earth; you hold life and death side by side in the same palm and you choose. I am a worm, mere dust and water, but you breathed upon me, and the dust and water produced a soul. Thus I shall speak! There are thousands of people in Sodom and Gomorrah who eat, drink, primp, laugh, and mock; there are thousands of minds down there that puff themselves up like serpents and sling their venom with a hiss toward heaven. But if forty righteous souls are to be found among them, Lord, will you burn them?"

"Names! I want names! Who are these forty?"

"And what if there are twenty, twenty righteous souls, Lord?"

"I want names! I am spreading my fingers to count."

"And what if there are ten, ten righteous souls, Lord? What if there are five?"

"Abraham, shut your impudent mouth!"

"Have pity, Lord! You are not only just, you are good. Woe betide if you were only omnipotent; woe betide if you were only just. We would all be lost. But you are good, Lord, and that is why men are still able to stand in the air."

"Do not kneel and stretch out your arms to clasp my knees. I have no knees! Do not start wailing in order to touch my heart. I have no heart! I am rigid, a solid piece of black granite; no hand can make an impression on me. I have arrived at my decision: I shall burn Sodom and Gomorrah!"

"Do not rush, Lord. Why rush when it's a question of killing. Wait! I found one!"

"Found what as you scratched in the soil, you worm?"

"A righteous soul."

"Who?"

"My brother Haran's son. Lot."

As I stood motionless on the sand dune, I felt my temples grating. Inside me I heard God's voice wrestling with the voice of man. For a moment it seemed that the air congealed and Lot stood before me—fierce and barefooted, with a flowing beard, an upright flame on his forehead. Not, however, the Lot of the Old Testament, the slave. This was a Lot all my own, a rebel who would refuse to obey God's command to flee and save himself. Instead, he would pity the charming, sinful cities and of his own free will throw himself into the fire to burn and perish with them.

"Tell him I'm not leaving!" he cried to Abraham. "I am Sodom and Gomorrah—tell him that—and I'm not leaving. Doesn't he say I am free? Doesn't he say (and boast about it no less) that he created me free? Well then, I do as I please. I'm not leaving!"

"I wash my hands of it, rebel. Goodbye."

"Goodbye, you old well of virtue; goodbye, lamb of God! And say to your boss, 'Greetings from old Lot.' Tell him something else too: that he isn't just, isn't good. He is omnipotent. Only omnipotent, nothing else!"

The sun had gone down by now. The light became a little more gentle, and my temples grew calm. Feeling as though I had just emerged from a desperate struggle, I drew a breath and glanced behind me. How had such a rebel risen from my bowels? It was terrifying. Where in my depths, behind God, had this savage, unsubduable soul been hiding? I had been with Abraham, the pious, obedient patriarch. How was it that now I had forsaken him, trampled on Holy Scripture, created a Lot such as this, and become one with him?

The impudent demon had been huddled deep down within me, waiting for my head to become unhinged for an instant and my mind to abandon the keys, so that it could open the trap door, leap out into the light, and begin straightway to act saucily toward God, its eternal adversary.

I had found it necessary to purge my bowels and expel the demons inside me—wolves, monkeys, women; minor virtues, minor joys, successes—so that I could remain simply an upright flame directed toward heaven. Now that I was a man, what was I doing but enacting what I had so ardently desired as a child in the courtyard of our family home! A person is born only once; I would never have another chance!

Night had already fallen when I arrived back in Jerusalem. The stars seemed like mouthfuls of fire suspended over the heads of mankind, but no one in Jerusalem's hallowed streets lifted his eyes to see them and perish with fright. The great fear was conquered by everyday passions, minor concerns, food, the pocketbook, and women. Thus the people were able to forget, still, and keep on living.

As I tossed and turned on my hard mattress, I thought to myself, The time has come for me to make a decision, to bring to completion what I divined as a child when the milk of God was still upon my lips.

At Mount Athos a monk had taken my hand and gazed at my palm; he said he wanted to read my fortune. His face was indeed a gypsy's: black and leathery, with thick goatlike lips and eyes that spit fire.

"I don't believe in your sorcery," I told him with a laugh.

"That doesn't matter," he answered. "What matters is that I believe."

He regarded the lines of my hand, its stars, crosses, and wrinkles. After much study he said, "Don't put your nose in other people's business. You were not made for action; keep your distance. You cannot struggle with men, not you, because at the very moment you are fighting, you keep thinking that your enemy might be right, and no matter what he does to you after that, you forgive him. Understand?"

"Continue!" I said. I was a little shaken, because I saw that although this monk had never seen me before, he was right.

He regarded my hand carefully once more.

"You are being devoured by many cares; you want a great deal and ask a great many questions. You are eating away your heart. But take my advice and do not be overanxious to find the answer. You must not go out to find it; it will come to find you. Listen to what I say, and rest at ease; it is coming. Let me tell you what my superior once told me: 'A monk searched all his life for God, and only when he was breathing his last did he realize that God had been searching all the while for him.' "

He bent over my hand again. Then he stared at me with bulging eyes. "You shall become a monk in your old age," he said. "Do not laugh. You shall become a monk."

Sometimes a false prophecy can be fulfilled; one must simply believe in it. I recalled that other prophecy uttered by the midwife when I was born and she regarded me in the light: "One day this child will become a bishop!"

Overcome by terror, I shouted, "No, no, I don't want to become a monk," and I drew back my hand as though I scented the danger.

I thought I had forgotten the monk's words after so many years, and then suddenly, on this night, they rose again into my mind. I tried to laugh but could not. The words seemed to have been working on me secretly all that time and pushing me precisely where I did not want to go. It was no longer a laughing matter.

I closed my eyes in order to fall asleep and escape. . . . Suddenly I was a rebel being pursued through the streets of a large city. I was captured, tried, and condemned to death. The executioner took me and made me march in front while he followed behind with the axe over his shoulder. I started to run. "Why are you running?" asked the executioner, who had begun to gasp for breath. "I'm in a hurry," I answered him, and as I said this, a warm breeze blew and the executioner vanished. It was not an executioner, it was a black cloud and it had scattered. I wanted to continue on but could not. A mountain rose up before me and blocked my path. It was solid rock, all flint, with a large red flag waving at the summit. I said to myself, If I want to go farther, I shall have to climb it. Well then, in God's name! Crossing myself, I began to ascend. But I was wearing hobnailed boots, and sparks flew as the hobs rubbed against the flint. I climbed and climbed, slipped, fell, regained momentum, climbed some more. And as I came closer and closer to the top, I saw that it was not a flag that waved at the summit, but a flame. I continued the ascent, my eyes riveted to the peak. No, it was not a flame either—I could see it clearly now—it was God. Not God the Father, however, but the other one, terrible Jehovah, and He was waiting for me.

My blood ran cold. For an instant I was ready to turn back, but I felt ashamed. "Onward, it's too late now to stop," I whispered to myself. "Aren't you afraid?" asked a feminine voice inside me. "Yes, I am afraid!" I shouted, so loudly and with such anguish that I awoke.

I sat up in bed. The dream was still sparkling between my eyelashes. I studied it, studied it again, but was unable to find an interpretation. Why a rebel? Why the executioner? Why the flag, the flame, and God? I shook my head. The answer comes when we stop asking the question, I told myself, growing calm. It comes when the question descends from our garrulous brains and invades our hearts and loins.

"O sweet font for he who thirsts. Thou art closed to all who speak, open to all who hold their peace. He who keeps silence, O font, comes, finds Thee, and drinks." These were age-old, eternal words, and on this day my lips whispered them with gratitude.

A religious procession was passing beneath my window. The air filled with incense and song. Suddenly I felt happy; some secret decision was ripening inside me in the darkness. I still could not see its features, but I had faith.

Getting up, I dressed myself and opened the window. The sky was blazing, the road beneath me overflowing with all kinds of people, all in a hurry. The air reeked of incense, putrescent fruit, and the heavy, repulsive stench of human beings. Balancing a basket of grilled corn on her head, a fat Arab woman hawked her wares in a shrill voice, her teeth flashing brilliantly white in the sunlight. The Jews, with their long greasy sideburns, slunk along the walls of the houses, their hooked noses dripping venom. Catholic, Orthodox and Armenian priests crossed one another's paths without exchanging greetings. Christ, in their hands, had degenerated to a flag of hate.

I went down to the street and walked about the town. I was viewing everything for the last time and saying goodbye. In a shop window I saw an old engraving of Mount Sinai. Saint Catherine stood in the middle with the royal crown on her head, and to her left and right, glued to her shoulders like a pair of colossal wings, were the two mountains, Sinai and Saint Episteme. In one hand she held a feather; with the other she tenderly stroked the wheel which had been the instrument of her martyrdom. Beneath, written in ancient Greek: "What are ye worth, ye remaining mountains? Why boast that ye are covered with plants, abounding in trees, and thick with milk? One and one only is the serried, massy, pious, thick, holy, honorable, virtuous, pure, heavenly, spiritual, angelic, and divine God-trodden Mount Sinai."

For a long time I was unable to take my eyes off this engraving. And the more I gazed at it, the more certain I became that if the dream had continued longer, if I had not shouted "I am afraid!" and awoke, the mountain which I was climbing would have become a pair of wings. For this mountain all of flint and sparks was my struggle's ascending road, and if I reached its limit, the struggle would become wings and I would be united with whatever blazed at the summit, be it a red flag, a flame, or God.

Dreams, childish yearnings, and absurd prophecies mixed with the reality of this picture of Sinai in front of my eyes. Suddenly the hidden decision ripening inside me found its features. "That is my road," I said aloud. "I've found what I am going to do: I shall go to Sinai. There my eyes will be opened!"

21

THE DESERT. SINAI

In my mind, Sinai, the mountain trodden by God, had gleamed for many years as an inaccessible peak. Before the famous monastery, built on top of the bush that "burned with fire but was not consumed," came the Red Sea, Arabia Petraea, the tiny harbor of Raïtho, the long journey by camel across the desert and the erratic course through the terrible, inhuman mountains where the groaning Hebrews had spent so many years.

Galilee, with its idyllic grace, harmonious mountains, blue sea, and tiny charming lake, extends smilingly behind Jesus' back and resembles Him as a mother resembles her son. It is a simple, lucid commentary beneath the text of the New Testament. In Galilee, God reveals himself as pacific, non-demanding, and jolly—like a fine human being.

But I had always been stirred by the Old Testament; it responded much more deeply to the needs of my soul. Every time I perused this raw Bible full of vengeance and thunderbolts, this book which steams if you touch it, just like the mountain to which God descended, I felt a burning desire to go and see these inhuman peaks where it was born, to see them with my own eyes and touch them.

I shall never forget a short and impulsive debate I once had with a girl in a garden.

"I'm disgusted with poetry, art, and books," I said. "They all seem without substance to me, made of cardboard. It's as though you were hungry, and instead of being given bread, wine, and meat, you were handed the menu, which you chewed up like a goat."

I don't know what had come over me to make me angry. Perhaps it was the fact that I fancied the girl who was standing in front of me, but could not touch her.

She resembled a Russian peasant lass: pale, with pronounced cheekbones and a broad mouth. As I looked at her, my anger increased. I was holding a rose, and I began to pluck out its petals.

"That's how our enfeebled souls satisfy their hunger—like goats!"

The girl winked her eye roguishly and answered with a laugh, "You speak angrily to me, but actually I agree with you. The only real book is the Old Testament, because it is not made of cardboard but is all flesh and bone, and dripping with blood. To my mind the Gospels are a cup of camomile tea for the simple-minded and bedridden. Jesus was truly a lamb; they slaughtered Him on the green grass at Eastertime and He bleated away docilely, without resisting. Jehovah is my God—severe, heavy Jehovah, dressed in the skins of the wild beasts He killed, like a barbarian coming out of the wilderness, a hatchet passed through His waistband. With this hatchet He opens my heart and enters."

She remained silent for a moment, her cheeks blazing. But the flames had not subsided, and she continued.

"Do you remember how He speaks to men? Have you seen how men and mountains melt in His hands, how kingdoms are engulfed beneath His foot? Man shouts, weeps, begs, hides in caves, burrows into ditches—struggles to escape. But Jehovah is planted in his heart like a dagger."

Once more the girl remained silent, as did I. But I felt the dagger in the depths of my heart.

That day marked the first kindling of my desire to see and touch the riverbed God had opened as He passed through the desert; of my desire to enter it as a person enters the lion's den. And now, glory be to God, the hour had come for me to satisfy this new hunger.

My passage seemed like a fleeting dream, a fiery and enchanting vision: Jerusalem to Suez, then Suez to Raïtho, the port of Arabia Petraea, whence I would depart for God-trodden Sinai. The mountains were pale blue, the water green, the harbor broad and open, with some red, yellow, and black caiques in the innermost recesses and a few poor cottages along the shore. Great tranquility. Two camels appeared on the quay, turned their heads for a moment toward the sea, swayed a little, and then with great rhythmical strides vanished between the houses.

A skiff with a white sail came to take me. In it was a chubby boyish monk. The Sinaitic fathers residing at Cairo had sent word of my arrival.

My heart was dancing as I set foot on the coarse sand. Could all this be a dream? The shore line was covered with large shells; the houses were constructed of lithoidal trees taken from the sea, of fossilized corals and sponges, of starfish and immense turtle shells. Several fellahs standing on the landing stage gleamed swarthily in their white jelabs; a small chocolate-tinted girl was playing in the sand, dressed in a brilliant shade of bougainvillaea.

Farther back were several European homes made of wood, with verandas, large colored umbrellas, doll-like gardens, and discarded tin cans strewn all about. Two Englishwomen sat on a green balcony; in this warm desert they seemed exceedingly pale, as though they had fainted.

The boyish monk who had come to fetch me explained that it was here in Raïtho that the quarantine of the Moslems returning from Mecca took place. At such times the deserted shore line filled with thousands of hadjis. There was great tumult, with tambours and hautboys, and hodjas sitting cross-legged on the sand reading the Koran in loud, incantatory voices.

We reached the dependency which the Sinaites maintained in Raïtho. From here we would take the camels and depart for the God-trodden mountain. The large courtyard was bounded by several cells, the guest quarters, a school for boys, another for girls, and the storerooms, kitchens, and stables. The chapel stood in the middle. But the greatest miracle of all in this Arabian desert was the warm, love-filled heart of Archimandrite Theodosius, the dependency's Superior. Greeks came only rarely to this wilderness, and Archimandrite Theodosius, a tall, ardent, stately Hellene from Tsesmés in Asia Minor, welcomed me as though he were welcoming Greece itself.

The whole of the exquisite ritual of sacred hospitality was performed, the ritual so familiar to me: the spoonful of jam, the Turkish coffee with a glass of cold water, the beautifully set table with its white perfumed tablecloth, the joy glowing in the faces of those who served the guest.

Through the window I could see the Red Sea glittering and the Thebaid mountains outlined in the distance, drowned in light. I spoke with the Superior about the "three score and ten palm trees" which the Scriptures allege were found in this tiny hamlet by the Hebrews after they crossed the Red Sea. I asked about the "twelve wells of water" as though inquiring about dear relatives living abroad. And when he told me that the palm forest still existed and the springs still flowed, I rejoiced.

I had tasted similar happiness very often in my life—after a fatiguing journey a glass of cold water, a simple goodly shelter, a human heart living unknown in an inglenook of the world, waiting warm and unspent for the stranger. And when the stranger appears at the end of the street, how this heart bounds and rejoices because it has found a human being! As in love, so in hospitality, surely he who gives is happier than he who receives.

The Archimandrite and I ate together at the cordial, hospitable table and conversed like two old friends pleased to be reunited. Here in the desert a multitude of questions had been born in him and he thirsted to have me answer them. I told him about large cities, the disbelief and anguish of contemporary man, the arrogance of the rich and destitution of the poor, the impotence of men of honor; then about the great upheaval taking place in Russia.

"Do those Muscovites out there believe in God?" the Superior asked apprehensively.

"No, they believe in man."

"In that worm?" said the Superior with scorn.

"Yes, in that worm, Father Theodosius," I replied obstinately, suddenly feeling the need to defend this worm.

A satanic desire had begun to rage within me. The serpent was climbing up the Tree of Knowledge and hissing. The monk listened greedily.

Thus, leading the serene eremite's heart into temptation, transforming his tranquility into apprehension, I repaid his hospitality in the highest possible fashion.

Along came Taëma, Mansour, and Aoua. Dressed in parti-colored jelabs, with turbans of camel's hair on their heads and long yataghans at their waists, they were the three camel drivers—supple thin-legged Bedouins with small eagle eyes—who were going to accompany me on the three-day, three-night journey to the monastery and protect me in case of danger. According to an ancient chronicle, Bedouins see twice the distance our eyes are able to reach, smell smoke from three miles away and identify what kind of wood is burning, distinguish between the tracks left in the sand by men and those left by women, and tell whether the women are married, unmarried, or pregnant.

They greeted us without speaking, placing their palms to breast, mouth, and forehead. Visible behind them in the courtyard were three camels laden with towering loads for the journey: provisions, blankets, and a tent. By this time I had learned a few words of Arabic, the most indispensable for the three days I was going to live with the Bedouins—their words for bread, water, fire, and God.

The camels knelt. Their gleaming eyes were very beautiful, but devoid of kindness. Their harnesses were decorated with orange and black tassels made of hair.

"Give the camels a few dates for their sweet tooth," ordered the Superior, and the young monk ran out, his fists filled with dates.

The Archimandrite and I embraced, our eyes but a hairbreadth from welling with tears.

We departed. Just a little beyond the monastery's dependency began the desert—gray, taciturn, and sterile.

The camel's sure, undulating rhythm transports your body, your blood takes on the rhythm of this undulation, and, together with your blood, so does your soul. Time frees itself from the geometric subdivisions into which it has been so humiliatingly jammed by the sober, lucid mind of the West. Here, with the rocking of the "desert ship," time is released from its mathematical, firm-set confines; it becomes a substance that is fluid and indivisible, a light, intoxicating vertigo which transforms thought into reverie and music.

Given over for hours on end to this rhythm, I began to understand why Anatolians read the Koran swaying to and fro as though on camelback. In this manner they impart to their souls the monotonous, intoxicating movement which leads them to the great mystic desert—to ecstasy.

Extending before us as far as the eye could see was a tempestuous rose-colored expanse. I supposed it was the sea. The three Bedouins came together, whispered secretly to one another, then separated again. We continued on. It was not the sea; all that rosy expanse was the desert, churned up by a fearful tempest which gave the burning sand clouds their rosy hue. Before long we entered the sandstorm. It took our breath away. Taëma cut short his song; the three Bedouins wrapped themselves tightly in their burnooses and covered their mouths and nostrils.

The sand rose up, striking our faces and hands, wounding them. The camels began to spin about, unable to keep their balance. Although the tortuous passage lasted three hours, I rejoiced secretly that I had been enabled to add this terrible desert whirlwind to my experiences.

The sun began to set; we had left the storm behind us and were finally nearing the mountains. Little by little the desert commenced to turn violet and be covered with shadows. Taëma, who had been going in the lead, stopped and gave the signal to set up camp. "*Krr! Krr!*" gurgled the Bedouin throats. The camels snorted. They knelt on their front legs, then fell back on their hindquarters, thundering like houses crumpling to the ground.

We unloaded them and pitched the tent, working all together. Aoua made a pile of the bits of wood he had taken such great care to collect along the route. He lighted a fire. Mansour, removing the casserole, rice, and butter from a sack made of braided straw, began to cook, while Taëma mixed fine cornmeal with water, thumped out the dough in the pan with his slender fingers, and prepared little pancakes resembling tortillas. The pilaf, meanwhile, started to give off a delicious aroma. Sitting together around the fire, we ate, made tea, then brought out our pipes and smoked, gazing sometimes at the dying embers, sometimes at the large disquieting stars suspended above our heads.

A strange sense of well-being flooded my body and soul. But I tried to bring all this romanticism—Arabia, the desert, the Bedouins—under control, and I scoffed at my heart for thumping away so excitedly.

Lying down inside the tent, I closed my eyes, and all of the muffled, inscrutable murmurings of the desert flowed into my mind. The camels were chewing their cud outside; I could hear their jaws grinding. The whole of the desert was chewing its cud like a camel.

The next day at dawn we began our journey through the mountains, those desolate, arid mountains which hate and repel human beings. Sometimes an ash-gray partridge beat its wings with a metallic sound in the black cavities of the rocks; sometimes a crow soared in circles over our heads as though it desired to smell if we had begun to exude the stench of cadavers, and then to pounce upon us.

All day long the camel's rhythm and Taëma's monotonous lulling song. The sun fell upon us like fire; the air trembled above the stones and our heads.

We followed the route which the Hebrews had taken three thousand years before in their flight from the rich land of Egypt. This wilderness we were traversing had been the terrible workshop where the race of Israel had hungered, thirsted, groaned, and been forged. With insatiable eyes I regarded the crags one by one, entered the sinuous ravine, imprinted the blazing mountain crests in my mind. I was reminded of how, once on the Greek coast, I had advanced for hours inside a cave filled with bulky stalactites, gigantic stone phalli which gleamed brilliantly red in the torchlight. Formerly the cave of a large river, it had been left empty because the river had altered its course over the centuries. The thought flashed through my mind that exactly the same had happened with this ravine we were now traversing beneath the sun. God—pitiless Jehovah—had dug out these mountain ranges in order to pass through.

Before He crossed this wilderness, Jehovah still had not firmly defined His identity, because His people had still not been firmly defined. The various Elohim were not one; they were innumerable spirits spread about in the air, all unnamed and invisible. They blew the breath of life into the world, procreated, descended upon women from on high, killed, flashed, thundered, came down to earth in the guise of thunderbolts. They had no homeland, belonged to no single person, nor to any single tribe. But gradually they took on flesh and became visible, preferably on huge rocks, prescribed sites of high elevation. Men smeared these rocks with lard, offered sacrifices, coated the rocks with blood. Whatever a man held dearest to himself—his first-born son, his only daughter—that he was obliged to sacrifice to God in order to creep into the Lord's good graces.

Over the centuries, with prosperity, the race slowly softened, became civilized. God softened also, became civilized. Animals were sacrificed to Him now instead of humans; He began to be given appearances within reach: snake, hawk, golden calf, winged sphinx. Thus in this rich and sated land of Egypt the God of the Hebrews commenced to vent His ferocity. But suddenly the hostile Pharaohs came, uprooted the Hebrews from their rich lands, and cast them into the Arabian desert. Hunger and thirst began, as did grumbling and rebelliousness. It must have been in this very vicinity that they halted one noontime when they were thirsty and famished, and cried out, "Would to God we had died by the hand of the Lord in the land of Egypt, when we sat by the fleshpots and when we did eat bread to the full!" And Moses, incensed, lifted his hands in despair and cried to God, "What can I do with these ungrateful people? In a moment they shall pick up stones and stone me!"

And God bent over His people and heard. Sometimes He sent them quails and manna so that they could eat; sometimes He sent a sword and cut them down. Day by day, the farther they advanced into the desert, the fiercer His countenance became, the more fiercely did He approach them. Nighttimes He became fire and marched at their head, daytimes a pillar of smoke. He crammed himself into the ark of the covenant; the Levites elevated Him with terror, and the hand that touched Him was reduced to ashes.

His countenance became defined ever more firmly. It grew harsh, took on the fierce appearance of Israel. He was no longer a group of nameless, invisible spirits scattered through the air without a homeland, no longer the God of the entire earth. He was Jehovah, the hard, vindictive, bloodthirsty God of only a single race, the Hebrew race. He had to be hard, vindictive, and bloodthirsty because He was passing through difficult times, was warring with the Amalekites, the Midianites, and the desert. He had to conquer them—by suffering, intriguing, killing—and save Himself.

This arid, treeless, inhuman ravine we were traversing had been Jehovah's fearsome sheath. Through here He had passed, bellowing.

How can anyone have a true sense of the Hebrew race without crossing this terrifying desert, without experiencing it? For three interminable days we crossed it on our camels. Your throat sizzles from thirst, your head reels, your mind spins about as serpent-like you follow the sleek tortuous ravine. When a race is forged for two score years in this kiln, how can such a race die? I rejoiced at seeing the terrible stones where the Hebrews' virtues were born: their perseverance, will power, obstinacy, endurance, and above all, a God flesh of their flesh, flame of their flame, to whom they cried, "Feed us! Kill our enemies! Lead us to the Promised Land!"

To this desert the Jews owe their continued survival and the fact that by means of their virtues and vices they dominate the world. Today, in the unstable period of wrath, vengeance, and violence through which we are passing, the Jews are of necessity once again the chosen people of the terrible God of Exodus from the land of bondage.

That noon we were finally going to reach the Sinai monastery. We had climbed to the Midian plateau, an elevation of more than 5,000 feet. The previous night we had spent in a Mohammedan graveyard, where we erected our tent in front of the sheik's tomb. We awoke at dawn. The cold was biting, snow had covered our tent. The whole of the plain stretched before us, brilliantly white. Dismantling the roof of a dilapidated hut in the graveyard, we lighted a fire. The flames tongued upwards. The four of us crouched around the fire to get warm. The camels came close too and stretched out their necks above us. We drank date raki and made some tea. Then the Bedouins spread a mat over the snow, knelt, and began to pray, their slender sunburned faces turned toward Mecca.

They were plunged in ecstasy, their faces radiant. It was with great respect that I watched those three buffeted, hungering bodies being so agreeably filled. Mansour, Taëma, and Aoua had experienced an Ascension; paradise had opened its gates and they had entered. It was their own paradise, the Mohammedan, Bedouin paradise of sun, white camels, and ewes grazing in green pastures, multicolored tents with women sitting cross-legged outside them, their heads thrown back in laughter, silver bracelets around their wrists and ankles, their eyes painted with kohl, their hair dyed with henna, two false beauty spots on their cheeks; and the meal was steaming: pilaf with milk, dates, white bread, and a jug of cold water; and there were three tents bigger than all the other tents, thirty-three camels faster than all the other camels, and three hundred and thirty-three women more ravishing than all the other women: the tents, camels, and women of Taëma, Mansour, and Aoua.

The prayer terminated; paradise closed its gates. The Bedouins descended to the Midian plateau, drew close to the fire without speaking, and cheerfully resumed their humble earthly tasks. After all, just how long could this life last? Paradise would follow, so best be patient.

Extending my hand to Taëma, who was sitting at my right, I recited to him in Arabic the hallowed Mohammedan cry: "There is one God, and Mohammed is his prophet." He jolted with astonishment; it was as though I had uncovered his secret. His face radiant with joy, he glanced at me and pressed my hand.

We set out. I proceeded on foot, no longer able to tolerate the camel's slow, patient rhythm. Mountains of red and green granite rose on either side of us. Now and then a jockey-like bird passed overhead, small and black, with a tiny white calotte. A file of camels appeared at the end of the road; the Bedouins uttered cries of joy, and we halted. "*Salaam aleikum*"—"peace unto you"—the two approaching camel drivers said in greeting. They clasped hands with our drivers; thc two pairs bent forward to each other and, cheek against cheek, spoke in hushed, lulling voices, prolonging the greeting. The simple, age-old stichomythy began: "How are you? How are your wives? Your camels? Where are you coming from? Where are you going?" The words *salaam* and *Allah* came again and again to their lips, and this encounter in the desert took on the sacred, elevated meaning which should always characterizc the encounter of man with man.

I have a heartfelt admiration for these children of the desert. Look how they live—on a few dates, a handful of corn, a cup of coffee! Their bodies are nimble, their shins are slender as a nanny goat's, their eyes like a hawk's. They are the world's most indigent people, and also the most hospitable. Though hungry, they never eat their fill, but save a little coffee, a little sugar, a handful of dates to offer to a stranger. At Raïtho the Superior told me how a small Bedouin woman stood gazing at an English tourist who had opened his tins of conserves and begun to eat. The Englishman offered her a mouthful, but she declined out of pride; then, suddenly, she swooned from hunger and collapsed to the ground.

The Bedouin's first love is his camel. I used to watch Taëma's, Mansour's and Aoua's delicate ear shells wag with anxiety whenever they heard one of the camels utter the slightest sigh. They would stop, adjust her saddle, examine her belly and hoofs, collect whatever desiccated grass happened to be available, and feed her. In the evening they unsaddled the camel and covered her with a woolen blanket; then they spread a cloth out on the ground and carefully removed any impurities from her grain.

There is an old Arab poem which extols the Bedouin's beloved companion:

The camel steps upon the desert and proceeds.
She is as solid as a coffin's planks; her firm thighs resemble a high fortress gate.
The traces of the cinch on her flanks are like dried-up lakes filled with pebbles.
Touch her there and you think you touch a rasp.
They are similar to the aqueduct built by a Greek engineer and covered by him with tiles!

We were hastening up the mountains, burning with desire to finally encounter the monastery. A bit of water in a natural basin, a few date palms, a stone hut, and a little farther on, a wooden cross implanted in the rock. Suddenly Taëma raised his arm.

"Derr!" he cried. The monastery!

Below us on an exposed stretch between two tall mountains appeared the celebrated monastery of Sinai, girded by high walls. I had greatly desired this moment, but now that I held the fruit of so much effort in my hand, I rejoiced quietly, without vociferation. Nor did I increase my pace. For a second I felt an impulse to turn back; there flashed through me the thrice-callous pleasure of not harvesting and enjoying this fruit of my desire. But then suddenly a warm breeze blew, carrying the aroma of blossoming trees. The human being in me triumphed, and I proceeded onward.

Now I began to distinguish the monastery's features more clearly, its walls and towers, the chapel, a cypress tree. We reached the monk's orchard, which lay outside the walls. Pulling myself to the top of the fence, I saw olive, orange, walnut, and fig trees, also huge divine almonds, all gleaming in the sunlight here in the very center of the desert! With the gentle warmth, the fragrance, the buzz of small insects, it was Paradise!

I enjoyed this face of God for a good while, the jovial one that loves men and is fashioned out of soil, water, and human sweat. For the past three days I had confronted His other face, the terrible unflowering one made all of granite. I had told myself that this, the fire that burns, the granite too hard to be incised by human desires, was the true God. But now as I leaned over the fence into this flowering orchard, I recalled with emotion the ascetic's saying: "God is a quiver and a gentle tear."

Buddha declares, "There are two kinds of miracles, those of the body and those of the soul; I believe in the second, not the first." The monastery of Sinai is a miracle of the soul. Built around a well in the middle of the inhuman desert, surrounded by rapacious tribes that profess a different religion and speak a different language, for fourteen centuries this monastery has towered like a citadel and resisted the forces, both natural and human, that have besieged it. I reflected pridefully that a superior human conscience exists here; human virtue, here, has subdued the desert.

It was only with difficulty that I succeeded in keeping my exultation in check. Here I was amidst the biblical peaks, on the elevated plateaus of the Old Testament! To the east lay the Mountain of Knowledge, where Moses embedded the serpent of brass. Behind this the land of the Amalekites and the Amorite Mountains. Northward the Kedar, Idumaea and the Thaiman Mountains, reaching to the Moab Desert. To the south, Cape Pharan and the Red Sea. Lastly, toward the west, the Sinai range with the Holy Peak where Moses conversed with God; and farther in the distance, Saint Catherine's. The monastery garden glistened amidst sun and snow. The olive trees rustled quietly, the oranges gleamed in their sober foliage, the cypresses rose up ascetically, black as pitch. The perfume from the blossoming almond trees came slowly and regularly, like the breath of God, making your nostrils and mind thrill with joy.

Truly, how had the monastic citadel been able to resist these enticing springtime puffs of wind? Over so many centuries how had it failed to crumple, one spring, to the ground?

I entered the monastery through the high fortress gate. In the center of a large courtyard stood the chapel, and next to it a small mosque with its slender minaret. Here, at long last, the cross and the crescent had joined. Round the periphery, covered with snow and gleaming in their whiteness, the cells, guest quarters, and storerooms. Three monks were sitting in the sun warming themselves. I stood for a long time and listened to them with absorption; their words echoed clearly in the air's great silence. Each was anxious to speak and relieve his mind. One told about the miracles he viewed in America—steamships, skyscrapers, women, brilliant illumination at night; the other how lamb was roasted on the spit in his home town; the third about Saint Catherine's miracles, how the angels took her from Alexandria and brought her here to the mountain peak, and how you could still see the imprint of her body on the rocks.

I climbed the tower to survey the environs. A pale young monk saw me and ran to bid me welcome. He turned out to be eighteen years old, and from Crete. Pierced as it was by the sun, the thick, curly fuzz on his cheeks had a chestnut-blond translucence. While we were conversing about our distant homeland, a sweet, peaceful old man of about eighty appeared, out of breath and puffing. With one foot in the grave, he no longer possessed the strength to desire either good or evil; his bowels were as Buddha wished them—emptied.

The three of us sat down in the sun on a long bench. The youth produced a handful of dates from beneath his shirt; he gave them to me, still warm from his body heat. The old man, touching my knee, began to relate how the monastery was built and how it had struggled for so many centuries. Seated as I was in the sun amidst these legendary mountains, the monastery's story seemed to me as simple and true as a fairy tale.

"The monastery was built by the Emperor Justinian around the well where the daughters of Jethro came to water their sheep, and just exactly on the site of the bush that burned with fire but was not consumed. Justinian dispatched two hundred families from Pontus and Egypt to settle near the monastery and service and protect it, to be its slaves. A century later along came Mohammed. He visited Mount Sinai; his camel's footprint is still preserved in a slab of red granite. The monks received him with great honor, which pleased Mohammed—may his bones fry in hell!—and led him to accord the monastery great privileges. These were written in Cufic script on the hide of a roe deer. As a seal he used the palm of his hand; he didn't know how to write, of course. The privileges say: "If a Sinaite monk takes refuge on the plain, or in the desert, the mountains, or a cave, I shall be there with him and shall protect him from all harm. I shall defend the Sinaites no matter where they happen to be—on land or sea, east or west, north or south. They shall not be obliged to pay tribute, nor shall they be conscripted or pay poll tax, nor shall their harvests be tithed. The wing of mercy shines over their heads. . . ."

As the old man spoke, his voice so removed from all human contact vivified the mountains and Byzantine walls surrounding me; the air filled with saints and martyrs. The Cretan adolescent at my side listened to the miraculous legend with gaping mouth, rapt in ecstasy. In the courtyard below, monks had emerged from their cells to weigh the corn which the Arabs had brought. The door to the kitchen was open, and through it I spied a long table loaded with huge red lobsters. A pale monk wrapped in a coffee-colored blanket was sketching a large marine conch.

"That's Father Pachomios," said the old man with a laugh. "He's half crazy, the poor idiot, and he draws pictures."

"The Apostle Luke was a painter too," I said, wishing to defend all artists.

"It's a terrible temptation, my child—God keep you from it. You've got to be an Apostle to resist."

He was right; I kept quiet. Rising, I descended to the courtyard. The monks were picking up the snow and playing with it like children. They were delighted that it had snowed, for this meant that the desert would produce grass, the sheep and goats would eat, and men would have their fill of bread.

Several slaves had come and seated themselves at the base of the monastery wall. They were smoking, gesticulating, conversing in loud voices. Among them were some filthy barefooted women wrapped in black robes, their hair done up over their foreheads in pointed buns, like the pommels of packsaddles, their faces covered from the nose downward by delicate chains, at the ends of which were shells and tiny silver piasters. Each of the women parted her robe and brought out an infant which she placed on the stones in front of her. All were waiting for the monks to appear and toss down their daily rations from above: three small round loaves of bread for each man, two for each woman and child. The rule was that they had to come in person to receive this food, and they had left their tents hours earlier in order to arrive on time. But these small loaves do not satisfy their hunger. They also collect grasshoppers, which they dry, grind, and knead into bread.

I was deeply moved as I regarded these distant brothers. For centuries they have surrounded these Byzantine walls, and the tiny loaves (made mostly of bran) have been thrown down to them like rocks. They live and die by threatening the monastery. Today, just as in the time of Jethro, only girls tend the sheep. No one molests them. When two young people fall in love, they slip away in secret and go to the mountains at night. The young man plays the flute, the girl sings; at no time do they touch each other. Then the boy comes down to attempt to purchase the girl. He seats himself outside his future father-in-law's tent, the girl arrives, he throws his burnoose over her and covers her. The boy's father comes along, as does the sheik. The two fathers grasp a palm leaf and pull it into two parts. Then the girl's father says, "I want a thousand pounds for my daughter."

"A thousand pounds!" exclaims the sheik. "But your daughter is worth two thousand. And the groom is willing to give this amount. . . . For my sake, however, allow him a five-hundred pound reduction."

"For the sheik's sake," the father replies, "I allow five hundred."

Meanwhile, the various relatives have been arriving one by one and seating themselves cross-legged in front of the tent. At this point they rise.

"Allow him a hundred more, for my sake."

"And another hundred," says someone else.

"And fifty . . ."

"And another twenty-five . . ."

Until finally the amount is lowered to one pound.

At that precise moment the women who have been grinding corn in a corner begin their cackling: "Lou . . . lou . . . lou . . . lou . . ."

The girl's father rises.

"For the sake of the women who grind the corn, I give my daughter for half a pound."

They eat, drink, and dance on the eve of the marriage, lavishing all they own.

Thus, for thousands of years, the customs of the desert have abided unshaken.

The young Cretan came and said to me, "The holy fathers are waiting for you in the reception hall. Go in, please."

Approximately twenty monks were seated in the large hall where guests are received. They stared at me with curiosity. I was going to kiss each one's hand, but there were so many of them that I decided this would be tedious, and kissed only the abbot's. Emaciated and severe, he sat in the middle without speaking. Once again the coffee, the spoonful of jam, a glass of date wine, the kindly age-old words—Where are you from? Who are you? Welcome!

The abbot, an ancient oak incised and carbonized by God's thunderbolts, regarded me, but I am certain that he did not see me. His eyes had begun to grow dim. They no longer distinguished the visible universe clearly; now they saw only the invisible one. He regarded me, and behind my shoulders he viewed great cities: the "world" that was wallowing in sin, vanity, impudence, and death.

I told him I was going through a crisis, and I asked permission to stay a few days at the monastery so that my soul could concentrate and reach a decision.

"Do you desire to find God?" asked the abbot. I realized that he saw me now for the first time; earlier he had been simply looking at me.

"I want to hear His voice," I answered. "I want Him to tell me which road to take. It's only here in the desert that the soul can hear Him."

"All voices can be heard here in the desert," said the abbot. "And especially two which are difficult to tell apart: God's and the devil's. Take care, my child."

Two monks entered the reception hall in order to see the new pilgrim and greet him. One was the guestmaster, a chubby soul with a curly beard and merry blue eyes; it was his job to look after strangers. The other had a weary, ironic smile; he was tall, with mustache, whiskers, and eyebrows as white as snow, and long-fingered hands also strikingly white. He did not speak to me, but simply stared, his eyes flickering and laughing. Laughing, or mocking? At that particular moment I could not tell; a few days later I could.

The abbot rose. Giving me his hand, he said, "God grant that you may find in the desert what you sought futilely in the world."

A monk ran to open the door for him. Walking heavily, with slow steps, he disappeared.

The guestmaster came up to me. "It's dinnertime," he said. "Come to the refectory, please."

The monks were seated around a long table with the abbot at the head. The monk who was serving brought in the meal—boiled lobsters and vegetables, with bread and a cup of wine for each. The fathers commenced to eat. No one spoke. The lector mounted a low pulpit and began to chant the commentary on the day's lesson, the return of the prodigal son.

Many times, in many different monasteries, I have experienced this liturgical rhythm of the collation. In this way the meal assumes its great and proper mystical significance. A rabbi once said, "In eating, the virtuous man liberates the God found in food."

The lector chanted with coloratura flourishes about the prodigal son: his torments and humiliation far from his father's home, how he ate carob beans like the swine, and how one day, unable to bear this any longer, he returned to his father . . .

In the midst of this deep mood of Christian piety I thought to myself, In another monastery more in keeping with today's spiritual unrest and rebellion they would have read the splendid conclusion which an apprehensive contemporary fashioned for this parable. The prodigal returns tired and defeated to the tranquil paternal home. That night when he lies down on the soft bed to go to sleep, the door opens quietly and his youngest brother enters. "I want to go away," he says. "My father's house has grown too confining." The brother who just returned in defeat is delighted to hear this. He embraces his brother and begins to advise him what to do and which direction to take, urging him to show himself braver and prouder than he did, and nevermore deign to return to the paternal "stable" (that is what he calls his father's house). He accompanies his brother to the door and shakes his hand, reflecting, Perhaps he will turn out stronger than I did, and will not return.

How can I ever forget that first night I spent in God's desert fortress? The silence had become ghostlike; it towered up around me as though I had fallen to the bottom of a dark dried-out well.

Then it suddenly turned to sound, and my soul began to tremble.

"What do you want here in my house? You are neither pure nor honest. Your glance flits first this way, then that. I don't trust you. You are ready to turn traitor at any minute. Your belief is an unholy mosaic of many disbeliefs. You do not realize that God sits waiting at the end of every road; you will always be in a hurry, will always become discouraged at the halfway point and turn back to take another road. The common people do not see Sirens or hear songs in the air. Blind and deaf, they sit bowed over in the earth's hold, and row. But the more elect, the captains, hear a Siren inside them—their soul—and gallantly follow her voice. What else, do you think, makes life worth while? The poor woebegone captains hear the Siren and do not believe, however. Entrenched behind prudence and cowardice, all their lives they keep weighing the pros and cons on a delicate assay balance. And God, not knowing where to throw them, desiring them neither to ornament hell nor defile heaven, orders them suspended between corruption and incorruptibility, upside down in the air."

The voice ceased. I kept waiting, my cheeks fiery red from shame and anger. And then somewhere—was it from the desert itself, I wonder—I gained the strength to lift my head rebelliously and object.

"I did reach the end, and at the end of every road I found the abyss."

"You found your own inability to go further. *Abyss* is the name we give to whatever we cannot bridge. There is no abyss, no end of the road; there is only the soul of man, which names everything in keeping with its own bravery or cowardice. Christ, Buddha, and Moses all found abysses. But they erected bridges and crossed over. For centuries now, human flocks have been crossing over behind them."

"Some people become heroes through God's decree, some through their own struggles. I struggle."

A frightening laugh broke out all around me, and also inside my vitals.

"Heroes? But to be a hero means to subordinate yourself to a rhythm transcending the individual. As for you, you are still full of anxiety and shiftlessness. Unable to subdue the chaos inside you and to create the one integral Word, you whine away in self-justification: 'The old forms are too confining . . .' But if you advanced further in thought or action, you would be able to reach the heroic boundaries wherein ten souls such as yours could fit comfortably and be able to work. If you received your impetus from known ecclesiastical symbols, you would be able to propel yourself into religious experiments of your own, and to give (you are seeking this but have not yet discovered it) a contemporary form to the age-old passions of God and man."

"You are unjust. Your heart knows no pity. I have heard you before, O merciless voice—every time I've halted at a crossroad to choose my path."

"And you shall hear me always: whenever you run away."

"I have never run away. I always advance, abandoning what I love, and my heart breaks in two."

"How long will you continue to do this?"

"Until I reach my summit. There I shall rest."

"There is no summit; there are only the heights. There is no rest; there is only struggle. Why are you astonished? Why do you stare like that with protruding eyes? Don't you know me yet? You think I am God's voice, do you? No, I am your voice. I travel with you always, never leaving you. Alas if I ever did leave you by yourself! Once, another time when I sprang angrily out of your bowels, you gave me a name which I have kept, because I like it. I am your Traveling Companion the Tigress."

The voice ceased. Recognizing it, I felt reassured. Why should I fear this Tigress? We always travel together. We have seen everything, enjoyed everything together. The two of us have eaten and drunk together in foreign lands; together we have suffered, together enjoyed cities, women, and ideas. When we return to our quiet cell laden with spoils and covered with wounds, this Tigress silently claws her way into the top of my head, where her lair is. She deploys herself adhesively around my skull, thrusts her talons into my brain, and the two of us, without resorting to words, ponder all we have seen, and yearn for all we have yet to see.

We rejoice that the whole of the visible and invisible world is a deep inscrutable mystery—incomprehensible, beyond the intelligence, beyond desire, beyond certitude. We chat together, my Traveling Companion the Tigress and myself, laughing because we are so hard, tender, and insatiable. We laugh at our insatiability, even though we know for certain that one evening we shall dine off a handful of dust and be sated.

O soul of man, O my Traveling Companion the Tigress: what a joy to live, love the earth, and look upon death without fear!

I got up at dawn, anxious to walk in the desert. The morning star still stood watch; a faint light had already invaded the mountain peaks. The partridges had awakened, and the entire mountain with the Holy Summit to which Jehovah had descended, rang with cackling. The sky had cleared, the low-lying snows had melted and been swallowed by the sand, but high on the mountains the snow glittered pinkly in the first beams of the sun. Not a single voice, no sign of water, no green grass. Inhuman solitude made of sand and God.

Surely only two kinds of people can bear to live in such a desert: lunatics and prophets. The mind topples here not from fright but from sacred awe; sometimes it collapses downward, losing human stability, sometimes it springs upward, enters heaven, sees God face to face, touches the hem of His blazing garment without being burned, hears what He says, and taking this, slings it into men's consciousness. Only in the desert do we see the birth of these fierce, indomitable souls who rise up in rebellion even against God himself and stand before Him fearlessly, their minds in resplendent consubstantiality with the skirts of the Lord. God sees them and is proud, because in them His breath has not vented its force; in them, God has not stooped to becoming a man.

Two prophets were once traveling in the desert and disputing. One claimed that God was fire, the other that He was a honeycomb. Though they shouted themselves hoarse, neither was able to bring the other over to his side.

Finally, the first pointed in exasperation to the mountain opposite them. "If I am telling the truth, the mountain will begin to shake."

And even as he said this, the mountain began to shake.

"That's no proof!" answered the second prophet scornfully.

"If I am telling the truth, an angel will descend from heaven and wash my feet."

And even as he said this, an angel descended from heaven, crouched, and began to wash his feet.

But the other shrugged his shoulders. "That is no proof," he said.

"If I am telling the truth, God will call out, 'It is true!' "

And even as he said this, a voice sounded from the heavens: "It is true!"

But the second prophet only shrugged his soulders again. "That is no proof," he said.

At that exact instant Elijah was passing by heaven. Seeing God laughing, he approached and asked, "Why are you laughing, Lord?"

God answered: "Because I am pleased, Elijah. Down below on earth I see two men talking, and they are my true sons."

As I went along I kept thinking with admiration of the two fierce prophets; it seemed to me that I could still see their footprints in the sand. Happy is the father deemed worthy of begetting such sons, I said to myself; happy the desert that saw walking upon it such lions out of God's jungle.

The next day, together with Father Agapios and Father Pachomios the painter, I climbed the Holy Summit, the sheer fortress where Moses saw God "face to face" and spoke with Him. From a distance the supremely abrupt ridge line looked like the mane of a wild boar. "What are ye worth, ye remaining mountains," asks Scripture, "ye mountains covered with grass, flocks, and cheeses? One and one only is the true mountain, Mount Sinai, where God descended and which He now inhabits."

Jehovah, Israel's fearsome sheik, sat atop this Hebraic Olympus, sat on His Summit as fire, making the mountain steam. No one could touch Him; no one could view Him face to face. Whoever saw Him died. Jehovah was identical with fire. He devoured whatever the Hebrews threw into the flames. And above all else, He loved to devour their children.

As we mounted the 3,100 steps leading from the mountain's foot to its top, we passed a low arched doorway opened into the rock. In the times when men trembled to touch the Summit, a confessor sat here and heard their confessions. Whoever climbed the Lord's mountain had to possess clean hands and an innocent heart; otherwise the Summit would kill him. Today the doorway is deserted. Soiled hands and sinful hearts are able to pass by without fear, for the Summit kills no longer.

We passed by.

Farther above us was the cave where the Prophet Elijah saw his great vision. He entered the cave, and God's voice thundered, "Tomorrow, go forth and stand before the Lord. A great and strong wind will blow over you and rend the mountains and break in pieces the rocks, but the Lord will not be in the wind. And after the wind an earthquake, but the Lord will not be in the earthquake. And after the earthquake a fire, but the Lord will not be in the fire. And after the fire a gentle, cooling breeze. That is where the Lord will be."

This is how the spirit comes. After the gale, earthquake, and fire: a gentle, cooling breeze. This is how it will come in our own day as well. We are passing through the period of earthquake, the fire is approaching, and eventually (when? after how many generations?) the gentle, cool breeze will blow.

Still farther above, Pachomios halted and pointed to a ledge. "This is where Moses stood on the day the Hebrews fought the Amalekites. As long as he kept his arms raised high, the Hebrews conquered, but when he grew tired and lowered them, the Hebrews were put to rout. Then two priests, Aaron and Hur, held his raised arms in place, until finally the last of the enemy was 'discomfited with the edge of the sword.' "

In Pachomios's guileless soul all these legends assumed an unequivocal significance; he stared in goggle-eyed amazement, as though telling about sacred monsters—dinosaurs and megatheria—that still roamed the mountains and could be seen by whoever was pure of heart.

Slender, sear Father Agapios led the way with youthful agility. He did not talk. Displeased by Pachomios' chattering, he was anxious to reach the top.

When he set foot on the Holy Summit, my heart shook. Never had my eyes enjoyed a more tragic, more extraordinary sight. Below us, Arabia Petraea with its deep purple mountains; in the distance the blue ranges of Arabia Felix and the bright green sea glittering like a turquoise. To the west, the desert steaming in the sun, and behind it, far in the background, the mountains of Africa. It is here, I reflected, that the soul of a proud or despairing man finds the ultimate happiness.

We entered the little chapel on the summit. Pachomios began scratching the walls with his fingernails, searching for the remains of ancient frescoes. He pointed triumphantly to the window's diminutive Byzantine columns and proudly summoned me to see the symbol of the Holy Spirit, two Byzantine doves with joined beaks. He was struggling to discover and reconstruct the old life, not wanting to allow the past to pass away. Here on this summit where God descended like an insatiable flame, this spirit of archaeological excavation annoyed me. I turned to the monk and asked him, "Father Pachomios, what do you imagine God is like?"

He gave me a perplexed look. Then, after reflecting a moment, he answered, "Like a father who loves his children."

"Shame on you!" I cried. "Here, on the top of Mount Sinai, do you dare talk in such a way about God? Haven't you read the Scriptures? The Lord God is 'a consuming fire'!"

"Why do you tell me that?"

"So you'll let Him burn all this—the past. Follow God's fire, Pachomios, and do not collect the ashes."

"Listen to my advice and stop working yourself up about the nature of God," said Father Agapios, finally parting his lips. "Don't touch fire, you'll be burned. Don't desire to see God, you'll be blinded."

Opening the sack which he was carrying on his back, he brought out a brace of roast doves, two lobsters, some walnuts and dates, a wooden jug filled with date raki, and a large loaf of whole-wheat bread.

"Dinner is served!"

Suddenly we realized how hungry we were. We set the food out on a stone bench at the spot where Moses' footprint, so it was said, could still be seen: a depression resembling the coffin of a small child. Forgetting the kissing doves, the ones of stone, Pachomios gave himself over to the roast doves with voracious appetite. Seldom have I seen a man put eyes, hands, and teeth into operation with such rapacity. He even took the tiny bones that remained, piled them in front of him, and began to lick them.

"The doves have come to life, Father Pachomios," I said with a laugh. "Go into the chapel and you'll see that they aren't there any more."

"Why laugh?" said Pachomios. "Everything is possible."

"Yes, and if the Holy Spirit was a dove, you'd eat Him too!" exclaimed Agapios, who did not care at all for the other's gluttony. Crossing himself, he gazed out over the desert and sighed.

"Why do you sigh, Father Agapios?" I inquired, longing to learn more about this strict monk who, despite his age, had climbed the mountain with such agility.

"How can I not sigh, my child," he replied, "when my hands, my feet—and my heart—are covered with mud? The hour is finally come when I must present myself before God—with what hands, what feet, what face? My hands are all bloody, my feet filled with mud. Who is going to cleanse them for me?"

"Christ will do it, Father Agapios," said Pachomios in order to comfort him. "Otherwise, why did He descend to earth? You should say to Him, 'Christ, here are my hands, here are my feet—wash them!' "

I laughed. Was this then God's work, to wash our feet?

Pachomios was offended. "Why do you laugh?" he demanded.

"With your permission, Father Pachomios," I replied, "I shall answer you with a parable. Once upon a time, in Arabia, there lived a king who was very, very cunning. Each morning he gathered his slaves together before dawn and did not permit them to begin work until he had commanded the sun to rise. One day a hoary sage went up to him and said, 'Don't you know that the sun does not await your command?' 'I know, I know, old master. But tell me, what kind of a god would we have if he could not become my instrument?' . . . Do you understand now, Father Pachomios?"

But while I was speaking, Pachomios had discovered a tiny bone with some lean meat on it. He gnawed away and did not answer.

I turned to Agapios in order the change the subject.

"How did you become a monk, Father Agapios?"

"How did I become a monk? It was not my wish, it was God's. When I reached the age of twenty, I was seized by a great yearning to don the robe. But the devil put obstacles in my path. What obstacles? you will ask. Well, just this: my affairs were going well, I was making money. And what does making money mean? It means forgetting God. I was a contractor; I built bridges, houses, roads, earned money hand over fist. As soon as I lose my money, I kept telling myself, I'll go and become a monk. God took pity on me. I played the stock market and lost my shirt. The Lord be praised, I said. I cut the cord and left. You know how they cut the cord on a dirigible and it rises to heaven? That's exactly how I left the world."

His pale face turned red. He remembered that he had saved himself from the world, and felt happy.

"So I came here. I had no idea where to go; God—infinite is His grace!—took me by the hand and brought me here. I came, but I was still young and hardy. Don't look at me now; I've grown old, have melted away, shriveled up like a raisin. In those days the blood was still boiling inside me. I couldn't sit with folded arms and do nothing. Praying gave me no relief, so I began to work. I built roads. All the roads we've come over are mine. Building roads is my assigned task here; that's what I was born for. If I go to heaven, it will be by the roads I build."

Wishing to ridicule his hopes, he laughed. "Pff! Heaven! Is that the way a man gets into heaven?"

Pachomios, soporific from overeating, had fallen half asleep, wrapped in a heavy blanket. He heard Agapios's last words and opened his eyes.

"You'll get in, Agapios," he said in a sweet voice, "you'll get in. . . . No need to worry."

Agapios chuckled. "You, to be sure, have everything just fine. No fear at all. You hold your brush and colors, paint paradise, and in you go. But what about me? With me, whew! it's build, build, build from out to out! I have to construct a road right to heaven's very gates or else I don't get in. Each with his own achievements."

He turned to me. "And what about you?"

"Me? I'm already in. In my mind I see heaven as a high mountain with a tiny chapel on the summit. And outside the chapel a stone bench, and on this bench a jug of date raki, two roast doves, some walnuts and dates; and two fine people as my companions, and all of us talking about paradise."

But Pachomios was shivering. Wrapping himself still more tightly in his blanket, he rose. His lips had turned blue. He bent over, picked up the jug, and drank the little raki that remained.

"For God's sake let's go back. We'll freeze to death here." Saying this he began the descent.

That night, alone in my cell, I began to leaf through the Old Testament, keeping the vision of the desert deeply in my mind.

Surely the desert is inhabited by no one, only by One, and this One neither forgives, smiles, nor pities. Panic is not the desert's potentate, nor is thirst, hunger, or exhaustion; nor any famished lion; nor death. God is.

As I perused the Old Testament, that bush that burned with fire and was not consumed, I imagined I was re-entering the frightening ravine which Jehovah carved out between the mountains in order to pass through. The Bible seemed to me like a many-peaked mountain range where the howling prophets, bound with cords, wrapped in tattered rags, were descending.

And while I was bent over the Bible, leaping from peak to peak as I turned its pages, I remembered the girl who once spoke to me so feelingly about the ruddy adolescent "of a beautiful countenance" whom God selected to be king despite the objections of men. The hoary prophet Samuel, who resisted and was twirled about in God's hands, filled my heart with distress. In order to soothe it, I got some paper and began to write. Such was the cowardly means to which I had already learned to stoop in order to exorcise my sorrows.

• • •

"Samuel!"

The hoary prophet with his leather girdle and patchwork tatters was gazing down at the city; he did not hear the Lord's cry. The sun stood a spar's length above the horizon. Sinful Gilgal was buzzing far below, wedged between the red rocks of Carmel with its sword-straight palms and thorny, fully ripened wild figs.

"Samuel!" God's voice rang out once more. "You have grown old, Samuel, my faithful servant. Can't you hear me?"

Samuel quivered. His thick eyebrows blended in wrath, his long forked beard blustered violently, his ears echoed like conches. The malediction whinnied in his entrails like an unbridled mare.

"My curse," he bellowed, extending his emaciated arm over the city which was laughing, singing, buzzing like a wasp's nest, "my curse upon all who laugh, upon the unlawful sacrifices which blur the face of heaven, upon the woman who beats her clogs against the cobblestones!

"Lord, Lord, have the thunderbolts in your palm of bronze been extinguished? You blew the sacred malady down upon the holy body of our king and he falls to the ground, foaming like a snail, puffing like a turtle. Why? Why? What did he do to you? I ask you—answer me! Loose a pestilence, then, on all men if you are just; pluck men's sperm out of their loins and squash it against the stones!"

"Samuel!" thundered the Lord a third time. "Be quiet, Samuel, and listen to my voice!"

The prophet's body began to tremble. And as he leaned for support against the bloody rock where the Almighty's victims were slaughtered, he heard all three of God's cries together. Lifting his arms high, he called, "I am here, Lord."

"Samuel, fill your pitcher with prophetic oil and go to Bethlehem."

"But Bethlehem is far away. A century's beating against the earth in your service has made my feet turn to rot. Mount someone else, Lord; I am no longer able."

"I'm not speaking to the flesh. That I detest and do not touch. I am speaking to Samuel!"

"Speak, Lord. I am here."

"Samuel, fill your pitcher with prophetic oil and go to Bethlehem. Without opening your mouth, without allowing anyone to accompany you, knock on Jesse's door."

"I have never been to Bethlehem. How shall I know which is Jesse's door?"

"I have marked it with a fingerprint made of blood. Knock on Jesse's door. Of his seven sons, choose one."

"Which one, Lord? My eyes have grown dim; I cannot see well."

"The moment you face him, your heart will bellow like a calf. That is the one you should choose. Push apart his hair, find the very top of his head, and anoint him King of Israel. . . . I have spoken!"

"But Saul will find out. On my return he'll lay a trap for me and kill me."

"What do I care? I have never valued the lives of my servants. Be gone!"

"No, I refuse!"

"Wipe the sweat from your face, Samuel. Steady your jaws so they stop rattling, and speak to me, to the Lord. You are gibbering, Samuel. Speak clearly!"

"I am not gibbering. I said, I refuse to go."

"Speak more softly. You are screaming, as though from fear. Why do you refuse to go? I trust Samuel will condescend to answer me. Are you afraid?"

"No, I am not afraid. Love keeps me from going. It was I who anointed Saul King of Israel. I loved him more than my own sons. I blew my soul between his pale lips; it was the spirit of prophecy, my spirit, that made him illustrious. He is my body and soul; I will not betray him!"

"Why do you fall silent? Is Samuel's heart emptied so soon?"

"Lord, you are almighty. Do not play with me. Kill me! You have no other choice—kill me!"

Samuel's eyes filled with blood. Clutching the rock, he waited.

"Kill me!" his heart bellowed once more inside him. "Kill me!"

"Samuel . . ." The Lord's voice was tender now; it seemed to be entreating him.

But the hoary prophet grew wilder and wilder.

"Kill me! Kill me! You have no other choice."

No answer. Midday passed; the sun declined. A swarthy barefooted boy appeared. He ascended the path and approached the prophet in terror, as though nearing the edge of a cliff. Placing the prophet's meal of dates, honey, bread, and a crock of water at the base of the rock, he left hastily with bated breath, descended to the city, and slipped into his family's mean cottage. His mother leaned over and hugged him.

"Still?" she asked, her voice trembling. "Still?"

"Yes," replied the boy. "Still battling with the Lord."

The sun fell behind the mountain. The evening star came to hover above the sinful city like a seed of fire. A pale woman saw it from behind her jalousie and cried out, "It is going to fall now and burn up the world!"

The stars flowed playfully, sparklingly over the prophet's

long locks, revolving with obedience on an invisible wheel. While he stood in their midst trembling, they pushed into his hair and beat against his temples like bulky hailstones.

"Lord . . . Lord . . ." he whispered toward daybreak. More than this he could not utter.

He took down the jug, filled it with prophetic oil, clutched his gnarled staff, and began the descent. His feet had sprouted wings; the dewdrops on his white beard were twinkling like stars. Two children playing on the doorstep of the first house scampered off the moment they were confronted with the prophet's patchwork tatters and green turban.

"He is coming, he is coming," they began to shout.

The dogs huddled in corners with their tails between their legs, a heifer lowed, dragging her neck along the ground, and a vehement gust of wind swept through the city from one end to the other. Doors were closed; mothers called their children and brought them in from the streets. Beating his staff against the stones, Samuel marched with huge strides in order to pass through. "I feel like a war hanging over men's heads," he murmured, "like a plague, like the Lord!"

Two shepherds with long crooks appeared on the path. As soon as they saw the prophet, they prostrated themselves on the ground.

"Command me to smash in their skulls, Lord. Speak to my heart; I am ready."

But no voice came to unsettle his mind, and he passed by, uttering heavy imprecations against the seed of man.

The sun was broiling; the dust beneath his feet rose and wrapped itself around him like a cloud. Feeling sudden thirst, he cried out, "Lord, give me something to drink."

"Drink!" replied a quiet voice next to him, a voice like babbling water.

Turning, he saw water dripping from a fissure in a ledge and accumulating in a hollow. He bent down, pushed apart his whiskers, and placed his mouth upon the water. The coolness descended to his heels, and his ancient bones creaked.

He resumed his march. The sun went down. He reclined against the base of a palm tree, put his right hand beneath his cheek, and fell asleep. The jackals gathered around him. Catching his scent, they fled in terror. The stars suspended themselves over him like swords. He awoke at dawn and set out once more. On the third day the plain appeared through a pass in the mountains, the River Jordan sparkling in its center like a sated, slow-moving serpent with green scales. Three additional days passed, and then suddenly the houses of Bethlehem gleamed snow-white behind the date trees.

A flock of doves passed over the prophet's head, hesitated for a moment, and all at once darted forward in terror toward the town.

At the large northern gate, with its oppressive stench of flocks, and its lepers and blind men begging for bread, the elders stood awaiting the prophet. Trembling, they mumbled among themselves.

"Leprosy will fall upon our village! God descends to earth only to ravage His creatures."

Steeling his heart, the oldest among them stepped forward one pace. "I shall speak to him," he said.

The prophet arrived in his cloud of dust, his rags flapping like a tattered war banner.

"What do you bring us, peace or slaughter?"

"Peace," replied the prophet, stretching forth his hands. "Go to your homes; empty the streets. I want to pass through by myself."

The streets were emptied, doors bolted. Striding into the village, Samuel inspected all the doors closely, running his fingers over them. At the very edge of the village, the very last house, he descried the fingerprint in blood. He knocked. The entire house shook, and old Jesse rose in terror to open the door.

"Peace unto your house, Jesse, health to your seven sons, and may your daughters-in-law bear male children. The Lord be with you!"

"His will be done!" answered Jesse, his lower jaw trembling.

A man appeared, filling the doorway. Samuel turned, and when he saw him, his eyes were pleased. The man was a giant with curly black hair, a broad hairy chest and legs as solid as columns of bronze.

"This is my eldest son, Eliab," said Jesse proudly.

Samuel said nothing; he was waiting for his heart to bellow. This must be the one, his mind kept saying. Surely this must be the one. Why don't you speak, Lord?

He waited a long time. But suddenly the terrible voice burst forth within him: "Why this grumbling? Your soul fancied him, did it? Well, I don't want him. I don't want him. I examine the heart, delve into the loins, weigh the marrow in the bones. . . . I don't want him!"

"Bring your second son," commanded Samuel. His lips had turned pale.

The second son came, but the prophet's heart remained mute, his viscera immobile.

"It's not him! Not him! Not him!" he kept bellowing as one by one he rejected six of the sons, riveting his eyes on their forcheads, eyebrows, mouths, investigating their backs, knees, midsections, and teeth as though they were rams.

Completely exhausted, he collapsed in a heap on the threshold.

"You have deceived me, Lord," he cried out in agony. "You are always crafty, always merciless; you do not pity mankind. Appear! It is I, Samuel, who call you. . . . Why don't you speak?"

Jesse, troubled, came up to him.

"There is still David, my youngest," he said. "He is tending the sheep."

"Have him called!"

"Eliab," said the father, "go and call your brother."

Eliab knit his brows, and the frightened father addressed his second son: "Abinadab, go and call your brother."

But this one refused also. They all refused.

Samuel rose from the threshold. "Open the gate. I'll go myself."

"Shall I describe his appearance so you can recognize him?" asked the old man.

"No. I recognized him sooner than his father or his mother!"

Stumbling over the stones, he began with curses to climb

the hillside, shouting, "I don't want to, I don't want to," as he proceeded.

The moment he perceived a youth standing among his sheep, a youth with flame-red hair which shone like the rising sun, he halted. His heart bellowed like a calf.

"Come here to me, David," he called commandingly.

"You come to me!" answered David. "I don't leave my sheep."

"It's him, it's him!" roared Samuel as he went forward, full of indignation.

Going close to him, he clasped his shoulder, dug his fingers into his back, examined his shanks, returned to the head.

The boy jerked his head away angrily. "Who are you? What do you mean by examining me?"

"I am Samuel, the Lord's servant. He tells me to go and I go; He tells me to cry out and I cry out. I am His foot, His mouth. His hand, His shadow upon the soil. . . . Bend down!"

Finding the top of the boy's head, he poured out the holy oil.

"I hate you, I do not want you; I love another. But the wind of the Lord passes above me, and look, against my will I lift my hand and pour the prophetic oil upon your scalp.

"David is anointed King of Israel! David is anointed King of Israel! David is anointed King of Israel!"

He hurled the sacred flask against the stones, shattering it.

"You have shattered my heart in the same way, Lord. I no longer want to live!"

Seven crows sped out of the heavenly depths, hovered in a circle close above him, and waited. Unwinding his green turban, the prophet spread it out on the ground as a shroud. The crows came closer, encouraged. The prophet covered his face with his patchwork tatters and did not move again.

• • •

With this vision of the man who vainly tries to oppose God, sleep carried me off, and I surrendered myself without resistance to the invisible hands. Thus the night, which I had so feared, passed happily and without dreams.

I descended to the courtyard at daybreak, fully rested. The monks, flitting by like wraiths in the half-light, disappeared one by one into the chapel. I went in with them to hear matins, huddling in one of the stalls. Two cressets were burning in front of the iconostasis—there was no other light—but I managed to make out Christ's austere figure in the dimness, and next to Him the tender, afflicted face of the Blessed Virgin. The air was redolent with wax and sweet-incense. Paschal laurels were still scattered over the paving stones.

What happiness is here, I thought to myself, what isolation! How distant is the reeling, bellowing world! Why flee from beneath this wing of Christ—to go where? Why drown in minor concerns and minor joys? The oyster is here, the oyster with the Great Pearl. I shall master my body, master my soul, prune away all the minor branches that drain off the strength of the crown; I shall remain nothing but crown, and shall rise. Before me I have a great Striver. I shall follow Him. He is climbing a terrible ascent; I shall climb it with Him.

I kept gazing at Christ's virile, ascetic figure in the gentle glow of the cressets. Perceiving the slender hands which maintained a firm grip on the world and kept it from falling into chaos, I knew that here on earth, for the full span of our lives, Christ was not the harbor where one casts anchor, but the harbor from which one departs, gains the offing, encounters a wild, tempestuous sea, and then struggles for a lifetime to anchor in God. Christ is not the end, He is the beginning. He is not the "Welcome!" He is the "Bon voyage!" He does not sit back restfully in soft clouds, but is battered by the waves just as we are, His eyes fixed aloft on the North Star, His hands firmly on the helm. That was why I liked Him; that was why I would follow Him.

What attracted me and gave me courage above everything else was how—with what striving and derring-do, what frantic hope—the person who found himself in Christ set out to reach God and merge with Him, so that the two might become indissolubly one. There is no other way to reach God but this. Following Christ's bloody tracks, we must fight to transubstantiate the man inside us into spirit, so that we may merge with God.

This dual nature of Christ had always been a deep, inscrutable mystery to me, and especially the yearning, so human, so superhuman, of Christ the man to attain to God, or, more exactly, to return to God and become identical with Him. This nostalgia, at once so mystical and so real, had opened large wounds in me and also abundant wellsprings.

From my youth onward, my principal anguish, and the wellspring of all my joys and sorrows, had been this: the incessant, merciless battle between the spirit and the flesh.

Within me were the dark immemorial forces of the Evil One, human and prehuman; within me too were the luminous forces, human and prehuman, of God—and my soul was the arena where these two armies clashed and met.

The anguish was intense. I loved my body and did not want it to perish; I loved my soul and did not want it to decay. I fought to reconcile these two antagonistic, world-creating forces, to make them realize that they are not enemies but, rather, fellow workers, so that they might rejoice in their harmony—and so that I might rejoice with them.

Every man is half God, half man; he is both spirit and flesh. That is why the mystery of Christ is not simply a mystery for a particular creed; it is universal. The struggle between God and man breaks out in everyone, together with the longing for reconciliation. Most often this struggle is unconscious and short-lived. A weak soul does not have the endurance to resist the flesh for very long. It grows heavy, becomes flesh itself, and the contest ends. But among responsible men, men who keep their eyes riveted day and night upon the Supreme Duty, the conflict between flesh and spirit breaks out mercilessly and may last until death.

The stronger the soul and the flesh, the more fruitful the struggle and the richer the final harmony. God does not love weak souls and flabby flesh. The spirit desires to wrestle with flesh which is strong and full of resistance. It is a carnivorous bird which is incessantly hungry; it eats flesh and, by assimilating it, makes it disappear.

Struggle between the flesh and the spirit, rebellion and resistance, reconciliation and submission, and finally—the supreme purpose of the struggle—union with God: this was the ascent taken by Christ, the ascent which He invites us to take as well, following in His bloody tracks.

This is the Supreme Duty of the man who struggles—to set out for this lofty peak which Christ, the first-born son of salvation, attained. How can we begin?

If we are to be able to follow Him, we must have a profound knowledge of His conflict, we must relive His anguish: His victory over the blossoming snares of the earth, His sacrifice of the great and small joys of men, and His ascent from sacrifice to sacrifice, exploit to exploit, to martyrdom's summit, the Cross.

I had never followed Christ's bloody journey to Golgotha with such intensity, never relived His Life and Passion with so much understanding and love as during my days and nights in Jerusalem, Galilee, and by the Dead Sea. Never with so much sweetness, so much pain, had I felt the blood of Christ falling drop by drop into my heart.

For in order to mount to the Cross, the summit of sacrifice, and to God, the summit of immateriality, Christ passed through all the stages which the man who struggles passes through. All—and that is why His suffering is so familiar to us; that is why we pity Him, and why His final victory seems to us so much our own future victory. That part of Christ's nature which was profoundly human helps us to understand Him and love Him and to pursue His Passion as though it were our own. If He had not within Him this warm human element, He would never be able to touch our hearts with such assurance and tenderness; He would not be able to become a model for our lives. We struggle, we see Him struggle also, and we find strength. We see that we are not all alone in the world; He is fighting at our side.

Christ's every moment is a conflict and a victory. He conquered the invincible enchantment of simple human pleasures; He conquered every temptation, continually transubstantiated flesh into spirit, and ascended. Every obstacle in His journey became an occasion for further triumph, and then a landmark of that triumph. We have a model in front of us now, a model who opens the way for us and gives us strength.

Blowing through heaven and earth, and in our hearts and the heart of every living thing, is a gigantic breath—a great Cry—which we call God. Plant life wished to continue its motionless sleep next to stagnant waters, but the Cry leaped up within it and violently shook its roots: "Away, let go of the earth, walk!" Had the tree been able to think and judge, it would have cried, "I don't want to. What are you urging me to do! You are demanding the impossible!" But the Cry, without pity, kept shaking its roots and shouting, "Away, let go of the earth, walk!"

It shouted in this way for thousands of eons; and lo! as a result of desire and struggle, life escaped the motionless tree and was liberated.

Animals appeared—worms—making themselves at home in water and mud. "We're just fine here," they said. "We have peace and security; we're not budging!"

But the terrible Cry hammered itself pitilessly into their loins. "Leave the mud, stand up, give birth to your betters!"

"We don't want to! We can't!"

"You can't, but I can. Stand up!"

And lo! after thousands of eons, man emerged, trembling on his still unsolid legs.

The human being is a centaur; his equine hoofs are planted in the ground, but his body from breast to head is worked on and tormented by the merciless Cry. He has been fighting, again for thousands of eons, to draw himself, like a sword, out of his animalistic scabbard. He is also fighting—this is his new struggle—to draw himself out of his human scabbard. Man calls in despair, "Where can I go? I have reached the pinnacle, beyond is the abyss." And the Cry answers, "I am beyond. Stand up!" All things are centaurs. If this were not the case, the world would rot into inertness and sterility.

As I walked hour after hour in the desert surrounding the monastery, God gradually began to liberate Himself from priests. Thenceforth, the Lord for me was this Cry.

With the passage of the days in this godly isolation, my heart grew calm. It seemed to fill with answers. I did not ask questions any more; I was certain. Everything—where we come from, where we are going, what our purpose is on earth—struck me as extremely sure and simple in this God-trodden isolation. Little by little my blood took on the godly rhythm. Matins, Divine Liturgy, vespers, psalmodies, the sun rising in the morning and setting in the evening, the constellations suspended like chandeliers each night over the monastery: all came and went, came and went in obedience to eternal laws, and drew the blood of man into the same placid rhythm. I saw the world as a tree, a gigantic poplar, and myself as a green leaf clinging to a branch with my slender stalk. When God's wind blew, I hopped and danced, together with the entire tree.

I kept speaking to my soul, asking it with anguish, Do you believe? Are you able to give of your entire being? Are you ready?

What I wanted was to comply with an austere rhythm, to enlist in an army which had set out to gain the supreme hope, to board in my turn the Christian Argo with its abstemious, destitute, virginal heroes—and we would heave out the red sail, and the mystic vine of the Eucharist would sprout from the mainmast, and we would cruise as pirates in order to snatch the golden fleece of immortality from God's shoulders! What I wanted was to triumph, in my turn, over triviality, pleasure, and death.

I roamed the desert for hours each day, aware that a hidden decision was slowing maturing inside me, a decision which still did not dare reveal itself by name. In the evenings when I returned, I found the monks outside their cells. The day's swelter had subsided, and they were inhaling the coolness of the approaching night.

Solitude is fatal to any soul which fails to burn with a great passion. If, in his solitude, a monk does not love God to the point of frenzy, he is doomed. The minds of several of the monks had tottered. These brothers had nothing to think about, nothing to desire. Half closing their eyes, they sat down in a row in the courtyard and waited for the hour when they would enter the chapel, the refectory, their cells—that was all. Their memories had grown murky, their teeth had fallen out, their loins ached. They were not men, but neither were they animals. Nor were they angels yet. They were neither male nor female, neither alive nor dead. In a stupor, their arms folded, they waited for death, just as bare stalks await the spring.

One of them kept recalling his wife, and spat incessantly. Another had a notebook and a little package of crayons beneath his shirt; every so often he brought them out and proceeded to draw the identical picture—Christ with breasts, nursing His Mother. A third, upon awakening each morning, went down to the courtyard to wash in the fountain, maniacally excoriating himself in order to remove the filth from the dreams he had during the night. And seated always in the same place in the yard, a closed book on his knees, was the strange monk who had come into the abbot's quarters with the guestmaster on the first day. He never spoke to anyone, and whenever he entered the yard, he lifted his eyes and observed me, his lips smiling sometimes with kindness—so it seemed to me—sometimes with mockery. On several occasions when I passed in front of him, he started to rise and was about to speak to me; but he always sat down again, the smile vanishing from his lips.

I enjoyed this divine solitude for seven days. On the seventh day the guestmaster, cheerful as always, came to my cell.

"The holy abbot sent me to ask where your soul stands, and what decision you have made."

"I kiss his hand," I replied. "I would like to go to confession before I answer him."

The guestmaster paused for a moment.

"Would you like to stay with us?" he inquired finally.

"I would like to stay with God, and here in the desert I feel Him closer to me than elsewhere. I'm afraid, however, that all the roots which bind me to the world still have not been plucked out. I shall confess to the abbot, and he will decide."

"Take care! The holy abbot expects a great deal from men."

"I expect a great deal from myself, Father. That is why I keep hanging back."

He hesitated just as he was opening the door to leave.

"Father Joachim gave me a message. He would like to see you."

"Father Joachim?"

"The old man who came to the reception hall with me to welcome you."

I was pleased. At last I would learn the identity of this strange, taciturn monk.

"When?" I asked.

"He says tonight, in his cell."

"Fine. Tell him I'll be there."

"He used to be a man of rank. He associates with no one, speaks only with God. He discovered your name and wants to see you. Address him with respect." With these words he strode across the threshold without waiting for my reply.

I tarried until night descended in earnest and the monks fell asleep. One by one the lights in the cells went out. Walking on tiptoe down the long cloister, I reached Father Joachim's cell. I stopped to catch my breath, for I had begun to pant as though I had been running. The light was on. I placed my ear against the door and listened intently. Silence. Just as I started to lift my hand in order to knock, the cell door opened and Father Joachim appeared. His head was uncovered, his white hair flowing over his shoulders. He had a thick knotted cord about his waist and was barefooted.

"Welcome," he said. "I hope no one saw you. Come in."

The walls were bare. In the corner a narrow straw mattress supported between a pair of iron bedsteads. Two stools, a tiny table, a jug in a niche in the wall. A thick bound volume on the table, obviously the Gospels, and a broad wooden cross on the wall opposite, painted not with Christ's crucifixion but with His resurrection. Rows of apples were suspended from the rafters, strung together into chaplets; the entire cell reeked of rotting fruit.

Father Joachim stretched out his arms. The cell was so narrow that they nearly touched the two walls. "This is my cocoon," he said, smiling. "I shut myself in here like a larva. I am waiting for the day when I shall emerge as a butterfly."

He shook his head. I could see him biting his narrow, moldered lips as he stood next to the lamp, which illuminated his long wizened face. His voice now was full of derision and bitterness.

"What else do you expect a poor larva to dream about? Wings!"

He fell silent. Turning, he looked at me. The derision had faded; his glance was that of a man who needed help.

"What do you think? Why does the larva dream of wings? Is it just his simple-minded innocence? Or his impudence? Or could his shoulders actually be tingling with the wings he is preparing?"

He made a rapid motion with his arm, as though he had a sponge in his hand and was erasing something.

"So far and no further!" he exclaimed. "We've gotten to deep waters very quickly—that's enough! . . . Take a stool and sit down. It was to tell you something else that I called you. . . . Well, sit down. Don't pay attention to me; I can't sit down."

He laughed.

"There is a heresy, you know, called 'Always on your feet.' I've subscribed to that heresy for years now, ever since my childhood."

"I, Father, belong to another heresy: 'Always uneasy.' I have been battling ever since my childhood."

"Battling with whom?"

I hesitated. Suddenly I was terror-stricken.

"With whom?" the monk repeated. Then, leaning over to me and lowering his voice: "With God?"

"Yes."

The old man riveted his eyes on me without speaking.

"Could this be a disease, Father? How can I be cured?"

"May you never be cured!"

He raised his hand as though to bless—or curse—me.

"Alas if you had to wrestle with your equal or inferior. But since you are wrestling with God, alas if you are ever cured of this disease."

He fell silent for a moment, and then: "Temptations come to us very often here in the desert. One night I had a strange temptation in my sleep. I saw myself as a great sage in Jerusalem. I could cure many different diseases, but first and foremost I was able to remove demons from the possessed. People brought patients to me from all over Palestine, and one day Mary the wife of Joseph arrived from Nazareth, bringing her twelve-year-old son Jcsus. Falling at my feet, she cried out tearfully, 'O illustrious sage, take pity on me and heal my son. He has many demons inside him.'

"I had the parents go outside. When I remained alone with Jesus, I caressed his hand and asked him, 'What is the matter, my child? Where does it hurt?'

" 'Here, here . . .' he replied, pointing to his heart.

" 'And what's wrong with you?'

" 'I can't sleep, cat, or work. I roam the streets, wrestling.'

" 'Who are you wrestling with?'

" 'With God. Who else do you expect me to be wrestling with!'

"I kept him near me for a month, addressed him ever so gently, gave him herbs to make him sleep. I placed him in a carpenter's shop to learn a trade. We went out for walks together and I spoke to him about God, as though He were a friend and neighbor who came in the evening to sit with us on our doorstep and chat. There was nothing impressive or difficult about these talks. We spoke of the weather, of the wheatfields and vineyards, the young girls who went to the fountain . . .

"At the end of a month's time, Jesus was completely cured. He no longer wrestled with God; he had become a man like all other men. He departed for Galilee, and I learned afterwards that he had become a fine carpenter, the best in Nazareth."

The monk glanced at me.

"Do you understand?" he asked. "Jesus was cured. Instead of saving the world, he became the best carpenter in Nazareth! What is the meaning, then, of 'disease' and 'health'? . . . Well, enough of all that—let's change the subject! . . . You seem tired. Sit down."

I sat down on a stool beneath the icon. I kept gazing at the monk's bare feet on the paving stones, their delicate bone structure, slender ankles, long aristocratic toes. The lamplight made them glow like ancient marble turned reddish blond by the sun.

He retreated two steps, then returned and stood in front of me, crossing his arms over his chest.

"Look up," he said in a caressing voice, as though speaking to a small child. "Regard me well. Don't you remember me?"

"I never set eyes on you in my life," I replied with astonishment.

"Nothing fades from a child's mind. Surely my face still exists somewhere deep down in your memory. Not this aged, shriveled one, but another—handsome, firm, and manly. Listen: I spent one summer in Crete, when you were not quite five years old. I was a wholesaler in those days, dealing in citrons, carob beans, and raisins. Your father was one of my suppliers. Is he still alive?"

"Yes, but he's old, bent, and toothless now. He sits on the couch all day long and reads the Prayer Book."

"Most unjust!" shouted the monk, raising his hands. "Bodies like his should never deteriorate; they should fall down dead all of a sudden while they are walking and the ground is crunching beneath them. Death is the work of God, the name of the spot where God touches man; but bodily deterioration is the treacherous, dishonest work of the devil. . . . Can it really be true that Captain Michael is old and decrepit?"

He remained silent for some time. His eyes had grown ferocious. But soon he took a breath and continued.

"Your father used to buy raisins, citrons, and carobs on account for me. I loaded ships and sent them to Trieste. I did very well, earned money hand over fist, and flung away just as much. I was a wild beast who could never have his fill of eating, drinking, and fornicating. I had sold my soul to Satan; my body was left masterless and unbridled. I sneered at God, called Him a bogeyman and scarecrow able to do nothing more than frighten away brainless sparrows and keep them from pecking in gardens. Each evening after I finished work, I devoted myself to shameless carousing until dawn.

"Now, try to remember: early one morning you were standing in front of your father's shop when all of a sudden you heard singing, laughter, and a coach-in-four speeding along at a frantic pace. Turning, you saw a half-dozen inebriated women—café singers—all shrieking and guffawing at the top of their lungs while they flung walnuts and figs at the people in the street. The driver was a majestic figure with a shiny top hat; he whipped the horses maniacally, and they whinnied with excitement and galloped. Then you felt afraid; you thought they were coming straight for you, and you screamed and ran to hide behind your father's apron. . . . Do you remember? Does it come back to you now? The drunken coachman was me. I had on a top hat, I tell you—a 'stove pipe'—and in order to tease you I directed the whip right at you and snapped it in the air. . . . Now do you remember?"

He bent over, placed his hand on my shoulder and gave me a shove.

"Do you remember?"

I had closed my eyes. While listening to him, I had been struggling to push aside the layer upon layer of memories stowed on top of my childhood years. Little by little the darkness thinned, and suddenly the four horses, the drunken "chanteuses," the frightening top hat, and the cracking of the whip above my head all bounded, fully alive, out of the deeps of my memory.

"Yes, yes," I cried. "I remember! And was it you, Father? You?"

But the old monk did not hear me. He had leaned against the wall and closed his eyes. It was thus, with lowered eyelids, that he continued.

"One morning I found I'd had enough. The fleshly round is not very extensive; it comes quickly to an end. You eat, drink, kiss, eat again, drink again, kiss again—and there is no place else to go. In the end, I tell you, I found I'd had enough. Remembering my soul, I stepped into a carriage and went to a monastery on Mount

Athos. I stayed three months. Prayer, fasting, matins, Divine Liturgy; work detail, barley bread, rancid olives, baked beans—I soon became sick of it all. I sent for the coachman again; he arrived and took me away. But what was I to do in the world now? It had not a single joy to offer me any more, not a single untasted sin. I returned to the monastery, but I instructed the coachman to remain nearby this time, to wait in the nearest village in case I should need him. And indeed before long I did need him. Once again I absconded from the monastery.

"My life had degenerated until it became unbearable. I was suspended between heaven and earth, swinging from one to the other and rejected by both. I went to an old ascetic who lived far from monasteries, in a cave dug into a cliff jutting over the sea, and had him confess me.

" 'What shall I do, holy Father? Give me some advice?'

"The old ascetic placed his hand on my head. 'Be patient, my child; do not be hasty. Haste is one of the devil's snares. Wait calmly, with faith.'

" 'How long?'

" 'Until salvation ripens in you. Allow time for the sour grape to turn to honey.'

" 'And how shall I know, Father, when the sour grape has turned to honey?'

" 'One morning you will rise and see that the world has changed. But you will have changed, my child, not the world. Salvation will have ripened in you. At that point surrender yourself to God, and you shall never betray Him.'

"That is exactly what happened. One morning I opened my window. Dawn was just breaking, the morning star still twinkling in the sky. The calm sea sighed lightly and tenderly as it broke along the shore line. We were still in the heart of winter, yet a medlar tree in front of my window had blossomed; its aroma was peppery, as sweet as honey. It had rained during the night; the leaves were still dripping, and the whole earth glittered contentedly. 'Lord, O Lord, what a miracle this is,' I murmured, and I began to weep. It was then that I understood: salvation had arrived. I came here to the desert and buried myself inside this cell with its humble bed, its jug of water, its two little stools. Now I am waiting. Waiting for what? God forgive me, but I really do not know very well. This doesn't bother me, however. Whatever comes will be welcome. I believe that in any event I shall come out ahead. If the afterlife actually exists, I will have managed to repent at the last moment. (Did not Christ give us His word that repentance even a split second before death brings salvation?) If on the other hand the afterlife does not exist, at least I will have enjoyed this life, squeezed the juice out of it and thrown it over my shoulder like a lemon rind. . . . Do you understand? What are you thinking about?"

"I was wondering why you invited me to your cell tonight, Father. Surely you wanted to tell me something else besides this."

He tilted the jug, filled a cup with water, and took a sip. Since he had been unaccustomed to talking for so many years, his throat must have grown parched.

"Of course I wanted to tell you something else, but first you had to learn who I was. Only thus can you understand what I want to tell you, and realize that I have the right to tell it to you."

He fell silent for a moment, but then, weighing his words, he added in a voice filled with emotion, "Not only the right, but the duty!"

I raised my eyes to look at him. He was standing stiff and straight now in the middle of the cell, like a column. I looked at him and marveled. What joys, what humiliations this man had tasted, what impudence he had displayed in challenging the Almighty. I marveled at how he had entered the desert without deigning to forget, how he had bravely allowed the caravan of his sins to follow behind him so that, full of confidence, he and they could march all together toward God.

He remained silent, apparently struggling to choose what to say and how to say it without wounding me. For he saw me squirming nervously on my stool.

"I want you to know," he declared at last, "that of all the world's joys—and it has many, curse it!—youth is the one I revere the most. When I see a young person in danger I feel that God's vanguard, indeed the whole of life, is in danger also. I run to help, as far as I am able—to help keep youth from perishing, in other words from going astray, shedding its flowers, and growing old prematurely. This is the reason I called you to my cell tonight."

I gave a start.

"What, am I in danger?" I asked, not knowing whether to become angry or break out laughing.

The old man moved his hand slowly back and forth to calm me.

"Be angry, laugh, get it out of your system—but listen carefully. I am talking to you out of bitter personal experience; it is your duty to listen. For seven days I have watched you circling God's flame like a nocturnal butterfly. I don't want to let you be consumed; no, not you, I repeat, but youth. I pity your cheeks which are still covered with fuzz, your lips which are still not surfeited with kisses or blasphemy, your guileless soul which darts forward to be consumed wherever it spies a glint of light. But I will not let you. You are at the edge of the abyss. I will not let you fall."

"Whose abyss?"

"God's."

The cell creaked as he pronounced that terrible word. Some invisible being had entered. Never had this word which I had uttered so often and so profanely, never had it provoked such fright in me. Alive once more inside me was the childhood terror I felt when I heard the word *Jehovah* issue as though from a dark clamorous cave, the same terror which the word *massacre* had aroused in me ever since my childhood.

I rose from the stool and huddled in a corner.

"Do not stop, Father," I murmured. "I am listening."

"Inside you there is a great devouring concern. I see it in your burning eyes, your incessantly fluttering eyebrows, your hands which grope in the air as though you were blind, or as though the air were a body and you were touching it. Take care. This anxiety can lead you either to madness or perfection."

I felt his glance pass into me and churn up my entrails.

"What anxiety? I don't know what anxiety you mean, Father."

"The anxiety about sainthood. Do not become frightened. You yourself are unaware of it because you are living it. Why do I tell you this? It is to enable you to realize what road you have taken, which direction you have chosen. To keep you from going astray. Though you have embarked on the most difficult of all ascents, you are in such a hurry to reach the top that you think you can accomplish this before you traverse the mountain's foot and sides, supposedly as if you were a winged eagle. But you are a man and don't forget it. A man—nothing more, nothing less. You have legs, not wings. Yes, I know: man's supreme desire is for sanctity. Well and good, but first we must traverse all the lower desires, we must learn to despise the flesh, and also the thirst for power, gold, and rebellion. What I mean is, we should live our youth and all the manly passions to the hilt, should disembowel all these idols and discover that they are overstuffed with chaff and air, should empty and cleanse ourselves so that we will never be tempted to look back. Then, and only then, should we present ourselves before God. . . . This is how the true Striver acts."

"I can never cease wrestling with God," I replied. "I shall be wrestling with Him even at the very last moment when I present myself before Him. I believe this is my fate. Not to reach my destination—this I shall never do—but to wrestle."

Coming close, he tapped me tenderly on the shoulder.

"Never cease wrestling with God. There is no better discipline. But do not assume that in order to wrestle with more confidence you must pluck out the dark roots inside you—the instincts. The sight of a woman frightens you to death. You say it is the Tempter —'Get thee behind me, Satan.' Yes, it is the Tempter, but if you wish to conquer temptation, there is only one way: embrace it, taste it, learn to despise it. Then it will not tempt you again. Otherwise, though you live a hundred years, if you have not enjoyed women, they will come whether you are sleeping or stirring and will soil your dreams and your soul. I have said it once and I say it again: whoever uproots his instincts uproots his strength—for with time, satiety, and discipline this dark matter may turn to spirit."

He glanced around him and stepped up to the window, as though afraid that someone might be listening. Then, coming close to me, he whispered in a hushed voice, "I still have something else to tell you. We are alone; no one can hear us."

"God can," I said.

"I fear men, not God. He understands and forgives, they do not—and under no circumstances do I want to lose the tranquility I found here in the desert. . . . Listen, therefore, and bear firmly in mind what I am going to tell you. I am sure that it will help you."

He stopped for a moment, half closed his eyes, and glanced at me through his eyelashes, as though weighing me.

"I wonder if you can stand it," he murmured.

"I can, I can," I answered with impatience. "Speak freely, Father."

He lowered his voice still more.

"Angels are nothing more—do you hear!—nothing more than refined devils. The day will come—oh, if only I could live to see it!—when men will understand this, and then . . ."

He leaned over to my ear. For the first time, his voice was trembling.

". . . and then the religion of Christ will take another step forward on earth. It will embrace the whole man, all of him, not just half as it does now in embracing only the soul. Christ's mercy will broaden. It will embrace and sanctify the body as well as the soul; it will see—and preach—that they are not enemies, but fellow workers. Whereas now, what happens? If we sell ourselves to the devil, he urges us to deny the soul; if we sell ourselves to God, He urges us to deny the body. When will Christ's heart grow sufficiently broad to commiserate not only the soul but also the body, and to reconcile these two savage beasts?"

I was deeply moved.

"Thank you, Father, for the precious gift you have given me."

"Until this moment I have sought a young man to whom I could entrust it before I died. Now, praise the Lord, you have come. Take it. It is the fruit of my entire apprenticeship to flesh and spirit."

"You are rendering up the flame of your entire life. Will I be able to carry it still further and turn it into light?"

"You should not ask if you will succeed or not. That isn't what matters the most. The only thing that matters is your struggle to carry it further. God reckons that—the assault—to our account and nothing else. Whether we win or lose is His affair, not ours."

Neither of us spoke for quite some time. The desert night with its innumerable disquieting voices passed outside the cell's tiny window. Jackals could be heard howling in the distance; they too were undergoing the pangs of love or hunger.

"It is the desert," murmured the old man, making the sign of the cross, "the goatsuckers and jackals, and farther away, the lions. And inside the monastery, the monks sleeping and dreaming. And in the sky above us, the stars. And everywhere, God."

He offered me his hand. "I have nothing else to tell you, my child."

Walking with weightless steps, I returned to my cell, my mind clear, my heart beating calmly. Father Joachim's words were a glass of refreshing water, and I had been thirsty. The coolness branched to the very marrow of my backbone.

Gathering together my things, I tied them into a bundle and threw them over my back. I opened the door. Day must have commenced, because the sky had turned milky and the smallest of the stars had begun to fade. Down in the ravine a partridge started cackling.

Deeply inhaling the hallowed dawn, I crossed myself and murmured, "In God's name."

I proceeded along the cloister walk once again. The light was still burning in the old man's cell. I knocked. I heard his bare feet sliding over the flagstones. He opened the door and looked at me. Seeing the bundle over my back, he smiled.

"I am leaving, Father," I said, bending over to kiss his hand. "Give me your blessing."

He placed his palm over my hair.

"Bless you, my son. Go, and the Lord be with you!"

22

CRETE

I HAD GROWN weary. I was young, after all, and youth's insatiability is burdensome. It will not condescend to acknowledge man's limits; it seeks much but is capable of little. Having struggled to attain these limits and grown weary of the struggle, I returned to the land of my fathers. I wanted to confront our mountains, see our aged standard-bearers with their tilted fezzes and broad laughter, and hear once more of wars and liberty. I wanted to tread my native soil in order to gain strength.

"Where are you coming from?" my father asked me.

"From far, far away," I replied, not breathing a word about my adventure of nearly taking vows at Sinai.

It was the second time an attempt of mine to attain sainthood had miscarried. The first time, you remember, was in my childhood when I went down to the harbor, ran to a captain who was preparing to weigh anchor, and begged him to take me to Mount Athos so that I could become a monk. The captain split his sides with laughter. "Home, home!" he shouted. Clapping his hands as though I were a pullet, he shooed me away. Now it had happened again. "Return to the world," Father Joachim had cried. "In this day and age the world is the true monastery; that is where you will become a saint."

It was to gather momentum that I returned to my native soil. Leaving Kastro, I walked out to the villages, where I ate and drank with shepherds and plowmen. I felt ashamed, seeing how the lazy, fraudulent life of the monastery was so strongly opposed by the whole land of Crete, this land which is incessantly battling, if not with floods and droughts, then with poverty, disease, or the Turk. And here I was trying to go against its will and betray it by becoming a monk! Father Joachim was right. The world is our monastery, the true monk he who lives with men and works with

God here, in contact with the soil. God does not sit on a throne above the clouds. He wrestles here on earth, along with us. Solitude is no longer the road for the man who strives, and true prayer, prayer which steers a course straight for the Lord's house and enters, is noble action. This, today, is how the true warrior prays.

A Cretan once said to me, "When you appear before the heavenly gates and they fail to open, do not take hold of the knocker to knock. Unhitch the musket from your shoulder and fire."

"Do you actually believe God will be frightened into opening the gates?"

"No, lad, He won't be frightened. But He'll open them because He'll realize you are returning from battle."

Never did I hear from an educated man words so profound as those I heard from peasants, especially from oldsters who had completed the struggle. Their passions had subsided within them; they stood now before death's threshold, tenderly casting a final, tranquil glance behind them.

One afternoon I encountered an old man on a mountain slope. He was wizened and gaunt, with snow-white hair, patched vrakes, and boots full of holes. As is the custom with Cretan shepherds, he held his staff extended across his shoulders. He kept climbing slowly, stone by stone, stopping every so often to gaze lingeringly at the surrounding mountains, the plain far below, and the band of sea visible in the distance between the walls of a ravine.

"Good afternoon, grandfather," I called to him from a distance. "What are you doing here all by yourself?"

"Saying goodbye, son, saying goodbye . . ."

"In this forsaken place? I don't see a soul here. Who are you saying goodbye to?"

The old man tossed his head angrily. "What forsaken place? Don't you see the mountains and the sea? Why did God give us eyes? Don't you hear the birds above you? Why did God give us ears? You call this place forsaken? These are my friends. We talk to each other; I call them and they answer me. I'm a shepherd. I have ranged for two generations in their company. But now the time for parting has come. It's evening already."

"But it's still early in the afternoon, grandfather," I said, assuming his sight had been dimmed by age. "It's not evening yet."

He shook his head. "I know what I'm talking about. It's evening, I tell you, evening. . . . Goodbye."

"You'll lay even Charon by the heels, grandfather," I said to encourage him.

He laughed. "I've already done so, confound it! Yes, don't you worry, I've already laid him by the heels, the old cheat. How? By not being afraid of him! . . . Goodbye. You lay him out too, my fine lad, and you'll have my blessing."

I couldn't bear to let him go.

"Give me your name, grandfather. I don't want to forget you."

"Well then, bend down and pick up a stone. Ask and it will tell you. It's old Manoúsos from Kavrohóri, that's what it will tell you. . . . All right, enough now! Pardon me. As you can see, I'm in a hurry. . . . Godspeed!"

So speaking, he resumed the ascent, stumbling because his sight was poor.

It is true that we cannot conquer death; we can, however, conquer our fear of death. This aged mountaineer was facing the end with serenity. The hills had enlarged and fortified his soul; he would not condescend to kneel before Charon. What he wanted from him was simply a few days' respite to give him time to take leave of his former companions—the fresh air, thyme, and stones.

But as I was walking one day near Phaistos, down below on the fertile plain of Messará, I saw another old man, a centenarian. He was sitting on the doorstep of his humble cottage, sunning himself. His eyes were like two red wounds; his nose was dripping, spittle was running from his mouth, and he smelled of tobacco and urine.

Upon my entrance to the village, one of the man's grandsons had spoken to me laughingly about his grandfather. I was told to go and see him because he had become a baby again; apparently he seated himself at the village tap each evening and waited for the young girls to come along to fill their jugs. "He cranes his neck the minute he hears their clogs," the grandson told me. "He is half blind and can't make them out very well, so he holds out his arms and calls, 'You there, who are you? Come here, my child, if you want my blessing. Come close and let me see you.'

"The girl goes up to him with a laugh, and the old codger thrusts his hand into her face. He strokes it greedily—you'd think he wanted to gobble it up—pets the nose, mouth, and chin insatiably, then tries to go down to the throat. But the girl won't let him. She lets out a screech, and off she runs amid peals of laughter. The old man is left sighing, his palm still open.

"And how he sighs! You've simply got to hear him. It's like a buffalo. I asked him one day, 'But why do you sigh, Grandpa? What's the matter with you?' And he answered me with flowing tears, 'What do you think is the matter with me, confound it! Don't you have eyes in your head? I'm sinking into the grave and leaving such beautiful girls behind! Oh, if only I were a king to have them all slaughtered so that I could take them with me!'

"Then, feeling full of reproach, he begins to sing a mantinádha, always the same one, in a hushed voice:

Alas! the times gone by; alas! the times so dear.
O to have them back, if only one day a year."

Listening to the grandson made me impatient to go and admire this centenarian oak. I was shown his cottage, where I found him sitting in the sun warming himself. Going up to him, I said, "Well, well, grandfather, I hear you're a hundred years old. Tell me, how has life seemed to you these hundred years?"

He looked up with inflamed, lashless eyes.

"It's like a glass of cold water, my child."

"And are you still thirsty, grandfather?"

He raised his hand high, as though to call down a curse. "Damn whoever isn't!" he said.

I stayed for three days in a monastery overlooking the Libyan Sea. I have always liked the anachronistic life of monasteries—the ancient rhythm governing them, the monks with their cunning or drowsy eyes, their bloated or empty bellies, their large hands clasping the pruning hook or spade at one moment, the Holy Chalice and paten at the next. I have always liked the odor of incense, the melismatics in the chapel at dawn and afterwards everyone progressing together to the great manger, the refectory, which reeks of offal and rancid olive oil. And in the evening the muted conversations on the monastery terrace, and the oppressive silences filled with the faraway echoes of the world. Only seldom did we talk about Christ. He was like a strict but absent master who had gone to heaven and left his servants by themselves in his castle, where they shamelessly invaded the larder, went down to the wine cellar, reclined on the soft beds—danced while the cat was gone. Ah, but should He appear suddenly at the door, how the tables would be overthrown, and what cries these befrocked suitors would emit, and how the Lord's bow would twang!

One day as I was sitting on the monastery terrace with one of the monks, I brought the conversation around to the saint I love so much, Francis of Assisi. The monk had never heard of him. He made a sour face (Francis was a Catholic saint, a heretic). But Greek curiosity won in the end.

"Fine and good, you tell and I'll listen." He crossed his hands over his abdomen, ready to condemn everything I said.

"This saint," I began, "used to say in his prayers to God: 'How can I enjoy heaven, Lord, when I know hell exists? Dear Lord, either take pity on the damned and put them in paradise, or let me go down to the inferno and comfort the sufferers. I'll found an order whose purpose will be to descend to the inferno and comfort the damned. And if we can't lighten their pain, we'll remain in hell ourselves and suffer along with them.' "

The monk burst out laughing. "Now let me tell you a nice story," he said. "Once upon a time a pasha invited a pauper to dinner. He placed a plate of olives in front of him and also a plate of black caviar. Without so much as glancing at the olives, the pauper attacked the caviar unstintingly and ate away. 'Have some olives too, brother,' the pasha said to him. 'Why, pasha effendi?' the other replied. 'What's wrong with caviar?'

"Understand? Paradise is the black caviar. I'm sorry, but as far as I'm concerned, your friend Francescis—whatdyacallim?—is just another idiotic Catholic."

On the day of my departure I rose before dawn and went to matins, longing to hear the monotonous quavering melody the monks offered to God, and the moving words, so full of contrition, which the faithful of ancient times had found to bid the Lord good morning before the break of day: "God, my God, before thee I come in the morning. My soul thirsteth for thee, flesh longeth for thee in a dry and thirsty land, where no water is . . ." I stood in a stall next to the window, through which I saw the

Libyan Sea far below me, boundless and untraveled, still white in the morning mist, and reaching out as far as the warm sands of Africa. The birds had awakened with the monks and begun their own melodizing to greet the light. In the middle of the courtyard the cypress's crown was already aglow, while the leaves of the orange tree next to it remained plunged in dark green obscurity. The semantrist had completed his round of the cells to wake the monks; now, entering the half-lighted chapel, he removed his flowing kalýmmafko and hung the wooden semantron next to the door. As he stood silhouetted in the doorway, his curly, raven-black beard and the hair falling free over his shoulders had a brilliant sheen. Tall, of blackish complexion, he was overflowing with youthfulness. What a shame that a body such as his had not been destined to embrace a woman and beget children. His sons and daughters would have beautified the world.

While I was meditating on how often the world's loss fails to bring about God's gain, a woman wrapped in a black wimple appeared timidly at the doorway, an infant in her arms. The abbot had warned me the day before, with a cunning smile, not to be scandalized when a newlywed from a nearby village came on the morrow to ask his blessing for her newborn son. She wanted to protect him from the evil eye; apparently he was extremely beautiful, and the bushy-browed glouters were putting a hex on him.

Stopping next to the door, she began to wait with bowed head for matins to finish and the abbot to approach with his aspergillum. The atmosphere seemed to change, the heavy monkish exhalations to mix with the woman's breath, the chapel to smell of milk and the laurel oil from the newlywed's freshly washed hair. The abbot's sluggish voice took on new life, just precisely at the moment he was chanting the joyous hymn: "It is the Lord God and He is revealed to us; blessed is he that cometh in the name of the Lord. . . ." The monks leaned forward in their stalls, turned, threw sidewise glances toward the door; two or three began to cough. The semantrist went up to the woman and whispered something in her ear. Without raising her head, she stepped forward two paces and sat down in the stall nearest the door. You could sense that everyone had lost his tranquility, and that all the monks now, and I with them, could not wait for matins to be over.

The sun had risen meanwhile. The yard filled with light; the oblique rays entered the chapel, making the holy icons and the monks' faces and hands gleam brightly. The monks stepped down from their stalls, all sighing "Praise the Lord, praise the Lord." The service had ended.

The abbot donned his stole and picked up the aspergillum. The semantrist stood behind him with the ciborium of holy water. The woman placed herself at the door, her whole body in the light. She had pushed away her black wimple now, revealing her entire face. Lifting her eyes, she looked at the abbot, who had rested his palm on the infant's tiny head and begun to pronounce the blessing. Afterwards, she fixed her gaze on the semantrist. Her large, black, sorrowful eyes, with their inexpressible sweetness, reminded me of the eyes of the Portaïtissa at the Iviron Monastery—the same sweetness, the same anguish of mother for son.

Suddenly the infant began to kick his tiny legs and bawl. In order to pacify him, the mother unbuttoned her bodice and drew out her breast. The infant snatched at the nipple and became quiet. It was a moment I shall never forget: the newlywed's bosom gleaming in its snow-white roundness, the air smelling even more strongly than before of milk, also ever so slightly of sweat, and the Libyan Sea stretched out, a rich blue now, behind the woman's shoulders. The abbot became tongue-tied, but just for an instant. God quickly conquered in him, and he completed the prayer without disgracing himself.

The devil had prodded me to speak to the semantrist. I went up to him in the courtyard, although I had no idea what to say.

"Father Nikódemos . . ." I began.

But he increased his pace and entered his cell.

An hour later I resumed my travels, on foot as I always preferred.

How many years have elapsed since then? Forty? Fifty? The monastery has faded from my memory and in its place, gleaming above the Libyan Sea, is nothing but the mother's round, white, immortal breast.

Nightfall overtook me the next day as I was nearing a village. I was hungry and tired from having walked all day over rocky barrens, but though I knew no one in the village, nor even had the slightest idea of its name, I felt at ease. I knew that no matter what door you knock on in a Cretan village, it will be opened for you. A meal will be served in your honor and you will sleep between the best sheets in the house. In Crete the stranger is still the unknown god. Before him all doors and all hearts are opened.

Night had already begun to descend as I entered the village. The doors were all shut; in the courtyards the dogs caught the intruder's scent and began to bark. Where should I go, at which door should I knock? At the priest's home, where all strangers find refuge. The priests in our villages are uncultivated, their education meager; they are incapable of any theoretical discussion of Christian doctrine. But Christ lives in their hearts, and sometimes they see Him with their eyes, if not by the pillow of a wartime casualty, then sitting beneath a flowering almond tree in springtime.

A door opened. A little old woman came out with a lamp in her hand to see who the stranger was who had entered the village at such an hour. I stopped. "Long may you live, madam," I said, sweetening my voice so that she would not be frightened. "I am a stranger and have nowhere to sleep. Would you be so kind as to direct me to the priest's house?"

"Gladly. I'll hold the lamp so you won't stumble. God—his holy name be blessed—gave soil to some, stones to others. Our lot was the stones. Watch your step and follow me."

She led the way with the lamp. We turned a corner and arrived at a vaulted doorway. A lantern was hanging outside.

"This is the priest's house," said the old woman.

Lifting the lamp, she threw the light on my face and sighed. She was going to say something, but changed her mind.

"Thank you, my fine woman," I said. "Sorry to bother you. Good night."

She kept looking at me, not going away.

"If you wouldn't mind a poor house, you could come and lodge with me."

But I had already knocked on the priest's door. I heard heavy steps in the yard. The door opened. Standing in front of me was an old man with a snow-white beard and long hair flowing down over his shoulders. Without asking me who I was or what I wanted, he extended his hand.

"Welcome. Are you a stranger? Come in."

I heard voices as I entered. Doors opened and closed, and several women slipped hastily into the adjoining room and vanished. The priest had me sit down on the couch.

"My wife, the papadhiá, is a little indisposed; you'll have to excuse her. But I myself will cook for you, lay the table for your supper, and prepare a bed so that you can sleep."

His voice was heavy and afflicted. I looked at him. He was extremely pale, and his eyes were swollen and inflamed, as though from weeping. But no thought of a misfortune occurred to me. I ate, slept, and in the morning the priest came and brought me a tray of bread, cheese, and milk. I held out my hand, thanked him, and said goodbye.

"God bless you, my son," he said. "Christ be with you."

I left. At the edge of the village an old man appeared. Placing his hand over his breast, he greeted me.

"Where did you spend the night, son?" he asked.

"At the priest's house."

The old man sighed. "Ah, the poor fellow. And you didn't catch wind of anything?"

"What was there to catch wind of?"

"His son died yesterday morning. His only son. Didn't you hear the women lamenting?"

"I heard nothing. Nothing."

"They had him in the inner room. They must have muffled their laments to keep you from hearing and being disturbed. . . . Pleasant journey!"

My eyes had filled with tears.

"What are you crying for!" exclaimed the old man in astonishment. "Oh, I see: you're young, you haven't got used to death yet. Pleasant journey!"

It's fine to be in Crete, but only to gain momentum. In a few months' time I felt constricted again. The roads narrowed, my family home shrank, the basil and marigolds in the yard lost their fragrance. Observing how my old friends had settled in, I was seized with terror. I vowed never to shut myself up inside the four walls of an office, never to come to terms with the good life, never to sign an agreement with necessity. I used to go down to the harbor and gaze at the sea. It seemed a doorway to freedom. O to open it and flee!

I began to pace up and down the house in sullen silence. My

father watched me and knit his brow. One day I overheard him say to my mother, "What's wrong with this son of yours? What bug is eating him? Instead of looking in front of him to grasp what is in arm's reach, he looks beyond to the unobtainable. For him, two birds in the bush are worth one in the hand. Call me a liar if our son isn't like those lunatics you read about in fairy tales, the ones who go to the ends of the earth supposedly to find the Fountain of Youth."

But he was crying over spilt milk. He expected me to open an office and begin acting as sponsor in village baptisms and weddings in order to win friends who would elect me to the legislature; also to write articles in the local newspaper and to bring out a pamphlet saying that the place was going to the dogs and that it was necessary by all means for new people to emerge and take over the helm.

One day, unable to restrain himself, he demanded, "Why do you go about doing nothing? When do you plan to open an office and get down to work?"

"I'm still not ready."

"What more do you need?"

I needed nothing, and yet I needed everything. I was still tormented by youth's insolence and greed; the Theban eremites with their yearning for the absolute were at work inside me (perhaps they still are), as were also the great voyagers who had enlarged the earth by traveling.

Gathering up courage, I repeated, "I'm still not ready. The University of Athens isn't enough. I have to pursue higher studies."

"And that means?"

I hesitated. My father was sitting in his usual corner on the couch, next to the courtyard window. He kept rolling and unrolling a cigarette, without looking at me. It was Sunday afternoon; the rays entering through the panes cast their light on his stern sunburned face and thick mustache, and on the scar across his forehead, which must have been caused by a Turkish sword.

"And that means?" he asked again, raising his head now to glance at me. "Do you want to go abroad?"

"Yes."

"Where?"

I think my voice was trembling. "To Paris."

My father remained silent for a few moments.

"All right," he said at last. "Go."

My father was wild and uneducated, but he never denied me anything when it was a question of my intellectual development. Once I overheard him say to a friend when he was in a good mood, "Who cares about the bloody vineyards, or the raisins, wine, and olive oil! Let my whole harvest turn into paper and ink for my son! I have faith in him." He made every sacrifice, seemingly hanging on me all his hopes for his own salvation, for if I were saved, he would be saved as well, and so would our entire obscure lineage.

While I was still a child, I once told him I wanted to learn Hebrew in order to read the Old Testament in the original. There were Jews in Megalo Kastro at that time; my father called the Rabbi, and they agreed that I should go to him three times a week to receive lessons in Hebrew. But the moment our friends and relatives heard, their hair stood on end and they ran to my father. "What are you doing!" they shrieked. "Have you no feelings for your son? Don't you know that on Good Friday those crucifiers put Christian children in a spike-lined trough and drink their blood?" My father finally grew weary of their screams and my mother's weeping. "We've got ourselves into a fine kettle of fish," he said to me one day. "Forget the Hebrew; you'll learn it when you grow up."

Whenever I told him I wanted to learn a foreign language, he said, "Fine, go ahead and learn it. But only on one condition: that you wear another undershirt." It seems I was delicate, and he must have been afraid. I learned three foreign languages before I left Crete, and was thus obliged to wear three additional undershirts. When I went to the university at Athens, I discarded them.

"All right, go," he said once more.

I could not contain my joy. I bent over to clasp his hand and kiss it, but he anticipated me and drew it back.

"I'm not a priest!" he exclaimed.

The next day I kissed my mother's hand. Bending over, she gave me her blessing and instructed me for the love of God not to turn Catholic. Then she hung an amulet around my neck. It contained a piece of the True Cross. It seems my grandfather had worn it in the wars and no bullet had touched him.

My father accompanied me to the harbor, glancing at me with uneasiness and curiosity from time to time out of the corner of his eye. He could not understand who I was, what I wanted, and why I shifted about, first here then there, instead of settling down in Crete.

"I think you're like your grandfather," he suddenly said to me as we were arriving at the waterfront. "I don't mean your mother's father, but mine, the pirate."

After a moment's silence, he continued. "But he rammed ships, killed and looted, amassed property. What about you! What ships are you ramming?"

We reached the harbor. He squeezed my hand.

"Goodbye, good luck, and mind what you're about!" He shook his head, not at all satisfied with his only son.

And truly, what ships was I ramming?

23

PARIS. NIETZSCHE THE GREAT MARTYR

Dawn. A fine gentle drizzle was falling. My face glued to the carriage window, I could see Paris passing in back of the rain's diaphanous net—passing, laughing amidst its tears, and welcoming me. I saw the bridges go by, and the multistoried soot-covered buildings, the parks and churches, the stark, leafless chestnut trees, the people walking hurriedly along the wide gleaming streets. Through the rain's hanging filaments I could see all of Paris's charmingly playful face, smiling and shining dimly, just as we glimpse the weaver behind the threads of the loom.

I asked myself what could be in store for me in this long-coveted city, and I took man's soul to task for its inability to predict the future, not even one hour in advance. In order to see ahead could the soul do nothing but wait for the unborn to be born? Was it drab and infirm, just like the flesh? I wondered if I would find in this great city what I was looking for. But what was I looking for? What did I wish to find? Did this mean that the guide with the crown of thorns was not enough for me, the guide who stood as a landmark on the elevated summit of a mountain made all of stones and blood, and showed me the way? Or could Father Joachim have been correct in urging me to pass through the entire earthly inferno and purgatory if I wished to reach paradise—to experience joy, pain, and sin, and afterwards to transcend joy, pain, and sin if I wished to be saved?

The light had lifted its head a little; a glabrous sun suspended itself in this strange sky composed of fog, melancholy, and inexpressible tenderness. How plucked the long-maned charioteer of Greece was in these foreign parts! Far away in his homeland he stripped everything and dressed it again in his light, making the soul gleam as secretless and visible as the body. The demons emerged from their dark cellars there; the light penetrated to the black marrow of their bones and turned them into creatures guileless and sweet of speech, like men. But here the sun was different, which is to say that the faces of the earth and the soul were different. We had to learn to love the new beauty's half-illumined forehead, discreet smile, and hidden significance.

This is God's new countenance, I reflected as I gazed avidly at the trees and houses, the mascaraed women, the somber churches. This is God's new countenance. I fall and worship His grace!

My first contact with this new earthly countenance was an intoxication which lasted for days, for weeks. The streets, parks, libraries, museums, the Gothic churches, the men and women in the theaters and on the streets, the fine snow that had begun to fall—all were intoxicated too, and they reeled in front of my enraptured soul until finally the drunkenness wore off and the world steadied itself once more and grew stable.

One day while I was bent over a volume in the Bibliothèque Sainte-Geneviève, a girl came up to me. She was holding a book containing a man's photograph and she had covered the bottom of the page with her hand in order to hide his name. Bending over and gazing at me in amazement, she pointed to the photograph.

"Who is he?" she asked.

I shrugged my shoulders. "How should I know?"

"But it's you—the very image! Look at the forehead, the thick eyebrows, the sunken eyes. The only difference is that he has a large drooping mustache and you don't."

I looked at the picture, startled.

"Well, who is he?" I said, trying to push aside the girl's hand in order to see the name.

"Don't you recognize him? Is it the first time you've seen him? It's Nietzsche!"

Nietzsche! I had heard of him, but still had not read any of his books.

"Haven't you read *The Birth of Tragedy* or *Zarathustra*? About Eternal Recurrence, the Superman?"

"Nothing, nothing," I answered shamefully.

"Wait a minute!" exclaimed the girl, and she flew off.

In a few moments she had returned with *Zarathustra*.

"Here," she said with a laugh. "Here's some solid, leonine nourishment for your brain—if you have a brain, and if it's hungry!"

That was one of the most decisive moments of my life. Owing to the intervention of an unknown university student, my destiny had laid an ambush for me there in the Bibliothèque Sainte-Geneviève. Waiting for me there was the Antichrist, that great fiery warrior all covered with blood.

At first he completely terrified me. Nothing was lacking: Lucifer's talons, fangs, and wings were all in evidence, as well as the impudence and arrogance, the unyielding mind, the rabid rage for destruction, the sarcasm and cynicism, the impious laugh. But his impetuosity and pride swept me off my feet, the danger intoxicated me, and I plunged into his work with fright and longing, as though entering a bustling jungle full of famished beasts and dizzying orchids.

Each day I could not wait for my classes at the Sorbonne to end and night to fall. I longed to go home and have the landlady come and light the fire so that I could open his books—they were all piled high on my desk—and begin to share his struggle. I had grown accustomed little by little to his voice, his halting breath, his cries of pain. I had not known—only now was I discovering this—that the Antichrist struggles and suffers just as Christ does and that sometimes, in their moments of distress, their faces look the same.

His pronouncements struck me as impious blasphemies, his Superman as the assassin of God. This rebel had a mysterious fascination, however. His words were a seductive spell which dizzied and intoxicated; they made your heart dance. Truly, his thought was a Dionysiac dance, an erected paean raised triumphantly at the most hopeless moment of the human and superhuman tragedy. In spite of myself, I admired his affliction, mettle, and purity, as well as the drops of blood which bespattered his brow as though he too, the Antichrist, were wearing a crown of thorns.

Although I did not have this consciously in mind at all, the two figures, Christ and Antichrist, gradually merged. Was it true, then, that these two were not eternal enemies, that Lucifer was not

God's adversary? Would evil eventually be able to enter the service of good and collaborate with it? In the course of time, as I studied the work of this prophet opposed to God, I mounted step by step to a foolhardy, mystical unity. The first step of initiation, I said, was this: good and evil are enemies. The second and higher step was: good and evil are fellow workers. The highest step, the highest I was able to reach at present, was: good and evil are identical! On this step I halted, shuddering from a terrible suspicion that flashed across my mind: perhaps this Saint Blasphemer was prodding me to join him in his blasphemy!

I passed the entire winter engaged in this battle. The contest became ever more obstinate and close-quartered as time went by; I inhaled the adversary's panting, deeply anguished breaths from an ever-decreasing distance, until hate began to change, be transformed, and without my knowledge the struggle turned into an embrace. Never in my life had I felt so tangibly and with such astonishment that hate, by passing successively through comprehension, mercy, and sympathy, can be transformed into love. The same can happen when good wrestles with evil, I reflected. It was as though they had formerly been united, were then separated, and now were struggling to meet once more. But the time of perfect reconciliation had apparently not yet arrived. If I could judge from my own experience, however, such a time would most assuredly come; that is, the day when recognition would be given to the adversary and also to his free participation in the great synthesis which is called "cosmos," in other words "harmony."

What moved me most of all, O Great Martyr, was your holy, tragic life. Disease served as your great enemy and also your greatest friend, the only one that stayed loyal to the death. It never permitted you to relax or remain where you were, never allowed you to declare: I am fine here, I shall go no further. You were a flame; you flared up, were consumed, left your ashes behind you, and departed.

Yea, I know whence I come.
Insatiable as flame,
I burn and am consumed.
Whatever I touch is turned to light,
Whatever I leave is turned to carbon.
Assuredly I am a flame.

When spring arrived and the weather grew a little warmer, I embarked on a pilgrimage to find and follow the drops of your still-warm blood on all the ascents of your heroic struggle and martyrdom.

One rainy morning I wandered through the fog, seeking you in the narrow, muddy lanes of your natal village. Then I found your mother's house in the small neighboring city with its superb Gothic church. During your periods of high fever you often took refuge there, to find peace in becoming her child once more. Next came the divine streets along the waterfront of Genoa, where you found so much pleasure in the sea, the sweetness of the sky, the humble people. You were so gentle and meek, so poor, so cheerful, that the little old women of the neighborhood called you a saint. And you made plans, you remember, to begin an exceedingly simple and tranquil life: "I resolve to be independent in such a way that my independence offends no one; to have a hidden tender-voiced pride; to sleep without cares, avoid drinking, prepare my own humble meals; to have no illustrious and imposing friends; not to look at women, read newspapers, or seek honors; to associate only with the choicest souls, and if I do not find any that are especially choice, then with the common people."

How moved I was while searching beneath the springtime sun in Engadine between Sils-Maria and Silvaplana, searching for the pyramidal rock where you were first overwhelmed by the vision of Eternal Recurrence! You cried out amid wailing and lamentation, "Even as bitter and insupportable as my life is, let it be blessed, and may it come again and again, innumerable times." For you were tasting that bitter joy of heroes, a joy which to paltry souls seems a martyrdom: to see the abyss in front of you and proceed toward it without condescending to feel afraid.

The surrounding peaks steamed bluishly in the sunlight. I heard a noise in the distance and saw a mountain of snow suddenly collapse. I recalled what your friend wrote to you: "In your books I seem to hear the distant sound of falling water."

On my way into Sils-Maria I turned to my right with a shudder as I was crossing the small footbridge with the humble cemetery next to it, because just as you had suddenly felt Zarathustra next to you, so I in the same way saw my shadow divide in two as I looked down at it—and there you were, walking at my side.

All of your exploits and tribulations rise into my mind, O Great

Martyr. Still full of youth and ardor, you persistently interrogated every hero in order to select one who would subdue your heart. The day came when you encountered Schopenhauer, the Brahman of the North. Seating yourself at his feet, you discovered the heroic, despairing vision of life: The world is my own creation. Everything, both visible and invisible, is a deceptive dream. Nothing exists but will—blind, without beginning or end, purposeless, indifferent, neither rational nor irrational. Nonrational, monstrous. When jammed into time and place it crumbles into innumerable forms. These it obliterates. Then it creates new forms and smashes them again, continuing for all eternity in this same way. There is no such thing as progress; destiny is not governed by reason; religion, morality, and great ideas are worthless consolations good only for cowards and idiots. The strong man, knowing this, confronts the world's purposeless phantasmagoria with tranquility and rejoices in dissolving the multiform, ephemeral veil of Maya.

All that you had previously divined, O future prophet of the Superman, was being organized now into a strict, well-knit theory, being elevated into a heroic vision. The poet, philosopher, and warrior at odds within your heart were becoming brothers. In music, solitude, and long walks the young ascetic was enjoying happiness for a certain time.

Once when a downpour caught you in the mountains, you wrote, "What do I care about moral precepts—do this, don't do that? How different are lightning, tempest, and hail—free forces devoid of moral teaching! How happy and vigorous are these forces which remain untroubled by thought!"

Your soul overflowed with heroic bitterness when, one day in the flower of your youth, destiny brought you face to face with your next guide after Schopenhauer, the man who gave you the harshest joy of your life—Wagner.

It was a great moment. You were twenty-five, ardent and retiring, with quiet gentle manners and fiery, deeply sunken eyes; Wagner fifty-nine, at the height of his powers, full of dreams and deeds, a natural force exploding over the heads of the younger generation. "I want a theater where I can create in freedom. Come and give it to me!" he called to the young. "I want a people that will understand me. You become my people! Help me—it is your duty. Help me, and I will glorify you!"

Art was the only deliverance. "In representing life as a game," Wagner wrote to King Louis II, "art transforms life's most frightening aspects into beautiful pictures, thus exalting and consoling us."

You listened attentively and turned the master's words into flesh and blood, fighting at his side. You cast your regard upon the pre-Socratic philosophers. Suddenly a great and heroic epoch surged up before you, an epoch full of extraordinary flashes of insight, terrifying legends, tragic thoughts, and tragic souls who conquered the abyss by covering it with cheerful myths. Here was no longer the idyllic Greece pictured for us by schoolmasters, the balanced, carefree land that confronted life and death with a simplehearted, smiling serenity. This serenity came at the end, the fruit of an ardent tree which had begun to wither. Chaos bellowed in Greek breasts before tranquility arrived. An unbridled God, Dionysus, led men and women in frenzied dances in the mountains and caves, and the whole of Greece danced like a maenad.

With the fever of tragic wisdom, you toiled now to fit the parts of your vision into a whole. Apollo and Dionysus were the sacred pair who gave birth to tragedy. Apollo dreams of the world's harmony and beauty, beholding it in serene forms. Entrenched in his individuation, motionless, he stands tranquil and sure amidst the turbulent sea of phenomena and enjoys the billows presented in his dream. His look is full of light; even when sorrow or indignation overcome him, they do not shatter the divine equilibrium.

Dionysus shatters individuation, flings himself into the sea of phenomena and follows its terrible, kaleidoscopic waves. Men and beasts become brothers, death itself is seen as one of life's masks, the multiform stalking-blind of illusion rips in two, and we find ourselves in breast-to-breast contact with truth. What truth? The truth that we all are one, that all of us together create God, that God is not man's ancestor but his descendant.

Entrenched in the fortress of Apollo, the Greeks struggled at first to erect a barrier against these uncontrollable Dionysiac forces that were arriving by all the routes of land and sea to fling themselves upon the Greek land. But they were unable to tame Dionysus entirely. The two Gods met in combat, neither subduing the other. Then they became friends and created tragedy.

The Dionysiac orgies were relieved of their bestiality; the

dream's restrained gentleness bathed them in splendor. But Dionysus remained tragedy's constant and only hero. All the heroes and heroines of tragedy are simply the god's masks—becalmed smiles and tears glowing in the Apollonian grace.

But then Greek tragedy abruptly vanished. It was murdered by logical analysis. Socrates, with his dialectics, killed the Apollonian sobriety and Dionysiac intoxication. In the hands of Euripides, tragedy degenerated into a human rather than a divine passion, a sophistical sermon to propagandize new ideas. It lost its tragic essence and perished.

But the Dionysiac intoxication survived, perpetuating itself in mystery cults and in man's great moments of ecstasy. Would it, you wondered, be able to dress itself ever again in the divine flesh of art? Would the Socratic spirit—in other words, science—keep Dionysus forever in chains? Or, now that human reason recognized its own limits, might a new civilization perhaps appear with Socrates as its symbol—Socrates at long last learning music?

The ideal of our civilization until this point had been the Alexandrian scholar. But the crown on science's head had begun to totter; the Dionysiac spirit was continually reawakening. German music from Bach to Wagner proclaimed its coming. A new "tragic civilization" was dawning; tragedy was experiencing a renaissance. How that world of illusion, Schopenhauer's dark desert, was being transformed! How everything dead and sedentary was being twirled about in the whirlpool of German criticism! "Yes, my friends," cried the young prophet, "learn to believe, as I believe, in the Dionysiac life and in the renaissance of Dionysiac tragedy. The Socratic age is finished! Take the thyrsus in your hands, crown yourselves with ivy, dare to become tragic beings, prepare yourselves for great struggles, and have faith in your god Dionysus!"

Such, O Nietzsche, were the universe-generating hopes you based on the work of Wagner. The new tragic civilization was going to spring from Germany. The new Aeschylus was alive and fighting in front of our eyes. He was creating, and he desired our aid.

But your prophecies awakened no response. The scholars scorned you, the younger generation remained unmoved. You grew bitter, doubts arose inside you, you began to wonder if it were possible for contemporary man to be ennobled. You fell ill, and at the university your students abandoned you.

Heartbreaking anguish. The poet in you covered the abyss with the flowers of art, but the philosopher in you, desiring to learn at all costs, scorned every comfort, even that of art. The first created, and found relief; the second analyzed, dissected, and found despair. Your critical intellect smashed the idols. What value does Wagner's art have? you kept asking yourself. It was without form, without faith; nothing but panting rhetoric devoid of sacred intoxication and nobility—exactly like the art of Euripides. Good for hysterical ladies, hypocrites, and invalids. Your demigod had degenerated now into a hypocrite. He had hoaxed you, failed to keep his word. Now he was working on Christian themes, writing *Parsifal.* The hero had been defeated, had collapsed at the foot of the cross—the very man who promised to create new myths and hitch the leopard of reason to the Dionysiac chariot!

Art covers the horrible truth with beautiful pictures and is therefore a consolation for cowards. This was your new cry. As for us, let us find the truth even if the world perishes in the process!

This new cry was antithetical to the first. The critic in you triumphed over the poet, truth over beauty. But now even Schopenhauer failed to satisfy the exacerbated needs of your mind. Life was not only the will to live, it was something more intense—the will to dominate. Life was not appeased simply by self-preservation, it desired to expand and occupy.

Art was no longer the purpose of life, but rather a short respite in life's struggle. Knowledge was higher than poetry, Socrates greater than Aeschylus. Truth, even though lethal, was superior to even the most brilliant and fertile of lies.

Your heart breaking in two, you wandered in sickness from place to place. Heat paralyzed you, snow wounded your eyes, wind flayed your nerves. Unable to sleep, you began to take sedatives. You lived in unheated rooms, comfortless and destitute. But the man who is sick, you kept saying with pride, has no right to curse life. Out of your pain arose, clear and unyielding, the hymn to joy and health.

You felt a great seed maturing inside you and devouring your bowels. As you were walking one day in Engadine, you suddenly halted. Terror-stricken, you had just reflected that time is illimitable, while matter is limited. Of necessity, therefore, a new moment would come when all these combinations of matter would be reborn precisely the same as before. Thousands of centuries from now a person like yourself, indeed your very self, would stand once more on that same rock and rediscover that same idea. And not only once, but innumerable times. Thus, there was no hope for a better future; there was no salvation. We would revolve forever the same, identical, on the wheel of time. In this way even the most ephemeral objects attained sempiternity and the most insignificant of our actions assumed an incalculable importance.

You plunged into an ecstasy of anguish. All this meant that your suffering was endless and the world's suffering incurable. But your ascetic's pride made you welcome the martyrdom joyfully.

You told yourself, A new work must be created, I have the duty to create—in order to preach the new gospel to humanity. But in what form? A philosophical system? No. The thought must pour out lyrically. An epic? Prophecies? Suddenly the form of Zarathustra flashed through your mind.

It was in the midst of this joyful anguish that Lou Salome found you. The fiery Slav with the trenchant intellect so full of excitement and curiosity bowed before you, Great Martyr, and listened insatiably. You lavished your soul on her and she, never sated, smilingly wrung it dry. How many years since you had opened your heart with such confidence, had enjoyed the fervor, turmoil, and productivity called forth in us by women, had felt your soft heart melting beneath your heavy martial armor! That evening when you entered your ascetic's cell, the air of your life was fragrant for the very first time with a woman's perfume, and you inhaled it deeply.

This sweetest of thrills followed you, O Ascetic, to the mountains where you had taken refuge. Breathlessly you awaited the woman's letter. One day she sent you eight verses. Your heart throbbing as though you were a twenty-year-old lad, you declaimed them aloud beneath the deserted fir trees.

Who can ever flee if grasped by you,
if you turn on him your earnest eye?
Fly I never will if seized by you,
nor believe you can only destroy.

You pass, I know, through every earthly being;
on earth no thing remains untouched by you.
Life without you would be beautiful,
and yet you too are worthy to be lived.

Immediately afterward came the fatal days of separation. You frightened the woman. You were like a benighted forest; in your darkness she failed to see the little god smiling at her with his finger to his lips. Your martyrdom—disease, abandonment, silence—began anew. You felt like a tree bowed beneath the weight of its fruit, and you longed for hands to come and gather up the harvest. Though you stood at the end of the road and gazed out over the cities of men below you, no one came. Is there no one to love me? you cried in your solitude; no one to insult or ridicule me? Where is the Church to call down its curses? Where is the State to take my head? I cry and cry—does no one hear?

Oh, this solitude, this separation from the person one loves! No, you said to yourself, never, never again may I relive these hours. I must open a door of salvation in the closed circle of Eternal Recurrence.

A new hope sprang up inside your bowels—a new seed, the Superman. The Superman constituted the world's purpose. He it was who held salvation in his hands and formed the answer to your old question of whether contemporary man could be ennobled. Yes, he could. And not by Christ, as that apostate Wagner was then preaching in his new work, but by man himself, by the virtues and struggles of a new aristocracy. Man was capable of begetting the Superman. Eternal Recurrence was strangling you. The Superman was the new Chimera which would exorcise life's horror. Not art any more, but energy. You took God for a windmill, O Don Quixote, and demolished Him.

"God is dead," you proclaimed, bringing us to the edge of the abyss. There is only one hope: Man must surpass his nature and create the Superman. Full administration of the cosmos will fall upon his shoulders then and he will have the power to undertake such a responsibility. God is dead, His throne vacant; we shall enthrone ourselves in His place. Do we remain all alone now in the world? Has the master passed away? So much the better! From now on we shall work not because He commands us to, not because we fear or hope, but because we ourselves want to work.

Eternal Recurrence was devoid of hope, the Superman a great hope. How could these two clashing world views be reconciled? Untold anguish. From that time onward your soul beat its wings over the abyss of madness. Zarathustra remained only a Cry. Abandoning this tragic poem in a half-completed state, you fought now to prove scientifically that life's essence was the will to power.

Europe is perishing, you cried. It must submit to the strict discipline of the leaders. Today's reigning morality is the work of slaves, a conspiracy organized by the weak against the strong, the flock against the shepherd. With cunning self-interest the slaves have turned values upside down; the strong person becomes bad, the sickly and weak good. They cannot endure pain, these slaves; they are philanthropists, Christians, and socialists. Only the Superman, who first of all acts harshly himself, is able to inscribe new commandments and give the masses new, superior goals.

The nature of these goals, the proper organization of the elect and the multitude, the role of war in this new tragic period of European history: these were the problems which harassed your final years of lucidity. Unable to answer them, your mind tottering, you devoted yourself again to your old Dionysiac poems, and with most bitter foreboding sang your swan song.

The sun is setting.

Soon you will no longer thirst,
O my burning heart.
A freshness is in the air,
I feel breaths from unknown mouths—
the great coldness comes. . . .

The air is strange and pure.
Did not this night cast
a wry and seductive
glance at me?
Keep strong, O my brave heart!
Do not ask why.

Eve of my life!
The sun is setting.

You saw what man is not permitted to see, and your sight was taken from you; you danced beyond human endurance at the brink of the abyss, and into the abyss you plunged.

The darkness quickly overwhelmed your mind. This darkness lasted eleven years, until your death. Sometimes you grasped a book in your hands and asked, "I wrote splendid books also, did I not?" And when you were shown Wagner's picture, you said, "I greatly loved that man."

Never had a more heart-rending cry sprung from a human breast. And never had I lived the life of a saint with such intensity, not even when I read the holy legends as a child. I believe that after my pilgrimage to the new Golgotha came to an end and I returned to Paris, my heart (more than my mind) had changed. To such a degree had I experienced this great atheist martyr's anguish, so severely had my old wounds begun again to rankle as I followed his bloody tracks, that I felt ashamed of my staid, well-ordered, cowardly life, which dared not destroy all its bridges behind it and enter, completely alone, the realm of utmost bravery and despair. What had this prophet done? What did he tell us, above all, to do? He told us to deny all consolations—gods, fatherlands, moralities, truths—and, remaining apart and companionless, using nothing but our own strength, to begin to fashion a world which would not shame our hearts. Which is the most dangerous way? That is the one I want! Where is the abyss? That is where I am headed. What is the most valiant joy? To assume complete responsibility!

Sometimes I suddenly felt his shadow next to mine as I strolled beneath Paris's chestnuts or along the banks of its famous river. We proceeded side by side in silence until the sun went down. He was always short of breath, gasping, and tinged with the smell of sulphur. It occurred to me that he must be returning from hell—my own breath caught in my throat and I began to gasp. But we did not wrestle now; we had become friends. He looked at me, and I perceived my face in the pupils of his eyes. Anguish is contagious, however. He had given me all his troubles. Together with him I had begun my own battle to match the unmatchable—to reconcile utmost hope with utmost despair, and to open a door beyond reason and certainty.

One evening as the sun was setting and we were about to part, he who never spoke to me turned and said, "I am the crucified Dionysus—I am, he is not!" His voice was full of envy, hate, and love.

My heart's calmness always returned when I went to hear Bergson's magical voice the following day. His words were a bewitching spell that opened a small door in the bowels of necessity and allowed light to pour in. But the wound, the blood, the giant sigh—all those elements so fascinating to youth—were missing, and I used to go and walk once more beneath the chestnuts in order to meet the other, the one who wounded.

In those days the wound never penetrated me deeply. I shared his hurts, but only superficially. Like Saint Francis, I was stamped with stigmata wherever the fierce prophet had a running wound; my skin turned black and blue, that was all. It was later, when the apocalyptic angels he had envisioned finally plunged down upon mankind, that my own wounds began to open. This was in London, I remember, many years later. Autumn had come again; I was sitting on a bench in some park. The air was filled with terror. Somewhere the Superman had been born; somewhere a bloodthirsty tiger imagined he was a Superman. Unable to fit in his lair any longer, he was possessed by the rage for domination. Genghis Khan wore an iron ring with two words engraved upon it: *Rastí Roustí*—"Might Is Right." Our age had donned this same iron ring. The demon of our age was like that legendary African king who mounted his highest tower with twelve women, twelve singers, and twenty-four goatskins of wine. He was as tall as a steeple, fat as butter, and covered with hair. The entire city shook with dancing and song; the oldest huts collapsed to the ground. At first the king danced. Then, growing tired, he sat down on a stone and began to laugh. Then he grew tired of laughing and began to yawn, and in order to pass the time he hurled from the tower first the women, then the singers, and finally the empty wineskins. But his heart felt no relief, and he began to bewail the inconsolable suffering of kings. . . .

A newsboy came along proclaiming the latest war communiqués. People stopped short in the street, as though their hearts had ceased beating. Some ran headlong toward their homes; they seemed anxious to see if their children were still alive.

A shadow came and sat down beside me on the bench. Turning, I shuddered. It was he. Who was the man who proclaimed that the essence of life is the longing to expand and dominate, and that only power is worthy of having rights? Who was the man who prophesied the Superman, and in prophesying him, brought him? The Superman had arrived, and here was his cowering prophet, struggling to hide beneath an autumn tree!

It was the first time I felt such a tragic sympathy for him. For it was the first time I saw so plainly that we are all the reeds of some invisible Shepherd, that we play whatever melody he blows into us, and not the melody which we ourselves desire.

I gazed at the sunken eyes, the sheer brow, the drooping mustache.

"The Superman has come," I whispered. "Is this what you wanted?"

He cringed even more, like a hunted and wounded beast attempting to hide. His voice rang out proud and sorrowful from the other bank. "Yes!"

I could feel his heart ripping in two.

"You sowed. Observe now what has been reaped. Do you like it?"

Once more from the other bank came a despairing, heart-rending cry. "Yes!"

Alone again, I rose from the park bench in order to leave. Just then a bomber roared over the blacked-out city. The airplane, imagined by Leonardo da Vinci as a kindly artificial bird which would carry snow from high mountain peaks in summertime and sprinkle it over cities to cool them, now passed overhead laden with bombs.

Similarly, I reflected—keeping the peaceful prophet of war always in my mind—similarly, thoughts spring from the human brain like skylarks at dawn, but as soon as man's rapacious glance falls on them, they are transformed into famished flesh-eating vultures. Their unfortunate sire calls out and protests in despair: "That is not what I wanted! That is not what I wanted!" But the vultures pass screechingly overhead, reviling him.

It was solid, leonine nourishment that Nietzsche fed me at this most critical, most hungry moment of my youth. I had waxed luxuriant, and now I found myself too constricted both by contemporary man in the state to which he had reduced himself, and by Christ in the state to which He had been reduced by man. Oh, how crafty of religion, I cried out indignantly, to transplant rewards and punishments into a future life in order to comfort cowards and the enslaved and aggrieved, enabling them to bow their necks patiently before their masters, and to endure this earthly life without groaning (the only life of which we can be sure)! What a jew-higgling Table of the Lord this religion is, where you lay out a farthing in this life and collect immortal millions in the next! What simplicity, what cunning, what usury! No, the man who either hopes for heaven or fears hell cannot be free. Shame on us if we continue to become intoxicated in the taverns of hope or the cellars of fear. How many years had I lived without comprehending this! It was necessary for the fierce prophet to come along and open my eyes!

Until now we had entrusted God with the full administration of the world. Could man's turn to undertake the responsibility have arrived—our turn to create a world, our own world, with the sweat of our brows? A satanic breeze of arrogance blew across my temples. I saucily declared that the time had come when man must receive into his breast all struggles and all hopes, must bring order out of chaos without expecting God's help—transform it, in other words, into a cosmos. We had to maintain our personal independence stiff and unbending so that we might be found standing on our feet amidst the contemporary world-wide delirium when the moment came for us to convert the inarticulate cries into a message which was simple and true—into a Gospel.

I heard this Gospel within me like a distant warbling, like the very first puffs of spring. My heart resembled the almond tree. While winter reigns around it and the sky above is everywhere dark, this tree, having already received the secret vernal mandates, suddenly appears before our eyes covered with flowers—covered with flowers in the heart of January, though it stands trembling in the icy wind. So too my fully blossoming heart stood trembling. A strong wind might blow and strip it, but little matter. It had done its duty, had cried aloud that it saw the spring.

One night I had a dream. Throughout my life dreams have always been infallible guides. All the problems tormenting my waking mind, twining and intertwining in a hopeless effort to discover a simple, certain solution, have been refined in my dreams. They throw off all superfluity, are reduced to the exceedingly simple essence, and this essence is liberated. During this entire period I was pierced through and through like Saint Sebastian by the arrows the tragic prophet of Eternal Recurrence had shot at me. My mind toiled in vain to discover, amid the darkness that surrounds and suffocates us all, what constitutes man's duty. Then, one night, I had a dream. It seemed I was at the shore's extreme edge, gazing outward. The ocean was pitch black, seething, full of terror, the sky above it similarly black, heavy, menacing. It kept descending lower and lower; in a moment it would touch the sea. Not a puff of breeze; the silence and stagnation were horrible. I was suffocating, unable to breathe. Suddenly a luminous white sail flashed in the narrow crack still left between sea and sky. It was a minuscule self-radiant skiff between the two darknesses, pressing forward swiftly, precipitously, in the suffocating calm, its sail bellied out to the bursting point. Extending my arms directly toward it, I cried, "My heart!" and awoke.

That dream was of great help to me throughout my life. What a shame I could not run to find the hopeless, despairing father of hope and inform him of the hidden meaning brought me in my sleep. Wasn't this the solution to all his anxieties? Hadn't he, amidst utmost despair, invoked this intrepid skiff which sails of its own wind, shines of its own light, and has no need of anyone?

How many times in moments of difficulty, when everything about me began to grow dark and my most precious friends and most assured hopes were abandoning me, had I not closed my eyes and seen this little skiff between my lashes? And my heart always took courage, leaped to its feet with a cry of "Luff the helm and do not fear," and ripped through the darkness!

The wounds opened in me by Nietzsche were deep and hallowed; Bergson's mystic salves could not heal them. They relieved them temporarily, but soon the sores opened again and bled—for as long as I remained young, what I desired most deeply was not the cure but the wound.

It was at this point that my battle with the Invisible became conscious and merciless.

Indignation had overcome me in those early years. I remember that I could not bear the pyrotechnics of human existence: how life ignited for an instant, burst in the air into a myriad of colorful flares, then all at once vanished. Who ignited it? Who gave it such fascination and beauty, then suddenly, pitilessly, snuffed it out? "No," I shouted, "I will not accept this, will not subscribe; I shall find some way to keep life from expiring." For I pitied man's soul and marveled at its achievements. How was this lowly silkworm able to extract such divine silk from its entrails?

The silkworm is the most ambitious of worms. Nothing but belly and mouth, it drags itself along, eating, soiling, eating again, a filthy pipe with two holes. Then suddenly all the food turns to silk. Man is the same. Heaven and earth sparkle, ideas sparkle with the precious silks in which he has clothed them; whereupon a huge foot suddenly comes and tramples the wonder-working worm.

Gone forever were the credulity and unsophisticated well-being of childhood. Now I knew that the heavens were a black chaos full of silence and indifference; I had seen what becomes of beauty and youth when they sink into the grave, and my soul no longer deigned to accept the consolation offered by agreeable, cowardly hopes.

Gradually, with unsure steps, I was nearing the abyss. But my sight was still untrained, and I dared not look it straight in the eye. My soul was still seething and unsettled. At times it stood up and challenged the destiny of man with juvenile bravura; at other times it shrank back and was overwhelmed by romantic melancholy.

Much later, very much later, I was able to stand with firm knees at the edge of the precipice and look down into the abyss fearlessly, and also with no trace of insolence.

What divine, untroubled nights of work and study in that tiny room far from home! Sometimes there were shouts and laughter in the street below, and love songs at midnight; sometimes just white peaceful snow on the rooftops. The lamp burning late into the night, a fire in the hearth, I bent over my books and relived the intellectual feats of mankind.

It was with such preoccupations, preoccupations belonging at the same time so eminently to youth and also so eminently to age, that my years in Paris were spent. My landlady began to suspect something and grow uneasy. She cast sidewise glances of disapproval at me and greeted me halfheartedly. One day she could restrain herself no longer.

"Once and for all, monsieur," she shouted, "how long is this state of affairs going to continue?"

"What state of affairs?"

"What state of affairs! Why, you come home early every evening, you never receive visitors, either men or women, you keep your light on past midnight. I suppose you think that's normal?"

"But I attend classes all day long at the university; at night I study and write. Isn't that permitted?"

"No, it is not. I've had complaints from the other tenants. You are hiding something. Such decorum, such isolation and silence—without a woman, good gracious, without a friend! You must be sick. Yes, you must be sick, or else, with all due respects, you're cooking up something. I'm sorry, but this simply cannot continue."

At first I was on the verge of anger, but I quickly realized that my landlady was right. When a person is orderly and quiet in a society which is unruly, immoral, and boisterous, when he welcomes neither men nor women into his room, he infringes the rules. He is not, and cannot be, tolerated. I have observed this all through my life. Since my life was always extremely simple, people considered it dangerously complicated. No matter what I said or did, they attached a different meaning to it, always trying to divine what was hidden and undivulged.

Later on, even my best friend could not believe such simplicity at first, and he found it insufferable when he finally did believe it. One night I was sitting in the yard gazing at the stars. For me the star-filled sky had always been the most heart-rending, the most disquieting, of sights. It gave me no joy whatsoever, nothing but fright; I could not look at it without panic invading my heart. My friend came out into the yard. "What are you doing there?" he asked me, astonished. "Ah, so you're not talking. Why not?" Coming closer, he leaned over me and saw the large tears that were flowing from my eyes. He burst into guffaws. "Liar! Hypocrite!" he shouted. "I suppose you'll tell me now that you're crying because looking at the stars is so moving. But you can't fool me, you Jesuit! You must be thinking of one of those tail-wagging females who keep fluttering around you."

And on another occasion as well, after this, when I came to know Panait Istrati in Russia and we were returning together to Greece, Panait stared at me during the entire journey. He kept examining me, but had no idea what conclusion to draw. In Athens he asked a journalist, who replied, "What can I say? He just isn't natural." "What does he do?" asked poor Panait, full of apprehension. "That's just it: nothing. He doesn't even smoke."

Such was my life in Paris during my three-year sojourn—peaceful and ardent, without a single external adventure, without student love affairs or student inebriation, without political or intellectual conspiracies. At the end even my landlady had grown accustomed to me. Believing that she had cracked my secret, she at last forgave the purity and decorum of my life, which formerly had been so incomprehensible to her.

"He must be enrolled in some religious order in his own country," I heard her say behind my back to one of the neighbors, a woman who likewise observed me morning and night with an uneasy eye. "He wants to, poor devil, yes he wants to, but it isn't allowed."

"If that's the kind of order he's in, why doesn't he resign?" asked the neighbor with irritation.

"Ah well, it's his one quirk," my landlady indulgently replied.

When I had packed my valises and was about to depart, she came into my room with her daughter Susan.

"Well, kiss my daughter now that you're leaving," said the mother, dying to tempt me.

"And not on the forehead," protested the daughter as she saw me approach. "Not on the forehead."

"Where, then?"

"Wherever else you like, poor devil!"

"On the mouth, you ninny!" screamed the mother, splitting with laughter.

I leaned over and kissed her on the cheek.

Before leaving Paris I went late one afternoon to say goodbye to Notre Dame. I shall always be grateful to this cathedral for moving me so very much when I first saw it. In our churches the dome strikes one as a graceful accord between finite and infinite, between man and God. The temple surges upward as though aspiring to reach heaven, but then, with pious resignation, it suddenly subordinates its impetus to saintly "measure," bows submissively, curves inward in the face of unattainable boundlessness and becomes a dome, pulling the Pantocrator down to its vertex.

The Gothic cathedral's rash aspiration struck me as altogether more self-esteeming. Notre Dame surges out of the ground, seemingly mobilizing all the stones of the earth in order to discipline them into terminating in a sharp, daring arrow which dashes into the sky like a lightning rod. Everything in this sacred architecture strives summitwards and becomes an arrow. No longer do we have the rectilinear, square logic of the Greek style, which places human order on top of chaos, perfectly balancing beauty with need and inaugurating a reasonable compact between man and God; instead, we have something vehement and irrational, a divinely inspired frenzy, which suddenly transports men and urges them to undertake an assault against the dangerous blue wilderness in order to pull the great Lightning Flash—God—down to earth.

Perhaps prayer and the human soul should be like this—who knows? Mobilizing our human hopes and fears, we ought to hurl them like arrows toward the unattainable superhuman heights. The human soul is impetus and pride; a cry amidst unbearable, cowardly silence; a lance which stands erect and unbending and does not allow the sky to fall upon our heads.

Gazing at this arrow that mounts fearlessly into the heavens, I felt my soul grow solid, stretch itself out, and become an arrow.

Suddenly I uttered a joyful shout. Was not Nietzsche's cry just the same? Was not it too an arrow darting into the sky, a lightning rod meant to seize God and pull Him down from His throne? How happy I was to be wandering in this way beneath the high Gothic arches at the hour of sunset, immersed in this Zarathustrian soul composed of stones, iron, lucent multicolored tracery, and the deep reverberations of an invisible, divinely enraptured organ!

In this way, slowly, with my heart full of questions and of frantic despair and hope, I bade farewell to Paris.

I was leaving; my heart had lost its sureness and peace. Who was the ascetic who declared, "You sit still and your heart is quiet, but if you hear so much as a sparrow's song, your heart no longer has its former peace"? And I—I who had heard the shrill cry of a savage hawk?

I was leaving Paris. The wounds on hands, feet, and side—all the wounds of the Crucifixion—had healed, but in their place and hurting me terribly was my soul, surging up within me all bloody and rebellious.

Always, whenever I reach some certainty, my repose and assurance are short-lived. New doubts and anxieties quickly spring from this certainty, and I am obliged to inaugurate a new struggle to deliver myself from the former certitude and find a new one—until finally that new one matures in its turn and is transformed into uncertainty. . . . How, then, can we define uncertainty? Uncertainty is the mother of a new certainty.

Nietzsche taught me to distrust every optimistic theory. I knew that man's womanish heart has constant need of consolation, a need to which that super-shrewd sophist the mind is constantly ready to minister. I began to feel that every religion which promises to fulfill human desires is simply a refuge for the timid, and unworthy of a true man. I asked myself if Christ's way was the one leading to man's salvation, or whether it was simply a well-organized fairy tale promising paradise and immortality with immense cleverness and skill, so that the faithful would never be able to learn if this paradise was anything more than the reflection of our own thirst. For we can determine this only after we die, and no one has, or ever will, return from the land of the dead to tell us.

We ought, therefore, to choose the most hopeless of world views, and if by chance we are deceiving ourselves and hope does exist, so much the better. At all events, in this way man's soul will not be humiliated, and neither God nor the devil will ever be able to ridicule it by saying that it became intoxicated like a hashish-smoker and fashioned an imaginary paradise out of naïveté and cowardice—in order to cover the abyss. The faith most devoid of hope seemed to me not the truest, perhaps, but surely the most valorous. I considered metaphysical hope an alluring bait which true men do not condescend to nibble. I wanted whatever was most difficult, in other words most worthy of man, of the man who does not whine, entreat, or go about begging. Yes, that was what I wanted. Three cheers for Nietzsche, the murderer of God. He it was who gave me the courage to say, That is what I want!

The Church of Christ in the state to which the clergy had brought it suddenly seemed to me an enclosure where thousands of panic-stricken sheep bleat away night and day, leaning one against the other and stretching out their necks to lick the hand and knife that are slaughtering them. Some tremble from fear they will be skewered for all eternity in raging flames, while others cannot wait to be slaughtered so that they may graze everlastingly in immortal springtime grass.

But the true man is not a sheep. Neither is he a sheepdog, a wolf, or a shepherd. He is a king who carries his kingdom with him and advances. Knowing where he is going, he reaches the brim of the abyss, removes the cardboard crown from his head, and discards it. Then he strips himself of his kingdom, and, completely naked like a diver, joins his hands together, also his feet, throws himself headfirst into chaos, and vanishes. Would I, I wondered, ever be able to confront the abyss with this tranquil, untrembling glance?

I wonder if such a cry has ever been heard on earth, a cry proud enough to scorn hope. Even Nietzsche gave way to terror for an instant. Eternal Recurrence struck him as an interminable martyrdom, and out of his fright he fashioned a great hope, a future savior, the Superman. But the Superman is just another paradise, another mirage to deceive poor unfortunate man and enable him to endure life and death.

24

VIENNA. MY ILLNESS

MY BODY was so fatigued, my soul in such a state of hypertension, that I closed my eyes in the railway car and did not so much as raise my lids to see the countries I was traversing. The bow had been so greatly overdrawn that I already heard the creaking of the cord stretched from one temple to the other inside me; it had reached the breaking point.

My temples ringing, the veins in my neck pounding, I felt the strength pouring out of my brain, loins, ankles—and perishing. I kept thinking to myself, So this is what death is like—calm, exceedingly compassionate; like entering a warm bath and slitting your veins. A woman, infant in arms, opened the door to enter the compartment where I was stretched out full length all alone. Seeing me, she immediately closed the door and fled in terror. My head must already have become a skull, I reflected; that's why the woman was frightened. Still, it's good that death did not strike me in the mind, as it did you, my master.

When we reached Vienna, I amassed all my strength in order to get off the train and buy a newspaper at the kiosk across the platform. But I slipped, struck an iron post, and collapsed unconscious to the ground.

After that I remember nothing. When I opened my eyes, I found myself in a large ward with rows of beds. It was night; a small blue light was burning above me. My head was bound in cotton and gauze. A white shadow with two great white wings, one at each temple, flitted weightlessly between the beds. It came up to me, placed its cool, gentle hand on my pulse, and smiled.

"Go to sleep," it said softly.

I closed my eyes; sleep descended upon me again, a strange, dense sleep. I felt submerged in tepid molten lead, my hands and feet so heavy that I could not budge them, as though my soul's wings had stuck together.

A dense sleep was what my entire sojourn in the sickbed seemed to me. For many days I refused to open my mouth and eat. I had melted away, was unable to lift myself up or move. Each day I felt myself sinking continually further and further—at first to the waist, then to the breast, then to the throat—into a tepid, soft mire which smelled of rotted leaves. I sensed it must be death.

From time to time I raised my head out of its torpor. My mind having issued once more into the light, I called the nurse. She, the white wings at her temples, came knowingly with pencil and paper in hand, ready to write. My mind was working, resisting, trying to keep itself from sinking into the mire along with the rest of me, and I had accustomed the nurse to coming so that I might say a few words to her—a haikai, whatever rose from chaos—and have her write them down. Many of those haikai went for nought; others I subsequently inserted in my writings after I emerged from the mire of death.

"I am ready," the sister said, taking my hand and smiling.

She always wrote with the paper resting on her knees—I remember her slim, brilliantly white hands. Closing my eyes, I dictated:

"*Hello there, man, you little two-legged plucked cock! It's true—never mind what people say—that the sun won't rise in the morning unless you crow.*"

The nurse laughed. "What things you concoct in your fever!" she said.

"Write: *A worm sleeps in God's heart and dreams that God does not exist.*

"Write: *If you open my heart, you'll find a steep, forbidding mountain and a man, all alone, climbing it.*

"And write this also: *'If you blossom now in midwinter, scatter-brained almond tree, the snow will come and destroy you.' 'Let it!' replies the almond tree every spring.*"

"That's enough, enough for today," the sister declared, seeing me grow pale.

"No, no, this too: *I enjoy seeing the mind knock at heaven and beg, and God refuse to open the gates and give it a piece of bread.*"

"Enough! Enough!" the nurse insisted.

"No, no, this too, so they'll know down there in Greece in case I die: *Wherever I go and wherever I stay, I hold Greece between my teeth like a laurel leaf.*"

I closed my eyes; my brain had been emptied.

"I'm tired, sister. . . ." I murmured, and I sank back down into the mire.

My life's joys and vicissitudes, the people I loved, the countries I had seen: all floated across my mind like clouds, halted momentarily, then immediately scattered and vanished, whereupon other clouds rose, sometimes from my right temple, sometimes from my left, according to how the wind was blowing.

In the midst of my fever one day, I remembered the Virgin of the Golden Steps, a Cretan monastery jutting over the Libyan Sea. What a day that had been, what a tender springtime sun, how the sea glittered as it made off toward the Barbary Coast! And the abbot, a squat, broadish, well-preserved, succulent old man with a forked white beard and twirled mustachios like a soldier, how full of good humor he was, how his mind scintillated! He took me for a stroll to view the monastery graveyard, where he showed me the tombs of the monks carved into the rock over the water. The sea spattered the black wooden crosses whenever there was a storm, and all the names engraved on them had been worn away. I started to turn back, since I found ambling among the tombs extremely unpleasant. But the abbot seized my arm, squeezing it until it hurt. "Come, come, my brave lad," he said to me laughingly, "don't be afraid. It's said the human being is the animal that thinks about death. But I disagree. No, the human being is the animal that thinks about life everlasting. Come and see!" He halted at an open, empty tomb. "Look, this is mine. Don't be afraid, lad. Come near. It's still empty, but it will be filled." He broke into peals of laughter. He himself had dug it out of the rock with a mattock and had also prepared the tombstone. "Look what I've engraved on it," he called to me. "Well, why don't you bend down and read? Stop being afraid, I tell you!" He knelt, brushed the dirt off the carved letters, and read: "Eh, Death, I'm not afraid of you!" He glanced at me; even his ears were laughing. "And why should I be afraid of him, the old impostor! He is a mule; I'm going to mount him and have him take me to God."

Some of man's richest hours, I believe, some of the freest, the most completely liberated from time, place, and rationality, are the hours of fever.

It was May when I was finally able to leave the clinic and emerge into the light. The lilacs were blooming in the parks; the women wore diaphanous dresses with floral designs; girls and boys exchanged whispers beneath the newly foliaged trees, as though they had great secrets to tell. On the afternoon of my discharge a gentle breeze was blowing, carrying with it the scents from the women's hair and powdered faces. I kept repeating to myself that this was the earth, the upper world. How very nice it was to be alive with all fives senses—the five doors through which the world enters—working well. How very nice to say, The world is fine, I like it.

The sun-washed earth aroused a feeling of tenderness in me, moving me greatly. I felt that I had just been born, had descended to the nether world for a moment, seen the horror, jumped up, opened my eyes, and found myself once more in the familiar, hallowed light, walking beneath the trees and listening to human laughter and talk.

I walked slowly. My knees still trembled; a colorful giddiness as sweet and tender as morning mist enveloped my mind; behind this mist I observed the world, half solid, half composed of dreams. I was reminded of an icon I saw once in some church, I don't remember which. The painting was divided into two levels. On the lower level a strong, blond Saint George mounted on a frenzied horse was nailing his lance into the horrible, writhing, frothing beast, which had its vermilion-colored mouth open and ready to eat him. The identical struggle raged on the upper level, except that Saint George, the horse, and the beast were made of delicate cloud ready to scatter and vanish into the air. As I walked with sagging knees through the parks and streets of Vienna, this upper level represented in the painting of the world was the one I saw, and I trembled lest a wind should blow and disperse it.

How was I to know that in just a few days this very wind would indeed blow and indeed disperse it!

Vienna is a charming, enticing city; one always remembers her as a beloved woman. Beautiful, flighty, coquettish, she knows how to dress and undress, how to surrender herself, and how to act perfidiously, not from hate or love, but in jest. She does not walk, she dances; she does not call out, she sings. She is stretched on her back along the banks of the Danube. The rain drenches her, the snow covers her, the sun warms her. You see her—she hides nothing—and you exclaim: Thalia, Aglaia, Euphrosyne, Vienna—the four Graces!

The first few days after my return to life I enjoyed this laughing city, including the light, the earth's fragrance, the conversations of men, and even more than these the refreshing water, the delicious bread, the fruit. I used to close my eyes on the balcony of my room and listen to the world's bustle. The world seemed like a beehive full of workers, drones, and honey, the springtime breeze like a tender, cool hand on my face.

But as my body filled out and my soul took up the reins again, all this gaiety gradually began to strike me as extremely shallow and frivolous; it went contrary to my deepest needs. One felt that all the men and women here were being tickled—this explained their constant laughter. But I considered man a metaphysical animal, so he seemed to me at the time. Laughter, insouciance, canzonettas, were treason and impudence. I reverted to my father, who deemed laughter a form of insolence, though without knowing why. I, however, knew why, and this was the only step the son succeeded in taking beyond his parent!

Beginning to sound inside me with ever-increasing clarity was the stern, merciless voice of the tragic prophet I loved. "For shame!" bellowed this inner voice. "Is this the solid, leonine mind I fed you? Didn't I instruct you not to stoop to consolations? Only slaves and cowards have hopes—you'd better become resigned to that fact. The world is a trap laid by Satan, a trap laid by God. Do not condescend to nibble the bait. Instead, die of hunger!" And then confidentially, in a softer tone: "I turned coward and failed. You succeed!"

At other times this voice rose up hissing and ironic: "What do you mean by swaggering about and proclaiming that you want whatever is most difficult, that you believe in the faith which won't stoop to consolations, while all the while you go on the sly and get drunk in those taverns of hope, the churches, bowing down to worship the Nazarene and beg 'Lord, save me' with extended hand! Take to the road—alone! March! Reach the end; there you'll find the abyss. Regard it—that's all I ask of you, to regard the abyss without becoming panic-stricken, that and nothing else. I myself did so, but my mind collapsed. You keep your mind firm and unshakable. Surpass me."

The human heart is a dark, unyielding mystery. It is a perforated jug with a mouth forever open; though all the rivers of the earth pour in, it will remain empty and thirsting. The greatest of hopes had not filled it. Would it be filled now by the greatest of despairs?

This was the direction in which the merciless voice kept urging me to go. I divined whose steps it was toiling to make me follow, steps which proceeded firmly and unhesitatingly to the abyss with neither delay nor haste, but a noble, majestic regularity. "He is the final Savior," the voice kept saying to me. "He delivers man from hope, fear, and the gods. Follow him! I myself failed to do so in time, for along came the Superman holding out a great hope for me, and I went astray. I had no chance to push him aside. But you push aside your superman, the Nazarene, and attain what I had no chance to attain—the utmost freedom."

The rasping voice kept urging me in this pitiless obstinate manner, and little by little the prophet of absolute, total redemption began to rise up noiselessly inside me. My entrails became a lotus flower upon which he sat cross-legged with two mystic wheels engraved on the soles of his feet, his fingers skillfully intertwined, and a black spiral between his brows, like a third eye. His mischievous, disquieting smile extended from his narrow lips to his monstrous ears, thence to his forehead, and then slid down like honey from that high cliff to invade his entire body, reaching clear to the soles of his feet, where the two wheels moved as though anxious to depart.

Buddha! I had read about his life and proud message of despair many years earlier, but had forgotten everything. Apparently I still was not ripe, and thus I failed to pay attention. His voice struck me then as an exotic bewitching sound issuing from the depths of Asia, from a dark forest filled with snakes and dizzying orchids. But I did not grow dizzy. Another voice, a familiar one of the utmost sweetness, kept calling inside me, and I marched forward with confidence to meet it. But now, in the midst of this city's cachinnation, here again came the sound of this exotic, bewitching flute! How I closed my eyes and welcomed it! The voice was more familiar now, as though it had never grown silent inside me, but had simply been covered over by the Christian trumpet of Judgment Day.

I had been strengthened without a doubt by the satanic prophet's leonine nourishment, for I began to feel ashamed of my attempts to cover the abyss with a gaudy stalking-blind. I still dared not confront it point-blank as it truly was: naked and repulsive. Christ, his arms held out compassionately, had placed Himself between the abyss and me to keep me from seeing it and being frightened.

I began to provoke my soul, to torment it. Although it desired to become entangled with the flesh and be granted a mouth and hands with which to kiss and touch the world, although it no longer desired to regard its envelope the body as an enemy, but rather to become friends with it so that the two could journey hand in hand, separating only at the grave—although the soul desired all this, I stood in its way. Which "I"? A demon inside me, a new demon—Buddha. This demon kept shouting, Desire is flame, love is flame, virtue, hope, "I" and "you," heaven and hell are flames. One thing and one thing only is light: the renouncement of flame. Take the flames that are burning you, take them and turn them into light. Then blow out the light!

In India, when the day's work finally ends and the shadows fall upon the rooftops, the village lanes, and the people's breasts, an aged exorcist leaves his hut to make the rounds of the village. The magic reed between his lips, he proceeds from door to door playing a melody sweet and lulling, like the charm which cures souls. It is the "tiger's melody," that is the name given it, and it is said to cure the day's wound. This was the melody I wished to hear more clearly, and in order to do so I locked myself in my room and leaned day and night over huge manuals, studying the sermons and teaching of Buddha.

"In the flower of my youth, with my curly black hair, at the very acme of contented youthfulness's joy, in the first pride of manly strength, I shaved my hair down to the roots, donned the yellow robe, opened the door of my house, and entered the desert. . . ."

Here began the struggles of ascetic discipline. "My arms came to resemble dried-out reeds. For nourishment I took only a single grain of rice from sunrise to sunrise, and do not suppose that rice was bigger then than now; it was exactly the same. My hindquarters became like the legs of a camel, my spine like a chaplet; my bones protruded like the framework of a dilapidated half-timbered hut. As water glitters at the bottom of a deep well, so gleamed my eyes. Like the gourd which dries in the sun and cracks, such was my head."

But salvation did not come from this harsh road of ascetic discipline. Going back to his village, Buddha ate and drank, seated himself beneath a tree, at peace, neither happy nor sad, and said, "I shall not rise from this tree, shall not rise from this tree, shall not rise from this tree, unless I find salvation."

His sight limpid, his spirit pure, he saw vanity, saw life emerge from the earth and disappear, saw the gods disperse like clouds in the sky, saw the entire cycle, and leaned back against his tree. And as he did so, the tree's blossoms began to fall upon his hair and knees, the Great Message upon his mind.

He turned left and right, before and behind; it was he himself who bellowed in beasts, who bellowed in men and gods. Love took possession of him, love and pity for his own self that was scattered and struggling throughout the world. All the suffering of earth, all the suffering of heaven, was his own suffering. "How can anyone be happy in this pitiful body, this skein of blood, bones, brain, flesh, mucus, sperm, sweat, tears, and excrement? How can anyone be happy in this body governed by envy, hate, falsehood, fear, anguish, hunger, thirst, disease, old age, and death? All things—plants, insects, beasts, men—proceed toward perdition. Look behind you at those who no longer exist; look ahead of you at those not yet born. Men ripen like grain, fall like grain, sprout anew. The boundless oceans grow dry, mountains crumble away, the North Star wavers, gods vanish. . . ."

Pity—that is the Buddhistic journey's unfailing guide. By means of pity we deliver ourselves from our bodies, demolish the partition, merge with Nothingness. "We are all one, and this one suffers—we must deliver it. If but a single trembling drop of water suffers, I suffer.

"The 'Four Noble Truths' dawn in my mind. This world is a net in which we have been caught; death does not deliver us, for we shall be reborn. Let us triumph over thirst, let us uproot desire, let us empty out our bowels! Do not say, 'I want to die,' or 'I do not want to die.' Say, 'I do not want anything.' Elevate your mind above desire and hope—and then, while yet in this life, you shall

be able to enter the beatitude of nonbeing. With your arm, you shall halt the Wheel of Rebirth."

Never had Buddha's form towered up before me bathed in such brilliant light. Formerly, when I considered nirvana identical with immortality, I saw Buddha as just another of Hope's generals, leading his army contrary to the thrust of the world. Only now did I realize that Buddha urges man to give consent to death, to love the ineluctable, to harmonize his heart with universal flux, and, seeing matter and mind pursue each other, unite, beget, and vanish, to say, "That is what I want."

Of all the people the earth has begotten, Buddha stands resplendently at the summit, an absolutely pure spirit. Without fear or sorrow, filled with mercy and good judgment, he extended his hand and, smiling gravely, opened the road to salvation. All beings follow impetuously behind him. Submitting freely to the ineluctable, they bound like kid goats going to suckle. Not only men, but all beings: men, beasts, trees. Unlike Christ, Buddha does not single out only humans; he pities everything, and saves everything.

In his heart he sensed the cosmos forming and vanishing—alone, without the aid of invisible powers. Ether condensed in his sun-baked skull and became a nebula, the nebula a star; the star, like a seed, formed a crust and put forth trees, animals, men, gods; then fire came into his skull and everything turned to smoke and perished.

I lived for many days and weeks plunged in this new adventure. What an abyss is the human heart! How the heartbeat breaks into palpitations and takes unforeseen routes! Was all my yearning and passion for immortality leading me then to absolute mortality? Or could it be that mortality and immortality were identical?

When Buddha rose from beneath the tree where for seven years he had struggled in his search for salvation, he went, saved now, and sat down cross-legged in the square of a large city. There, surrounded by lords, merchants, and warriors, he began to speak, preaching salvation. At first all these unbelievers ridiculed him, but gradually they felt their bowels emptying, felt themselves purged of desire, and little by little their festively white, red, and blue garments turned yellow, like Buddha's robe. I, in the same way, felt my bowels emptying and my mind dressing itself in the yellow robe.

One night when I went out to take a short walk in the Prater, Vienna's large park, a girl of the painted sisterhood stepped up to me beneath the trees. Frightened, I increased my pace, but she overtook me and caught hold of my arm. She exuded a heavy scent of violets; in the light I could make out her blue eyes, painted lips, and half-exposed breasts.

"Come with me . . ." she whispered, winking her eye.

"No! No!" I cried as though in danger.

She released my arm. "Why not?" she asked.

"I'm sorry but I don't have time."

"Are you crazy?" said the girl, glancing at me with sympathy. "What are you, a monk? No one is looking."

Buddha is looking, I was about to reply, but I restrained myself. The girl's eye, in the meantime, had caught sight of another solitary stroller, and she ran off to accost him. I took a deep breath. Feeling as though I had escaped a great danger, I returned post-haste to my room.

I had submerged myself in Buddha. My mind was a yellow heliotrope and Buddha the sun; I followed him as he rose, reached the zenith, and disappeared. "Water sleeps, but souls do not," an old Rumelian once said to me. It seemed to me during those days, however, that my soul had entered a beatific sleep, submerged in Buddhist imperturbation. Just as when you dream and know you are dreaming, and all you see in your sleep, whether good or bad, arouses neither joy, sorrow, nor fear in you because you know that you will awake and all will be dispelled, so in this same way, feeling neither joy nor fright, unperturbed, I watched the phantasmagoria of the world pass before my eyes.

In order to prevent the vision from dispersing with great rapidity, in order to solidify perfect salvation with words so that my soul could feel it in a tangible way, I commenced to write a dialogue between Buddha and his beloved disciple Ananda.

• • •

Barbarians had descended from the mountains and blockaded the city. Buddha sat cross-legged beneath a blossoming tree, smiling. Ananda had leaned his head on Buddha's knees and closed his eyes to keep the world's phantasmagoria from leading his thoughts astray. Around them stood a multitude of auditors who longed to become disciples; they wanted to hear the words of salvation, but as soon as they learned that the barbarians were waging war, they became incensed.

"Get up, Master," they cried. "Lead us to repel the barbarians. The secret of deliverance you can tell us afterwards."

Buddha shook his head. "No, I refuse to come."

"Are you tired?" shouted the others angrily. "Are you afraid?"

"I have completed the journey," replied Buddha, his voice beyond fatigue and fear, beyond patriotism.

"Well then, let us go ourselves and defend the soil of our fathers!" cried all the rest, and they turned toward the city.

"Go with my benediction," said Buddha, lifting his hand to bless them. "I went where you are going, went and returned. I shall be sitting here beneath this flowering tree, waiting for you also to return. Then only, when we all sit beneath the same flowering tree, each word that I speak and each word that you speak will have the same meaning for all of us. Now it is still much too soon. I say one thing and you understand something else. We do not speak the same language. So, pleasant journey! . . . Till we meet again!"

"I do not understand, Master," said Sariputta. "Are you speaking to us in parables again?"

"You will understand upon your return, Sariputta. As I told you, now is much too soon. For years I have lived the life and suffering of mankind; for years I have filled out and ripened. Before this I never attained such complete freedom, my companions. And why did I attain this freedom? Because I made a great decision."

"A great decision?" asked Ananda. Raising his head, he bowed to kiss the sole of Buddha's holy foot. "What decision, Master?"

"I do not wish to sell my soul to God, to what all you others call God; I do not wish to sell my soul to the devil, to what all you others call the devil. I do not wish to sell myself to anyone. I am free! Happy the man who escapes the claws of God and the devil. He, and he alone, is saved."

"Saved from what?" asked Sariputta, sweat dripping from his forehead. "Saved from what? Some words remain on your lips, Master. They are burning you."

"No, Sariputta, they are not burning me, they are cooling me.

Forgive me, but I do not know if you have the endurance, if you can hear them without becoming terror-stricken."

"Master," said Sariputta, "we are going off to war and may never return, may never see you again. Disclose these final words to us, your last. . . . Saved from what?

Slowly, heavily, like a body falling into the abyss, the words fell from Buddha's compressed lips. "From salvation."

"From salvation!" exclaimed Sariputta. "Saved from salvation? Master, I do not understand."

"So much the better, Sariputta. If you understood, you would be frightened. Nevertheless, I want you to know, my companions, that this is my form of freedom. I have been saved from salvation!"

He fell silent. But now he was no longer able to restrain himself. "I want you to know that every other form of freedom is slavery. If I were to be born again, I would fight for this great freedom, for salvation from salvation. . . . Enough, however. It is still too early for us to speak. We shall say it all when you return from war—if you return. Farewell!"

He took a deep breath. Seeing his disciples hesitate, he smiled. "Why do you stay?" he asked. "Warfare is still your duty. Off with you then, off to fight. Farewell!"

"Until we meet again, Master," said Sariputta. . . . "Come, let's go, and may God be with us!"

Ananda did not move. Buddha eyed him with satisfaction out of the corner of his eye.

"I am going to stay here with you, Master," said the disciple, coloring strongly.

"From fear, Ananda, my beloved?"

"From love, Master."

"Love is no longer enough, my faithful companion."

"I know that, Master. As you spoke, I saw flames licking your mouth."

"They were not flames, Ananda, they were my words. Do you understand those superhuman words, my young, faithful friend?"

"I think I do. That is why I remained with you."

"What do you understand?"

"Whoever says salvation exists is a slave, because he keeps weighing each of his words and deeds at every moment. 'Will I be saved or damned?' he tremblingly asks. 'Will I go to heaven or to hell?' . . . How can a soul that hopes be free? Whoever hopes is afraid both of this life and the life to come; he hangs indecisively in the air and waits for luck or God's mercy."

Buddha placed his palm on Ananda's black hair.

"Stay," he said.

They remained silent for some time beneath the flowering tree, Buddha slowly, compassionately caressing the beloved disciple's hair.

"Salvation means deliverance from all saviors. This is the supreme freedom, the highest, where a man breathes only with difficulty. Do you have the endurance?"

Ananda had bowed his head. He did not speak.

"In other words, now you understand who is the perfect Savior . . ."

He fell silent for a moment, but then, twisting between his fingers a blossom which had fallen from the tree: "It is the Savior who shall deliver mankind from salvation."

• • •

With the twenty-six letters of the alphabet (the only stones and concrete I have) I paved the new road leading to salvation. Now I knew, and knowing, I regarded the world tranquilly, without fear, because now it could no longer deceive me. Leaning out of my window, I looked at the men, women, and cars, at the stores loaded with meat, groceries, drinks, fruit, books—and smiled. All these were just so many variegated clouds; a gentle breeze would blow and they would be dispelled. The Tempter's power had begotten them; now human thirst and hunger were holding on to them for an hour or two, as long as possible before the breeze blew and scattered them.

Going outside to the street, I mingled with a wave of people all running somewhere in a great hurry. I ran with them; I no longer had anything to fear. They are wraiths, I reflected, a mist composed of dewdrops. Why be afraid of them? Why not go along and see what they're doing? Reaching a movie theater with red, blue, and green lights, we went inside and enthroned ourselves in velvet-cushioned seats. At the far end was a bright screen over which anxious shadows were hurriedly passing. What were they doing? Kissing, killing, being killed. Next to me sat a girl. Her breath smelled of cinnamon. I felt her bosom heave as she respired. From time to time her knee touched mine. I shuddered, but did not draw away. She turned and glanced at me for an instant, and in the half-darkness of the auditorium I thought I saw her smile.

Soon I had enough of watching these shadows, and I got up to leave. The girl got up also. At the exit she turned again and smiled at me. We struck up a conversation. The moon shining above us, we headed toward the park and sat down on a little bench. It was summer; the night was sweet as honey, the lilacs fragrant. Couples kept passing; others were embracing, stretched out on the grass. A nightingale hidden deep in the lilacs began to sing above our heads, and my heart stood still. It was not a bird; it must have been some cunning goblin. I had heard this same voice once before, I believe—when climbing Psiloríti—and I knew what it was saying. Extending my hand, I rested it on the girl's hair.

"What's your name?" I asked her.

"Frieda," she replied, laughing. "Why ask? My name is 'Woman.' "

At that point something terrible escaped my lips. The words I spoke were not my own; they must have belonged to one of my ancestors—not my father, who despised women, but someone else. The moment I uttered them, I felt overcome by terror. But it was too late.

"Frieda, will you spend the night with me?"

The girl calmly replied, "Not tonight. I can't. Tomorrow."

Feeling relieved, I rose in great haste. We parted. I walked hurriedly back to my room.

And then something incredible happened, something which makes me shudder even now when I recall it. Man's soul is truly indestructible, truly august and noble, but pressed to its bosom it carries a body which grows daily more putrescent. While on my way back home, I heard the blood mounting to my head. My soul had become enraged. Sensing that my body was about to fall into sin, it had bounded to its feet, full of scorn and anger, and refused to grant permission. The blood continued to flow upward and mass in my face, until little by little I became aware that my lips, cheeks, and forehead were swelling. My eyes soon grew so small that nothing remained but two slits, and it was only with difficulty that I managed to see anything at all.

Constantly stumbling, I increased my pace and ran anxiously homeward in order to look in the mirror and see what state I was in.

When I finally arrived and turned on the light and looked, I emitted a cry of terror. My entire face was swollen and horribly disfigured; my eyes were barely visible between two overflowing masses of florid flesh, and my mouth had become an oblong slot incapable of opening. Suddenly I remembered the girl Frieda. Being in such a disgusting state, how could I see her the next day? I wrote out a telegram: "Can't come tomorrow, will come the day after," and fell onto my bed in despair. What disease can this be? I asked myself. Was it leprosy? As a child in Crete I often saw lepers with their swollen, blood-red, constantly desquamating faces, and now I recalled what horror they had roused in me—so much that one day I had said, "If I were king, I would take all the lepers, hang stones around their necks, and heave them into the sea." Was it possible that the Invisible (*an* Invisible) had remembered my inhuman words and sent me this horrible disease as a punishment?

That night I did not get a moment's sleep. I was anxious for dawn to come, for I said to myself that perhaps the trouble would pass by morning, and I continually investigated my face to see if the swelling had begun to subside. At daybreak I jumped out of bed and ran to the mirror. An appalling mask of flesh was glued to my face; the skin had commenced to burst open and exude a yellowish-white liquid. I was not a man, I was a demon.

I called for the chambermaid in order to give her the telegram. She screamed and hid her face behind her palms the moment she opened the door and saw me. Not daring to come close, she snatched the telegram and left. A day went by, two, three; a week, two weeks. Every day, afraid that the girl might come to my room and see me, I dispatched the same telegram: "Can't come today, will come tomorrow." I felt not the slightest pain, but I could not open my mouth to eat; my only nourishment was milk and lemonade, which I sucked in through a straw. Finally I could stand it no longer. I had read several psychoanalytical works by the famous disciple of Freud, Wilhelm Stekel, and I went to seek him out.

My psyche had inflicted this disease on me, though I did not know why. This much I divined: my psyche was to blame.

The learned professor began to hear my confession. I related my life history: how I'd been searching for a path of salvation ever since my adolescence; how I followed Christ for many years, but lately had found His religion too unsophisticated, too optimistic, and had left Him to follow the path of Buddha. . . .

The professor smiled.

"To search in order to find the world's beginning and end is a disease," he said to me. "The normal person lives, struggles, experiences joy and sorrow, gets married, has children, and does not waste his time in asking whence, whither, and why. But you did not finish your story. You are still hiding something from me. Confess everything."

I related how I met Frieda, and said we had arranged a tryst.

The professor burst into shrill, sarcastic laughter. I glanced at him with irritation. I had already begun to hate this man, because he was examining my secrets beneath his indiscreet magnifying glass, and struggling to force open all the barred and padlocked doors inside me.

"Enough! Enough!" he said, beginning to titter again in his sarcastic way. "This mask will remain glued to your face as long as you stay in Vienna. The disease you have is called the ascetics' disease. It is extremely rare in our times, because what body, today, obeys its soul? Have you ever read the saints' legends? Do you remember the ascetic who left the Theban desert and ran toward the nearest city because the demon of fornication had suddenly mounted him, and he felt compelled to sleep with a woman? He ran and ran, but just as he was about to pass through the city gates, he looked down and saw with terror that leprosy was spreading over his body. It was not leprosy, however; it was this disease, the same one you have. With such a revolting face, how could he present himself before a woman? What woman would find it possible to touch him? So he ran back to his hermitage in the desert and gave thanks to God for having delivered him from sin, whereupon God, according to the legend, forgave him and scraped the leprosy off his body. . . . Do you understand now? Plunged as it is in the Buddhist Weltanschauung, your soul—or rather what for you goes by the name of *soul*—believes that sleeping with a woman is a mortal sin. For that reason it refuses to permit its body to commit this sin. Such souls, souls capable of imposing themselves to so great a degree on the flesh, are rare in our age. In my entire scientific career I have encountered only one other such case, that of an extremely upright, extremely pious Viennese lady. She loved her husband very much, but he was away at the front, and she chanced to meet a young man and fall in love with him. One night she was ready to surrender herself, but suddenly her soul rose up in revolt, opposing her. Her face became repulsively swollen, just as yours is now. In desperation she sought me out. I reassured her. 'You'll be cured when your husband comes back from the war,' I told her, and indeed, as soon as her husband returned, in other words as soon as the danger of sin was past, her face regained its original beauty. Your case is the same. You will be cured as soon as you depart from Vienna and leave Frieda behind you."

I did not believe it. Scientific fairy tales, I said to myself, leaving in a state of stubborn vexation. I'll stay in Vienna, I'll stay and get better. . . . I remained for another month, but the mask did not melt away. I continued to send the daily telegram to Frieda: "Can't come today, will come tomorrow." This tomorrow never arrived, however. One morning, having grown weary of the whole business, I got out of bed with the resolute determination to leave. I took my valise, descended the stairs, emerged into the street, and headed for the station. It was early morning and a cool breeze was blowing. Working-class men and women were racing to their jobs in merry flocks, still munching mouthfuls of bread. The sun had not come down into the streets yet. Several windows were being opened; the city was awakening. I walked with weightless steps, in a fine mood; I was awakening just like the city. I felt my face losing its burden as I proceeded. My eyes were being freed, they could open now. The swelling in my lips began to subside, and I started whistling like a child. The cool breeze passed over my face like a compassionate hand, like a caress. When I finally reached the station and took out my pocket mirror to look at myself, what joy, what good fortune! The swelling in my face had entirely disappeared; my former features—nose, mouth, cheeks—had returned. The demon had fled; once more I was a human being.

Ever since that day I have realized that man's soul is a terrible and dangerous coil spring. Without knowing it, we all carry a great explosive force wrapped in our flesh and lard. And what is worse, we do not want to know it, for then villainy, cowardice, and falsehood lose their justification; we can no longer hide behind man's supposed impotence and wretched incompetence; we ourselves must bear the blame if we are villains, cowards, or liars, for although we have an all-powerful force inside, we dare not use it for fear it might destroy us. But we take the easy, comfortable way out, and allow it to vent its strength little by little until it too has degenerated to flesh and lard. How terrible not to know that we possess this force! If we did know, we would be proud of our souls. In all heaven and earth, nothing so closely resembles God as the soul of man.

25

BERLIN

FROM VIENNA I hopped to Berlin. Although Buddha had quenched many of my inner thirsts, he was unable to extinguish my thirst to view as many more parts of the earth and as many more seas as I possibly could. He had given me what he himself termed the "elephant eye"—the ability to see all things as if for the first time and greet them, to see all things as if for the last time and bid them farewell.

I kept telling myself that the world was a specter and that men were wraiths, dew-beings, ephemeral children of the dew. Buddha, the black sun, had risen and they were melting into nothingness. But pity took possession of my soul, pity and love. If only I could hold those specters at the edge of my vision for a moment longer and keep them from expiring! Every last bit of my heart, I felt, had not been wrapped in the yellow robe. A blood-red heartbeat still remained; pounding obstinately, it refused to let Buddha take full possession of me. Inside me a Cretan was lifting his hand in revolt and refusing to pay even a brass farthing of tribute to the peaceable conqueror.

It was at Berlin that I came to realize all this. As I close my eyes now to recall my sins in that disagreeable city (mortal sins for a follower of Buddha), my memory overflows with laughter, fiery words, wonderfully warm nights passed with no thought of sleep, blossoming chestnut and cherry trees, insatiable Jewish eyes, the acrid smell of female armpits—and I am unable to place things in their proper order.

I thumb through yellowed notebooks in an an effort to remember what came first, what next, what vows we swore, what caused the separation. . . . Great indeed is the strength of the letters of the alphabet, those twenty-six miniature soldiers that stand at the edge of the cliff and defend man's heart at least for some little time, preventing it from falling and drowning in the black, bottomless eye of Buddha!

October 2. I've been wandering for three days now through Berlin's endless, monotonous streets. The chestnut trees have lost their leaves; there is a frigid wind; my heart has turned to ice. Today I passed a great doorway with a sign written in large letters: "Congress of Educational Reform." It was snowing and I was cold, so I went in. The hall was full of teachers, a great crowd of men and women. I searched for a place to sit. Suddenly I saw an orange blouse gleaming between gray and black suit jackets. Just as the insect is attracted by the color of the flower, so I, in the same way, moved toward the girl with the orange blouse. The seat next to her was vacant; I sat down. One of the teachers was gesticulating deliriously—he shouted himself hoarse, drank a little water, calmed down somewhat, then worked up steam again, all about how he was going to change the school curriculum and forge a new German generation which would disdain both life and death. Here was yet another savior; he was struggling to save the world by conquering it.

I turned to my neighbor. Her hair was blue-black, her immense eyes black and almond-shaped, her nose slightly hooked. Her skin was swarthy, the color of old amber, with a slight splotchiness in the face. Leaning over, I asked her, "Where do you think I'm from?"

"From the land of the sun," she replied, blushing strongly.

"That's right, from the land of the sun. I'm suffocating in here. Shall we go out and take a little walk?"

"Yes, let's."

Once out in the street, she jumped, laughed, and shouted like a child given a new toy.

"My name is Sarita, and I'm Jewish and I write poems."

We went into a park. The yellow leaves massed on the ground craunched beneath our feet. I placed my palm on her hair; it was warm, and soft as silk. Without speaking, the girl stopped and craned her neck as though listening intently to something.

"Your hand gives off a force," she said. "I feel like a jug being filled at the fountain."

It was nearly noon. "Let's go and eat," I suggested. "A thick soup, nice and hot—to warm us."

"This is a Jewish fast day. It's a sin to eat. I'm just as hungry and cold as you are, but it's a sin."

"Let's sin then, so that we can repent afterwards and be pardoned by terrible Jehovah, your god."

She seemed annoyed to hear me refer to her god in this jocular way.

"And who is your god?"

This made me wince. Instantaneously I sensed that I too was sinning against my god. All this time I had forgotten that those eyes, that hair, that amber skin was nothing but a specter, and I did not blow, did not want to blow, to dispel it.

"Dionysus?" asked the girl with a laugh. "The great drunkard?"

"No, no, someone else, someone even more terrible than your Jehovah. . . . Don't ask!"

I should have gotten up at that moment and left, but I pitied my body, pitied hers, and stayed.

"Recite one of your poems," I said in order to divert my thoughts.

Her face beamed. Her voice became extremely caressive and embittered.

Exiles who have not realized yet
that exile is a home.
When we stride in new cities,
home walks next us like a sister.

Exiles who have not realized yet
that in our exiled hearts,
should a smile be granted us,
the Song of Songs begins.

Her eyes had filled with tears.

"Are you crying?" I asked, leaning close to her.

"No matter where you touch a Jew," she answered, "you find a wound."

October 3. If only man could really preserve the intoxication! If only Dionysus were an omnipotent god! But the intoxication rapidly disperses, the mind clears, and the warm, firm flesh becomes a specter once again. The next day my brain woke up. Eying me with disdain and severity, it shouted, Infidel, traitor, inconstant betrayer! I am ashamed to live and travel with you. Perhaps Buddha can forgive you, but I cannot. Do not step again into the orange-tinted snare.

Nevertheless, first thing in the morning I took the same route and returned to the Congress. I looked, but the orange color was nowhere to be seen. Though I wanted to rejoice, I could not. Once more I heard the big-sounding bombast. Many of the listeners were eating apples to calm their hunger; others were bent over taking notes, not missing a single word. Suddenly I had the presentiment of something like a warm breath behind me: a face ferreting me out and riveting its eyes upon me. Turning, I saw her at the far end of the hall. She was wearing a shabby shawl, dark olive in color, and had turned up her collar of napless fur because the room was cold. She smiled at me, her face beaming like a marble bust in sunlight.

I did not turn to see her a second time. I attempted to make my exit, but she overtook me in the corridor and gave me a slim volume of her poems. She laughed and cavorted, her intoxication of the previous day not having dissolved. But I was anxious to part with her and leave. The moment I began to bow in order to give her my hand, I saw her eyes regarding me questioningly, uncertainly, with just a shade of fear. Her body had grown even smaller, more hunched; she had shrunk into herself. My heart breaking with sympathy, I seized her by the upper back and kneaded her skinny shoulders. She screeched from contentment and pain.

"Why are you hurting me?" she asked, trying to escape.

"Because you're made from other soil, because you have another god, because all night long I was thinking of you. I wanted to ask you some questions—but you must tell the truth."

"Why shouldn't I tell the truth? I'm not afraid of it. I'm a Jew."

"What does your god order you to do, what duty does he impose on you? Before we go any further, this is what I must know."

"Hate—that is the primary duty. Are you satisfied?"

Her features had suddenly become contorted. Although her thick lips no longer spoke, they still trembled. Two yellow eyes and the gaping jaw of a tigress became visible behind the beautiful dark-complexioned face.

"Are you satisfied?" she hissed once more, provokingly.

I remembered Buddha's saying: "If we answer hate with hate, the world will never be free of hate."

"Hate," I replied, "is the servant that walks in front and cleans the road so that the master may pass."

"And who is the master?"

"Love."

The Jewess laughed sarcastically. "That's what your Christ bleats. As for us, our Jehovah commands, If someone knocks out one of your teeth, knock out a whole jawful in return! You are a lamb, I am a wounded she-wolf; we can never mix. It's a good thing we realized this before we joined our lips."

"What have you got against the world? Why do you want to destroy it?"

"I doubt that you've ever gone hungry; no, not you. You've never slept beneath a bridge, never had your mother murdered in a pogrom! In short, you have no right to ask. This world—your world—is unjust and venal, but our hearts are not. I want to help my comrades destroy it and build a new world, one which will not bring shame upon our hearts."

We strolled beneath the denuded trees. A few leaves still hung on at the crowns, but an icy gust came to shank them, and they settled on our heads and shoulders. The Jewess was shivering; her gloves were full of holes, her blouse made of cotton, her down-at-heel shoes on the verge of wearing through. I cast a sidewise glance at her eyes for a moment and saw with fright that they were pinned on me, burning with the hatred which filled them.

What this girl must have gone through in order to talk with such hate! Perhaps, I said to myself, it was because she feared for an instant that she might fall in love with a man from the enemy camp.

Her lips had turned blue with cold; her teeth were chattering. Feeling ashamed, I took off my fur overcoat and swiftly cast it across her shoulders before she had time to escape. She shook herself angrily, trying to throw it off, but I held it firmly on her and implored her to keep it.

She halted, as though unable to catch her breath. She had

ceased to resist. I felt my body heat leaving my overcoat and penetrating slowly, deeply, into her body. Her lips became red again; little by little her face regained its beauty. She leaned her arm on me. Her knees must have become paralyzed.

"It's good to be warm," she murmured. "Life seems to change."

My eyes nearly brimming with tears, I reflected, A little warmth, a little bread, a roof over your head, a kind word, and hate vanishes. . . .

We had reached her house.

"When shall I see you again?" I asked her.

"Take your coat," she said. "I've just come to understand why everyone who has a fur coat talks the same way you do. Take it, because my heart is about to give out."

"Not your heart, Sarita. Your hate."

"They're the same. God bless cold and hunger. Without them I'd be engulfed in comforts. In other words, dead—a carcass. Goodbye!"

She did not offer me her hand. Opening her purse, she took out her key to unlock the door.

"When shall I see you again?" I repeated.

But her face had become a yellow mask of hate once more. Without answering, she opened the door and vanished into the darkness.

I never saw her again.

I locked myself in my room. My heart had turned into a sack of caterpillars. Suddenly the world had taken on flesh and bones again; it seemed truly to exist. The five thirsts had opened in my body and I began calling on Buddha to come and exorcise the Tempter. Once there was a great saint who after forty years of ascetic discipline still could not reach God. Something stood in his way preventing him. At the end of forty years he understood. It was a little jug which he greatly loved because it cooled the drinking water he stored in it. He smashed the jug and was immediately united with God.

I knew—knew that in my case the little jug was the girl's small irresistible body. If I in my turn wished to be united with God, I would have to obliterate this body which stood in the way. When a wild wasp slips into a beehive to pillage the honey, the workers rush upon it, swaddle its entire body in a net of fragrant wax, and smother it. My net of wax consisted of words, verses, meter. With these hallowed winding sheets I would enwrap Sarita and prevent her from pillaging my honey.

The blood began to throb at my temples. I assembled my far-scattered thoughts, struggling to concentrate my strength on one body, one voice, two black insatiable eyes. I wanted to exorcise them, for they were separating me from Buddha.

Mobilizing words, I placed myself at their head and set out for war. I wrote, but the more I wrote the more my purpose shifted and my yearning broadened. Sarita fell further and further behind, grew increasingly smaller until she vanished, and an ascent flashed before me, a rocky ascent with a red track upon it and a man who was climbing—a simple hieroglyph done in a minimum of strokes. I recognized it as my life. Deciphering it, I saw how naïvely and with how many hopes I had set out; and which were the various way stations I halted at momentarily to catch my breath and work up new momentum—the self, the race, mankind, God; and how I suddenly discerned the supreme peak above me—the Silence, Buddha. Finally, I saw the yearning which began to rage inside me, the yearning to extricate myself forever from all deceptions, both mundane and celestial, and to succeed in reaching this desolate, uninhabited peak. . . . When I picked up and read the pages I had written—they were scattered on the floor—I was seized by terror. I had wanted to write an exorcism to obliterate Sarita, and instead I had written an exorcism to obliterate the entire cosmos! Buddha sat immobile and self-assured at the summit, watching my struggles at the base of the ascent and smiling with compassion and kindness.

Having established order over the age-old questions, having found words and solidified the answer, I felt at ease. Rising, I went outside to shake the numbness off my body, which had been locked indoors for so many days. Night had fallen; people must have already finished eating supper. As it was neither raining nor snowing, they had poured out into the streets. I saw colorful lights over a large entranceway, and multicolored placards announcing: "Dances of Java." From inside I heard grave music full of passion. Men and women were entering. I entered too.

Of all the sights my soul has enjoyed, the dance and the star-filled heavens have always stood supreme. Never have wine, women, or even ideas thrown me so completely into a ferment—body, mind, and soul—as have these two. Thus I was delighted that on this night, after so many days of ascetic fasting, not only was my flesh going to shake off its numbness and enjoy itself, but also my mind and soul—all three of the co-travelers.

When I entered the hall, I found the dance already in progress. The lights were out, except for the mysterious blue-green spot which illuminated the stage, making it appear like the bottom of some far-distant oriental sea. A swarthy, delicately built adolescent wearing strange, stunning ornaments and a gold-green costume—like a male insect in summer rut—was dancing in front of a wheat-dark, thin-boned little woman. While she remained motionless, he danced and danced, displaying his litheness to the female, and how much strength and grace he had, and how worthy he was—he and no one else—of being chosen to couple with her and produce a son, so that these great virtues of litheness, strength, and grace might be transmitted to this son instead of perishing. The female stood immobile, looking at him, weighing him, trying to decide. Suddenly she did decide, and she threw herself into the dance. Frightened, the man stepped aside; now it was his turn to stand motionless and rapt, looking at the woman. She danced and danced in front of the terror-shaken man, opening her arms and pushing aside her veils so that her body glowed blue-green at one moment, faded away at the next. She approached him, pretending to fall into his embrace. He emitted a cry of triumph and spread his arms, but the woman escaped each time with a hiss and danced out of his reach.

Be it animals, birds, or humans, at each whirl of the dance the ephemeral masks are thrown off and behind all of them the same face is always revealed, the eternal face of love. As I watched the Javanese couple, I asked myself whether another dance beyond this one of love, the dance, let us say, of God, would be able in its whirling to throw off this love mask as well. What terrifying face, I wondered, would then be revealed? I was struggling to capture the final face behind every mask, but could not do so. Would it, I wondered, be empty air—the face of Buddha? . . . The two dancers, the man and woman, had joined by this time; they were dancing arm in arm now in a transport of ecstasy, leaping into the air, falling, surging high again, struggling amidst gasps of desire to surpass human boundaries.

Leaving, I roamed the streets until after midnight. Scattered snowflakes had begun to fall; I welcomed them with a feeling of relief, for they cooled my burning lips. New questions were rising inside me. The dance that evening had opened the old wellsprings in my bowels, the ones I thought had been stanched. I realized that the entrails of a Cretan are not easily emptied. Inside me were terrible ancestors who had not eaten as much meat or drunk as much wine as they craved, nor kissed as many women as they desired, and now they were bounding up fiercely in order to prevent me—and themselves—from dying. Truly, what business did Buddha have in Crete, what could he hope for . . . in Crete?

I gazed at the snowflakes eddying in the light of the streetlamps; they reminded me of the Javanese man and woman I had seen that evening, of the innumerable men and women who enact the dance—the pursuit, the battle, the desire—and in the final figure unite in order to engender a son and insure their immortality. The thirst for immortality is far more invincible than the thirst for death.

Completely exhausted, I lay down to go to sleep. And as frequently is my good fortune when my waking mind is tormented with questions and unable to find a way out, along came slumber to simplify them all and transform them into a tale. Such is the crown of the dormant stock of truth when it blossoms.

I dreamed that I was climbing a mountain. I had my crook across my shoulders in the manner of Cretan shepherds, and I was singing. I remember it was a folk song I loved very much:

I sowed a pepper seed on Margaro's lips.
It sprouted thickly, became a giant plant
—mown now by Greeks, carried by Turks,
and threshed by Margaro astride her mount.

Suddenly an old man darted out of a cave. His sleeves were tucked up, his hands covered with clay. Placing his finger on his lips to silence me, he commanded in a stern voice, "Stop singing! I want quiet! Can't you see I'm working?" (Here he indicated his hands.)

"What are you making?" I asked him.

"Can't you see for yourself? Inside this cave I am fashioning the Redeemed."

"The Redeemed? Who is redeemed?" I cried, and the old wounds began to flow again inside me.

"He who perceives, loves, and lives the totality!" replied the old man, hurriedly burrowing again into his cave.

"He who conceives, loves, and lives the totality . . ." All the next day I kept repeating those words from my dream, never tiring of them. Was this God's voice, I wondered, the voice which can be heard only at night when the loquacious brain has finally closed its mouth? I had always placed faith in the advice which the hours of darkness give us. Surely the night is more profound and holy than that nincompoop the day. The night takes pity on man.

Several days went by. As so often in my life, those two sleepless demons the Yes and the No were wrestling and scuffling inside me. Every time I find an answer to the questions tormenting me, I always accept it with uneasiness because I know that this answer, without fail, will spawn new questions. Thus the hunt conducted by the two demons inside me has no end. It seems that each answer hides future questions in the folds of its temporary certainty. That is why I always view its coming not with relief but with hidden disquietude.

Christ had hidden the seed of Buddha, thrust deep down within Him. What, I wondered, was Buddha hiding, wrapped deep inside his yellow robe?

One rainy Sunday I was promenading slowly in a museum, looking at fierce African masks made of wood, hide, and human skulls. In an effort to unravel the mystery of masks, I said to myself, The mask is our true face; we are these monsters with their bloody mouths, hanging lips, and horrifying eyes. A repulsive mask howls behind the beautiful features of the woman we love, chaos behind the visible world, Buddha behind Christ's gentle face. Sometimes in the terrible moments of love, hate, or death the deceptive charm vanishes and we view truth's frightening countenance. With a shudder I remembered the Irish lass inside that little chapel atop the Cretan mountain. As my lips touched hers, it seemed that her face turned to rot and oozed away, revealing a horrible, tormented, swooning monkey which filled me with disgust and fright. Ever since that day I have restrained myself, though with difficulty, from baring the true faces of mankind, because then love, courtesy, and mutual understanding would disappear. I pretend to believe in mankind's faces, and in this way I am able to live with my fellow human beings.

Every morning before daybreak these aborigines who carved the masks raced up the nearest hill and called the sun—entreated it—to appear, trembling lest by some chance it might fail to come again. Rain for them was full of male spirits who entered the earth and made it fruitful; lightning flashes were the angry glances of the invisible Chief. The leaves on the trees spoke, just like the lips of men, and several aged women understood what they said. A river, when these aborigines crossed it, drew them to it in order to drown them, but they gathered up momentum, strode through the current with utmost speed, and doubled over in laughter when they reached the opposite bank, because they had come through safely. All things spoke, hungered, heard, had gender, coupled. The air was densely filled with spirits of the dead; in order to push them aside these people spread and churned their arms when they walked, as though they were swimming. This is why they saw the real so clearly behind the apparent, why they bared the eternal mask behind the ephemeral face.

A girl came, stood next to me, and began looking, like myself, at the masks. For a moment I was ready to leave, for I always feel a certain annoyance when I am alone, looking at something which moves me, and someone else comes to look at it too. She was short and chubby, with high bosom, strong chin, hawklike nose, and eyes with huge eyelashes.

Turning, she cast a protracted, searching glance at me, as though I too were a mask.

"Are you an African?" she asked me.

I laughed.

"Not entirely," I replied. "Only my heart."

"Your face too," she said. "And your hands. . . . I'm Jewish."

"A terrifying race," I said to tease her. "Dangerous. Apparently it wants to save the world. . . . Are you still awaiting the Messiah?"

"No. He's come."

"The Messiah?"

"Yes, the Messiah."

I laughed again. "When? Where? What's his name?"

"Lenin."

Her voice had suddenly become deep, her eyes somber.

Lenin! For an instant it seemed that all the masks in front of me stirred and clapped open their massive jaws. Without speaking, the girl glanced out through the window at the blackened sky.

Yes, Lenin was another new savior, I reflected, another new savior created by the enslaved, hungry, and oppressed to enable them to bear slavery, hunger, and oppression—another new mask for mankind's despair and hope.

"I know another Messiah who delivers man from hunger and also from satiety, from injustice and also from justice. And what is most important, from all Messiahs."

"And his name is . . ."

"Buddha!"

She smiled disdainfully, then said in an angry voice, "I've heard of him. He's a ghost. My Messiah is made of flesh and blood."

She had flared up. The acrid odor of her sweating body mounted from her open blouse. For an instant my eyes turned leaden.

"Do not be angry," I said, touching her arm. "You're a woman, I'm a man; we can come to understand each other."

She glared at me through half-closed eyes, her brows quivering.

"This place is a graveyard," she said, looking now at the masks, the wooden gods, the strange, exotic armor all around us. "A graveyard. I'm suffocating in here. It's raining outside. Come, let's get wet!"

We spent hours in the rain walking beneath the trees of the large park. She had returned from Russia just a few days before—from paradise—and her whole being was steaming with love and savage hate. Her name was Itka.

I listened to her. At first I offered objections, but I soon realized that faith rules from an elevated level above man's head, and that reason is unable to touch it. I let her go on speaking, therefore, let her demolish and rebuild the world.

Evening drew on. The pedestrians thinned out; lights were lit.

Houses, men, and trees suddenly appeared to be drowning in the illumined rainfall.

"I'm tired," said the girl, leaning on my arm. "Let's go to my room."

Leaving the park, we proceeded through narrow lanes and reached a working-class neighborhood.

"You'll meet three friends of mine. Tonight we'll all have tea together. One is a painter. She wrestles with her pigments, makes something, then rips it up. She is searching, but she doesn't know what for. 'When I've found it,' she says, 'then I'll discover what I'm after.' Her name is Dina and she's Jewish. The other is an actress. She's searching just like Dina. She enters every character she plays, but when she comes out again, she tears herself to pieces. Her name is Lia; she's Jewish too. The third is very beautiful, also very affected and spoiled. Her rich father keeps giving her money and she orders evening gowns, buys perfume, chooses the men she wants, and sleeps with them. Her name is Rosa; she isn't Jewish, she's Viennese. I like her, I don't know why . . ."

She fell silent for a moment, but then: "Maybe because I'd like to resemble her. Who knows?"

I pretended that I had not heard, but inside myself I was secretly delighted to hear the voice of the eternal feminine surging above ideas, above all theories about destroying and rebuilding the world.

The friends were already there. Rosa had brought sweets and fruit. The table was set and they were waiting, Rosa applying lipstick, stretched out on the divan, while the other two read greedily from a newspaper they held open in front of them. People were seething again, the world was feverish.

As I watched the four savage souls around me, I kept thinking, Bless my fate for always throwing me among Jews; I believe they suit me much better than Christians.

The three girls let out a cry when we entered. They had not expected a man.

"I don't even know his name," Itka said with a laugh. "I found him in the Ethnological Museum. He's a mask."

Rosa shifted her position; the air filled with scent. The aura of warm breaths and impatient youth made me ill at ease. I don't know why, but being in the midst of so many female breasts, so many insatiable eyes and painted lips, filled me with shyness and fear. I would have preferred to leave, but the tea was brought and we seated ourselves on pillows on the floor, our knees touching. Now, so many years later, I remember nothing from that entire evening—that evening which weighed so heavily upon my life—except Itka talking with ardor about Moscow, the red capital of the world, and Rosa laughing and redoing her lips because she had drunk tea, and the other two girls staring goggle-eyed and saying nothing.

Night fell. The three girls got up to leave. I got up with them, but Itka squeezed my arm and signaled me to stay. I stayed. That night Buddha began to grow pale within me. I realized that night that the world is not a specter; that the body of woman is warm, hard, and filled with the waters of immortality; that death does not exist.

I stayed with her for many nights. She did not utter a single word about love, the heart not daring to distract our hallowed, naked games with its sighs and vows. Nothing but bodies now, like animals, we battled and then rolled headlong into sleep, exhausted and joyous. Ah, Buddha, Buddha! I kept thinking, and I laughed. What a relief when the flesh does not embroil itself in spiritual concerns but remains on earth, pure and unsullied, like an animal! Christianity soiled the union of man and woman by stigmatizing it as a sin. Whereas formerly it was a holy act, a joyous submission to God's will, in the Christian's terror-shaken soul it degenerated into a transgression. Before Christ, sex was a red apple; along came Christ, and a worm entered that apple and began to eat it.

I gazed with admiration at this fiery girl. The entire night she was an insatiable male-eating beast with every bit of her soul turned into flesh, the entire day a flame of the utmost purity. She reminded me of an extraordinary woman, likewise either all body or all soul: Saint Teresa. One day the nuns of her convent saw her voraciously gorging herself with a roast partridge. The simple-hearted nuns were scandalized, but Saint Teresa laughed. "At prayer-time, pray," she said, "at partridge-time, partridge!" She gave herself completely to each of her acts, nourishing her body and her soul with equal voracity.

Itka played with me all the night, but when day came, she puckered her brows and eyed me with hatred. "Aren't you ashamed to be comfortable and well off?" she kept asking me. "Not to be hungry, not to shiver in wintertime, not to have shoes which are worn through? Aren't you ashamed to stroll through the streets and say to yourself, 'The world is fine, I like it'?"

"I don't say, 'The world is fine, I like it.' I say, 'The world is a phantasmagoria. Hunger, cold, shoes (with or without holes) are phantasmagorias. A breeze will blow and dispel them all!' That's what I say!"

She charged me in a frenzy and sealed my mouth with her palm.

"Silence! Silence! I don't want to hear a word more! Can it be true then that all you who are well off don't have hearts with which to feel compassion? Don't any of you have eyes to see with? Come and see!"

Taking me, she led me through the proletarian quarter. Everyone knew her. Slipping into the wretched hovels, she showed me the hungry children, the weeping mothers, the unemployed men sitting there in silence biting their lips. When I asked them questions, they eyed me from tip to toe and then turned away their faces.

"Why don't they talk?" I demanded of Itka. "Why?"

"They are talking, they're bellowing—but how can the likes of you hear them? Never fear, however. One day you'll hear them well enough!" She riveted her eyes upon me, hoping to see that mankind's suffering had penetrated.

But I answered mockingly, "What a shame that I too don't suck some kind of gumdrop to sweeten my breath, one of those delicious products of mankind's confectionery art: God, fatherland, or your favorite, Karl Marx. Once I met the happiest man in the world; he sucked two gumdrops at once, Christ and Marx. By being a fanatic Christian and also a fanatic communist he solved all of life's problems, both the mundane and the celestial."

I had begun in jest, but as I spoke, I felt compassion and bitterness weighing down my soul. Out of a false sense of self-respect, however, I did not wish to divulge this, and I persisted in opposing her and taking pride in my refusal to find consolation by sucking gumdrops.

"I don't want any such comforts. Every faith promising rewards and happiness seems to me a cowardly consolation, good for dotards, weaklings, and vegetarians."

"I'm not a dotard, and I'm not a cripple or a vegetarian," my companion angrily retorted. "Stop your swaggering. Your Buddha is a gumdrop just like the rest. And what's more, I want you to know that I never want to hear you or see you again!"

Tossing her head in a furor, she abandoned my arm, turned into the first street we came to, and left me.

But in the evening her thick Jewish lips would be smiling. "Whatever we said during the day—water over the dam," she used to declare with a laugh. "Now it's nighttime!"

We parted each morning. She went to the factory where she worked; I had acquired the habit of taking solitary walks through the slums. I did not want to go there any more in Itka's presence, for when I was with her, my self-respect made me resist and keep my heart closed. When I was alone, however, man's suffering ceased to be a phantasmagoria. It was no longer a shade, but a real, famished body that wailed and bled.

Lord God, do not give man all he can endure! I had never known that so much suffering, so much hunger and injustice existed in the world. Never until this time had I confronted this horrible face of need at such close hand. Another table of laws was in force here, with hate as the primary duty. The Ten Commandments had to change here; they had already changed. Love, hate, war, and morality had taken on new meanings. One day I saw an emaciated young woman lying on the pavement. Her tattered dress had crept up indecently, revealing her nudity. Feeling sorry for her, I stopped to tell her to pull down her dress. "You are not decent," I said. She shrugged her shoulders, and a sarcastic laugh rent her lips. "I'm hungry and you talk about being decent. Modesty is for the rich."

I could not bear so much horror—cheeks hollowed out from hunger, tiny children digging in garbage pails to find a scrap of refuse to eat, their abdomens green and swollen, their shanks nothing but bones wrapped in yellow hide. Some leaned on crutches because their legs were unable to support them; and some had beards growing on their unfledged cheeks.

Unable to stand it any longer, I averted my eyes to keep from seeing—because I felt ashamed.

This I remember well: before compassionating mankind, I felt this inner shame. I was ashamed to see mankind's suffering while I toiled to transform all this horror into a spectacle both ephemeral and vain. I told myself that none of this was true. I must not be led astray into believing, like some simple, naïve person. No, hunger and satiety, joy and sorrow, life and death—all were specters! I said this over and over again, but as I saw the hungry, crying children and the women with their sunken cheeks and their eyes so filled with hate and pain, my heart gradually began to melt. It was with great emotion that I observed this unforeseen change within me. At first, shame throbbed in my heart, afterwards compassion—I began to feel the suffering of others as my own suffering. Next came indignation, then the thirst for justice, and above all else, a sense of responsibility. I am to blame for all the hunger and injustice in the world, I told myself; the responsibility is mine.

What should I do? I saw that my duty was shifting. The world was broadening, need getting out of hand, and duty felt imprisoned and suffocated in one small body, one small soul. What should I do? Which direction should I take? Deep within me already I knew what I ought to do, but I dared not reveal it. This road seemed against my nature, and I was not certain whether man, by means of love and effort, was capable of surpassing his natural disposition. But I meditated the question. Did he, I wondered, have so much creative force? If he did, then he was left with no possible justification if in critical moments he neglected to smash his limitations.

During those difficult days when I was toiling against my nature to surpass my odious self and to take pains to relieve human suffering, a surpassingly noble example of sacrifice and love came to my mind—it seemed as though he wished to show me my way. I recalled something he said one day: "We must always heed the cry of a man who calls for help."

When I first entered Assisi's narrow lanes during my pilgrimage to Italy and heard the bells ringing cheerfully (it was vespertime) from the campanile of the Church of Saint Francis, the poor man of God, and from the tiny Convent of Saint Clare, I felt inexpressibly happy. Staying at the palazzo of the elderly Countess Erichetta, I remained in this holy city for many months, not wanting to leave. Now, in these difficult days when my soul was fighting to rise a little higher, my heart opened and out rushed Assisi. The ragged, barefooted son of Bernardone rose up into the light during these critical days, stepped in the lead, and indicated my road with his hand. It was not a road, it was a rocky, precipitous ascent. But the air all about bore the sweet fragrance of sainthood.

I remembered the cloudy day when I climbed della Verna, the mountain of Francis's martyrdom and glory. A strong, icy wind was blowing; the rocks were gray and bare, devoid of grass, the barren trees all black. The region groaned cheerlessly, tormented and harsh—nothing but poverty, bareness, and desolation. Darkness was approaching, the light sparse and lusterless, and the summit still loomed high above me. I tried in vain to concentrate my desire and invoke all my strength, sensing a panic taking hold of my frozen, famished body, which was about to be benighted in this wilderness. Then suddenly the miracle took place. This inhuman, unflowering region around me seemed to have been displaced, seemed to have mounted the mystic step which all reality secretly yearns to mount, and I sensed that here about me was poverty—Franciscan poverty—harsh toward the body, merciless toward man's agreeable habits and his slothful, so exceedingly declivous pleasures.

It was this selfsame saint who mortified his flesh, denied the pleasures of the five senses, and threw ashes upon his food when he felt the inner devil of gluttony licking his chops. He plunged into icy streams in the heart of winter, kept vigils at night, went hungry and cold—tormented his body of clay so excessively that, pitying it on his deathbed, he turned and said, "Forgive me, Brother Ass, for I tormented you very much."

But this poverty was Franciscan, that is to say, certain of its wealth, of the mystic springtime it was preparing and the warm fruit-laden summer concealed within. Suddenly the starkly bare mountain of Verna laid itself open in my mind on this evening; it became the exquisite landscape of our inward paradise, verdant, fragrant, covered everywhere with bees and butterflies, and I began now to climb the metamorphosed mountain again and to shout, "Be thou blessed, Sister La Verna! Sister Poverty!"

Spring came. How could I possibly leave? I was happy living opposite the little Convent of Saint Clare, in the palazzo of the old Countess Erichetta, who was so pervaded by Franciscan joy and grace. Never had I experienced the identity between Saint Francis and the spring so deeply, for of the three great Franciscan precepts of Poverty, Chastity, and Obedience, none is so completely in harmony with Francis's pure, forever renascent soul as the great springtime precept of Chastity. Springtime in any other region would have awakened man's charmed, nostalgic soul to the memory of youth, and a woman he loved, and his tiny daughter; it would have generated resentment: why should nature be renascent while men found it impossible to recapture their youth. It would have made man's soul envy the mountains and valleys because they "await not death, nor know old age." Spring in Assisi, however, necessarily and cheerfully assumes the form of Francis. This Umbrian soil, the soil that had the good fortune to produce such a fruit, grows broader and richer; it ushers in a twofold, threefold spring in which every Assisian flower, without in any way losing its happy destiny, is elevated into a sacred symbol of the blossoming of the human soul.

Francis was one of the first, *the* first consummate flower to rise out of the discord-tilled winter of the Middle Ages. His heart was simple, happy, and chaste; his eyes, like those of children and great poets, always saw the world for the first time. Francis must have often gazed at an insect, a simple flower, a spring of water, and found his eyes flooding with tears. What a sight this is, he must have thought to himself, what joy, what divine mysteries are flowers, water, and insects! After so many centuries, Francis was the first to see the world with virgin eyes. All the heavy, unwieldy scholastic armor of the Middle Ages fell away, and body and soul remained naked, delivered over to all the shivers of spring.

I visited Assisi a second time a few months later, unable to keep myself away. The Umbrian plain with its abundant vineyards, fig plantations, and olive groves was laden with fruit now. I walked across it, proceeding by myself once more from village to village, enjoying the splendidly fruitful soil in mute tranquility: the sacred, fecund earth which had borne the pain of plow and spade with silent resignation, and now was reclining restfully and contentedly, its lap overflowing with fruit. You sensed that it was content and tranquil because it had done its duty. Bound to eternal laws, passing with confidence and patience through all the stages of meditation and suffering, it had achieved this rich autumn harvest of its virtue.

Suddenly, without any conscious effort, I found myself once

more experiencing the profound meaning of Obedience, the third fundamental Franciscan precept. To obey a harsh signal and abandon ourselves with confidence to the high forces around and within us, visible and invisible, unshakable in our faith that these know everything and we nothing—this is the one and only road to fertility. All the others are sterile and deceptive, because they do not lead anywhere, but simply bring us back to the miserable, accursed self after vain and presumptuous meanderings.

Thus it was that Francis rose again from this land he so adored. I saw him lying on the ground just as on that dawn when the friars discovered him couched on the soil of Saint Clare's garden, chanting the praises of sun, fire, water . . . and dying. He was happy. He had bound himself to eternal law, filled his hands with fruit, and like a good worker, was returning to his Lord.

During those months when I wandered through Assisi's lanes and outlying fields, or gazed at the paintings in the Poor Man's great palazzo, I remember that I kept struggling to experience such a spring and autumn myself, as far as I was able to. What insatiable, unsubmitting years of youth those were! Each morning, joyous and despairing, I went out at the break of dawn to roam this sacred region. I felt what every young man must feel, what must have been felt by the Spartan lad who held the fox next to his bare flesh and neither spoke nor screamed though his body was being torn apart—he suffered, proud in the knowledge that he had succeeded in mastering his pain.

Without my so wishing, however, my face doubtlessly must have divulged my struggle and pain, because one morning as I was leaving the city through the Saint Clare gate, I was stopped by a thin, lanky man whose blond hair had begun to turn gray. Though I had often seen him roaming like myself through this region which attracted so many pilgrims, we had never exchanged a word. We simply smiled politely at each other whenever our paths crossed, and continued on without speaking—treading more lightly, in a way of speaking, as though neither wished to disturb the other's solitude and tranquility.

But this morning the unknown stranger halted, looked at me, and after hesitating a moment, asked, "Would you like to walk together a little?"

"Yes, I would."

After we had proceeded a few paces, I said to him, "I'm from Greece. I came to Assisi and fell in love with Saint Francis."

"I'm from the other end of Europe," replied the stranger. "From Denmark. I too fell in love with Saint Francis. I have been living for years here in Assisi, unable to leave him. My name is Jorgensen."

I gave a start. "The one who wrote the brilliant book about Francis?"

Jorgensen smiled bitterly and nodded. "Who can ever do justice to Saint Francis? Not even Dante. Do you know the eleventh canto of the *Paradiso?*"

I was delighted. Those very days I had developed an overwhelming love for this canto, and as I took my solitary walks through Assisi's streets or the surrounding countryside, I often murmured its opening lines:

O insensate care of mortals,
How false are the arguments which
Make thee downward beat thy wings!

Together we began to recite the marvelous Italian, suddenly united in brotherhood beneath the great wing of poetry. We took the high road above the ravine with its lavish vineyards and olive groves. The sun had risen now, lighting the world and filling it with long-sweeping shadows. We remained silent for quite some time. Finally my companion turned to me and asked, "Why do you love Saint Francis?"

But he immediately regretted what he had done. "Forgive me," he said. "I have been indiscreet."

"I love him for two reasons," I replied. "First, because he is a poet, one of the greatest of the pre-Renaissance. Bending over even the most insignificant of God's creatures, he heard the immortal element they have inside them: melody."

"And second?" asked Jorgensen.

"Second, I love him because by means of love and ascetic discipline his soul conquered reality—hunger, cold, disease, scorn, injustice, ugliness (what men without wings call reality)—and succeeded in transubstantiating this reality into a joyous, palpable dream truer than truth itself. He discovered the secret so sought after by medieval alchemists: how to transubstantiate even the basest metal into pure gold. Why? Because for Francis the "philosopher's stone" was not something inaccessible and external to man which could be found only by throwing natural laws into confusion; it was his own heart. Thus, through this miracle of mystical alchemy, he subdued reality, delivered mankind from necessity, and inwardly transformed all his flesh into spirit. Saint Francis, for me, is the great general who leads the human flocks to unconditional victory."

"Is there nothing else?"

"I know what you want to ask me," I replied. "No, nothing else. General and poet—nothing else."

We fell silent again, but soon Jorgensen remarked, "That is not enough." Though he started to raise his hand as though wishing to touch my shoulder and soothe me on account of his blunt declaration, he held it in mid-air and repeated even more decisively this time, "No, that is not enough."

I was going to respond, but I restrained myself from fear I might say something rude.

"That is why your face appears so worried," said Jorgensen, as though continuing a silent thought. "You are still struggling, you have not achieved deliverance, and this struggle day after day is exhausting you. This is the reason I stopped you this morning and spoke to you."

"And supposedly you can help me in my struggle?" I asked in a voice which in spite of myself came out full of anger and irony.

I felt ashamed. Sometimes we speak before our souls have time to gain the upper hand over the body.

"Control yourself," said Jorgensen. "I cannot help you. Every person has to find his own road and save himself. From what? From the ephemeral. Save himself from the ephemeral and find the eternal."

Still irritated, I said, "Judging from your serene face, calm, sure gait, and ever-gentle tone of voice, you have already found your road. Doubtlessly you look upon the rest of us with sympathy, maybe even with condescension—the rest of us who are still struggling. Perhaps you were born privileged, with balanced faculties, and never knew any struggle."

Jorgensen halted and glanced at me for a moment. Extending

his hand resolutely this time, as though to a drowning man, he seized me by the arm.

"You are still young," he said. "I was young once, and I know. You are impatient, you still lack humility, you still will not deign to call for help. Allow me to tell you something: No, I was not born privileged. I know the meaning of anguish, struggle, and arrogance extremely well. When I was young like yourself, I had great satanic ambitions. I wrote novels full of sensuality, passion, and irony. In time, art became too constricting for me. Devoting myself to science, I turned into a fanatical advocate of Darwinism and every antichristian idea. I wanted to smash church, state, morality—all the shackles. At life's center I enthroned the self. 'War against the age-old enemy,' I proclaimed. Age-old enemy was my name for God. I wrote, I made speeches everywhere; I ran and ran, banner in hand. But suddenly I halted and fell silent. An unforeseen and inexplicable malaise had begun to perturb my heart. I knew neither how it came nor whence—perhaps it was inside me all the while, awaiting its hour. Leaving Denmark in order to escape my friends and my old habits, I traveled to Germany, then came down to Italy and entered Assisi."

He smiled.

"That was thirty years ago. The past thirty years I have spent here in Assisi, beneath Francis's shadow. God be praised!"

"And? . . ." I said, deeply moved. "I haven't read any of your other books—only *Saint Francis*."

"So much the better. I published an *Itinerary* in which I spoke (rather, tried to speak) of the emotion I felt at seeing the ancient cities with their castles, churches, paintings. . . . I'd gone before this to a Benedictine monastery, but it frightened me, and I left at once, the very next morning. Although the calm, beatific communion of cenobites seemed so sweet and attractive to me, so completely opposite to the life I had been leading, although it enabled me for the very first time to see which road leads to happiness, I hesitated to take this road. . . ."

Jorgensen turned and pointed with fervent joy to holy Assisi with its ancient walls, moldering acropolis—the Rocca Grande—and huge three-leveled fortress-like church of Saint Francis.

"Shall we return and see it?" he asked.

We took the road leading back to Assisi. Lean, fiery-eyed peasants kept passing us, preceded by pairs of oxen, the celebrated all-white oxen of Umbria, plodding with heavy gait beneath the yoke, their twisted horns garlanded with ripe ears of grain. A young peasant girl with raven-black hair and a silver voice greeted us cheerily.

"*Pax et bonum!*" Jorgensen responded, returning her "Good morning" in the Franciscan manner.

He pointed to the great basilica at Assisi's foot. Inside it, Francis's tiny little chapel, the Porziuncola, was to be found. "There in the Porziuncola," he said, "I fell on my knees for the first time, involuntarily, as I gazed at the Saint with the five wounds in his body. But I felt ashamed, and got up angrily and left. What made me kneel, what happened to me, I kept asking myself in a rage. But at the same time, an inexplicable sense of peace invaded my deepest being. Why, why, I asked myself again, why should I feel such relief? And truly, this happiness exceeded anything I had tasted in my life up to that point. But despite this, something inside me did not want to believe. It scorned everything supernatural and placed its confidence in only one thing: the human intellect, in whatever the intellect said. This was what stood at the doorway to my heart and prevented the miracle from entering."

"Well—and then?" I asked impatiently, seeing my companion fall silent once more. "How did deliverance come to you?"

"Calmly and without noise, as it most always does. Just as a fruit ripens and grows sweetly succulent, so my heart ripened and became sweetly succulent. Suddenly everything seemed simple and certain to me. The agonies, hesitations, and battles all ceased. I sat at Francis's feet and entered heaven. Francis, Francis himself, is the Brother Gatekeeper who opened the door for me."

We were finally nearing Assisi. The sun shone on the city's blood-tinted, half-crumbled citadel; Saint Clare's diminutive, silver-voiced bell began to toll merrily, cacklingly, like a highland partridge.

"You must forgive me for talking so much about myself," said Jorgensen. "Consider it a confession. I am more advanced in years than you and I enjoy confessing to my juniors—because that is the only kind of confession, perhaps, which can be of any benefit."

In order to hide my emotion, I said laughingly, "Ah, if only Francis were truly the gatekeeper of heaven—what joy! He would usher in saints and sinners, believers and infidels, even millionaires. Yes, and even the most repulsive of animals: rats, worms, hyenas."

"That would be anarchy," said Jorgensen without smiling. "Not only anarchy, but injustice."

We passed beneath the fortress gate. The Convent of Saint Clare was on our left, the house where I was staying on our right.

"I'll come up with you for a minute to say hello to the old countess," said my companion. "I remember her when I first came—the most beautiful noblewoman in Assisi. She was widowed at a young age and never remarried. I remember that she used to mount a white horse and inspect her estate—the olive groves and vineyards. If she had lived in Saint Francis's time, she might have become his Saint Clare."

"I wonder if she shares your religious belief."

"Don't you see her face?" Jorgensen answered. "It is radiant!"

We mounted the steps. It was chilly in the huge deserted palazzo and a fire was burning in the countess's room. Her servant Ermelinda had begun to set the small low table and bring coffee, milk, and whole-wheat bread to her mistress. Seeing us, she added additional cups. We sat down.

Yes, the aged aristocratic face was truly radiant; the large, velvety, raven-black eyes had remained untouched by time. The door leading to the garden was open; a blossoming rose bush glittered in the sunlight.

"Where did you two go so early in the morning?" inquired the countess. "I'm sure you were talking about Saint Francis."

"How did you know?" asked Jorgensen, glancing at me with a smile.

The countess laughed. "Because a moment ago when I went out into the garden, I saw you in the distance headed this way, and you were both wrapped in flames!"

How clearly those days in Assisi came back to me, complete in every detail! I had not requested Francis's aid, yet here he was running to show me the way. If only I could find the strength! When I glimpsed him embracing lepers in the distance, I was overwhelmed with nausea and fright; when I saw him going about barefooted to preach, his face radiant with beatitude as people hooted, drubbed, and stoned him, my heart stood up to resist. Though I was conscious of my abasement, I kept telling myself, Anything but that! Better to perish suddenly in an abrupt martyrdom. . . . To face jeering and derision day in and day out exceeded my endurance.

Direct contact with human beings I had always found irksome. I was eager to help them as much as I could, but from a distance. I did so with great pleasure, I loved them all and sympathized with them all, but from a distance. Whenever I came near, I found it impossible to tolerate them for long, they felt the same about me, and we parted. I have a passionate love for solitude and silence; I can gaze for hours at a fire or the sea without feeling any need for additional companionship. These two have always been my most faithful, most beloved comrades; whenever I fell in love with some woman or idea, it was because in them I found the principal characteristics of fire and the sea.

And furthermore (I told myself in order to justify my incapacity to follow Francis's ascending road), how can a Poor Man of God—another supernal Don Quixote, with equal artless simplicity, equal purity and love—how can such a man possibly reappear on earth in these times of Mammon and Moloch in which we live?

I said this over and over in order to console myself. I did not know that a new Poor Man of God had already made his appearance on earth; the lepers surrounding this one were Negroes. If I had learned about him during those critical, transitional days in Berlin which were urging me out of Buddhist inaction and into revolutionary action, I would have felt even more ashamed of my cowardice. I learned about him much—very much—later, when it was no longer possible, nor perhaps advisable, for me to change my life; when I had already taken an entirely different road in order to carry out my duty.

I was overcome with emotion on that August afternoon when I took the narrow road leading to the minuscule village of Gunsbach in the Alsatian forests. The Saint Francis of our day opened the door personally when I knocked, and offered me his hand. His voice was deep and peaceful; he looked at me, smiling from beneath his thick gray mustache. I had seen old Cretan warriors just like him—full of kindness and indomitable will.

The moment was well favored by destiny. Our hearts opened to each other. We stayed together until nightfall, talking about Christ, Homer, Africa, lepers, and Bach. In the late afternoon we set out for the village's tiny church.

"Let us remain silent," he said to me along the way, deep emotion having suffused his rough face.

He was going to the organ, to play Bach. He sat down. . . . That moment, I believe, was one of the happiest of my life.

On our way back, seeing a wildflower at the edge of the road, I stopped to pick it.

"Don't!" he said, restraining my hand. "That flower is alive; you must have reverence for life."

A tiny ant was parading on the lapel of his jacket. He took hold of it with untold tenderness and placed it on the ground, off to one side so that no one would trample it. Though he said nothing, the words "Brother Ant" were on the tip of his tongue, the tender words of his great-grandfather from Assisi.

When night came, we finally parted. I returned to my solitude, but that August day never sank below my mind's horizon. I was no longer alone. With unshakable assurance, this striver measured out his road in firm, youthful paces at my side. Though his road was not mine, I found it a great comfort and severe lesson to see him mounting his ascent with so much conviction and obstinacy. From that day onward I was convinced that Saint Francis's life had not been a fairy tale; I felt certain thereafter that man could still bring miracles down to earth. I had seen the miracle, touched it, spoken with it; we had laughed and kept silence together.

After that day my heart could nevermore distinguish between these two deeply enticing figures so far removed in transitory time, so closely united in eternity, that is to say in God's bosom. They resemble each other like two brothers: Saint Francis of Assisi and Albert Schweitzer.

The same tender, vehement love for nature. The hymn to Brother Sun and to Sisters Moon, Sea, and Fire echoes day and night in their hearts. Both hold the leaf of a tree at their fingertips, and, raising it into the light, see on it the miracle of the entire created universe.

The same tender reverential fellow-feeling for men, snakes, ants—everything that lives and breathes. Both see life as sacred;

both shudder with joy as, bent over the eyes of every living thing, they see the Creator reflected there in His entirety. Gazing at the ant, the snake, the human being, they make the joyous discovery that all things are brothers.

The same compassion and kindness (expressed in action) for everything that suffers. Both chose lepers, the deepest and most horrible abysm of wretchedness and pain; one white lepers, the other the black lepers of Africa. I said compassion and kindness, but I should have said *Metta;* only this Buddhist word faithfully expresses the sentiment engendered in these two brothers by human suffering. In kindness and compassion there are two: the sufferer and he who compassionates the sufferer. In Metta, on the other hand, there is absolute identification. When I see a leper, I feel that I myself am that leper. The ninth-century Mohammedan mystic Sari-al-Sakadi formulated this consummately: "Perfect love exists between two people only when each addresses the other with the words, 'O myself!' "

The same divine lunacy—renouncing the joys of life, sacrificing the small pearls in order to obtain the Great Pearl, abandoning the level road which leads to an easy happiness, and taking the savage uphill road which mounts between two chasms to divine lunacy. The lunacy of freely choosing the impossible.

The same guileless humor is seen in both: laughter gushing from the depths of a benevolent heart; joy, the dearly beloved daughter of a soul overflowing with riches; power to see and accept the countenance of everyday reality with tenderness and comprehension. The laughterless Spartans raised an altar to the god of laughter; the utmost austerity continually invoked laughter, for this alone is capable of helping a deep soul to endure life. . . . God endowed these two brothers with gleeful hearts, and because He did so, they journey gleefully to the summit of their endeavor, to God.

The same passionate love for music. What Thomas of Celano said about the one applies perfectly to the other: "An extremely thin partition separated Brother Francis from eternity. That is why he always heard the divine melody—through this delicate partition." Listening to this melody, both feel a jubilation approaching ecstasy. "If the angels who played the viol in my dreams had drawn their bows over the strings just once more, my soul would have torn itself away from my body, so unbearable was the beatitude." Thus spoke the first; the second, I am sure, must feel the same extremity of beatitude when playing Bach.

Both have in their grasp the philosopher's stone which transubstantiates the basest of metals into gold, the gold into spiritual essence. They take disease, hunger, cold, injustice, ugliness—reality at its most horrible—and transubstantiate these into a reality yet more real, where the wind of spirit blows. No, not of spirit; of love. And in their hearts, like the sun over great empires, love never sets.

But I learned all this too late; I did not know it during those crucial days in Berlin. When I viewed the human miracle in his tiny Alsatian hamlet, my fingers were already smudged with ink; I had been carried away by the profane mania to convert life into words, similes, and rhymes, had degenerated (I still don't know how) into a pen-pusher. What befell me was precisely what I most scorned: to satisfy my hunger with paper, like a nanny goat.

These two Poor Men of God were able to help me in only a single respect, the inestimable one of showing me that man is able, and has the duty, to reach the furthest point of the road he has chosen. (Who knows, perhaps at the end of the road all the various strivers will meet.) Thus they became models for me, lofty examples of persistence, patience, and hope. God bless them, for these two heroes of exploit taught me that only by means of hope can we attain what is beyond hope.

Encouraged by them, I made an attempt to conquer my nature; I pursued the path urged upon me by Itka's compassion, indignation, and smarting words. I did this for quite some time, and I do not regret it. When I returned to my natural path, I felt that my heart had become filled with human suffering and that the sole way to save oneself is to save others. Or to struggle to save others —even that is sufficient. I learned as well that the world is real, not a specter, and that man's soul is dressed in flesh—not in wind, as expounded to me by Buddha.

But while I toiled to make my decision, I remember, my brain offered great resistance. It was still wrapped in Buddha's yellow robe. What you intend to do is futile, it kept saying to my heart. The world as you crave it, where no one will suffer from hunger, cold, or injustice, does not exist and never will exist. But I heard my heart answering from deep within me: Though it does not exist, it shall exist because I want it to. I desire it, want it at every beat of my heart. I believe in a world which does not exist, but by believing in it, I create it. We call "nonexistent" whatever we have not desired with sufficient strength.

My heart's answer threw me into turmoil. If everything it said was true, what a fearful responsibility man bears for all the world's injustice and opprobrium!

The rhythm of events accelerated before many days had passed, perhaps because my soul was at last ready. Episodes followed one upon the other, pushing me. At any other time I would have considered them mere spectacles; now they were like flesh of my flesh.

One morning before we had gotten up, we heard a vague, boundless clamor, a remote lowing, as though far in the distance a herd of cattle on their way to the slaughterhouse had already felt the red bands around their necks and begun to bellow.

Itka jumped out of bed, wrapped herself in her threadbare overcoat, and without turning to look at me, hurtled down the stairs. The bellowing came continually closer. I flew to the window and opened it. Weightless flakes of snow were falling outside. In Greece the mountains and beaches would have gleamed in the morning sun, but here the light which crept over the snow-covered asphalt was sick and muddy.

Not a person, not a dog; the street completely deserted. Off in the distance, everywhere in the air, this deep bellowing which drew nearer and nearer. I waited. Little by little the street grew lighter. Two crows came and perched on an ice-encrusted tree without uttering a sound. They were waiting too.

Suddenly I saw a tall, bony woman with free-flowing hair dart into the far end of the street. She was not walking; she was leaping as though in a dance, a black banner flapping above her head. All at once behind her an army of men, women, and children appeared, wading through the snow in ordered formation, four abreast, pressing forward. The muddy light struck them. You saw nothing but pale, incensed faces with black holes for eyes, as if a thick army of blind, worm-eaten skulls had risen from the grave.

The light had grown a little stronger now; I was able to see more clearly. Across the street several shopkeepers were taking out their keys to open their stores, but as soon as they caught sight of the savage army, they replaced the keys in their pockets and glued themselves to the wall. The woman saw them. Striding across the sidewalk, she went up to them and flapped the black banner curtly over their heads. A hoarse voice rent the air.

"We are hungry!"

At that same moment she glanced up toward my window and opened her mouth. Divining the words she was about to utter, I became terrified, and without being fully aware of what I was saying, I began to shout, "Quiet! Quiet!"

I slammed the window shut and glued myself against the wall of the room—I was just like the shopkeepers. Completely discomposed, I murmured, "They are hungry . . . they are hungry; the Hunger Army . . ."

That entire day I could not—dared not—go outside for fear that along my way I might meet the woman with Hunger's black banner. This time she would be quick enough to hurl the grievous, insupportable words at me. I knew what words these would bc; that was why I felt afraid and ashamed.

Itka arrived around noontime, pale and out of breath. Tossing her threadbare overcoat on the floor, she began to pace up and down the narrow room. I was huddled in a corner waiting. I could hear her heavy respiration. Turning suddenly, she pointed at me.

"You're to blame! You!" she screamed. "You and everyone like you: the well-meaning, well-fed—and indifferent. You need to know hunger and cold, to have children who are hungry and cold, to want to work and be refused work! That's what I expected from you, not this sauntering from city to city to gape at museums and old churches and weep when you look at the stars because they seem so very pretty or frightening. Poor fool, just lower your gaze, look at the child dying at your feet!"

She fell silent for a moment, and then: "You write poems. You speak in your turn—have the effrontery to speak—about poverty, oppression, and villainy. By transforming our pain into beauty you get it out of your system. Damn beauty, when it makes a man forget human suffering!"

Two tears flew from her eyes. I went close; I wanted to touch her, to calm her by resting my hand upon her hair. But she winced, pushed me away, and cried, "Keep your hands off me!"

The glance she gave me was filled not only with resentment and scorn, but with hate.

The blood rose to my head.

"What do you expect me to do?" I cried angrily. "What *can* I do? . . . Leave me alone!"

"No, I won't leave you alone! You'd like me to leave you alone, you'd like to escape. But I won't! You cannot hate, is that it? Well, I'll teach you. You cannot fight? I'll teach you."

An attempt at laughter marred her face. It was not laughter, it was an unbearable convulsion of the flesh. She stepped close to me.

"Do you know the oriental proverb: 'Whoever mounts a tiger can never again dismount'? You mounted a tiger—me—and I shall never let you dismount!"

Opening a small cupboard, she brought out some bread, a little butter, several apples. She lit the kerosene burner and prepared tea. Not breathing a word, we sat down on two stools (all the room possessed), drew a little table near us, and began to eat. I observed her palpitating eyebrows. She kept lifting her cup in order to drink and then forgetting herself with her arm in mid-air. Her mind was elsewhere; some thought was tormenting her. I chewed away with bowed head, terribly ashamed. For I sensed with humiliation that this woman was stronger than I.

We finished our meal. She raised her head and looked at me. Her eyes were flickering now, her lips had reddened.

"Forgive me for speaking so nastily—but I've just come from the Hunger Army."

Rising, she went to the window and closed the tattered curtains. A peaceful, compassionate light poured into the room. She pushed the little table to one side, making space. Then she went to the divan and drew back the covers. I followed her, out of the corner of my eye. As she was unbuttoning her blouse she turned to glance at me.

"Are you sleepy?" I asked her, laughing.

"No," she answered. Her voice had grown murky. "Come!"

The next day she rose before dawn and hastily packed her tiny valise. Coming to the divan, she awakened me.

"I'm going," she said.

I shuddered. "Going? Going where?"

"Far away. Don't ask. Goodbye until we meet again."

"When?"

She shrugged her shoulders. Wrapping a scarf tightly around her hair, she stooped and picked up her little valise. Then she looked at me. Her blue eyes were hard and dry, her thick lips smiling.

"Thanks for all the nights," she said. "We performed our duty to the flesh very thoroughly. Buddha is done and finished; we exorcised him. . . . Why look at me like that? Are you sorry?"

I said nothing. A most bitter sweetness had settled in my vitals. All those nights and days were mixing together inside me and filling my entrails with joy and anguish.

"Are you sorry?" she asked again.

She had reached the door and was extending her hand to open it.

"Yes, I am sorry," I replied with irritation. "You demolished Buddha for me; my heart is empty."

"So you need a master, do you?" She laughed ironically.

"Yes, I do. Better a master than anarchy. Buddha gave a rhythm to my life, a purpose. He put a bridle on the demons inside me. But now . . ."

She wrinkled her brows. She was no longer laughing.

"Comrade," she said (it was the first time she had called me comrade), "your heart has been emptied and cleansed; it is ready. That's what I wanted. I have faith in you—don't listen to what I say when I'm angry. You are an honest man and one who is uneasy. I have faith in you. . . ."

She reflected a moment, then added, "No, not in you but in the Cry of our times. Be quiet and you'll hear it. Goodbye."

She opened the door. I heard her hasty steps as she descended the stairs.

"Be quiet and you'll hear it!" Those words of Itka's escorted me many days and nights. Keeping quiet, I listened intently, trying to hear. I attended lectures given by the friends of Russia, read their books and pamphlets, wandered late at night through the working-class sections of Berlin. I viewed the poverty and nakedness, heard sinister conversations, breathed in an atmosphere filled with indignation. Sorrow and compassion took possession of me at first, then anger, and finally the bitter certainty that I myself was responsible, that the fiery Jewess was right. The fault was mine! Why? Because I did not rise up to shout, because I saw, pitied, and straightway forgot, because I lay down at night and slept in a warm bed, without thinking of those who lacked a roof over their heads.

One of Francis of Assisi's disciples found his shivering master walking naked one night in the heart of winter. "Why do you go naked in such cold, Father Francis?" he said to him in astonishment. "Because, my brother, thousands upon thousands of brothers and sisters are cold at this moment. I have no blankets to give them to make them warm, so I join them in their coldness."

I recalled the Poor Man of God's words, but only now did I realize that to join others in their coldness was not enough. One had to cry out, "Forward all together, everyone who is hungry, everyone who is cold. There are scores of extra blankets. Take them and cover your nakedness!"

Little by little I began to divine the all-embracing, panhuman significance of the bloody experiment taking place in Russia's boundless land, her boundless soul. My mind began to tolerate and accept the revolutionary slogans which formerly had seemed so extremely naïve and utopian to me. As I gazed at the famished faces, sunken cheeks, and clenched fists, I began to have a presentiment of man's divine privilege: by believing in a myth, desiring it, imbruing it with blood, sweat and tears (tears alone are not sufficient, nor is blood, nor sweat), man transforms that myth into reality.

I was terrified. For the first time I saw how creative man's intervention is, and how great his responsibility. We are to blame if reality does not take the form we desire. Whatever we have not desired with sufficient strength, that we call nonexistent. Desire it, imbrue it with your blood, your sweat, your tears, and it will take on a body. Reality is nothing more than the chimera subjected to our desire and our suffering.

My heart began to throb for the hungry and oppressed. Their patience had given out; they had begun the assault. It seemed that all my Cretan blood scented revolution and commenced to seethe. I saw freedom and slavery before me again—the eternal adversaries —and Crete rose up inside me and whooped.

Could this be the Cry I was waiting to hear? Perhaps. In the decisive moments of my life Crete has never failed to rise up within me and whoop.

One evening, tired of the day's horrible sights, I bent over my desk and began looking through a book on Renaissance art in an attempt to forget all I had seen, heard, and suffered while roaming since early morning. More than wine or love, more underhandedly than ideas, art is able to entice man and make him forget. Art takes the place of duty; it fights to convert the ephemeral into the eternal and to transubstantiate man's suffering into beauty. What does it matter if Troy was reduced to ashes and Priam and his sons killed? In what way would the world have benefited, and how much poorer man's soul would be, if Troy had continued to live in happiness and if Homer had not come along to convert the slaughter into immortal hexameters? A statue, a verse, a tragedy, a painting—these are the supreme memorials man has erected on earth.

Supreme, but also the most dangerous for everyday human suffering. Art makes us scorn the petty everyday concern for food, and even for justice; we forget that this is the root which nourishes the immortal flower.

The early Christians were right in not wanting their artists to make the Virgin beautiful in sacred paintings. Seduced by her beauty, we forget that she is the Mother of God.

Suddenly there was a knock on the door. I opened it. A telegram from Moscow! I read it again and again, rubbing my eyes from disbelief. I held it up to the lamp and examined it, as though it concealed a dangerous secret which I wished to discover in the light before making my decision. This little piece of paper might be a message from destiny coming to change my life, I reflected. In my interests or against them? Who can trust destiny? It is not blind, it blinds.

Should I go or not? The telegram invited me to travel to Moscow to represent Greek intellectuals at the great tenth anniversary of the revolution. Pilgrims would be speeding to the red Mecca from all over the world. Who had made this invitation possible by mentioning my name? Why had I been chosen? Three days later I understood. I received a short letter from Moscow. It was a teasing summons from Itka:

> *All hail, you pseudo Buddhist with a full stomach, you aristocrat, you amateur sufferer! Until now you have sought God's countenance, deserting one false god to go to another false god. Come here, my poor friend, to find the countenance of the true god, the countenance of man. Come if you want to be saved. The world we are building is still a mere framework. Bend down in your turn, add a stone, build; Buddha is fine, fine indeed—for graybeards!*

Night had fallen by now. I rose and opened the window. Outside all was peaceful. The snow had stopped. From some bell tower a clock chimed sweetly in the frigid air. The trees in the street below me glistened, coated with icicles. And as my gaze began to lose itself in the nocturnal haze, Russia suddenly unfurled before me, vast, buried in whiteness, with its warm, lighted isbas, and its sleighs that slide over the snow. Steam rose from the horses' nostrils, and I even heard the cheerful little bells tinkling on their necks. Beyond, at the snow's edge, gilded domes flashed brilliantly, crowned not by crosses but by red flags like conflagrations. I recalled a half mad Athonite monk who used to tell me, "Every man and every object is crowned by a cluster of flames. If these flames go out, the man and the object perish." He was right. Russia too, I reflected, was crowned by a cluster of flames. If these flames went out, Russia would perish.

I closed the window with great haste. I had decided to depart for Moscow.

26

RUSSIA

MIRACLE butts against reality, makes a hole, and enters. When the time was ripe, Lenin gathered together his rags and tatters, made a thick package of his manuscripts, tied all his worldly possessions into a bundle, and bade farewell to his landlord, the Swiss cobbler who had rented him a room in his house in Switzerland.

"Where are you going, Vladimir Ilich?" said the landlord, holding Lenin's hand and regarding him with pity. "What madness makes you want to return to Russia? What will you do there? Do you suppose you'll find a room in Russia—or work? Take my advice, Vladimir Ilich, and stay here in peace."

"I have to go, I have to," Lenin replied.

"Have to? Why?"

"I have to," Lenin calmly repeated.

"But you paid all your rent and the month is not over yet. You realize of course, that I'm not going to refund the difference."

"It doesn't matter," Lenin answered him. "Keep it. I have to leave."

And he left. He set foot on Russian soil with his little cap, his clean frayed shirt, his shabby coat—an army of one, stubby, pale, and unarmed. Over against him: the boundless Russian land, the sinister, brutalized muzhiks, the roisterous aristocrats, the all-powerful priesthood, the fortresses, palaces, prisons, and barracks, the old laws, the old morals, and the knout. The fearful empire, armed to the teeth. There he stood with his little cap, his tiny Mongolian eyes staring fixedly into the air, while inside him a dancing, whistling demon gnashed his teeth and spoke.

"All this is yours, Vladimir Ilich. I give it to you—free! Just say one phrase, say the magic phrase I've been dictating to you for so many years: 'Workers of the world, unite!' Say it, and czars, gold braid, goat-bearded priests, well-dressed, well-fed pot-bellies—with one puff they'll all fall down on their backs. March over their carcasses, Vladimir Ilich! Forward, lad, march over their carcasses and climb. Nail the red flag to the Kremlin. Smash in their skulls with the hammer; slit their throats with the sickle!"

"Who are you?" Lenin kept asking him, listening with clenched fists to the demon inside him. "Tell me your name. I want to know who you are."

"I am the Miracle," replied the demon, and with his horns he butted Russia.

Until now few men have been able to look at Russia with clear, impartial eyes, unable to see its many-faceted countenance of abundant shadow and light as one unified sphere. A great gulf divides the Slavic soul from the Western. The Russian is able to harmonize inner contradictions which are incompatible to the European's rationality. The European places ratiocination above everything else, limpid ratiocination subjected to a rational scale of values. The Russian places the soul above everything else, the dark, rich, contradictory, intricate force which pushes man beyond rationality to violent, irresponsible passion. In him the blind creative forces still have not crystallized into a rational hierarchy. The Russian is still tightly glued to the soil; he is filled with earth and world-engendering darkness.

I considered Lenin's face, that face so filled with light and flame. Before me I saw the dark dough—the muzhik—which this obstinate mind had undertaken to knead. I yearned with ever-increasing vehemence to view the two primordial, implacable enemies and allies, Spirit and Matter, wrestling inside the Kremlin's closed, bloody arena.

The snow was falling thickly; it blanketed the entire tilled plain. Beneath the snow the sown wheat took its nourishment. The muzhiks moved tranquilly, without haste, as though eternal. Now and then a pitch-black crow winged silently by, headed for human habitation, to eat.

I waited many hours for the train, surrounded in the station by Mongolian faces, slanting eyes, beards filled with the shells of melon seeds, two women fortunetellers tossing cards, an elderly muzhik pouring tea into a little saucer and sucking it up thunderously with animalistic joy, Chinese mothers wrapped in filthy quilts, their infants bound to their backs or hanging from their necks like kangaroos—a warm human mass which sweated and reeked. The air smelled everywhere like a stable, perhaps like the stable of Bethlehem.

Midday came, evening bore down; we waited. The faces were grave and peaceful around me. No one darted outside to see if the train was coming or not. Everyone waited, certain that today, or tomorrow, the train would appear without fail. They did not count the hours with a watch. They knew that time is a nobleman, a great duke, and they were afraid to contradict him.

Toward dawn the train's whistle sounded in the distance. All the people rose and gathered their bundles, once more without any haste. An old graybeard who had stretched out at my side and snored the whole night long looked at me now and winked triumphantly, as though to say, Well, my little old man, how silly of you to get all excited because the train didn't come, and grumble and not sleep a wink all night. Look, here it is. It came!

Snowing again. Hamlets; tiny churches with green pointed domes; smoke motionless above the rooftops. More crows, lowering sky, snow. I looked and looked; my eyes had taken on a remote bluish depth, like the eyes of all who live in boundless plains. I looked, and suddenly round gilded domes appeared faintly in the distance against the gray-black sky.

It was about noontime; we were finally coming near, arriving finally at the new Jerusalem of the new god, the Worker, in the heart of Russia—perhaps the heart of today's world. Moscow!

Itka was waiting for me at the station. When she saw me, she laughed. "You've fallen in the trap, but don't be afraid. It's a big trap; no matter how much you walk in it you won't find its bars. That's what it means to be free. Welcome!"

I roam from dawn to dusk, gazing with insatiable eyes at this multicolored, multispermous chaos—Moscow. The whole of the Orient is poured out over the snow. Anatolian peddlers wearing weighty turbans; Chinese with leathery, monkey-like skin selling oxhide belts and little toys of wood and paper. Every inch of sidewalk taken up by men and women vociferously retailing fruit, smoked fish, infants' bibs, drawn fowl, statuettes of Lenin. Young girls hawk newspapers, a cigarette in their mouths; women workers go by, red kerchiefs on their heads. Fat, coarse women with Mongolian cheekbones and eyes. Half-naked children wearing dome-shaped astrakhan hats. Cripples who drag themselves along the sidewalk with outstretched hand and grovel before each passer-by. The muzhiks pass in their orange-colored cowhides, their beards thick and clotted like maize, and the air everywhere around them smells as though a herd of cows had passed.

Churches with green and gilded domes. Skycrapers. "Workers of the world, unite!" inscribed on the streets, the churches, the trams; and in red paint on the walls of a huge church, "Religion is the opiate of the masses!" Toward evening, above all this disorderly din, the deep Russian chimes suddenly resound with utmost sweetness, the chimes for the vesper service, which persists in remaining alive. . . . Chaos—that is one's first impression of Moscow.

The second is fright. In no other city of the world can you see these hard, resolute, morose faces, the flaming eyes, compressed lips, the tension and violent fever. You feel as though you have moved to a somber medieval town full of towers and battlements, where the knights are donning their armor behind barricaded doors as the enemy approaches. The atmosphere is filled with savage preparation for war. A great menace and a great hope hang over every head. Something lurks in the air here, giving rise to fear. A fiery cherubim all eyes and sword sits on the Kremlin towers like a medieval chimera on a Gothic campanile, keeping sleepless watch over Moscow with thousands of eyes, thousands of swords.

A company of red soldiers suddenly flew into the street from around a corner, their faces ferocious and rapt. The pavement shook, the pedestrians raced to get out of the way, a chubby little woman with a basket of apples shrieked from fear, and the apples spilled out and rolled over the snow, brilliantly red. The soldiers marched with heavy steps; they were wearing the pointed hat of the Mongols, and gray greatcoats which reached their feet. The officer marching in front was the first to begin to sing. I saw him as he passed in front of me. His mouth was in epileptic spasm, the veins of his throat swollen to the breaking point, sweat flowing down his cheeks. For some time he sang all alone; he seemed to be dancing as he marched, so uncontrollably ecstatic was the rhythm of his body. He sang all alone, but suddenly the soldiers took up the song, and the frozen street burst everywhere into flame and resounded like a battlefield. A faint shudder ran down my spine. Future reality—who could tell?—knifed through me like a lightning flash. The Russians had made their appearance in a great city, London or Paris, and were pillaging it. Which is the most bloodthirsty and carnivorous of beasts? A new faith. Which is the most herbivorous? A faith that has grown old. We had entered, now, the new faith's maw.

That same evening I met the most mystical and voluptuous of muzhik poets, Nikolai Kliuev. Scanty blond beard, receding hairline; he must have been forty, and looked seventy. His voice was muted, caressing.

"I'm not one of those Russians who busy themselves with politics and cannons," he said to me with secret pride. "I am part of the golden lode which makes fairy tales and icons. The true Russia depends on us."

He stopped; he seemed to regret having spoken so frankly. But his inner pride had carried him away. Unable to restrain himself, he continued. "Bulls and bears cannot smash the door of fate; the heart of a dove, however, smashes it."

He filled his glass with vodka and began to drink it sip by sip, clacking his tongue with contentment. Once more he regretted his words. Half closing his eyes, he glanced at me.

"Don't listen to me. I don't know what I'm talking about. I am a poet."

The eve of the great day: the Russian Revolution was celebrating its gory birth. White, black, and yellow pilgrims had come from all over the world. In other ages, the dark-skinned races of the East would have descended similarly on Mecca, the yellow race would have gathered similarly at Benares in mute antlike swarms. The earth's centers were shifting. Today all eyes, of both friends and foes, willingly or unwillingly, whether with love or hate, were pinned on Moscow.

In the center of Red Square the contemporary Holy Sepulcher of the new Jerusalem was hooded with snow. Four-abreast in densely packed rows, thousands of pilgrims were waiting for the squat door to open. Men, women, infants, they had come from the ends of the earth to see and do homage to the red czar who lay fully alive beneath the ground. I had come with them. No one spoke. We waited for hours in the snow and cold, our eyes riveted to the Holy Sepulcher. Suddenly a great hulk of a man moved in front of the squat door; the red guard had opened the tomb.

Slowly, by fours, without speaking, the multitudes plunged into the black entrance and vanished. I vanished with them. We descended gradually into the earth, the air heavy with the respiration and stench of people. Suddenly the drab, bovine faces of the two muzhiks preceding me became radiant, as though struck by a subterranean sun. I craned my neck. Far, far below, the large crystal which covered the sacred relics could at last be seen; flashing beneath it was the livid, bald pate of Lenin.

He lay fully alive in his gray worker's blouse, covered from the waist down by the red flag, his right hand clenched, his left opened upon his breast. His face was rosy and smiling, his short beard exceedingly blond. An air of serenity filled the high heated crystal. The Russian masses stared ecstatically, with the precise gaze they had employed just a few years earlier when they viewed the rosy, blond face of Jesus upon the gilded rood screens. This man was also a Christ, a red Christ. The essence was the same: humankind's eternal essence, made of hope and fear. Nothing had changed but the names.

I emerged onto the snow-covered square in a pensive mood. How very much this man had struggled, I reflected, full of admiration. How very much he had endured in his exile—poverty, betrayals, calumny. How even his dearest friends, frightened by his faith and obstinacy, had abandoned him! Inside that bald pate which I saw beneath the crystal, behind those small eyes, now extinguished, Russia with her villages and cities, her boundless plains, wide slow-moving rivers, and desolate tundras, had cried out and demanded freedom.

Because he was Russia's strongest and therefore most responsible soul, he believed that she was calling him, imposing on him the duty to save her. Why, after all, had she fashioned this strongest soul out of her struggles and blood and tears, if not to commit the terrible, fatal task to it?

While I paced pensively back and forth in Red Square, Itka, who had been assigned to me as a guide, kept speaking to me, and I marveled at her youthfulness and faith. As she spoke, her entire body turned to flame, just like El Greco's saints.

"Don't ask me about Lenin," she protested. "What can I say?

Where can I begin? He isn't a man any more, he's a slogan. He has lost human characteristics and become a legend. Children born during the revolutionary years are called Lenin's children; the mysterious old man who comes on New Year's Day laden with gifts which he distributes to the children is no longer Saint Nicholas or Saint Basil, he is Lenin. All the muzhiks and little old women of the masses need a superhuman comforter, a protector; the women hang Lenin's hallowed figure on their new iconostases and light a lamp for him. In the remotest villages of Russia, everywhere from the Arctic Ocean to the tropical settlements in Central Asia, the simple folk—fishermen, plowmen, shepherds—spend their nights carving Lenin's figure while they talk, laugh, and sigh. The women embroider him in all manner of silks, the men whittle him in wood, the children sketch him on the walls with a piece of charcoal. Once he received his portrait from a small village in the Ukraine—a mosaic made from grains of wheat, with lips of red pepper.

"Lenin has become a slogan for all of us, educated and uneducated alike. For us, the great man does not hang suspended above the masses that engendered him; he issues from his people's bowels, with the sole difference that what the masses shout inarticulately he formulates into an integrated message. The moment this message has been formulated, there is no longer any possibility for it to scatter and perish. It becomes a slogan. And a slogan means action!"

"What about Stalin?" I demanded, longing to hear about this savage mustachioed figure with the foursquare sluggish body, the all-cunning eye, the grave, measured gestures. What species of sacred monster was Stalin?

Itka remained silent for a moment, as though counting her words lest one too many escape her. You could sense that she had entered a forbidden zone. Finally she found what to say, and spoke.

"Lenin is the light, Trotsky the flame, but Stalin is the soil, the heavy Russian soil. He received the seed, a grain of wheat. Now, no matter what happens, no matter how much it rains or snows, no matter how much it fails to rain or snow, he will hold that seed, will not abandon it, until finally he turns it into an ear of wheat. He is patient, obstinate, sure of himself, and he has unbelievable endurance. I'll relate just a single incident from his youth, when he was a worker in Tiflis, and you'll understand what I mean.

"In those times (they seem like a fairy tale to us now) the Russian grand dukes, when they got drunk, lined the muzhiks up in their parks and used them for target practice. But the workers had begun to organize, and the czarist police arrested the working-class leaders at frequent intervals, imprisoned them, exiled them to Siberia, or killed them. One day the workers who unloaded freight cars at Tiflis declared a strike. Either you improve our living conditions so we can live like human beings, they said, or else we stop working. The police descended upon them, arrested some fifty, and lined them up in a field outside of Tiflis. The czarist soldiers formed ranks, each holding a knout garnished with spikes.

"One by one the workers bared their backs and passed in front of the rank while each soldier brought down the knout with all his might. Blood spurted, the pain was unbearable; many found it impossible to pass along the entire rank, and they swooned. Several fell down dead.

"Came the turn of the workers' leader. He threw off his shirt and bared his back, but before beginning his ordeal, he bent down to the ground, picked a tender blade of grass and passed it between his teeth. Then he proceeded to cross in front of the line of soldiers, slowly, bolt upright. The knout fell upon him maniacally, the blood spurted from his wounds, but he did not open his mouth, did not utter a sound. The incensed soldiers set about determinedly to do away with him; each struck two times, three times. But from him, not a sound. He passed the entire rank without bending, without groaning, and when he reached the last soldier, he removed the blade of grass from between his teeth and gave it to him. 'Take this to remember me by,' he said. 'Look, I didn't even bite it. My name is Stalin!' "

Itka glanced at me and smiled.

"Every Russian has been holding that blade of green grass between his teeth for years now, struggling not to bite it. . . . Now do you understand?"

"Yes," I replied with a shudder. "Life is violent, extremely violent—"

"But the human soul is more violent still," said Itka, and she squeezed my arm, as though wishing to give me courage.

I held my head high as I listened to fervid Itka's words. I felt as though the distant, impetuous breath of the steppes were blowing over me. An eastern wind full of destruction and creation had set my mind in a whirl.

What moved me supremely, and each day to a greater degree, was this: Never before had I seen the Invisible so visibly as here in the clamorous cities and on the snow-covered plains of Russia. When I say the Invisible, I do not mean any priestly version of God, or metaphysical consciousness, or absolutely perfect Being, but rather the mysterious force which uses men—and used animals, plants, and minerals before us—as its carriers and beasts of burden, and which hastens along as though it had a purpose and were following a specific road. You feel surrounded here by the blind forces which create sight and light.

Beyond all reasoning, beyond learned bickering, beyond economic needs and political programs, above Soviets and commissars, it is the spirit of our times which operates and directs here, the gloomy, drunken, merciless spirit of our times. All, from the most bestial muzhik to the saintly figure of Lenin, are its conscious or unconscious collaborators. This spirit is higher than programs, higher than leaders, higher than Russia. It blows above them, leaves them behind, and mobilizes the world.

When I came to this terrifying laboratory, I posed philosophical questions to the faithful who were constructing the new Russia. I was still governed by the futile, genteel concerns of the urbanite who has eaten to satisfaction and possesses the leisure to discuss and play. I did not see the visible world; I wanted to see the invisible one. Obviously I was coming from the daffodil-covered meadow of Buddha.

It is said that the aged Socrates was strolling one morning in the agora waiting for the first young man, so that he could stop him, engage him in conversation, and carry away his soul. But that morning, instead of a young man, he saw an elderly Indian sage appear from the East. This sage had set out on foot, years before, to find Socrates. The moment he saw him, he threw himself at his feet, clasped his knees, and said, "Buddha, O sage delivered from the mundane, conquerer of life and metamorphosis, sovereign over the gods, white elephant who treads and rips asunder the deceptive stalking-blind of vanity; O body beyond the eye and ear, beyond smell, taste and touch, incline the bowl of alms which you hold and spill me like a drop into the ocean of nonbeing. Master, extend your hand and show me the road of everlasting disaster."

And Socrates, politely concealing the ironic smile occasioned by these barbarous words, answered, "Stranger, if I understood correctly, you speak of gods and eternity. I am going to bring you to a friend of mine, a hierophant at Eleusis. He knows how the world came into being, where we come from, and whither we are going, and that the stars are larger than the Peloponnesus. He knows, in addition, that God is an egg gleaming in Erebus, and he will teach you the spell for the white cypress. . . . As for me, I'm sorry, but I concern myself only with this world, and with man."

How Stalin would have laughed, I reflected, had I entered the Kremlin the next day and asked him the old Indian's questions!

Daybreak. I lean out my window. Outlandish constellations—hammers, sickles, red stars—phosphoresce in the obscure dawn with their multicolored lightbulbs. I struggle to discern the letters of the red inscriptions which belt the streets. The light gradually increases, and I spell out, "Workers . . . seven-hour . . . Lenin . . . world-wide revolution . . ."

I hurriedly dress myself. I meet all the races of mankind in the hotel corridors as I descend from floor to floor—a multitude of invited workers, both manual and intellectual. I bow deeply as I encounter the Japanese writers, the delegates from Persia and Afghanistan, two hodjas from Arabia, three young Indian university students and two charming Indian women with orange-colored cashmere shawls. On the first floor I exchange greetings with two gigantic Mongols and three diminutive supersubtle Chinese generals; in their words and eyes I feel all the dangerous, seething agitation of Asia.

We race to be in time for the beginning of the ceremony. Extreme cold, gray sky, steam flowing from nostrils and mouths. Red Square is already full. The government officials stand in a row above Lenin's Holy Sepulcher; opposite them, on benches arranged amphitheatrically in rising tiers, the invited guests from the world over. The troops in ranks, motionless; the masses behind them make a dense, muffled din like a remote subterranean earthquake. The ground shakes beneath your feet. In the background, the beloved cathedral of Ivan the Terrible, with its many domes and many colors, protudes like a ghost in the morning fog.

The diminutive Chinese generals are packed in around me, decorations on their chests. Also some Indian men and women, the Japanese intellectuals, and a Negro of gigantic proportions, a gold ring in his ear. We look at one another tenderly, smile, and tacitly voice our affection. A Japanese poet squeezes my hand. I know only a single word of Japanese—*Kokoró*—which means "heart." Placing my hand over my heart, therefore, I lean to his ear and say, "*Kokoró!*" whereupon he emits a cry of joy and falls into my arms.

Suddenly—martial trumpets. We all jump to our feet, faces beaming. Cavalry units of Circassians, Caucasians, Mongols, and Kalmucks press by, the commander in front with a naked sword held upright, the cavalrymen following in ethnic costume, with lances and multicolored banners. They salute Lenin's tomb and disappear. One on top of the other, in compact waves, come the infantry, artillery, the sailors of the Baltic and the Black Sea, the air force, the Moscow guard, the Gay-Pay-Oo, the workers with their leather blouses and short rifles, the women workers with their red kerchiefs and rifles over their shoulders. Next, the astonishing, interminable people's parade. Three slow-moving red rivers spill out of the three sides of the gigantic square. Students go by, then pioneers, communist youth, peasants, Asians on camels, Chinese with a colossal cloth dragon which opens and closes its jaws. On a float a large globe choked by chains, and a child striking the chains with a hammer and breaking them; afterwards a series of floats with disabled veterans waving their crutches in the air and cheering. Mothers pass holding their infants. The hours roll by; suddenly the sun pierces the fog and the myriad faces gleam, the eyes sparkle. The whole square shakes from cheering and the marchers' heavy tread. The Indians in front of me remove their orange-colored shawls and unfurl them in the air.

I look around me. Everyone is weeping. I look again, but see nothing; my eyes have been dimmed by tears like all the rest. Falling upon the slender Chinese general at my side, I hug him as tightly as I can, and we both weep. The Negro dashes forward and clasps the two of us in his arms. He is weeping also, and laughing. . . . How many hours did this divine intoxication last? How many centuries? This was the second great day of my life, the loftiest of all. The first was when Prince George of the Hellenes set foot on Cretan soil. As I squeezed the Chinese general in my arms, as the Negro squeezed the two of us, I felt that boundaries were crumbling away, that names, countries, and races were vanishing. Weeping, laughing, embracing, man was uniting with man. A lightning flash had illuminated their minds and they had seen: all men are brothers!

I too felt my tiny heart cry out, like the boundless land of Russia. I vowed that my life would finally take on singleness of purpose, that I would free myself from slavery's myriad forms, triumph over fear and falsehood, and help others to free themselves from fear and falsehood. Men had committed injustice long enough; I would tolerate it no further. We must give clean air, toys, and education to all the children of the earth, freedom and tenderness to the women, courtesy and kindness to the men, and a grain of wheat to that tail-wagging jade, man's heart.

This is the voice of Russia, I told myself, and I vowed to follow it to the death.

Vows of a man in love. I meant what I said; I was determined to give up my life. I understood for the first time what joy must be felt by those who are stoned, burned, and crucified for an idea. This was the first time I had experienced the meaning of brotherhood so deeply, the meaning of "all men are one." I realized that there is a gift higher than life, and a force which conquers death.

I knew of Panait Istrati's heroic life of tribulations and had read his stories, so full of oriental charm, but as yet I had never seen him. One day I received a crumpled, smudged piece of paper covered with large, hastily written letters: "Come and see me. My father was Greek, my mother Romanian. I am Panait Istrati."

I knocked on the door of his room at Moscow's Hotel Passage. I was truly delighted at the prospect of seeing a man who knew the meaning of struggle. I had conquered the distrust which takes hold of me each time it is a question of making a new acquaintance, and I went to this man, to Istrati, full of confidence. He was lying in bed sick. The moment he caught sight of me he sat up and shouted joyfully in Greek, "Good to see you. By God, good to see you!"

The initial contact, the decisive one, was cordial. Each of us observed the other as though attempting to divine something—

like two ants groping with their antennae. Istrati's much-buffeted face was slender and deeply creased. His lustrous gray hair fell unkemptly over his forehead, like a child's. His eyes gleamed, full of roguery and sweetness; his hircine lips hung down voluptuously.

"I read the speech you gave at the Congress the other day," he said to me. "I liked it. You laid it into them—just what they deserved. Those idiotic Westerners! They think they're going to prevent the war with their little pacifist penholders! Or else, if war does break out, they think the workers will revolt and throw away their arms. Hooey! I know the workers only too well! They'll drag themselves to the slaughter all over again and start killing. Yes, you laid it into them nicely, I tell you. Another world war is going to break out whether we like it or not, so let's be ready!"

Looking me straight in the eye, he extended his bony hand and squeezed my knee.

"They tell me you're supposed to be a mystic," he said with a laugh. "But I can see you've got a weather eye open and that your tummy doesn't get filled just with fresh air. That's what it is to be a mystic, eh? Well, what do I know about it? Words, words! Give me your hand."

We clasped hands, both laughing. He flew out of bed with a bound. There was something of the wildcat in this man's abrupt, nimble movements, rapacious eyes, fierce grace. He lit the kerosene burner and placed the briki on it.

"One medium-sweet!" he cried in a waiter's singsong.

Memories of Greece arose in him, and his Cephalonian blood began to boil. He started to sing some ancient songs he had heard in the Greek quarter of Brăila:

O to be a butterfly,
and fly near you . . .

Greece was rising from his vitals. The prodigal son yearned to return to the land of his fathers now. Suddenly, full of passion, he made his decision: "I'm going back to Greece!"

He had grown tired. Coughing, he returned to bed and sipped his coffee.

Sitting up in bed and lighting one cigarette after the other, he began to talk with passionate slovenliness about Russia, then about his work and its principal hero, Adrian Zographi, who suffers because he searches for a friend all his life and does not find one. His desires are undisciplined, his heart insurgent, his mind incapable of regulating chaos.

I regarded Istrati with much love and compassion. I sensed that his life was undergoing a decisive change but that he still had not settled to himself which road to take. He kept looking at me with his tiny inflamed eyes, as though seeking my aid.

"Adrian, the hero of your books, is you," I said to him with a laugh. "Identical! You're not the revolutionist you think you are; you're the *homme révolté!* The revolutionist has system, order, and coherence in his activity, a bridle on his heart. You are a rebel and find it very difficult to remain faithful to one idea. Now that you've set foot in Russia, however, you must put things in order inside yourself and come to a decision. You have a responsibility to do so."

"Leave me alone!" he cried, as though I had grasped him by the throat. But a moment later he asked me in an anguished tone, "Are you sure?"

"The Romanian Adrian Zographi is dead," I declared, and I caught hold of Istrati's emaciated arm, as though wishing to console him. "Long live the Russian Adrian Zographi! Panait, it's time you left Brăila's narrow districts. The world's anxiety and hope have broadened, and Adrian has broadened as well. Let the personal, disorderly rhythm of his life join with the world-wide rhythm of Russia, so that it may finally acquire coherence and faith. The time has come to put into effect the lofty equilibrium which Adrian—and Panait—sought in vain for so many years, because now it can base itself not on the inconsistent destiny of a single individual, but on the dense struggling masses of a colossal people."

"Enough!" cried Istrati, irritatedly. "Enough! What devil brought you here? I've thought about all you've said day and night as I've lain here on my bed. But you don't ask if I can. You shout 'Jump' at me, but you don't ask 'Can you?' "

"We'll see, Panaitáki," I replied. "Don't get excited. Jump, and we'll see how far you get."

"Good God, this isn't a game! How can you talk like that? It's a question of life and death."

"Life is a game and so is death," I said, rising. "A game—and whether we win or lose depends on just such a moment as this."

"Why did you get up?"

"I'd better go. I'm afraid I've tired you."

"You're not going anywhere! You'll stay, we'll eat, and in the afternoon we'll go out somewhere together."

"Where?"

"To see Gorki. He sent a message; he's expecting me. Today I shall see this celebrated European Istrati for the first time."

His embittered voice revealed a childish envy of the great model.

He jumped out of bed and dressed himself. We went outside. He kept a tight grip on my arm.

"We shall become friends," he kept saying to me. "Yes, we shall become friends, because I already begin to feel the need of giving you a punch in the nose. You'd better learn that I can't feel friendship without punches. We've got to quarrel now and then and crack each other's skulls—do you hear? That's the meaning of love."

We entered a restaurant and sat down. He took a tiny vial of olive oil from around his neck, where it hung like a talisman, and poured the oil into his thick meat soup. Next, he sprinkled the soup with ample pepper from a little box which he removed from his waistcoat pocket.

"Oil and pepper!" he said, licking his lips. "Just like in Brăila."

We ate with zest. Istrati was recalling his Greek little by little; each time a word rose out of his memory he clapped his hands like a child.

"How do you do!" he shouted at each word. "How do you do! And how are you today?"

He kept his wits about him, however, and every few minutes looked at his watch. Suddenly he got up. "It's time," he said. "Let's go."

Calling the waiter, he purchased four bottles of good Armenian wine, filled his overcoat pockets with little packages of mezédhes, loaded his cigarette case to overflowing, and we were off.

Istrati was excited; he was about to see the great Gorki for the first time. He doubtlessly expected hugs, tablefuls of food, tears, laughter, and conversation followed by more conversation, then, hugs and more hugs all over again, without end.

"You're excited, Panait," I said to him.

No answer. Irritated, he quickened his pace.

We reached a large building and climbed the stairs. I kept looking at my companion out of the corner of my eye; I enjoyed watching his slender, gangling body, his workingman's hands that had known so much labor, his insatiable eyes.

"Can you control yourself now that you're going to see Gorki?" I asked him. "Can you keep from launching into hugs and shouting?"

"No!" he replied angrily. "What do you think I am, an Englishman? How many times do I have to tell you that I'm a Greek, a Cephalonian. I shout, I hug, I give of myself. Your worship can play the Englishman if you like. . . . And if you must know," he added a second later, "I prefer to be alone. I find your presence annoying."

The words were hardly off his tongue when suddenly there stood Gorki on the landing, a cigarette butt glued to his lips. He was huge and heavy-boned, with sunken jaws, prominent cheekbones, small blue eyes that looked anxious and afflicted, and an indescribably embittered mouth. Never in my life had I seen so much bitterness on a man's mouth.

Istrati mounted the stairs three at a time the moment he saw him, and seized his hand.

"Panait Istrati!" he shouted, ready to fall upon Gorki's broad shoulders.

Gorki offered his hand calmly, without speaking. He regarded Istrati with an expression which betrayed not the slightest sign of either joy or curiosity.

After a moment, he said, "Come in."

He went first at a calm pace, Istrati following behind nervously, the mezédhes and the four bottles of wine protruding from his overcoat pockets.

We sat down in a small office full of people. Gorki spoke nothing but Russian, and it was difficult to start the conversation. Istrati began to bibble-babble with great excitement. I do not remember what he said, but I shall never forget the ardor of his discourse, the tone of his voice, and his broad gestures and fiery eyes.

Gorki answered calmly and succinctly in a sweetly modulated voice, incessantly lighting cigarettes. His embittered smile gave his peaceful talk a deeply concentrated air of tragedy. You sensed in him a man who had endured much and who continued to endure much, a man who had seen sights so horrible that nothing, neither the Soviet celebrations and cheering, nor the honors and glory he had received, could ever again efface them. Flooding up behind his blue eyes was a calm, incurable sadness.

"My greatest teacher was Balzac," he said. "When I read him, I remember, I used to lift the pages to the light, look at them, and exclaim with dismay, 'Where can a person find so much strength? Where can he find the great secret?' "

"What about Dostoevski and Gogol?" I asked.

"No, no. Of the Russians, only one: Leskov."

He fell silent for a moment.

"But above all—life. I suffered greatly, and I developed great love for everyone who suffers. Nothing else."

He remained silent, following with half-closed eyes the blue smoke from his cigarette.

Panait brought out the bottles and placed them on the table; he brought out the packages and packets of mezédhes. But he lacked the courage to open them. He realized that it was not fitting. The atmosphere he expected had not developed. He had expected something quite different. He thought the two tormented heroes of trial would drink and shout, utter grand speeches, sing and dance until the very earth commenced to thunder. But Gorki was still plunged in his trials, still nearly without hope.

He rose. Several of the young men present had called him, and he shut himself up with them in the adjoining office.

"Well, Panait," I asked when he was gone, "what do you think of the master?"

Istrati opened a bottle with a spasmodic movement.

"We don't have any glasses," he said. "Can you drink from the bottle?"

"Yes."

I took the wine.

"Here's to!" I said. "Man is a desert beast, Panait. Each man is surrounded by a gulf, and there are no bridges anywhere. Don't get upset, Panaitáki. Didn't you know this?"

"Hurry up and drink so I can have my turn," he said disgustedly. "I'm thirsty."

He wiped his lips. "I knew it. But I keep forgetting."

"That's your great virtue, Panait. Alas if you didn't know it—you'd be an idiot. And knowing it, alas if you didn't keep forgetting—you'd be cold and insensitive. Whereas now you're a real man—warm, full of absurdities, a skein of hopes and disappointments—to the death."

"Well, we've seen Gorki now. That's that!" He replaced the bottles in his pockets, collected the packages and packets, and we left.

On our way he said to me, "I thought Gorki extremely cold. And you?"

"I though him extremely embittered. Inconsolable."

"He should have screamed, drunk, and wept to lighten his burden!" growled Panait indignantly.

"Once, when the dear ones of a certain Mohammedan emir were killed in a war, the emir issued an order to the men of his tribe: 'Do not weep or scream, lest your sorrow be lightened?' That, Panait, is the proudest discipline a man can impose on himself. And that is why I liked Gorki so very much."

The next day I went by Moscow's great Cathedral, and entered. The boundless temple which had been the boast of czarist Russia was empty, unlighted, and unheated, the multicolored processions of gilt-haloed saints freezing in the desolate winter darkness. The little old lady who kept watch at the offertory table over an empty plate containing not a single kopeck was not sufficient to warm this whole sacred, shivering flock with her breath, which issued like smoke from her mouth and nostrils.

Suddenly, I heard the angelic-sweet voices of men and women singing psalms in the women's gallery high above. Groping about, I found the marble spiral staircase and began to mount. Above me I could discern two or three little old men and women in the dimness. Wearing shawls, they were mounting also, gasping for breath.

When I reached the head of the stairs, I found myself in a warm alcove, a chapel all of gilt, with lighted tapers, kneeling people, and the sanctuary filled with deacons, priests, and prelates dressed in gold, dressed in silk.

I shall not forget that alcove's warmth and sweetness. The men were for the most part old, with side whiskers; they seemed like former noblemen, or like doormen in noble houses. The women had their hair cowled with snow-white wimples. Christ glittered on the iconostasis, well fed and rubicund, his breast covered with decorations—human hands, eyes, and hearts of silver and gold.

I remained standing amid the kneeling crowd. I found it impossible to contain my emotion. All this assemblage seemed to me like a heart-rending farewell, as though some extremely beloved person were going away on a distant, dangerous journey, and his friends were seeing him off. . . . The last believers were taking bitter leave of their God's beloved form while the first believers in the terrible Mystery's new form were charging without mercy and smashing the old, infirm idols. . . . We live in a crucial, merciless moment in which an old religion is dying and a new one being engendered in the blood.

The times through which we are passing—and even more terrifying, those through which our children and grandchildren will pass—are difficult ones. Difficulty, however, has always been life's stimulant, awakening and goading all our impulses, both good and bad, in order to make us overleap the obstacle which has suddenly risen before us. Thus we sometimes reach a point much further than we had hoped: by mobilizing all our forces, which otherwise would have remained asleep or acted reluctantly and without concentration. For these mobilized forces are not merely our own personal ones, nor are they merely human. The forces released within us in the forward propulsion we develop in order to jump are a threefold unity: personal, panhuman, and prehuman. At the instant when man contracts like a spring in order to undertake the leap, inside us the entire life of the planet likewise contracts and develops its propulsion. This is when we clearly sense that simplest of truths which we so often forget in comfortable, barren moments of ease: that man is not immortal, but rather serves Something or Someone that is immortal.

When the liturgy terminated and the last believers began to go slowly down the marble staircase, I was approached by a pale, weakish young man. He had a short blond beard, tired blue eyes, and kept coughing. He engaged me in conversation.

"Are you one of us?" he asked excitedly. "You didn't betray Christ?"

"I don't betray Him if He doesn't betray me," I answered.

"Christ never betrays," said the youth, astonished at my words. "He never betrays; He is only betrayed. But come, it's cold out; let's go to my house and have some hot tea."

His father was a former nobleman who owned a large mansion and had been crowded now into two rooms, the rest being filled with working-class families. He had been given the least sunny rooms because, unlike the workers, he did not have small children, and the workers' children needed to enjoy the sun. The young man worked in a factory in order to live, but he was a poet, and he wrote verses whenever he had a little time.

"Right now I am writing a long poem," he said. "A dialogue—Christ talking with a worker. It is morning; the factory whistles are blowing; it's snowing out, very cold. The men and women are running to their factories, shivering, their bodies deformed by toil. My worker takes Christ by the hand and conducts Him on a tour of the factories, the coal mines, the harbors. Christ sighs.

" 'Why all these damned? What have they done?'

" 'I don't know,' the worker answers him. 'You tell me.'

"He takes Him next to his damp shack with its fireless hearth and his hungry, crying children. The worker shuts the door, clutches Christ by the arm, and cries, 'Rabbi, how should we behave toward Caesar? What is his, that we may give it him, and what is ours, that we may take it!' "

The young man stopped, out of breath. He kept moving his hands back and forth, vehemently, anxiously.

"Well?" I asked. "What was Christ's reply?"

"I don't know," answered the last believer, looking around him fearfully. "I don't know yet; or more exactly, I don't know any more."

The young man collapsed into a disemboweled armchair and hid his face behind his hands. "Why? Why?" he groaned.

He too asks, I reflected, asks and finds no answer. I wonder if Christ is capable of answering. Why doesn't he ask Lenin?

"Why don't you ask Lenin?" I demanded of him. Involuntarily I spoke with anger.

"I did."

"And what was his reply?"

" 'Workers of the world, unite!' I jumped up in a rage: 'But I'm asking about the soul, Vladimir Ilich, about God, about eternity!' "

"And?"

"Lenin shrugged his shoulders and laughed. 'Bourgeois . . . ' he murmured, and he crushed his cigarette butt beneath his heel."

The forest is large, the wind is right.
Forward, Be-Kou, take up your bow!
This way, that way, this way, that way!
A boar! Who kills the boar,
O poor Be-Kou? Be-Kou!
But who eats it, O poor Be-Kou?
Forward, cut it in pieces. You shall eat the guts.
Bam! An elephant rolled to the ground!
Who killed it? Be-Kou.
Who shall get the precious tusks, O poor Be-Kou?
Patience, Be-Kou. They'll give you the tail.
(*Pygmy song*)

The more the days went by, the more I felt Russia's mysterious fascination penetrating deeper and deeper within me. It was not simply the exotic spectacle of the hyperborean winter which fascinated me, nor my first view of Slavic life—the people, palaces, churches, troikas, balalaikas, and dances everywhere around me. It was something else, something more mysterious and profound. Here in the Russian air I felt the two primordial world-generating forces openly, almost visibly, clashing. So much did the surrounding atmosphere of war penetrate to your very vitals that like it or not you threw yourself into the struggle with one of these world-generating forces or the other, and fought. What I myself had tasted so sharply in my own microscopic existence I saw merciless and terrible here in Russia's vast body. It was the same struggle, the precisely identical battle, with the same eternal adversaries: light and darkness. Thus my own struggle gradually became one with Russia's struggle. Russia's deliverance would be my deliverance as well, for light is one and indivisible, and wherever it triumphs or is defeated, it also triumphs or is defeated inside you.

From the instant I finally arrived inwardly at this identification, Russia's fate became my fate. I was struggling and agonizing at her side. Feeling too constricted in Moscow now, I set out to see the entire vast arena at first hand—from Murmansk on the Arctic to Bokhara and Samarkand, from Leningrad to Vladivostok—everywhere the primeval enemies and allies were wrestling.

Each man bears his cross; so does each people. The majority carry it on their shoulders until they die; there is no one to crucify them. Happy the man who is crucified, for he alone shall enjoy a resurrection. Russia was being crucified. As I roamed her various republics and villages, I shuddered from sacred awe. Never had I seen such struggle, such agony upon the cross, never so many hopes. For the first time I realized how difficult it is for a man to decide to take a step forward in order to conquer his former love, former God, age-old habits. Although all these had once been spirit urging him to ascend, they had turned to leaden matter in the course of time and had collapsed halfway along in the journey. Now they kept the new creative breath from passing.

Millions of muzhiks were resisting. They did not understand, did not want to be saved. They held nails and nailed them into the Mother. Working the soil generation after generation, they had turned to soil, they hated the flame. The hungry, wounded workers—all flame, they—were pushing the crude masses to join the path of deliverance, sometimes by means of gentle coaxing, sometimes by violence.

And the peoples of the world stood, prudent and well fed, around the Russian arena where light and darkness were engaged in battle. "Finished! Russia is finished!" they guffawed, because the prudent and well-fed can never understand the invisible resurrectional forces of the Crucifixion. But as Christ said, in order for the grain of wheat to become an ear of wheat, it must descend to earth and die. Russia was suffering similarly—like a grain of wheat; like a great idea.

One of the apocryphal Gospels relates how the beloved disciple John had an astounding vision as he stood weeping before the Crucified. The cross was not of wood but of light, and crucified upon it was not a single man but rather thousands of men, women, and children, all groaning and dying. The beloved disciple trembled, unable to capture and immobilize any of the innumerable figures. All kept changing, running, disappearing; some returned a second time. Suddenly they all vanished, and nothing remained on the cross but a crucified Cry.

This vision writhes before us today. Today's savior, however, is not one man but an entire people. All of Russia, millions of men, women, and children, are being crucified and are suffering. They disappear, they flow, you cannot distinguish one definite figure; but out of these innumerable deaths surely the Cry will remain.

Nothing else is needed; this is how the world will be saved anew. What does "will be saved" mean? It means finding a new justification for life because the old one has vented its strength and can no longer support the human edifice. Happy the man who hears the Cry of his times (each epoch has its own Cry) and works in collaboration with it. He alone can be saved.

We live our epoch and consequently do not see it. But if in time the new idea which is being crucified today really does enkindle and renew the world, then we have already entered the first circle of fire. Centuries from now this epoch of ours will possibly be called a middle age, not a renaissance. Middle age—in other words an interregnum. One civilization becomes exhausted, loses its creative strength and crumbles; a new Breath carried by a new class of men toils with love, rigor, and faith to create a new civilization.

The creation of this new civilization is not assured; in no creative act is anything assured beforehand. The future may be a total catastrophe; it may be a pusillanimous compromise. But it may also be a triumph for the creative Breath. In that case our own transitional period is one in which we are experiencing the excruciating labor pains of a civilization in process of birth.

Nothing is certain. For that very reason every people, every individual, has a great responsibility in our amorphous, uncertain age, a greater responsibility than ever before. It is in such uncertain, possibility-filled times that the contribution of a people and of an individual can have incalculable value.

What, then, is our duty? It is to carefully distinguish the historic moment in which we live and to consciously assign our small energies to a specific battlefield. The more we are in phase with the current which leads the way, the more we aid man in his difficult, uncertain, danger-fraught ascent toward salvation.

When I completed my full pilgrimage and remained in Bokhara a few days in order to rest, I felt the beloved sun finally striking me after Siberia's inhuman gelidity, warming my spine and my soul. I had arrived a little before noon. Torrid heat, but the streets had been watered down and the air smelled of jasmine. Mohammedans with colorful turbans were sitting beneath canopies of straw matting drinking refreshing sherbets. Chubby youngsters with open shirt fronts were singing passionate oriental amanédhes, installed on high stools in the cafés. Feeling extremely hungry and thirsty, I bought a melon and sat down in the shade cast by the celebrated Kok-Kouba mosque. I placed the melon on my knees, cut it into slices, and began to eat. Its aroma, its sweetness, reached to my very bones. I was like the wilted rose of Jericho; I dove into this melon's coolness and was revived.

A little girl went by, about seven years old, her back covered by a multitude of tiny, tiny braids with a shell, turquoise, or bronze half-moon tied to each in order to ward off the evil eye. As she passed in front of me, her hips swung like those of a mature woman, and the air smelled of musk.

At noontime the green-turbaned, white-bearded muezzin climbed the minaret opposite me, placed his palms to his ears, gazed at the heavens, and began in a sweet, sonorous voice to call the faithful to prayer. While he was calling, a stork sailed through the burning air, came to the minaret's tip, and perched there on one leg.

I sat with open ears listening; with open eyes looking. I savored the sweeter-than-sweet, aromatic fruit. I was happy. I closed my eyes, but afraid that I might fall asleep and lose all this happiness, I opened them again. Bokhara's celebrated square, the Registan, stood deserted in front of me. Each spring, once upon a time, maniacal pilgrims descended upon this city from every Mohammedan land and bewailed Hasan and Hosain, Ali's two unjustly murdered sons. Caravans arrived laden with spices, apples, dates, and sacred prostitutes; young boys came mounted on white horses, with white doves in their fists, their shaven heads powdered with ashes and chaff; behind them the frenzied faithful in their brilliant white jelabs, striking their heads with their yataghans until the blood ran onto their twirled mustaches, their beards and white robes. They lamented forty days and forty nights, bellowing Hasan! Hosain! Hasan! Hosain! Afterwards, still lamenting, still covered with blood, they reclined beneath the blossoming trees and copulated with the sacred prostitutes.

But now Registan Square was deserted and the marvelous,

colorful mosque lay half in ruins. They were ghosts; the cock had crowed, and they had vanished.

Toward what did men direct all this divine mania, this tumult and wailing? What was its purpose?

My soul felt overwhelmed with bitterness. I had grown weary of resurrecting the dead. In order to sleep and escape, I closed my eyes. I had a dream. Two stormy lips, woman's lips, suspended themselves in the air without a face. They moved, and I heard a voice: "Who is your God?" "Buddha," I unhesitatingly replied. But the lips moved again: "No, no. Epaphus!"

I jumped to my feet. All the hidden labor going on for the past three months in the cellar of my mind, all had been uncovered. The trap door to my vitals opened, and I saw. The whole of that time I had been agonizing and struggling like a serpent amidst thorns, toiling to change garment, to put forth a new one. I had been in pain without knowing why. Now, here was this dream: Buddha was the old garment, Epaphus the new.

Epaphus, the god of touch, who prefers flesh to shadow and like the wolf in the proverb does not wait upon the promises of others when it is a question of filling his belly. He trusts neither eye nor ear; he wants to touch, to grasp man and soil, to feel their warmth mix with his own, feel them become one with him. He even wants to turn the soul into body so that he can touch it. The most reliable and industrious of all the gods, who walks on earth, loves the earth, and wishes to remake it "in his own image and after his likeness"—that was my god.

Russia had performed her miracle noiselessly, without words. Like the serpent whose new garment has not yet developed and which is cold and creeps into the sun to warm itself, so too my soul crept into the new sun. When I awoke, I was no longer the same person, because formerly I had not known, and now I knew. I kept asking myself how a dream could change a man's life. It does not change it, I replied; it simply announces that the change has taken place.

Toward what do men direct all the frenzied efforts they feel compelled to make? What is the purpose? Formerly I would have smiled beatifically and answered, "Phantasmagoria. The world does not exist. Injustice, hunger, joy, sorrow, and effort do not exist. Everything is a specter. Blow, and all will be dispelled."

Now, however, I jumped to my feet with a feeling of relief. Dusk had begun to descend over Registan Square. I raised my head. "What is the purpose? Do not ask. No one knows, not even God, for He advances along with us, He too, searching and being exposed to danger; He too is given over to the struggle. Hunger and injustice exist in the heart, as does an abundance of darkness. These things you see are not specters; no matter how much you blow, they will not be dispelled. They are flesh and bone. Touch them; they exist. Don't you hear a cry in the air? They are crying. What are they crying? Help! To whom are they crying? You! You: every man. Rise up. Our duty is not to ask questions, but to clasp hands one and all and mount the ascent."

The world had changed when I stopped in Berlin again and then in Vienna on my way back to Greece at the end of those three months. No, not the world—my eyes. The brazen dances, barbaric modern music, mascaraed women, mascaraed men, the cuttingly ironic smile, the lust for gold and kisses—everything that had formerly seemed so strange and enticing to me, now called forth nausea and horror. I saw that they were portents of the end. An oppressive stink hung in the air, as though the world was rotting. Sodom and Gomorrah must have smelled the same.

So too must have Pompeii just before it was reduced to ashes. I felt the condemned city of pleasure rise suddenly into my thoughts one night as I roamed through Vienna's brightly illuminated streets that teemed with women and laughter. I was very young when I first saw Pompeii, and incapable then of discovering the fearful message it has for us. Nor did I seek this message. At that time it never entered my mind that Pompeii's fate could one day be our fate as well. The world for me then was still firmly, cozily glued to the shoulders of Christ. But now? . . . I decided to make a slight detour on my return trip, in order to see Pompeii again.

The sky was lightly overcast, the springtime grass had blanketed the thresholds and courtyards; the streets were the way I like them, deserted. I roamed all by myself in the empty city, whistling.

The houses were open, without doors, without owners. Taverns, temples, theaters, and baths—all deserted. Still preserved on the walls in faded colors were nude dancers, moronic-looking cupids, cocks, dogs, and shameless depictions of intercourse between humans and animals.

A voice suddenly rang in my ear: "May my god likewise enable me to walk in Paris and London, talking Russian to the comrades!" I shuddered; a terrible foreboding traversed my spine.

Pompeii's larders had been full; its women brazen, freshly bathed, and sterile; its men faithless, ironic, and tired. All the god-denying gods—Greek, African, Asian—were there in a cowardly swarm, herded into one democratic flock of wickedness. Smiling cunningly, they divided up offerings and people. The whole city lay stretched on its back at the foot of Vesuvius, guffawing unconcernedly.

I ascended a rise and looked. Now, after so many years and so much struggle, I understood. Blessings upon this sinful city for bringing us the message that the entire world is a Pompeii shortly before the eruption! What is the use of such a world with its brazen women, faithless men, with its villainy, injustice, and disease? All these sharp merchants, anthropophagic triggermen, these priests trading god in retail, these panders and eunuchs—why should they live? Why should all these children grow up to occupy the places their parents occupied in the taverns, factories, and brothels? All this matter prevents the spirit from passing. Whatever spirit this world once possessed was expended in creating a brilliant civilization—ideas, religious, arts and crafts, sciences, deeds. Now this world has vented its strength. Let the barbarians come to clear the obstructed road and open a new riverbed for the spirit.

I see multitudes of the oppressed and hungry charging the laden tables where the masters sit stupefied from heavy eating and drinking. The chimera ignites those who are making the assault; the others, the ones who are sitting, suddenly hear the noise. They turn. At first they laugh; then they grow pale, look down anxiously, and perceive, perceive that their slaves and servant girls, the sharecroppers, the workers, the barefooted, are rising. A sacred moment! The greatest feats of thought, art, and action were begotten during these times of man's headlong ascent.

The masters band together to resist, and they do resist. But the entire momentum of our times is against them. They have eaten, drunk, created a civilization, lost their vigor. The moment has come for the final form of their duty: they must vanish.

As soon as the new tables are laden, the slaves will begin to grow fat and stupefied in their own turn. Other tyrannized multitudes will rise from the soil, with Hunger and the Chimera, the soul's generals, once more leading the way. And this regular rhythm will continue forever, without cease.

This is the law; only in this way can life renew itself and advance. All living organisms (and ideas and civilizations are living organisms) feel the irresistible inner need, and beyond this the obligation, to grasp and assimilate whatever they can from their surroundings, making this their own—to rule, if they can, the world. And a new idea is the most famished and grasping of all beasts.

But at the same time another law begins to operate, the pitiless law that by however much the living organism carries out its duty to expand and rule, by so much, and more, does it approach its downfall. Hubris is perhaps the only sin which the universal harmony considers mortal and does not forgive. The culmination of an organism's power is fated to engender its destruction.

There is also this incomprehensible fact: precisely because the living organism has accomplished its duty, that is why it is annihilated. If it had not carried out this duty, it would have lived—vegetated—for a much longer time, without bothering others, without being bothered itself.

It would seem that this disastrous duty was embedded in the organism's heart to help it disappear once it has completed its mission to overtop and conquer, to disappear lest it stand in the way of another living organism which begins to lift its hand in revolt and wishes, in its turn, to rule the world. It would seem that a great explosive *élan* exists in life's every molecule, as though each such molecule had compressed into it the impetus of life in its entirety, ready to explode at every collision. Life liberates its inner yearnings in this way, and advances.

This law seems unjust to us at first and throws us into a rage. But if we bend over to look more closely, we are overcome with admiration. Thanks to this law the barbaric force loses its almighty strength. The strong man does not swell up inordinately with cheek and insolence, for while on the one hand this law of harmony prods him to expand his might to the utmost, on the other it reminds him that each moment he advances in the service of the All, he advances toward his own personal annihilation.

The Bolshevik leaders do not know this, nor should they. Destiny places a blindfold over their eyes to keep them from seeing where they are headed. If they saw, their *élan* would decrease.

I fight to embrace the entire circle of human activity to the full extent of my ability, to divine which wind is urging all these waves of mankind upward. I bend over the age in which I live, that tiny, imperceptible arc of the vast circle, and struggle to attain a clear view of today's duty. Perhaps this is the only way a man can carry out something immortal within the ephemeral moment of his life: immortal because he collaborates with an immortal rhythm.

I feel most deeply that a man given over to the struggle ascends from minerals to plants, from plants to animals, from animals to man, and then fights for liberty. The struggler assumes a new appearance in every decisive age. Today he is the leader of the rising proletariat. He shouts Justice! Happiness! Liberty! giving the comrades slogans and encouraging them, while no one possesses the terrible secret that justice, happiness, and liberty keep growing ever more remote.

It is right and useful, however, that all who struggle for an ideal should believe they will reach it and that as soon as they do reach it, happiness will reign thoughout the world. In this way the spirit acquires a stout heart and gathers up courage for the endless ascent. It is just the same when the carter places a handful of fodder before the mouth of his horse. The horse, pulling the heavily loaded cart, stretches its neck and eats a stalk, but the fodder grows ever more remote. The horse follows, struggling to reach it, and thus advances and mounts the ascent.

I am overcome with respect. In the midst of these dark masses I clearly discern the Cry of the Invisible that is ascending and prodding mankind to ascend with it. Had I lived in other times, I would have discerned this Cry within the masses of nobles, burghers, manufacturers, and merchants who were rising then, and would have allied myself with them. Men are caught up in an eternal assault higher than themselves, an assault which pushes them upward, leaves them when they are finally exhausted, and dashes to other raw material that has not lost its vigor.

We have a duty to follow and aid this eternal assault in our own epoch, to work in collaboration with it. Today it has seized upon the multitudes who slave and hunger; these multitudes today are its raw material. The masses cannot apprehend this merciless Assault. They give it tiny appellations to enable them to render it intelligible to their narrow minds and agreeable to their everyday needs.

They name it happiness, equality, peace. But the invisible Struggler, leaving these lures to hearten the masses, battles harshly, mercilessly, to pierce through minds and bodies and create a message of liberty out of all the contemporary cries of wrath and hunger.

It is extremely dangerous to lean over and see. You may be terror-stricken then, because you will discover an appalling secret: the Struggler is not interested in men; he is interested in the flame which kindles men. His course is a red line which perforates men as though they were a chaplet of skulls. I follow this red line; of all things in the world it alone interests me, even though I feel it passing through my own skull, piercing and smashing it. Of my own free will I accept necessity.

But let us stop at human boundaries; only inside them can we work and do our duty. Let us not advance beyond them to the brink, because the abyss yawns at the brink, and our blood might run cold. Standing at the brink with his calm, venomous smile is Buddha, the great prestidigitator who blows and makes the world disappear. But we do not want the world to disappear, nor do we want Christ to load it on His shoulders and transfer it to heaven. We want it to live and struggle here with us. We love it just as the potter loves and desires his clay. We have no other material to work with, no other solid field over chaos to sow and reap.

27
THE CAUCASUS

I WAS still in Italy when I received a telegram from the Ministry of Social Welfare in Athens asking if I would consent to undertake the Ministry's General Directorship, with the specific mission of going to the Caucasus, where more than a hundred thousand Greeks were in danger. I was to try and find some means by which they could remove to Greece and be saved.

It was the first time in my life I had been presented with the opportunity to engage in action, to wrestle with living, flesh-and-blood men instead of having to struggle any longer with theories, ideas, Christs, and Buddhas. I was delighted. I had grown weary of this shadowboxing, of wandering from place to place carrying questions and seeking an answer. The questions kept constantly renewing themselves; the answer kept constantly shifting. Question had heaped upon question, serpent upon serpent, asphyxiating me. The moment was ripe to test whether action, by slicing its sword through the insoluble knots of speculation, was alone capable of giving an answer.

I consented for another reason as well: I pitied my eternally crucified race, once more endangered in the mountains of Prometheus, the Caucasus. Once more the State and Violence had nailed not Prometheus now but Greece herself to the Caucasus. This was her cross and she was calling, calling not on the gods but on men, her children, to save her. Thus, identifying today's adversities with Greece's eternal suffering, elevating the contemporary tragic vicissitudes into symbols, I consented.

I left Italy, stopped at Athens, took ten choice colleagues with me (mostly Cretans), and departed for the Caucasus to see at first hand how these thousands of people might be saved. On the south, the Kurds were nailing horseshoes onto every Greek they caught; on the north, the Bolsheviks were descending with fire and the axe. Naked, hungry, ill, the Greeks of Batum, Sukhumi, Tiflis and Kars stood in the middle and awaited death, the noose growing ever tighter around their necks. Once again it was the State on the one hand, Violence on the other—the eternal allies.

What a great joy to depart for a difficult objective surrounded by ardent and honest colleagues. We left the Greek coast behind us; one morning Constantinople came palely into view on the shadowy horizon.

A gentle rain was falling; the white minarets and black cypresses pierced the fog like masts from a sunken city. Saint Sophia, the palaces, and the half-crumbled imperial walls were lost in the silent, despairing rain. Crowding all together at the ship's bow we struggled to make our gaze bore through the thick mist in order to see.

One of my companions cursed. "Damn her, the whore! Sleeping with Turks!" His eyes filled with tears.

"*Over the years, in time, she'll be ours once more,*" murmured another.

But my heart remained unmoved. Had I traversed these mythical waters on another occasion, my mind would have blazed up luxuriantly with fairy tales and folk songs, with violent desires, and I would have felt large warm tears from the icon of the Blessed Virgin upon my palms. On this day, however, the entire legendary city seemed like an extremely distant, extremely improbable reflection of desire, like a creature made of mist and fancy.

For two days we gazed at Constantinople from a distance, waiting for the sea to grow calm so that we could depart. I was glad the rain kept me from seeing her, glad the huge Turkish guards who came on board did not permit us to disembark and set foot on the holy Turkified soil. All this accorded very well with my soul's bitter, headstrong disposition, and with my pretentious idiot of a heart that did not wish to reveal its pain.

More rain. Constantinople kept continually sinking. But then the sea turned bright green, the waves gradually decreased, and finally, on the morning of the third day, we departed. We went through the Bosporus. The dense orchards grew increasingly more sporadic, the houses decreased, the coasts of Europe on our left and Asia on our right took on a more savage aspect. We entered the terrible Black Sea. A strong wind again; the salty sea odor. The waves dashed forward, arching their backs frothily and whinnying like the white steeds of Homer. Gathered together in my cabin, we talked of Greece—immortal, much-buffeted Greece of the thousand wounds—and of our responsibility not to disgrace her in the distant parts where we were going.

I am not going to report here the vicissitudes of our mission. My companions and I spent a month visiting the cities and villages where Greek souls were scattered. We passed through Georgia and entered Armenia. Those very days the Kurds had captured some Greeks again, three this time, and had shoed them like mules. They had reached the vicinity of Kars; we heard their cannons night and day.

"One of us," I said, "must remain in Kars to assemble all the Greeks—men, women, and children, plus their livestock and implements—and act as leader to bring them to Batum harbor. I have already sent in my report requesting boats to come with cargoes of foodstuffs, clothing, and medicine. They'll take the mass of people back on the return trip. Who wants to stay in Kars? Let there be no mistake—his mission will be dangerous."

The Greek notables of Kars were gathered around us and listening, hanging on our lips.

All ten of my companions jumped forward; they all wanted to stay. I chose the most striking in appearance, a dearly beloved former classmate of mine who had been wounded in past wars. He was a stalwart, all insouciance and gusto, and he enjoyed playing jokes with danger.

"You stay, Heracles," I said. "And may the God of Greece be with you!"

"You must all forgive me if I kick the bucket," he replied with a laugh. "And may God forgive you!"

We shook his hand and left him. A few weeks later he appeared at Batum covered with dust, black as coal, his clothes ripped to shreds. He was marching in the lead, and behind him in a great troop came the Greeks of Kars with their oxen, horses, and implements, and in their midst the priest with the silver-bound Gospels from the church, and the elders hugging the holy icons in their arms. They had pulled up roots and were at last headed for free Greece to throw down new ones.

We, in the meantime, had assembled all the Greeks of Georgia. One morning I heard cries, shouts of joy, rifleshots. I ran to the harbor. The first Greek ships had appeared to take the people away.

It was a difficult struggle. We were emaciated from fatigue, worry, sleepless nights. Sometimes I threw quick, furtive glances at the wild, legendary mountains, the tranquil plains, gorgeous stock of people here with their large oriental eyes, indomitable sweetness, and carefree laughter-loving souls. They drank and danced, kissed and killed one another with thrice-noble grace, like colorful insects.

I did not have time, but neither did I wish, to direct my train of thought away from the grave duty which had brought me here. I saw hungry, desperate men, women, and small children herded together around me and gazing into my eyes. They were waiting for me to bring them salvation. How could I betray them? "Don't be afraid, brothers," I kept telling them. "We're all in this together; I'll be saved or lost with you!" Sometimes I spoke to them about our tormented race which had been besieged for centuries by barbarians, hunger, poverty, earthquakes, and discord. These forces wanted to put an end to her, but she was immortal. Behold how she had lived and flourished for thousands of years! . . . Thus, having Greece in their minds, these poor souls managed to persevere.

There was only one evening when I came within a hairsbreadth of betraying them. I remember it with shame: an evening by the sea in Batum, in an intimate garden strewn with coarse white pebbles and surrounded by rattans which had sprouted sinuous crimson-colored flowers. Those days I was tormented by unbearable anxiety. There was still no sign of additional boats. Would they come or wouldn't they? Would all these souls hanging around my neck be saved? A few days earlier I had been introduced to Georgiana Barbara Nikolaevna, and this evening she invited me to this intimate garden because she saw how deeply troubled I was and felt sorry for me. She was the most beautiful woman I had ever met. No, not beautiful; something else which cannot be contained in words—eyes green and dangerously bewitching, like a snake's; voice a shade husky, all promise, denial, and sweetness. When I looked at her, my mind grew turbid; prehuman grunts rose from my loins; deep black caverns opened inside me and disgorged primeval shaggy ancestors, who bellowed as they set eyes on Barbara Nikolaevna.

I set eyes on her as well, thinking to myself, This moment will never come again; this woman will never be found again. Countless ventures, coincidences, accidents, and fates worked for millions of years for this woman and man to be born and for them to couple on a Caucasian seashore, inside this garden with its blossoming rattans. Were we going to let this divine instant escape us?

The woman turned, half closing her eyes. "Nikolai Mikhailovich, have you come to take me away?"

I was terror-stricken. The woman had dared to say what I longed to say but dared not.

"Take you away? Where to?"

"Far from here. I'm tired of my husband. I'm suffocating here, wilting. I pity my body, Nikolai Mikhailovich, I pity my body. Come, take me away."

I clung tightly to the chair on which I was sitting. A caique had cast anchor in front of us, and I was afraid I might leap up, seize her by the middle, and bring her on board so that we could flee. I battled to resist.

"And what about my duty, Barbara Nikolaevna, the thousands of souls waiting for me to save them?"

With a swift movement the woman undid the silk ribbon around her head; her bluish hair poured down over her shoulders. Puckering her lips with irritation, she exclaimed sarcastically, "Duty! There is only one duty, let me tell you! Only one: not to let happiness escape you—to seize it by the hair. Seize me by the hair, Nikolai Mikhailovich! No one is looking."

I gazed at the sea. Inside me all the devils were wrestling, not a single angel. Fate stood in front of me waiting. A long moment passed. Suddenly the woman jumped up, livid.

"Too late!" she said. "You failed to accept at once, failed to seize me by the hair. You weighed the profit and loss. Too late! Now, even if you accept, I won't! Your health, Nikolai Mikhailovich! Bravo! You're an honest little crumb, what's known as a real pillar of society. Here's to your health and happiness."

Saying this, she emptied her glass of tart Armenian wine.

Now, thousands of years later in my miserable old age, I close my eyes and the rattans sprout up again, the Black Sea pounds my temples, Barbara Nikolaevna comes and sits down opposite me, not in a chair this time, but cross-legged on the white pebbles. I look at her and ask myself, Was I wrong in not seizing the divine moment by the hair?

I sigh and answer, No, and I don't regret it.

I left the Caucasus two weeks later. The final days were extremely bitter. True enough, the ships had begun to leave with the mass of people. I saw my intervention in the realm of action bearing fruit; I could already picture these industrious Greeks throwing down roots in Macedonia and Thrace, our old lands that had been devastated under the barbarian heel. They would cover them with wheat, tobacco, and little Greeks. I should have been content. But a hidden worm was working my heart and gradually puncturing it. As yet I was unable to distinguish my new anxiety's countenance with any clarity; I simply felt its bitterness.

Just as I was about to board ship, an old man from Pontus came up to me.

"I'm told you're educated, boss. I'd like to ask you something if you don't mind. The Lydians who fought in the Trojan war, were they Greeks?"

I was flabbergasted. I had never dreamed that this of all things could be a problem to torment the man.

"Greeks?" I replied. "Not at all. They were Lydians, from Asia Minor."

The old man shook his head. "The others were right then when they told me you'd renounced our national traditions. Goodbye!"

That was the final voice I heard in the Caucasus.

Afterwards I often thought of this old man from Pontus. Gradually I began to understand that it does not matter very much what problem, whether big or small, is tormenting us; the only thing that matters is that we be tormented, that we find a ground for being tormented. In other words, that we exercise our minds in order to keep certainty from turning us into idiots, that we fight to open every closed door we find in front of us. "I cannot live without certainty," says the person who is in a hurry to settle down, to find firm ground on which to stand, to eat without seeing the innumerable hungry, gaping mouths behind the food he devours. "I do not wish to live without uncertainty, nor can I," cry others who do not eat with an easy conscience, do not sleep without nightmares, do not say, This world has no defects, may it remain the same forevermore! These others, God bless them, are the Lord's salt; they keep the soul from rotting. I laughed and mocked when I heard the old man from Pontus with his comical anxiety. But now, my brother, my companion in struggle, if I could see you again I would fall into your arms!

The ship was filled with human beings uprooted from their land; I was on my way to transplant them in Greece. People, horses, oxen, kneading troughs, cradles, mattresses, holy icons, Bibles, picks, shovels—all were fleeing the Bolsheviks and Kurds and traveling toward free Greece. It is in no way shameful to say that I was deeply moved. I felt as though I were a centaur and that this ship with the great troop on it was my body from the neck down.

There was a light swell on the Black Sea; the dark indigo surge smelled like watermelon. To our left the coast and mountains of Pontus, which once upon a time had been ours; to our right, the vast sparkling sea. The Caucasus had faded into the light, but the old men sat at the stern with turned backs, unable to tear their eyes away from the beloved horizon. The Caucasus had vanished, they were a specter which had been dispelled; yet deep in the old men's pupils they remained stationary and unsetting. It is difficult, exceedingly difficult for the soul to tear itself away from its homeland, from the mountains and seas, the beloved people, the poor little beloved house. The soul is an octopus and all these are its tentacles.

I sat at the bow on a coil of rope. Assembled around me were men and women, some from Kars, some from Sukhumi, and still other persecuted Greeks from Taigan. Their suffering had no end; each was impatient to relate it all and unburden himself. I listened, secretly admiring the endurance of the Greek race, for in the midst of their lamentations for loved ones who had perished, homes which had been burned, and the hunger and fright they had suffered, one of them would suddenly loose an indelicate joke, whereupon all the calamity would vanish, and heads would once again be lifted high. While a chubby young woman was bewailing her husband who had been killed, a colossus with a drooping coal-black mustache extended his immense paw and touched her on the shoulder.

"Stop crying. Marioritsa," he said. "Even if only two people remained in the world—you and me, let's say—the Greek land would fill up again with children!"

He swept his eyes over the deck.

"Do you know where the hope of the world lies, brothers? In the head, you'll say? No, farther down! In the heart, you'll say? No, no, farther down, brothers, farther down!"

He cast a rapid glance toward the woman.

"Eh, by God, if I wasn't ashamed in front of the ladies, I'd show you, I would, where the hope of the world lies! . . . So stop your crying, will you!"

The women blushed; the men laughed.

"Thodorís, there's no one comes near you," they exclaimed. "Bless you for making us laugh."

One man only sat off to the side and did not talk. This man did not laugh, did not relate his sufferings; he seemed reluctant to unburden himself. He had a monstrous body, bull neck, and great long paws that must have reached to his knees. His opened shirt revealed a chest covered with hair. Never had I seen a man who so closely resembled a bear.

When the others had all scattered and lain down on their tatters to go to sleep, this man remained staring at the sea, his thick neck craned forward. I went up to him, aware that a disquieting power sprang from this unmoving human bulk.

"You didn't talk," I began, in order to open a conversation.

He turned to look at me, then extended his hand. His bones creaked.

"Talk? To say what? To describe my suffering and find relief? I don't want to find relief."

Falling silent, he rose as if wishing to go away, but then he sat down again. I felt him struggling inwardly. He did not want to talk, but his heart was overflowing. Besides, night had descended and we were alone. He softened a little.

"You saw the mountains and forests in the Caucasus, didn't you? I roamed them, all alone, for years. I was called the wild boar because I kept company with no one. I never went to the café, never went to church. As I said, I roamed the mountains and forests all alone. I devoured the mountains stone by stone. I was a quarrier, lumberjack, and charcoal-maker—naked and poor, but I was young, strong as an ox, and had no need of anyone. One day, however, I felt my strength choking me as I was climbing a mountain, and to keep myself from bursting I began to hack away at the mountain, to hew beams from the biggest pines, and build a house. I built it next to a spring—doors, windows, everything. It was ready. Men and women came from the nearby village to see it. They brought wine and food. But I just sat on a stone and looked at it. A girl came and sat down by my side. She looked at it too. And while we were both looking at it, my head went dizzy. The next morning I found myself a married man."

He sighed.

"I found myself a married man. The dizziness passed. My mind returned from the high mountains.

" 'What are we going to eat, wife?' I said to her. 'I can't feed one, how am I going to feed two? And what about the children?'

" 'Don't worry,' she said. 'Let's go to church.'

" 'What do you expect me to do in church? I'm not going.'

" 'Let's go, I tell you.'

"We went. We crossed ourselves, felt encouraged.

" 'Now let't go and work our field,' said my wife.

" 'Field? What field, you idiot? Stones, you mean!'

" 'We'll smash the stones, crush them, make soil.'

"We went. We smashed the stones, made soil, planted our crop.

" 'Now let's go and prune the olive trees,' my wife said to me this time.

" 'What olive trees? Those dry sticks?'

" 'Let's go, I tell you.'

"We went. We pruned the dry sticks. We planted, pruned, filled ourselves with bread, lined our innards with olive oil. May God sanctify my grandfather's bones. 'No need to fear being poor and naked,' he used to tell me, 'provided you have a good wife.' "

Once more he fell silent. Seizing one end of the rope, he began to sleave it with his nails, like a wildcat. I could hear his teeth gnashing in the darkness.

"And after that, after that?" I asked him, troubled.

"Enough! You expect me to describe my suffering like all those others?"

"What about your wife?"

"Enough, I tell you!"

He wedged his head between his knees, and did not speak again.

"Human tears can turn all the world's water mills, but God's mill they do not turn." I was once told this in a Macedonian village by a centenarian who had squatted on the doorstep of his poor shack in order to warm himself in the sun. Love and compassion are man's daughters, not God's. What unbearable suffering this boat was carrying and bringing to Greece! But time, all blessings upon it, takes pity on us. Time is a sponge, and it erases. The new crop of spring grass quickly covers the tombstones, and life pantingly resumes the ascent.

The heavens were filled with stars. My beloved constellation Scorpio, with its twisted tail and red eye, issued in fury from the sea. Around me was the suffering of man, and above me the star-filled sky, mute and inhuman, full of menace. Surely all those luminous spots must have a hidden meaning. Surely this thousand-eyed Argus guarded some terrible secret. But which? I did not know. The one thing I felt deep down within me was that this secret had not the slightest connection with man's heart. It seemed that two separate kingdoms existed in the cosmos: the kingdom of man and the kingdom of God.

With such conversations, such meditations, we crossed the Black Sea. We saw Constantinople in the distance again, bathed in sunlight this time and filled with orchards, minarets, and ruins. My fellow voyagers crossed themselves emotionally and did obeisance to her; one man leaned over the bow and called out, "Courage, mother. Courage!" When we arrived opposite the Greek coast, the priest from Sukhumi, who was among those traveling with us, rose, slipped on his stole, and lifted his aged arms to heaven. "Lord, Lord," he cried in a loud voice, so that God would hear him, "save your people, help them cast roots in new soil, so that they may turn the stones and wood into churches and schools, and glorify your name in the language you love!"

We skirted the coasts of Thrace and Macedonia, weathered the Holy Mountain, and entered the port of Salonika. My assignment had lasted eleven months. Shiploads of people and livestock kept arriving continually from the Caucasus; new blood was entering the veins of Greece. I went around Macedonia and Thrace choosing fields and villages from those left by the Turks when they departed. The new owners took possession and began to plow, plant, and build. I believe that one of man's most legitimate pleasures is to toil and see his toil bearing fruit. Once a Russian agronomist took Istrati and myself to a stretch of desert near Astrakhan. Spreading his arms, he triumphantly embraced the boundless sands. "I have thousands of workers," he said. "They plant a type of long-rooted grass which holds the rain and soil. In a few years this entire desert will be an orchard." His eyes were beaming. "Look! Do you see the villages, orchards, and water everywhere around you?" "Where?" cried Istrati in astonishment. "Where? We don't see anything." The agronomist smiled. "You'll see it all in a few years," he said, and he drove his walking stick into the sand, as though taking an oath.

Now I saw that he was right. I looked around me similarly at the devastated soil my fellow voyagers were dividing among themselves, and saw it abounding in people, orchards, and water. And I heard the bells from the future churches, the children playing and laughing in the schoolyards . . . and here was an almond tree in bloom before me: I must reach out and cut a flowering branch. For, by believing passionately in something which still does not exist, we create it. The nonexistent is whatever we have not sufficiently desired, whatever we have not irrigated with our blood to such a degree that it becomes strong enough to stride across the somber threshold of nonexistence.

When everything finally ended, I suddenly felt how tired I was. I could not stand on my feet, could not eat, sleep, or read; I was exhausted. I had mobilized all my forces up to that time, as long as the great need lasted; the soul had buttressed the body and kept it from falling. But immediately the battle ended, this inner mobilization dissolved, the body remained undefended, and fell. Not before I had accomplished the mission entrusted to me, however. Now I was free. I submitted my resignation and immediately turned my face toward Crete. I wanted to tread her soil and touch her mountains again in order to gain strength.

28

THE PRODIGAL RETURNS

When a man returns to his country after many years of wandering and struggle abroad, leans against the ancestral stones, and sweeps his glance over the familiar regions so densely populated with indigenous spirits, childhood memories, and youthful longings, he breaks into a cold sweat.

The return to the ancestral soil perturbs our hearts. It is as if we were coming back from unmentionable adventures in new, forbidden regions and suddenly, there in our sojourn abroad, we sensed a weight on our hearts. What business do we have here with the pigs, eating acorns? We gaze behind us to the land we left, and sigh. Remembering the warmth, the peace, the prosperous well-being, we return like the prodigal son to the maternal breast. In me this return always caused a secret shudder, a foretaste as though of death. It seemed I was coming back to the long-desired ancestral clay after life's jousts and prodigalities; as though darkly subterranean, inescapable forces had entrusted a man with the execution of a specific charge, and now on his return a harsh voice rose from the great bowels of his earth and demanded, Did you carry out your charge? Give an account of yourself!

This earthen womb knows unerringly the worth of each of her children, and the higher the soul she has fashioned, the more difficult the commandment she imposes on it—to save itself or its race, or the world. A man's soul is ranked by which of these commandments it is assigned, the first, the second, or the third.

It is natural that each man should see this ascent, the ascent his soul is obliged to follow, inscribed most deeply upon the soil where he was born. There is a mystical contact and understanding between this soil which fashioned us, and our souls. Just as roots send the tree the secret order to blossom and bear fruit so that they themselves may receive their justification and reach the goal of their journey, so in the same way the ancestral soil imposes difficult commandments upon the souls it has begotten. Soil and soul seem to be of the same substance, undertaking the same assault; the soul is simply maximal victory.

To refuse ever to deny your youth, right up to extreme old age, to battle all life long to transubstantiate your adolescent flowering into a fruit-laden tree—that, I believe, is the road of the fulfilled man.

The soul knows full well (even though it pretends to forget many times) that it must render account to the paternal soil. I do not say "fatherland," I say "paternal soil." The paternal soil is something deeper, more modest, more reserved, and it is composed of age-old pulverized bones.

This is the terrestrial—and unique—Last Judgment, where your life is weighed within your still-living entrails. You hear the strict, righteously judging voice rise from the soil of your forebears, and you shudder. What answer can you give it? You bite your lips and think, Oh, if only I could live my life over again! But it is too late. The opportunity is given us once and for all, once in all eternity. Never again.

The childhood memories which fly out from every direction serve to increase the pain all the more. A thick crust has enwrapped our upward-gushing souls, immobilizing them into humps, wrinkles, and humiliating habits. This soul which longed in the acutely quavering blaze of youth to conquer the world, which felt too constricted in its splendid adolescent castle, now sits shivering in one corner of a body all shriveled and leathery. In vain does ancient and modern wisdom admonish it to submit with understanding and patience to the law of necessity. This wisdom tells it by way of cowardly consolation that plants, animals, and gods all surge forward, conquer, are conquered, and decline in exactly the same way. But an exacting soul will not deign to accept such consolations. How can it? It was born precisely to declare war against this law of necessity.

The return to our homeland is a decisive event. The comfortable, treacherous crust bursts, the trap door opens, and all the once-possible identities we have killed—all the better selves that we could have become and failed to become out of laziness, misfortune, and cowardice—revive like unwanted ghosts and jump into our consciousness.

This ordeal becomes even more unbearable when a person's paternal land is recalcitrant and unmanageable, when its mountains and seas—and the souls fashioned from such crags and brine—do not permit him to settle into manageable ease for even an instant, to feel sweet contentment and say, "Enough!" This Crete has something inhumanly cruel about it. I do not know if she loves her children and torments them accordingly; all I know is that she flogs them until blood flows.

One day Sheik Glailan, son of Harassa, was asked, "What must the Arabs do to keep from declining?" He replied, "All will go well as long as they gallop forward with the sword in their hands and the turban on their heads." As I inhale the Cretan air and gaze at the Cretans, I can think of no other people on earth who have followed this proud Arabian commandment more faithfully.

At life's most decisive moment—when the young man pushes aside the multitude of possibilities open to him, selects one and one only, identifies his destiny with it, and enters adulthood—at that moment three Cretan incidents saved (no, did not save; attempted to save) my soul. Perhaps they will save other souls, and therefore I will be forgiven if I cite them. They are very simple, with a thick peasant rind; but whoever can crack this rind will taste three mouthfuls of solid, leonine brains.

• • •

1) A shepherd from Anóghia, a wild, rocky village on the flanks of Psiloríti, used to hear his fellow villagers relate signs and wonders about Megalo Kastro. In this city, so it went, you could find all the goods of the world: horse beans by the ladleful, sacks of salted codfish, barrels and barrels of sardines and smoked herring; shops, moreover, chock-full of boots, and others with muskets for sale, as many as you liked, and gunpowder and penknives and daggers; still others whose ovens disgorged peelful after peelful of bread each morning, white bread in long thin loaves. And in addition, so it went, at night there were women who did not murder you, as Cretan girls did, if you touched them, and their flesh was as white and tasty as the long thin loaves.

The shepherd's mouth watered as he listened to all these miracles, and Megalo Kastro beamed in his imagination as a Cretan paradise, full of codfish, muskets, and women. He listened and listened, and one noontime, unable to stand it any longer, he belted his wide cummerbund tightly around him, slung his best provision sack, the embroidered one, over his shoulder, took hold of his shepherd's staff, and plummeted down Psiloríti. In a few hours he was face to face with Kastro. It was still daylight, and the fortress gate stood open. The shepherd halted on the threshold. One stride and he would be in paradise. But suddenly his soul leaped to its feet. It seemed to feel itself straddled by desire; it was no longer doing what it wished, no longer free. Ashamed, the Cretan knit his brows. He would stand on his self-respect.

"If I want, I go in; if I don't, I don't," he said. "I don't!"

Turning his back on Megalo Kastro, he headed again for the mountain.

2) A handsome young stalwart had died in another Cretan village, in the White Mountains. His four best friends rose and said, "Shall we go and keep the deathwatch by him, to let the women rest from their lamenting?"

"Yes," they all replied in strangulated voices.

He had been the village's best pallikári, twenty years old, and his death was a dagger thrust in their hearts.

"Someone brought me some raki today," one of the friends remarked. "It's mulberry raki, and that can bring even the dead back to life! What do you say, boys, shall I fill a bottle and take it along?"

"My ma did her baking today. Shall I take a couple of barley rolls?"

"I have some pork sausages left. Shall I bring along a good string of them?"

"Me, I'll provide the glasses," said the fourth. "And a couple of refreshing cucumbers."

Each took his provisions and thrust them beneath his short shepherd's cloak of frieze. Come nightfall, all four entered the dead man's house.

Adorned with basil and marjoram, the deceased was laid out in his casket, which stood on trestles in the middle of the house. His feet faced the door; around him the women were wailing the dirge.

"Go and get some sleep, ladies," said the friends, bidding them good evening. "We'll keep vigil by him."

The women retired to an inner room, bolting the doors. The friends went to the stools, placed the raki and mezédhes at their feet, and gazed tearfully at the deceased. They did not speak. A half-hour went by; an hour. Finally one of them lifted his eyes from the corpse.

"What say, boys, shall we have a drink?"

"Why sure!" they all replied. "We're not stiffs, are we? Let's drink!"

They bent down and picked up the food. One of them lighted some paper and broiled the sausages. A delicious odor invaded the death chamber. They filled the glasses and, enlacing them in their fists to keep them from making noise, "clinked" them vigorously.

"God forgive him. . . . Here's to our turn!"

"To our turn! God forgive him!"

They tossed off one raki, two, three, ate the mezédhes, reached the bottom of the bottle, began to feel jolly.

They gazed at the corpse again. Suddenly one of them leaped to his feet.

"What say, boys"—he indicated the corpse with a sidewise glance—"wanna vault him?"

"Let's!"

Turning up their wide, loose-fitting foufoúles, they stuffed the ends into their cummerbunds so they would not be hindered in running. Then they transferred the casket to the threshold and opened the door leading to the courtyard.

Pftt! Pftt! They spat into their palms, took a running start, and began to vault the corpse.

3) And this final incident:

Easter Sunday, shortly before daybreak. In the mountains of Crete, Father Kaphátos races from village to village resurrecting Christ with mercurial speed because there are many villages having only this one priest, and he must perform the resurrection in all of them before daybreak. Sleeves rolled up, weighted with his vestments and the heavy silver-bound Bible, he clambers over the rocky furze-covered mountains, runs through the holy night gasping for breath, reaches one village, shouts the *Christos anesti*—Christ is risen—and then dashes to the next village, his tongue hanging out of his mouth.

In the final village, a little hamlet wedged between two crags, the people are assembled in the diminutive church. They have lighted the cressets and adorned the icons and portal with laurels and myrtles they carried from the ravine. Their candles remain unlit in their hands; they are waiting for the Great Word to come so that they can light them.

Just then they hear a crunching of pebbles in the silence, as though a horse were hastily climbing the mountainside and the stones cascading down.

"He's coming! He's coming!"

They all fly outside. The east is already tinted rose; the skies are laughing. Heavy breaths are heard, the sheep dogs bark with joy, and then all at once from behind a frizzled oak—shirt unbuttoned, drenched with sweat, flushed from running, engrossed in the many Christs he has resurrected—out springs old, black, dwarfish Father Kaphátos, his unbraided hair flowing.

The sun is at that very instant emerging from behind the mountain's crest. Taking a leap, the priest lands in front of the villagers and spreads his arms:

"*Christos anéstakas*, lads!" he shouts.

The familiar, trite word *anesti* had suddenly seemed small, cheap, wretched to him; it was incapable of containing the Great News. The word had broadened and proliferated on the priest's lips. Linguistic laws had given way and cracked in the wake of the soul's great impetus, new laws were created, and lo! in creating the new word, this morning, the old Cretan felt for the first time that he was truly resurrecting Christ—all of him, in every inch of his great stature.

• • •

Love of liberty, the refusal to accept your soul's enslavement, not even in exchange for paradise; stalwart games over and above love and pain, over and above death; smashing even the most sacrosanct of the old molds when they are unable to contain you any longer—these are the three great cries of Crete.

In these three incidents, what fills the soul with pure unadulterated joy is the fact that philosophers or moralists are not speaking here, men who fabricate and promulgate difficult, elevated theories in their spare time, away from all danger. Rather, we have simple souls, Cretan peasants who follow the impulses of their bowels and, without growing short of breath, ascend the highest peaks man is capable of attaining: liberty, scorn of death, creation of new laws. Unveiled to our eyes here is man's thrice-noble origin, for we see how the two-legged beast, in following other than intellectual roads, succeeded in becoming human. Our journey to the fatal intellectual Golgotha thus becomes more loaded with responsibility because now, looking at the Cretans, we know that if we fail to become human, the fault is ours, ours alone. For this lofty species—man—exists, he made his appearance on earth, and there is no longer any justification whatever for our deterioration and cowardice.

In Crete, a person who will not deign to deceive either himself or others encounters face to face, to a degree found nowhere else, the single-breasted goddess, the Amazon, who shows favor to no one, who sits on the knees of no one, neither gods nor men: the goddess Responsibility.

For many days I roamed the old beloved lairs where I had spent my youth. Promenades by the edge of the sea. In the evenings the same cool breeze blew that used to blow through my hair when it was black; the same perfume of jasmine, basil, and marjoram arose when I went through the narrow lanes at twilight and the doors stood open and the housegirls began to water the flowerpots in the courtyards.

Breeze, perfume, and sea possessed immortal youth; only the houses had aged, and also my former friends. Many of them I did not recognize; many did not recognize me. They stared at me for a moment—I reminded them of someone, but of whom? Weary of trying to remember, they passed on. Only one raised his arms in astonishment as he saw me and halted.

"Is that you, my old friend?" he cried. "Look at you—what happened!"

It was my former bosom friend, the third of the group which had founded the Friendly Society. He appeared well fed, and had an empty pipe in his mouth so that he could inhale the aroma, hoax himself, and break the habit of smoking. He looked me over, examined me, then clasped me indulgently in his arms.

"How skinny and black you've become! Your cheeks are sunken, your forehead covered with crests and troughs; your eyebrows have luxuriated like thorns and your eyes spit fire. What happened to you? How long will you keep on burning, how long will you roam the world?"

"As long as I'm still alive—when I can't change any more, and I stand dead and beatified, with an unlighted pipe in my mouth, making fun of the living."

"I'm old, am I? I'm dead?" said my friend, breaking into a hissing, mocking laugh.

I said nothing. The thought of my old friend suddenly filled me with sorrow and indignation. How I had loved him! In those days of youth's divine, comic haughtiness when we roamed Kastro's streets until dawn, with what conviction and vehemence we demolished and rebuilt the world! The walls of our small city constricted us, the ideas we learned from our teachers constricted us, we found it impossible to subside comfortably into man's customary joys and aspirations. "Let's smash the frontiers," we said constantly. Which frontiers we did not know. We simply kept spreading our arms, as though we were suffocating.

Now my friend's arms were at his side and he found no trouble in breathing. If he still had an unlawful desire left, he was fighting to drown it by smoking a tobaccoless pipe.

"Why did you go to Russia, to do what?" my father asked me on the night of my arrival.

He eyed me furiously, restraining his anger only by force. For years he had been expecting me to open an office and begin touring the villages to act as sponsor in baptisms and weddings. My friends would multiply, and then I would declare my candidacy and be elected to the Boule. But now, instead, he saw me roaming the world. Rumor had it, furthermore, that I wrote books. The last time I'd seen him he had asked me, "What kind of books—fairy tales, love letters, amanédhes? For shame! Eunuchs and monks are the only ones who write. Settle down at long last in your own territory; you're a man, work at a man's job."

Now he regarded me out of the corner of his eye and said, "Maybe you've turned Bolshevik on me—is that it? No God, no country, no honor. Forward, dogs, and no holds barred!"

I told myself that this was a good time to explain what was happening in Russia, what kind of a new world was being built there. So I began to relate in simple words how neither rich men nor poor existed in Russia any longer. Everyone worked and everyone ate; there were no masters and serfs now, everyone was a master. A new humanity existed there, a superior morality, a more honorable honor, a new family. Russia had taken the lead and was showing the way; the whole world was going to follow her, so that justice and happiness might finally reign on earth.

I had worked up steam and begun to preach. My father listened in silence. He kept rolling a cigarette, unrolling it, rolling it again, without deciding to light it. I thought to myself, He understands, thank God. Suddenly he raised his arm with irritation and I fell silent.

"All you say is well and good," he declared, shaking his head. "But what if it really happens?"

In other words: Go ahead, talk, talk—if you think it's worth the trouble. They're just words—twaddle—they can't do any harm. But take care, wretch, you don't go turning them into action!

Would that I really could have turned those words into action! But I was afraid I could not. In me the fierce strength of my race had evaporated, my great-grandfather's pirate ship had sunk, action had degenerated into words, blood into ink; instead of holding a lance and waging war, I held a small penholder and wrote. Contact with people annoyed me, diminished my strength and love. Only when I was by myself and contemplating man's destiny did my heart overflow with compassion and hope.

Upon returning from the world-engendering Soviet laboratory, however, I gathered up courage. Now I said to myself, Man can conquer his incompetence and imperfections, can't he? Of course he can! Shame on me then to sit passively and accept what nature has given me. I shall rebel!

And just precisely at the instant I needed him, a rich uncle came along and gave me a sum to have me stop wandering shiftlessly around the world, as he put it, and instead apply myself zealously to my work, open a law office, be elected to the Boule, perhaps one day even be asked to head a ministry, and thus glorify my ancestral name. After all, I was the first of our lineage to be educated, the first to open a book and read. Therefore, I had a duty to carry out.

I turned this over and over in my mind. No, I still could not shut myself up in an office—I was suffocating. I would find some other way to enter the practical life. But which? I had no idea. I recruited workers in my imagination. Together, we would harness ourselves to a job, eat the same food, wear the same clothes. There would be no boss and workers; the workers would not be workers but co-workers, with exactly the same rights as myself.

Having just returned from Russia, I too wished to make this microscopic attempt to emerge from my ivory tower and work with human beings.

Just then—as if fate was in a mood to play games—I made the acquaintance of an elderly mineworker named Alexis Zorba.

29

ZORBA

MY LIFE'S GREATEST BENEFACTORS have been journeys and dreams. Very few people, living or dead, have aided my struggle. If, however, I wished to designate which people left their traces embedded most deeply in my soul, I would perhaps designate Homer, Buddha, Nietzsche, Bergson, and Zorba. The first, for me, was the peaceful, brilliantly luminous eye, like the sun's disk, which illuminated the entire universe with its redemptive splendor; Buddha, the bottomless jet-dark eye in which the world drowned and was delivered. Bergson relieved me of various unsolved philosophical problems which tormented me in my early youth; Nietzsche enriched me with new anguishes and instructed me how to transform misfortune, bitterness, and uncertainty into pride; Zorba taught me to love life and have no fear of death.

If it had been a question in my lifetime of choosing a spiritual guide, a *guru* as the Hindus say, a *father* as say the monks at Mount Athos, surely I would have chosen Zorba. For he had just what a quill-driver needs for deliverance: the primordial glance which seizes its nourishment arrow-like from on high; the creative artlessness, renewed each morning, which enabled him to see all things constantly as though for the first time, and to bequeath virginity to the eternal quotidian elements of air, ocean, fire, woman, and bread; the sureness of hand, freshness of heart, the gallant daring to tease his own soul, as though inside him he had a force superior to the soul; finally, the savage bubbling laugh from a deep, deep wellspring deeper than the bowels of man, a laugh which at critical moments spurted redemptively from Zorba's elderly breast, spurted and was able to demolish (did demolish) all the barriers—morality, religion, homeland—which that wretched poltroon, man, has erected around him in order to hobble with full security through his miserable smidgen of life.

When I think what nourishment books and teachers fed me for so many years in an attempt to satisfy a famished soul, and of the solid, leonine brain fed me by Zorba for just a few months, I find it difficult to endure my bitterness and indignation. How can I avoid heartfelt excitement when I recall the words he spoke to me, the dances he danced for me, the santir he played for me on that Cretan shore where we spent six months digging with a mass of laborers, supposedly to find lignite? We both knew full well that this practical aim was dust to mislead the eyes of the world. We waited anxiously for the sun to set and the laborers to stop work, so that the two of us could lay our dinner out on the beach, eat our delicious peasant meal, drink our tart Cretan wine, and begin to talk.

I rarely opened my mouth. What could an "intellectual" say to an ogre? I listened to him tell me about his village on the flanks of Mount Olympus, about snow, wolves, komitadjis, Saint Sophia, lignite, women, God, patriotism, death—and when words became too constricting for him and he felt suffocated, he leaped to his feet and began to dance on the shore's coarse pebbles. Spare, vigorous, with a tall, erect body and small circular eyes like a bird's, he danced with inclined head, and shrieked and stamped his big feet on the shore line, sprinkling my face with sea water.

If I had listened to his voice—not his voice, his cry—my life would have acquired value. I would have experienced with blood, flesh, and bone what I now ponder like a hashish-smoker and effectuate with paper and ink. But I did not dare. I watched Zorba dance and whinny in the middle of the night, heard him call me to leap up in my own turn from the agreeable haven of prudence and custom in order to depart with him on great voyages from which there was no return, and there I sat, motionless and shivering.

I have been ashamed many times in my life because I caught my soul not daring to do what supreme folly—the essence of life—called me to do. But I never felt so ashamed of my soul as I did in front of Zorba.

The lignite enterprise went to the devil. Laughing, playing, conversing, Zorba and I did all we could to reach the catastrophe. We did not dig to find lignite; that was a pretext meant for the naïve and prudent—"to keep them from barraging us with lemon rinds," Zorba always said, bursting into laughter. "As for us, boss" (he used to call me boss and laugh), "we have other aims, great ones."

"What are they, Zorba?" I asked him.

"It seems we're digging to see what devils we have inside us."

In no time we devoured what my poor dear of an uncle had given me to open (supposedly) an office. Dismissing the workmen, we roasted a lamb, filled a little barrel with wine, spread our meal at the water's edge, the site of our quarry, and began to eat and drink. Zorba took up his santir. Stretching his elderly throat, he commenced an amané. We ate and drank. I can never remember being in such good spirits. "God forgive the dear departed," we shouted. "God forgive the late enterprise—and long life to ourselves! To the devil with lignite!"

We parted at dawn. I headed for paper and ink again, incurably wounded by the bloody dart which, not knowing what else to call it, we term *spirit*; he went north and landed in Serbia, near Skopje, at a mountain where it seems he unearthed a rich vein of magnesite, wrapped various nabobs around his little finger, purchased tools, recruited workers, and began to open galleries in the earth again. He dynamited boulders, constructed roads, brought water, built a house and, succulent old man that he was, married a pretty, fun-loving widow named Lyuba, and had a child by her.

Whereupon one day I received a telegram: "Found most beautiful green stone. Come immediately. Zorba." It was the period when the first distant rumblings of the Second World War could be heard, the tempest which had already begun to drive down upon the earth. Millions of people trembled as they saw the oncoming hunger, slaughter, and madness. All the devils in men were awake and thirsting for blood.

It was in those venomous days that I received Zorba's telegram. At first I grew angry. The world was perishing; honor, man's soul, life itself, were in danger, and here of all things was a telegram asking me to set out and travel a thousand miles to see a beautiful green stone! Beauty be damned! I said. It is heartless, and cares nothing for man's pain.

But I suddenly felt afraid. My anger had already evaporated; now I had the horrible feeling that this inhuman cry of Zorba's corresponded to another inhuman cry inside my own being. A savage vulture within me was beating its wings in order to leave. But I did not leave; once more I did not dare. I did not depart to make the journey, did not follow the divinely brutal inner cry, did not perform a valiant, preposterous act. Following the cold human voice of reason, I took up my pen and wrote to Zorba, explaining to him . . .

He answered me: "Forgive me for saying so, boss, but you're just a pen-pusher. Here you had the chance of a lifetime to see a beautiful green stone, and you didn't see it. By God, sometimes when I have nothing better to do, I sit down and ask myself, Is there a hell or isn't there? But yesterday when I received your letter, I said, There sure is a hell for certain pen-pushers!"

Years went by, long, terrible years in which the times gathered momentum and seemed to go mad, years when geographical frontiers danced and states expanded and contracted like accordions. Zorba and I lost each other in the storm. Now and then, only, I received a brief card from him, from Serbia: "I'm still alive. It's devilishly cold here, so I had to get married. Turn the card over to see her little mug. Quite a piece, eh? Her belly is a trifle inflated because she's already getting a little Zorbadhaki ready for me. Her name is Lyuba. The overcoat I'm wearing with the fox-fur collar is part of my wife's dowry. They're an odd breed; she also gave me a sow with seven piglets! Love and kisses, Alexis Zorba, ex-widower!"

Another time he sent me an embroidered Montenegrin cap from Serbia. It had a silver bell on its pompon. "Wear it, boss," he wrote to me, "when you write the hooey you write. I wear the same cap when I work. People laugh. 'Are you crazy, Zorba?' they ask. 'Why do you wear that bell?' But I chuckle and refuse to answer them. The two of us, boss, we know why we wear the bell."

Meanwhile, I had harnessed myself again to paper and ink. I had come to know Zorba too late. At this point there was no further salvation for me; I had degenerated into an incurable pen-pusher.

I began to write. But no matter what I wrote—poems, plays, novels—the work always acquired, without conscious effort on my part, a dramatic *élan* and form—full of mutually clashing forces, struggle, indignation, revolt, the pursuit of a lost equilibrium; full of portents and sparks from the approaching tempest. No matter how much I struggled to give a balanced form to what I wrote, it quickly assumed a vehement dramatic rhythm. In spite of my wishes, the peaceful voice I desired to emit became a cry. That is why I kept finishing one work, finding that it did not unburden me, and desperately beginning another, always with the hope of being able to reconcile the dark and luminous forces which were then in a state of war, and of divining what form their future harmony would take.

Dramatic form makes it possible for creative literature to formulate the unbridled forces of our times and of our souls by incarnating them in the work's vying heroes. As faithfully and intensely as I could, I attempted to experience the important age in which I happened to be born.

The Chinese have a strange malediction: "I curse you; may you be born in an important age." We have been born in an important age full of kaleidoscopic experiments, adventures, and clashes, not only between the virtues and the vices, as formerly, but rather—and this is the most tragic of all—between the virtues themselves. The old, recognized virtues have begun to lose their authority; they are no longer able to fulfill the religious, moral, intellectual, and social demands of the contemporary soul. Man's soul seems to have grown bigger; it cannot fit any longer within the old molds. A pitiless civil war has broken out in the vitals of our age, has broken out, whether consciously or unconsciously, in the vitals of every man abreast of his times—a civil war between the old, formerly omnipotent myth which has vented its strength, yet which fights desperately to regulate our lives a while longer, and the new myth which is battling, still awkwardly and without organization, to govern our souls. That is why every living man is racked today by the dramatic fate of his times.

And the creator most of all. There are certain sensitive lips and fingertips which feel a tingling at a tempest's approach, as though they were being pricked by thousands of needles. The creator's lips and fingertips are of this kind. When the creator speaks with such certainty of the tempest which is bearing down upon us, what speaks is not his imagination but the lips and fingertips which have already begun to receive the tempest's initial sparks. We must reconcile ourselves heroically to the fact that peace, carefree joy, and so-called happiness belong to other ages, past or future, not to our own. Our age has long since entered the constellation of anguish.

In formulating this anguish, however, I was fighting without conscious effort to surpass it and find (or create) a form of deliverance. In what I wrote, I often took my pretext from ancient times and legends, but the substance was modern and living, racked by contemporary problems and present-day agonies.

But I was tormented and enticed less by these agonies than by certain still-indefinite, vacillatory hopes whose countenances I struggled to stabilize, the great hopes which enable us to hold ourselves still erect and to gaze confidently before us, past the tempest, at the destiny of man.

I was troubled by concern not so much for present-day man in his state of decomposition as—this above all—for future man in his state of composition and gestation. I reflected that if today's creative artist formulated his deepest inner presentiments with integrity, he would aid future man to be born one hour sooner, one drop more integrally.

I kept divining the creator's responsibility with ever-increasing clarity. Reality, I said to myself, does not exist independent of man, completed and ready; it comes about with man's collaboration, and is proportionate to man's worth. If we open a riverbed by writing or acting, reality may flow into that riverbed, into a course it would not have taken had we not intervened. We do not bear the full responsibility, naturally, but we do bear a great part.

Writing may have been a game in other ages, in times of equilibrium. Today it is a grave duty. Its purpose is not to entertain the mind with fairy tales and make it forget, but to proclaim a state of mobilization to all the luminous forces still surviving in our age of transition, and to urge men to do their utmost to surpass the beast.

The heroes in ancient Greek tragedies were no more or less than Dionysus's scattered limbs, clashing among themselves. They clashed because they were fragments. Each represented only one part of the deity; they were not an intact god. Dionysus, the intact god, stood invisible in the center of the tragedy and governed the story's birth, development, and catharsis. For the initiated spectator, the god's scattered limbs, though battling against one another, had already been secretly united and reconciled within him.

They had composed the god's intact body and formed a harmony.

I always considered that in just this way the future harmony must be elevated in today's tragedy, above the enmity and battle, intact amid the fragmented, antagonistic heroes. This is an extremely difficult task, perhaps one still incapable of achievement. We find ourselves in a moment of universal destruction and creation in which even the most valiant individual attempts are in most cases condemned to miscarry. These miscarriages are fertile, however—not for us, but for those yet to come. They open a road and aid the future to enter.

As I wrote in the peace of my family home, wrote away in a transport, this terrible responsibility never left my mind. Verily, in the beginning was the Word. Before action. The Son, only Son, of God; the spermatic Word which creates both the visible and invisible world.

Gradually, exultantly, I found myself engulfed in ink. Great shadows jammed around the pit of my heart and sought to drink the warm blood which would bring them back to life—Julian the Apostate, Nicephorus Phocas, Constantine Palaeologus, Prometheus. Great tormented souls that had suffered and loved exceedingly in their lives, and had impudently contended against God and destiny. I fought to drag them up from Hades in order to glorify their pain and struggle—mankind's pain and struggle—in front of living men. In order to gain courage myself.

I know that what I write will never be artistically consummate, because I intentionally struggle to surpass the boundaries of art, and thus harmony, the essence of beauty, is distorted.

The more I wrote the more deeply I felt that in writing I was struggling, not for beauty, but for deliverance. Unlike a true writer, I could not gain pleasure from turning an ornate phrase or matching a sonorous rhyme; I was a man struggling and in pain, a man seeking deliverance. I wanted to be delivered from my own inner darkness and to turn it into light, from the terrible bellowing ancestors in me and to turn them into human beings. That was why I invoked great figures who had successfully undergone the most elevated and difficult of ordeals: I wanted to gain courage by seeing the human soul's ability to triumph over everything. This is what I knew, what I saw: the same eternal battle which had broken out before my eyes when I was a child was still breaking out uninterruptedly inside me, breaking out uninterruptedly in the world at large. It was the inexhaustible motif of my life. This is why in all my work these two wrestlers, and these alone, were always the protagonists. If I wrote, it was because my writings, alas, were the only means I had to aid the struggle. Crete and Turkey, good and evil, light and darkness, were wrestling uninterruptedly inside me, and my purpose in writing, a purpose at first unconscious and afterwards conscious, was to do my utmost to aid Crete, the good and the light, to win. My purpose in writing was not beauty, it was deliverance.

I chanced to be born in an age when this struggle was so intense and the need of help so imperative that I could quickly see the identity between my individual struggle and the great struggle of the contemporary world. We were alike in our battle to be delivered, I from my dark ancestors, it from the old iniquitous world, both from darkness.

World War II had been declared, the whole earth had gone mad. Now I plainly saw that each age has its demon. This demon governs, not we. The demon of our age is a bloodthirsty carnivore, as is always the case when a world rots and must disappear. It seems that an inhuman, superhuman Mind aids the spirit to deliver itself from putrescent man and ascend; when it sees a world stepping in the way, it dispatches the carnivorous demon of havoc to demolish this world and clear a road, always a bloody one, so that the spirit may pass.

Now, without respite, I saw and heard the world around me being demolished. Everyone saw it being demolished. The purest souls tried to resist, but the demon puffed upon them and they lost their wings.

I took to the Cretan mountains again when war was declared, knowing that only there could I find, not peace or consolation, but the pride a man needs in difficult moments to keep him from becoming worthless. Once I saw an aged campaigner sitting on the church stoop one Sunday after the service and advising young men in the stratagems of manly valor. "Look fear straight in the eye if you can," I heard him say, "and the fear will feel afraid and run away." I took my staff, therefore, slung a rucksack over my shoulders, and headed for the mountains. It was the time when the

Germans were forcing their way into Norway and fighting to subjugate it.

One midday I heard a savage voice high above me as I was traversing the foot of Psiloríti. "Hey, neighbor, wait a minute! I want to ask you something!"

Lifting my head, I perceived a man draw away from a boulder and come tumbling down. He descended with giant strides from rock to rock; the stones rolled away under his feet, a great clamor began, the entire mountain seemed to be tumbling down with him. Now I could distinctly see that he was an immense, elderly shepherd. I stopped and waited for him. What could he want with me, I asked myself, and why such eagerness?

He came close to me, halting on a rock. His uncovered chest was hairy and steaming.

"Hey, neighbor, how is Norway getting on?" he asked with panting breath.

He had heard that a country was in danger of being enslaved. He had no real idea what Norway was, where it was located or what kind of people lived there. The one thing he clearly understood was that liberty was in danger.

"Better, grandpa, better. No need to worry," I answered.

"Thank God," roared the old shepherd, making the sign of the cross.

"Want a cigarette?" I asked him.

"Bah! What do I want with a cigarette? I don't want anything. If Norway's all right, that's enough for me!"

Saying this, he swung out his crook and climbed up again to find his flock.

The Greek air is truly holy, I thought to myself; surely freedom was born here. I do not know if the ordeal of a remote and unknown land fighting for its freedom could have been experienced with as much anguish and disinterestedness by any other peasant or shepherd in the world. Norway's struggle had become this Greek shepherd's struggle, because liberty, for him, was like his own daughter.

Such was the combative assignment I gave my duty as I wrote in the peacefulness of my family home, trying to play my part in the eternal battle. But sometimes I abandoned paper and ink in order to take the olive- and vine-surrounded road which leads to Knossos. When this unforeseen Cretan miracle first rose like spring out of the soil, when I first saw the stone stairways, the columns, courtyards, and frescoes, I was overwhelmed by inexpressible gladness and sorrow for this extraordinary world which had perished, for the doom of every human exploit: to maintain itself a split second in the light and then plunge into chaos for all eternity. To the degree to which the royal palace was reconstructed, loomed again in the Cretan sunlight, and the bullfights and the women with high, exposed breasts, painted lips, and curled unruly tresses came to life again on the half-demolished walls, to this same degree a Last Judgment loomed before me; age-old unknown ancestors rose from the soil, the men mute, jolly, and cunning, the women wearing skirts embroidered with stars from the sky, stars from the sea, flowers from the earth, and dandling God's poisonous snakes in their arms.

But one day when I took the verdurous road again, reached the Last Judgment's sacred hill, and strolled for hours among the crumbling miracles, one painting shook me above all. It was as though I had seen it for the first time. Doubtlessly, this painting must have corresponded to my soul's present concerns and hopes; that was why I understood its hidden meaning on this day for the first time. Numerous fish were cruising in the water with lifted tails, frolicking happily, whereupon a flying fish in their midst suddenly spread its little fins, took a leap and bounded out of the sea in order to breathe air. Too big for its slavish piscine nature it was, too big to live all its life in the water. It suddenly longed to transcend its destiny, breathe free air, and become a bird—for a flash only, as long as it could endure. But that was enough; this flash was eternity. That is the meaning of eternity.

I experienced great agitation and fellow feeling as I gazed at this flying fish, as though it was my own soul I saw on that palace wall painting which had been made thousands of years before. "This is Crete's sacred fish," I murmured to myself, "the fish which leaps in order to transcend necessity and breathe freedom." Did not Christ, the ICHTHYS, seek the same thing: to transcend man's destiny and unite with God, in other words with absolute freedom? Does not every struggling soul seek the same thing: to smash frontiers? What good fortune, I reflected, that Crete should have been perhaps the first place on earth to see the birth of this symbol of the soul fighting and dying for freedom! The flying fish—behold the soul of struggling, indomitable man!

I observed the flying fish venture the fatal leap out of the water, observed the svelte, narrow-waisted man and woman playing happily with the bull in the stone-paved arenas, observed the lioness sleeping peacefully among the lilies, and struggled to find their hidden meaning. What was the source of such valor and joy? What prayer were the woman's triumphant arms offering, and to whom—those bare arms entwined by black snakes? This indestructible thirst for life and this heroic fearless smile in the face of danger and death awakened fatal ancestral feats of derring-do in me, long-desired encounters with death. Bull and man, death and the soul, seemed to be friends; both naked, both anointed like athletes with aromatic oil, they were playing for one hour, two hours, as long as the sunlight lasted. Shaken and disturbed, I reflected that it is here in this terrible moment of confrontation between the Cretan and the abyss that Crete's secret lies concealed. I had to find this secret.

Christ, Buddha, and Lenin had paled inside me; I had been swept away by the soil of Crete. Without looking behind me now, I lifted my eyes to gaze with longing and fright upon an invisible peak still enveloped in clouds—a God-trodden peak of Sinai where, armed with thunderbolts and stern commandments (such was my presentiment) my God had his abode.

I sensed new strength, new responsibility, swelling my veins. My soul seemed to have been enriched along with the Cretan soil; it felt kneaded from more of the age-old laughter and tears. Once again I realized how intensely and with what secret assurance soil feels its correspondence to the soul. Similarly, a flower must surely have an inner awareness of the mud which rises from its roots and is transformed into aroma and color.

I saw my soul expanding in my blood like a mysterious miniature of Crete. It had the same contour of a three-masted schooner; it lived through the same centuries, the same terrors and joys, cruising in the middle of the three continents—the three violent, spermatic winds—of saintly Asia, ardent Africa, and sober Europe. The conscious or unconscious longing I had for years awoke even more imperatively inside me now: the longing to harmonize these three disparate desires and drives, and to reach the supreme exploit—the synthesis, the sacred trihypostatic Monad.

In me, the world-wide religious symbol of the Holy Trinity was transposed to another, less symbolic plane. It became burning imperious reality, an immediate, supreme duty. "This or nothing!" was the inner vow I took in a moment of rapture. This Trinity was not given me ready-made from on high; I had to create it myself. This was my duty, this and only this! I told myself that it was not for nought that Crete was situated in the middle of three great Breaths, not for nought that my soul assumed Crete's contours and destiny. It was my duty to take what Crete had cried out over the centuries, with her people, her mountains, the frothy seas around her, with her body and soul, in her sleeping hours and waking hours, to take this and turn it into an integrated message. Was I not her son? Was I not of her soil? Was it not she, now when I confronted her most ancient splendor, who had commanded me to find the hidden meaning of her struggle, and why she had been crying out for so many centuries, and what—what Cretan message all her own—she was toiling to deliver to mankind?

I took the road leading back to my house. When did I pass the olive groves and vineyards, when did I enter Megalo Kastro and reach home? I saw nothing. The flying fish kept desperately leaping in front of my eyes. I thought to myself, would that I could fashion a soul able to leap and to smash man's boundaries if only for a split second, able to escape necessity if only for a split second, to leave joys, sorrows, ideas, and gods behind it, and to breathe unsoiled, uninhabited air!

A letter with a mourning band on the envelope was awaiting me at home. It bore a Serbian stamp; I understood. I held it in my trembling hand. Why should I open it? I had surmised the bitter news at once. "He's dead, he's dead," I murmured, and the world grew dark.

For a long time I looked through the window at the descending night. The pots in the yard must have been watered that evening; the soil was fragrant. The evening star suspended itself from the acacia's thorny branches like a drop of dew. The evening was lovely; life seemed very sweet to me. For an instant I forgot the sorrowful letter I held in my hand.

Suddenly I realized that in regarding the world's beauty I had been attempting to forget death. Feeling ashamed, I ripped the envelope open with a violent movement. At first the letters danced, but then they settled little by little into immobility, and I was able to read:

> *I am the village schoolmaster. I am writing in order to inform you of the sad news that Alexis Zorba, who ran a magnesite mine here, passed away last Sunday at six o'clock in the evening. He called for me during his death agony and said, "Come here, teacher. I have a certain friend in Greece. When I die, write him that I'm dead and that I was in my right mind to the very last, all my wits about me, and was thinking of him. And that no matter what I did, I don't regret it. Tell him I hope he stays well, and that it's high time he put some sense into his head. . . . And if any priest comes to confess me and give me communion, tell him to make himself scarce, and may he give me his curse! I did this, that, and the other thing in my life, yet I did very little. Men like me should live a thousand years. Good night!"*

I closed my eyes and felt the tears rolling slowly, warmly down my cheeks. "He's dead, dead, dead . . ." I murmured. "Zorba is gone, gone forever. The laughter is dead, the song cut off, the santir broken, the dance on the seaside pebbles has halted, the insatiable mouth that questioned with such incurable thirst is filled now with clay, never will a more tender and accomplished hand be found to caress stones, sea, bread, women. . . ."

I was carried away, not by grief, but by anger. "Unjust! Unjust!" I cried. "Such souls should not die. Will earth, water, fire, and chance ever be able to fashion a Zorba again?"

Although I had gone without news from him for many months, I had not been worried. It was as though I believed him to be immortal. I said to myself, How can a fountain like that ever run dry? How can Charon force such a cunning antagonist to bite the dust? At the last moment won't he find a laugh, a dance, a maneuver to trip up Charon and escape him?

I was unable to close my eyes that entire night. Memories had set out in haste, one straddling the next, to ascend anxious and panting into my mind, as though they wished to gather Zorba up from the ground and air in order to keep him from scattering. Even the most insignificant incidents connected with him gleamed clear, quick-moving, and precious in my memory, like colorful fish in a transparent summertime ocean. Inside me nothing of his had died. It seemed that whatever Zorba touched had become immortal.

All night long I kept thinking, What can I do, what can I do to exorcise death—his death?

The trap door to my vitals swung open and the irate memories sprang out, jostling one another in their haste to encircle my heart. Working their lips, they called me to gather Zorba up from earth, sea, air, and bring him back to life. Was this not the heart's duty? Did not God create the heart for this very purpose: to resurrect dear ones, bring them back to life?

Resurrect him!

The human heart is surely a deep, closed, blood-filled pit. When it opens, all the thirsting, inconsolable shades we have loved run to drink and be revived; they grow continually denser around us, blackening the air. Why do they run to drink the blood of our hearts? Because they realize that no other resurrection exists. On this day Zorba was running in front of all the rest with his great strides, pushing aside the other shades, because he knew that, of all those I loved in my life, I loved him most.

By morning I had made my decision. I felt suddenly calm, as though the resurrection had already begun inside me, as though my heart were a Magdalene speeding to the tomb and resurrecting.

I had remained in bed later than usual. The cheerful springtime sun entered my room and illuminated the beloved bas-relief above my bed. My father had found this relief somehow and had hung it over my head while I was still a child. I do not believe in coincidence; I believe in destiny. This bas-relief divulged the secret of my life with astonishing simplicity, perhaps the secret of Zorba's life as well. It was a copy of an ancient tombstone carving. A naked warrior, who has not abandoned his helmet, not even in death, is kneeling on his right knee and squeezing his breast with both palms, a tranquil smile flitting around his closed lips. The graceful motion of the powerful body is such that you cannot distinguish whether this is a dance or death. Or is it a dance and death together?

Even if it is death, we shall transform it into a dance, I said to myself, encouraged by the happy sun falling upon the warrior and bringing him to life. You and I, my heart, let us give him our blood so that he may be brought back to life, let us do what we can to make this extraordinary eater, drinker, workhorse, woman-chaser, and vagabond live a little while longer—this dancer and warrior, the broadest soul, surest body, freest cry I ever knew in my life.

30

WHEN THE GERM OF "THE ODYSSEY" FORMED FRUIT WITHIN ME

THE MYTH of Zorba began to crystallize inside me. At first it was a musical agitation, a new rhythm, as though the blood had begun to circulate more rapidly in my aorta. I felt feverish and giddy, a mixture of pleasure and vexation difficult to disentangle, as though some undesirable foreign body had entered my blood stream. My entire organism was roused to charge forward and expel it, but the foreign body resisted, entreated, put out roots, and gripped first one organ then another, not wishing to leave. It had become a seed, a hard grain of wheat; it seemed to feel that the ears and bread imprisoned within it were in danger, and it fought desperately to keep itself—and them—from perishing.

I went out and walked for hours in the fields, I swam in the sea, I returned to Knossos again and again. Like the horse which shakes itself and struggles to be rid of the ravenous horsefly that has alighted upon it, I too shook myself and kicked. In vain. The seed continually sprouted new roots and took possession.

At that point the second secret processing began inside me. By nourishing that seed and watering it with my blood I would make it part of my own vitals, thus subduing it by assimilating it. This was my only hope of release. The seed which entered me as a conqueror had to be united with me, so that both of us might become victors and vanquished.

Words, rhymes, and similes began immediately to run around the intruding seed, to encompass it and nourish it like an embryo.

Faint memories revived; submerged joys and sorrows, laughter, gushing conversations all ascended. Our many days together crossed in front of me like graceful white doves, full of gurgles. The memories ascended a story higher than truth, two stories higher than falsehood. Zorba metamorphosed gradually and became a legend.

At night I did not have the courage to go to bed; I felt the seed working away in my sleep. In the night's hallowed calm I listened intently as it nibbled and nibbled the leaves of my heart of hearts like a silkworm desiring to turn them into silk.

I rambled through Kastro's narrow streets at night. The ancient memories kept springing out from every corner. I met myself as a child walking all alone and not wanting to play with other children, then as an adolescent promenading with his friends on the Venetian ramparts above the sea—it was the hour of dusk and there was a gentle breeze laden with salt from the sea, jasmine from the neighborhood's tiny gardens, and perfume from the girls who were promenading too, laughing and taunting us because they longed to have us turn and look at them, whereas we were discussing God and whether or not the soul was immortal. . . . And whenever the moon was full and clear, a deep bewitching intoxication overcame me. The doors and roof tiles of the houses became intoxicated too. Stones, wood, fountains, and bell towers doffed their thick bodies, relieving themselves of the weight which crushed them during the day. Now their souls beamed naked in the moonlight.

The first rains of autumn came. Sky descended to earth; the seeds raised their heads in the furrows and gazed upward rejoicingly. Finding my family home too confining now, I fled all alone to a little deserted house belonging to one of my friends. It stood by the water's edge, outside the city: a square enclosed courtyard with high walls, containing two lemon trees, a cypress, and several pots of basil and marjoram; a ponderous street door made of three layers of planking like a fortified gate, with a massive unliftable bolt, which to be drawn required both your hands and all your strength. What deep happiness when I did draw it, barred the door, and remained alone with no one able to set foot in my solitude! "I'll hold you tightly beneath my arm when I enter heaven, and you shall enter with me," I said to the bolt, looking at it with gratitude. Some will hold the tools they worked with to earn a living, some the lances they fought with, some the pens they wrote with, some will hold their sweethearts by the hand. I shall hold this bolt.

What a pleasure to be alone, to hear the sea sighing beyond your threshold, to have the first rains burst upon the lemon trees and cypresses of your courtyard—and to feel a seed eating you in the very, very middle of your vitals!

Zorba reposed inside me like a chrysalis, swaddled in a hard, transparent shell. He did not move. But I sensed an inscrutable, terribly mysterious process continuing night and day, secretly, noiselessly, inside that mute chrysalis. Its collapsed veins were gradually filling, its desiccated flesh softening—the shell was about to split at any minute near the shoulders, and the immature, curled, still-impotent wings to appear. Stretched inside the chrysalis was a grub which had been swept away by a sudden divine madness and wished to emerge as a butterfly. And I, I heard the first rains, heard the earth crack and receive the downfall, heard the wheat germs drinking and swelling in the ground, heard them throwing out all-powerful green grapples to hook into the soil, afterwards lifting the ground and rising into the light to become wheat and bread for people to eat in order to stay alive and keep God from dying. Listening intently, I heard the spirit which stands by every tiny blade of grass to help it grow and accomplish its duty on earth. Here in my impregnable solitude I sensed that even the most insignificant of God's creatures—a grain of wheat, a worm, an ant—suddenly recalls its divine origin, is possessed by a God-inspired mania, and wishes to mount step by step in order to touch the Lord; the wheat, worm, or ant to touch Him and stand at His side along with angels and archangels, it too an angel, an archangel.

Having met Zorba when he still cast a shadow on the earth, and knowing that neither his body, nor song, nor even his dance was big enough to contain him, I wondered with great expectation what kind of wild beast would burst forth when its hour came and shatter the transparent swaddling bands which held it immobile now in my bowels. What beast, what insatiable desolation, what unslackening, unhoping flame? If a worm, a good-for-nothing worm, wanted to become a butterfly, I said to myself, what then would a Zorba want to become!

These were unforgettable days of holy meditation. The rains fell, the clouds melted, the sun appeared freshly bathed. The lemon flowers had formed fruit, and the sacred still-green lemons glittered on the trees. The stars rose at night, revolved above my head, and fell in the west. Time ran like immortal water; I felt my head sailing above time and the flood with confidence and assurance, like the Ark, laden with every kind of seed: animals, birds, men, gods. Mobilizing all my memories, retraveling all my travels, bringing back to mind all the great souls to whom I had lighted candles in my life, dispatching wave after wave of my blood to nourish the seed within me, I waited. I fed this seed with the precious honey I had collected from a lifetime of boring into the most fragrant and venomous of flowers. For the first time I tasted the true meaning of paternal love, and what a fountainhead of eternity a son is. Just as the pearl is a sickness and at the same time the oyster's supreme accomplishment, so too I felt turmoil and fever in my blood, and at the same time a secret message from profound sources that I had arrived—was about to arrive—at the most decisive moment of my life. On the basis of this seed, this son, my fate would be determined.

Autumn passed, winter began. I sauntered in the plowed fields around my hideaway, admiring how patiently the grassless earth retained its own seed and waited with confidence for the coming of spring. I too waited patiently, together with the soil. I felt I had switched sex, as though I were a woman like the earth, nourishing my seed, the Word, and waiting. I said to myself, O if only I can incarnate all my anguishes and hopes in this Word and leave such a son behind me when I open earth's door to depart!

I recalled an ascetic I had encountered one day on Mount Athos. He was holding a poplar leaf up to the light and looking at it, the tears flowing from his eyes. Surprised, I stopped and asked him, "What do you see in that leaf, holy Father, that makes you cry?"

"I see Christ crucified," he answered. Then he turned the leaf over and his face beamed with joy.

"What do you see now that makes you so happy?" I asked him this time.

"I see Christ resurrected, my child."

If only the creator could likewise see all his anguishes and hopes even in the most humble detail of this world, in an insect, a shell, a drop of water, and not only his own anguishes and hopes, but those of the entire cosmos! If only he could see man crucified and man resurrected in every heartbeat, could sense that ants, stars, ghosts, and ideas all issue from the same mother as we do, that we all suffer and all hope the day will come when our eyes will be opened and we shall see that we all are one—and be saved.

I shall never forget those mystical months of waiting. The lemon leaves rustling, a bee flying, the sea which did not grow calm but kept sighing and knocking at my door, a crow passing over the roof of the house—all hurt me and made me cry out, as though my body had been flayed by some god and could not tolerate even a breath of wind.

Until finally one day I could stand it no longer. I had known well enough for years that the only way for me to escape intense pain or joy and to retrieve my freedom was to bewitch this pain or joy with the magic charm of words. In tropical countries an extremely thin, threadlike worm pierces the human skin and eats it. Along comes the exorciser. He plays his long magic flute; the spellbound worm appears, uncurls little by little, and emerges. Such also is the flute of art.

The sunbathed halcyon days of January had arrived, the days which God in his infinite goodness had purposely wedged into the heart of winter so that the poor unfortunate sea birds could lay their eggs with assurance and deposit them on the rocks. One morning during those halcyon days I dove into the sea, swam, worked up heat, came out, and dried myself in the sun. Seldom in my life had I tasted such bodily relief, such spiritual bliss. I returned to the house, took the penholder (this is my flute) and with a gentle shudder, leaned over the paper.

I wrote, I crossed out. I could not find suitable words. Sometimes they were dull and soulless, sometimes indecently gaudy, at other times abstract and full of air, lacking a warm body. I knew what I planned to say when I set out, but the shiftless, unbridled words dragged me elsewhere. My plan burgeoned with rank luxuriance, overflowing the mold in which I had placed it and shamelessly invading more space and time. It changed, changed again; I could not stabilize its countenance. And my soul changed with it, changed again; I could not stabilize it either.

In vain I toiled to find a simple idiom without a patchwork of ornaments, the idiom which would not overload my emotion with riches and deform it. Who was the thirsty Mohammedan mystic who lowered the bucket into a well in order to pull up water and drink? He hauled up the bucket. It was filled with gold. He emptied it. He lowered the bucket again and drew it up. It was filled with silver. He emptied it. "I know you are full of treasures, Lord," he said. "But just give me some water to drink. I'm thirsty." He lowered the bucket again, brought up water, and drank. This is how the Word should be—without ornaments.

Realizing that the time still had not arrived, that the secret metamorphosis inside the seed still had not been completed, I stopped.

Once, I remembered, I had detached a chrysalis from the trunk of an olive tree and placed it in my palm. Inside the transparent coating I discerned a living thing. It was moving. The hidden process must have reached its terminus; the future, still-enslaved butterfly was waiting with silent tremors for the sacred hour when it would emerge into the sunlight. It was not in a hurry. Having confidence in the light, the warm air, in God's eternal law, it was waiting.

But I was in a hurry. I wanted to see the miracle hatch before me as soon as possible, wanted to see how the body surges out of its tomb and shroud to become a soul. Bending over, I began to blow my warm breath over the chrysalis, and behold! a slit soon incised itself on the chrysalis's back, the entire shroud gradually split from top to bottom, and the immature, bright green butterfly appeared, still tightly locked together, its wings twisted, its legs glued to its abdomen. It squirmed gently and kept coming more and more to life beneath my warm, persistent breath. One wing as pale as a budding poplar leaf disengaged itself from the body and began to palpitate, struggling to unfold along its entire length, but in vain. It stayed half opened, shriveled. Soon the other wing moved as well, toiled in its own right to stretch, was unable to, and remained half unfolded and trembling. I, with a human being's effrontery, continued to lean over and blow my warm exhalation upon the maimed wings, but they had ceased to move now and had drooped down, as stiff and lifeless as stone.

I felt sick at heart. Because of my hurry, because I had dared to transgress an eternal law, I had killed the butterfly. In my hand I held a carcass. Years and years have passed, but that butterfly's weightless carcass has weighed heavily on my conscience every since.

Man hurries, God does not. That is why man's works are uncertain and maimed, while God's are flawless and sure. My eyes welling with tears, I vowed never to transgress this eternal law again. Like a tree I would be blasted by wind, struck by sun and rain, and would wait with confidence; the long-desired hour of flowering and fruit would come.

But look, I was at that very moment breaking my vow. Though Zorba's chrysalis still had not matured, I was in a hurry to open its shroud. Ashamed of myself, I tore up everything I had scrawled on the paper and went outside to lie at the edge of the sea.

I remembered something Zorba once said: "I always act as though I were immortal." This is God's method, but we mortals should follow it too, not from megalomania and impudence, but from the soul's invincible yearning for what is above. The attempt to imitate God is our only means to surpass human boundaries, be it only by a hair, be it only for an instant (remember the flying fish). As long as we are imprisoned in our bodies, as long as we are chrysalises, the most precious orders given us by God are: Be patient, meditate, trust.

I watched the sun go down; the deserted island opposite me glowed rosily, happily, like a cheek after a kiss. I heard the small songbirds returning drowsily to go to sleep, tired after a full day's hunting and singing. Soon the stars would rise to take their places one by one, and the wheel of night would begin to turn. Midnight would come, dawn would come, the sun would assuredly appear, and the wheel of day would commence its round.

A divine rhythm. Seeds in the ground, birds, stars—all obey. Only man lifts his hand in rebellion and wants to transgress the law and convert obedience into freedom. This is why he alone of all God's creatures is able to sin. To sin—what does that mean? It means to destroy harmony.

Feeling that a trip would give me the patience to wait, I boarded a caique which called at the graceful Aegean isles of Santorin, Naxos, Paros and Mykonos. I have said this and I say it again: One of the greatest pleasures man is capable of being granted in this world is to sail the Aegean in spingtime when a gentle breeze is blowing. I have never been able to conceive how heaven could be in any way different. What other celestial or mundane joy could be more perfectly in harmony with man's body and soul? This joy reaches as far as exaltation but it does not go beyond—praise the Lord—and thus the beloved visible world does not vanish. On the contrary, the invisible becomes visible, and what we term God, eternity, and beatitude board our caique and sail along with us. Close your eyes at the horrible hour of death, and if you see Santorin, Naxos, Paros, and Mykonos, you shall enter heaven directly, without the soil's intervention. What are Abraham's bosom and the immaterial fetches of the Christian heaven compared to this Greek eternity composed of water, rocks, and a refreshing north wind?

I rejoiced that I was a man, a man and a Greek; thus I could feel the Aegean my own, my own ancestral heritage—instinctively, without the distorting interference of abstract thought—and could sail among the islands from one happiness to the next without overstepping the boundaries of my soul. These divine islands gleamed like a partridge's downy breast; they frolicked and changed colors at every instant in the shade and sunlight, sometimes dark brown, sometimes sprinkled with gold dust, densely planted with roses in the morning, immaculate lilies at noon, and warm violets at the hour when the sun decides to set.

This honeymoon-like voyage lasted two weeks. When I returned to the little house on the seashore, my mind had settled in place and my heart was beating calmly. Christ, Buddha, and Lenin, my life's three great and beloved pirates, had not vanished; they were phosphorescing in memory's crepuscule like decorative hieroglyphics with an exalted significance that has been surpassed.

Not a single intellectual concern had distracted me during the entire course of my journey; not a single dream had come in my sleep to remind me that I had creative agonies to resolve and that I could not resolve them. I saw, heard, and smelled the world with carefree simplicity, as though my soul had become body too, as though it too saw, heard, and smelled the world in a state of well-being.

Who were the two artists of ancient times who competed to see who could paint the visible world most faithfully? "Now I shall prove to you that I am the best," said the first, showing the other a curtain which he had painted. "Well, draw back the curtain," said the adversary, "and let us see the picture." "The curtain is the picture," replied the first with a laugh.

During this entire voyage of mine on the Aegean I had sensed with profundity that the curtain is truly the picture. Alas for him who rips the curtain in order to see the picture. He will see nothing but chaos.

I remained plunged in solitude's austere silence for many additional days. It was spring; I sat beneath the blossoming lemon tree in the courtyard, joyfully turning over in my mind a poem I had heard at Mount Athos: *"Sister Almond Tree, speak to me of God." And the almond tree blossomed.*

Truly, the curtain embroidered with blossoms, birds, and men—this must be God. This world is not His vestment, as I once believed; it is God himself. Form and essence are identical. I had returned from my Aegean pilgrimage holding this certainty, this priceless booty. Zorba knew this, but could not say it. He danced it. I thought to myself, If only I can transform this dance into words!

And as I thought this, my mind cleared. I realized that I had been seeking God all those years while never noticing that He was right in front of me, just like the fiancé who thinks he has lost his engagement ring, searches anxiously for it everywhere, and does not find it because he is wearing it on his finger. Solitude, silence, and the Aegean were secretly, compassionately collaborating with me. Time passed above me, it too one of my collaborators, and ripened the seed in my entrails. Together with the birds and stars I yoked myself to the eternal wheel and for the first time in my life, I believe, felt what true liberty is: to place oneself beneath God's—in other words harmony's—yoke.

Creation, like love, is a seductive pursuit filled with uncertainty and fluttering heartbeats. Every morning when I went out for this mystical pursuit, my heart throbbed with anguish, curiosity, and a strange satanic arrogance which resembled (I don't know how or why) deep, untellable humility. For without having this at all in mind, from the very first days I fearfully realized which was the invisible—perhaps nonexistent—bird I was hunting. The mountains were filled with partridge, the passes with turtledoves, the lakes with wild duck. But I, scornfully bypassing all this delicious flying flesh, was hunting the uncatchable bird which from time to time I heard flapping its wings in my heart of hearts, the bird made so far of wings only. I was struggling to give this bird a solid body so that I could catch it.

In the beginning I could not assign this bird a name, perhaps did not want to, for I knew full well that a name imprisons the soul, cramps it so that it can fit inside a word, obliges it to take whatever it has of the inexpressible, all the most precious qualities for which no substitute can be found, and abandon them outside this name's boundaries.

But I quickly understood that such anonymity makes the hunt much more difficult. I was unable to localize my prey anywhere and set a trap for it. The invisible presence hovered everywhere in the air, everywhere and nowhere. The human being cannot support absolute freedom; such freedom leads him to chaos. If it were possible for a man to be born with absolute freedom, his first duty if he wished to be of some use on earth would be to circumscribe that freedom. Man is able to bear working only in a fixed, circumscribed arena. I had to submit to this human incapacity if I wished to surpass it. Thus, with the full, bitter awareness that I was narrowing my desire, I needed to bequeath a name to the mysterious bird I had set out to hunt, a name with boundaries as movable as possible, with hedges as transparent as possible, so that I could see, even if dimly, what was happening behind and around it.

This need worked within me secretly, day and night. Fortunately, my mind was unaware; all this went on behind its back. One morning I got up and the bird's name gleamed unforeseen and terrible in the air. It was not a bird, it was a cry from innumerable mouths. All at once I recognized it. This cry was what I had been hunting—the Cry of the future. I was tormenting myself and making war for its sake, I had been born for its sake. All the rest—my joys and sorrows, my journeys, my virtues and vices—were nothing more than my progress toward this Cry. Christ, Buddha, and Lenin had been stations en route. I had to go by way of them; it was they who marked out the passings of the hidden bird, they who functioned as beaters to help me flush the Cry.

Had nothing gone to waste, then? Considered separately, each of my intellectual ramblings and sidewise tacks seemed wasted time, the product of an unjelled, disordered mind. But now I saw that considered all together they constituted a straight and unerring line which knew full well that only by sidewise tacks could it advance over this uneven earth. And my infidelities toward the great ideas—I had abandoned them after being successively fascinated and disillusioned—taken all together these infidelities constituted an unshakable faith in the essence. It seemed that luck (how shall we call it? not luck, but destiny) had eyes and compassion; it had taken me by the hand and guided me. Only now did I understand where it had guided me and what it expected me to do. It expected me to hear the Cry of the future, to exert every effort to divine what that Cry wanted, why it was calling, and where it invited us to go.

My blood coursed up to my head, babbling all with joy. Taking my pen, I inscribed at the very top of a page the happy motif of the final, definitive work I was beginning:

Greetings, man, you little two-legged plucked cock! It's really true (don't listen to what others say): if you don't crow in the morning, the sun does not come up!

A cool, playful flame had perched on my head; I felt it waving like a red feather in the breeze. It was a mysterious, chirping bird, a fiery helmet with magical power to increase the warrior's ferocity and hope. Beating with impatience, my heart was about to gather up momentum, but when it saw the gulf in front of it (the gulf? or God?), it turned coward. The wretched flesh had not the slightest appetite for adventure. Comfortably installed in that peaceful little house with the lemon trees and the sea and the ponderous bolt, it kept backing away and shrieking. But an invisible eminence higher and truer than my true body surged above my head and ruled me. I had become a ship and was preparing to cut across the main. Nailed to my prow was a mermaid with one hand resting upon her breast, the other extended commandingly, straight forward. She was not a Nike, she was the Great Cry, and she pointed my way between sky and sea.

All the words, tales, and jokes I knew—all entered the ship. I took aboard my dearest friends, the most disparate stalwarts my imagination possessed, also ample provisions, ample goatskins of wine, and a goodly number of ancient gods crudely carved in wood, to help me pass the time. The sails bellied; we put out to sea.

Where should we lay our course? I had nothing in my mind; my temples were open, and all four winds were blowing with equal strength. Between my fingers I held a hard lump of clay, the future. I kneaded it, gave it a form—man, god, devil—then destroyed it and fashioned another. The forms ran off my fingertips, solidified for a moment in the air, and flowed back into chaos. You must not say I was playing; I was not playing, I was agonizing—toiling to bequeath my soul's countenance to the clay.

Since I had no clear idea which my soul's countenance was or how it looked, the struggle was a difficult and desperate one. I was battling to find this countenance by fashioning the clay. I had no confidence in the mind, for this can discern nothing but the body, the body's firm outlines. It does not see the flame which shimmers around the body and leaps from the scalp and is battered by the wind like a banner. This, precisely this, is the soul. Therefore, I allowed only mystic forces to guide my fingers.

Concentrating for three days, silent and immobile like a fakir, I relived my life. Nothing had perished. Even the most insignificant details—a flowering pomegranate tree near Kalamata, a fragrant Santorinian melon so big I could hardly put my arms around it, a swarthy little girl selling jasmine in Naples, the joyously triumphant clamor from the wooden clogs of a widow dancing at a wedding in the courtyard of her house, the two great arcs formed by the eyebrows of a Circassian woman in Moscow—all, all rose from the trap door of memory and filled my loins with happiness. When I went to bed at night, I continued my travels in my sleep, with the sole difference that these same travels hovered in the air at night, relieved of the weight of truth and composed of a more buoyant, more precious substance.

Is there anything truer than truth? Yes, legend. This gives eternal meaning to ephemeral truth. All my wanderings were joining together in harmony now, being compressed into a single all-precious journey which knew full well whence it had set out, why, and where it was going. Each stopping point was not a meaningless whim of chance, but rather the application of destiny's plan.

All my journeys had become a red line beginning from man and ascending in order to reach God, in other words the supreme summit of hope.

On the fourth day, as I was fighting to see how far the red line marking my ascension had reached up to now, I was suddenly overcome by sacred awe. This red line had not been inscribed by my blood; someone else was ascending, someone else's blood was flowing from his wounds and tracing a red course over land and sea—someone incomparably higher than me, a gigantic ancestor, a sea-fighter and mountaineer. I was no more than his shadow, the faithful shadow following him. I did not perceive him; I simply heard his sigh or thunderous laughter from time to time. I would look around me then and see no one. But I felt his immense breath hanging over me.

My eyes full of his presence (not the eyes of clay, the others), I bowed over my paper. But now the blank page was not a mirror to reflect my face, as it had been previously. I saw another face for the first time, that of the great Fellow Voyager, and I recognized him immediately. Wearing a pointed sailor's cap, he had an eagle's piercing glance, short curly beard, tiny quick-darting eyes as seductive as a snake's, and eyebrows slightly puckered, as though he were weighing with his sight a ram he had a fancy to steal, or a wind-laden cloud which had suddenly emerged from the sea, or his own strength against the strength of the immortals, before deciding whether a display of his valor or his wiles would be to his best advantage.

Strength lies in wait on his face, silent and motionless, ready to pounce. He is an athlete who reveres death and wrestles with it carefully and skillfully, without shouts or insults, looking it straight in the eye. Both anointed with oil, both completely naked, they wrestle in the light, observing the intricate rules of battle. Though the great Fellow Voyager knows full well who his opponent is, he does not fall prey to panic. Raising his eyes, he regards death's face as it flows and takes on innumerable faces—sometimes a woman on the sandy shore holding her breast and singing, sometimes a god who raises tempests and wishes to drown him, sometimes a thin column of smoke above the roof of his house. Licking his lips, he enjoys all of death's faces and wrestles with them, hugging them greedily.

It was you—you! How could I do anything but recognize you at once, O Shipcaptain of Greece, grandfather, beloved ancestor! You with your pointed cap, your ever-shrewd insatiable mind that creates myths and relishes lies as works of art; ravisher, pighead, masterful blender of human prudence and divine folly, proudly erect on the ship of Greece and not abandoning the helm for how many thousands of years already and how many thousands to come!

I see you on every side; my mind reels. Sometimes you seem like a hundred-year-old patriarch, sometimes a stalwart with curly blue hair sprinkled with sea salt, sometimes an infant grasping the two breasts of earth and sea, and suckling. I see you on every side and struggle to compress you into a word, to immobilize your countenance and declare, "I've got you, you won't get away!" But you smash the word (how could you ever fit inside it!), slip out of my clutches, and I hear you laughing in the air above me.

What names did I not set as traps to catch you! I addressed you as God-swindler, God-battler, God-abolisher, God-deceiver, seven lives, multiple mind, subterfuge mind, fox mind, crossroad mind, mind of many summits, right-left mind, heart-deceiver, heart-battler, heart-knower, house-closer, soul abductor, soul guide, acrite, world traveler, world-harvester, bow mind, fortress-builder, fortress-abolisher, sea-fighter, ocean breast, dolphin, man of five minds, double-triple will, leader, solitary, fowler, majestic three-masted schooner of hope!

And once in the very, very beginning when I did not know you, in order to keep you from going away, I set in your path what I thought was the most masterful trap of all—Ithaca. But you burst into laughter, took a deep breath, and Ithaca was reduced to a thousand pieces. That was when I understood—thanks to you, homeland-abolisher—that Ithaca does not exist. The only thing that exists is the sea, and a barque as tiny as a man's body, with Mind as captain. This captain stands in his osseous cabin. Both male and female, he sows and gives birth; gives birth to the world's sorrows and joys, its beauties, virtues, adventures, all its bloody, beloved phantasmagoria. He stands motionless with his eyes fixed in the direction of death's cataract, which drags his little barque toward it and insatiably pays out its five famished tentacles over land and sea. "Whatever we've still time for," he cries, "whether a glass of cool water, a breeze on our temples, a woman's warm breath, an idea, whatever falls our way, let's act quickly, lads—we can't possibly lose!"

I had been struggling for a lifetime to stretch my mind until it creaked at the breaking point in order to bring forth a great idea able to give a new meaning to life, a new meaning to death, and comfort to men.

And now, look! With the aid of time, solitude, and the blossoming lemon tree, the idea had turned into a tale. What joy! The blessed hour had arrived, the grub had become a butterfly.

A rabbi of ancient times, Rabbi Nahman, had taught me years before how to know when the hour had come for me to open my mouth and speak, take up my pen and write. He was a simple, cheerful, sainted man who used to advise his disciples how they too could become simple, cheerful, and sainted. But one day they fell at his feet and complained: "Dear Rabbi, why don't you talk like Rabbi Zadig, why don't you sort out great ideas and construct great theories, so that people will listen to you in a transport, their mouths agape? Can't you do anything but speak with simple words like an old grandmother, and tell tales?"

The good rabbi smiled. It was quite some time before he replied. Finally he opened his mouth.

"One day the nettles asked the rosebush, 'Madam Rosebush, won't you teach us your secret? How do you make the rose?' And the rosebush answered, 'My secret is extremely simple, Sister Nettles. All winter long I work the soil patiently, trustfully, lovingly, and have only one thing in mind: the rose. The rains lash me, the winds strip off my leaves, the snows crush me, but I have only one thing in mind: the rose. That, Sister Nettles, is my secret!"

"We don't understand, Master," said the disciples.

The rabbi laughed. "I don't understand very well myself."

"Well then, Master?"

"I think I wanted to say something like this: When I have an idea, I work it for a long time, silently, patiently, trustfully, lovingly. And when I open my mouth (what a mystery this is, my children!), when I open my mouth, the idea comes out as a tale."

He laughed once more.

"We humans call it a tale," he said, "the rosebush calls it a rose."

I had never faced my father with a feeling of tenderness. The fear he called forth in me was so great that all the rest—love, respect, intimacy—vanished. His words were severe, his silence even more severe. He seldom spoke, and when he did open his mouth, his words were measured and well weighed; you could never find grounds to contradict him. He was always right, which seemed to make him invulnerable. I often used to think, Oh, how I wish he'd be wrong for once; perhaps then I'd steel my heart and contradict him. But he never gave such an occasion, and this is something for which one could never forgive him. An oak he was, with a hard trunk, rough leaves, bitter fruit, and no flowers. He ate up all the strength around him; in his shade every other tree withered. I withered in his shade similarly. I did not want to live beneath his breath. Frantic revolts broke out within me when I was young; I was ready to throw myself into dangerous adventures, but I thought of my father each time and my heart turned coward. This is why I was forced to write down all I wished I had done, instead of becoming a great struggler in the realm of action—from fear of my father. He it was who reduced my blood to ink.

When I returned to the little house on the seashore three days later, I felt an untellable, profane sense of relief. A weight, a shadow, had been lifted from me. The mysterious, invisible string tying me to submission and fear had been cut. Now I could say, write, and do what I wanted; I was no longer obliged to render account to anyone. The guardian was gone, the eye that saw and never forgave had set, the slave contract was ripped in two. I was free now, emancipated.

Too late, however. I had already taken a road. I did not choose it, it chose me. All the other roads before and behind me had been blocked. I had settled down into fixed habits, fixed sympathies and antipathies; now it was too late to make an abrupt about-face and change battlefronts. I had to go the whole way along the road I had taken, and reach the end. That and nothing else. Now, however, I had a great advantage. I had been unburdened; at last I could walk at ease and in the manner I myself wished: singing, laughing, halting, playing. I no longer felt either shame or fear before anyone. I had feared only one man in my life: my father. Now whom was I to fear? When I raised my eyes as a child and looked at him, he seemed a giant to me. As I grew older, everything around me shrank: men, houses, trees. He alone remained always as I had seen him in my childhood: a giant. Towering in front of me, he blocked my share of the sun. In vain did I avoid staying in my father's house, in the lion's den. Though I became shiftless, traveled, threw myself into difficult intellectual adventures, his shadow always remained between me and the light. I voyaged beneath a never-ending solar eclipse.

There is much darkness in me, much of my father. All my life I have fought desperately to transubstantiate this darkness and turn it into light, one little drop of light. It has been a harsh struggle without pity or respite. Had I tired for even an instant and allowed an interval in the hostilities, I would have perished. And if sometimes I emerged victorious, what agony that entailed, how many wounds! I was not born pure, I have fought to become so. Virtue, for me, is not the fruit of my nature, it is the fruit of my struggles. God did not give it to me, I have had to labor in order to conquer it by the sword. For me, virtue's flower is a pile of transubstantiated dung.

This war never came to an end. I have not been completely vanquished so far, nor have I completely triumphed. I struggle continually. At any moment all of me may perish; at any moment all of me may be saved. I am still crossing the Hair Bridge that swings above the abyss.

I undressed, dove into the sea, and swam. I felt the sacrament of baptism in all its deathless simplicity on that day, understood why so many religions consider water and the bath, in other words baptism, the indispensable, presupposed condition of initiation before a convert begins his new life. The water's coolness penetrates to the marrow of his bones, to the very pith; it finds the soul, and this, seeing the water, beats its wings happily like a young sea gull, washes itself, rejoices, and is refreshed. The simple everyday water is transubstantiated; it becomes the water of eternal life and renews the man. When the convert emerges from the water, the world seems changed to him. The world has not changed, it is always wonderful and horrible, iniquitous and filled with beauty. But now, after baptism, the eyes that see the world have changed.

When I emerged from the sea, the sun was setting. Opposite me, the two uninhabited islands had pinkened, as though day was breaking. The gentle ripples murmured tenderly upon the white pebbles; the whole ancient shore smiled contentedly. A fishing skiff passed with gleaming oars which left a wake of melted gold wherever they struck and wounded the water. Inside the boat the fisherman sighed heavily, and his sigh resounded in the evening silence, full of complaint and carnal passion. Young and companionless as he must have been, he found the sea's beauty so unendurable that only his Ahh! could contain it.

The tiny islands were violet now, the sea growing darker. Feeling the nocturnal sweetness upon their lids, the night birds opened their eyes; they were hungry. Two bats flew silently above me with gaping beaks, in pursuit of prey. They had once been mice (the experts did not know this, the peasants did) but they had entered a church, eaten Christ's body in the consecrated wafers, and developed wings. As I regarded their mouselike bodies in the semi-darkness, once more I was overcome with admiration for the world's secret harmony. Men and animals are governed by the same utterly simple laws. The adventures of the human soul and of Sister Bat are equivalent. The human soul was also a mouse at one time. It ate Christ's body, partook of God in communion, and developed wings.

I know of no animal more disgusting than the mouse, no bird more disgusting than the bat, no edifice of flesh, hair, and bones more disgusting than the human body. But think how all this manure is transubstantiated and deified when God is embedded in it—the seed which develops into wings.

I return to the house; this thought comforted me the entire night. At daybreak my father came to me in my sleep, his motionless face beaming and filled with gentleness. He stood before me in the middle of a green pasture, extraordinarily high and transparent, as though composed of cloud. And as I gazed at him and began joyfully to open my mouth to pronounce the kind word I had never uttered while he was alive, a gentle breeze blew (was it a breeze, or perhaps my own breath?), the cloud stirred, attenuated, lost its former human shape, and dispersed everywhere over the grass, like morning frost.

When I awoke, I found the sun in my room, filling my bed. Propping myself on my elbows to look through the window, I saw the sea laughing and raising tiny breasts so that the warm rays could caress them. This was another divinely beautiful day. Each morning the world rediscovers its virginity; it seems to have issued fresh from God's hands at that very instant. It has no memory, after all; that is why its face never develops wrinkles. It neither recalls what it did the day before nor frets about what it will do the day after. It experiences the present moment as an eternity. No other moment exists; before and behind this moment is Nothing.

Sitting in front of the window to receive the sun squarely upon my chest, I bent over the blank page. It was not a blank page, it was a mirror in which I saw my face. I knew that all I wrote, no matter what, would be a confession. This was the critical hour of the Last Judgment. Standing before the invisible Judge, your heart begins shamelessly to cry out its sins: I stole, I murdered, I lied, I coveted my neighbor's wife, fashioned a whole troop of gods, worshiped them, smashed them, fashioned others. I had the impertinence to wish to surpass the human being and do what You were unable, or did not wish, to do. I conspired with all the luminous and tenebrous forces I had at my disposal, in order to drive You from Your throne, sit there myself and establish a new order in the world—less injustice and hunger, more tender-voiced virtue, more militant love.

I felt my heart crying out inside me. It had ample complaints, it disagreed with God, and the time had come for it to prepare a report and inform Him, mincing no words now, of its indignation and pain. The years were rolling by, after all, and I with them; clay must not stop up my mouth before I spoke out. Every man has a cry, *his* cry, to sling into the air before he dies; let us waste no time, therefore, lest we be caught short. It is true that this cry may scatter ineffectually in the air, that there may be no ear either below on earth or above in heaven to hear it. No matter. You are not a sheep, you are a man, and that means a thing which is unsettled and shouts. Well then—shout!

Do not turn coward, I told myself, do not think that since you are an ephemeral animal you cannot interfere in the government of the cosmos. Alas! if you only knew your strength, you would already have overstepped human limits.

Spring came and found me still wrestling and toiling to tame those wild mares: words. Though thousands, millions, of years have passed since man's first dawn, the technique of enticing the invisible has remained forever the same, the rules of the hunt have not changed. We still use the same artifice, the same self-interested prayers; we entreat, threaten, ambush the invisible with the same coarse wiles—for the soul cannot spread free wings, overladen as it is with body, but is obliged to follow the pathways of the flesh, on foot.

Primitive men in caves struggled to paint the wild beast they longed to catch. They did this because they were hungry; they had no intention whatsoever of producing art or unremunerative beauty. The beast's outline which they depicted with paints or with incisions in the rock was a magic charm for them, a mystical trap which would draw the beast to it, whereupon the animal would enter and be caught. That was why it was so absolutely necessary for the outline to be as faithful as possible, so that the hunted beast could be deceived more easily.

In the same way, I was setting words as traps, setting them with all the cunning I possessed, so that I could capture the uncapturable Cry which kept advancing in front of me.

Suddenly the dividing wall of exploration and effort crumbled noiselessly. Just as savages upon discovering the name of the god or devil tormenting them are able to pass a bit between his jaws, mount him, and apply the spurs to make him carry them where they wish, so I too in giving a name to my hero felt his strength penetrating me just as the horse's strength penetrates the rider, and I began to plunge impetuously forward.

Everything unfolded before my eyes—empty shadows pining for me to give them my blood so that they could form bodies; the hero's travels and adventures; wars, massacres, conflagrations, love affairs, mystical encounters with great souls, and finally at the journey's very end a long and narrow coffin-like skiff and in it two aged oarsmen, two elderly stalwarts, my hero and Charon. And the waves of the Cretan main, swelling in mid-sea, flashing and guffawing in the sunlight as they rolled one after the other and ran in flocks to break murmuringly upon the pebbles of the beach, these became octameters, and my brain's sun-washed hem received them and laughed like a Cretan shore line.

As the days and weeks went by I was ever-anxious for dawn to come so that I could bend over the blank page again and see what my hero was going to do today, where he would go, how he would wrestle with the luminous and tenebrous forces blowing from the horizon's entire arc and bellying out his sail. Not even I knew what lay in store. I waited, unrolling the myth from inside me in order to learn. I wrote without a mental plan; other forces governed me, forces which had their seat, not in the head, but around the loins. These guided my hand and obliged the brain to follow and establish order.

Never had I experienced the silkworm's mute agony and relief with such a sense of identification. When all the mulberry leaves it has eaten are finally transformed inside it and turned to silk, then the creative process begins. Swaying its head from side to side, it plucks out its entrails with a convulsive shudder, withdraws the silk, tiny thread by tiny thread, and with patience and mystic wisdom knits—white, gold, all of precious substance—its coffin.

There is no sweeter agony, I believe, no more urgently imposed duty than for the entire worm to turn to silk, the entire flesh to spirit. Nor is there any undertaking more in keeping with the laws reigning in the workshop of God.

31

THE CRETAN GLANCE

THE ENTIRE TIME a person creates, he has the morning sickness of the woman nourishing a son with her vitals. I found it impossible to see anyone. The slightest noise made my entire body quake; it was as though Apollo had flayed me and my exposed nerves were being wounded by mere contact with the air.

The octameters rolled clamorously one behind the other and spread sealike over the paper. Stationary in my chair, I was experiencing the exploits and ordeals of Odysseus. He had weighed anchor for the great journey from which there is no return; his minuscule island, insignificant little wife, and simple-minded, well-meaning son were too constricting for him now. Disgusted, he picked up and left. He stopped at Sparta and abducted Helen, who felt constricted in her own right by the peaceful life. Going down to Crete and joining the barbarians, he burned the decadent palace. But he was suffocating, even this great archisland constricted him, and he shaped a course southward once more. I myself had boarded his ship; I was journeying with him, a mermaid figurehead on his prow. My mind had become a perfect sphere, a terrestrial globe on which, in red ink, I marked the ports we had called at and those which still remained—to the ends of the earth. I knew everything, absolutely everything; I saw everything and guided the way. The terrible route shone with utter clarity inside me; but what a struggle to lock that entire vision inside words without letting even a single drop spill out!

The creator wrestles with a hard, invisible substance, a substance far superior to him. Even the greatest victor emerges vanquished, because our deepest secret, the only one that deserves expression, always remains unexpressed. This secret never submits to art's material contours. We suffocate inside every word. Seeing a blossoming tree, a hero, a woman, the morning star, we cry, Ah! Nothing else is able to accommodate our joy. When, analyzing this Ah! we wish to turn it into thought and art in order to impart it to mankind and rescue it from our own dissolution, how it cheapens into brazen, mascaraed words full of air and fancy!

But alas, there is no other way for us to impart this Ah!—the only bit of immortality in us—to mankind! Words! Words! For me, alas, there was no other salvation. Under my authority I had nothing but twenty-six lead soldiers, the twenty-six letters of the alphabet. I will proclaim full mobilization, I said, raise an army, and battle against death.

I know perfectly well that death is invincible. Man's worth, however, lies not in victory but in the struggle for victory. I also know this, which is more difficult: it does not even lie in the struggle for victory. Man's worth lies in one thing only, in this: that he live and die bravely, without condescending to accept any recompense. And I also know this third requirement, which is more difficult yet: the certainty that no recompense exists must not make our blood run cold, but must fill us with joy, pride, and manly courage.

As I wrote, I saw that two words kept reappearing and refusing to go away, even though I did not want this, indeed tried to avoid it. The words were *God* and *ascent*. What is God: the supreme chimera, the supreme hope, or the supreme certainty? Or perhaps the supreme uncertainty? Although I had been struggling for years, I still could not decide how to answer this tragic question definitively. Inside me the answer kept changing in accordance with the valor, trust, or discouragement my soul felt in its meditations upon God. I was never firmly certain at which of these three Sirens—the Chimera, Hope, or Certainty—I should halt and render up my soul. All three of their songs bewitched me equally, and the more I heard of any one of these songs the less I desired to proceed and perish further on.

All my life, however, I was sure of one thing: that one road, and one road only, leads to God—the ascent. Never the descent or the level road, only the ascent. My inability to distinguish the contents of that word *God* with any clarity, that word so soiled and overused by men, made me hesitate many times, but I never hesitated regarding the road which leads toward God, in other words toward the supreme peak of man's desire.

There is this as well: I was always bewitched by three of God's creatures—the worm that becomes a butterfly, the flying fish that leaps out of the water in an effort to transcend its nature, and the silkworm that turns its entrails into silk. I always felt a mystical unity with them, for I always imagined them as symbols symbolizing the route of my soul. It is impossible to express the joy I experienced when I first saw a grub engraved on one tray of the delicate golden balances discovered in the tombs of Mycenae and a butterfly on the other—symbols doubtlessly taken from Crete. For me, the grub's yearning to become a butterfly always stood as its—and man's—most imperative and at the same time most legitimate duty. God makes us grubs, and we, by our own efforts, must become butterflies.

I experienced equal joy and excitement at seeing the flying fish on the frescoes of Knossos, seeing it soar above the sea on the wings it had developed. I sensed my identification with extremely remote ancestors. Now, thousands of years later, I was faithfully following in their footsteps: I too was transforming Cretan earth into wings.

And once in a tiny country chapel on a Greek island I saw (saw? or perhaps dreamed that I saw?) an icon of the Virgin to which the faithful had coupled a frame of thorns. They had strewn silkworm eggs over this frame, the eggs had opened, and the tiny wonder-working worms which emerged had been fed daily on mulberry leaves. The worms had accomplished their duty on the day I saw the icon, had transubstantiated the mulberry leaves and turned them into silk. The Virgin was framed with white cocoons. I thought to myself, O if only I could remain in front of her until spring to see the cocoons break open and the fuzzy white butterflies—the "souls" as the peasants call them—encompass the Mother of God with their glossy, microscopic eyes!

A faithful Christian would have said to me, "What you saw was not a dream. You did not see worms, you saw us—human beings. As soon as we accomplish our duty upon earth, we shall enter the grave and emerge therefrom as souls to flap our wings around the Mother of God for all eternity. God gave us eyes, and with these eyes we see that He sent us the silkworm to point out our way.

The sacred, prophetic symbols disconcert our hearts for a moment, but we dare not take the next step: to believe, and convert hope into certainty."

In the morning the world was resplendent and steaming. A violent squall had broken out during the night; the parched soil had received the celestial waters and been refreshed. When I went to my window, I found the earth and sea sweetly fragrant, the sky freshly washed and sparkling, brilliantly white from the sun's radiance. My breast, like a parcel of land, had been refreshed as well; like parched soil it had received the entire nighttime squall. The joy I felt was so great that I found it impossible to bend over my paper on this day and turn the world into octameters. Opening the door, I went outside.

It was August, the most openhanded and beloved of months, a robust paterfamilias who, with armfuls of succulent fruit, strolls in the melon fields and vineyards, spattered with sediment from the wine-making—a holy double-chinned, triple-bellied, vertical-tailed Satyr, great is his grace! who enjoys and eternally vintages his vineyard, Greece.

These are our native gods, the true ones, the immortals. Beneath such a sun, before such a sea, among such mountains, how could other gods—without bellies, without joy, without vine-leaves at their temples—have been born, how could they have thrived? And how could the sons and daughters of Greece have believed in a paradise different from this earthly paradise?

I had entered the vineyards. Young girls were vintaging, their faces tightly wrapped in white wimples to keep them from being burned by the sun. They raise their heads when a person passes, and you glimpse nothing but two large pitch-black eyes flickering in the sunlight and filled with visions of men.

I had allowed my body to take whatever path it wished. The fact that it was guiding me and not I it gave me great pleasure. I had confidence. The body is not blind unwrought material when bathed in Greek light; it is suffused with abundant soul which makes it phosphoresce, and if left free, it is able to arrive at its own decisions and find the correct road without the mind's intervention. Conversely, the soul is not an invisible airy phantom; it has taken on some of the body's sureness and warmth in its own right, and it savors the world with what you might call carnal pleasure, as though it had a mouth and nostrils and hands with which to caress this world. Man very often lacks the persistence to maintain all of his humanity. He mutilates himself. Sometimes he wishes to be released from his soul, sometimes from his body. To enjoy both together seems a heavy sentence. But here in Greece these two graceful, deathless elements are able to commingle like hot water with cold, the soul to take something from the body, the body from the soul. They become friends, and thus man, here on Greece's divine threshing floor, is able to live and journey unmutilated, intact.

Finding a tap along the way, I halted. A bronze cup was hanging from a delicate chain. I was thirsty. The water refreshed me right down to my heels, and my bones rattled. I stood beneath an olive tree for a moment. Crickets had glued their bellies to its trunk and begun to sing; they suddenly fell silent, frightened at the sight of this colossal cricket. Two peasants came by, their little donkeys laden with grapes. "Long life to you!" they greeted me, placing their palms over their breasts. Grape stems hung from their beards; the entire road smelled of must. Opposite me I saw cypresses and black crosses jutting above a whitewashed enclosure; it was the calm cloister where the dead reposed, my father among them. Picking an olive leaf, I placed it between my teeth and bit into it. My mouth filled with bitterness.

I left the olive's shade and set out again, quickening my pace. It was then that I saw where my body was taking me—toward the age-old forebears with the large almond-shaped eyes, thick voluptuous lips, and tiny ringlike waists, the forebears who thousands of years before had played with that mightily powerful god the bull.

Man can feel no religious awe more genuine and profound, I believe, than the awe he feels when treading the ground where his ancestors—his roots—repose. Your own feet sprout roots which descend into the earth and search, seeking to mingle with the great, immortal roots of the dead. The tart fragrance of the soil and camomile fills your vitals with tranquility, and also with a desire for free submission to the eternal laws. Or if death's sweet fruit has still not ripened inside you, you grow incensed and rise up in revolt, refusing to be deprived of light, struggle, and life's great troubles at such an early juncture. In this case you stride with all haste over this soil composed of ancestral bones and brains, before your feet put forth roots, and you fly outside again into the hallowed palaestra, into the light.

The emotion I felt in walking over the ancient grounds of Knossos was so superabundantly rich, so embroiled with life and death, that I find myself unable to analyze it clearly. Instead of sorrow and death, instead of tranquility, stern commandments rose from the decomposed mouths. I felt the dead hanging in long chaplets from my feet—not to lower me into their cool darkness, but rather to take hold of something and rise into the light with me in order to recommence the battle. Unquenchable joy and thirst, together with the living bulls bellowing in the pastures of the world above, the sea salt and the perfume of grass, had penetrated the earth's crust for thousands of years and prevented the dead from dying.

I gazed at the bullfights painted on the walls: the woman's agility and grace, the man's unerring strength, how they played with the frenzied bull, confronting him with intrepid glances. They did not kill him out of love in order to unite with him, as in oriental religions, or because they were overcome with fear and dared not look at him. Instead, they played with him, obstinately, respectfully, without hate. Perhaps even with gratitude. For this sacred battle with the bull whetted the Cretan's strength, cultivated his bodily agility and grace, the fiery yet coolheaded precision of movement, the discipline of will, the valor—so difficult to acquire—to measure his strength against the beast's fearful power without being overcome by panic. Thus the Cretans transubstantiated horror, turning it into an exalted game in which man's virtue, in direct contact with mindless omnipotence, received stimulation and conquered—conquered without annihilating the bull, because it considered him not an enemy but a fellow worker. Without him, the body would not have become so flexible and strong, the soul so valiant.

Surely a person needs great training of both body and soul if he is to have the endurance to view the beast and play such a dangerous game. But once he is trained and acquires the feel of the game, every one of his movements becomes simple, certain, and leisurely; he looks upon fear with intrepidity.

As I regarded the battle depicted on the walls, the age-old battle between man and bull (whom today we term God), I said to myself, Such was the Cretan Glance.

And suddenly the answer invaded my mind, and not only my mind but also my heart and loins. This was what I had been seeking, what I wanted. I had to fill the eyes of my own Odysseus with this Cretan Glance. Our age was a ferocious one. The Bull—the dark subterranean powers—had been let loose; the earth's crust was cracking. Courtesy, harmony, balance, happiness, life's sweetness—all these were virtues and joys which we had to be brave enough to bid adieu; they belonged to other ages, past or future. Every age has its own countenance. The countenance of our age was ferocious, and delicate souls dared not look it straight in the eye.

Odysseus, he who sailed upon the octameters I was writing, had to be made to view the abyss with such a Cretan Glance—without hope and fear but also without insolence—as he stood proudly erect at the very brink of the precipice.

My life changed from that day onward, the Day of the Cretan Glance, as I named it. My soul discovered where to stand and how to cast its gaze. The terrible problems tormenting me grew calm; they smiled, as though springtime had come and the wild perplexities, like vernal thorns, had been covered with flowers. It was a tardy, unforeseen juvenescence. Like the ancient Chinese sage, I seemed to have been born a hoary, decrepit old man with snow-white beard. As the years went by, the beard turned gray, then gradually blackened, then fell off, and in my old age a tender adolescent fuzz spread across my cheeks.

My youth had been nothing but anxieties, nightmares, and questionings; my maturity nothing but lame answers. I looked toward the stars, toward men, toward ideas—what chaos! And what agony to hunt out God, the blue bird with the red talons, in their midst! I took one road, reached its end—an abyss. Frightened, I turned back and took another road; at its end the abyss once more. Retreat again, a new journey, and suddenly the same abyss yawned before me anew. All the routes of the mind led to the abyss. My youth and maturity had revolved in the air around the two poles of panic and hope, but now in my old age I stood before the abyss tranquilly, fearlessly. I no longer fled, no longer humiliated myself—no, not I, but the Odysseus I was fashioning. I created him to face the abyss calmly, and in creating him, I strove to resemble him. I myself was being created. I entrusted all my own yearnings to this Odysseus; he was the mold I was carving out so that the man of the future might flow in. Whatever I yearned for and was unable to attain, he would attain. He was the charm that would lure the tenebrous and luminous forces that create the future. Faith moves mountains; believe in him and he would come. Who would come? The Odysseus I had created. He was the Archetype.

The creator's responsibility is a great one; he opens a road that may entice the future and force it to make up its mind.

I looked at the Cretan sea, at the waves that towered proudly, flashed for a moment in the sun, and sped to give up the ghost with a chuckle upon the pebbles of the beach. I felt my blood following their rhythm as it left my heart and spread to my fingertips and the very roots of my hair. I was becoming a sea, an endless voyage full of distant adventures, a proud despairing poem sailing with black and red sails over the abyss. And at the poem's summit was a seaman's cap, beneath the cap a rough sunburned forehead, two black eyes and a mouth frosted with salt spray, and lower down two huge, callused paws that gripped the helm.

He could not—we could not—fit any longer within the constricting homeland. Choosing the island's most unsubmissive souls, we seized what we could from our homes, boarded a ship, and departed. Where to? The wind would blow and show us our route. Southward! To Helen, who was pining away on the banks of the Eurotas, constricted just like ourselves by security, virtue, and the comfortable life. To the great archisland of Crete, which was withering because potency had departed the loins of its rulers; raising her arms in the middle of the sea, she was calling the barbarians so that she might have children by them. To Africa, to the ends of the earth, to the everlasting snows, to death!

At first the blue bird with the red talons went in the lead, but it quickly tired and we left it behind us, remaining free in the empty air, without a guide bird. From time to time great immortal souls dug their claws into our ship's rigging and warbled in an effort to entice us, but we burst into laughter, and they became frightened and left. Sometimes we heard a terrible cry spurt up from the sea's bottom: "Stop! Where are you going? Enough!" and we leaned over the gunwale and shouted back at it, "No, not enough, not enough! Keep still!" And one evening Death came and curled up on the prow. He was dressed like us, in fox pelts, with a pointed blue cap crowned by a red pompon; he had a snow-white beard, and his face, chest, arms, and thighs were furrowed with cicatrized wounds. He smiled at us tenderly. We understood. We were finally approaching the end of our voyage.

Stretching out supine on the boat's deck, we closed our eyes and saw: above the continents and seas we had traversed, above the men we had encountered, the women we had kissed, above earth, water, fire, and flesh was another voyage where the boat was made of clouds, and the continents, seas, and people of silken threads which had emanated from our entrails. And still higher, on the highest level of all, our cloud boat scattered, our silken threads dissolved. The world's apparitions vanished, and nothing remained on this highest level but a mute, blind, stationary sun, blacker than blackness. It's probably God, we said to ourselves, who knows, it is probably God. . . . We tried to raise our hands in order to greet Him, but we could not.

While I was writing this *Odyssey* on my Cretan shore line, the infernal powers were preparing the second great war. A wind of insanity blew over the human race, the earth's foundations creaked, and I, bending over my paper and listening to the clamor made by waves, people, and infernal powers, held on to my soul for dear life in order to keep panic from overcoming me. I strove to divine—and to entice with well-ordered, harmonious words—the man who lay beyond the massacres and tears, beyond today's ape man. Though he remained a specter hanging in mid-air, I felt as I leaned over and wrote, that I was transfusing my own blood into him. I was being emptied, he being filled, and his body began to solidify little by little, to move, and come.

I had entered a deep dream. Truth's lower level had vanished, the solid one whose entire area rests against the earth; and tonguing upward high in the air, like a fire blown by a strong wind, was the most elevated level of truth, the soul of man.

I worked all day, slept all night. Never in my life have I been able to work at night; I am like a solar clock. *Sine sole sileo*—without the sun I am silent. The night, with its dreams, its silence, with the dark doors it opens in me, prepares my work for the following day.

The supreme benefit for me at this point is time. When I see people going for strolls or lolling about aimlessly or squandering time in vain discussions, I feel like going to the street corner and extending my hand like a beggar in order to entreat, "Alms, good Christians, grant me a little of the time you are losing—one hour, two hours, whatever you prefer."

The day was finally declining. I crossed my arms, leaned my head back against the wall, and watched the setting sun. I felt neither joy, sorrow, nor fatigue. Just a sense of relief, as though my entrails had been emptied, as though I had shed all my blood, as though I was the hard transparent garment left by the cricket on the olive trunk when it hatches. A tiny skiff with a red sail was returning from fishing; I could discern the glittering fish on its deck. A tiny island opposite me had filled with violets. The diminutive, desolate chapel of the Crucified gleamed whitely at the mountain's summit, like an egg; the light clung to its whitewashed walls and did not wish to leave.

I heard the grating of pebbles on my right; someone was striding hastily over the shingle and approaching. I turned. A pointed cap flashed in the purple dusk and the acid smell of human sweat suffused the air. Moving to one side on the stone bench where I was seated, I made room for him to sit down near me.

"Welcome," I said. "I've been expecting you."

Bending over, he picked up some seaweed the surf had thrown up, and placed it between his lips.

"Here I am," he said. "I'm glad to see you."

The blue, fluffy night was descending from the sky, ascending from the sea. Behind us, on land, the night birds took wing amidst the olive trees; the two great, deathless cries of love and hunger sounded in the black silence. The tiny beasties hiding deep in the squat bushes were hungry too, they too wanted love, and a great dirge rose from the ground.

We remained silent; each could hear his heart beating reposefully. It seemed that all those hidden nocturnal yearnings, all those clashing voices were being harmonized in passing through our vitals.

The joy and sweetness were so great that tears suddenly began to flow from my eyes; ancient, mystical words rose from my vitals and toddled over my lips:

Death and birth are one, my lads,
One the heartache and joy.
One to land and sail away,
One the hello and goodbye!

I turned to the silent companion on my right.

"Are we moving, Captain Odysseus?" I asked. "Have we arrived? Time, as though changed into eternity, seems to have stopped; space is rolled up in my palm like an ancient parchment charted with lands and seas. Deliverance—what we call deliverance and desperately extend our arms toward heaven to reach—has become a sprig of basil behind my ear. Don't you smell its scent in the air?"

My companion inhaled deeply and smiled.

"You have been delivered from deliverance," he said. His voice was crusty, hoarsened by the sea wind. "You have been delivered from deliverance—and that is man's supreme feat. Your term in the service of hope and fear is over; you have leaned over the abyss, have seen the world's apparition turned upside down, and have not been frightened. We have leaned together over the abyss, precious companion, and have not been frightened. Do you remember?"

The terrible journey sprang into my mind, the sea thundered from one temple to the other; my memory swelled and I viewed, re-viewed, re-enjoyed how we wrenched ourselves away from son, wife, fatherland, the comfortable life, how we left virtue and truth behind us, how we passed between the Scylla and Charybdis of God without losing our ship, how we made for the open sea with bellying sails and valiantly shaped our course for the abyss.

"It was a fine trip," I said, heartfeltly touching my companion's knee. "Now we have arrived."

"Arrived?" he asked in surprise. "What does that mean?"

"I know. It means: now we are leaving."

"Yes, now we are leaving. Without a boat, without the sea, without a body."

"Free."

"No, freed from freedom. Beyond."

"Beyond? Where? My mind is incapable of containing that."

"Beyond freedom, my companion. Have courage!"

"I am afraid to follow you. My strength reaches just so far; farther I cannot go."

"No matter, Father. You did your duty: you begot a son higher than you. You stay here as a buoy; I shall go farther."

Rising, he tightened his belt and glanced out beyond him into the darkness. A star spilled forth and rolled tearlike down night's cheeks. A wind rose from the earth; the waves neighed in the silence like awakening horses. He offered me his hand.

"Are you leaving?" I cried, as though my own soul were leaving.

Bending over, he kissed my right shoulder, my left shoulder, then both my eyes. His lips covered me with brine. He smiled, and his voice issued with tenderness, playfully.

"Who was the ascetic who sought God for forty years and could not find him? Some dark object loomed in the middle, hindering him. But one morning he saw: it was an old fur which he loved dearly and did not have the heart to discard. He threw it away, and all at once he saw God in front of him. . . . You, dear companion, are my old fur. Farewell!"

I was terrified. His final words seemed to come from far, far away, from the other bank. I jumped to my feet and searched in the darkness. No one.

EPILOGUE

I KISS your hand, beloved grandfather. I kiss your right shoulder, I kiss your left shoulder. My confession is over; now you must judge. I did not recount the details of daily life. Rinds they were. You tossed them into the garbage of the abyss and I did the same. With its large and small sorrows, large and small joys, life sometimes wounded me, sometimes caressed me. These habitual everyday affairs left us, and we left them. It was not worth the trouble to turn back and haul them out of the abyss. The world will lose nothing if the people I knew remain in oblivion. Contact with my contemporaries had very little influence on my life. I did not love many men, either because I failed to understand them or because I looked upon them with contempt; perhaps, also, because I did not chance to meet many who deserved being loved. I did not hate anyone, however, even though I harmed several people without desiring to. They were sparrows and I wished to turn them into eagles. I set about to deliver them from mediocrity and routine, pushed them without taking their endurance into account, and they crashed to the ground. Only the immortal dead enticed me, the great Sirens Christ, Buddha, and Lenin. From my early years I sat at their feet and listened intently to their seductive love-filled song. I struggled all my life to save myself from each of these Sirens without denying any one of them, struggled to unite these three clashing voices and transform them into harmony.

Women I loved. I was fortunate in chancing to meet extraordinary women along my route. No man ever did me so much good or aided my struggle so greatly as these women—and one above all, the last. But over this love-smitten body I throw the veil which the sons of Noah threw over their drunken father. I like our ancestors' myth about Eros and Psyche; surely you liked it too, grandfather. It is both shameful and dangerous to light a lamp, dispel the darkness, and see two bodies locked in an embrace. You knew this, you who hid your beloved helpmate Jeronima de las Cuevas in love's divine obscurity. I do the same with my Jeronima. Intrepid fellow athlete, cool fountain in our inhuman solitude, great comfort! Poverty and nakedness—yes, the Cretans are right in saying that poverty and nakedness are nothing, provided you have a good wife. We had good wives; yours was named Jeronima, mine Helen. What good fortune this was, grandfather! How many times did we not say to ourselves as we looked at them, Blessed the day we were born!

But we did not allow women, even the dearest, to lead us astray. We did not follow their flower-strewn road, we took them with us. No, we did not take them, these dauntless companions followed our ascents of their own free will.

One thing only we pursued all our lives: a harsh, carnivorous, indestructible vision—the essence. For its sake what venom we were given to drink by both gods and men, what tears we shed, what blood, how much sweat! Our whole lives, a devil (devil? or angel?) refused to leave us in peace. He leaned over, glued himself to us and hissed in our ears, "In vain! In vain! In vain!" He thought he would make us freeze in our tracks, but we repulsed him with a toss of our heads, clenched our teeth, and answered, "Just what we want! We're not working for pay, we have no desire for a daily wage. We are warring in the empty air, beyond hope, beyond paradise!"

This essence went by many names; it kept changing masks all the while we pursued it. Sometimes we called it supreme hope, sometimes supreme despair, sometimes summit of man's soul, sometimes desert mirage, and sometimes blue bird and freedom. And sometimes, finally, it seemed to us like an integral circle with the human heart as center and immortality as circumference, a circle which we arbitrarily assigned a heavy name loaded with all the hopes and tears of the world: "God."

Every integral man has inside him, in his heart of hearts, a mystic center around which all else revolves. This mystic whirling lends unity to his thoughts and actions; it helps him find or invent the cosmic harmony. For some this center is love, for others kindness or beauty, others the thirst for knowledge or the longing for gold and power. They examine the relative value of all else and subordinate it to this central passion. Alas for the man who does not feel himself governed inside by an absolute monarch. His ungoverned, incoherent life is scattered to the four winds.

Our center, grandfather, the center which swept the visible world into its whirl and fought to elevate it to the upper level of valor and responsibility, was the battle with God. Which God? The fierce summit of man's soul, the summit which we are ceaselessly about to attain and which ceaselessly jumps to its feet and climbs still higher. "Does man battle with God?" some acquaintances asked me sarcastically one day. I answered them, "With whom else do you expect him to battle?" Truly, with whom else?

That was why the whole of our lives was an ascent, grandfather —ascent, precipice, solitude. We set out with many fellow strugglers, many ideas, a great escort. But as we ascended and as the summit shifted and became more remote, fellow strugglers, ideas, and hopes kept bidding us farewell; out of breath, they were neither willing nor able to mount higher. We remained alone, our eyes riveted upon the Moving Monad, the shifting summit. We were swayed neither by arrogance nor by the naïve certainty that one day the summit would stand still and we would reach it; nor yet, even if we should reach it, by the belief that there on high we would find happiness, salvation, and paradise. We ascended because the very act of ascending, for us, was happiness, salvation, and paradise.

I marvel at the human soul; no power in heaven and earth is so great. Without being aware of it, we carry omnipotence within us. But we crush our souls beneath a weight of flesh and lard, and die without having learned what we are and what we can accomplish. What other power on earth is able to look the world's beginning and end straight in the eye without being blinded? In the beginning was not the Word (as is preached by the souls crushed beneath lard and flesh) nor the Act, nor the Creator's hand filled with life-receiving clay. In the beginning was Fire. And in the end is neither immortality nor recompense, paradise nor the inferno. In the end is Fire. Between these two fires, dear grandfather, we traveled; and we fought, by following Fire's commandment and working with it, to turn flesh into flame, thought into flame—hope, despair, honor, dishonor, glory, into flame. You went in the lead and I followed. You taught me that our inner flame, contrary to the nature of the flesh, is able to flare up with ever-increasing intensity over the years. That was why (I saw this in you and admired you for it) you became continually fiercer as you aged, continually braver as you arrived ever closer to the abyss. Tossing the bodies of saints, rulers, and monks into the crucible of your glance, you melted them down like metals, purged away their rust, and refined out the pure gold: their soul. What soul? The flame. This you united with the conflagration that engendered us and the conflagration which shall devour us.

The prudent accused us of making the angelic wings excessively large, and of having the audacity to wish to shoot the arrow beyond human frontiers. But we were not the ones who wished to shoot the arrow beyond human frontiers; a devil inside us—let us call him Lucifer, for he brings light—kept urging us on. He it was who wished to overstep the limits in order to go we knew not where. All we knew was: higher. Like Saint George, who carried on his horse's rump the young princess whom the dragon wished to devour, this devil carried life, the life which was stifled and endangered inside every living thing, and which desired to escape in order to save itself. Monkeys must have felt the momentum of the universe inside them in this same way, urging them to stand on their hind legs, even though the pain made them howl, and to rub a pair of sticks together to produce a spark, even though the other monkeys derided them. This is how ape man was born, how man was born; this, grandfather, is how the indestructible, merciless force kicked against our breasts as well: in order to save itself from man, and continue beyond. Why do you think we writhed and suffered so much among men? "We refuse to go further," they cried. "Clip your wings, do not shoot the arrow so high. You don't fear God, don't listen to reason. Sit down!" But we did not talk, we worked. We worked on our wings, stretched our bow. We ripped open our vitals to let the devil pass.

"I like neither the angels you paint nor the saints," the Grand Inquisitor of Toledo scolded you one day. "Instead of making people pray, they make them admire. Beauty inserts itself as an obstacle between our souls and God."

You laughed, thinking tacitly, But I do not want to make people pray. Who told you I wanted to make people pray? . . . You did not speak, however.

And someone else, this time a painter and personal friend,

shook his head when he saw "Toledo in the Storm." "You trample the rules," he declared. "This is not art. You have overstepped the boundaries of reason and entered the realm of madness."

You smiled (how was it you did not explode with anger?) and answered him: "Who told you I produce art? I do not produce art, I do not care about beauty. Reason is too constricting for me, and so are the rules. Like the flying fish, I leap out of safe, secure waters and enter a more ethereal atmosphere that is filled with madness."

You fell silent for a moment and glanced at the Toledo you had painted: wrapped in black clouds, cleft by thunderbolts, with its towers, churches, and palaces which had been delivered from their bodies of stone to emerge from the blackness as phantoms dressed in disquieting splendor. You looked at them and your nostrils began to quiver, inhaling brimstone. After reflecting in silence for a moment, you cried out in pain, digging your ten nails into your breast, "What devil is in me? Who set fire to Toledo? I really do inhale a wind filled with madness and death, I mean filled with freedom."

The only one able to comprehend the divine frenzy was a poet (no matter if he was also a monk), Father Hortensio Felix Paravicino. He saw the menacing darkness, the savage thunderbolts, the great wings, the saints whose bodies had melted away and become blazing candles, and one day he seized your paint-bespattered hand and kissed it. "You make snow itself burst into flame," he said. "You have overstepped nature, and the soul remains undecided in its wonderment which of the two—God's creature or yours—deserves to live." At the last of these words, his voice began to tremble.

You listened, smiling and unperturbed, to the insults and commendations. If you frequently pretended to be angry, the anger was a superficial storm on your face; the depths beneath remained motionless. Because you were aware of the great secret, you had neither hope, fear, nor vain self-conceit. Men scuffle with those two great phantoms good and evil (who knows, perhaps they are the two aspects of God). The most ignorant say that good and evil are enemies. Others rise one step higher and say that good and evil are allies. Still others, embracing the game of life and death upon this terrestrial crust with an all-encompassing glance, rejoice at the harmony and say: Good and evil are One.

But we, grandfather, are aware of the great secret. We reveal it, and who cares if no one believes! So much the better if they do not. Man is infirm, he needs consolations. If he believed, his blood would run cold. What secret? That this One does not exist.

One day I went to your house in Toledo, grandfather, so that I too could view the saints, apostles, and nobles you painted. How you unburdened them of the weight of the flesh and made them ready to turn to flame. Never in my life had I seen more flaming flames. This is how the flesh is defeated, I reflected, this is how the precious essence is preserved from disintegration, not our feet and hands of clay, not our blond or black hair, but the precious essence which battles inside this sack of skin and which some call soul and others flame.

If you had still been dressed in your flesh, grandfather, I would have brought you some honey, myzíthra, and oranges as gifts from Crete; also Harídhemos, that fine rebecist with the basil behind his ear, to sing you the three mantinádhes you adored:

Luff the helm, embrace your faith come what come may,
Who cares if a project thrive or if it decay!

A job before you, luff and do not fear,
Pay out your youth to it with never a tear.

I am the son of lightning, grandson of thunder's howl;
At will I flash and thunder, at will I fling down hail.

But you had turned to flame. Where could I find you, how could I see you, what gift could I bring you to make you remember Crete and rise from the grave? Only flame is able to find favor in your sight. Oh, if only I could turn to flame and join you!

You perched for thirty-seven years upon this ledge which is Toledo. For thirty-seven years you must have stepped onto this terrace where I now stand, and watched the muddy Tagus flow beneath the double-arched Alcántara Bridge, watched it flee, proceed to pour into the ocean and perish. Your mind flowed with it, your life flowed also, proceeded to pour into death and perish. Bitter, rebellious cries rose from your bowels. So far I have done nothing, nothing, you thought to yourself, clenching your fists (you did not sigh, you became angry). I have done nothing. What can the soul accomplish with paints and canvas? It does not suit me to perch here at the end of the earth mixing colors, fooling with a brush, and painting saints and crucified Christs. These decalcomanias do not unburden my soul. The world is narrow, life is narrow, God is narrow; I should have taken up fire—fire, sea, winds, and stones—in order to build the world as I wanted it: equal to my own stature!

The sun began to set, the rooftops turned to gold, the river darkened, the evening star plummeted from the mountain. The lamps had been lighted in your house; your old faithful servant Maria Gomez was setting the table. Jeronima, the dear companion of your sleeping and waking hours, stepped onto the terriace and touched your hand ever so lightly, lest she frighten you. "It is dark now," she said. "You have worked all day and eaten nothing. Don't you pity your body? Come . . ."

But you had called a halt now to your creation of the world and had bounded to Crete. Striding over the Cretan mountains, you did not hear the gentle voice, did not feel the white hand. You were not quite twenty years old. The air smelled of thyme. Singing the three mantinádhes you adored, a kerchief with long fringes girding your raven-black hair, a marigold behind your ear, you were going to the celebrated monastery of Vrondíssi to paint the Marriage of Cana, which the abbot had commissioned from you.

Your mind was overflowing with blue, crimson, and green paints. The bride and groom were enthroned on high stools decorated with carvings of two-headed eagles. The marriage tables were ready, the guests eating and drinking; the rebecist sat in their midst playing his instrument and singing sprightly marriage songs. Christ was rising—He had drunk, His cheeks were ablaze—and placing a silver florin on the musician's forehead . . .

Suddenly the beloved voice came to you, as though from far in the distance. You heard it. "I am coming," you answered. Smiling, you followed the woman who was compassionately returning you to earth. But the Marriage of Cana had luxuriated in your mind, the belled rebec of Crete had tinkled and wailed inside you, and lo, the everyday meal seemed like a wedding feast! You kept two musicians in your employ; you summoned them, O bridegroom, to play the lute and guitar while you ate, so that your humble food and wine could become a marriage feast of Cana. And when you had finished eating, you too rose (you remembered the picture you had painted in your mind) and with lordly generosity placed two golden ducats on the musicians' foreheads.

For you lived like a lord. You were a lord. Having nothing but scorn for prudence, you squandered all you earned from your art. Friends and enemies alike censured and scolded you. "What do you want with a twenty-four-room house?" they demanded. "What do you want with musicians? Why don't you condescend to load your icons on your back like all the others, and make the rounds of churches and monasteries to sell them?"

They called you high-nosed, disdainful, freakish. You blazed up in anger if a single word was uttered against you; you flew into a rage when asked how many ducats you expected for one of your paintings. "My paintings are not for sale," you answered. "They cannot be bought. Works of art like mine are beyond the reach of any purse. I am simply leaving them in pawn with you. When I feel like it, I shall return your ducats and take back my painting."

"Where are you from?" the judges asked you. "Why did you come to Toledo? Who are you?" But you interrupted them. "I am not obliged to answer," you said, "and I am not going to answer." When they did not force you, however, you inscribed your name wide and broad on your paintings, and below it, with magisterial pride, the title CRETAN.

And when that venom-nosed King Philip panicked at the sight of the Saint Maurice you had painted for him, you bit your lips and deigned neither to supplicate nor to take the edge off your colors. Instead, enveloped in flames, you took your wrath, pride, and unyielding art with you and scampered off to Toledo.

It was a great moment. A pure, righteous conscience stood on one tray of the balance, an empire on the other, and it was you, man's conscience, that tipped the scales. This conscience will be able to stand before the Lord at the Last Judgment and not be judged. It will judge, because human dignity, purity, and valor fill even God with terror.

Forgive me, grandfather, for being unable to control myself. I felt such great admiration for the thrice-noble moment when you strode across the Escorial's threshold and departed with head held high, leaving the world's great and small profits scornfully behind you, that I dared to make that moment fast in verse and meter in order to keep it from fleeing. I write my homage in black ink, in red ink, and hang it in the air:

Curled on a ledge beneath the sweltry
blaze, the king—the worm—observes
with lingering gaze the masons
towering his desolate foursquare
coffin all around them. Cell,
palace and tomb, the savage rough-hewn
granite bellows coarse and nude
upon the barren crag. His lathery
mouth was moldering, the unrighteous
judge's wax-white face and wizened
body slowly decomposing—
when suddenly from the mountain's mane
down swoops with joyful shriek a starving
vulture upon the torpid form:
thirty years before, it smelled
the stench. The comely youth, the Cretan,
feels the stalker bird depart
his mind to pounce upon the monarch.
In the cavern of his ear reverbrates
still the hissing wrath-filled lash
which drove him from the temple of his
dreams: "The King rejects Saint Maurice!"
The air stirred and tingled—flames on
every side; arms and angels;
the breasts catch fire, rapt in God;
the spears are spindling sun-washed lilies;
flowers spring from flame-hot stones;
enamel, ruby, emerald the shields;
lion-like prowls the light and consumes;
in heaven, with their misty stature,
the stalwarts march in file like wraiths in
early gusts. The youth, with vigorous
frenzied fingers, kneads a clod of
ardent Cretan cistus gum,
his hand forever fragrant. Noon;

shimmering air above the stones.
The slender acrite sees a new
creation flashing vaguely in the
light—celestial and barely seen
its form. As an upright wing which spreads
with creaking force, so shakes, immured,
the monastery, and mankind's ponderous
bastion, the languid body, an azure
window opens toward the sky.
Birds the angels, plummeting to the
reason's forge; like rosy apples
the king's black tidings dangle;
from chaste heaven's garrets the mind-vulture hurtles
mutely down to the Cretan's brain,
an archangel with a mouthful of fire.
Children pass, like embers after
evening rain, and monks, and virgins,
and lords with sunken cheeks, and mothers
consecrated to their sons: their
gods. His hands are burning to begin.
Vague desires are stifling him; with
insatiable span-length bites he measures
out the ethereal canvas in the air.
The paints flow thick and simmer briskly
in his brain before the hand
can seize them. Virile angels plunge,
swarms of meteors burst at the heads.
Like martial flags returning in tatters,
the apostles torch into his mind;
keys they hold, and fires, the beloved
a massive snake-embossèd chalice.
Upon him, bowed, the youth feels God
descend as clumps of fire; he howls,
his body sacrificed upon
the cross. Seething earth. Like a lion's
tongue, grace divine voraciously
licks the stones. The unborn mass
enwraps his flanks, a briskly vibrant
dance. His fingers spark, and one

by one he lights the tips, heads of
slender flame on doubly man-sized
candles. With otherworldly brilliance,
like a pearly corona of moon,
earth's trembling upper level beckons him.
"I shall bow out the body: let it crack!
God, a magnet high in the clouds,
draws me to the dance floor thrice-
ethereal. But the King, that venomous
figwort, ejects me from his dreary
henroost; he sees the light and panics.
Damn you! goodbye, and learn, you fleshly
sieve, that art is not submission
and rules, but a demon which smashes the molds.
I leave you to sweep up cunt-hair with your
putrid eunuch daubers." So he
spoke. Sunward to the granite
turning, those precious indurated
jewels his eyes he fixes on the
stylite crags. He smelled the cistus;
Crete the fondled tigress slipped
and spread throughout his vitals' sounding
darkness. Heavy cares, desires
proud and manly, drum his breast,
the bee-swarm buzzes in flowering thyme, and
Vrondíssi belovèd enters his mind.
Ablaze, Psiloríti steams;
icy waters pound the marble
fountain; bridge raised high, the tingling
rebec wails its lively reels.
The sea brine on his lips, he still
can hear—O hidden treasure—the deacon-
ascetic at Kastro's harbor before
he sailed, his agèd master's double
admonition: "Kyriákos,
anointed you were with flame of prophecy,
do not fall in affluence's
pit, a pot-licker in regal
courts. Blaze untried trails and advance!"

O proud capricious heart, when crafty
hope was offering sweet and slavish
dreams, why did you hide and fail to
lash me with a furious heel
to make us leave? Back, heart! Back home!
He spoke. His soul cavorted like a
leopard. Isolation rose—a
fortress. God blazed starlike at his
brows; following, he turned to flee.
A virifying mantinádha
came to tip the scales of his will:

A JOB BEFORE YOU, LUFF AND DO NOT FEAR,
PAY OUT YOUR YOUTH TO IT WITH NEVER A TEAR.

I shed tears for my youth? Not I!
Patience is stifling me. I've had enough!
We, O heart, were made to violently
open freedom's unalloyèd
wings and be consumed on upper
roads! A sword we hold in our hands: the
light! Turn sunward to Crete, freedom
to find, and holy isolation!
Speedily, he turns to the right,
toward his father's house at the distant
haven. Psiloríti's proudful
summit flapped kerchief-like above
his mind; Messára plain stretched wide
and verdant with its genial orchards.
But suddenly he springs to his feet;
two frightening hands have seized him. Wings,
the roaring of wings he hears, and—Oh,
the great effulgence!—his eyes brim over
with stars. Flames incorporeal,
green and gold, fleetingly lick
his scalp, and brimstone, lightning, scorching
gusts. An archangel leaps upon him,
a warm south wind, his wings redolent
of cistus; clasps the youth to his burly
breast, kicks the ground, straight upward

zooms, and hurtles through the azurean
depths. The youth is pale in the fierce
torrential light. He firmly binds his
Cretan kerchief, and black eyes open,
lips stoutly clenched, beholds in the
torrid sun, earth's lower level
melt. A carcass in the solar
glare the mausoleum, ants the
builders scouring it. Highlands whistle,
roads meander; bent at the angelic
prow he reaps the light, desire's
summit. Earth's invisible stature
rose. His inner-archangel's breast had
thrust him on the virgin crests, on
savage freedom's single hope,
this world's most exalted garret,
Upper Crete, the secret homeland!

I wandered all day through Toledo's narrow lanes. I sniffed brimstone in the air, as though a thunderbolt had fallen. The wind still smelled of wild beast more than three centuries after your passage, as though a lion had come this way. How frightening and joyful it is to walk and feel a great soul furiously beating its wings above you!

At night when I went to bed, grandfather, and my entrails were filled with your breath, sleep came and took me away. Was it sleep, or a three-masted schooner with hoisted sails? I boarded it, and just as I was about to turn and ask the captain where we were going, we had anchored at Megalo Kastro, in Crete. The stone of the winged Venetian lions was turning rose in the afternoon sun, Saint Mark's banner was waving over the great tower, the wharf smelled of wine, olive oil, lemons, and oranges. Next to the harbor gate Geronimo's tavern was buzzing, filled with drunken Venetian and Genoese sailors, and with the brazen women who frequent the waterfront. We sat down behind a barrel, the two of us, off to one side. Grilled oysters and crabs were brought us as mezé; we emptied and refilled our glasses repeatedly, without speaking, each gazing into the other's eyes.

We were both young, you twenty, I seventeen. Though we

loved the same girl, we did not quarrel, for we were unqualified friends. At night we both sang beneath her closed window, relieving our heartache with mantinádhes, you carrying a lute, I a guitar. Our two voices blended, yours deep and virile, mine still immature, and we left the girl free to choose, behind her closed window. At dawn we parted, you to take up your brush without sleeping, and to paint colossal-winged angels who bounded out of their frames, as was your custom; while I, overcome with fatigue, went home to sleep and dream that the window opened and a red apple fell into my palm.

And now we gazed at each other in the tavern and did not speak, because you were going to depart the following day at dawn. We drank in order to forget the pain of separation.

It was nearly midnight when we rose to leave the tavern. We had been drinking tart Malevyzian wine, and our minds had opened, branched out, and invaded the entire world.

"The world is ours, brother Meneghí," I said. "Let's go."

We clasped each other around the waist to keep from stumbling. I felt your breath on my cheek. For how long, I asked myself, for how long? Dawn would come in just a few hours, and the beloved breath would leave me, would never fall upon me again! But I was young. I endured the pain, and my eyes did not fill with tears.

We passed through the harbor gate, turned to the right, and mounted the Venetian walls which encircle the city. The moon hung sadly over us, fully round. Only the biggest stars had been able to resist its radiance; these flashed in the milky speechless sky, while the Cretan sea bellowed on our right.

You stopped, beloved companion, and extended your arm. "Look," you said to me, "look at the water. It is charging to devour the walls and expel the Venetians. Can't you see? Look well—those aren't waves, Meneghàki" (that was the teasing nickname you gave me), "they are horses, a terrifying cavalry brigade!"

I laughed. "They're waves, Meneghí, they aren't horses."

You shrugged your shoulders. "You see with the eyes of clay, I with the others. You see the body, I the soul."

"Perhaps that explains why we are such good friends and do not wish to part. Does the soul wish to part from its body?"

We were reminded of the separation and felt sick at heart.

"Come," you said, squeezing my arm. "Don't talk about parting."

We proceeded for quite some time, beneath the moon, but our minds rested on the separation. The two of us were toiling to find some way to divert our thoughts lest we fall prey to tears. We were ashamed to weep; we had both read the holy legends, had envied the saints' steadfastness under pain—their eyes which remained dry even though they were parting forever from their dearest loved ones—and we had vowed to imitate them.

"What are you thinking about?" you asked me in order to conjure away the silence.

"Nothing," I replied, trying to hide my feelings. "Well yes, how wild the Cretan sea is, that's what I was thinking. And now that I have mentioned it, I feel like going down to the shore and fighting with the waves, even if I drown."

"Youth thinks itself immortal, that is why it challenges death," you answered, and you clasped my hand as though wishing to restrain me from descending to the shore.

I was pleased; the pressure of your hand seemed very tender to me. Though my pain at losing you increased, I feigned disinterest and suggested that we bring our conversation down to everyday needs in order to forget for a moment that we were parting.

"How are you going to live there in foreign lands, Meneghí?" I asked. "You don't know a soul, not a soul knows you, your star has not begun to shine yet. The ducats your brother Manoúsos gave you are not very many, and I know how openhanded you are. You'll spend them in no time, and after that? Aren't you afraid?"

"Don't bother yourself about me, Meneghákí," you replied. "No matter how little I have, it is enough; no matter how much, it is not enough. Do you understand what I'm saying?"

"No."

You laughed like a child. "Neither do I. Anyhow, that's the way it is."

But you saw that I was uneasy. Placing your hand on my shoulder, you said to comfort me, "Don't worry, Meneghákí, I won't go under. I have great goals in my mind, great power in my hands. I shall contend with the most formidable of them out there in Europe where I'm going, in order to force my soul either to win or perish. You'll see, you'll see. And first of all I'm going to have it out (don't be alarmed) with Michelangelo. The other day I saw a small copy of the Last Judgment he painted at Rome. I don't like it."

Your eyes in the moonlight were spitting flames; your voice had grown husky. Stooping, you picked up a rock and slung it down at the sea, as though you wished to indicate your strength by stoning the waves.

"Why look at me like that? Do you think I drank too much wine and became drunk? I am not drunk. No, I don't like it. He resurrects the flesh; the world fills with bodies again. I'll have none of them! I'll paint another Last Judgment, I will. With two levels. Lower level: graves—they're opening, and worms as large as a man's body are coming out, anxiously, with lifted heads, as though smelling the air. Upper level: Christ. Christ, all alone. He leans over, blows on the worms, and the air fills with butterflies. That's the meaning of resurrection—the worms must become butterflies, and not simply come back to us and be turned into immortal worms."

Raising my eyes, I glanced at you in the moon's magic light. The air around your flaming head had filled with butterflies.

I was opening my mouth to speak (this Last Judgment seemed excessively heretical to me), but you had worked up momentum and were anxious to tell me your secrets in time—daybreak was almost upon us, and we would soon be forced to part. I do not believe you were addressing me any more; you were soliloquizing as you went.

"They paint the Holy Spirit descending upon the Apostles' heads in the form of a dove. For shame! Haven't they ever felt the Holy Spirit burning them? Where did they find that innocent, edible bird? How can they present that to us as spirit? No, the Holy Spirit is not a dove, it is fire, a man-eating fire which clamps its talons into the very crown of saints, martyrs, and great strugglers, reducing them to ashes. Abject souls are the ones who take the Holy Spirit for a dove which they imagine they can kill and eat."

You laughed.

"Some day, God willing, I shall paint the Holy Spirit above the Apostles' heads, and then you'll see."

Falling silent, you moved your arm swiftly up and down, as though painting the future Pentecost in the air.

"Can't you turn the fire into light?" I asked. But I regretted my words immediately, for your face darkened.

"You and your mania for light!" you replied, knitting your brows—the way you glanced at me, for a moment I thought you were angry. "What's your hurry? That is none of our business. This is the earth, not a cloud, and the earth is made of bodies with flesh, fat, and bones. Let us turn them into flame. So much we can do, more we cannot. That is enough! Fire sleeps even in a dead stump, and in the leaf of a tree, and in the most splendid and silken of royal cloaks—sleeps and waits for man to awaken it. Wake the fire! That is man's duty! A flame penetrates stones, people, angels. That flame is what I want to paint. I don't want to paint the ashes. I am an artist, not a theologian. The moment I want to paint is the moment when God's creatures are burning, just before they turn to ashes. If only I arrive in time—I ask nothing more—if only I arrive in time. That is why you see me gasping and hurrying so; I want to arrive before they turn to ashes."

"Quiet!" I exclaimed. I felt your body enveloped in flames. "Be still, my companion. I am afraid."

"Do not be afraid, Meneghiáki. Fire is the Virgin Mother; it bears the immortal son. What son? Light. Life is purgatory; we burn. It is paradise's job to take the flame we have prepared for it and to turn that flame into light. Let us allow paradise to do that."

You fell silent again, but in a moment: "That, I want you to know, is how men collaborate with God. Certain people call me a heretic—let them. I have my own Holy Writ, and it says what the other either forgot or did not dare to say. I open it and read in Genesis: God made the world and rested on the seventh day. At that point He called his final creature, man, and said to him, 'Listen to me, my son, if you want my blessing. I made the world, but I neglected to finish it. I left it in the middle. You continue the creation. Ignite the world, transform it into fire, and render it unto me. I shall turn it into light.' "

With the clear air and grave talk, we had begun to feel sober. We seated ourselves on a rock and gazed at the sea. Sunward, the skies had already started to whiten at the horizon's hem. Below us, the sea was still dark and roaring. It seemed to me when I turned for an instant, Meneghí, that you were wrapped in flames.

"You are a merciless inquisitor," I said. "You torture and kill the body in order to save the soul."

"You call it soul, I call it flame," you answered me.

"I love the body. The flesh seems holy to me, it too is from God. And don't become angry if I tell you something else: the flesh has a glimmer from the soul, and the soul has a fleshly fuzz. They live together in harmonious balance like two young girls who are good friends and neighbors. You smash the sacred balance."

"Balance means stagnation, and stagnation means death."

"But in that case life is ceaseless denial. You deny what succeeded in opposing dissolution by achieving a balance. You smash this, and seek the uncertain."

"I seek the certain. I rip apart the masks, lift up the layers of flesh. I say to myself, Something immortal exists beneath the meat, it cannot be otherwise. This is what I am seeking, this is what I am going to paint. All the rest—masks, flesh, beauty—I gladly present to the Titians and Tintorettos, and I hope they enjoy them!"

"You want to surpass Titian and Tintoretto? Do not forget the Cretan mantinádha: 'If you build your nest too high, the branch will break!' "

You shook your head.

"No, I do not want to surpass anyone. I am alone, isolated."

"You are extraordinarily proud of yourself, Meneghí. Like Lucifer."

"No, I am extraordinarily alone."

"Take care, my dear friend! God punishes arrogance and isolation."

Without replying, you cast a final glance at the bellowing sea and swept your gaze over the still-sleeping city. The first cocks crowed. You rose.

"Come," you said. "It is dawn."

You clasped me around the waist again, and we resumed our walk. You were mumbling some words, opening and closing your mouth. You obviously wished to disclose something to me, but felt hesitant. Finally you could not restrain yourself.

"What I am going to tell you is distressing, Menegháki. Forgive me. You can say I am drunk."

I laughed. "Now that you're drunk you have the perfect opportunity to say what you shrink from saying when you are sober. The Malevyzian wine is talking, not you. . . . Well?"

Your voice resounded extremely deep and embittered in the pale dawn.

"One night I demanded of God, 'Lord, when are You going to pardon Lucifer?' and God answered, 'When he pardons me.' Do you understand, my young friend? Some day if you are asked who is God's greatest collaborator, you should say Lucifer. If you are asked who is the most sorrowful of God's creatures, you should say Lucifer. Lastly, if you are asked who is the prodigal son whose father waits for him with open arms, having killed the fatted calf, you should say Lucifer.

"I am revealing my most hidden secrets to you because I want you to know that if I am too late, or unable, to accomplish all I have in mind to accomplish, you must continue the struggle. Continue it without fear, never forgetting the savage injunction Cretan gives to Cretan: Pay out your youth to it with never a tear! That is what it means to be a man, to be truly brave: a pallikari. That is the holy flame's ultimate desire.

"Do you give me your word? Can you do it? Your courage will not grow faint? You will not look behind you and say, 'Prosperity is a fine thing, and so is a woman's embrace, and so is glory'? . . Why don't you speak?"

"The charge you give me is a heavy one, Meneghí. Couldn't man's duty be made a little less bitter?"

"Yes, but not for you or me. There are three kinds of souls, three kinds of prayers. One: I am a bow in your hands, Lord. Draw me lest I rot. Two: Do not overdraw me, Lord. I shall break. Three: Overdraw me, and who cares if I break!

"Choose!"

I awoke. The bells of the neighborhood church, Santo Tomé, were tolling matins; day had begun. Cries echoed in the street, women's heels clacked on the cobblestones, a young cock crowed raucously in the courtyard. Toledo was awakening. My dream still clung to my eyelashes; I could still hear the final, merciless word which had filled me with terror and shaken me out of my sleep. Choose!

Beloved grandfather, how much time—a flash or three centuries—has passed since that night when I slept in Toledo and you, scenting the arrival of a Cretan in your neighborhood, rose from your grave, turned into a dream, and came to find me? In the atmosphere of love, who can distinguish a flash from eternity? A life has slipped by since then. Black hair has whitened, temples have sunk, eyes grown dim. I was never able to determine in whose hands, God's or the devil's, the bow creaked. But I rejoiced at feeling a power, very much greater and purer than my own, continually arming me with arrows and shooting. All wood is from the true cross because all wood can be made into a cross. Similarly, all bodies are sacred because all bodies can be made into a bow. My entire lifetime I was a bow in merciless, insatiable hands. How often those invisible hands drew and overdrew the bow until I heard it creak at the breaking point! "Let it break," I cried each time. After all, you had commanded me to choose, grandfather, and I chose.

I chose. Now the twilight casts its haze upon the hilltops. The shadows have lengthened, the air has filled with the dead. The battle is drawing to a close. Did I win or lose? The only thing I know is this: I am full of wounds and still standing on my feet.

Full of wounds, all in the breast. I did what I could, grandfather. More than I could, just as you directed. I did not want you to feel ashamed of me. Now that the battle is over, I come to recline at your side, to become dust at your side, that the two of us may await the Final Judgment together.

I kiss your hand, grandfather. I kiss your right shoulder, I kiss your left shoulder.

Grandfather, hello!